INTERNATIONAL ENCYCLOPEDIA OF ENVIRONMENTAL POLITICS

INTERNATIONAL ENCYCLOPEDIA OF ENVIRONMENTAL POLITICS

Edited by
John Barry and E. Gene Frankland

London and New York

First published 2002
by Routledge
11 New Fetter Lane, London EC4P 4EE

Simultaneously published in the USA and Canada
by Routledge
29 West 35th Street, New York, NY 10001

Routledge is an imprint of the Taylor & Francis Group

© 2002 Routledge

Typeset in Baskerville by Taylor & Francis Books Ltd
Printed and bound in Great Britain by TJ International Ltd,
Padstow, Cornwall

British Library Cataloguing in Publication Data
A catalogue record for this book is available from the British Library

Library of Congress Cataloging in Publication Data
International encyclopedia of environmental politics / edited by John Barry
and E. Gene Frankland.
p. cm.
Includes bibliographical references and index.
1. Environmental policy–Encyclopedias. I. Barry, John. II. Frankland, E.
Gene.
GE170 .I55 2001
363. 7dc217
2001019754

ISBN 0–415–20285–X

The *International Encyclopedia of Environmental Politics*
is dedicated to the memory of Dick Richardson
who was the main initiator and driving force
behind this monumental project until his
untimely death in September 1997.
Dick was an active member of the green movement
and was a parliamentary candidate for the UK Green Party.
He was also a highly respected academic who helped
to create the academic field of environmental politics
in the 1980s and 1990s through his various activities
as a writer, conference organizer, and as a
tireless member of various national, European
and international academic networks.
Dick also founded and maintained an important archive
on European green parties (located at the
University of Teeside where he worked).
It is a great pity he is not alive to see his labours
finally bear fruit in this encyclopedia.
He is sorely missed by colleagues, friends,
his wife Marianne, and his four children.

Contents

Editorial team

General editors

John Barry
Queen's University Belfast, Northern Ireland

E. Gene Frankland
Ball State University, Muncie, Indiana, USA

Associate editors

Tony Affigne
Providence College, USA

Robyn Eckersley
University of Melbourne, Australia

Hazel Henderson
St Augustine, Florida, USA

Lettie McSpadden
Northern Illinois University, USA

Joan Martinez-Alier
Universitat Autonoma de Barcelona, Spain

Benoît Rihoux
Université Catholique de Louvain, Belgium

Chris Rootes
University of Kent, Canterbury, UK

Wolfgang Rüdig
University of Strathclyde, Scotland

Vandana Shiva
Research Foundation for Science, Technology and Ecology, India

Vaclav Smil
University of Manitoba, Canada

Editorial assistant

Jon E. Fitch
Ball State University, Muncie, Indiana, USA

List of contributors

Tony Affigne
Providence College, USA

Susan Baker
University of Cardiff, Wales

Jenny Barker
Forum for the Future, UK

Rod S. Barratt
The Open University, UK

John Barry
Queen's University Belfast, Northern Ireland

Gerry Bates
University of Sydney, Australia

Brian Baxter
University of Dundee, Scotland

Theodore L. Becker
Auburn University, USA

Sharon Beder
University of Wollongong, Australia

Lynn G. Bennie
University of Aberdeen, Scotland

Roberto Biorcio
Università degli Studi di Milano, Italy

Andrew Blowers
The Open University, UK

Ingolfur Blühdorn
University of Bath, UK

Christopher J. Bosso
Northeastern University, USA

Daniel Boy
Maison des Sciences de l'Homme, France

Nik Brown
University of York, UK

Ton Bührs
Lincoln University, New Zealand

Verity Burgmann
The University of Melbourne, Australia

Stephen Burnley
The Open University, UK

Ben Campbell
University of Manchester, UK

David Carlisle
University of Aberystwyth, Wales

Sverker Carlsson
Goteborg University, Sweden

Alan Carter
Heythrop College, University of London, UK

Neil Carter
University of York, UK

List of contributors

Paula Casal
Keele University, UK

Paul Chandler
Ball State University, USA

Steve Charnovitz
Wilmer, Cutler & Pickering, USA

Peter Christoff
University of Melbourne, Australia

Alice H. Cooper
University of Mississippi, USA

Kate Crowley
University of Tasmania, Australia

Michael S. Cummings
University of Colorado at Denver, USA

Nicole Dando
Brighton, UK

Marius de Geus
University of Leiden, The Netherlands

Elizabeth R. DeSombre
Colby College, USA

Thomas M. Dietz
German Green Party

Andrew Dobson
Keele University, UK

Brian Doherty
Keele University, UK

Peter Doran
Sustainable Ireland, Northern Ireland

Robyn Eckersley
University of Melbourne, Australia

James Eflin
Ball State University, USA

Paul Ekins
Keele University, UK

Lorraine Elliott
Australian National University, Australia

Marcus Enoch
The Open University, UK

Daniel C. Esty
Yale University, USA

Florence Faucher
University of Stirling, Scotland

Jon E. Fitch
Ball State University, USA

Tony Fitzpatrick
University of Nottingham, UK

Susan L. Flader
University of Missouri, Columbia, USA

James Flynn
Decision Research, USA

Erich G. Frankland
Casper College, USA

E. Gene Frankland
Ball State University, USA

J. George Frynas
Coventry Business School, UK

Robert Garner
University of Leicester, UK

Brendan Gleeson
University of Western Sydney, Macarthur, Australia

Alan Greer
University of the West of England, UK

Lori Gruen
Stanford University, USA

Yrjö Haila
University of Tampere, Finland

Meira Hanson
Hebrew University Jerusalem, Israel

Paul G. Harris
Lingnan University, Hong Kong

Kathryn Harrison
University of British Columbia, Canada

Charles Hauss
George Mason University, USA

Tim Hayward
University of Edinburgh, Scotland

Lamont C. Hempel
University of Redlands, USA

Hazel Henderson
St Augustine, Florida, USA

Horace Herring
The Open University, UK

Martin Horak
University of Toronto, Canada

Peter Hough
Middlesex University, UK

Janet Hunter
Northern Arizona University, USA

Mark Imber
University of St Andrews, Scotland

Detlef Jahn
Universitaet Greifswald, Germany

Andrew Jamison
University of Aarhus, Denmark

Manuel Jiménez
Juan March Institute Madrid, Spain

Christopher B. Jones
Eastern Oregon University, USA

Stanley R. Keil
Ball State University, USA

Aynsley Kellow
University of Tasmania, Australia

Richard L. Knight
Colorado State University, USA

Robert J. Koester
Ball State University, USA

Maria Kousis
University of Crete, Greece

Michael E. Kraft
University of Wisconsin-Green Bay, USA

Priya A. Kurian
University of Waikato, New Zealand

Chunglin Kwa
University of Amsterdam, The Netherlands

Volkmar Lauber
University of Salzburg, Austria

Penelope Law
British Association of Nature Conservationists, UK

David C. LeBlanc
Ball State University, USA

Joan Leach
Imperial College London, UK

Enrique Leff
Mexico City, Mexico

Heather Leslie
Oregon State University, USA

Les Levidow
The Open University, UK

Andrew Light
New York University, USA

Nicholas Low
University of Melbourne, Australia

Thomas Lowe
Ball State University, USA

David Lowry
Surrey, UK

Paul Lucardie
Rijksuniversiteit Groningen, The Netherlands

John McCormick
Indiana University-Purdue University in Indiana-polis (IUPUI), USA

Alistair McCulloch
Edge Hill College of Higher Education, UK

Lettie McSpadden
Northern Illinois University, USA

Joan Martinez-Alier
Universitat Autonoma de Barcelona, Spain

Masatsugu Maruyama
Higashiyamanashigun, Japan

Mary Mellor
University of Northumbria at Newcastle, UK

Daniel Mittler
University College London, UK & Friends of the Earth Germany (BUND), Germany

Elizabeth Moore
University of Toronto, Canada

Peggy Morgan
University of Oxford, UK

Mokbul Morshed Ahmad
Dhaka University, Bangladesh & National University of Ireland, Galway, Ireland

Jon Mulberg
University of Reading, UK

Stephen Mumme
Colorado State University, USA

Niamh Murnaghan
University of East Anglia, UK

Eric Neumayer
London School of Economics, UK

Peter Newell
University of Warwick & Institute for Development Studies, UK

Kenneth Omeje
University of Nigeria, Nigeria

David Ostergren
Northern Arizona University, USA

Ed Page
Keele University, UK

Joy A. Palmer
University of Durham, UK

Matthew Paterson
Keele University, UK

David Pepper
Oxford Brookes University, UK

John Pichtel
Ball State University, USA

Stephen Potter
The Open University, UK

John Proops
Keele University, UK

Derrick Purdue
University of the West of England, UK

Barry G. Rabe
University of Michigan, USA

Kevin Radaker
Anderson University, USA

Dick Richardson
University of Teeside, UK

Benoît Rihoux
Université Catholique de Louvain, Belgium

Michael Rodi
Universitaet Greifswald, Germany

Chris Rootes
University of Kent, Canterbury, UK

Dieter Rucht
Wissenschaftszentrum Berlin, Germany

Wolfgang Rüdig
University of Strathclyde, Scotland

Amandeep Sandhu
University of Victoria, Canada

Raymond H. Scheele
Ball State University, USA

David Scrivener
Keele University, UK

Benjamin Seel
University of Kent at Canterbury, UK

Paul Selman
Cheltenham & Gloucester College of Higher Education, UK

Gill Seyfang
University of East Anglia, UK

Eric Shibuya
Colorado State University, USA

Sandrine Simon
The Open University, UK

Vaclav Smil
University of Manitoba, Canada

Denis Smith
University of Sheffield, UK

Graham Smith
University of Southampton, UK

Zachary A. Smith
Northern Arizona University, USA

Ispurwono Soemarno
University of Melbourne, Australia

K. Ravi Srinivas
Madurai, India

Piers H.G. Stephens
University of Manchester, UK

Aki Suwa
University College London, UK

Anna Syngellakis
University of Portsmouth, UK

Caroline Thomas
University of Southampton, UK

Paul B. Thompson
Texas A&M University, USA

Matthew P. Tunno
Northern Arizona University, USA

Cédric van de Walle
Université Libre de Bruxelles, Belgium

Warren Vander Hill
Ball State University, USA

Paula Vandergert
Forests Monitor, UK

Roberto Verzola
Quezon City, Philippines

Norman J. Vig
Carleton College, USA

Bruno Villalba
University of Lille, France

Eduardo Viola
University of Brasilia, Brazil

Derek Wall
University of Bath, UK

Gert-Rüdiger Wegmarshaus
European University Viadrina Frankfurt (Oder),
Germany

Ian Welsh
University of Cardiff, Wales

Damian White
University of East London, UK

Andrew Whitworth
University of Leeds, UK

Marcel Wissenburg
University of Nijmegen, The Netherlands

Aaron T. Wolf
Oregon State University, USA

David Wood
University of Newcastle upon Tyne, UK

Douglas Wood
Staffordshire University, UK

Matthew Wyman
Keele University, UK

Stephen C. Young
University of Manchester, UK

Charles Ziegler
University of Louisville, USA

Introduction

The *International Encyclopedia of Environmental Politics*, like all such publishing projects, has been a long time in coming. With over 500 entries and over 160 authors from all around the world, there were times when as editors we felt we had taken on a hopeless task. However, the opportunity to compile and to present a map of international environmental politics from 'A to Z', was a privilege and an exciting and attractive prospect for us both. Indeed we were keenly aware of the responsibility for compiling and documenting a comprehensive encyclopedia of a rapidly changing subject. With no other comparable encyclopedia upon which to draw, compiling, editing and producing this present work was in part a voyage into the unknown, the mapping of a new territory, and in part the bringing together, in one volume, of the diversity of views, perspectives, issues and debates which together make up international environmental politics.

However, as with all maps, when using this encyclopedia readers should remember that 'the map is not the territory'. Like all written accounts of a quickly changing subject area, we are only too aware of the limitations of any encyclopedia's claim to comprehensiveness; there are, for example, doubtless some entries which individual readers may either not find or find not done to their particular taste. But in a work of this kind, and within the constraints of the space we had available to fill, such shortcomings are practically unavoidable. For example, although we have tried our best to be genuinely 'international', inevitably, as a survey of the entries and contributors indicates, there is a bias towards European, North American and Australasian environmental politics. We hope, however, to have included sufficient entries about other countries, concerns, issues and debates so that what we have produced can be characterized as 'international environmental politics'. Our criteria for individual country entries were: population size, geographical size, environmental problems and significance in development of environmental politics. As it was not possible to include all countries in a single-volume work, we also commissioned regional entries to address problems shared by specific sets of countries.

We have actively solicited a diversity of perspectives and views on international environmental politics, and have tried not to present a 'party line'. While there are entries about issues, groups or people by those associated with or closely related to the 'green' political movement or perspective (or 'ecological' or 'environmental' depending on the terminology used), we hope to have succeeded in producing an encyclopedia of international *environmental* politics and not an encyclopedia of international *green* politics. That is, the aim of this encyclopedia is to serve as an introduction and resource for the study of the many dimensions of the 'politics of the environment', rather than the different aspects of just one political or ideological take on the subject.

As editors we are committed to a view of environmental politics as something that necessarily demands an interdisciplinary approach. Thus the encyclopedia has been compiled and structured with this in mind, largely within and between the social sciences and humanities (including politics, international relations, geography, sociology, history, economics, law, philosophy, cultural studies, development studies, anthropology), though with appropriate entries on some 'natural science' themes and issues.

We hope to have produced a useful guide to the complex, important, contested and fascinating world of international environmental politics, a politics which as we stand at the threshold of a new century and millennium, with controversial technological developments such as 'genetic engineering', continuing loss of 'biodiversity', the potentially catastrophic effects of 'global warming', and the beginnings of a concerted global resistance movement to the environmental, economic and cultural dangers of economic 'globalization', is set to increase in significance and importance.

Acknowledgements

Our 10 Associate Editors were an appreciated source of professional and personal support, particularly in suggesting and/or writing entries and/or suggesting possible contributors. In particular, we would like to thank Benoît Rihoux, Wolfgang Rüdig, Chris Rootes and Lettie McSpadden for work above and beyond the call of Associate Editor duty.

We would also like to acknowledge the unfailing support, encouragement (and good humour!) of the various people at Routledge without whom this project would never have been completed – Fiona Cairns, Mina Gera-Price and, last but not least, Dominic Shryane, our development editor, for all his help.

John Barry, Queen's University Belfast,
Northern Ireland
E. Gene Frankland, Ball State University,
Muncie, Indiana, USA
March 2001

How to use this encyclopedia

This encyclopedia has been written, structured and organized explicitly as a 'first place' to start one's search or research into the different issues, topics and debates in international environmental politics. The entries have been written by experts in their fields, from a variety of professional and ideological backgrounds, in a jargon-free style in order to communicate the main issues. Most entries (particularly the larger entries) have a 'Further reading' section which readers can use to further their study and/or research in the particular area. It has been structured to enable readers to find relevant entries quickly and with extensive cross-references (provided both in the text and the *see also* sections at the end of many entries), and a comprehensive index, the reader can quickly locate other relevant entries in the encyclopedia.

There are four entry sizes:

- *150-word entries*: Short, definitional entries or short biographical ones on significant individuals or groups.
- *750-word entries*: These offer a more in-depth overview and analysis of particular issues (such as **air pollution** or **greenwashing**), individuals (such as **Rachel Carson** and **Mohandas Gandhi**), groups (such as **Greenpeace**), country level entries (**Italy**, **Pakistan** or **Philippines**), to institutions such as **labour/trades unions**.
- *1,500-word entries*: These offer comprehensive overviews and in-depth analyses of a variety of important topics in international environmental politics. These range from some of the major institutions of international environmental politics (such as the **United Nations Environment Programme** to **World Trade Organization** and **multinational and transnational corporations**), to major environmentally damaging and controversial projects such as **The Three Gorges Project** in China to **genetic engineering**, and the regional environmental politics of **South East Asia** to general issues such as **forest management**.
- *3,000-word entries* These cover major topics of international environmental politics and these article-length entries give original and expert views on the environmental politics of and within large countries such as **China**, **India**, and **Russian Federation/Former Soviet Union**. This category also has entries on more theoretical/ethical topics such as **deep ecology** and **sustainable development**.

Thematic entry list

African environmental politics

African Green Parties, Federation of
Maathai, Wangari (Kenya)
Nigeria
North Africa and Middle East
Ogoni People (Nigeria)
Sahel
South African environmental politics
Sub-Saharan Africa

Agriculture/food production

agribusiness
agriculture
agroecology
Common Agricultural Policy
famines
fisheries
food quality, politics of
green revolution
mad cow disease/BSE
organic farming
pesticides

American environmental politics

Abbey, Edward
Association of State Green Parties
Atomic Energy Commission
Bari, Judi
Berry, Wendell
Bookchin, Murray
Brower, David
Burford, Anne Gorsuch
Carson, Rachel
Citizens' Clearinghouse for Hazardous Wastes

Citizens Party
Clean Air Act
Clean Water Act
Commoner, Barry
Council on Environmental Quality
Cuyahoga River
Daly, Herman
Department of the Interior
Douglas, William O.
Dust Bowl
Earth First! (US)
Ehrlich, Paul
Emerson, Ralph Waldo
Endangered Species Act
Environmental Defense Fund
environmental law/litigation
Environmental Protection Agency
Everglades
Exxon Valdez oil spill
Foreman, Dave
Gibbs, Lois
Gore, Albert
Great Lakes International Joint Commission
green parties, US
Hardin, Garrett
Henderson, Hazel
Hetch Hetchy Dam
Inglehart, Ronald
Jefferson, Thomas
Leopold, Aldo
Love Canal
Lovins, Amory and Hunter
Marsh, George Perkins
Marshall, Bob
MOVE
Muir, John

Mumford, Lewis
Nader, Ralph
NAFTA (North American Free Trade Agreement)
National Audubon Society
National Environmental Policy Act
National Wildlife Federation
Natural Resources Defense Council
Nature Conservancy
net energy
Odum, Eugene
Pinchot, Gifford
political action committees
Price–Anderson Act
Reagan, Ronald
Rifkin, Jeremy
Roosevelt, Theodore
Ruckelshaus, William
Sagebrush Rebellion
Santa Barbara oil spill
Sierra Club
Sierra Club v. Morton
Silkwood, Karen
Simon, Julian
snail darter case
Spaceship Earth
spotted owl controversy
Spretnak, Charlene
Superfund
takings
Thoreau, Henry David
Three Mile Island accident
Watt, James
White, Lynn, Jr
wise-use movement
Worldwatch Institute
Yucca Mountain and nuclear wastes
Zahniser, Howard
Zero Population Growth

Asian environmental politics

Aral Sea
Bangladesh
China
East Asia
Indonesia
Japan
Japanese nuclear power industry

Lake Baikal
Pakistan
Philippines, the
South East Asian environmental politics
Three Gorges project

Australian environmental politics

Australian environmental groups
Australian environmental law and policy
Australian regulatory agencies
Franklin Dam
green bans
Singer, Peter
Tasmanian Greens

Belgium

Aelvoet, Magda
Agalev
Belgium
Ecolo
Lannoye, Paul

Biodiversity and conservation

biodiversity
biopiracy/bioprospecting
CITES (Convention on International Trade in
    Endangered Species)
conservation biology
coral reefs
ecology
endangered species
exotic species
forest management
landscape
mangroves
national parks
whaling
wildlife management

British environmental politics

Alarm UK
anti-roads movement
Blueprint for Survival
Brent Spar controversy

British environmental law and policy
British nuclear power industry
British regulatory agencies
Campaign for Nuclear Disarmament
Council for the Protection of Rural England
Department of the Environment, Transport and
   the Regions
Earth First! (UK)
Environment Agency
Forum for the Future
Goldsmith, Edward
Green Party (UK)
Inspectorate of Pollution
mad cow disease/BSE
McDonald's/'McLibel'
Mill, John Stuart
National Trust
New Economics Foundation
Parkin, Sara
public inquiries
Ramblers' Association
Robertson, James
Royal Society for the Protection of Birds
Scotland
Sellafield/Windscale
Soil Association
Wales, Party of

Canadian environmental politics

Canadian environmental law and policy
Canadian environmental ministries/agencies
Canadian Greens
Great Lakes International Joint Commission
James Bay hydroelectric project

Chinese environmental politics

China
Three Gorges Project

Countries and regions

Amazonia
Antarctica
Arctic
Bangladesh
Belgium

Brazil
Central American environmental politics
Chile
China
Denmark
East and Central Europe
East Asia
European Union
Finland
France
Greece
India
Indonesia
Italy
Japan
Latin American environmental politics
Luxembourg
Mexico
Netherlands, the
New Zealand
Nigeria
North Africa and Middle East
Norway
Pakistan
Philippines, the
Russian Federation/Former Soviet Union
Scotland
South African environmental politics
South East Asian environmental politics
Spain
Sub-Saharan Africa
Sweden

Energy

energy conservation
energy crisis
fossil fuels
nuclear energy
renewable energy
soft energy path
solar energy

Environment and health

asbestos
DDT
dioxin

health and the environment
lead poisoning
mercury poisoning
PCBs

Environmental non-government organizations, groups and movements

Alarm (UK)
anti-nuclear movements
BUND (German Federation for Environment and Nature)
Campaign for Nuclear Disarmament
Chipko Andolan Movement
Climate Action Network
conservation movement
Earth First! (UK)
Earth First! (US)
Environmental Defense Fund (US)
environmental movements
Forum for the Future
Friends of the Earth
Greenpeace
international non-governmental organizations
monkey-wrenching
MOVE
NABU (German Nature Protection Association)
National Audubon Society
New Economics Foundation
New Left
new politics
new social movements
non-violent direct action
peace movements
Peoples' Global Action
Rainbow Warrior
Robin Wood
Royal Society for the Protection of Birds
Sea Shepherd Conservation Society
Sierra Club
wise-use movement
Women's Environmental Network
World Conservation Union
Worldwatch Institute
Zapatistas/Chiapas
Zero Population Growth

Environmental political ideologies and ideas

anarchism/eco-anarchism
bioregionalism
doomsayers
eco-feminism
eco-socialism
eco-terrorism
ecological modernization
education, environmental
enclosure
environmental history
environmentalism and ecologism
environmentalism of the poor
Gaia hypothesis
green political theory
Limits to Growth
Luddites
noble savage, myth of
precautionary principle
Romanticism
social ecology
steady-state economy
stewardship
voluntary simplicity
utopia/ecotopia

Ethical issues

animal rights
anthropocentrism
biotechnology
cloning
deep ecology
distributive justice
eco-centrism
eco-philosophy/eco-sophy
environmental ethics
environmental pragmatism
factory farming
genetic engineering, animals
genetic engineering, crops
genetic engineering, humans
human rights
humanism and the environment
intergenerational justice
intrinsic value
Leopold, Aldo
religions and the environment

Watt, James (US)
White Jr., Lynn (US)
Zahniser, Howard (US)

International environmental agreements, conferences

Basel Convention
Framework Convention on Climate Change
International Convention on the Law of the Sea
international environmental law
Kyoto Conference/Protocol
Montreal Protocol
Rio Conference 1992
Stockholm Conference
World Heritage Convention

International/global environmental issues

environmental management
global environmental governance
global warming
globalization
indigenous peoples
militarism and the environment
ozone depletion
population movement and control
sustainability
sustainable development
tourism, environmental impact of
tradeable emission permits
urbanization
whole Earth photograph

Italian environmental politics

Italian green parties
Italy
Meana, Carlo Ripa di
Seveso disaster

Latin American environmental politics

Amazonia
Brazil
Brazilian Green Party
Central American environmental politics
Chile

Federación de Partidos Verdes de Las Américas
Latin American environmental politics
Max-Neef, Manfred
Mendes, Chico
Mexico
Partido Verde Ecologistica de Mexico
Zapatistas/Chiapas

Law and the environment

common law/torts
community-right-to-know laws
international environmental law

Oil/nuclear/chemical disasters/problems

Aral Sea
Bhopal disaster
Brent Spar controversy
chemical industry
Chernobyl
Cuyahoga River
Exxon Valdez oil spill
Kyshtym nuclear accident
mercury poisoning
Sandoz spill
Santa Barbara oil spill
Seveso disaster
Three Mile Island
oil pollution
Oilwatch

Political economy/economic issues

anti-environmentalism
business and the environment
capitalism
citizens' income
co-operatives
cost-benefit analysis
debt-for-nature swaps
development
ecological debt
ecological economics
ecological footprint
ecological modernization
eco-taxes
eco-tourism

environmental economics
environmental refugees
environmental security
externalities
free-market environmentalism
Global Climate Coalition
greenwashing
International Monetary Fund/neoliberalism
labour/trade unions
land reform
less developed countries
life cycle analysis
MAI (Multilateral Agreement on Investment)
multinational and transnational corporations
NAFTA
natural capital
newly industrializing countries
North/South divide

Political and social theory

civil society
communism
counter-culture
critical theory
democracy
disenchantment of nature
Enlightenment
federalism and decentralization
future studies
intentional communities
issue–attention cycle
liberalism/liberal democracy
mass media and the environment
NIMBY (Not In My Backyard)
paradigms
policy networks
political opportunity structures
post-industrial society
post-materialism
post-modernism
prisoners' dilemma
progress
public opinion and the environment
resource mobilization theory
sociobiology

Pollution problems/issues

acid rain
air pollution
Basel Convention
Bhopal disaster
brownfield sites
Danube Circle
hazardous and toxic waste management
municipal solid waste
ocean dumping
polluter pays principle
Seveso disaster
water pollution

Property rights

quality of life
social economy, informal economic activity in
structural adjustment programmes
World Bank
World Trade Organization

Resource environmental problems/issues

biodiversity
biopiracy/bioprospecting
common pool property resources
fossil fuels
non-renewable resources
recycling

Russian Federation/Former Soviet Union

Aral Sea
Lake Baikal
Chernobyl (Ukraine)
Kyshtym nuclear accident
Russian Federation/Former Soviet Union
Russian nuclear power industry
Russian green parties and movements

Science and technology

appropriate technology
biotechnology
civic science
entropy
environmental research and development

epistemic communities
genetic engineering, animals
genetic engineering, crops
genetic engineering, humans
net energy
risk assessment
technology
technology assessment
technology transfer

State or international environmental organizations

Agenda 21
Alliance of Small Island States
Brundtland Commission
Commission on Sustainable Development (United Nations)
Council on Environmental Quality
Department of the Environment, Transport and the Regions
Environment Agency
Environmental Protection Agency
European Environment Agency
European Environment Bureau
Global Environment Facility
Inspectorate of Pollution
International Atomic Energy Authority
United Nations Environmental Programme
United Nations Fund for Population Activities

World Health Organization
United Nations Development Programme
World Conservation Union
World Resources Institute
World Wide Fund for Nature

Transport

air transportation and infrastructure
car industry
transportation

Water environmental issues

Aral Sea
Arctic
Aswan Dam
Baltic Sea
coastal zone management
dams/hydroelectric power
Danube Circle
Great Lakes International Joint Commission
Hetch Hetchy Dam
Lake Baikal
Narmada Valley development programme
Three Gorges project
water politics
water pollution
wetlands

A

Abbey, Edward

b. 29 January 1927, Pennsylvania, USA;
d. 14 March 1989, Oracle, Arizona

Author and activist

Edward Abbey, a distinguished writer of books and articles on nature and the environment, is unique as one who refused to consider himself an environmentalist, even though virtually all of his published work shows a love of wild places. Indeed, he resisted all efforts to identify him with any organized group or movement. A self-described agrarian anarchist, Abbey's career included time as a bus driver, park ranger, social worker, and cowboy. These varied experiences helped to give him a world view that was extremely critical of contemporary American society. His clarion call was for life to be brought back to the firm reality of Mother Earth. One means to that end which received a great deal of notoriety, was '**monkey-wrenching**', from Abbey's 1975 book, *The Monkey Wrench Gang*, which advocated the direct defence of the earth, and was championed by such groups as **Earth First!**

See also: anarchism

Further reading

Abbey, E. (1968) *Desert Solitaire*, Tucson: University of Arizona.

WARREN VANDER HILL

acid rain

Acid precipitation or, better yet, acid deposition are more accurate descriptions than the commonly used term 'acid rain': any precipitation (fog, sleet, snow) can be acid, and there is also a great deal of dry-deposited acidifying compounds. Oxides of sulphur (SO_x) and nitrogen (NO_x) are precursors of acidifying compounds: sulphates and nitrates produced by their oxidation have to be balanced by hydrogen ions (H^+) to form strong (that is fully dissociated) acids, for instance sulphuric acid (H_2SO_4) and nitric acid (HNO_3), which are the two most important acidifying compounds. Acidity is expressed as the concentration of H^+ in solution on a logarithmic scale (pH).

Downwind precipitation from large SO_2 sources can have episodic acidity below pH 3, comparable to that of vinegar (pH 2.9), and annual averages in the worst affected areas of eastern North America, western and Central Europe have ranged between pH 4–4.5, with individual rains having pH even less than 3.5. But in all arid and semiarid regions average precipitation pH is higher thanks to huge quantities of dust containing neutralizing base cations (mostly Ca^{2+} [calcium], K^+ [potassium] and Mg^{2+} [magnesium]).

Although the first systematic studies of the phenomenon are R.A. Smith's writings of the 1850s, widespread modern attention to this environmental degradation began with the Swedish studies of the late 1960s which concluded that long-range atmospheric transport of air pollutants from coal-burning countries of western and Central Europe had been causing acidification of aquatic ecosystems, leaching of toxic metals from soils, and reduction of forest growth over much of southern Scandinavia. **Sweden** made its concerns about long-distance acidification the case study for the first United Nations Conference on the Human Environment in 1972. A number of multinational European studies followed during the rest of the 1970s, and in 1981 the USA began its decade-long National Acid Precipitation Assessment Program (NAPAP).

Coal-fired electricity-generating plants and smelters of colour metals are the largest sources of SO_x whose subsequent atmospheric oxidation generates sulphates; their long-range transport can affect ecosystems hundreds of km downwind. Effects of high acid deposition are usually seen first in surface waters. Aquatic acidification affects biota both directly and through its changes of soil and substrate chemistry, above all due to increased concentrations of aluminum and heavy metals. Chronic acidification dissolves aluminum hydroxide, a reaction which helps neutralize further pH declines but which puts large amounts of Al^{3+} (aluminium) into the water. These ions irritate fish gills and destroy their protective mucus. Acidification also mobilizes abnormally high levels of all heavy metals. Acid-sensitive organisms include fish (minnows, dace, lake and rainbow trout, and roach), many amphibians, gastropods, crustaceans, and invertebrates.

Forests, especially coniferous trees, are also at risk. During the early 1980s it appeared that an unequivocal causal link between acid deposition and large-scale deterioration of coniferous forests had been clearly established in Germany – but subsequent research revealed a much more complex reality, with acid deposition being just one of several contributing factors. Acid deposition also accelerates corrosion of metals (iron, steel, nickel-plated steel and zinc are most susceptible) and deterioration of limestone, marble, and mortar: among the thousands of affected structures the two most famous ones are the Parthenon and Taj Mahal. But prevailing levels of acid deposition in North America and Europe have not caused any measurable reductions of crop yields.

Because of the long-range transport combined with seasonally varying winds, most European countries are both sources and receptors of acidifying compounds. That is why the European SO_2 control strategy opted for virtually continent-wide uniform emission cuts rather than for an array of specific, and easily contestable, national quotas. For many years before the signing of a bilateral treaty in March 1991 acid deposition had been a highly contentious issue in US–Canadian relations.

Conversions from coal to cleaner fuels (above all to natural gas) and flue gas desulphurization have brought major cuts of SO_x emissions in both Europe and North America, and as a result many of the previously affected aquatic ecosystem on both continents have been recovering. At the same time, emissions of NO_x from large stationary sources as well as from transportation have been increasing steadily. The situation is very different in Asia, where modernizing economies are burning increasing amounts of **fossil fuels**. Large areas of **China** now have rains as acid as they used to be in Europe during the 1970s, and Chinese emissions are bringing acid deposition to South Korea and **Japan**; acid rains are now being also recorded in northern **India**.

Further reading

Firor, J. (1992) *The Changing Atmosphere*, New Haven, CT: Yale University Press.

Longhurst, J.W.S. (1991) *Acid Deposition: Origins, Impacts, and Abatement Strategies*, Berlin: Springer.

Smil, V. (1997) *Cycles of Life*, New York: Scientific American Library.

VACLAV SMIL

Aelvoet, Magda

b. 4 April 1944, Steenokkerzeel, Belgium

Politician

Magda Aelvoet has been a key figure in Belgian environmental politics since the late 1970s. She began her professional career in a series of development non-governmental organizations until 1985, when she joined government.

From 1979 onwards, she played a leading role in the process which led to the creation of the Flemish Green Party **Agalev** in 1982. She was elected to the Senate in 1985 and in 1987, and then to the House of Representatives in 1991. In 1994, she became an MEP and vice co-president, then co-president (in 1996) of the **Green Group in the European Parliament**.

Following the Greens' breakthrough in June 1999, she became the first Flemish green minister at the federal level, in charge of environment, public health and consumer affairs. From the outset, she has had to tackle difficult issues attracting strong media coverage, such as the management of the **dioxin** scandal (large-scale contamination of the food chain).

BENOÎT RIHOUX

African Green Parties, Federation of

The Federation of African Green Parties was set up in May 1998 during the third Congress of the African Green Co-Ordination (formally constituted in Niamey in 1994). It gathers about 20 parties from the African continent, with a majority of West African green parties. Its aim is to reinforce **democracy** and **sustainable development** in Africa, to develop co-operation among African green parties, to strengthen the co-operation with the American and the **European Federation of Green Parties** agreed in May and December 1998 respectively. Its delegates are regularly participating in Euro-African meetings financed mainly by the German Heinrich Böll Foundation, the Swedish Green Forum and the French Greens. Its activities have increased at the end of the 1990s with the electoral success of green parties in Burkina Faso (the first two African green ministers in November 1999) and Guinea-Bissau (one minister in February 2000).

See also: sub-Saharan Africa

CÉDRIC VAN DE WALLE

Agalev

Agalev is the Belgian Flemish-speaking green party (see **Belgium**). Along with its French-speaking counterpart **Ecolo**, it has become one of the most institutionalized and successful green parties worldwide.

The historical roots of *Agalev* can be traced back to a small Christian counter-cultural 'self-improvement' group, created in 1970 by a Jesuit priest in the Antwerp suburbs. From 1973 onwards, this group, called *Anders Gaan Leven* ('Live Differently'), began to be involved in protest actions in connection with environmental issues. In the process, some local sections as well as *Aktiegroepen* ('action groups') were set up.

At the 1974 parliamentary elections and the 1976 local elections, the movement chose to endorse 'green lists' of candidates running on the tickets of established parties. As this proved totally ineffective, the first lists under the *Agalev* name were fielded in the 1977 and 1978 elections. By then, an explicitly *political* group had been created within the movement, which began to attract more politics-orientated activists.

After a first encouraging result at the 1979 European elections (2.3 per cent), the real breakthrough occurred when the *Agalev* list (not yet a 'party') obtained 4 per cent and 3 national parliamentary seats at the November 1981 elections. Hence, there was strong structural pressure to create a real party (*Agalev*), formally separated from the movement, which was done in February 1982.

As *Ecolo*, *Agalev* institutionalized and professionalized rather quickly, making further progress at the 1985 and 1987 legislative elections (11 national parliamentary seats by then). An acceleration of this process took place from 1989 onwards, as the party continued its electoral development – though less spectacularly than *Ecolo* – in 1989 and 1991, and as the public financing of political parties increased significantly. Throughout the whole period, the party never experienced any major factional conflicts.

From April 1992 to July 1993, *Agalev* and *Ecolo* temporarily joined the ruling majority in order to support the country's institutional reforms (federalization) in Parliament. It was expected that the

Greens would obtain, in exchange, the introduction of **eco-taxes** on various products. However, as soon as the institutional reforms were passed, the eco-taxes were slowly but surely dismantled, a clear political defeat for the Greens. Partly as a result of this, *Agalev* suffered its first electoral setbacks, both in terms of percentage and seats, at the 1994 European and 1995 legislative elections. Unlike *Ecolo*, this did not cause any major factional conflicts, though three 'historical' leaders did leave the party and joined the Socialists or Christian Democrats in 1994 and 1995.

Following this more difficult period, quite similarly to *Ecolo*, but in a less spectacular way, *Agalev* was able to capitalize on the whole series of scandals and affairs which shook the country from 1996 onwards. It made a breakthrough at the June 1999 general (11.4 per cent; a total of 27 parliamentary seats at the federal and regional levels) and European (11.9 per cent, 2 seats) elections.

Hence, from July 1999 onwards, *Agalev* has joined a 'rainbow coalition' with Liberals and Socialists, both at the federal and regional levels (with *Ecolo* at the federal level, and with the Flemish regionalists in Flanders). Altogether, it has obtained 4 governmental positions covering a broad range of portfolios (mainly public health, consumer affairs, social affairs, environment, agriculture and third-world aid). This presence in power constitutes yet another stage of development for the party, implying quite a lot of challenges, in terms of internal organization, strategy and effective policy impact. *Agalev* has had to accept some compromises on which it had kept a high profile before the elections, stirring some unrest among its rank-and-file. The presence of green ministers during the 'rainbow' legislature has also been marked by quite a few striking initiatives and subsequent controversies.

See also: Ecolo

Further reading

Hooghe, M. and Rihoux, B. (2000) 'The Green Breakthrough in the Belgian General Elections of June 1999', *Environmental Politics* 9,3: 129–36.

Kitschelt, H. and Hellemans, S. (1990) *Beyond the European Left: Ideology and Political Action in the Belgian Ecology Parties*, Durham, NC and London: Duke University Press.

Rihoux, B. (1995) 'Belgium: Greens in a Divided Society', in D. Richardson and C. Rootes (eds) *The Green Challenge. The Development of Green Parties in Europe*, London: Routledge.

—— (1999) 'Agalev: la transformation inachevée d'un "parti-mouvement" en un parti de pouvoir', in P. Delwit and J-M. De Waele (eds) *Les partis verts en Europe*, Brussels: Editions Complexe.

—— (2000) 'Ecotaxes on the Belgian Agenda, 1992–5 and Beyond: Environment and Economy at the Heart of the Power Struggle', in S. Young (ed.) *The Emergence of Environmental Modernisation*, London: Routledge.

BENOÎT RIHOUX

Agarwal, Anil

b. 1948, India

Academic and environmentalist

Born in 1948, Anil Agarwal is one of the most influential environmentalists in **India**. Trained as a mechanical engineer, he founded the NGO Centre for Science and Environment (CSE) in Delhi in 1980. From that base, he published and continues to publish a series of 'Citizens' Reports on the State of India's Environment', and also videos and other materials originating from environmental groups and scientists around the country. The CSE defends the idea of community rights as the basis for sustainable resource management. Anil Agarwal also edits together with Sunita Narain, *Down to Earth*, a monthly periodical on environmental issues whose influence extends much farther than India. Anil Agarwal and Sunita Narain became well-known worldwide when one year before the so-called Earth Summit of 1992, they published a booklet, *Global Warming: A Case of Environmental Colonialism*, arguing for equal property rights on carbon sinks.

JOAN MARTINEZ-ALIER

Agenda 21

Agenda 21, signed at the United Nations Conference on Environment and Development (UNCED; see **Rio Conference 1992**), is perhaps the most thorough and ambitious attempt at the international level to specify what actions are necessary if development is to be reconciled with global environmental concerns. With its adoption by all the nations represented at UNCED, it is intended to guide nations towards sustainable development into the twenty-first century. However Agenda 21 is non-binding and has no legal status in international law.

The document is the result of long and protracted negotiations between virtually all political, social and economic interest groups in the run-up to UNCED and at the conference itself. The text is often contradictory because of the need to find compromises on controversial issues such as population control, reduction of **fossil fuel** usage and the nature of North–South debt. It is not surprising that the final text did not appear until September 1992 – four months after the Conference.

Agenda 21 consists of four sections. The first highlights the interconnectedness of environmental problems with social and economic issues such as poverty, health, trade, debt, consumption and population. The second stresses the need to manage physical resources such as land, seas, energy and wastes. The third section argues that the role of major social groups needs to be strengthened in decision-making processes. Partnership with women, indigenous populations, local authorities, non-governmental organizations (NGOs), workers and **labour/trade unions**, business and industry, scientists and farmers are all discussed. The final section focuses on the means of implementation, highlighting the role of governments and non-governmental agencies in funding and technical transfer.

The significance of Agenda 21 and the Rio process divides greens – some argue that it should be seen as an important turning point in the move towards more sustainable practices, others that it was simply 'greenwash'(see **greenwashing**) and that the UNCED actually subverted the **environ-**mental **movement** and reinforced existing political and economic relations.

Critics point to the fact that there were no firm and binding commitments on important issues such as debt, **structural adjustment programmes**, population (see **population movement and control**), and financial and technological transfer, and that fundamental questions about the structure of the capitalist system, the role of **multinational and transnational corporations** and global militarism were completely ignored (see **militarism and the environment**). There may be reference to consumption levels in Agenda 21, but there are no specific targets and action plans to actually reduce these levels in more economically prosperous nations. Contradictions abound in the text between the need for carefully planned change and the frequent celebration of the free market. This highlights the continued international domination of the North and the Bretton Woods institutions and the marginalization of alternative visions of development. One Third World diplomat famously remarked: 'What was unsaid at UNCED eclipsed what was said'.

Whilst not wishing to downplay the criticisms of Agenda 21, it is possible to find green principles embraced within the document, such as improved co-operation between states and other actors; the defence of equal rights, empowerment and education of individuals and communities; increasing the capacity of institutions to manage the changes that **sustainable development** requires; and the need for increased financial and technological assistance for the South. Even after such protracted negotiations, it is perhaps surprising to find such a strong theme of democratic renewal running through the document. At all levels of governance, local to international, the development of new institutional forms that increase participation by all major groups is taken to be fundamental. The third section of the document, 'Strengthening the Role of Major Groups' argues the case for the involvement and participation of all social groups within decision-making processes.

Agenda 21 has been a catalyst for activity at international, national and local level. In the wake of the Earth Summit, the United Nations

Commission on Sustainable Development (CSD) was established to monitor the implementation of Agenda 21. A number of national governments have responded to the commitments made at the Earth Summit, publishing sustainable development strategies and presenting evidence to the CSD (see **Department of the Environment, Transport and Regions**).

Chapter 28 of Agenda 21, 'Local Authorities' Initiatives in Support of Agenda 21' recognizes that as the level of governance closest to the people, local authorities will play a vital role in educating, mobilizing and engaging with the public in the promotion of sustainable development. Local authorities are called upon to 'enter into a dialogue with its citizens, local organizations and private companies and adopt "a local Agenda 21" '. The effect on localities has been mixed, with some local authorities, especially in the UK, embracing the opportunity that Local Agenda 21 offers as a restatement of the importance of local **democracy** to sustainable development.

See also: North/South divide

Further reading

Connelly, J. and Smith, G. (1999) *Politics and the Environment*, London: Routledge.

Lafferty, W.M. (ed.) (1999) *Implementing LA21 in Europe*, Oslo: ProSus.

O'Riordan, T. and Voissey, H. (1997) *Sustainable Development in Western Europe: Coming to Terms with Agenda 21*, London: Frank Cass.

URL: http://www.ecouncil.ac.cr/ (website of the Earth Council).

URL: http://www.iclei.org/ (website of International Council for Local Environmental Initiatives).

URL: http://www.igc.org/habitat/agenda21/ (full text of Agenda 21).

GRAHAM SMITH

agribusiness

Agribusiness is the integration of farming with upstream (inputs) and downstream (processing, distribution, sale and marketing) sectors. It is the culmi-

nation of the transformation of **agriculture** from a local activity of production and supply of food and fibre into a globalized vertically integrated industrial sector, the agro-food system, dominated by transnational corporations (TNCs) (see **multinational and transnational corporations**).

Occurring largely since the Second World War (WW2), this transformation was prefigured in the American 1930s 'New Deal' programme; the USA has remained the driver of agricultural restructuring followed by other northern nations. WW2 saw the state take control of agriculture, aiming to increase production and provide food security. State-sponsored 'productivism' persisted after the war, including: subsidies for agricultural expansion, intensification through introduction of new mechanical and chemical inputs; research and development; and planning policies to facilitate spatial reconstruction of farmlands – larger fields, centralized storage facilities, and increased livestock stocking densities. The countryside provided a non-proletarianized labour supply – an unspoken 'social contract' with the state. This regime provided ideal opportunities for the growth of firms specializing in new agricultural technologies and in processing and distribution. Since the 1970s, such firms have merged into larger, more powerful conglomerates, increasingly able to direct agricultural change. Control of the agro-food system became concentrated with a few TNCs, e.g., Nestlé (processed foods), Cargill (trade, transport and distribution) and DuPont (agro-chemicals, biotech, packaging).

Northern agriculture has evolved a dual structure. On the one hand are large industrial farms, tied to upstream suppliers through a 'technological treadmill' of dependency on changing chemical technologies, partial advice and training, and credit, supplied by TNCs; this replacement of what was provided by separate farming activities with technological inputs is called 'appropriation'. Downstream, farmers are often tied to processors and distributors by 'contract farming', whereby the entire production of a farm is sold in advance to a firm, which will 'add value' to the product through processing and packaging; this is known as 'substitution'. These vast farms are often subsidized by the state through policies like the EU **Common Agricultural Policy** and employ fewer permanent farmers, although certain agribusiness sectors (e.g., soft fruit) rely on large numbers of low-paid casual workers. On the other hand peasant agriculture and traditional family farms are left struggling to survive. The inputs needed to increase productivity are either too expensive, leading to stagnant yields or indebtedness, or inappropriate to geophysical surroundings. Their former markets are captured by contract-produced processed food sold through supermarkets.

Concurrent social changes, such as increased female employment and higher earnings, increased consumption of food products, and domestic freezer technology, speeded the commoditization of food and the differentiation of food types and brands. Rising consumer expectation and sophisticated marketing demanded year-round supplies of fresh produce, necessitating energy- and chemical-intensive glasshouse cultivation, and restructuring of agriculture in peripheral northern regions and **less developed countries** (LDCs).

The export of the northern agribusiness model to LDCs via credit-funded technological transfer and aid money forced peasants into low-wage agricultural labour, into city-edge slums, or onto marginal lands making hunger ever-present while national production was increasing; and contributed to the destruction of fragile ecosystems, such as **rainforests**. Dependency on the North increased with the **green revolution**, which introduced fast-growing, high-yield and more chemical-resistant seed varieties, supplied by TNCs.

The net result of these rapid and mutually reinforcing global processes of technological, social, economic and political change, has been huge increases in food output world-wide, but inequitable distribution. Agribusiness has also broken agriculture from dependence on natural cycles, **biotechnology** accentuating this trend; TNCs are increasingly able to control the foundations of agriculture through patenting of plant and animal varieties. Agro-chemicals have polluted water, and reduced **biodiversity** in field-edge ecosystems; despite the banning of the most toxic, notably **DDT**, in the North, they remain in use elsewhere. Longer supply chains have generated increased transport and related pollution and disturbance.

The creation of larger fields has caused soil erosion. **Factory farming** has led to pollution from slurries and greenhouse gases, and unethical treatment of animals. 'Food scares' have also proliferated, where agribusiness has produced health risks for consumers.

See also: agriculture; factory farming; food quality, politics of; land reform; landscape; organic farming

Further reading

Goodman, D. and Redclift, M. (1991) *Refashioning Nature: Food, Ecology and Culture*, London: Routledge.

McMichael, P. (ed.) (1994) *The Global Restructuring of Agro-Food Systems*, Ithaca, NY: Cornell University Press.

The Ecologist (1996) Special Issue: 'Food Insecurity: Who Gets to Eat?' 26,6: 243–316.

Ward, N. and Almås, R. (1997) 'Explaining Change in the International Agro-Food System', *Review of International Political Economy*, 4,4: 611–29.

DAVID WOOD

agriculture

Including crop and livestock farming, grazing, horticulture and silviculture, agriculture constitutes the most extensive human use of the Earth's landmass. Prior to the twentieth century, environmental politics were almost exclusively dominated by debates over agriculture and agricultural land use. Although the negative effects of overgrazing and soil-depleting crop farming have been known since antiquity, environmental impacts of agricultural production were not a prominent focus of political concern throughout most of human history.

Two competing themes occur in controversy over agricultural land uses. *Agrarians* argue that agriculture has moral and political significance beyond mere food production. *Modernizers* hold that agriculture is but one economic sector among many, and that like any sector, agriculture should be regulated to promote efficient food production.

For much of European history, these themes co-existed, and even complemented one another. In the twentieth century they became competitors, especially with respect to the role of environmental factors.

Agrarianism is evident in the political writings of Plato and Aristotle. Because tree and vine crops represent a lifetime investment of labour and capital, landowning agrarians had a great personal stake in protecting their farms from interlopers. They became the backbone of Athens' military power and government. As Athens grew in sea power, trade brought new sources of wealth to the city, but also a call to extend the right of citizenship to merchants. Agrarians argued that traders would be inclined to expend the city's wealth on opportunistic schemes, and would leave when resources were exhausted. The argument was the basis for the belief that farmers make the best citizens.

Agrarian themes were especially evident in the early days of political economy. In England, James Harrington's *Oceana* (1656) argued that military power depended on a robust farming population. In France, Montesquieu's *De l'Esprit des Lois* (1748) argued that soil and climate are determinants of national character. In Scotland, Adam Smith and Ferguson theorized a history of political institutions based on the transition from hunting to grazing, then to farming and finally the industrial state. The physiocrats argued that agriculture was the sole basis of new wealth and called for a reform of the French tax system, which discouraged the use of new farming technologies. In the USA, Thomas **Jefferson** argued for policies that would favour agricultural development over manufacturing.

English **enclosure** was the most hotly contested of all agricultural issues during the formative period of political economy. Common pastures and small land holdings were confiscated, consolidated and given over to more intensive production practices. Enclosure was vigorously opposed by Gerrard Winstanley who led political protests and published an agrarian tract entitled *The Law of Freedom in a Platform* (1652), and a century later by George Ogilvie, who continued the argument in *Essay on the Right of Property in Land* (1782). Enclosure was defended by John Locke,

whose *Second Treatise of Government* (1689) states: '[H]e that encloses land, and has a greater plenty of the conveniences of life from ten acres, than he could have from an hundred left nature, may truly be said to give 90 acres to mankind'. During a second period of enclosure Arthur Young's *Annals of Agriculture* (1784) extolled all manner of increase in agricultural production. Locke and Young sounded the call for enclosure in the name of modernization (though Young recanted his former praise of enclosure during his declining years).

These debates were formative for environmental politics that emerged centuries later. They laid down many of the basic terms for political debate about private property, and especially property in land. In tying the property right to efficient use, Locke implicitly linked his theory of property to the cause of modernization. The agrarians held that land and agriculture support a nexus of reciprocal relationships, and that this balance of interests underwrites the integrity and legitimization of the rural community. On the agrarian view, **property rights** presumed duties to aid others and to use the land according to principles of stewardship.

Karl Marx is sometimes read as expressing admiration for the moral economy of agrarian societies. Whether that interpretation can be sustained or not, there is no doubt that Marx was among the first to appreciate the environmental consequences of modernization and the capital-intensive technologies it spawned. Volume I of *Capital* includes numerous references to farming, while volume III returns with an extended discussion of soil fertility and its likely fate in a capitalist agriculture (see **capitalism**).

By the twentieth century, agrarian claims about the moral and spiritual superiority of rural folk were allied with a form of social conservatism in the national politics of European and North American states. Max Weber castigated the agrarian leagues in Germany as the antithesis of liberalism, pointing to English agriculture as the model for a rational state (see **liberalism/ liberal democracy**). A. Whitney Griswold's *Farming and Democracy* (1948) offered a comparative analysis of agrarian rhetoric and national development in the USA, England and France. Griswold quotes an unnamed British Minister of Agriculture approvingly: 'Some say that agriculture is necessary for security, others that agriculture is a way of life; more still that the countryside must be preserved, because it breeds healthy and virile manhood. For my part I believe that the test by which agriculture must stand or fall is the job which it is its primary function to perform, that is the production of food economically and as efficiently as possible' (1948: 83).

Modernization and the industrial sector view of agriculture became dominant during a time when provincialism, racism and xenophobia of agrarian movements were allied with the twentieth century's most repressive political movements. Yet large industrial farming interests were never slow in their appeal to agrarian sentiments when seeking government subsidies. The obvious cynicism with which agrarian rhetoric came to be used discredited the agrarian tradition further, especially in North America. Any linking of agriculture to moral or political virtue continues to be derided by liberals as 'agrarian fundamentalism'.

Agriculture's engagement with environmental politics has been shaped by the rise of the modernisers' industrial sector model of agriculture, as well as by neoliberal conceptions of private property. As would be the case with any industrial sector, environmental problems such as pollution and resource pollution will be analysed as external costs – costs borne not by producers but by society as a whole. The goal of liberal environmental politics is to require that these costs be contained through regulation or incentive payments. Liberal environmental politics does not question the overall goal of efficiency, but merely demands that environmental costs be accounted for in determining whether a particular mode of agriculture is indeed efficient.

There is little doubt that industrial agriculture has lived up to the image of a polluting industry. Efficient production has reduced food costs worldwide, but industrial farming methods are beset with environmental **externalities**. Rachel **Carson**'s *Silent Spring* (1962), the book sometimes credited with starting the environmental movement, lists a host of environmental insults associated with agricultural **pesticides**. Chemical fertilizers contaminate surface water. Mechanization has been

tied to soil loss worldwide, and large animal production units concentrate animal waste in holding facilities that are both offensive and vulnerable to catastrophic (if mostly local and temporary) forms of environmental pollution. Furthermore, preservationism and **eco-centrism** within **environmental movements** can conspire with industrial efficiency model of agriculture in an ironic way. If the primary goal of the environmental movement is to set aside as much land as possible for wild nature, it follows that the lands used for food and fibre production must be farmed as intensively as possible.

Agricultural politics are deeply influenced by local history and culture. Nevertheless, the contrast between agrarian and industrial efficiency approaches to agricultural policy has influenced agriculture world wide. European colonies tended toward modernization of export crops, and did not organize subsistence production to seek democratic or environmentally sustainable goals. The **green revolution**, a large agricultural development project launched by the Rockefeller Foundation in the late 1940s, aimed to bring the technology of industrial agriculture to the developing world. It was criticized for causing the collapse of local community institutions.

As the twentieth century drew to a close, two developments augur a shift in the environmental politics of agriculture. One is widespread opposition to the use of **biotechnology** to genetically engineer new plant and animal varieties. The second is the gradual rise of sustainable agriculture. Both movements are committed to an environmentally sound agriculture and challenge the modernizer's idea that agriculture is inherently incompatible with environment. Rather than pursuing the regulation of agriculture, advocates of sustainable agriculture dedicated themselves to the establishment of environment-friendly farming practices and public policies. However, many environmental groups do not readily embrace advocates of agricultural reform, in part because their neo-agrarian rhetoric continues to seem anti-liberal and deeply problematic. Thus the political contest between agrarian and modernizing visions of agriculture continues.

See also: eco-centrism; environmental ethics;

environmental management; environmental movements; genetic engineering, animals; genetic engineering, crops; sustainable development

Further reading

Browne, W.P. (1988) *Private Interests, Public Policy and American Agriculture*, Lawrence, KS: University of Kansas Press.

Council on Agricultural Science and Technology (CAST), 4420 West Lincoln Way, Ames, IA 50014–3447, USA. URL: http://www.cast-science.org.

Montmarquet, James A. (1989) *The Idea of Agrarianism: From Hunter–Gatherer to Agrarian Radical in Western Culture*, Moscow, ID: University of Idaho Press.

Thompson, Paul B. (1995) *The Spirit of the Soil: Agriculture and Environmental Ethics*, London: Routledge.

Thompson, Paul B. and Stout, Bill A. (eds) (1991) *Beyond the Large Farm*, Boulder, CO: Westview Press.

Worldwatch Institute, 1776 Massachusetts Ave. NW, Washington, DC, 20036–1904, USA.
URL: http//www.worldwatch.org (various reports on agriculture and environment).

PAUL B. THOMPSON

agroecology

Agroecology, as a science, studies agro-ecosystems: the flow of nutrients and water, the interplay between agricultural and 'wild' **biodiversity**. The word refers also to a movement which favours 'low-input' **agriculture**, composting of waste, pest management based on insects rather than chemicals. In Europe and the USA, this is a neo-rural movement which started in the 1960s and 1970s, with roots in the 1920s ('biodynamic' agriculture). However, in the world at large there are still hundreds of millions of agroecologists. Movements for peasant agroecology are increasing, with help from northern academics (Miguel Altieri, Steve Gliessman) and activists (RAFI, GRAIN). This is not so new, Albert Howard's 'Agricultural Testament' of 1948, a bible of Agroecology, was inspired by knowledge acquired in **India**. The claim for

Farmers' Rights (recognition and payment for *in situ* co-evolution of agricultural biodiversity) is part of the agroecology movement, as in the late 1990s also the campaigns against Monsanto, Novartis, Cargill and other 'seed' multinationals.

JOAN MARTINEZ-ALIER

air pollution

Air pollution results from excessive concentrations of various gases or aerosols (liquid or solid airborne particulate matter) emitted either from natural sources or from human activities. Volcanic eruptions, wind erosion of soils, desert storms, and wildfires are the largest natural sources of particulate matter (PM). Some volcanoes also release large amounts of sulphur dioxide (SO_2) and wildfires produce plenty of carbon monoxide (CO) and nitrogen oxides (NO and NO_2, commonly labelled NO_x). Some forests are large sources of volatile organic compounds (VOC), and bacterial metabolism produces numerous gases, above all methane, NO_x, hydrogen sulphide, and dimethylsulphide. However, only large volcanic eruptions, major wildfires and intensive dust storms generate high ground-level concentrations of natural air pollution. Normally, VOC from some forests cause only locally or regionally reduced visibility, and most biogenic gases are present in the atmosphere only in trace amounts.

Anthropogenic air pollutants in preindustrial societies were primarily emitted from inefficient combustion of biomass (woody and crop residues), and later coal, in households and in small manufactures, and from deliberate burning of forests and grasslands. The latter practice continues in many tropical regions, resulting in recurrent, and often prolonged, episodes of very high levels of air pollutants blanketing large areas (most notably in **Brazil**, in parts of **sub-Saharan Africa** and in **Indonesia**).

Coal combustion was the largest source of anthropogenic air pollutants in all industrializing countries of Europe and in North America, and it still holds this primacy in **China** where the fuel supplies more than 70 per cent of all commercial energy. PM and SO_2 are the two most objectionable pollutants that are released during coal combustion in large quantities. Combination of their high levels creates the classical (London-type) smog marked by greatly reduced visibility (particularly in areas of high humidity), higher frequency of respiratory ailments and, during the most severe episodes (as in London in 1952 or in New York in 1966), by increased mortality of sensitive individuals (infants and elderly with chronic lung and cardiovascular diseases).

Worldwide substitution of coal by hydrocarbons (liquid fuels produced by refining of crude oils and natural gases) has helped to lower emissions of PM and SO_2, but it has resulted in rising emissions of NO_x (above all from efficient high-temperature combustion in electricity-generating plants and in internal combustion engines), CO (mainly from inefficient combustion in motor vehicles), and VOC. Atmospheric oxidation of SO_2 and NO_x produces sulphates and nitrates which are responsible for **acid rain**. In all permanently or seasonally sunny regions emissions of NO_x, CO and VOC undergo a complex sequence of atmospheric reactions producing photochemical smog. Ozone (O_3), an aggressive, cell-damaging oxidant, is one of the main products of these photochemical reactions. High O_3 levels are responsible for higher incidence of asthma, emphysema and bronchitis, for reduced yields of many crops (wheat, corn, soybeans), and for damage to forests and materials (particularly to rubber and synthetics).

Coal-derived PM from large sources can be effectively controlled by electrostatic precipitators which can be up to 99.9 per cent efficient – but they still leave behind particles smaller than 10 m which are most likely to reach lungs and to cause chronic damage. SO_2 from large sources can be removed by flue gas desulphurization, but this expensive process is used widely only in the world's richest nations. Air pollution from vehicles can be controlled by catalytic convertors that remove all but small fractions of generated CO, NO_x and hydrocarbons. However, growing numbers of vehicles and longer travel distances mean that the most polluted regions have not been able to clean up their air, merely to prevent further rapid deterioration of their air quality. Expansion of megacities and higher density and intensity of urban traffic have created regional, rather than merely local, air pollution problems.

Most of the air pollution research and regulatory and control efforts during the twentieth century have been concentrated on outdoor pollutants; only recently have we come to appreciate that indoor air pollution poses health risks that are often much higher than those of outdoor air. Indoor air pollution is particularly acute in rural areas of Africa, Latin America and Asia where low-efficiency combustion of biomass fuels in poorly ventilated rooms results in very high levels of fine PM and carcinogenic organic compounds, and hence in high prevalence of chronic respiratory diseases. Even many modern air-conditioned buildings have considerable air pollution problems due to inadequate air exchange and build-up of emissions from chemicals used in construction, carpeting and furniture.

See also: Clean Air Act

Further reading

Arya, S.P. (1998) *Air Pollution Meteorology and Dispersion*, New York: Oxford University Press.

Boubel, R.W. *et al.* (1994) *Fundamentals of Air Pollution*, San Diego: Academic Press.

Lipfert, F.W. (1997) *Air Pollution and Community Health*, New York: John Wiley.

Warner, C.F. *et al.* (1997) *Air Pollution: Its Origin and Control*, Menlo Park, CA: Addison-Wesley.

VACLAV SMIL

air transportation and infrastructure

Since 1960, world passenger air travel has grown at an average of 9 per cent and air freight at 11 per cent each year. Between 1995 and 2015, the British Government expects the passenger numbers passing through UK airports to rise by between 87 and 192 per cent.

This prediction suggests that London airports alone will need extra capacity to cater for 100 million more passengers by 2015, as many as already use Heathrow, Gatwick, Stansted and Luton combined each year. An extra 79 million passengers – five times the current throughput of Manchester Airport – are expected to use regional airports by the same year. As a consequence, major expansions are underway and planned to all of Britain's international and regional airports. These are often strongly opposed, not only because of the land they take up – the paved area of Heathrow Airport is equivalent to 200 miles of three-lane motorway – but also due to the impacts of associated developments and traffic generation effects.

Noise is another long-established concern. In the UK, aviation is the second most widespread form of noise disturbance, found at 62 per cent of sites (compared to 92 per cent of sites for road and 15 per cent for rail). Complaints of aircraft noise made to Environmental Health Officers rose six-fold between 1984/5 and 1994/5.

At the global level, aviation is the fastest growing source of carbon dioxide (CO_2) emissions. Currently, aircraft generate 3.5 per cent of global CO_2, a figure predicted to rise to 14 per cent by 2050. But, this is only half of air transport's climate change impacts. Flying aircraft are responsible for 60 per cent of the NO_x found in the ozone layer, as well as several secondary products that help damage it. Despite this, emissions from international air travel are excluded from the Kyoto Climate Change Convention because they cannot be easily allocated to a specific country (see **Kyoto Conference/Protocol**). More locally, aircraft use a large amount of fuel upon takeoff and in the vicinity of major airports this can be the major source of NO_x, Volatile Organic Compounds, and Particulates (see **air pollution**).

To date, unlike with road travel, attempts to reduce the environmental problems of air travel have merely accepted the rapid growth in demand. While the use of quieter turbofan engines has significantly reduced noise levels and although the fuel consumption per passenger/kilometre is half that of 20 years ago, these improvements have been insufficient to match the rise in the amount of air travel and so emissions and places affected by noise have risen. Furthermore, though there could be some gains from introducing 600-seater super-jumbo jets, further major improvements in fuel economy are not envisaged. Changes to air traffic control with a more direct routing of flights could cut fuel use and flying more slowly would also improve fuel economy, if it were acceptable. The ozone problem could also be mitigated were aircraft to fly lower and avoid sensitive polar areas, but fuel consumption would rise.

The root of the overall problems is that air travel, like road transport, does not cover its external environmental costs and is thus priced lower than its true cost. Indeed, the situation is worse than for road transport as fuel for aircraft is not taxed. To do so would require an international agreement: these at the moment tend to focus on competition and deregulation issues, which increase demand for air travel and cut prices further. Although some countries like the UK have introduced airport departure taxes, these have been opposed by the air industry and are at too low a level to have a demand management effective.

Developing alternatives to short-haul air trips has been advocated. The most obvious alternative is high-speed trains which, running at 300–350km/h, can be competitive with air for up to 1,000km. However, on their own all that such developments do is to expand the travel market for both rail and air. For example, although Eurostar now holds two-thirds of the London–Paris and 45 per cent of the London–Brussels market, its main effect has been to increase travel between these cities. Thus energy use and emissions have grown.

Overall air transport represents one of the most disturbing and intractable environmental challenges, and is one that is the most hidden or ignored.

Further reading

Friends of the Earth (2000) *Plane Crazy*, Friends of the Earth, Atmosphere and Transport.

Pearce, F. (1998) 'Air on a Green String', *Green Futures*, March/April, pp. 35–6.

MARCUS ENOCH AND STEPHEN POTTER

Alarm UK

Alarm UK was an organization that developed out of ALARM (All London Against the Road Menace), an alliance of local residents' associations, environmental organizations and public transport pressure groups that campaigned against 1988 road plans for London. To join, groups were required to campaign against all new road schemes in London rather than just the one in their particular area. Alarm UK was launched in 1991 as a national umbrella body operating on the same principle. Its main function was to provide a co-ordinating support network supplying technical information, tactical advice and human and material resources for local groups opposing new road-building schemes announced in the Thatcher government's *Roads for Prosperity* programme. Alarm UK had a decentralized structure that allowed affiliated groups autonomy of action and it supported direct action as well as procedural challenges such as the fighting of public inquiries.

See also: anti-roads movement

BENJAMIN SEEL

Alliance of Small Island States

The Alliance of Small Island States (known as AOSIS) was formed in 1990 at the Second World Climate Conference in Geneva, led by the President of the Maldives. It is an alliance of states which are particularly vulnerable to one of the main impacts of **global warming**, sea-level rise. For some of these states, such as the Maldives or Kiribati, sea-level rise threatens their very existence. The Alliance has consistently proposed the most ambitious cuts in carbon dioxide emissions, and also an insurance fund to compensate those most adversely affected by the impacts of global warming.

MATTHEW PATERSON

Amazonia

Amazonia is a tropical region of South America occupying approximately 6 million square kilometres, one-third of the total area of the continent. It is named after mythical women warriors of European lore and is defined geographically as the watershed of the Amazon River, the world's second

longest river and greatest single source of fresh water. While half this region lies within **Brazil**, the river itself rises in Colombia as the Rio Negro, and in Peru as the Rio Solomões, which together form the Rio Amazonas. Amazonia further extends into Bolivia, Venezuela, and Ecuador. The region supports over half the world's remaining tropical **rainforests** and, by some estimates, over half the earth's terrestrial **biodiversity**. It has been sparsely occupied by **indigenous peoples** for several thousand years and has become the destination of growing numbers of homesteaders since the early 1970s.

See also: biopiracy/bioprospecting; forest management; Mendes, Chico; World Bank

PAUL CHANDLER

anarchism/eco-anarchism

Ecological politics burst onto the scene in the late 1960s – a period when anarchism enjoyed a major revival of interest. It is not surprising, then, that much of the impetus and original shaping of environmental political thought came from eco-anarchists. And eco-anarchism remains a hugely important strand within present-day political ecology.

Anarchists value anarchy; and the word 'anarchy' derives from the Greek for 'without rule'. In other words, anarchists value a society that is literally without rulers. As 'without rule' is not cognate with 'without rules', most anarchist theorists consider it a mistake to confuse 'anarchy' either with 'chaos' or with 'anything goes'. In other words, upon closer inspection, anarchism turns out to be very different to how it tends to be caricatured by its opponents or to how it is portrayed in popular stereotypes.

How, then, might 'anarchism' be best construed? Anarchism is a political philosophy which holds that a condition of anarchy is preferable to one 'with rule'. How, then, might we best construe 'anarchy'. Perfect anarchy would appear to be a condition of perfect political equality – in other words, a situation where political power is equally distributed. Anarchism is, therefore, perhaps best viewed as a variety of political egalitarianism.

However, many would not unreasonably regard perfect political equality as unfeasible. But political egalitarianism need not be so extreme. Rather, we might better think of political egalitarianism as the normative opposition to certain substantive inequalities in the exercise of political power, without assuming that perfect political equality could ever be attained. But many who would not regard themselves as anarchists would also view themselves as political egalitarians, so construed. What would distinguish anarchists from others is the additional empirical belief that the significant political inequalities that ought to be opposed are, in the modern world, generated by, embedded within or sustained by the state.

Thus modern-day anarchists principally oppose the state. They believe that a stateless society is both possible and preferable to a state-dominated one. Most anarchist thinkers would also insist that this does not entail a lack of co-ordination nor a complete lack of services presently supplied by the state. Anarchists frequently point out that stateless societies have lived in harmony (and in harmony with nature) for millennia. Moreover, anarchists often point out that many of the services currently provided by the state have been provided effectively by very different groupings or institutions to the state, many of them informal. It is the coercive nature of the state that anarchists most oppose. And, anarchists frequently argue, many of the welfare functions of a modern state can quite conceivably be provided without being incorporated into a coercive, militaristic system, such as states have at their core.

Anarchists also usually hold specific views about the route that would need to be taken towards an anarchist society. Most anarchists argue against authoritarian Marxists that neither a Leninist vanguard party nor a 'transitional state', such as the dictatorship of the proletariat, could be deployed effectively to bring about a politically and economically egalitarian society. Most anarchists hold that a political vanguard would soon turn into a new state, and that a so-called 'transitional' state would eventually consolidate its power and would not relinquish it.

Eco-anarchism is one of the many variants of anarchism. Eco-anarchists claim that there is some important connection between the state and environmental problems, and see an anarchist society as the most likely solution to them. For example, one eco-anarchist theory runs as follows: States are usually in military competition with some other state. In order to remain militarily competitive, they must continually develop their military capacity. But this demands technological development that fits the needs of military development (for example, nuclear power stations to provide the raw materials for nuclear weapons). It also demands a highly productive technology to generate the surplus the state needs to acquire in order to pay for its military needs. This means that states have an interest in choosing and then stabilizing economic systems that are as efficient as possible at generating a high surplus and at producing the innovative technology that is especially suited to its ever-growing military requirements. Such a theoretical perspective, in placing the primary emphasis on the state, has been labelled 'the State-Primacy Theory'. And this has been argued to cash out into 'an environmentally hazardous dynamic', for the highly productive economy which the state requires and the kind of **technology** it needs to be developed are bound to be resource- and energy-consumptive in the extreme, as well as highly polluting. Hence, on this variety of eco-anarchism, the state is viewed as being centrally implicated within the major environmental problems that we face, and a necessary condition for solving those problems is therefore argued to be some form of stateless society.

See also: Bookchin, Murray; capitalism; green political theory; social ecology

Further reading

Bookchin, M. (1974) *Post-Scarcity Anarchism*, London: Wildwood House.
—— (1980) *Toward an Ecological Society*, Montreal: Black Rose.
Carter, A. (1999) *A Radical Green Political Theory*, London: Routledge.
Marshall, P. (1993) *Demanding the Impossible: A History of Anarchism*, London: Fontana.

Taylor, M. (1982) *Community, Anarchy and Liberty*, Cambridge: Cambridge University Press.

ALAN CARTER

animal rights

Animal rights as both an idea and a social movement dates back to the nineteenth century, but is particularly associated with developments that have occurred since the 1960s. Animal rights can be distinguished from animal welfare by its espousal of the moral equivalence between humans and at least some non-humans. As a result, the animal rights movement seeks the abolition, as opposed to the regulation, of vivisection and the raising and killing of animals for food. While the animal rights movement is not synonymous with illegality and direct action, some activists regard the moral imperatives as so compelling that they are prepared to engage in such tactics, usually under the umbrella of the Animal Liberation Front (ALF).

The concept of animal rights is not entirely a modern phenomenon. The rights of animals were proclaimed by the little known nineteenth century thinker Henry Salt and mainstream British political theorists such as Jeremy Bentham and John Stuart **Mill** entertained the idea of increasing the moral status of animals (Clarke and Linzey, 1990). Abolitionist anti-vivisection organizations had emerged in both Britain and the USA by 1900. However, it was not until the 1960s and 1970s in Britain, and slightly later in the USA, that the theory and practice of animal rights became prominent. These two decades saw the creation of a number of new animal rights-based groups – such as Animal Aid – the revitalization of the existing anti-vivisection organizations and a sustained, and to some degree successful, attempt by animal rights activists to radicalize that bastion of moderate welfarism, the Royal Society for the Prevention of Cruelty to Animals (Garner, 1993). A remarkably similar pattern occurred in the USA where the animal rights baton was carried in particular by an organization called People for the Ethical Treatment of Animals (Jasper and Nelkin, 1992).

One cause and effect of the rise of a reinvigorated animal rights movement has been the interest shown in the subject by a new generation of academic philosophers. There are two key distinctions in the realm of ideas. The first is between, on the one hand, advocates of animal welfare and, on the other, advocates of the view that animals should be given a much higher moral status. The second concerns the *type* of moral theory employed once it is accepted that at least some animals have a moral status more or less equivalent to humans. The major distinction in this latter category is between the rights-based approach of philosophers such as Tom Regan (1984) and the utilitarian argument for animal liberation provided by Peter **Singer** (1990).

Since the first distinction identified above has been of much greater relevance in informing political practice, it is worthwhile exploring it in more detail. There are very few thinkers who would want to argue that humans have no moral obligations towards animals. Most now accept that animals have, at the very least, sentiency – the capacity to experience pleasure and pain – and therefore it is accepted that what is done to them matters to them directly. Accepting that animals have moral standing, however, is not equivalent to moral equality and, for animal welfarists, greater moral weight should be accorded to humans because of our greater intellectual capacities, described collectively as full-personhood, moral agency or autonomy. As a result, it is argued, we are entitled to exploit animals for our purposes but only if the benefits are regarded as non-trivial and if animals are treated as humanely as possible in the process.

What is regarded as 'non-trivial', of course, will be a matter of opinion, and this explains why there is a *politics* of animal welfare. As a result it is not necessary to establish that animals have rights to justify many improvements in the way they are treated. For example, the end of cosmetic testing in Britain can be and, for many, was, justified on the grounds that inflicting suffering on animals in order to test the safety of yet another lipstick or eye-shadow is illegitimate because trivial. For most, on the other hand, inflicting suffering on animals in medical research, if there is a realistic expectation of some significant benefit for humans and/or other animals, remains legitimate.

Ideas have played a central role in the development of the animal protection movement, determining not only objectives but also, to some degree, strategy. If one perceives that animals have rights then their routine exploitation becomes a fundamental injustice requiring urgent remedies. As a reflection of this, the animal rights movement is associated with intensive grassroots activism in general and an, albeit small, part of the movement is prepared to engage in various forms of direct action, typically under the auspices of the ALF. The roots of the ALF date back to the late 1960s when a faction in the Hunt Saboteurs Association, disillusioned by the limited impact of non-violent civil disobedience, broke away and began engaging in more extreme types of direct action. This group, under the leadership of Ronnie Lee, renamed itself the Band of Mercy in 1972 and, four years later, became the ALF.

There are now versions of the ALF in many different countries. In Britain, ALF 'cells' have been responsible for thousands of actions, ranging from small-scale damage inflicted on butchers, meat wholesalers and furriers, laboratory break-ins where equipment may be destroyed, information taken and the animals released and, at the other end of the spectrum, the use of car bombs and incendiary devices. Estimates of the ALF's membership vary from 250 to 2,500 but it is clear that only a tiny proportion of activists are willing to engage in illegal activities and the more extreme forms are the responsibility of a handful of people. What can be said is that some of the most vehement opponents of the ALF can be found in the leadership of the animal rights movement and most animal rights activity is of the traditional law-abiding variety characteristic of cause groups.

A number of factors have to be considered in an assessment of the degree to which direct action in pursuit of animal liberation is justified. A preliminary question concerns the utility of direct action. Here, it is necessary to consider issues such as the effect of direct action on the behaviour of those targeted, as well as public opinion and, in turn, politicians (Garner, 1998). In general, parti-

cularly in Britain, direct action would not seem to have affected negatively the public's attitude to animal issues, although this would undoubtedly change if a human fatality were to occur as a result of an ALF action. On the positive side, ALF laboratory raids have been invaluable sources of information on the vivisection industry and, as in the case of the raid on the head-injury laboratory at the University of Pennsylvania in 1985 which uncovered appalling cruelties inflicted on non-human primates, can have an immediate and dramatic public and political impact (Blum, 1994).

Three additional questions suggest themselves. First is the nature of the direct action. There is clearly a significant moral and political difference between relatively innocuous activities such as sit-ins and trespass even when it involves minor criminal damage, on the one hand, and actions that threaten human life on the other. A second consideration is the nature of the political system within which the direct action has taken place. Bypassing the normal channels of decision-making becomes more appropriate if those channels do not give a fair hearing to a particular interest. Rightly or wrongly, it is common for animal rights activists to complain that the institutional exploiters of animals – the medical and scientific establishment, the pharmaceutical industry and agribusiness interests – operate a blocking veto preventing the introduction of animal protection measures which will damage their interests.

Finally, of crucial importance, in explaining both the willingness of animal rights activists to undertake direct action and their case for doing so, is the moral dimension. An acceptance of the position that, at least some, animals have a moral status equivalent to humans makes our infringement of their fundamental interests an issue that overrides the democratic niceties of majority rule. Indeed, there is a strong case for arguing that, if one accepts the moral equality of humans and animals, then a democratic polity demands the protection of the rights of the latter as much as those of the former.

See also: agribusiness; environmental ethics; green political theory; non-violent direct action; Singer, Peter; vegetarianism

References

Blum, D. (1994) *The Monkey Wars*, New York: Oxford University Press.

Clarke, P. and Linzey, A. (eds) (1990) *Political Theory and Animal Rights*, London: Pluto Press.

Garner, R. (1993) *Animals, Politics and Morality*, Manchester: Manchester University Press.

—— (1998) 'Defending Animal Rights', *Parliamentary Affairs*, 51, 3: 458–69.

Jasper, J. and Nelkin, D. (1992) *The Animal Rights Crusade*, New York, Free Press.

Regan, T. (1984) *The Case for Animal Rights*, London: Routledge.

Singer, P. (1990) *Animal Liberation*, London: Cape, 2nd edn.

Further reading

Garner, R. (1998) *Political Animals: Animal Protection Politics in Britain and the United States*, Basingstoke: Macmillan.

Ryder, R. (2000) *Animal Revolution*, Oxford: Berg.

ROBERT GARNER

Antarctica

Public interest in the Antarctic continent has grown since the mid-1980s in response to scientific research conducted there concerning stratospheric **ozone depletion** and the increasingly stark evidence of the effects of global climate change in Antarctica. On the international diplomatic level, the 'Question of Antarctica' featured regularly on the agenda of UN General Assembly sessions from the mid-1980s until the early 1990s, reflecting the political controversy which embroiled the existing arrangements for the governance of the continent in the wake of closed negotiations over the future exploration and exploitation of Antarctica's non-renewable resource potential.

The origins of these arrangements lay in the fear of a 'fatal collision' over conflicting sovereignty claims in Antarctica in the 1950s, at which time twelve states undertook scientific research in the continent, seven of which had already made territorial claims there. Entering into force in 1961, the 1959 Antarctic Treaty signed by these twelve states revolved around a *modus vivendi* on the sovereignty question, whereby existing territorial claims were 'frozen' for the Treaty's duration, without prejudice to the right of the non-claimant states to make a claim themselves should the Treaty be abandoned. The Treaty's other key provisions concerned non-militarization, scientific co-operation, mutual access to scientific bases and consensus decision-making by the Consultative Parties. Though the Treaty was open to accession by any state, the requirement that any new Consultative Party demonstrate its interest in Antarctica through conducting substantial scientific research there constituted a formidable entry barrier to membership of the 'Antarctic club'. By 1997 there were 27 Consultative Parties to the Treaty. Primarily a conflict-avoidance mechanism, and hardly mentioning environmental matters, the Antarctic Treaty implied that this selective multilateralist regime would act as a worthy steward of the continent in the interests of humankind as a whole.

Conservation issues soon became one of the main foci of regulatory activity in the Antarctic Treaty System (ATS) developing around the Treaty, resulting in a range of agreed measures, recommendations and conventions (e.g. the 1972 Convention for the Protection of Antarctic Seals; the 1980 Convention on the Conservation of Antarctic Marine Living Resources). While the constructive evasion of the sovereignty issue had made it possible for the states to respond to problems as they arose, including environmental issues, it severely constrained the speed and ambitiousness of the regime's policy-making process and dictated the absence of any centralized procedures for monitoring and enforcing compliance with the rules that were produced. Campaigning in the 1980s by a transnational NGO network – the Antarctic and Southern Ocean Coalition (ASOC) – and the activities of **Greenpeace** in Antarctica in the late 1980s focused attention on the poor record of compliance with the weak environmental rules of the ATS.

Concern over the future fate of the Antarctic environment was one of the two driving forces behind the serious external threats facing the Antarctic Treaty System in the 1980s. While environmentalists questioned the effectiveness of the ATS in protecting the Antarctic environment, several developing countries, led by Malaysia, argued that Antarctica is a 'Common Heritage of Mankind' and should, to meet the demands of equity, not be controlled by an exclusive club of states. The resort to the common heritage argument was inspired by the distributional issues raised by the efforts of the Consultative Parties to agree amongst themselves on how to regulate future minerals operations in the area before any such activity could destabilize the sovereignty compromise at the heart of the ATS. The above-mentioned NGO mobilization in favour of a permanent ban on minerals activity within an Antarctic 'World Park' was, similarly, a reaction to these negotiations and their product – the 1988 Convention on the Regulation of Antarctic Mineral Resources Activities (CRAMRA). The environmentalist argument helped to persuade three of the claimant states to 'defect' from the CRAMRA consensus and advocate a minerals ban as part of comprehensive environmental protection convention for Antarctica. Despite reservations over the desirability of a long-term minerals ban, the remaining staunchly pro-CRAMRA states rapidly agreed to a 50-year moratorium as part of the 1991 Protocol on Environmental Protection to the Antarctic Treaty (PREP). The possibility that the breakdown of consensus might, at best, strengthen the case for 'globalizing' Antarctic governance or, more tragically, lead to the reinvigoration of territorial conflict and the collapse of the whole ATS weighed more heavily than the desire to keep the minerals option open.

The entry into force of PREP in 1998 constituted a consolidation of, and marked improvement upon, the existing environmental protection and conservation elements of the Antarctic Treaty System. Defining Antarctica as a natural reserve devoted to peace and science, the Protocol's objective is the comprehensive protection of the Antarctic environment and its dependent and associated ecosystems. It provides for mandatory, detailed rules and a Committee for Environmental Protection to advise the Antarctic Treaty Consultative Meetings. The ATS survived the equity- and environmentally-driven challenges provoked by the CRAMRA episode and adapted to the greater salience of environmental issues on the global political agenda

since the 1980s. It has developed a distinctly more 'green' tinge. As the sovereignty-driven need to preserve consensus persists, it remains to be seen whether the ATS will improve much upon its past track record protecting the environment of this 'frozen continent'.

See also: Arctic; international environmental law

DAVID SCRIVENER

anthropocentrism

Anthropocentrism literally means 'human-centredness'. Originally used to characterize a worldview in which humans, rather than God, provided the central focus of reference and reverence, the term has increasingly come to be applied to attitudes, values or practices which give exclusive or preferential concern to human interests at the expense of the interests or well-being of other species or the environment.

Those who have sought to justify anthropocentrism have traditionally emphasized distinctive characteristics of humans – such as having a soul, rationality or language – that set them apart from the rest of nature and make ethics an exclusively human matter. Yet these justifications have come under increasing attack in recent years.

Criticism of the factual basis of anthropocentrism has come from natural scientific findings which undermine humans' former views of themselves as the centre of the universe, the purpose of creation, or the 'measure of all things', showing them instead to be a product of evolutionary physiological and biological processes, to have considerable affinities with other creatures, and to have a vulnerable dependence on ecological conditions of existence.

Ethical criticism of anthropocentrism in part draws the consequences of the scientific critique: if humans can no longer be thought to occupy a special and privileged position in the world, this calls into question their prerogative to use natural creatures and the environment however they see fit. The critique also captures increasingly widespread moral intuitions that many creatures are relevantly similar to humans and that other natural phenomena have value in themselves and not merely for us. Thus, the principled objections to anthropocentrism find increasing application in practice. Many human practices can be criticized on these grounds, including those which involve cruelty to animals, destruction of habitats, endangering species, upsetting ecosystemic balances, and so on. Nevertheless, there are also practical problems involved in avoiding anthropocentrism: a concern with human interests is in some ways inescapable and legitimate; applied ethics also has to deal with 'hard cases' where vital human interests oppose those of non-humans. Moreover, general criticisms of human-centredness can overlook how harm to and exploitation of non-human nature may be caused and benefited from by particular groups of humans at the expense of other humans. Furthermore, there are also conceptual difficulties: some stem from the paradox that overcoming anthropocentrism in science is achieved by increasing rather than decreasing humans' cognitive detachment from the rest of nature; others from the recognition that there are limits to how much humans can actually know about what is good for non-humans.

Some of these difficulties can perhaps be overcome by drawing distinctions between types of anthropocentrism: for instance, between 'strong' forms which are rejected because they involve unjustifiable human preferentiality, and 'weak' forms which are accepted because they allow only the unobjectionable features. Other difficulties might also be avoided by using a more extensive and nuanced range of terms – including such ideas as speciesism and human chauvinism – to characterize morally unacceptable ways of relating to the non-human world (Hayward, 1998).

If the generalized critique of anthropocentrism can sometimes be excessively sweeping, its underlying impetus nevertheless serves to open up important questions about the relationship between humans and non-human nature and to foreground their problematic aspects.

Reference

Hayward, T. (1998) *Political Theory and Ecological Values*, Cambridge: Polity Press.

TIM HAYWARD

anti-environmentalism

Anti-environmentalism refers to the way that corporations and conservative groups in society have sought to counter the gains made by environmentalists, to redirect and diminish public concern about the environment, to attack environmentalists, and to persuade politicians against increased environmental regulation.

Anti-environmentalism has been a response to the rise of environmental consciousness and awareness first in the late 1960s and early 1970s and then again in the late 1980s and early 1990s. It is a backlash against the success of environmentalists in raising public concern and pressuring governments to protect the environment.

Between 1965 and 1970 environmental groups proliferated and environmental protection, especially pollution control, rose dramatically as a public priority in many countries. As environmental concern grew, so did distrust of business institutions, which were seen to be the cause of environmental problems such as air and water pollution. Governments worldwide responded with new forms of comprehensive environmental legislation aimed at regulating and constraining environmentally damaging business activities.

Businesses found that their past ways of dealing with government no longer sufficed. The scope of political conflict widened. Throughout the 1970s corporations became politically active, particularly in the USA. In response to government regulations, brought on by the activities of environmentalists and public interest groups, businesses began to co-operate in a way that was unprecedented, building coalitions and alliances and putting aside competitive rivalries.

Corporations adopted strategies that public-interest activists had used so effectively against them – grassroots organizing and coalition building, telephone and letter-writing campaigns, using the media, research reports and testifying at hearings. To these strategies corporations added huge financial resources and professional advice.

Corporations also put large amounts of money into advertising and sponsorships aimed at improving the corporate image and putting forward corporate views. Much of this advertising and public relations activity was on environmental issues (see **greenwashing**).

Corporations managed to achieve a virtual moratorium on new environmental legislation in many countries throughout the late 1970s and most of the 1980s. However, towards the end of the 1980s public concern about the environment rose again, reinforced by scientific discoveries regarding phenomena such as **ozone depletion** and weather patterns that seemed to indicate that **global warming** had already begun. Local pollution events, such as medical waste washing up on New York beaches and sewage pollution on Sydney beaches, also contributed to the public perception of an environment in decline.

Amidst all this public concern, regulatory agencies in various countries got tougher and new laws were enacted. This induced a new wave of corporate political activity. This time corporations were able to take advantage of the new PR techniques and information technologies available for raising money, building coalitions, manipulating public opinion and lobbying politicians.

It was during the 1990s that the application of public relations to environmental concerns really came into its own. The coalition building which began in the 1970s continued to grow. Some corporations went beyond their corporate allies in their organizing efforts, hiring specialized public relations firms to set up front groups and create the impression of grassroots support for corporate causes so as to convince politicians to oppose environmental reforms.

Environmental public relations or greenwashing has become big business for PR firms. US firms now spend hundreds of millions of dollars each year on greenwash and strategic counselling – shaping public and government perceptions of environmental problems and finding ways to counter environmentalists and environmental regulations.

The use of front groups enables corporations to take part in public debates and government hearings behind a cover of community concern. These front groups lobby governments to legislate in the corporate interest; to oppose environmental regulations; and to introduce policies that enhance corporate profitability. Front groups also campaign to change **public opinion** so that the markets for corporate goods are not threatened and the efforts of environmental groups are defused. The names of corporate front groups are carefully chosen to mask the real interests behind them.

Apart from helping corporations form front groups and artificial coalitions, public relations firms help them to gather information on environmentalists and journalists. Techniques for dealing with environmental activists and the media depend on knowing who they are and how they operate. Several public relations firms specialize in supplying this sort of information and this is sometimes done by infiltrating environmental groups and spying on them.

Public relations firms also help corporations to deal with environmentalists by getting the more moderate and mainstream ones on their side, through donations and job offers and working out deals with them. Those unwilling to co-operate are subject to marginalization and alienation. Such environmentalists are branded as extremists and terrorists and have been subject to dirty tricks campaigns that have attempted to falsely pin violent actions on them.

Public relations firms have also become proficient at helping their corporate clients convince key politicians that there is wide public support for their environmentally damaging activities or their demands for looser environmental regulations. Using specially tailored mailing lists, field officers, telephone banks and the latest in information technology, these firms are able to generate hundreds of telephone calls and/or thousands of pieces of mail to key politicians, creating the impression that there is wide public support for their client's position. Artificial grassroots coalitions created by public relations firms for this purpose are referred to in the industry as 'astroturf' (after a synthetic grass product).

Industry interests have been able to turn the disaffection of rural and resource industry workers, farmers and small business people into anti-environmental sentiment. Nowhere has this been as spectacularly achieved as in the USA with its **'wise-use' movement**. The 'wise-use' movement attained grassroots support through enrolling thousands of people in the USA who are worried about their future and feel individually powerless to do anything about it. A similar coalition was formed in Canada called the Share Movement.

The 'wise-use' movement is a broad ranging, loose-knit coalition of hundreds of groups in the USA which promotes a conservative agenda. Many groups within the movement receive substantial industry funding and support but the movement prefers to portray itself as a mainstream citizens movement. Indeed its extended membership includes farmers, miners, loggers, hunters and landowners as well as corporate front groups.

Opposition to environmentalists is the glue that holds the disparate elements of the 'wise-use' movement together. Wise-use groups have successfully attracted rural workers and landowners to their groups by arguing that environmental protection costs jobs, threatens their land, and that environmentalists care more about animals and plants than people. Some wise-use groups actively sabotage environmentalists.

The movement draws membership from people who are pro-development, anti-big government, opposed to environmentalists, or just plain worried about their future economic prospects. It has been an influential political force in the American landscape. Its ability to turn out a couple of hundred vocal protesters for key meetings and hearings has a significant impact on decision-makers.

Conservative think tanks have also turned their attention to environmental issues and the defeat of environmental regulations. They sought to cast doubt on the very features of the environmental crisis that had heightened public concerns at the end of the 1980s including ozone depletion, greenhouse warming and industrial pollution.

Think tanks opposed environmental legislation in a variety of ways. In the USA they attempted to hamstring the regulatory process by advocating legislation that would ensure regulatory efforts became too expensive and difficult to implement, through insisting on **cost-benefit analysis** and **risk assessment** of proposed legislation and compensation to state governments and property owners for the costs of complying with the legislation (see **takings**). Worldwide these think tanks promoted free market techniques, such as tradeable property and pollution rights, pricing mechanisms, tax incentives, and voluntary agreements, for dealing with environmental degradation.

Whilst corporations amplified their own voice through the use of front groups, think tanks and public relations firms, they intimidated their opponents with the threat of law suits. Every year thousands of environmentalists and ordinary citizens are sued for circulating petitions, writing to public officials, speaking at, or even just attending, public meetings, organizing a boycott and engaging in peaceful demonstrations. The law suits have been labelled 'Strategic Lawsuits Against Public Participation' or SLAPPs by University of Denver academics Penelope Canan and George Pring.

Such cases seldom win in the courts. The charges often seem extremely flimsy and the damage claims outrageously large. The purpose of a SLAPP is to harass, intimidate and distract one's opponents. They win the political battle, even when they lose the court case, if their victims and those associated with them, stop speaking out against them.

References

Beder, S. (1997) *Global Spin: The Corporate Assault on Environmentalism*, Devon: Green Books.

Helvarg, D. (1994) *The War Against the Greens: The 'Wise-Use' Movement, the New Right, and Anti-Environmental Violence*, San Francisco: Sierra Club Books.

Rowell, A. (1996) *Green Backlash: Global Subversion of the Environment Movement*, London and New York: Routledge.

Stauber, J. and Rampton, S. (1995) *Toxic Sludge is Good For You! Lies, Damn Lies and the Public Relations Industry*, Monroe, Maine: Common Courage Press.

Further reading

Deal, C. (1993) *The Greenpeace Guide to Anti-Environmental Organizations*, Berkeley, CA: Odonian Press.

Ehrlich, P. and Ehrlich, A. (1996) *Betrayal of Science and Reason: How Anti-Environmental Rhetoric Threatens Our Future*, Washington, DC and Covelo, CA: Island Press.

Hager, N. and Burton, B. (1999) *Secrets and Lies: The Anatomy of an Anti-Environmental PR Campaign*, Nelson: Craig Potton Publishing.

SHARON BEDER

anti-nuclear movements

Social movements against the civil use of nuclear technology were an important agent of social and political change in the last three decades of the twentieth century. They contributed to a widespread stop of nuclear construction but also to the emergence of many other new political organizations, in particular green parties.

History

Protest against the civil use of nuclear technology was essentially a phenomenon of the 1970s. Earlier, criticism of nuclear technology was predominantly focused on its military use; only some individuals and very small local groups had then protested against the development of nuclear facilities intended to produce energy. Anti-nuclear protest became a major social movement in the 1970s when the expansion of nuclear building programmes coincided with the publicizing of expert challenges to nuclear safety. Concern about nuclear safety found resonance in a public that had just been sensitized to the new environmental issues in the late 1960s and early 1970s. The emergence of major local protest movements against particular sites chosen for nuclear installations, and the often harsh police reactions against local protesters, also inspired the political heirs of the student movement and other 'radical' forces to embrace the nuclear energy issue. The late 1970s saw major demonstrations in many countries, normally at nuclear sites, often escalating into violence. Anti-nuclear energy mobilization waned somewhat in the early 1980s when radical politics was dominated by protest against nuclear weapons and other environmental issues such as **acid rain**. The **Chernobyl** accident of April 1986 led to a further protest wave in western Europe. In many eastern European countries, environmental and anti-nuclear protest became one important platform of nation-

alist movements against the Soviet Union. By the late 1980s and throughout the 1990s, anti-nuclear protest movements had declined or disappeared altogether in most countries. However, in some countries local and national opposition to new nuclear projects remains important and continues to mobilize many people, for example in Taiwan and in Germany.

Organization and tactics

A broad range of individuals and groups has been involved in anti-nuclear movements. One can distinguish between five types of groups that, to varying degrees, became important parts of anti-nuclear mobilization: 'alternative', anti-nuclear scientists; local opposition groups; environmental groups; the political left, and green parties.

Substantial protest against nuclear energy in the 1970s benefited from the rise of anti-nuclear experts, mainly in the USA, who challenged the claims of the nuclear sector about the safety of the industry. The propagation of their views in the early 1970s coincided with the major expansion of nuclear construction programmes in many countries and the rise of strong local protest groups. In addition, many countries had seen the development of student politics and the '**New Left**' in the late 1960s, creating a potential for radical politics, as well as the rise of environmental concern and a new generation of environmental organizations in the early 1970s.

Local protest had an important catalyst effect and defined many of the key battle grounds of the anti-nuclear movement in the 1970s. Local opposition tended to occur at planned nuclear sites in predominantly rural areas untouched by **industrialization** with a strong community spirit and/or a local political culture open to protest activity. Local conflicts with police often attracted the attention of the radical Left and/or environmentalists who had previously taken little interest in the nuclear issue. In countries with strong local mobilization and an unresponsive state, anti-nuclear protest radicalized strongly in the 1970s, with site occupations, blockades and battles with security forces becoming a major part of movement activity. While this often placed the issue high on the political agenda, these tactics generally failed to achieve any substantial results. In the 1980s and 1990s, mass protest remained important only in isolated cases where the traditions of the 1970s were maintained locally. The main change was that large environmental organizations, such as **Greenpeace** or **Friends of the Earth**, became dominant. Local opposition tended to fade away once a nuclear plant was built. In some countries, green parties, often set up as a direct result of anti-nuclear mobilization, were the major anti-nuclear player. The tactics involved varied from country to country according to the legal and political opportunities available, but, in general, the development of 'alternative' energy strategies and the mobilization of anti-nuclear expertise became an important part of anti-nuclear strategy.

Policy impacts

Anti-nuclear movements were highly successful in countries where the nuclear industry was not firmly established, in particular where the country had no substantial indigenous nuclear construction industry and where no or very few nuclear power stations were operating at the time of the political challenge emerging, i.e. in the late 1970s and in 1986 following Chernobyl. Cases of countries abandoning any nuclear plans in these circumstances include the Republic of Ireland, **Denmark**, **Norway**, and **Luxembourg**, **Greece**, **Austria** and **Italy**. Austria had built a nuclear station but a referendum in 1978 narrowly won by the anti-nuclear movement prevented it from opening. Italy also abandoned nuclear energy in 1986 in a referendum held after the Chernobyl accident, remaining the only country with operating nuclear reactors to make and implement a political decision to close them down. In many of these countries, strength of mobilization and **political opportunity structures** were not so important, as vested nuclear interests were quite weak and politicians of several parties were only too happy to represent the public's wishes.

Anti-nuclear movements were at least partially successful where mobilization against a well-established industry was very strong but only if there were significant political opportunities for the opposition to use. Examples include the case of Sweden where a referendum in 1979 decided to phase out nuclear energy, but only in the medium term. In Germany, strong anti-nuclear mobilization and opportunities to hassle the industry in the courts as well as through exploiting special regional interests in a federal system led to some partial success. The de facto moratorium on new nuclear construction was, however, also economically motivated. Anti-nuclear movements were generally not successful in reversing nuclear policies where very strong vested interests in nuclear energy combined with limited resources available to the anti-nuclear opposition, even when anti-nuclear mobilization was very strong, such as in France.

Overall, nuclear construction came to a halt in most countries during the 1980s, mainly for economic rather than for political reasons. Nevertheless, the anti-nuclear movement contributed to making nuclear projects financially unviable in some cases, and also hampered nuclear activities by helping to create, in many countries, a climate of public opinion that was very sceptical of and often openly hostile to nuclear technology.

The anti-nuclear movement has generally failed, however, in promoting the conditions to phase out existing nuclear installations and remove the nuclear option from the range of energy policy options in the future. Once the construction of nuclear stations was completed, public mobilization became much more difficult. Some of the policies put forward by ecologists, such as energy conservation, speed limits, and higher energy taxes, proved consistently unpopular with electorates. The rise of global environmental issues, such as **global warming**, provided new opportunities for ecological and green groups to argue for a new energy policy, but it also opened new opportunities to the nuclear side which has been trying hard to promote nuclear energy as a solution to limiting climate change.

The surviving nuclear industry has been difficult to target, as popular mobilization has generally faded away once planned projects were cancelled. Proposals to phase out existing plants invoke strong opposition from nuclear employees and the hostility of industry demanding huge compensations for lost earnings. Not surprisingly, where political decisions to phase out nuclear power have been made (e.g. in Germany, Belgium and Sweden), the time scales involved are very generous to nuclear operators.

Political impacts

While their exact impact on the commercial development of nuclear power is difficult to ascertain, there can be few doubts about the impact of anti-nuclear movements on political discourses, and political organizations in the environmental field. In many countries, anti-nuclear protest galvanized a radical ecological movement in the 1970s that mobilized very many people. Among the chief beneficiaries were national environmental movements, in particular Friends of the Earth and, later, Greenpeace, which established themselves quite firmly with a mass membership in the 1980s and 1990s. The nuclear issue in some cases also helped to reshape the area of radical and New Left politics that had first emerged in the 1960s. By drawing many of these groups into anti-nuclear and ecological politics, the movement was politicized and, in some countries, became the catalyst for green electoral politics. The formation of green parties in the 1970s and 1980s was often a direct result of anti-nuclear politics (e.g. in Sweden and Germany). Even where the foundation of the party had other origins, opposition to nuclear energy is one issue that provides part of the political identity of green parties across the world. Concerns over nuclear accidents and other safety issues, for example nuclear waste, have benefited green parties electorally on many occasions.

Once national environmental groups and green parties became the major actors in the anti-nuclear field, they needed to mobilize alternative expertise to support their policies. Here, anti-nuclear movements have impacted as well in a substantial way in terms of promoting the formation and growth of a new infrastructure of ecological, anti-nuclear research establishments, providing independent inputs into energy and environmental decision-making.

There are signs that the impact of past nuclear conflicts is waning, however, in the early twenty-first century. For some greens and environmental-ists, nuclear power is an 'old' issue that represents division and conflict and thus stands in contrast to the more consensus-orientated, inclusive approaches that are favoured to address the issues of environmental **sustainability**. Co-operation with business in environmental circles and coalition compromises in green politics have moved many of the political heirs of anti-nuclear protest away from the political margins and closer to the political establishment. The mobilizing potential of anti-nuclear protest remains undiminished, however. With the nuclear waste question remaining unresolved and the possibility of nuclear interests staging a recovery in the coming decades, anti-nuclear movements may yet revive to challenge the political establishment, including its new green members, again.

See also: Chernobyl; nuclear energy/nuclear waste management; political opportunity structures

Further reading

Dawson, J.I. (1996) *Eco-Nationalism: Anti-Nuclear Activism and National Identity in Russia, Lithuania and Ukraine*, Durham, NC: Duke University Press.

Falk, J. (1982) *Global Fission: The Battle over Nuclear Power*, Melbourne: Oxford University Press.

Flam, H. (ed.) (1994) *States and Anti-nuclear Movements*, Edinburgh: Edinburgh University Press.

Joppke, C. (1993) *Mobilising against Nuclear Energy*, Berkeley, CA: University of California Press.

Kitschelt, H. (1986) 'Political Opportunity Structures and Political Protest: Anti-Nuclear Movements in Four Democracies', *British Journal of Political Science*, 16: 57–85.

Kriesi, H., Koopmans, R., Duyvendak, J.W. and Giugni, M.G. (1995) *New Social Movements in Western Europe: A Comparative Analysis*, London: UCL Press.

Mez L. (ed.) (1979) *Der Atomkonflikt*, Berlin: Olle & Wolter.

Nelkin, D. and Pollak, M. (1982) *The Atom Besieged: Anti-nuclear Movements in France and Germany*, Cambridge, MA: MIT Press.

Opp, K.D. and Roehl, W. (1990) *Der Tschernobyl-Effekt: Eine Untersuchung über die Ursachen des politischen Protests*, Opladen: Westdeutscher Verlag.

Rucht, D. (1994) *Modernisierung und neue soziale Bewegungen: Deutschland, Frankreich und USA im Vergleich*, Frankfurt: Campus.

—— (1995) 'The Impact of the Anti-Nuclear Power Movement in International Comparison', in M Bauer (ed.) *Resistance to New Technology*, Cambridge: Cambridge University Press, pp. 277–92.

Rüdig, W. (1990) *Anti-Nuclear Movements: A World Survey of Protest against Nuclear Energy*, Harlow: Longman.

—— (2000) 'Phasing out Nuclear Energy in Germany', *German Politics*, 9: 43–80.

Welsh, I. (2000) *Mobilising Modernity: The Nuclear Moment*, London: Routledge.

WOLFGANG RÜDIG

anti-roads movement

In the UK the anti-roads movement arose in opposition to a major road-building programme announced by the Conservative government in 1989. By 1997 the programme had been reduced to a third of its original size. The protest movement certainly played an important part in making road-building controversial, but its role in reducing the scale of road-building also needs to be set alongside the pressure on the government to make cuts in public spending and the appearance of a number of official reports critical of the rationale of road-building.

The movement had two distinct wings. The first was made up of local campaigns against specific road projects. Many of these groups had opposed a particular local road scheme for many years but had exhausted all legal avenues of opposition, including **public inquiries**. The social profile of these groups varied according to the character of the local community and included both urban and rural, middle-class and working-class campaigns. Accounts of individual campaigns tell a story common to many local environmental campaigns of groups that began with a purely defensive and **NIMBY** strategy becoming more political in their criticism of the undemocratic character of decision-making.

By 1996 there were around 300 local groups affiliated through a co-ordinating group called

Alarm UK. This group, like **Citizens' Clearinghouse for Hazardous Wastes** (US), was grassroots based and did not seek to impose policies on its constituent local groups. Alarm provided briefings and tactical advice to its members, concentrating on avoiding the dangers of being drawn into the officially sanctioned forum for public participation, the public inquiry. In the years from 1989 to 1993 there were a number of quiet successes for local anti-roads campaigns such as the cancellation of new roads in Preston, Crosby, Hereford, Norwich and Calder Valley.

The second wing of the movement was represented by counter-cultural groups of protesters who took direct action against construction sites. British **Earth First!** groups had been formed in 1991 and they provided the core upon which the new **non-violent direct action** (NVDA) movement was based. The first major direct action protests against roads were at Twyford Down on the route of the M3 in Hampshire in 1992. Although this campaign and most other campaigns failed to prevent the roads being built, the protests were widely covered in the media. There was particular interest in the alliances between dread-locked and body-pierced radicals and 'ordinary' local people. The tactics used to occupy sites threatened with destruction also attracted attention and served to delay construction and increased the costs of road-building. Adapting tactics first used by NVDA groups in Australia and the USA, protesters constructed defences in trees and houses and also, in a British innovation, in underground tunnels. These tactics were all used to make protesters vulnerable and to exploit the fact that evictors could not use excessive force in removing protesters.

By 1995 many NVDA protesters wanted to expand their repertoire to include more offensive actions. One result was the spread of reclaim the streets (RTS) actions. These seized streets back from motor vehicles in order to hold parties. After beginning in London, they took place in most major cities and later spread to other countries. The main aim of this action was to show how cars colonized public space and restricted freedom.

Successive years of major cuts in the roads programme were followed by new legislation, sponsored by **Friends of the Earth** and the **Green Party UK**, in 1998 committing the government to seek ways to reduce road traffic. What had been a radical idea was now government policy. Alarm UK was dissolved as there were now too few local road schemes for it to be necessary.

The movement was novel in that until the 1990s Britain had a very centralized and quiescent **environmental movement** which had been unable, or unwilling, to mount major protests. Both wings of the movement emerged independently of the major environmental movement organizations. Although by 1996 Friends of the Earth began to play a more prominent role in anti-roads campaigns, this was after the movement had already become important politically.

In a decade when all the major political parties in Britain emphasized the importance of economic growth, the anti-roads movement came to represent the most important voice critical of dominant views of **progress**. The NVDA groups moved on to other issues where the pattern of alliances with local groups was replicated, such as the expansion of airports, quarries, housing on greenfield sites and others of more national concern such as trial sites for genetically modified crops (see **genetic engineering, crops**). It is probably more accurate to define it as an alliance between two different networks than as a single movement. By the end of the decade the counter-cultural groups had become more anti-capitalist and more concerned with issues of global political economy.

Further reading

Doherty, B. (1999) 'Paving the Way: The Rise of Direct Action against Road-Building and the Changing Character of British Environmentalism', *Political Studies*, XLVII, 275–91.

Seel, B., Paterson, M. and Doherty, B. (eds) (2000) *Direct Action and British Environmentalism*, London: Routledge.

Wall, D. (1999) *Earth First! and the Origins of the Anti-Roads Movement*, London: Routledge.

BRIAN DOHERTY

appropriate technology

Appropriate technology represents an American attempt to bridge some of the principles in E.F. Schumacher's intermediate technology to the USA. The term 'intermediate technology' was seen as inferior and thus not palatable to most Americans, so appropriate technology evolved as a term. Appropriate **technology** attempts to achieve a balance between technology, environmental, social, cultural and economic values. One of the most basic principles of appropriate technology revolves around the establishment of an environmentally sound, ecological worldview. With regard to resources, appropriate technology is intensive in the use of abundant factors, such as labour, readily available natural resources and other locally produced inputs. It tends to be frugal in the use of scarce factors, such as capital, energy, highly trained personnel and natural resources from far removed locations. There are a number of independent organizations in the USA that were founded on these principles. The New Alchemy Institute, Woods Hole, Massachusetts, the Institute for Local Self-Reliance in Washington, DC, the Farallones Institute in Berkeley, California and the Social Ecology Program at Goddard College are a few examples. The Centre for Alternative Technology, Machynlleth, Powys, Wales serves as an international example.

Further reading

Darrow, K. and Saxenian, M. (1986) *Appropriate Technology Sourcebook*, Stanford: Volunteers in Asia.

THOMAS LOWE

Aral Sea

Formerly the world's fourth largest inland lake, located in Central Asia between northern Uzbekistan and Kazakhstan. In one of the greatest human-induced environmental catastrophes ever, it is expected completely to disappear by 2010. The primary cause is the use of water from its feeder rivers to increase cotton production in the region from the 1950s onwards. Consequences include local climate change, desertification and the destruction of agricultural land, plant and animal life. Frequent dust storms are estimated to have added five per cent to the amount of particulate matter in the Earth's atmosphere. Surrounding land is poisoned by salinization, and water supplies by runoff of agro-chemicals. This has created an immense public health crisis. Post-Soviet economic decline, dependence on hard currency from export crops, and competition for scarce resources between the five newly independent states make prospects for any effective action to reverse the decline remote.

MATTHEW WYMAN

Arctic

Unlike **Antarctica**'s role as a laboratory for co-operative science, during the Cold War the potential for circumpolar co-operation in the Arctic was frozen by the Arctic's strategic importance, with the exception of Polar Bear conservation. Yet in the early 1990s co-operation between the eight states with Arctic territory (Canada, **Denmark/Greenland**, **Finland**, Iceland, **Norway**, **Sweden**, the **Russian Federation/Former Soviet Union** and the USA) developed rapidly, alongside nongovernmental links. Environmental problems featured prominently in the agenda-setting process in most of these circumpolar interactions, reflecting concern over threats to the relatively pristine Arctic environment, their often regional transboundary implications and the Arctic's role as a 'sink' for pollutants originating far away from the region itself (such as POPs – persistent organic pollutants).

In the Rovaniemi Declaration on the Protection of the Arctic Environment (1991), the Arctic states agreed to exchange information, co-ordinate research and explore the possibilities for common action on environmental issues in the region through a joint Action Plan to realize the objectives of the accompanying Arctic Environmental Protection Strategy (AEPS). The AEPS was then operationalized through five expert-level working groups, each addressing priority areas of concern: monitoring and assessment; conservation; seas;

emergencies; and, somewhat later, sustainable development. Improving the common knowledge base about the condition of, and threats to, the Arctic environment and on the adequacy of existing international environmental agreements was seen as a necessary (though hardly sufficient) precondition for the Arctic states to co-ordinate their responses at the regional level or to act in concert in wider international or global policy forums. Moreover, opinions diverged over the relative merits of forming new Arctic-specific arrangements or, alternatively, seeking action through larger international regimes. Consequently, the AEPS – and its successor since 1996, the Arctic Council – took a programmatic approach to environmental co-operation, with little effort to develop aspects of a regulatory regime at the circumpolar level and evolved in a lightly institutionalized, precariously funded, piecemeal manner.

The output of one of the Working Groups – the Arctic Monitoring and Assessment Programme (AMAP) – contributed the most to a common knowledge base for future policy action. The 1997 *Arctic Pollution Issues: A State of the Arctic Environment Report* with supporting technical data, and AMAP's continuing work in monitoring trends, provided the ammunition for Arctic states to push in global forums for more urgent action on a range of long-range transboundary pollutants, most notably persistent organic pollutants. However, the recent formation of a global POPs Convention revealed that 'common victimhood' does not guarantee a common 'Arctic' negotiating stance in the face of competing, more central, national economic interests.

The working group on Conservation of Arctic Flora and Fauna (CAFF) produced general and species-specific strategies, most notably for a Circumpolar Protected Areas Network. The working group on the marine environment (PAME) analysed the adequacy for Arctic marine environmental protection of existing, wider international regimes, produced Arctic Offshore Oil and Gas Guidelines and drafted a Regional Programme of Action on land-based activities in an attempt to mobilize external assistance for cleaning up pollution 'hotspots' in the Russian Arctic. The emergencies working group (EPPR) assessed the adequacy for the Arctic of existing international agreements on emergency notification and response, conducted a risk analysis of facilities and activities posing a risk of significant accidental pollution in the region. Environmental Impact Assessment Guidelines for the Arctic were developed.

Canada's proposal for a regional political body to oversee the various strands of circumpolar co-operation and promote **sustainable development** in the region eventually overcame US resistance and led to the establishment of the Arctic Council in 1996. The momentum of circumpolar co-operation was then slowed by protracted debate over the Council's Rules of Procedure and the Terms of Reference for the Sustainable Development Programme (SDP) that was to complement the pollution- and conservation-orientated programmes inherited from the AEPS. Sustainable development's transition from a divisive concept to a unifying theme for the Council's activities has been slow and incomplete, not least due to the concern in many environment ministries that development-orientated activities would compete with environmental programmes for attention and resources.

By the tenth anniversary of the Rovaniemi Declaration in 2001, the Arctic Council was initiating concrete pollution prevention and remediation projects under its Action Plan to Eliminate Pollution of the Arctic, while overall priorities were beginning to emerge under the sustainable development rubric, centred around human health, children and youth, and capacity-building. The impact of the AEPS/Arctic Council on the state of the Arctic environment has probably been quite small. The most notable feature of this modest intergovernmental forum has been the novel status achieved by five Indigenous Peoples' Organizations of the region as Permanent Participants, setting them above Observer states and nongovernmental groups and affording them a direct role in articulating the Arctic consensus. Finland's successful Northern Dimension initiative in the **European Union** now promises to inject more resources into addressing the region's problems – not least the nuclear safety threats emanating from Russia's Kola Peninsula – while raising potentially distracting though unavoidable issues of co-ordination.

See also: Antarctica; international environmental law

DAVID SCRIVENER

asbestos

Asbestos is a generic term for the minerals: chrysolite (white asbestos), actinolite, amosite (brown asbestos), anthophyllite, crocidolite (blue asbestos) and tremolite. Health risks occur primarily through inhalation of asbestos fibres dispersed in air.

Progressive regulations have prohibited the importation, supply and use of asbestos, but thousands of tonnes were used in buildings in the past. Common uses included sprayed asbestos for fire control; lagging for thermal insulation and asbestos-cement products such as corrugated sheets and rainwater gutters. Regulations laying down practices for all work with asbestos have been in place for many years, but the continued existence of the materials, especially in building stock, will present technical difficulties long into the future. The legacy of past use is evident in continuing asbestos-related diseases and the legal judgement in the UK in October 1995 when liability for compensation was awarded against a company that closed a particular factory using asbestos some 37 years previously.

ROD S. BARRATT

Association of State Green Parties

The Association of State Green Parties (ASGP) is the national federation of green parties in the USA. ASGP organized the June 2000 Green Party Convention in Denver, Colorado, where green parties from 40 US states nominated Ralph Nader and Winona LaDuke for president and vice president. ASGP's member parties are autonomous. Each state party elects two delegates to a policymaking Co-ordinating Committee, which meets twice annually. The ASGP Platform Committee wrote the national green programme approved at the 2000 convention. ASGP's International Committee named US delegates to green conferences in Rio de Janeiro, Paris and Oaxaca, and co-ordinated US involvement in the 2001 Global Greens meeting in Canberra, Australia.

In mid-2000 ASGP represented the green parties of Arkansas, Arizona, California, Colorado, Connecticut, District of Columbia, Delaware, Florida, Georgia, Hawaii, Massachusetts, Maine, Michigan, Minnesota, Nevada, New Jersey, New Mexico, New York, Ohio, Oregon, Pennsylvania, Rhode Island, Tennessee, Texas, Utah, Virginia, Wisconsin, and Wyoming.

TONY AFFIGNE

Aswan Dam

The Aswan Dam complex consists of the Low Dam, a gravity-type masonry dam completed by Britain in 1902, and upstream the larger High Dam, a rock-fill dam completed with Soviet assistance in 1970. The older dam has been superseded by the new one, but still serves as a traffic crossing and additional flood control. The High Dam was proposed in 1953 by Gamal Abdel Nasser, but was not begun until after the 1956 war. It was intended to provide for Egypt's economic **development** through hydroelectric production (it provides 40 per cent of Egypt's electricity), agricultural irrigation of nearly seven million acres, water storage shared with Sudan, improve downstream navigation, and flood control.

The complex has also contributed to decreasing soil fertility downstream with the annual loss of millions of tons of silt, increased reliance on costly artificial fertilizers, increased salinity downstream, erosion of the Nile delta region, increased earthquake probability due to Lake Nasser's weight, and water loss through seepage and evaporation. The initial decline in marine fisheries has rebounded since the 1980s, and the dam has emerged as integral to Egypt's economy and national pride.

Reference

White, G.F. (1988) 'The Environmental Effects of the High Dam at Aswan', *Environment* 30(7): 5–40.

ERICH G. FRANKLAND

Atomic Energy Commission

In the aftermath of the destruction of Hiroshima and Nagasaki and with tensions increasing between the USA and the Soviet Union, the US Congress enacted the Atomic Energy Act in 1946, thus establishing the Atomic Energy Commission (AEC). The AEC's primary purpose at the outset was to oversee the fledgling US atomic weapons programme; there was little discussion of the potential peaceful utilization of the atom. Congress subsequently passed the 1954 Atomic Energy Act, which was geared toward the development of a private commercial nuclear industry. Through this legislation the AEC was assigned several roles: to oversee nuclear weapons development, to promote private utilization of atomic energy, and to protect the public from the hazards of commercial nuclear power.

The AEC evolved to actively support a strong relationship between government and industry, encouraging the private sector to expand the applications of atomic power. By 1955 the AEC offered to conduct research and development on nuclear reactors, to subsidize industry research, and to provide financial incentives for the use of government nuclear feedstock.

Due to heightened public anxiety about possible risks from nuclear radiation, the AEC drafted regulations and licensing procedures stringent enough to ensure power plant safety but flexible enough to allow for ongoing advancements in nuclear technology. Rules were drafted addressing radiation protection standards, safeguarding of fissionable materials, reactor operator qualifications, and procedures for licensing privately owned reactors.

From its inception, the AEC was criticized for its competing responsibilities of developing and regulating nuclear technology. In 1974 Congress divided the AEC into the Energy Research and Development Administration and the Nuclear Regulatory Commission (NRC). The NRC began operations in 1975, performing many of the same licensing and rulemaking functions that the AEC had originally conducted. The NRC also assumed new regulatory and administrative responsibilities. Very significantly, the NRC was given power to make binding decisions on regulatory issues. As a result, pressures for energy development had a less significant impact on decisions relating to safety issues.

In the wake of the Three Mile Island (TMI) nuclear accident, the NRC temporarily suspended granting operating licences for plants that were in the commissioning and construction stages (see **Three Mile Island accident**). The NRC's activities shifted away from licensing new plants to overseeing the safety of currently operating plants. In addition the NRC conducted a comprehensive review of radiation protection regulations. Based upon recommendations and research findings, the NRC tightened several regulations, including one which restricted public exposure to radiation to 100 millirems per year, down from the previous limit, 500 millirems per year.

In mid-1980 the NRC issued the first full-power operating licence since TMI. Over the next ten years it granted operating licences to over 40 additional reactors.

Partly as a result of the oil shocks of the 1970s, nuclear power became increasingly attractive to many politicians and utilities. Furthermore, new plant designs were proposed that markedly reduced the risks of accidents.

The lengthy and tedious licensing procedures for new reactors were significant barriers to utilities considering the construction of a nuclear plant, however. This created an incentive for streamlining the regulatory process. The NRC facilitated licensing procedures by replacing the original two-step process with a simpler, one-step system. The procedure established an incremental approach in which the detail required in the application varied according to the relationship of the specific system to plant safety. Ultimately, the objective of the NRC's action was to ensure public safety while providing flexibility in the development of new designs.

The NRC has also extensively reviewed issues involving nuclear materials safety and nuclear

energy safeguards. The protection of nuclear materials from theft continues to be a major concern of the agency. The NRC has evaluated safety issues related to the building and operation of repositories for high-level and low-level radioactive waste. In 1990, the NRC proposed procedures in which small quantities of low-level radioactive materials were exempted from federal regulations.

Controversy over high-level waste disposal, and continued concerns over the probability of a major reactor accident remain at the forefront for NRC scientists, engineers and policymakers.

See also: nuclear energy/nuclear waste management; Yucca mountain and nuclear wastes

Further reading

Jones, C. (2000) *The US Nuclear Regulatory Commission and How it Works*, Washington, DC: US Nuclear Regulatory Commission.

Rolph, E.S. (1979) *Nuclear Power and the Public Safety: A Study in Regulation*, Lexington, MA: Lexington Books.

Walker, J. (2000) *A Short History of Nuclear Regulation, 1946–1999*, Washington, DC: US Nuclear Regulatory Commission.

JOHN PICHTEL

Australian environmental groups

The contemporary Australian psyche is very much defined by the character of its natural environment, by its coastline, mountains, rainforests and desert heartland. Before European invasion and settlement, Aboriginal Australians had lived out an intimate connection with their ancient land in body and spirit for over 50 thousand years. Just such a transpersonal connection is the aspiration of many environmentalists. But environmentalism and aboriginal activism have rarely intersected, the exceptions being instances of joint 'green–black' opposition to uranium mining in the remote Northern Territory. The environmental impact of the Aborigines was so slight that Australia was declared 'terra nullius', the 'empty land', by the Europeans and remained so until the High Court's

1992 Mabo decision. The Aboriginal community has thus been more preoccupied with achieving recognition of its prior settlement and ill-treatment by the colonialists and their successors than with environmentalism. It is now accepted that the Aborigines had a modifying environmental impact, and that they historically traversed or inhabited virtually the whole Australian continent.

The environmental degradation of Australia is thus only two centuries old. It began with its Europeanization and the importation of inappropriate cultivation practices, and invasive foreign plant and animal species. The environment was rolled back as the settlers carved out the colonies with a frontierist zeal that is still recognizable. Indeed, the pioneering view of nature-as-frontier and wilderness-as-wasteland that displaced the intrinsic valuing of the **indigenous peoples** persists today. Australia remains the most dependent of the Organization for Economic Cooperation and Development (OECD) nations upon natural resource exploitation, with its balance of payments reliant upon **agriculture** and **mining** in particular. It has endured possibly the highest rate of ecosystem destruction by the fewest people over the briefest period of time. Australia enjoys a low population, limited air pollution, clean drinking water and healthy coastal regions in remote areas, but it suffers from serious ecological problems. These include native habitat and species destruction, urban environmental problems, poor inland water management, **ozone depletion**, land degradation and clearing, old growth forest destruction, and a raft of complex **environmental justice** issues for indigenous Australians.

Despite this, Australia is one of the few places in the world still characterized by mega-diversity. This is owed in no small part to its conservationists, environmentalists and green parties, for securing the world heritage listing of over two dozen natural areas. No other nation comes close to this record. The protection of the Kakadu National Park, Great Barrier Reef, and Tasmanian Wilderness alone has secured Australia's reputation as a premier eco-tourist destination. However this protection is relatively recent, and would not have succeeded had it not built upon earlier waves of activism that began with the pre-federation

romanticists, scientists and natural historians. Here we find the oft-neglected roots of contemporary environmentalism that are well over a hundred years old despite the accounts of '**new social movement**' theorists. The first conservation efforts began less than a century after European occupancy with the philosophical and scientific societies, wildlife groups and field naturalists. Early activism achieved the declaration in 1879 of Australia's first National Park, south of Sydney, and with it, the beginnings of what was to become an extensive park system throughout the country.

Natural historian and botanist Baron Ferdinand von Mueller, one of Australia's first conservationists, delivered moving speeches advocating the preservation of nature in the late 1800s. These speeches were influenced not only by the European Romantics but by the American preservationists, G.P. **Marsh**, author of *Man and Nature*, in particular. Hutton and Connors (1999) credit von Mueller's contemporaries with campaigning for national parks, fauna protection, forest preservation, soil and water conservation. After federation of the colonies in 1901, scientific environmentalism and conservation waned only to re-emerge in the 1920s and 1930s with the proliferation of recreational walking clubs and their national parks campaigning. However, the natural resource-based developmentalism of the state governments, their mining and logging programmes especially, was to place many newly protected areas under threat of revocation in the 1940s and 1950s. The campaigns organized in response to these threats were the precursors to the more successful, higher profile activism of the late 1960s and 1970s.

In the 1960s and 1970s, conservationists thwarted agricultural development of the Little Desert, mining on the Great Barrier Reef, sand mining on Queensland's Fraser Island, and had Australia sign the **World Heritage Convention**. The Australian Conservation Foundation was founded in 1965, and from elitist beginnings evolved into a respected national lobby group. Tasmanian conservationists lost their battle to save Lake Pedder in Tasmania's wilderness, but changed Australia's conservation politics forever by founding the world's first state-based green party, the United Tasmania Group, in 1972. The Commonwealth Government then enacted cornerstone environmental legislation giving itself expansionist powers against state developmentalism. In the wake of Lake Pedder's loss, environmentalism achieved a national profile that elicited institutional responses throughout the 1970s at all levels. Conservation groups flourished with memberships increasing ten-fold over the next two decades. Again this laid the foundation for future successes, including the halting of Tasmania's Franklin River dam in early 1983. The 1980s then became the green decade of world heritage declarations, commercial **whaling** moratoriums, arid land protection, and Australia's push to protect **Antarctica**.

However the green decade has subsequently proved to be an aberration from natural resource-based developmentalism, and from the economic rationalism that defined the federal Labour government (1983 to 1996). The world heritage listings and Commonwealth intervention against the threats to protected areas continued into the 1990s, but the mood was different. Many of federal Labour's environmental protections until then had been expedient, aimed at achieving crucial green preferences at election time. When the billion dollar Wesley Vale pulp mill proposal was thwarted in 1989 by Tasmanian conservationists, causing five green politicians to achieve the balance of power in the Tasmanian Parliament, the business backlash began. By the early 1990s the populist, expediently green Labour Prime Minister Bob Hawke had been deposed by his long-time Treasurer, Paul Keating, who then began to devolve environmental politics and power back to the States. About this time, in August 1992, conservationists from Tasmania, New South Wales and Queensland founded the Australian Greens. They were later joined by greens from the Australian Capital Territory, the Northern Territory, Victoria, and South Australia, and informally co-operate with Western Australian Greens.

Australia has had a distinguished history of green political activism, beginning with the '**green bans**' of the New South Wales Builder Labourer's Federation led by Jack Mundey between 1971 and 1977. At this time, the United Tasmania Group was campaigning as a political party whose successors twice achieved the balance of state

parliamentary power in the Tasmanian House of Assembly (1989–91 and 1996–8 respectively). This early activism had the effect of uniting Australia's traditional political antagonists, the Labour Party and the Liberal–National Coalition, in their resistance of the social, economic and environmental challenges of conservation politics. The founding of green politics was a logical consequence of this bi-partisan developmentalist alliance. Democrat Dr Norm Sanders was Australia's first green parliamentarian, followed by the Independent Dr Bob Brown, who has been a driving force in conservation politics. Dr Gerry Bates subsequently joined Dr Brown as a Green Independent parliamentarian. The Tasmanian Greens were founded after the election of Green Independent Wesley Vale campaigners Christine Milne, Di Hollister and Lance Armstrong in 1989.

Nationally, Jo Vallentine of the short-lived Nuclear Disarmament Party won a Senate seat in 1984, which she held subsequently as a Western Australian Green until 1992. She stood down in favour of Christabel Chamarette, who was joined in 1993 by a second Western Australian Green Senator, Dee Margetts. Dr Bob Brown was elected to the Senate in 1996, and eventually served as the sole Australian Green in a political climate that has all but eclipsed green politics. The Liberal–National Coalition was also elected federally in 1996, displacing Labour after its thirteen years in power. Under Prime Minister John Howard, the Coalition has pursued a conservative, devolutionary environmental agenda. Through its $1.25 billion Natural Heritage Trust, it has encouraged a re-definition of environmentalism as a local, less politically driven, more 'hands-on', co-operative ecological restoration project. This has proved to be both empowering by broadening environmental consciousness across Australia, and disempowering by fracturing environmentalism between those operating at the strategic, national level and those who have narrowed their focus. Whether this narrow focus persists will depend largely on whether the devolution of environmental powers and politics back to the States resolves the developmentalist threats to the Australian environment.

See also: Australian environmental law and policy; Tasmanian Greens

Further reading

Brown, B. and Singer, P. (1996) *The Greens*, Melbourne: Text Publishing Company.

Hutton, D. and Connors, L. (1999) *A History of the Australian Environment Movement*, Cambridge: Cambridge University Press.

Lines, W. J (1991) *Taming the Great South Land: A History of the Conquest of Nature in Australia*, North Sydney: Allen and Unwin.

Walker, K. and Crowley, K. (eds) (1999) *Australian Environmental Policy: Studies in Decline and Devolution*, Sydney: University of New South Wales Press.

KATE CROWLEY

Australian environmental law and policy

Environmental law in Australia generally prohibits any potentially destructive activities that may have been permitted at **common law**, but then sets up an administrative scheme for the issue of licences to permit such activities under conditions.

The purpose of the law is:

- to set up government regulatory structures for natural resources management. (These include the creation of regulatory authorities, such as environment protection authorities; and the creation of specialist courts and tribunals to hear both merits appeals and enforce the law.)
- to enable members of the public to take part in strategic planning, project evaluation and law enforcement;
- to provide government regulators with management tools to control environmentally significant activities;
- to require persons proposing to carry on environmentally significant activities to seek permission from government regulators. (The permitting authority may be either central government, e.g., for permits to access public forests and **fisheries**, or local government, e.g., for development control.)
- to provide that non-compliance with the law will attract liability for a range of administrative, criminal and civil sanctions.

The structure of environmental legislation

Legislation commonly incorporates all or a combination of the following:

- a definitions or interpretation section (sometimes called a 'dictionary') defining key terms or concepts in the legislation;
- a statement signifying to what extent the legislation may affect or interact with other legislation;
- a statement that the Crown is bound by the legislation;
- a statement that the legislation is not to affect the availability of civil (common law) remedies;
- a statement of the objectives of the legislation;
- a statement of the objectives of the statutory authorities created by or operating under the legislation;
- a statement of the functions of those statutory authorities;
- provisions which empower the creation of instruments of management or control such as policies, plans, notices and conditional licensing by statutory authorities;
- provisions which identify relevant criteria which govern the exercise of specific functions;
- provisions which impose certain duties on decision-makers to do certain things, such as to have regard to stipulated instruments of management or stipulated criteria;
- provisions for enforcement of the legislation.

Legislative tools for environmental management

Some of the common management tools include the following:

State policies State policies aim to ensure that consistent planning or environmental controls are imposed throughout a state; and that a co-ordinated and integrated approach is taken to development which might require the input of a number of permitting authorities.

Management plans, strategies and programmes These are a central feature of resource management, and commonly provided for in environmental planning, **national parks**, wildlife, forests, water, land degradation and fisheries legislation.

Property and conservation agreements and covenants These enable resource-based agencies to make legal agreements with private landowners, to provide for financial or equivalent management incentives (for example grants for fencing).

Guidelines These effectively indicate criteria that should or must be followed in applying for permits of various kinds, and in environmental assessment of proposals or in decision-making.

Codes of practice Codes of practice may be developed by particular industry sectors or by the regulatory authorities. They generally appear in the form of industry codes for best practice directed to particular industries or activities and may be supported by more detailed guidelines.

Economic incentives These may be offered as an inducement to the promotion of good resource management, for example grants and rates relief in conjunction with property or conservation agreements; or as an encouragement towards the achievement of better standards of resource management, for example through the imposition of the **polluter pays principle** and load based licensing. Credit trading schemes offer another form of economic incentive.

Declarations of protected areas This is a common device for conservation and management. Such declarations normally cover only public land. For privately owned land, conservation or property agreements are likely to achieve a more satisfactory negotiated solution.

Conservation or land management notices and orders These enable land management agencies to prohibit certain activities or compel private or public landowners to carry out conservation or land management works on their land; and may enable the agency to enter onto land and carry out such works and recover costs from the landowner.

Conditional leases Leases of crown land may be issued subject to conditions of management.

Conditional licensing It is common in all environmental protection legislation to allow a competent authority to permit by licence activities which otherwise would be illegal. Conditions under which activities may be carried out may then be imposed by the authority. Any breach of the licence, or carrying on an activity without a licence where one is required, is regarded as a criminal offence.

Further reading

Bates G.M. (2001) *Environment Law in Australia*, Sydney: Butterworths, 5th edn.
Bates G.M. and Lipman Z (1998) *Corporate Liability for Pollution*, Sydney: Law Book.
Farrier D. (1999) *Environmental Law Handbook (NSW)*, Sydney: Redfern Press.

GERRY BATES

Australian regulatory agencies

The significant environmental regulatory agencies in Australia are located at the level of state and territory governments, although in some instances limited powers have been devolved onto local government. This is because the Constitution reserves to the states those powers not explicitly allocated to the Commonwealth government.

This constitutional arrangement has occasionally produced tensions, as state governments have generally been seen as more developmentalist in their orientation, often exhibiting a reluctance to impose strict environmental regulation lest they induce industry to relocate to other states. As a result, conflict has often been displaced to the Commonwealth level, where the national government has occasionally acted to resolve conflicts, using powers such as that over trading corporations, trade and commerce or external affairs. In 1999 the Commonwealth government (with the Environment Protection and Biodiversity Conservation Act 1999) regularized the conditions under which matters would be subject to Commonwealth development approval, in which case the Department of Environment and Heritage would become involved.

This in many ways marked the end-point of a process of redefinition of state and Commonwealth powers in relation to the environment which had commenced in the late 1970s and early 1980s with the cases involving sand mining on Fraser Island and the Tasmanian dams case. While the Commonwealth intervened decisively in these cases and others involving the Wesley Vale pulp mill proposal and the Wet Tropics, the 'New Federalism' of Prime Minister Bob Hawke in the early 1990s saw a growing reluctance on the part of the Commonwealth to assert greater authority, perhaps reflecting a belief that it lacked the capacity to govern effectively a land mass the size of Australia.

New Federalism produced an Intergovernmental Agreement on the Environment, the most significant result of which was perhaps the establishment of the National Environmental Protection Council, an intergovernmental body which has been effective in developing harmonized national approaches to many environmental problems with the development of National Environmental Protection Measures (NEPMs) and a National Pollutant Inventory (NPI). Western Australia was initially reluctant to join this body, fearing that harmonized output standards would be developed which might be appropriate in the more heavily industrialized states but which would be unduly harsh for its circumstances. These difficulties have been overcome by ensuring that harmonization has largely been of ambient standards rather than output standards.

The state regulatory agencies themselves have evolved considerably in response to political demands for environmental management, reflecting both the capacity in federal systems for experimentation in institutional approaches and eventual convergence on what has been perceived as the most effective model. This has been the establishment of an 'Environmental Protection Authority' or EPA in which holistic consideration is given to environmental pollution, including preventative measures (such as cleaner production techniques), rather than responsibility for discharges into air and water or into or onto land residing with different agencies, as had often been the case.

The EPA approach was introduced into Victoria in 1970 and Western Australia shortly thereafter, but New South Wales persisted for many years with a State Pollution Control Commission before

adopting an EPA in 1991. In 1998, Queensland established an EPA, but this was an 'agency' rather than an 'authority'. It is essentially a traditional government department, and enjoys little independence, unlike the EPA in Victoria, where successive governments have come to accept that there are some advantages in having transparent decision-making at some remove from politicians, both in terms of 'blame avoidance' on their part and predictability for industry having to make investment decisions.

The situation in Queensland perhaps reflects the persistence of a developmentalism embedded in the state government machinery which is present to a lesser extent in other states, including the similarly resource-dependent Western Australia, and which sees regulation of environmental aspects left to the mining agency which has as its principal role the fostering of **mining**. A similar lingering commitment to developmentalism persisted in Tasmania in the form of provision for ministers to grant exemptions from the requirements of the Environment Protection Act 1973, which successive ministers duly did for the worst polluters. This was removed by the Labour government which came to power as the result of the Accord with the Greens in 1989. Tasmania is now alone among the Australian states in not having an EPA, with environmental responsibilities residing with the Department of Primary Industries, Water and Environment.

Most states have also gathered the management of land and water resources into a single agency – Natural Resources and Environment in Victoria, Land and Water Resources in New South Wales. Because they often brought conservation and **forest management** functions together, these agencies have sometimes been embroiled in controversy, especially in the case of the Department of Conservation and Land Management in Western Australia, where there has been continuing conflict over logging of native forests.

AYNSLEY KELLOW

Austrian Greens

The Austrian Greens' roots go back to the early 1980s when two green parties were launched in the aftermath of the successful movement against nuclear power plants in 1978. The United Greens (*Vereinigten Grüne Österreichs*, VGÖ) were a moderate to conservative bourgeois party organized along conventional lines. The Alternative List (*Alternative Liste Österreichs*, ALÖ) was a leftist party aligned with the grassroots–democratic model of the *Die Grünen* (the German Greens). In the parliamentary election of 1983, the parties competed against each other and neither won seats. The opposition to the Hainburg hydroelectric project in 1984–5 caused the Greens to take off nationally. A coalition of green parties and groups formed around the presidential candidacy of Freda Meissner-Blau (who won a respectable 5.5 per cent of vote), and it continued as an electoral alliance in the 1986 parliamentary election, winning 4.8 per cent and 8 seats. In 1987 the Green Alternative Party ('Greens') was launched as the ALÖ and most of the VGÖ merged. Soon dissidents resurrected a rump VGÖ, which survived (with covert assistance from the major parties) into the mid-1990s. The Greens won 4.8 per cent of the vote in the 1990 parliamentary election; their breakthrough came in 1991 when they won 9.1 per cent in the Vienna election.

The Austrian Greens have never[1] sought to become a membership party. Officially they have reported a direct membership of 2,000 (independent observers have estimated no more than 800 activists/members) in the 1990s. Continuous public quarreling marked the early history of the party. However, intra-party strife did not follow the German cleavage of *Fundis* (fundamentalists) versus *Realos* (realists) because there was little prospect of sharing power nationally with the Social Democrats (*Sozialistische Partei Österreichs*, SPÖ). There were regional tensions between the western and the eastern parties (especially Vienna's more leftist party). In 1992 the Greens began a series of reforms, initiated by national figures, to move away from the grassroots-democratic model of party organization. For example, they abandoned the rule separating parliamentary membership and party leadership. In 1994 Madeleine Petrovic was allowed to chair the parliamentary group and to become federal party speaker (leader). Also the party, which never embraced the German Greens'

rule of midterm rotation, eased restrictions on the number of consecutive terms that parliamentarians could serve.

Surveys indicate that in the 1990s green voters were motivated primarily by the party's stance on ecology and secondarily by its stance against the established parties' cartel. The Greens drew heavy support from those 18–29 years old, with above average education, and who resided in large cities. Its programmes have emphasized: **ecological modernization** (including tax reform); opposition to the **European Union** on ecological and democratic grounds (after Austria's entry in 1995 the party accepted the EU, but have opposed the 'euro' common currency and any militarization of the EU); defence of the **human rights** especially of women (the party has a gender quota) and immigrants; and opposition to NATO membership. The party did well in the 1994 parliamentary election (7.1 per cent) with Petrovic as its media 'super-star', but she stumbled in the 1995 parliamentary campaign, some leftist voters shifted to the SPÖ as the barrier against the right-wing threat posed by Jörg Haider of the Freedom Party (*Freiheitliche Partei Österreichs*, FPÖ), and the Liberal Forum (a splinter from the FPÖ) competed with the Greens for social liberals' votes. The party was back to square one (4.8 per cent). However, as disenchantment set in with the EU, its votes picked up in the 1996 election to fill Austria's European Parliament seats (6.8 per cent) and went even higher in the 1999 EP election (9.3 per cent).

In the 1999 parliamentary election, the Greens scored their best ever result, winning 7.4 per cent of the vote. Many observers have given their new federal speaker (and parliamentary group chair), Alexander Van der Bellen a large portion of the credit for his party's surge since 1996. Van der Bellen, who is a professor of economics at the University of Vienna, has performed with a distinctive 'anti-politician' style blending competence, straightforwardness, and modesty, which appeals to the centre. As party leader, he has gone a long way in consolidating the Greens and ending the public venting of intra-party quarrels. Further professionalization of the party will be likely under his leadership. The political landscape since 1999 has changed in a way favourable to the prospects of the Austrian Greens. With the Liberal Forum gone from parliament and the SPÖ (still lacking credibility as a reformist force) forced into opposition by the new coalition of Christian Democrats (*Österreichische Volkspartei*, ÖVP) and Haider's FPÖ, the Greens seem well positioned as 'the' reformist opposition party, raising speculations about whether there might be a SPÖ/Green coalition option in Austrian national politics.

Further reading

Frankland, E.G. (1995) 'The Austrian Greens: From Electoral Alliance to Political Party', in W. Rüdig (ed.) *Green Politics 3*, Edinburgh: Edinburgh University Press, pp. 192–216.

Lauber, V. (1997) 'The Mixed Fortunes of the Austrian Greens in the Mid-1990s', *Environmental Politics*, 6(1) (spring): 185–92.

Van der Bellen, A. (1999) 'Grüner Wahlerfolg und eisiger Wind von rechts', *Schrägstrich* (German Greens' federal party magazine) 11–12: 22.

E. GENE FRANKLAND

B

Bahro, Rudolf

b.1935, Berlin, Germany; d.1997, Berlin

Green thinker, politician and activist

Rudolf Bahro was a communist dissident, an early member of the German Greens and a leading proponent of spiritual green political thought and action. Soon after he was deported from East to West Germany in 1977, Bahro became involved with the nascent German Greens (*Die Grünen*), and strongly identified with the 'eco-socialist' wing of the green movement, arguing for a synthesis of green and socialist ideals and aims. However, throughout the early 1980s, Bahro became an increasingly vocal spokesperson for the 'fundi' or fundamentalist wing of the party. He left the party in 1985. In the mid-1980s, in keeping with his disillusionment with *Die Grünen* and 'normal' democratic politics, he began to speak less in political terms and more in religious/spiritual terms. Bahro had come to the view that if the greens were to address the ecological crisis by radically changing society, they had to focus their efforts on the psychological, cultural and spiritual levels. Some accused him of flirting with fascism, authoritarian spirituality and linking ecological politics to right-wing/conservative/nationalistic values and principles. He has been portrayed as believing that the ecological crisis is resolvable only through authoritarian, non-democratic means. Standing above Bahro's later analysis of and political prescriptions for the ecological crisis seem to be modern, green descendants of Plato's Guardians, dedicated, knowledgeable and wise elite stewards who will guide society in the right direction away from ecological, spiritual and cultural disaster, who govern without any democratic input from the people. The increasingly authoritarian dimension of Bahro's thought and strategy for dealing with the ecological crisis is what many find most worrying.

Further reading

Barry, J. (2000) 'Rudolf Bahro', in Palmer, J. (ed.) *50 Key Environmental Thinkers*, London: Routledge.

JOHN BARRY

Baltic Sea

Environmental protection was one of the first areas in which the states of the Baltic Sea region were able to co-operate with the onset of pan-European detente in the early 1970s. The 1974 Helsinki Convention on the Protection of the Marine Environment of the Baltic Sea Area established the Helsinki Commission (HELCOM) to draw up non-binding recommendations on specific measures to prevent and reduce pollution of the Baltic Sea. Its initial focus on shipping and scientific co-operation in assessing the sea's quality status gradually widened to include reducing pollutant inputs from land-based sources. Regular national reporting on implementation of Recommendations began in the mid-1980s. The 1988 HELCOM goal of a 50 per cent reduction of total discharges into the Baltic Sea was followed by the approval of a Joint Comprehensive Environmental Action Programme (JCP) and agreement on a more inclusive and demanding Convention (1992 Helsinki Convention). In identifying 'hot spots' for remedial action, HELCOM now stressed the dependence of environmental improvements on the success of economic restructuring in the former East Bloc. The JCP became part of the environmental action programme of the Council of Baltic Sea States (CBSS) established in 1992 to promote **democracy**, economic **development** and environmental improvement in the formerly Communist Baltic rim states. The European Commission plays an increasingly important role in the CBSS, further encouraged by the successful Finnish initiative to introduce a 'Northern Dimension' into the policies of the **European Union**.

See also: Finland; international environmental laws/treaties; Russian Federation/Former Soviet Union

DAVID SCRIVENER

Bangladesh

Bangladesh is one of the few countries in the world where the amount of poverty is concentrated among so many people in so small an area and with so bleak an outlook. All available arable land has been utilized for many decades, but ownership is very unevenly distributed. Programmes against poverty have, since independence, changed greatly. Still they continue to succeed in employing the middle **class** and providing fine political rhetoric, not in reducing poverty. During 1990–4 the average annual population growth rate was 1.7 per cent, lower than the 2.4 per cent per annum of the 1980s, but still high for a poor country. This decline will have very little impact on the growth of the labour force in the short or medium term, because the new entrants in the labour force up to the year 2010 have already been born.

Even given full labour absorption in crop production, there will remain a large surplus of labour for whom gainful employment opportunities need to be created in the non-crop sector, where the growth of employment has been very limited.

The modern industrial sector cannot absorb the surplus labour because of its narrow base, its capital intensive nature and a host of other techno-economic factors. Moreover, urban-based **industrialization** provides little relief to the rural populace. Compared to many other Low Income Economies Bangladesh has failed to generate sufficient employment in the non-farm sector.

Apart from the economic misfortune, Bangladesh is located in one of the worst environmental corners in the world. In other words, it is located in one of the most disaster-prone areas of the world. Its coasts are susceptible to cyclones, most of which are almost near the sea-level. Except for a few Pleistocene terraces, the whole country is a flood plain. So, a severe flood may inundate around 50 per cent of the land area of this densely populated country.

Floods affect not only the **agriculture** of the country but the livelihoods of the majority of the population. Although it helps irrigation since only 20 per cent of the croplands are artificially irrigated, moderate to severe flooding drives many small and medium farmers to leave villages and find a room in the mushrooming urban slums in Bangladesh. The responses to these environmental disasters have been two-fold. First, due to the weakness of the state and its lack of resources, international donor and aid agencies have funded the construction of many embankments and barrages along the major rivers. Cyclone shelters for the coastal people have been built in the same way. Second, a large number of non-governmental organizations (NGOs) have been working in post-disaster relief and development work targeting women (see **international non-governmental organizations**). NGOs provide services like microcredit, education, health awareness and skill-training. Donors who want to help the poor in Bangladesh prefer the NGO channel due to its efficiency compared to the state.

A major environmental disaster that has recently struck Bangladesh is contamination by arsenic in almost one-third of the tube-wells of the country. This is ironic since every effort has been made to motivate the people to drink 'safe' water from wells instead of rivers, canals or ponds. Leaving aside the cause of this disaster, the mitigation and cure for this have shown little success. Another example is the environmental impact of shrimp cultivation in the coastal areas which was driven by the short-term goal of gaining foreign currency through export. The net effect of this project is the encroachment of salinity in the croplands and loss of livelihoods of many farmers. Some NGOs in Bangladesh and in the West tried to highlight this issue again with little success.

The response to the environmental effects of these structural measures to mitigate floods has been rather muted. Donors and the elite in Bangladesh prefer them because these constructions bring money and employment to both sides. **Civil society** and NGOs in Bangladesh have been more involved in national issues like women's rights, fair election and rights of the sex workers or slum dwellers. Bangladesh has no major environmental movements like the **Chipko Andolan Movement** or Narmada Bachao in its neighbouring **India** (see also **Narmada Valley development programme**). One reason could be the absence of public awareness towards the environmental time bomb on which Bangladesh is sitting. Another reason could be that the poor and their NGOs are busy with their short-term goal of meeting their basic needs, ignoring the vision and mission of a long-term **sustainable development** which is not found at the top of their agenda.

MOKBUL MORSHED AHMAD

Bari, Judith Beatrice

b. 7 November 1949, Baltimore, Maryland, USA; d. 2 March 1997, Willits, California

Environmental and labour activist

A drop-out from the University of Maryland, Judi Bari worked as a grocery clerk and a postal worker, and became a labour union activist. In 1979 she moved to California where she worked as a carpenter. In 1988 she joined the **Earth First!** direct action campaign to preserve old growth forests. But she also continued her labour activism by finding common cause with timber workers. Bari opposed the 'tree-spiking' tactics of Earth First! because of the threat of injuries to workers. In

1990, in response to Louisiana-Pacific's 'liquidation logging', she proposed that its forest lands be seized by Mendocino County and be managed by a worker co-operative. Bari stood out among radical environmentalists through her efforts to build worker–environmentalist alliances.

In spring 1990, Bari and Darryl Cherney co-organized 'Redwood Summer' to bring thousands of university students to the old growth forests for nonviolent resistance to logging.

On 24 May 1990, Bari and Cherney were car bombed in Oakland, California; Bari was nearly killed. The FBI had them under surveillance as 'eco-terrorists', (see **eco-terrorism**) and the Oakland police arrested them for knowingly transporting a bomb. After a media smear campaign, the authorities, lacking credible evidence, dropped the charges and closed the case. In 1991, Bari and Cherney filed a civil rights lawsuit against the FBI and the Oakland Police (which is still in progress). Despite her disabilities, Bari continued to speak out and to organize **non-violent direct action** against the giant timber companies. In 1997 Bari succumbed to breast cancer.

Further reading:

Bari, J. (1994) *Timber Wars* Monroe, Maine: Common Courage Press.

E. GENE FRANKLAND

Basel Convention

Signed in 1989 and ratified in 1992, the Basel Convention regulates the transboundary movements of hazardous wastes. By 2000 the Convention had 132 parties, not including the USA, the world's largest generator of hazardous waste.

Measures adopted in 1989 include:

1 A system of Prior Informed Consent whereby the transboundary movement of hazardous waste can only occur after the notification of and consent from the 'competent authority' in the importing country.
2 The export of hazardous waste to countries who have banned such imports domestically is illegal. **Antarctica** is included in this.

3 Exports of hazardous waste to non-parties is illegal unless they are subject to a comparable convention.

A subsequent measure, adopted in 1994, bans the export of hazardous waste from Organization for Economic Co-Operation and Development (OECD) states to non OECD states.

PETER HOUGH

basic income

A basic income (BI), or citizens' income, is a proposal to reform the tax and benefit systems that has wide implications for economic, employment and social policies. A BI would be periodically received by everyone as a right of citizenship and unconditionally, i.e. without reference to marital or employment status, employment history and intention to seek employment. It would replace most benefits, tax reliefs and allowances, and could be age-related, e.g. with a higher BI for elderly people. BI therefore represents an alternative both to means-testing and to the social insurance principle.

Although BI has a long history, the idea has only gained widespread support since the 1970s. It has been defended from all parts of the ideological spectrum, although for different reasons and with different implications for its specific design and implementation. All supporters agree that a BI would have the following advantages: it would be more effective than existing policies at guaranteeing a minimum income for all; it would embody the equal rights of all citizens; it would tackle poverty and unemployment traps; it would enhance individuals' freedom and security; it would be easy to understand and administer. However, BI's critics allege that the proposal: ignores the obligations of citizenship; would either be too expensive or, if it were to be made affordable, would not itself provide enough to live on; will never attract enough political and popular support.

Green theorists and parties have been among the most prominent supporters of BI because it takes the emphasis away from paid employment and could help to facilitate an increase in free time. In general, green social policies would be organized around a much broader conception of welfare than prevails at present and would abandon a 'productivist' ethic of growth for growth's sake. Accordingly, a BI could make three significant contributions to an environmental society. First, it could help to slow Gross Domestic Product (GDP): if a BI were to be high enough then many people might be encouraged to opt out of the formal economy into the third sector. Second, because it would be unconditional a BI might embody an ethic of common ownership, the idea that a basic level of the wealth created through the use of natural resources should be distributed equally to all. Finally, a BI is a visionary yet practical proposal that, by addressing specific social problems, could encourage people to support other green reforms.

However, there are those within the green movement who criticize the BI idea. First, the transformatory potential of BI might be quite low. For instance, it might not slow GDP growth down because the substantially high level at which a BI would need to be paid to make this happen is impracticable and unsustainable. Second, even if people were freed from the formal economy this does not necessarily mean that they would work and live within the third sector; the fact that a BI would be unconditional might promote environmentally *damaging* activity. Finally, a BI would have to be centrally administered and so seems to contradict the social and economic decentralization that most greens favour.

Whilst offering counter-arguments to these criticisms, supporters of BI accept that it should not be regarded as the sufficient condition of a green society. Therefore, BI tends to be regarded as one element of a wider 'policy package'. This package includes the kind of **eco-taxes** for which those such as James **Robertson** have argued, with BI counter-acting for the potentially regressive effects of these taxes. In addition, **Gorz** (1989) anticipates that a minimum income would constitute a 'second cheque' to compensate for the fewer hours that he recommends people should have to work in the future. Initially, he also believed that those receiving this cheque should first have to perform a minimum numbers of working hours, although he has now acknowledged the benefits of an unconditional income that is more consistent with BI (Gorz, 1999: 85–93). Finally, those such as Claus Offe (1996) have made links between BI and the kind of informal, co-operative economies of which LETS (Local Employment and Trading Systems) are one possible prototype.

See also: distributive justice; New Economics Foundation; Rifkin, Jeremy; risk society

References

Gorz, A. (1989) *Critique of Economic Reason*, London: Verso.
—— (1999) *Reclaiming Work*, Cambridge: Polity Press.
Offe, C. (1996) *Modernity and the State: East, West*, Cambridge: Polity Press.

Further reading

Fitzpatrick, T. (1999) *Freedom and Security*, London: Macmillan.
Van Parijs, P. (ed.) (1992) *Arguing for Basic Income*, London: Verso.

TONY FITZPATRICK

BBU

BBU, the German Federal Association of Citizen Action Groups for Environmental Protection, is a loose network of formally and informally organized citizen action groups focusing on environmental issues. It was founded in 1972 as the first national umbrella organization of the fledgling German environmental movement. In contrast with older conservationist organizations the BBU was clearly associated with political ecology and the **new social movements**. It paved the way for other more formally organized ecologist social movements as well as the German Green Party. Due to the informal organizational structure, exact figures about membership are notoriously difficult to come by. Until the late 1980s the BBU claimed to represent about 200 local groups. In the 1990s the unbureaucratic and decentralized structures became an obstacle in so far as they proved inappropriate for contemporary campaigning strategies. They are also unsuitable for modern techniques of fundraising and membership recruitment. In recent years the BBU has become increasingly marginal with its future being uncertain.

INGOLFUR BLÜHDORN

Belgium

The Kingdom of Belgium is a small (30,545 square kilometres) and densely populated country (about 10.2 million inhabitants). It also features a high density of transportation, industrial infrastructures and urban or suburban built surface, and hence a high degree of human pressure on the natural environment. Furthermore, it is an extremely busy continental transit zone in terms of passenger and freight **transportation**. The modalities of human pressure on the environment however vary greatly between subregions which feature older heavy industries (such as the East–West industrial basin which spans the whole of Wallonia, the southern region), and subregions which feature a fast-growing service sector and/or high-tech economic activity.

Before the 1960s, the environment was not considered a major political issue. A large number of national nature protection organizations already existed. From the second half of the 1960s onwards, a large number of very diverse groupings sprang up, mainly in reaction to some local infrastructure-building schemes. In 1971, a national federation of environmental organizations was created, then in 1974 separate federations in Wallonia (*Inter-Environnement Wallonie*), Flanders (*Bond Beter Leefmilieu*) and the Brussels area, gathering an increasing number of organizations. Intense debates opposed more moderate groups (directed towards nature protection) and more radical ecologist groups. A particularly divisive issue was **nuclear energy**, as the authorities pursued a very ambitious building scheme of nuclear power plants. Eventually, many activists from the more radical movements, such as the Belgian section of **Friends of the Earth**, became involved in politics and were among the founding fathers of the two green parties.

In the course of the 1970s, environmental politics and policies began to institutionalize. The first significant pieces of legislation, regarding water protection, were passed in 1971. The next year, a specific ministerial committee was set up, as well as parliamentary committees. The first 'environment' ministerial portfolio was created in 1973. However, the real burst of environmental legislative production occurred in the 1980s and early 1990s. It coincided with the country's gradual transformation from a unitary to a federal system. In 1980, 1988 and 1993, most environment-related prerogatives were transferred to the three regions (Flanders, Wallonia and Brussels). Some important prerogatives have however been maintained at the federal level, such as the definition of emission norms, nuclear and energy policy, international conventions and agreements and some aspects of public health. From 1997 onwards, **sustainable development** has become a full policy domain, with the creation of a specific federal advisory body and ministerial portfolio.

Environmental policies and politics have become increasingly institutionalized. From the early 1980s onwards, the two green parties (**Ecolo** and **Agalev**) became stable parliamentary parties, and contributed notably to agenda-setting. In addition, a whole range of administrative units and specialized agencies were created at the national and – increasingly – regional levels, with regards to nature protection, waste management, water management, pollution control, etc. Third, a series of advisory bodies, comprising representatives from the socio-economic sectors and environmentalist groups were set up in order to monitor the elaboration and implementation of various policies. In the process, many environmental organizations have become much more moderate and reform-orientated. However, some organizations, such as the Belgian branch of **Greenpeace**, still resort to more extra-institutional actions. Furthermore, from the second half of the 1990s onwards, more radical groups emerged, advocating direct action (such as *GAIA*, an animal-rights organization), or even **eco-terrorism** (such as a Belgian extension of the Animal Liberation Front; see **animal rights**).

Many environment-related issues have stirred controversy. This is not only the case with nuclear energy and countless **NIMBY**-style problems. The most recurrent issues have probably been the building of high-speed railways, the management of waste dumpsites, and the increasingly conflict-laden problem of underground water poisoning by nitrates from industrial **agriculture** (especially in Flanders). From 1992 onwards, the **eco-taxes**, brought on the agenda by the Greens, were a major issue, but their implementation scheme was eventually dropped. From the second half of the 1990s onwards, issues related to food and consumer protection became increasingly salient, culminating in the 'dioxin scandal' (a broad contamination of the food chain) in 1999.

Further reading

Bursens, P. (1997) 'Environmental interest representation in Belgium and the EU: Professionalization and Division of Labour within a Multi-Level Governance Setting', *Environmental Politics* 6(4): 51–75.

Gobin, C. (1986) 'L'Etat belge et la problématique de l'environnement', *Courrier Hebdomadaire du CRISP* 1109.

Rihoux, B. (2000) 'Ecotaxes on the Belgian Agenda, 1992–5 and Beyond: Environment and Economy at the Heart of the Power Struggle', in S. Young (ed.) *The Emergence of Environmental Modernisation*, London: Routledge.

Rihoux, B. and Molitor, M. (1997) 'Les nouveaux mouvements sociaux en Belgique francophone : l'unité dans la diversité?', *Recherches Sociologiques* 28(1): 59–78.

Walgrave, S. (1994) *Nieuwe sociale bewegingen in Vlaanderen. Een sociologische verkenning van de milieubeweging, de derde wereldbeweging en de vredesbeweging*, Leuven: SOI/KULeuven.

BENOÎT RIHOUX

Berry, Wendell

b. 5 August 1934, Port Royal, Kentucky, USA

Author and ecology advocate

Wendell Berry is a farmer, teacher, writer, and

ecology advocate who, during the last few decades, has become an internationally known voice of the modern **environmental movement**. In his essays, poems, short stories, and novels, Berry writes with eloquence and passion about the importance of his attachment to the land, the human connection to the soil, and the value of family and community while, at the same time, criticizing the rise of corporate **agriculture** and our increasing loss of personal identity. In a quiet, measured style, this farmer-teacher poses such important questions as, 'What is this place? And, What is its nature?' His life is a unique combination of a long-time academic and farmer who works the land with horses and produces his own food and fuel.

Further reading

Berry, W. (1993) *Sex, Economy, Freedom and Community*, New York: Pantheon Books.

WARREN VANDER HILL

Bhopal disaster

On 3 December 1984, the world's worst ever industrial accident occurred at Bhopal, India. During the production of the pesticide Carbaryl, the plant, owned by the American multi-national corporation Union Carbide, accidentally released 40 tonnes of the highly toxic chemical methyl-isocyanate (MIC) used in the production process. At least 2,500 people living near the plant were killed and around 180,000 other people have since suffered from a range of long-term health effects and birth defects.

As an intermediate chemical, MIC did not feature on the *International Register of Potentially Toxic Chemicals* of the **United Nations Environment Programme** (UNEP), and Indian authorities were unaware that it was being stored. Investigations proved that safety standards at the plant were weak and that previous fatal accidents had occurred. Years of legal wrangling following the accident have seen Union Carbide pay $470 million to the Indian government in an out-of-

court settlement, and 600,000 Indian citizens claim compensation.

PETER HOUGH

biodiversity

Biodiversity refers to the global variety of life forms, or their genes, as a natural resource. The concept was invented in the mid-1980s to articulate the extinction crisis of wild species of plants and animals, and whole eco-systems, such as tropical **rainforests**. Similarly, gene pools within **agriculture** were shrinking rapidly, with domesticated crop and animal varieties and whole farming systems disappearing. Most biodiversity exists in the tropical Third World. Poor farmers and **indigenous people** in the South depend on agricultural and natural diversity to maintain a varied agriculture and secure food supply. Biodiversity became enshrined in international law as the Convention on Biological Diversity at the Earth Summit in Rio de Janeiro in 1992. Critics suggested that the sudden eagerness to protect genetic diversity coincided with the development of the **biotechnology** industry in northern countries which could potentially turn genes into profits.

See also: biopiracy/bioprospecting; endangered species

DERRICK PURDUE

biopiracy/bioprospecting

The development of **genetic engineering** from the mid-1970s and the extension of **property rights** to include gene patenting has led to a search for patentable genes as a basis for marketable products, usually pharmaceuticals. Biopiracy and bioprospecting both refer to this attempt to locate genes and to capture them as unique property; where the two terms differ is on the legitimacy of such an exercise.

The idea of bioprospecting is related to Prospect Theory, which has been used as an argument to justify patenting. Prospect Theory owes its name to the gold prospectors of the 'Wild' West in America. By analogy with mineral claims, it is argued that private property is more efficient than common property and that patents will encourage patent owners to co-ordinate research and development. Prospecting takes private property into previously unclaimed territory, which on closer inspection is usually the common property of another society. Bioprospecting is not purely about locating genes, but also about making and settling claims to ownership.

Searching for usable genes in an eco-system can be done by systematically scanning large numbers of local organisms, or by working from the knowledge held by local people, embodied in their current usage of whole plants or parts thereof. Using this local knowledge, scientists are then able to isolate active ingredients and the genes controlling the production of the active ingredients. Once such a gene has been isolated, it is possible to acquire a patent whether or not this gene is transferred to another organism.

A series of bioprospecting deals have been struck between companies and indigenous communities, the most famous of which between Merck & Co. Ltd and INBIO, a not-for-profit organization in Costa Rica. Merck acquired the rights to any product they could produce from genetic scanning of the Costa Rican National Forest (Reid *et al.* 1993). Bioprospecting deals have been put forward as equitable models of co-operation and benefit sharing with local communities.

In the run up to signing the **World Trade Organization** trade agreement, northern (particularly American) companies made much of the 'piracy' of their intellectual property rights, when their copyrighted computer programs were copied by South East Asian companies. Non-governmental organizations (NGOs) have ironically reversed the charge of piracy to coin the term biopiracy for the patenting of natural and agricultural products in the South by northern companies.

A series of cases have emerged of northern companies laying claim to novel products derived from plants already in use in the South. Turmeric, bringal (aubergine), basmati rice and various part of the Neem tree have long been in use in **India** for nutritional and medicinal reasons. All have

been patented by northern companies. Legally, a patent cannot be granted on an invention that is already in the public domain. Yet, this public domain tends to refer to established similar technologies not traditional uses. This type of patenting has been called biopiracy on the grounds that to claim a monopoly of the knowledge and **property rights** to these genes involves theft of genes that are already owned collectively and of the knowledge embodied in their usage. The objection is not against using these genes, but in creating monopoly rights to their use. Patents enclose the genes and the knowledge of their use from public access, even by those who were already using them prior to the patent. In the case of seeds this kind of patenting would prevent farmers from saving seed and re-planting it, or from using it to develop new varieties. Seed companies may introduce DNA markers, so that future generations derived from their patented seed may be identified in order to prosecute farmers.

See also: genetic engineering, crops

Further reading

Baumann, M, *et al.* (1996) *The Life Industry: Biodiversity, People and Profits*, London: IT Publications.

Reid, W, *et al.* (1993) *Biodiversity Prospecting: Using Genetic Resources for Sustainable Development*, Washington: World Resources Institute.

DERRICK PURDUE

bioregionalism

Bioregionalism could be viewed as one of the most radical versions of green decentralist thought. Central to this current is the notion that a key cause of the 'ecological crisis' is that modern industrial societies have obscured or lost contact with the extent to which they are reliant on and embedded in ecosystems. It is maintained that modern human beings have lost a sense of place and belonging to the land, demonstrating little real knowledge or appreciation of the immediate specific locale where they live. The bioregional project thus necessitates that this detachment is reversed by human beings becoming, as Kirkpatrick Sale argues, 'dwellers on the land', living as close to **nature** as possible and letting the rhythms of the land, its soils, winds, patterns and limits enter into human social life.

The idea of a bioregion suggests the Earth has certain contours or boundaries that are dictated by natural rather than human dictates, by attributes of flora, fauna, water, climate soils and land forms. Bioregions can thus be defined by measures of native vegetation, soil contours and watershed. Bioregionalists argue it would be appropriate for those seeking to build sustainable societies and economies to (a) most modestly attend to working with this 'grain of nature' (b) more commonly and more radically, seek wholesale redesign of human political boundaries and social forms so they are tailored to fit the unique natural boundaries of the bioregion.

Many bioregional writers have focused on envisaging how human beings might cultivate a deeper sense of place and awareness of ecosystems boundaries and vulnerabilities. Such writings often overlap with ecotopian themes present in **deep ecology**, **eco-feminism** and even currents of social ecology (see **utopia/ecotopia**). Bioregionalist ideas have also proved highly influential in attempts to develop an ecological aesthetics through 'green' art and drama. Work in green architecture over recent times has also sought to fashion distinct bioregional architectural styles through using building materials specific to a locality.

More explicitly, political forms of bioregionalist thought have also been influential in green politics. At the pragmatic end, resource management agencies in the USA have reorganized their field operations under offices defined by bioregions rather than state boundaries. European green parties have also deployed bioregional ideas in their commitment to a 'Europe of the Regions' which aspires to create a more decentralist, non-nationalist view of an alternative Europe to that of the existing **European Union**. Perhaps the most radical advocacy of bioregional ideas though has emerged in the USA, through the writings of Kirkpatrick Sale.

Mirroring the concerns of much eco-anarchism, radicals like Sale suggest that bioregionalism is ultimately incompatible with the current nation state system (see **anarchism/eco-anarchism**). Demanding that nation states be replaced by political units divided by bioregional boundaries, the preferred unit of bioregional radicals is invariably 'human scale' communities that are underpinned by self-sufficient economies which have abandoned elaborate networks of continental dependency. Sale also argues, (in a manoeuvre similar to **Bookchin**), that bioregional political values would be grounded in the natural values of diversity and decentralization. Yet, in a fashion quite unlike **social ecology**, it is maintained that truly autonomous bioregions will very likely develop highly disparate political systems, some of which may not be democratic.

Bioregionalists maintain that reliance on local sources could free economies from boom and bust cycles and distant political crises rather from resulting in impoverishment. Moreover, far from facilitating authoritarianism, bioregional communities would be freed from the systematic control and violence of distant and uncontrollable national bureaucracies. They would thus be marked by a sense of place, community and comradeship. Other green critics though have remained unconvinced. Social ecologists have insisted on the importance of confederal relations to avoid parochialism and poverty and the importance of defending a universal justification for direct **democracy**. Ecosocialist currents have equally warned of possible eco-fascist articulations of bioregional thought through 'blood and soil' ideology (see also **eco-socialism**). The extent to which radical bioregionalist thought falls into a form of geographical determinism and naive naturalism is a further issue. A sustainable society clearly needs to attend to its natural conditions and contexts to flourish. However, the extent to which this factor should completely determine human social and political life is clearly much more open to question.

See also: green political theory; sustainability

Further reading

Andruss, V., Plant, C. and Plant, J. (1991) *Home! A*

Bioregional Reader, London: New Society Publications.

Berg, P. and Dasmann, R. (1978) *Reinhabiting a Separate Country*, New York: Planet Drum Foundation.

Sale, K. (1985) *Dwellers on the Land: The Bioregional Vision*, San Francisco: Secker and Warberg.

DAMIAN WHITE

biotechnology

'Biotechnology' usually refers to modern techniques, e.g. genetic engineering, cloning or **xenotransplantation**. In prevalent definitions of biotechnology, however, its specificity has been rhetorically dissolved into the entire human history of biological intervention, e.g. yoghurt, beer brewing, bread-making, etc. In that vein, a widespread definition is 'any technique that uses living organisms (or parts of organisms) to make or modify products, to improve plants or animals, or to develop micro-organisms for specific uses'. An alternative definition is 'the application of organisms, biological systems or biological processes to manufacturing and service industries' – phrases which acknowledge the new commercial and technological context. Novelty has been downplayed in arguments that genetic engineering results in familiar, predictable products which therefore warrant no special regulation for environmental or health risks. By contrast, novelty is emphasized in arguments that biotechnology products are 'inventions' which therefore warrant patent rights.

See also: genetic engineering, animals; genetic engineering, crops; genetic engineering, humans

LES LEVIDOW

Black Forest

The Black Forest is a mountainous wooded area in the south west of Germany. Like other forests, it is of great cultural importance to Germans. Therefore, the revelation – in the 1980s – that over half of the Black Forest was dying from **acid rain** caused a public outcry. The dying Black Forest became a powerful symbol for a growing environmental movement. **Robin Wood** formed to stop what became known in Germany as 'Forest Death'. Regular reports on the state of the Black Forest drove environmental policy measures such as the fitting of scrubbers to coal power plants. Today, the majority of trees in the Black Forest remain sick. However, the rapid decline of the 1980s has been halted, leaving an inaccurate public perception that the Black Forest has been saved.

See also: acid rain; forest management

DANIEL MITTLER

Black Triangle

The Black Triangle refers to the border region of (formerly East) Germany, Poland and the Czech Republic, which faces a particularly grave **air pollution** crisis. The region has a high concentration of coal power stations, which burn high-polluting, locally mined lignite coal. SO_2 and NO_x concentrations, in particular, are very high in the area. They have killed most forests and have caused an epidemic of respiratory diseases and cancers among the local populations. Air pollution was at its worst before 1989, when food grown in East German gardens in the region was classified as 'toxic waste' and many coal plants operated very inefficiently. For example, one East German plant had not been upgraded since 1929! Post-1989, matters have improved marginally. Sadly, they have done so only through the closure of the most toxic plants, which has in turn resulted in very high unemployment.

DANIEL MITTLER

Blueprint for Survival

Blueprint for Survival was a radical ecological manifesto issued by the editors of the British magazine, *The Ecologist*, in January 1972. Through skilful PR it attracted extensive publicity, and in conjunction with the ***Limits to Growth*** report, stimulated much public debate in the UK about 'ecodoom'. The blueprint attracted criticism for its pessimism about the consequences of economic growth and technological change and also from anarchist writers concerned about the Blueprint's emphasis on the need for stability, the family and small communities (see **anarchism/eco-anarchism**).

The blueprint, through its fame, has become the most discussed environmental text of the 1970s, and to many writers becomes the starting point of the **environmental movement** in the UK. However, it is not an original work, but an amalgamation of previous work by the Conservation Society, the *Limits to Growth* report and its predecessor report, *Man's Impact on the Environment*, and Edward Goldsmith's edited book, *Can Britain Survive?* (1971).

HORACE HERRING

Bookchin, Murray

b. 14 January 1921, New York, USA

Political and social theorist

Over the course of his long career, Murray Bookchin has been known variously as a theoretician, political activist, environmental educator, historian of the left, labour organizer, and sometime public intellectual. He is best known, however, as the founder and leading figure of the school of anarchist political ecology known as **social ecology**. In addition to authoring over a dozen volumes on the subject, Bookchin also co-founded the Institute for Social Ecology in 1974 in Plainfield, Vermont, USA.

Born into the raucous intellectual climate of left sectarian politics in New York City between the World Wars, Bookchin was for many years active first in the youth wing of the Communist Party, then in Trotskyist circles and finally as a left-libertarian anarchist. While writing on a number of political issues of his day, his first work on the environment in the 1950s culminated eventually in his first book, published under the name Lewis Herber, *Our Synthetic Environment* (1962).

Bookchin's writings and debates with social activists during the 1960s and 1970s are published in *Post-Scarcity Anarchism* (1971) and *Toward an*

Ecological Society (1980). A more recent collection of articles entitled *The Modern Crisis* was published in 1986. In 1982 Bookchin published perhaps his best known book, *The Ecology of Freedom*. The positions developed in *The Ecology of Freedom* and his other publications have been further elaborated on in *The Rise of Urbanization and the Decline of Citizenship* (1987) summarized in *Remaking Society* (1989), and extended theoretically in *The Philosophy of Social Ecology* (1990, revised edition, 1995).

In general, Bookchin's social ecology posits a spontaneous and teleological evolution of matter towards increasing complexity and consciousness. Echoing Peter Kropotkin's evolutionary theory, in Bookchin's view, the link between the evolution of external nature and social nature is profound. The natural processes that we find in animal and plant evolution involving symbiotic participation reappear as distinctive social processes in human evolution. Human societies, though a continuation of natural evolution, are however quite different from the animal communities from which they evolved, since they produce institutions involving structures of contrived and constructed social rigidity. The initial evolution of human institutions is seen by Bookchin to have generated 'organic' preliterate societies in which internal social relations and relations with the external world were organized around mutualistic practices which supported social and ecological differentiation. Historically, the conditions within which these societies existed are seen to have been disturbed by nascent, increasingly institutionalized social relations of domination and hierarchy.

Relations of hierarchy and domination, for Bookchin, are inherently social and institutional. Relationships of hierarchy and domination, as institutions, can only be found in human societies, and, for Bookchin, cannot be said to exist in animal communities. Domination, as a coercive social relation, is seen to work against spontaneity and, unlike other social relations in organic societies, counters the processes of evolution. Given Bookchin's distinction between animal and plant communities and human societies, domination becomes the primary destructive relationship within society in that it destroys social 'participation and differentiation'.

The ecologically destructive character of hierarchy and domination emerges from ideologies of the domination of nature which spring from the real domination of human by human. On Bookchin's view, the history of social and natural evolution has become the history of two competing logics: the logic of spontaneous mutualistic ecological differentiation and the logic of domination which works against everything represented by the other. Bookchin's historical work explores how these two logics work themselves out as spontaneous organic societies are transformed into cities, city-states, nations, nation-states and capitalist political economies increasingly organized through domination and hierarchy. Out of this view of history, Bookchin builds a thoroughgoing positive theory of the reconstruction of society. Foremost among the steps necessary for the reconstitution of a more organic society and **nature** is a rebuilding of local human association and the reconstruction of human beings within a libertarian political eco-community. Re-empowering communities and people demands the abolition of the state, and the nation-state in particular.

The preferred social relationship for decision-making for Bookchin is democratic politics, not logistical administration. Bookchin envisions human scale communities linked in confederations. He advocates for these communities a strong form of direct **democracy**. For Bookchin, it is only through social institutions such as citizens' assemblies and the municipalization of property that we can overcome the social and ecological consequences of the centralized state, modern market economies, and the technologies they spawn. Overcoming these institutions is a necessary condition for re-establishing social and ecological differentiation.

See also: anarchism/eco-anarchism

Select bibliography

Bookchin, M. (1971) *Post-Scarcity Anarchism*, Montreal: Black Rose Books.
—— (1980) *Toward an Ecological Society*, Montreal: Black Rose Books.
—— (1982) *The Ecology of Freedom*, Palo Alto, CA: Cheshire Books.
—— (1986) *The Modern Crisis*, Philadelphia: New Society Publishers.
—— (1987) *The Rise of Urbanization and the Decline of Citizenship*, San Francisco: Sierra Club Books.
—— (1989) *Remaking Society*, Montreal: Black Rose Books.
—— (1990) *The Philosophy of Social Ecology*, Montreal: Black Rose Books.

Further reading

Chase, S. (ed.) (1990) *Defending the Earth : A Dialogue Between Murray Bookchin and Dave Foreman*, Boston: South End Press.
Herber, L. (1962) *Our Synthetic Environment*, New York: Harper & Row.
Light, A. (ed.) (1998) *Social Ecology after Bookchin*, New York: Guilford.

ANDREW LIGHT

Brazil

Brazil's people assert with confidence that 'Brazil is the country of the future'. Their belief is based on more than national pride. Brazil is the largest nation in South America in terms of population, land area, and economic productivity. With the exception of **fossil fuels**, it is rich in natural and cultural resources. It was spared the worst of the twentieth century's strife. Economic **globalization** has resulted in large technological, industrial, and service sectors within its economy and a growing middle **class**. Its people, including many of its poor, have experienced a generation of improving standards of living. Beyond all this, the people of Brazil have great confidence in a largely unsettled and beckoning frontier, **Amazonia**.

Brazil is also the country of a less confident future that reflects its past more than its potential. Before the European Age of Discovery, Brazil was inhabited by diverse societies of **indigenous peoples**, although no sedentary or imperial societies like the Mayan, Mississippian, Incan, or Aztec. The end of these Brazilian societies began in 1500 with the arrival of the Portuguese navigator Pedro Álvarez Cabral. The Portuguese sought trade wealth in new sea routes to Asia, but had to content themselves with plundering the natural and cultural wealth from this so-called New World. One form of this wealth, the fiery red-orange '*pau-brasil*' or 'ember-wood', gave Brazil its name. With time the Portuguese penetrated Brazil's southern and central interior to discover gold, silver, diamonds, emeralds, and other precious stones. Being adventurers rather than miners or settlers, the Portuguese first subdued and coerced what they could of the native population and then transported and enslaved people from Angola, Mozambique, and other parts of Africa to do the dangerous, heavy labour of resource extraction and the tedious, menial chores of daily life. As the quickest mineral and timber wealth disappeared, slavery was ended in 1888 and independence from Portugal gained in 1889. By independence an agrarian society re-creating Medieval European feudal patterns of concentrated land ownership had spread throughout Brazil's Atlantic states and into landlocked Minas Gerais. Since the 1970s this same pattern has extended further into the deep interior states of the Mato Grosso and Amazonia.

Other legacies of its colonial past persist in Brazil. The rubber boom of the first half of the twentieth century and the 'Brazilian miracle' of rapid **industrialization**, **urbanization**, and economic growth in the 1960s and 1970s improved the lives of many, but extreme concentrations of income, education, land ownership, and other real and personal wealth continued. In 1970 the hope for the social safety valve of 'land without men for men without land' led then-President Emilio Garrastazu Medici to begin the Trans-Amazon Highway with funding from the **World Bank**. Many landless rural poor migrated to the Amazon from the south and north-east seeking homes and farms and many unskilled urban young followed Brazil's old dream of quick wealth. In the ensuing land rush indigenous land claims were commonly ignored, as were the indigenous dispersed resource management practices. European diseases afflicted masses of indigenous populations, many homesteads failed on the productive but fragile soils, and most of the get-rich-quick dreams died. Soon enough land claims began passing into the hands of the same landowners from whom the poor had fled years earlier. A few Brazilians, notably the late

Chico **Mendes**, understood and resisted this process, but poverty, ignorance, violence, and Brazil's powerful landowning and governing elites have continued to promote and support it.

At the same time as the Amazon concerned the popular media and the scientific press, a far greater migration from Brazil's older rural areas to its urban industrial centres went relatively overlooked. The rapid population growth of the 'miracle' years began to slow as rural homelessness grew, especially in the south and south-east. Rural areas where a large family had been an economic advantage lost the young to the cities. Urban population growth has led to widespread unemployment and other social ills. Today, Brazil's post-miracle urban and educated elites embrace their natural heritage with symbolic First-World-style **environmentalism**, best illustrated by the 1992 Earth Summit (see **Rio Conference 1992**) but maintain their social and physical distance from Brazil's Third World poverty that is the greatest threat to that heritage.

See also: Brazilian Green Party; land reform; newly industrializing countries; population movement and control; property rights; rainforests

Further reading

Clastres, H. (1995) *The Land-Without-Evil*, Champaign, IL: University of Illinois Press.

Rambali, P and Holt, H. (1995) *In the Cities and Jungles of Brazil*, Hyattsville, MD: Daedalus Books.

PAUL CHANDLER

Brazilian Green Party

The Brazilian environmental movement began in the mid-1970s. Inspired by its North American and western European counterparts, it combined the fight to protect the environment with demands for political democratization. At the beginning of the democratic regime in 1985, there were three positions taken by environmentalists on the creation of a Green Party: a small group thought a Green Party was desirable and viable in the short term; most environmentalists believed a Green

Party was desirable, but not viable in the short or mid-term; and a small group emphasized that a Green Party was undesirable since it would create difficulties instead of helping the work of the environmental movement. The group committed to the creation of a Green Party, concentrated in the state of Rio de Janeiro, launched it on the back of an alliance with the Workers Party in the state governor elections of 1986. In spite of the fact that the Green Party had some visibility during the electoral campaign, most of the environmentalists in the state of Rio remained reluctant about it.

The foundational programme of the Brazilian Green Party was similar to that of the German Green Party, *Die* **Grünen**. Brazilian Greens strongly criticized both **capitalism** and socialism and proposed an alternative ecological society based on decentralized economy, **appropriate technologies**, a clean environment, grassroots democracy and development of post-materialist values (see **Inglehart, Ronald**). Brazilian Greens proposed to overcome the irrational **consumerism** of the upper and upper-middle classes and the extreme poverty of around 40 per cent of the population.

Between 1988 and 1996, the Green Party participated in several municipal, state and national elections, most of the time with very poor performance, gaining less than 1 per cent of the votes. The Green Party never had more than one representative elected to the National Congress. However, there were some good performances: in small towns the party received 10–30 per cent of the vote, and in the city of Rio de Janeiro the Green Party has consistently received over 3 per cent of the votes. Alfredo Sirkis, national president of the Green Party and member of the Rio City Council, was elected City Secretary of the Environment between 1993–6. In this capacity, Sirkis gained a national profile by pioneering several projects combining environmental protection and poverty mitigation.

In the 1998 general elections the Green Party tried to profit from the prestigious and high visibility of Sirkis, launching him as presidential candidate supported by many candidates on a variety of levels. The results of the election were a major fiasco for the Green Party: Sirkis won 0.2 per cent of the votes, only one national representa-tive was elected to the National House, and a couple more were elected to State Houses.

By the beginning of 2000, the Green Party was present in most metropolitan areas, some middle-sized cities, and some towns. The party is badly organized and its continuity is strongly in doubt, particularly since in the future it will have to deal with a more restrictive electoral law. Fourteen years after its foundation, the Brazilian Green Party has been a failure, both in terms of its organizational development and its electoral performance. Among the countries (Europe, Australia, Americas) where there have been serious attempts over the last two decades to develop a Green Party, Brazil's case is probably the least successful. Six factors have contributed to the failure of the Green Party: the Brazilian political culture and electoral system does not favour the formation of new parties based on substantive political platforms; the party was formed in a way that implied a progressive detachment from the environmental movement; the party's leadership had an excessively loose idea about party organiza-tion; the party had a utopian programme and failed to transform general principles about **sustainable development** into a concrete and viable set of public policies; the party did not have a specifically designed programme for the metropolitan areas where most of its potential electors were concen-trated; and within the party there was not enough investment in adapting the European idea of a Green Party to the Brazilian reality. In most countries where green parties developed there has been a corresponding development of the environ-mental movement. In Brazil, on the contrary, there has been a strong dissonance: the environmental movement has become progressively stronger and has some capacity to shape political culture, public institutions and the corporate world; the Green Party, however, has had almost no effect in most dimensions of society, except perhaps in the city of Rio de Janeiro, where it has had some influence in re-shaping public policies.

See also: Brazil; environmental movements; environmentalism of the poor

Further reading

Viola, E. (1997) 'The Environmental Movement in

Brazil: Institutionalization, Sustainable Development and Crisis of Governance, Since 1987', in MacDonald, N. and Stern, O. (eds) *Latin American Environmental Policy in International Perspective*, Boulder, CO: Westview Press.

 EDUARDO VIOLA

Brent Spar controversy

The 14,500-tonne Brent Spar was operated by Shell Oil in the North Sea as an oil storage and loading buoy until 1991. After cost- and environmental-analysis, the company decided that the 'best practicable environmental option' for disposal of the platform was to sink it in the deep ocean. A number of environmental activists disagreed. The controversy centred on potential hazards to the ocean environment versus the cost and dangers of dismantling the structure on land; accounts of the amount and type of hazardous materials contained in the buoy differed widely. **Greenpeace** activists occupied the Brent Spar in protest until they were forced off, and others bombed Shell filling stations in Europe. Deep ocean disposal eventually proved politically unacceptable. The structure was dismantled on land and sections of it used as the base of a quay in Norway, at a cost of $41 million, twice the original estimate. One impact of the controversy was to alert Shell and other companies to the need to consider the opinions of environmental activists.

Further reading

McCulloch, A. (1996) 'Shell, the Brent Spar and Greenpeace: A Doomed Tryst?' *Environmental Politics* 5(1): 122–9.

ELIZABETH R. DeSOMBRE

British environmental law and policy

The environment – by almost every measure – has long been a relatively minor issue on the British policy agenda, driven more by the concerns of successive governments to appease vested interests (notably industry, farmers and landowners) than by a desire to develop a rational and integrated response to **environmental management**. While postwar British political debates have focused on issues such as unemployment, health care, welfare, education and foreign policy, they have touched only rarely on the environment. Ever cautious and pragmatic, recent British governments have been slow to recognize the environment as a distinct policy area, unwilling to provide environmental agencies with adequate power or funding, and reluctant to support international attempts to control pollution without absolute certainty of the links between cause and effect. Because Britain is a small, crowded, post-industrial society, its most pressing environmental concerns revolve around managing the relationship among its people, industry, and what remains of nature in a country with one of the highest population densities in Europe (about 640 people per square mile). The most important policy debates have long tended to focus on two key areas: land-use planning and pollution control (see **land use regulation/planning**).

Postwar policy on the first of these was driven by the Town and Country Planning Act of 1947, which provided Britain with one of the most comprehensive land-use planning systems in the world, and required that all proposed development be subject to planning permission from local authorities. Unfortunately, farming was largely excluded from planning requirements, and Britain's postwar drive to greater self-sufficiency in food quickly brought damaging change to the countryside, including the use of intensive agricultural techniques, **factory farming**, chemical fertilizers and **pesticides**, the removal of forests and hedgerows, and the 'reclamation' of ecologically important **wetlands** and grasslands.

Meanwhile, as the cradle of the industrial revolution, Britain has had a longer history of **air pollution** and **water pollution** than any other country. While it took a number of early initiatives to deal with these problems, they tended to be *ad hoc*, to be decided through negotiation with affected interests, and to avoid setting targets and standards. It was not until 1956 that a national Clean Air Act was passed, and most other pieces of law on air pollution have come in response to the requirements of **European Union** (EU) law; they included the Road Traffic Acts of 1972 and 1974 (emissions from road vehicles), the Control of Pollution Act of 1974 (quality of motor fuels and fuel oil), and the Environmental Protection Act of 1990 (introducing the concept of integrated pollution control). Meanwhile, environmental quality objectives for water were introduced only with the 1989 Water Act and the 1991 Water Resources Act.

Superficially, Britain appears to have an impressive community of government agencies with responsibilities for environmental management, and an impressive body of law to back up their work. In truth, lethargic political responses to environmental problems have meant that the work of many of these agencies is confused and divided, with much of the responsibility for environmental policy left in the hands of quasi-governmental agencies rather than being addressed directly by central government. Furthermore, much of the responsibility for promoting public awareness, generating pressure for legislative change, and overseeing policy implementation has fallen to the environmental lobby.

Until 1970, there was no single or comprehensive authority for environmental regulation in Britain. This was addressed to some extent by the creation of the Department of the Environment (DOE), but this was more a reorganization of government machinery than the creation of a new department with new powers. Its creation brought the word 'environment' more centrally into cabinet discussions, but many key environmental responsibilities were left with other departments and with local authorities. For example, energy policy remained with the Department of Energy and the Central Electricity Generating Board (both now defunct), while pollution issues were addressed in part by a new advisory Royal Commission on Environmental Pollution (RCEP) established in 1969.

The role of the DOE has been further weakened by the responsibilities of other government departments for policy areas with critical environmental significance (for example, transport, energy supply, housing, and trade). Among the most influential of these is the Ministry of Agriculture, Fisheries and Food (MAFF), which arguably plays a more central role in British environmental policy than the DOE, and certainly has more influence over wildlife and countryside issues. Among other things, it is responsible for implementing the EU's **Common Agricultural Policy**, which has long focused on improving the efficiency of European farmers, which has – in turn – been at the heart of threats posed to the British countryside.

Rural management and nature conservation issues have meanwhile come under the aegis of a cluster of specialized quasi-governmental agencies (QGAs). Foremost among these were the Nature Conservancy Council (NCC, created in 1949), and the Countryside Commissions for Scotland and for England and Wales (created in 1968, and responsible for amenity). Despite vocal opposition from environmental non-governmental organizations (NGOs; see **international non-governmental organizations**), the NCC was broken up in 1991 into English Nature, Scottish Natural Heritage, and the Countryside Council for Wales, and a Joint Nature Conservation Committee was created to promote co-ordination and to deal with Britain-wide issues.

Britain's state forests, meanwhile, come under the jurisdiction of the Forestry Commission. In addition to protecting and expanding forests, developing afforestation, and supplying timber and forest products, the Commission is responsible for overseeing forestry and forestry research. It too has been criticized by some environmental groups for suggesting that the interests of commercial forestry and wildlife conservation are compatible, for providing grant-aid for the removal of ancient woodland, and for promoting fast-growing, commercial conifer plantations (see also **wildlife management**).

Institutional arrangements for air and water pollution control underwent several changes in the 1980s and 1990s, not because the government recognized the weakness of the existing system and the need for integration, but because of a combination of the requirements of EU law, changes in economic policy, and legal concerns over the arrangements made for controlling pollution from Britain's newly privatized energy and water supply industries. The first major change came in 1987 with the establishment of Her Majesty's **Inspectorate of Pollution** (HMIP), created in an attempt to develop a unified approach to pollution abatement. In 1988, prompted mainly by the requirements of EU law, the DOE finally made the case for a system of integrated pollution control, a recommendation which formed the basis of the 1990 Environmental Protection Act.

In response to plans by the Thatcher government in the late 1980s to privatize the water and energy supply industries, a new National Rivers Authority (NRA) was created in 1989 to monitor the quality of river water, and a Drinking Water Inspectorate to monitor standards in drinking water. Similarly, when the electricity supply industry was privatized in 1989, a new Office of Electricity Regulation (Offer) was created to act as a watchdog over the two new generation companies, PowerGen and National Power; its remit included environmental pollution. Meanwhile, the Department of Energy (created during the energy crisis of 1973) was abolished in 1992.

In 1990, the Environmental Protection Act extended a number of existing policy initiatives, and either confirmed or introduced new institutional changes. The most significant outcomes of the Act included further promotion of the concept of integrated pollution control, and reorganization of waste disposal procedures, involving the creation of Waste Regional Authorities and Waste Disposal Authorities. The Act covered a broader range of issues than any previous piece of environmental law, and attempted to bring some order to a system that had become enormously complex. In 1995, the Environment Act replaced the HMIP, the NRA, the Waste Regional Authorities and parts of the DOE with a new **Environment Agency**. Sponsored by the reorganized **Department of the Environment, Transport and the Regions** (created in 1997), it concerns itself mainly with air and water pollution control, waste management, and radioactive waste disposal. Initial impressions suggested that the creation of the Environmental Agency simply followed the British tradition of disjointed and incremental institutional change.

Alongside the government agencies and the EU, the most consistent source of pressure for change in British environmental policy has come from interest groups. Britain has what may well be the oldest, best-organized, and biggest (per capita) community of environmental interest groups in the world, with a membership of more than five million. Much of the growth in its size and levels of activity has come since the mid-1980s, and the groups with the fastest growth have been those that are either more activist (such as **Greenpeace** and **Friends of the Earth**) or which have international interests (such as the **World Wide Fund for Nature**, WWF).

See also: British regulatory agencies; Council for the Protection of Rural England; public inquiries

Further reading

Grey, T.S. (ed.) (1995) *UK Environmental Policy in the 1990s*, Basingstoke: Macmillan.

Lowe, P. and Ward, S. (eds) (1998) *British Environmental Policy and Europe*, Basingstoke: Macmillan.

McCormick, J. (1991) *British Politics and the Environment*, London: Earthscan.

Robinson, M. (1992) *The Greening of British Party Politics*, Manchester: Manchester University Press.

JOHN McCORMICK

British nuclear power industry

The British nuclear power industry, originally established to make atomic weapons, subsequently flourished, then faltered, as a civil programme for generating electricity until a slow decline began with the decommissioning of the early reactors. Its rise and decline has reflected changing commercial, technical and political circumstances.

The first reactors were for plutonium production for military purposes at Windscale (Cumbria), followed in 1953 by two full-scale military nuclear power stations, at Calder Hall (near Windscale), which also became the first station to produce power for the national grid (in 1956) and at Chapelcross (Dumfriesshire), together with a fast breeder reactor at Dounreay in northern Scotland.

The concept, though not necessarily the practice, of 'Atoms for Peace' was announced with *A Programme of Nuclear Power* (Cmnd 9389) heralding a series of nine Magnox (gas-cooled, graphite moderated using natural uranium) power stations at remote sites in southern England (6), Wales (2) and Scotland (1).

These stations were complemented by a series of Advanced Gas-Cooled Reactors (AGRs) using slightly enriched uranium, commissioned during the 1970s and 1980s both at existing sites and in new locations including two in urban areas thereby demonstrating confidence in their safety features. The British nuclear energy programme was completed with the opening, in 1995, of the Sizewell B station, a Pressurized Water design, the largest of all with a capacity of 2000MW. At its peak, in 1999, nuclear energy was generating 87.67TWh of electricity, nearly 28 per cent of the total available in the UK from major domestic electricity producers.

In its early days British nuclear energy represented new and innovative technology, the prospect for politicians and the public of unlimited electricity 'too cheap to meter' and a secure, safe and clean source of energy. One by one these claims have proved unfounded.

Technically, the British programme is a hybrid of different reactor types. There was little consistency in design, substantial cost overruns and a failure to secure export orders. The industry has been beset by long lead times, in the case of Dungeness B 19 years from order to completion. By the time Britain abandoned its own technology in favour of a proposed series of stations based on the American pressurized water reactors (PWR), the nuclear programme was already in decline and only one PWR, Sizewell B, was built. Hopes that had been pinned on fast breeder technology using depleted uranium to breed plutonium were dashed when the programme at Dounreay was abandoned and the prototype reactor closed down in 1994.

Throughout its history it has been difficult to assess the comparative economic performance of nuclear energy given its high capital costs, subsidies and linkage to the military nuclear programme and reprocessing. Justification depended to an extent on the need for energy security and diversity in a sector threatened by coal strikes and oil price rises in the 1970s and 1980s. But, by the 1990s, both fossil and nuclear energy were being supplanted by gas, a more flexible and cheaper source of supply.

In its early years nuclear energy encountered few political problems. The military programme was shrouded in secrecy and the first civil reactors were approved after very short **public inquiries** (Hinkley Point two days, Bradwell three). Public concerns about issues of safety, environment and nuclear waste had developed by the 1970s and 1980s and the **Three Mile Island accident** (1979) and **Chernobyl** (1986) transformed public attitudes to safety. In this changing political context the Sizewell B inquiry, lasting 340 days during the mid-1980s, became the forum for debate on environmental, economic and safety issues facing the industry.

By that time, the political conditions for the industry had become unfavourable. The problems created by nuclear energy, the reprocessing of spent fuel and the management of radioactive wastes, had become key political issues leading to conflicts over proposed repository sites and casting doubt over the future of the Sellafield reprocessing plant. These conflicts had revealed the power of local communities, combined with environmental groups, to open up a policy process hitherto confined to the closed relationship between the industry and government. Failure to find acceptable ways of managing wastes over the long term had become a major obstacle to the further development of nuclear energy (see also **hazardous and toxic waste management**; **Sellafield/Windscale**).

While public confidence in the industry has diminished, economic circumstances have proved decisive in its decline. Privatization of nuclear energy (with the exception of the Magnox stations) in the 1990s exposed the industry to competition. The commercial prospects for any further commercial development of nuclear power are poor. Nor is it likely, in view of its high costs, lead times and long-term risks that nuclear power will provide an answer to the problem of **global warming**. More likely it will gradually fade away. Already a programme of decommissioning the Magnox stations has begun and by 2010 all but two will have closed. The AGRs will probably have disappeared by 2030 leaving Sizewell as the sole survivor of a once ambitious programme.

See also: militarism and the environment; nuclear energy/nuclear waste management

Further reading

Blowers, A., Lowry, D. and Solomon, B. (1991) *The International Politics of Nuclear Waste*, London: Macmillan.

Openshaw, S. (1986) *Nuclear Power: Siting and Safety*, London: Routledge and Kegan Paul.

O'Riordan, T., Kemp, R. and Purdue, M. (1988) *Sizewell B: An Anatomy of the Inquiry*, London: Macmillan.

ANDREW BLOWERS

British regulatory agencies

The principal environmental protection agency in England and Wales is the **Environment Agency** which was established in 1996 with the merger of Her Majesty's **Inspectorate of Pollution** (HMIP), the National Rivers Authority (NRA) and local government's Waste Regional Authorities (WRAs). The Environment Agency is one of many QUANGOs (quasi-autonomous non-governmental organizations) in the UK, with policy and financial oversight coming from the **Department of the Environment, Transport and the Regions**. The equivalent agency in Scotland is the Scottish Environmental Protection Agency (SEPA) which has also taken over local authorities' environmental health functions and responsibilities. A separate agency, the Health and Safety Agency, retains certain responsibilities which impinge on environmental protection, for example, the regulation of nuclear installations and industrial hazards.

The Environment Agency is one of the largest environmental protection agencies in the world, employing around 9,500 staff, with a budget of £500 million a year, much of it raised from charges on industry, commerce and anglers. The merger of HMIP and NRA allows the Environment Agency to operate integrated pollution control (IPC) – making holistic assessments of environmental impacts to air, land and water. In principle the Environment Agency has a formal, transparent, arms-length relationship with industry, operating to strict objectives and standards and able to take an anticipatory and preventative approach to pollution control. One of the most interesting duties of the Environment Agency is the promotion of **sustainable development**, which goes well beyond traditional pollution control responsibilities. This raises the potential of conflict with the government when the Environment Agency believes that the government's policies are detrimental to sustainable development.

The establishment of the Environment Agency brings to an end the tradition of fragmentation within pollution control in the UK. Historically, pollution control authorities tended to focus on a single medium, irrespective of impacts outside their competence and jurisdiction. These authorities were created incrementally, often in response to contingent problems, beginning with the Alkali Inspectorate in 1863. This led to an unacceptable situation in which there was a variety of different agencies, incoherent structures and often overlapping responsibilities. This not only had detrimental environmental consequences, but caused problems for industry, since it had to deal with more than one agency, some interested in specific aspects of plant operation, others only concerned with 'end-of-pipe' emission levels.

The traditional 'style' of pollution control in the UK was based on secretive and discretionary collaboration between public officials and representatives from industry, resulting in 'negotiated consents' based on very loose national guidelines and principles. The politics of pollution control in many ways mirrored the rest of British policy-making and political culture, with a close and confidential relationship between government and its agencies and the industrial and economic sector.

A more zealous approach to enforcement was developed by the NRA, established in 1989 with the privatization of the water industry in England and Wales. In part, this was a result of the NRA being a completely new Inspectorate and not an amalgamation with inherited practices and associations with industry. In contrast, HMIP, established in 1987 was an amalgamation of four earlier inspectorates. The inclusion of the NRA's functions means that the Environment Agency has responsibilities beyond simply pollution control – it also has responsibilities for flood defence, regulation of rivers and ground water, protection and improvement of water stocks, and promotion of water-based activities – a unique combination of traditional pollution control, river management and conservation roles.

In practice, the new Environment Agency has had to come to terms with the merging of different philosophies and approaches to pollution control. The principle of formal, arms length authorization has been difficult to achieve since much of the knowledge required for control is held by industry. There are concerns about a return to more discretionary practices. There has also been disappointment about the relatively low number of prosecutions and the level of fines handed out to polluting companies in the courts. The Agency argues that it is only going to prosecute those companies that blatantly disregard their responsibilities and once in court it is not the Agency, but rather magistrates and judges who need to be more zealous in applying deterrents. In 1998, there was only one company fined more than £100,000: ICI was fined £300,000 for polluting groundwater at its site in Runcorn, Cheshire.

The 1999 Integrated Pollution Prevention and Control (IPPC) Act heralds a new approach to pollution control that will take the Environment Agency beyond IPC – a shift in focus away from emission standards and towards waste and pollution prevention. The objective of IPPC is to prevent or solve pollution problems rather than transferring them from one part of the environment to another. The British Government played a central role in the development of the European Directive which forms the basis of this Act and it opens the door for much more contact between regulator and industry – a hybrid between the more pragmatic, traditional approach and a more formal objective-led European approach.

Further reading

Carter, N. and Lowe, P. (1995) 'The Establishment of a Cross-Sector Environment Agency', in

Gray, T. (ed.) *UK Environmental Policy in the 1990s*, Basingstoke: MacMillan, pp.38–56.

Environment Agency website: URL: http://www.environment-agency.gov.uk.

Jordan, A. (1993) 'Integrated Pollution Control and the Evolving Style and Structure of Environmental Regulation in the UK', *Environmental Politics*, 2(3):405 27.

Skea, J. and Smith, G. (1998) 'Integrated Pollution Control', in Lowe, P. and Ward, S. (1998) *British Environmental Policy and Europe*, London: Routledge, pp.265–82.

O'Riordan, T. and Weale, A (1989) 'Administrative Reorganization and Policy Change: the Case of Her Majesty's Inspectorate of Pollution', *Public Administration*, 67: 277–94.

Weale, A. (1992) *The New Politics of Pollution*, Manchester: Manchester University Press.

GRAHAM SMITH

Brower, David

b. 1 July 1912, Berkeley, California, USA;
d. 5 November 2000, Berkeley

Environmental activist

David Brower, former executive director of the **Sierra Club** (1959–69), founder and president of **Friends of the Earth** (1969–79), and founder and chairman of the Earth Island Institute (1982), is one of America's best known environmentalists and mountaineers.

Brower's early memories of his childhood include family outings into the Sierra Nevada range, a place that actually terrified him until he was in his early twenties and successfully climbed a number of peaks. His early years were a time of great trauma for young David. When he was eight years old, his mother went blind and soon thereafter his father lost his job at the University of California. David and his three siblings were forced to sell newspapers and help manage family apartments which were the Browers' only source of income.

At age 16, he entered the University of California with no particular academic interest. However, the family's difficult financial circumstances forced him to leave in his second year. He got a clerk's position at a local company and on one of his vacations went on a long trip to the Sierra wilderness, a time that seems to have had a transforming influence on his life. In 1933, he joined the Sierra Club, his membership application sponsored by the renowned photographer Ansel Adams. Over the next two years, Brower spent more time in the wilderness and less at his clerk's position from which he was eventually fired. He found employment at Yosemite, ending up as publicity manager and from there, moved to an editorship at the University of California Press in 1941. Here he met and married fellow editor Anne Hus, and they subsequently had four children.

Following service in the Second World War with the US Army's renowned Tenth Mountain Division, Brower went back to his position at the California Press and spent a good deal of time writing the *Sierra Club Handbook*, first published in 1947. The turning point in Brower's career occurred in 1952 when the Sierra Club's board named him its executive director.

In the years since 1892, when the activist and preservationist John **Muir** had founded the organization, the Sierra Club had become a passive, conservative group of primarily west-coast, wealthy, 'posey-pickers', as one observer noted. That was all to change as Brower led a group of the Club's 'young Turks' to take a much more aggressive stand. Brower expanded the membership to a much more national base as he urged on the faithful to become foot soldiers in the fight to preserve **nature**. Indeed, what this charismatic, determined, charming and difficult man accomplished was to help set up the American environmental movement's first organization for influencing electoral politics and using the courts to protect the environment. Moreover, his experience as a writer and editor had certainly helped make him aware of the importance of using printed words and beautiful photographs to influence the public.

The Brower-led Sierra Club entered the national environmental picture in the 1950s with a high-profile, public campaign to save Dinosaur National Monument. Utilizing an extensive programme of lobbying and mobilization, this effort also featured *This is Dinosaur*, the first book-length publication in environmental history that sought to publicize a park or wilderness and to assist in a preservation campaign. Indeed, such publications became part of a Sierra Club series and served as one of Brower's most important contributions to the environmental movement.

After the Dinosaur battle, Brower continued to lead Sierra in such notable national lobbying efforts as opposition to a proposed dam in the Grand Canyon, the fight to save California's redwood groves, and support for the Wilderness Act, among others. Called by one writer the 'archdruid' of the **conservation movement**, Brower was tireless in testifying before committees of all kinds on behalf of his passionate beliefs.

By the late 1960s, however, Brower's high profile, aggressive style had put him at odds with the Sierra Club's directors. Following an internal fight, he resigned and formed a rival group, Friends of the Earth (FOE), which gave him a platform to continue to work on his preservationist agenda, but with the added dimension of making FOE the first international environmental organization. However, by the early 1980s, Brower had alienated many in FOE's leadership and he decided to move on. This time he founded the Earth Island Institute (1982) which became involved in extensive publishing activity and continued the fight to protect natural resources and wildlife, a battle that, for him, as Earth Island's chairman, continued until his death in November 2000.

Further reading

Brower, D. (1991) *Work in Progress*, Salt Lake City: Peregrine Smith.
McPhee, J. (1971) *Encounters with the Archdruid*, New York: Farrar, Straus and Giroux.

WARREN VANDER HILL

brownfield sites

Brownfield sites refers to areas that have been contaminated for years by industrial wastes that are now abandoned. Before the passage of laws mandating the safe treatment of hazardous waste, factory workers disposed of wastes in the cheapest, most convenient manner. Often they poured liquid waste on the ground behind the plant or into the nearest stream. Sometimes wastes were placed in holding ponds until part of the liquid was evaporated; often they were contained in 50 gallon drums stacked in abandoned buildings or in trenches dug for them on the corporation's property. In this way the soil and ground water in many traditional industrial sites became highly contaminated.

Most of these sites are located in urban areas although even small towns have abandoned petrol stations where a leaking underground storage tank has contaminated the groundwater. After recognizing the danger these sites pose to urban populations in close proximity, industrialized nations passed new laws regulating the manner by which hazardous waste may now be disposed of and mandating the cleanup of old sites. In the USA, many such sites have been placed on the Superfund priority list (see **Superfund**) and started on an expensive remediation programme for which any and all former, present and future users and owners may be jointly liable for cleanup costs (see also **hazardous and toxic waste management**).

One unintended consequence of Superfund was to make it so expensive to clean up a brownfield, that industrial and commercial developers tended to forsake the cities and develop new plants in greenfields far removed from urban centres. In many cases it cost more to clean up one of these brownfields than to build a new plant in a formerly unused greenfield, which has not been contaminated in the past. The potential liability of many parties has created an unwillingness on the part of financial institutions to lend money for brownfield development until these sites have been successfully remediated.

Concerned about the loss in employment and tax revenue from the abandonment of these sites, urban planners and city mayors have negotiated with federal and state regulators to find less expensive ways of redeveloping brownfields. Environmental groups too have urged the reuse of urban sites rather than degrading formerly unpolluted areas and pushing urban sprawl into the countryside. In attempting to reuse valuable urban land, regulatory agencies at state and federal levels have become more flexible about the standard of cleanliness required to bring a brownfield back into commerical or industrial use as long as the community where it is located is satisfied. It is less important that contaminated dirt be incinerated on a lot where plans call for an industrial plant with a concrete floor covering the entire area than it is for a lot slated for use as a school playground.

As new generations of workers have returned to the cities the demand for urban residential space has expanded, and former warehouses are being transformed into condos and apartment buildings. In every case the brownfield site must be carefully analysed and cleaned of materials formerly stored and used there which are considered dangerous to the new residents. In each case a standard of cleanliness appropriate to the new use must be agreed upon to facilitate the return of industry to the cities. Hence a movement has been started to rehabilitate and restore brownfields to economic use and avoid the proliferation of future such sites.

References

Environmental Protection Agency (US) (1996) *Basic Brownfields Fact Sheet* , Region 5, Office of Public Affairs.

LETTIE McSPADDEN

Brundtland, Gro Harlem

b. 20 April 1939, Oslo, Norway

Physician, politician

Gro Harlem Brundtland studied medicine and public health in the USA, before returning to Norway, and working at the Ministry of Health from 1965 to 1974. An active member of the social democratic party from her youth, she was appointed Minister of the Environment in 1974, and served for five years in that capacity. She became leader of the social democratic party and Norwegian prime minister in 1981, the first woman ever to hold that post. She served as prime minister for a total of ten years (1981, 1986–9 and 1990–6), resigning in 1996 to become director-general of the **World Health Organization** (WHO) in 1998. In 1983 Brundtland was asked by the UN secretary-general to chair the World Commission on Environment and Development, which, in 1987, produced the report, *Our Common Future*, in which the doctrine of **sustainable development** was brought to the attention of the international community.

See also: Brundtland Commission

ANDREW JAMISON

Brundtland Commission

Known officially as the World Commission on Environment and Development (WCED), the Brundtland Commission was created by a September 1983 United Nations General Assembly resolution. This called for the creation of an independent commission charged with addressing the question of the relationship between environment and **development**, and with listing 'innovative, concrete and realistic' proposals to deal with the question. The Commission held its first meeting in Geneva in October 1984, and was chaired by Gro Harlem **Brundtland**, the former prime minister of Norway. The Commission had 23 members: twelve from less developed countries, seven from industrialized western countries, and four from the Communist bloc.

The Commission noted that an unprecedented growth in pressures on the global environment made grave predictions about the future commonplace, and that a more prosperous, just and secure future demanded policies aimed at sustaining the ecological basis of development, and at changing the nature of co-operation between governments, business, science, and citizens. The Commission selected six key policy areas on which to focus (population, food security, species and ecosystems, energy, industry, and human settlements) and examined them each from the perspective of the year 2000. A secretariat was set up in Geneva, and between October 1984 and February 1987, the Commission sponsored more than 75 studies and reports, held meetings or public hearings in ten

countries, and garnered the views of a wide selection of individuals and organizations. In 1987, the report of the Commission was published as *Our Common Future*. The report concluded that environment and development were inextricable, and that policy responses were handicapped by the fact that existing institutions tended to be independent, fragmented, too narrowly focused, and too concerned with addressing effects well beyond national frontiers. Greater international co-operation was needed, but international agencies – notably those that were part of the UN system – were under siege at the time they were most needed.

Furthermore, the Commission concluded, environmental policy was too often accorded a secondary status, and environmental agencies often learned of new initiatives in economic, trade, or energy policy (with possible consequences for resources) long after the effective decisions had been taken. It was time that 'the ecological dimensions of policy [were] considered at the same time as the economic, trade, energy, agricultural, industrial, and other dimensions – on the same agendas and in the same national and international institutions' (WCED, 1987: 21). The Commission had several specific recommendations:

- national environmental protection agencies needed urgent strengthening, particularly in **less developed countries**;
- the work of the **United Nations Environment Programme** needed to be reinforced and extended, notably through increased funding;
- environmental monitoring and assessment needed better focus and co-ordination;
- policy-makers needed to work more closely with non-governmental organizations and industry;
- law and international conventions needed strengthening and better implementation;
- the UN should work towards a universal declaration and later a convention on environmental protection and sustainable development.

Perhaps the most lasting effect of the Commission was to draw new attention to the idea of sustainable development, which it defined as development that 'meets the needs of the present without compromising the ability of future generations to meet their own needs' (WCED, 1987: 8). While this was little more than a reformulation of the old idea of conservation, the idea of **sustainable development** has since been central to the goals of **environmental management** in industrialized and less developed countries alike. It was also central to the agenda at the UN Conference on the Environment and Development, held in Rio de Janeiro in 1992 (see **Rio Conference 1992**). The work of the Commission was promoted between 1987 and 1995 by the activities of the 'Center for Our Common Future', and the follow-up to proposals made by the Commission has since been monitored by the Commission on Global Governance, based in Geneva. The findings of the Commission have also been at the core of the work of a large network of research institutes and non-governmental organizations working on issues related to sustainable development.

See also: Brundtland, Gro Harlem; global environmental governance; international non-government organizations; Rio Conference 1992; sustainable development; United Nations Commission on Sustainable Development; United Nations Environment Programme; United Nations Development Program

Reference

World Commission on Environment and Development (1987) *Our Common Future*, Oxford: Oxford University Press.

JOHN McCORMICK

Bulgarian Green Party

Founded in April 1989, the Bulgarian Green Party, Ecoglasnost, has its origins in opposition to transboundary pollution from a Romanian chemical plant in Ruse. Ecoglasnost played a key role in mobilization against the communist regime. In December 1989 it formed, with other dissident political groups, the independent Union of the Democratic Forces (UDF) (*Sayuz na demokrati hnite sili*). After the elections of 1990, Ecoglasnost entered government (Prime Minister 1991; Minis-

ter of Finance 1990). However, economic decline and frequent changes of government have impeded the development of green party activism. The Political Club Ecoglasnost (*Politicheski Klub Ekoglasnost*) was founded in March 1990 as Ecoglasnost's political wing. In 1991, following disputes over the new Bulgarian constitution, most of the Ecoglastnost members of parliament were expelled from the UDF. This led to a split within Ecoglasnost and the formation of the National Movement Ecoglasnost (*Dviženie Ekoglasnost*). A Green Party (*Zelena Partija*) was also founded in December 1989 from Ecoglasnost. Aleksandar Karakachanov, (Mayor of Sofia), has been its Chair since its foundation. The Party has joined various parliamentary coalitions. The 1991 split in the UDF also triggered a split in the Green Party, leading to the formation of the Conservative Ecological Party.

SUSAN BAKER

BUND

BUND (Bund für Umwelt und Naturschutz Deutschland), the German Association for Environment and Nature Protection, is one of the main environmental pressure groups in Germany, with almost 230,000 members. It was founded in 1975 as a national lobbying group, including amongst its founder members the Bavarian Association for Nature Protection which was originally founded in 1913. Initially, the BUND set itself apart from the radical tactics of the anti-nuclear movements of the 1970s, concentrating on nature protection issues and traditional lobbying work. With the decline of **new social movements** in the 1980s, the BUND increased its national profile. Expanding from its traditional concerns on nature protection, the BUND campaigned on an anti-nuclear platform from 1980 and subsequently moved to address the whole range of national and international environmental issues (see **anti-nuclear movements**). In 1989, it became the German affiliate of **Friends of the Earth** International. The strength of the BUND is the combination of a strong grassroots organization, with more than 2,000 active local groups, with forceful national campaigning coordinated by a national office, which has been located in Berlin since 2000. The BUND has a democratic internal structure, with an annual conference electing the association's leadership and deciding on the BUND's general policy direction.

WOLFGANG RÜDIG

Burford, Anne Gorsuch

b. 21 April 1942, Asper, Wyoming, USA

Government administrator

Anne Gorsuch Burford was appointed by President Ronald **Reagan** to head the **Environmental Protection Agency** (EPA) and served from 1981 to 1983. A hard-driving, no-nonsense conservative from Colorado, Burford arrived in Washington with a specific right-wing agenda about ways she wished to change the nation's environmental policies, and little experience in the ways to get that done. Her goal, she openly boasted, was to advocate Reagan's policy of 'industrial revitalization', which meant trying to lessen the 'regulation overburden' that environmental legislation had placed on industry. Burford surrounded herself with like-minded political appointees, but her agenda soon ran aground when a series of congressional investigations uncovered illegal activities, cronyism, and overly friendly deals with chemical waste violators. Left on her own by the administration, she resigned in March 1983, leaving a dispirited EPA whose programmes had been badly damaged.

WARREN VANDER HILL

Bürgerinitiativen

While electoral democracy with strong competing parties and high voter turnout was apparent in the Federal Republic of Germany in the 1950s–60s, studies indicated that citizenship was largely passive. This was to change in the 1970s, when *Bürgerinitiativen* (citizen action groups) sprang up all over West Germany. A citizen action group is 'an *ad hoc* group of citizens that lobbies decision-makers on a special policy issue' (Dalton, 1993). Citizen action groups

are non-partisan, loosely organized coalitions. They emerge as a response to a specific problem involving a collective good, may use unconventional protest tactics as well as conventional lobbying/litigating tactics, and challenge the technocratic expertise and/or policy priorities of politicians and bureaucrats. They typically disband after a few months or years. West German opinion polls in the 1970s found declining public satisfaction with the established parties and increasing public involvement with citizen action groups (to the point where such participation overshadowed membership figures in the three Bonn parties). Party elites worried that proliferating grassroots activism could undermine the legitimacy of representative institutions.

Many of the citizen action groups dealt with environmental problems. In 1972 the **BBU** (Federal Association of Citizen-Action Groups for Environmental Protection) was created by 16 citizen action groups to co-ordinate and support local efforts; in the late 1970s the BBU had about 1,000 groups under its umbrella. Activists from the **anti-nuclear movements** and from the BBU were key players in the alliance that launched *Die Grünen* in 1980. Although environmental politics in the following decades with the Greens' electoral successes has become more focused within the parliamentary system, citizen action groups have remained a feature of German politics at the state and local levels. In fact, recent years have seen occasions when environmental citizen action groups have mobilized against policy compromises that the Greens have made regarding nuclear wastes transport and infrastructure developments (e.g., highways and airports) in order to preserve coalitions with the Social Democrats.

Reference

Dalton, R.J. (1993) *Politics in Germany* New York: Harper Collins, 2nd edn.

Further reading

Helm, J. (1980) 'Citizen Lobbies in West Germany', in P.M. Merkl (ed.) *Western European Party Systems*, New York: Free Press.

E. GENE FRANKLAND

business and the environment

Business attitudes to environmental issues have changed significantly over the years. Environmental protection has traditionally been seen by businesses as the responsibility of governments and environmental regulation something to be fought against. The late 1980s saw a change in this approach, especially amongst large industrial businesses that began to recognize their responsibility for environmental pollution. At the time of the **Rio Conference** (Earth Summit) in 1992 more corporate leaders had accepted **environmental management** as a key business issue, forming organizations such as the Business Council for Sustainable Development (BCSD) and the World Industry Council for the Environment (WICE) to compile voluntary guidelines on environmental best practice for business.

Throughout the 1990s environmental issues have progressively moved up the corporate agenda through the adoption of business practice in eco-efficiency, voluntary agreements and environmental auditing/reporting. From the mid-1990s leading businesses have moved from addressing pure environmental management issues to embrace the concept of sustainable development. Reflecting this change, the BSCD and the WICE merged in 1995 to form the World Business Council for Sustainable Development (WBCSD) a coalition of some 140 international companies united by a shared commitment to sustainable development.

Many factors have played a part in changing business' attitudes to the environment including: increased niche market demand for green products, enhanced reputation from environmental best practice, pressure from employees to work for companies they can be proud of and the rising costs of **eco-taxes** and regulation. However, the most dominant argument used by government, non-governmental organizations (NGOs) and businesses themselves is that environmental management is not a question of scaling down economic activity, it is rather a challenge to do more with less and generate increased profit through cost savings (Forum for the Future (FFF), 1999–2000). This whole argument has been captured in the concept of eco-efficiency.

The concept and definition of eco-efficiency was first pioneered by the BCSD and progressively developed by its successor organization the WBCSD between 1992 and 1995. Eco-efficiency is reached by the delivery of competitively priced goods and services that satisfy human needs and bring quality of life, while progressively reducing ecological impacts and resource intensity throughout the life-cycle, to a level in line with the earth's estimated carrying capacity (WBCSD, 1996).

The WBCSD established the following seven core elements of eco-efficiency:

1 reducing the material intensity of goods and services
2 reducing the energy intensity of goods and services (see **energy conservation**)
3 reducing the dispersion of any toxic materials
4 enhancing material **recycling**
5 maximizing sustainable use of renewable resources
6 extending product durability
7 increasing the service intensity of goods and services

Many businesses have found that the eco-efficiency approach has been profitable due to real improvements in productivity, both in the economic and environmental sense. One of the most celebrated successes is that of 3M, whose 'Pollution Prevention Pays' programme is estimated to have saved the company $482 million since its introduction in 1975, as well as eliminating over 500,000 tonnes of pollutants and waste materials. The company achieved further savings of $650 million through energy conservation. Baxter Healthcare's commitment to eliminate sending waste to landfill by 1995 spurred the company to develop a major recycling capacity. As a result, it has recorded a net profit of $1.7 million on this activity alone. Dow Chemical's WRAP initiative ('Waste Reduction Always Pays') is one of the longest-standing corporate pollution control programmes. Its aim is to cut the consumption of raw materials and energy, and the production of waste, for every product. All Dow plants have to compile an 'inventory of process losses' to air, land and water. These are used to provide a ratio of waste per product per site. WRAP has resulted in significant savings in the form of materials recovered and reused, and reduced waste transport, treatment and disposal costs. Moves to cut the usage of one particular reactant, in part by recycling it for further applications, slashed consumption by 80 per cent and saved the company $8 million each year (FFF, 1999–2000)

Alongside the rise of business eco-efficiency programmes has been a large growth in the number of companies signing up to a standardized environmental management system. These provide business with standard guidelines for the development of an internal system to manage and continuously improve their environmental performance. Certification to the system by an independent auditor signals to the outside world that the business is committed to good environmental practice. The British Standards Institute (BSI) pioneered the development of environmental management standards for business in 1992 through the development of BS7750. The EU Eco-Management and Audit Scheme (EMAS) followed in 1995 and in 1996 the International Standards Organization (ISO) developed ISO14001 which has rapidly become the dominant global standard for business environmental management systems, officially subsuming BS7750 in 1998. Experts predict that the number of business registrations to ISO14001 will rise to around 30,000 by the end of 2000.

However, a key criticism of environmental management systems is that they do not provide businesses with a complete framework for decision-making about **sustainability**. ISO14001 and EMAS will tell you how to do things right; but they won't tell you how to do the right things. A company could in theory undertake all the actions necessary to meet a certified environmental management standard and still produce highly polluting goods (FFF, 1999–2000). In response to this a UK project called SIGMA (Sustainability: Integrated Guidelines for Management), a partnership of NGOs, business and the government, was launched in July 1999 to create a strategic management framework for sustainability, the next generation of business-management systems.

This project is symptomatic of a wider shift amongst large proactive businesses in the late 1990s to move from a pure environmental focus to embrace the wider concept of **sustainable development**. This has been motivated by a recognition that to survive, companies of the future will have to be sustainable in the true sense of the word – economically profitable, environmentally sound and socially just. Debates around the changing face of corporate social responsibility have been at the centre of this shift.

There is now widespread acceptance amongst business leaders that the way in which a company accounts for its activities, and to whom, is a crucial component of its licence to operate. Whilst, traditionally companies have only been answerable to their shareholders, the Centre for Tomorrow's Company reports that 40 per cent of business leaders now believe that a company cannot succeed unless it has accountability that goes wider than shareholders to embrace stakeholders such as employees, suppliers and communities. The high profile examples of Shell and the **Brent Spar controversy**, Nike and child labour, Monsanto and GM crops (see **genetic engineering, crops**) show how **civil society** can effectively revoke a company's licence to operate if it is deemed to be engaging in ethically unsound and irresponsible practices.

Companies are increasingly recognizing that to win and maintain their licence to operate from civil society they need to actively engage in dialogue with their key stakeholders and provide them with more accessible and transparent information on both their economic and social performance as well as on environmental performance. Corporate environmental reporting is on the increase amongst larger businesses. In 1999 a survey by the Pensions Investment Research Consultants (PIRC) showed that 81 per cent of the FTSE 350 disclose information in some form on environmental issues, 92 per cent of the FTSE 100 disclose information on environmental issues and 79 per cent on community and social issues. However, for leading companies the emphasis on reporting has moved from producing separate environmental reports to integrated sustainability reporting covering economic, environmental and social performance.

The Global Reporting Initiative, a coalition of NGOs, experts and multinational corporations, is developing standard guidelines for corporate sustainability reporting worldwide (see also **multinational and transnational corporations**). Draft guidelines were published in March 1999 and June 2000 and have been piloted by 20 leading multinational businesses.

It is important to note that the significant changes in business attitudes to the environment identified above are restricted to the realm of large companies. The vast majority of small and medium sized enterprises (SMEs), have either yet to be affected in any direct and significant way or are only just starting to engage in environmental issues through the supply chain influence of larger companies.

References

Forum for the Future (1999–2000) *Sustainability Learning Networks Background Briefings*, Cambridge Programme for Industry, 33–64

World Business Council for Sustainable Development (1996) *Eco-Efficient Leadership for Improved Economic and Environmental Performance.*

Further reading

Cairncross, F. (1995) *Green, Inc*, London: Earthscan

Global Reporting Initiative (June 2000) 'Sustainability Reporting Guidelines' at
URL: http://www.globalreporting.org.

Lovins, A., Lovins, H. and Hawken, P. (1999) *Natural Capitalism*, London: Earthscan.

World Business Council for Sustainable Development Website:
URL: http://www.wbcsd.ch.

JENNY BARKER

C

Campaign for Nuclear Disarmament

The Campaign for Nuclear Disarmament (CND) was formed in 1958 to campaign against nuclear weapons. It quickly became a mass protest movement, symbolized by the annual march from London to the Atomic Weapons Establishment at Aldermaston. CND's greatest influence was at the height of the Cold War in the early 1980s when a decision was made to site American cruise and Pershing missiles in Britain, and when, under the hawkish leadership of **Reagan** and Thatcher, the threat of a nuclear conflict increased. At this time, too, the Labour Opposition adopted unilateral nuclear disarmament. However, Conservative electoral dominance in the 1980s, a warmer climate between the USA and the Gorbachev-led Soviet Union, multilateral disarmament progress, and, ultimately, the collapse of the Soviet Union, significantly reduced CND's role. CND still exists, in a much-reduced capacity, still campaigning against Britain's independent nuclear capacity.

See also: anti-nuclear movements

ROBERT GARNER

Canadian environmental law and policy

Canada is a federal country, with both federal and provincial governments active in environmental law and policy. Since Canada's constitution does not explicitly allocate authority with respect to the environment, federal and provincial environmental authority tends to be associated with other subjects that are mentioned in the constitution. The federal government's authority with respect to coastal and inland **fisheries**, as embodied in the federal Fisheries Act, historically has been the basis for federal water pollution control. Uniform technology-based discharge standards have been promulgated under the Act for several categories of industry. A second major federal statute, the Canadian Environmental Protection Act (CEPA) was passed in 1988 and amended in 1999. The Act, which is predicated primarily on the federal government's criminal law power, takes a cradle-to-grave approach to toxic substances management, authorizing a broad range of regulatory measures should a substance be deemed to present a potential risk to human health or the environment. However, to date relatively few regulations have been issued under the Act. A third federal environmental law is the Canadian Environmental Assessment Act, which was proclaimed in 1995. The Act mandates review of private and public projects that involve federal lands or federal funding, or that could have an impact on other matters of federal jurisdiction.

Provincial governments also have clear and broad constitutional authority with respect to natural resources and the environment, both as the owners of public lands ('Crown lands') and by virtue of their legislative authority with respect to 'property and civil rights' within their borders. Each provincial government has its own statutes concerning matters such as pollution control, **endangered species** conservation, and environmental assessment. However, differences in the scope and enforcement of provincial environmental laws reflect the diverse ideologies of provincial governments, from social democratic to neo-conservative, and resource disparities among the provinces, which range in size from Prince Edward Island with a population of just over 100,000 to Ontario with over 11 million residents.

Federal and provincial governments co-ordinate their environmental policies through the Canadian Council of Ministers of the Environment. Historically, provincial governments have taken the lead in environmental policy, including taking responsibility for enforcement of both their own and federal standards. However, the federal government asserted a more independent role in the late 1980s in response to both growing public concern for the environment and a series of high-profile court decisions through which environmentalists forced the federal government to abide by its own environmental impact assessment regulation. This renewed federal assertiveness generated conflicts between the federal government and the provinces, not least because provincial governments were the proponents of some of the projects the federal government was forced by the courts to evaluate. However, as public attention to the environment declined in the early 1990s, federal and provincial Ministers sought to restore harmony. The resulting Canada-Wide Accord on Environmental Harmonization, signed by the federal government and all provinces but Quebec in 1998, sought to rationalize federal and provincial roles with respect to environmental policy. Fearing that rationalization would involve the lead role once again falling to provincial governments eager to exploit their natural resources, Canadian environmental groups strongly opposed the Accord.

It is noteworthy that in keeping with parliamentary traditions Canadian environmental statutes at both the federal and provincial level tend to grant considerable discretion to Cabinet. The Minister or Cabinet is typically authorized, but not required, to take a broad range of actions. As a result, with the exception of the rather exceptional litigation concerning environmental assessment noted above,

citizen suits have not been a common feature of Canadian environmental policy landscape. Nor has litigation by the state been prominent. Federal and provincial governments alike have historically pursued an informal, negotiated approach to regulatory enforcement. Although many have expressed a commitment to more rigorous enforcement in recent years, the impact of that shift has been largely undermined by funding cuts and federal and provincial governments' embrace in recent years of informal voluntary approaches as an alternative to formal environmental regulation. Among the most prominent voluntary programmes are the Accelerated Reduction/Elimination of Toxic Substances programme, and the Voluntary Challenge and Registry for greenhouse gases.

See also: Canadian environmental ministries/agencies; Canadian Greens

Further reading

Boardman, R. and Van Nijnatten, D. (eds) (2001) *Canadian Environmental Policy: Ecosystems, Politics and Process*, Toronto: Oxford University Press.

Harrison, K. (1996) *Passing the Buck: Federalism and Canadian Environmental Policy*, Vancouver: UBC Press.

Parson, E.A. (ed) (2001) *Governing the Environment*, Toronto: University of Toronto Press.

KATHRYN HARRISON

Canadian environmental ministries/agencies

Responsibility for environmental policy is shared by Canada's federal and provincial governments as a result of the Constitution. Since the 1970s, environmental departments have been created at the federal and provincial levels. Their resources have risen and fallen dramatically, determined largely by shifts in political commitment, fiscal policy, and change in the party in power. The intergovernmental nature of environmental policy has become more prominent since the mid-1980s.

The federal department, Environment Canada, was created in 1971 in response to rising public concern about environmental degradation. The federal government leads in international environmental issues including climate change and water quality in the Great Lakes (see **Great Lakes International Joint Commission**). Court rulings since the late 1980s have reinforced federal jurisdiction over matters such as **water pollution** and environmental assessment. Several other federal departments have responsibilities that involve them in environmental policy. Environment Canada was intended to co-ordinate federal environmental policy. However, governments have often treated it as a junior ministry. It has lacked the tools to act as a central agency, greatly weakening its co-ordinating capacity. The result has been overlap, gaps, and turf wars, resulting in numerous administrative arrangements within the federal government.

Environment Canada enjoyed a heightened profile during the late 1980s and early 1990s when environmental issues grew in importance. The department had more influential ministers and was given new legislative tools including the Canadian Environmental Protection Act (1988) which extended federal authority into areas such as regulation of toxic substances (see **Canadian environmental law and policy**). The ambitious 1990 Green Plan was initially funded with (Cdn) $3 billion, but was wound down a few years later with only (Cdn) $847 million spent. The arrival of the Liberal government (1993) resulted in a lower priority on environmental issues through the 1990s. Environment Canada had its annual budget cut 30 per cent to (Cdn) $503 million while staff dropped from 5,700 to 4,300. In the mid-1990s, the first independent Commissioner of Environment and Sustainable Development was appointed to report periodically on the federal government's environmental record.

Each of Canada's thirteen provinces and territories has a department responsible for environmental policy. Environmental programmes vary by province, but usually include efforts to protect water and air quality and to encourage waste reduction. Ontario is Canada's largest province by population with a territory of 413,000 square miles. In the late 1990s, the resources of Ontario's environmental department were dramatically reduced after the election of a Conservative government. By 1999–

2000, staff was at 1,400, down from 3,300 in 1995. Annual spending was at (Cdn) $223 million, down from a peak of (Cdn) $711 million in 1991–2.

Quebec is Canada's second largest province by population with a territory of 595,000 square miles. In 1998–9, its environmental ministry had 2,891 staff and a budget of (Cdn) $275 million. Nova Scotia, one of Canada's smaller provinces by population, has a territory of 21,000 square miles. In 1999–2000, its environmental department had 235 staff and a budget of (Cdn) $16 million. Shared jurisdiction has resulted in hundreds of environmental agreements between the federal and provincial governments. In several cases, the federal government sets standards while provinces enforce. Since 1964, there has been an institutional mechanism for intergovernmental co-ordination. The Canadian Council of Ministers of the Environment, created in 1988, now fills this role. Overall, the contribution of federalism to strengthening environmental protection appears to be mixed (see **federalism and decentralization**). In the 1990s, national unity concerns encouraged federal efforts to increase provincial responsibility for environmental activities, causing concern among Canadian environmental groups. They believe provinces place greater priority on developing natural resources to create employment than on environmental protection.

There was also an increased effort in the 1990s to reduce intergovernmental conflict through harmonization. In 1998, the Canadian Accord on Environmental Harmonization was signed by all provinces except Quebec. Under the accord, national environmental standards will be set through interprovincial agreement and provinces will have responsibility for enforcement and environmental assessments. Canadian environmental groups have expressed scepticism about the accord, believing that it will lead to the weakening of environmental protection.

See also: Canadian Greens

Further reading

Brown, P. (1992) 'Organizational Design as Policy Instrument: Environment Canada in the Canadian Bureaucracy', in R. Boardman (ed.)

Canadian Environmental Policy: Ecosystems, Politics, and Process, Toronto: Oxford University Press.

Doern, B. and Conway, T. (1994) *The Greening of Canada: Federal Institutions and Decisions,* Toronto: University of Toronto Press.

Harrison, K. (1996) *Passing the Buck: Federalism and Canadian Environmental Policy,* Vancouver: University of British Columbia Press.

Skogstad, G. (1996) 'Intergovernmental Relations and the Politics of Environmental Protection in Canada', in K. Holland, F. Morton, and B. Galligan (eds) *Federalism and the Environment: Environmental Policymaking in Australia, Canada, and the United States,* Westport: Greenwood Press.

ELIZABETH MOORE

Canadian Greens

Environmental groups long predate the emergence of green parties in Canada. Relatively strong support among Canadians for environmental groups has not yet translated into visible electoral success for green parties. In the early 1990s, it was estimated that Canada had at least 1,800 environmental groups, not including small local groups. There are several national groups, some of which are Canadian branches of international groups. Examples include **Greenpeace** Canada, the World Wildlife Federation of Canada, **Friends of the Earth** Canada, the **Sierra Club** of Canada, the **Nature Conservancy** of Canada, the Canadian Wildlife Federation (CWF), and the Canadian Nature Federation (CNF). The CNF is perhaps Canada's oldest environmental organization, dating to 1939. The CWF is among the largest organizations with 500,000 supporters in 2000. Greenpeace was founded in Canada in 1971; its Canadian membership in 2000 was at 130,000. Overall, it was estimated that between one and two million Canadians belonged to an environmental group in the early 1990s.

Canadian environmental groups are active in a wide range of issues. They vary significantly in the size of their memberships, their strategies, and available resources. Few command impressive budgets; most rely heavily on volunteers. Financing comes largely from individual membership fees and donations. Some groups receive funding from government and industry, often to accomplish specific projects. The federal environment ministry has provided regular funding for the Canadian Environmental Network, an umbrella organization. Groups frequently work together to pool resources and increase credibility. Strategies include media campaigns, direct lobbying, demonstrations, boycotts, and increasingly, the use of the courts. For example, the Sierra Legal Defence Fund was established in 1990 to provide legal services to environmental groups.

Canadian environmental groups have had greater success in raising public awareness than in achieving policy change. However, they have often succeeded in adding a more explicit environmental dimension to policy issues. They have been consulted more consistently during policy-making since the late 1980s, in part through procedural innovations such as multi-stakeholder consultations and roundtables. The challenge is that their issues place them in direct conflict with major economic sectors given the ongoing, although declining, importance of natural resources (forestry, **mining**, **fisheries**, **agriculture**) to the Canadian economy. The shared jurisdiction of provincial and federal governments for environmental issues further complicates the task of advocacy.

Green parties emerged in Canada at the provincial and federal levels in the early 1980s. The Green Party of British Columbia was the first green party in North America, formed in February 1983. The Green Party of Canada was created that same year and ran 60 candidates in the 1984 federal election. In the late 1990s, the Green Party of Canada had fewer than 4,000 members. Canadian green parties have yet to achieve significant electoral success. In the 1997 Canadian federal election, the Green Party ran 79 candidates and received 0.4 per cent of all valid votes. Regionally, support was highest in British Columbia (2 per cent), Alberta (0.4 per cent), and Ontario (0.4 per cent). The Green Party of British Columbia has won a handful of municipal seats since 1990. In the 1996 provincial election, it received 2 per cent of all votes. The Green Party of Ontario received 1.7 per cent of all votes in the 1999 Ontario provincial election.

Explanations for the lack of electoral success include that the environmental platforms of the mainstream parties are judged sufficient by Canadians, green party platforms are too radical, and the nature of the electoral system. Green parties in Canada have advocated electoral reform, calling for a move to proportional representation which would translate green votes into a greater likelihood of seats in legislatures. Green parties have also not had strong alliances historically with Canada's major left-wing party, the New Democrats. The electoral platforms of Canadian green parties are comprehensive and call for significant policy change. For example, they have called for the introduction of economic indicators that account for the social and environmental costs of products and services; tax reform that includes replacing income and consumption taxes with environmental taxes to increase employment, favour locally owned businesses, and encourage sustainable industries; phasing out the use of **fossil fuels** and **nuclear energy** to be replaced with **renewable energy** sources; replacing welfare payments and employment insurance with a guaranteed income supplement; and reduction of military spending.

See also: Canadian environmental law and policy; Canadian environmental ministries/agencies

Further reading

Lyon, V. (1992) 'Green Politics: Parties, Elections, and Environmental Policy', in R. Boardman (ed.). *Canadian Environmental Policy: Ecosystems, Politics, and Process*, Toronto: Oxford University Press.

Wilson, J. (1992) 'Green Lobbies: Pressure Groups and Environmental Policy', in R. Boardman (ed.) *Canadian Environmental Policy: Ecosystems, Politics, and Process*, Toronto: Oxford University Press.

ELIZABETH MOORE

capitalism

Depending on one's ideological perspective, capitalism is either the root cause of the environmental crisis both globally and locally, or an essential part of the solution to it. These positions frame a continuum of views and perspectives regarding the relationship between capitalism and the environment.

For those who see capitalism as the cause of environment problems, the various structures and properties of the capitalist organization of the economy and society (private property, production for profit, **consumerism**, commodification, **globalization**, materialism, its 'big is better' and 'more is good' mentality and **anthropocentrism**, to name but a few of its ecological vices) systematically lead to environmental degradation, socioeconomic inequality, poverty, the waste of scarce resources, pollution and conflict and the removal of intrinsic ethical value from the non-human world. The relentless pursuit of profit, an in-built imperative to continual economic growth and the accumulation of capital and the search for new sources of profit (by privatizing or commodifying what was once a commonly owned or unowned 'free' good), all lead to descriptions of capitalism as possessing an 'environmentally destructive dynamic' (Carter, 1993), that is systematically and structurally incapable of being 'reformed' or 'tamed' along more environmentally sensitive lines. Those who reject capitalism on the basis of arguments such as these include 'eco-anarchists' such as social ecologists, eco-socialists and eco-Marxists (see **anarchism/eco-anarchism**; **eco-socialism**), those in the developing world who subscribe to the '**environmentalism of the poor**', environmentally inspired critics of **globalization** and those concerned about the social and environmental impact of large multi-national corporations, some eco-feminists, deep ecologists and those within the **environmental justice** movement (see also **multinational and transnational corporations**; **eco-feminism**; **deep ecology**). Though their reasons often differ as to why they reject and/or criticize capitalism, one of the key shared points is that capitalism stands condemned ecologically speaking as it is a growth-orientated socio-economic system which is incompatible (i.e. unsustainable) within the 'limits to growth' character of the global biosphere. It stands condemned on ethical grounds as it unequally and unjustly distributes the 'goods' of capitalist economic **development** within and between nations, as well as unevenly and unjustly distributing the environmental 'bads' (pollution, ecosystem degradation) of that same process.

Defenders of the environmentally positive aspects of capitalism point out that while the 'creative destruction' (to use a term from Joseph Schumpeter) of capitalism has caused environmental problems, like Achilles' lance, it can heal the wounds it inflicts. Basically the argument here is that the wealth created by capitalist development enables a society to clean up and improve the environmental damage caused in the production of that wealth. Another argument often used by **free-market environmentalism** is that many of the environmental problems that exist are as a result of unclear private **property rights**, inefficient state ownership and/or regulation, and the lack of an existing market for the particular environmental good or bad in question. Proponents of 'market solutions' to environmental problems assert that environmental problems exist because the environmental **externalities** of production (pollution, environmental degradation, **global warming**, desertification etc.) are not included in the price and cost calculations of firms. For example, **environmental economics** seeks ways to 'internalize' these environmental costs so that the market price of goods and services more accurately reflects its real cost (in terms of its environmental impacts). A final argument used by free market environmentalists is that private ownership of land leads to an 'in-built' incentive for the owner not to degrade it, unlike 'unowned' public or state-owned land which is abused precisely because the cost is not borne by those who abuse or unsustainably manage it (Anderson and Leal, 1991).

Between these two positions on the environmental assessment of capitalism lie those who while being critical of the ever-present environmentally destructive dynamics of capitalism, nevertheless for pragmatic or ideological reasons, conclude that the best way forward is to seek the 'greening of capitalism' in some way. We can dismiss the free market environmentalist position which is really not concerned with the environment and the achievement of environmental aims (such as **sustainable development**). Rather, it ought to be regarded as a right-wing attempt to denounce

and pre-empt some imputed 'left-wing' or socialist implications of the environmentalist position, in terms of such things as sustainable development requiring a degree of state planning and regulation, especially of private corporations, as well as having implications about the private ownership of land, and the positive relationship between socio-economic equality/justice and a more sustainable society (Eckersley, 1993; Barry, 1999). Those who adopt a more defensible attempt to 'green' or 'ecologically reform' capitalism include proponents of **ecological modernization**, and green liberal and social democracy (see **liberalism/liberal democracy**).

One thing that is clear is that capitalism as a global phenomenon does indeed stand guilty as charged on its environmental crimes against humanity and non-humanity, and the real question is whether a sustainable future lies somewhere 'beyond' capitalism or in a 'greener' less 'unfettered' and more managed variety of capitalism, and equally whether there exists sufficient public and democratic support for this transition.

See also: environmental justice; externalities; social ecology; World Trade Organization

References

Anderson, T. and Leal, D. (1991) *Free Market Environmentalism*, Boulder, CO: Westview Press.

Barry, J. (1999) *Rethinking Green Politics: Nature, Virtue and Progress*, London: Sage.

Carter, A. (1993) 'Towards a Green Political Theory', in Dobson, A and Lucardie, P (eds) *The Politics of Nature*, London: Routledge.

Eckersley, R. (1993) 'Free Market Environmentalism: Friend or Foe?', *Environmental Politics*, 2:1.

JOHN BARRY

Capra, Fritjof

b. 1 February 1939, Vienna, Austria

Theoretical physicist

Capra's *Tao of Physics* (1975) drew parallels between eastern mysticism and the 'new physics' of quantum mechanics. *The Turning Point* (1982) expanded these into a critique of mechanistic worldviews based on 'outdated' Newtonian physics; reductionist approaches incompatible with the uncertain holism of the physical world, which thereby contributed to environmental damage and spiritual alienation. Capra argued for a holistic philosophy, manifested in alternative therapies, decentralized authority and environmental awareness, supported scientifically and spiritually by the new physics. In *The Web of Life* (1996), he directly related these conclusions to the philosophy of **deep ecology**. He has however been criticized for inferring from physics a naturalistic, even mystical view of society and environmentalism, unmindful of cultural and economic structures.

ANDREW WHITWORTH

car industry

The car industry has been one of the central focuses of many environmental critiques. It has often been taken as a key ideological target. This is in part because of the environmental impacts of the car. Cars produce a range of pollutants, including carbon dioxide, nitrogen oxides, volatile organic compounds, and a range of other gases which produce urban **air pollution**. This pollution causes large-scale environmental change like **global warming**, as well as micro-level impacts such as on human, animal, and plant health. Cars also consume substantial amounts of natural resources, in particular oil (both in use and in asphalt production), steel, aluminium, lead, platinum, and rubber.

A car-based society has also radically altered the way space is organized. Urban space in particular has been systematically reconstructed to make allowance for the space required to move people about in cars. Cars take up huge amounts of space which could be used for other purposes. The highest figure is for Los Angeles, where two-thirds of all land space is devoted to car use – driving and parking. For the USA as a whole, 10 per cent of available arable land is taken up by roads and parking places. Many suggest that this suburbanization has become a self-reproducing trend, as the reorganization of towns and cities to make car-

based mobility more possible has meant that increasingly a car has moved from being a luxury to a necessity (e.g. **Gorz**, 1980: 69–77)

In this context, the car industry has been a persistent focus for environmental policy-makers. Conversely, the car industry has generally lobbied against regulation. Such debates began in the mid-1960s over safety concerns (Ralph **Nader**'s book *Unsafe at Any Speed* (1965) catalysed this debate), fuel economy, regulation of fuel emissions (lead in petrol, catalytic converters, nitrogen oxide emissions, in particular), and most recently global warming.

But the practical environmental consequences of the car are not the only reason it has been a focus of green critique. Cars have been extremely important in symbolic terms in projecting a modernist social vision. Cars have both been sold through key ideological terms in twentieth-century modernity – individualist notions of freedom, placelessness and mobility, speed, power, comfort – and they have also been key in helping to reproduce capitalist modernity. Green values contradict directly these ideologies – valuing place and community in particular, rejecting the valorization of speed and power – so the car has thus been a useful concrete symbol around which to advance the green critique. Key examples of this can be found in **Illich** (1974), Gorz (1980) and Sachs (1992).

In this context, political resistance to the car and to a car-based society has emerged. This has tended to be either against road building, or directly against the domination of urban spaces by cars. The former has tended to be either to protect rural areas against encroachment by roads – for example preventing road building into wilderness areas, or protection of particular rural places from destruction by road building – or it has been to do with preventing the way in which road construction in urban areas, particularly of urban freeways, often destroys the communities through which such roads go. From the late 1950s through to the mid-1970s (at least) in the USA, there was much resistance to such urban building. International resistance by many diverse groups has been organized to road building projects such as the Trans-Amazonian Highway. The most recently famous have been the roads protests in the UK, which captured a great deal of public support and arguably helped to transform public policy on road building.

Other more general protests against car culture have been primarily organized around the reclamation of public spaces for purposes other than transit – often organized under the banner of 'Reclaim the Streets'. Roads have been occupied, and parties held on them, showing that cities and towns could be organized on an alternative basis based much more around community and sustainability. Similarly, Critical Mass refers to organized cycle rides in cities designed to disrupt car traffic and show the possibilities of alternative means of organizing transport in urban areas. In many cases, these protests simultaneously ask the public to imagine a world organized much more along green lines, showing the importance and utility of the car and its critiques for environmental politics.

See also: anti-roads movement; transportation; urbanization

References

Gorz, A. (1980) 'The Social Ideology of the Motor Car', in *Ecology as Politics*, London: Pluto.

Illich, I. (1974) *Energy and Equity*, London: Calder & Boyars.

Sachs, W. (1992) *For the Love of the Automobile*, Berkeley: University of California Press.

Further reading

Freund, P. and Martin, G. (1993) *The Ecology of the Automobile*, Montreal: Black Rose Books.

MATTHEW PATERSON

Carson, Rachel

b. 27 May 1907, Springdale, Pennsylvania, USA; d. 14 April 1964, Silver Springs, Maryland

Nature writer and ecologist

Rachel Carson was a prizewinning author who initially earned a national reputation as a writer of books about the seashore and oceans, but in the last years of her life, researched and wrote *Silent Spring* (1962), a study that alerted the nation to the danger of the indiscriminate use of **pesticides** and has been called the most influential work of American environmental commentary.

The youngest in a family of three children, Carson was born in rural Pennsylvania where her mother introduced her to the beauty of the natural world while also encouraging Rachel's interest in reading and music. She attended Pennsylvania College for Women on a scholarship where she intended to study English. However, a Biology professor inspired her to change her major and she graduated in 1929 with a zoology concentration. Carson continued her education at Johns Hopkins University completing a zoology master's degree in 1931 and supporting herself during the next few years with teaching at Hopkins, the University of Maryland, and summer research grants at Woods Hole, Massachusetts. Carson also continued her interest in scientific writing, publishing feature pieces in the *Baltimore Sun*. However, the economic problems of the Great Depression and the need to provide for her elderly parents forced Carson to leave teaching and look for a higher paying position. In 1936, she became an aquatic biologist with the US Bureau of Fisheries, only the second woman to work for the agency in a non-clerical position.

Carson's life turned again in a literary direction when the *Atlantic Monthly* published one of her essays, 'Undersea', in 1937. Encouraged to expand the work into a book, four years later she published *Under the Sea Wind* which received fine reviews but, more importantly for Carson's career, caught the attention of the oceanographer William Beebe who became a life-long friend and supporter.

During the 1940s, Carson advanced at Fisheries, but she and her family still had difficulty making ends meet. Aware of recently declassified oceanographic material on the geological formation of the oceans, she decided to write a book on this subject. With a contract from Oxford University Press in hand, she devoted most of her spare time and vacations to research and writing on her new project. Assisted by fellowship funds, Beebe's contacts, and an agreement with the *New Yorker* to publish half of her manuscript, Carson completed the book in 1951. Within months, reviews and sales of *The Sea Around*

Us made her a national literary figure with all of the acclaim associated with that stature.

Much more important, the success gave her the financial freedom to leave her government position and to devote the rest of her life to writing. In 1955, she published *The Edge of the Sea*, which was also a critical and financial success, and began work on a nature book for children, *The Sense of Wonder*.

However, in 1958, her life – and ours – changed forever. Carson received a letter from a friend, who inquired about the possible effects that spraying **DDT** (dichloro-diphenyl-trichoroethane) might be having on the insect and bird populations near her Massachusetts home. This innocent inquiry was to result in a book, *Silent Spring* (1962), that many have compared in its far reaching impact to *Uncle Tom's Cabin*.

Originally a nineteenth-century German discovery, DDT was reinvented as a pesticide by the Swiss chemist, Dr Paul Muller, in 1939. It quickly became one of the 'miracles' of the Second World War used to fight typhus and malaria, but its miraculous reputation carried over into peace time where it was commonly used by state and local governments to help eradicate insects.

Carson's research acknowledged that pesticides could be helpful if used properly, but that the widespread use of DDT was nothing short of a national disaster. The result of this would indeed be a 'silent spring' as DDT contamination killed off song birds which she saw as only the beginning of a nature-altering calamity. Her solution was biological controls, but her critics, especially in the pesticide-producing chemical industry, condemned her as an uninformed alarmist. The loud controversy over *Silent Spring* eventually reached the federal government with the result that many pesticides, including DDT, were banned and others were subject to greater control. However, Carson lost a long, difficult fight against cancer before these victories were achieved, though she finished *The Sense of Wonder*, which was published posthumously, shortly before her death.

Further reading

Carson, R. (1962) *Silent Spring*, Boston: Houghton, Mifflin.

Lear, L. (1997) *Rachel Carson: Witness for Nature*, New York: Henry Holt.

WARREN VANDER HILL

Central American environmental politics

Environmental politics in Central America is an evolving phenomenon focused on a broad and growing variety of disputes. The oldest, most widespread, and seemingly most enduring are the disputes over land ownership and **property rights** between several groups of **indigenous peoples** and various other claimants, including governments, state-supported and **multinational and transnational corporations**, and local landed elites. These disputes involve Mayans in Guatemala, Belize, and Chiapas and Oaxaca states in southern **Mexico**; Miskitos in Nicaragua; Borucas in Costa Rica; and Talamancas in Costa Rica and Panama. Land and property-rights conflicts have combined with state militarism (see **militarism and the environment**), Marxism and **communism**, movements for social justice, the international drug trade, and differences in socio-economic **class** as well as ethnicity to generate organized violence in El Salvador, Nicaragua, Honduras, Panama, Guatemala, and Mexico.

While the older disputes are legacies of Central America's history of Spanish imperial colonialism, according to local and international **environmental movements**, the newer ones are the products of the neo-colonialism of First World **capitalism**. These disputes emerged in the 1970s over preservation of **rainforests** and **biodiversity**, the use of **pesticides**, the impacts of **ecotourism**, industrial pollution, and the role of the **World Bank** in **sustainable development**. They enjoy much greater press attention than the old disputes, due mainly to their appeal to well-travelled and educated European, North American, and local elites and the usefulness of the USA's power and proximity as an ideological and rhetorical foil.

Costa Rica illustrates many of the origins and current trends in the region's newer environmental

politics. Unlike its neighbours, Costa Rica overcame the worst of the region's history of militarism
and concentrated land ownership in the late 1940s
when its new constitution abolished the nation's
military and included provisions permitting people
to gain property rights to unused land merely by
moving on to it and either building a home or
cultivating a crop. The nation's people and
economy flourished, achieving First World standards of literacy, life expectancy, public health and
sanitation. While violent conflicts from the old
disputes engaged several of its neighbours in the
1970s and 1980s, Costa Rica enjoyed both peace
and widespread economic security and prosperity.
This invited foreign investment and permitted the
development of Costa Rica from an export-
orientated economy dependent on bananas, coffee,
chocolate, beef, and ornamental plants to one in
which tourism became the largest single source of
income and employment. In recent years Belize
and to a lesser extent Mexico and Guatemala have
tried to copy the example and develop their
infrastructure for such environmental tourism (see
eco-tourism).

Peace, material and social **progress**, and its
tropical ecosystems have made Costa Rica an
attractive destination for First World tourists,
scientists, students, and even expatriate pacifists.
American Quakers fleeing Cold War fears arrived
in the 1950s, acquired tracts of cheap agricultural
land, and with their new neighbours in the ensuing
years created the Monteverde Cloud Forest
Reserve and with the contributions of Scandinavian school children purchased the Children's
Eternal Rainforest. North American and European
biologists and ecologists came in the 1960s and
1970s to establish large, well-funded tropical
ecology field schools and research institutions in
La Selva, Siquirres, and Turrialba. These institutions have grown so in influence that they have
gained the prestige to make the careers of tropical
ecologists and even the authority to certify whether
the tropical forest products grown and harvested
throughout the region are managed sustainably
and are therefore legal to sell in Europe. All this
local, regional, and international environmentalism
flourished, especially in the press, and culminated
in Costa Rica's Earth Charter.

Other manifestations of the new environmental
politics have come in law suits brought before the
World Court by private landowners to stop the use
of pesticides by export banana producers in Costa
Rica; international negotiations and treaties to
remove and clean up dangerous military ordnance
and wastes in Panama and reduce industrial air
and water pollution in Mexico; designations of
World Heritage and Biosphere Reserves in Belize,
Guatemala, Costa Rica, and Mexico. Still, the new
First World politics of Central American environmentalism has failed to combine and integrate
itself with the old Third World politics of
indigenous property rights and social justice. This
being the case, the poverty that remains the
greatest long-term threat to the region's environment goes largely unaddressed.

See also: distributive justice; globalization; land
reform; Mexico; Zapatistas/Chiapas

Further reading

Faber, D. (1993) *Environment under Fire: Imperialism
and the Ecological Crisis in Central America*, New
York: Monthly Review Press.

PAUL CHANDLER

chemical industry

The chemical industry of the world generates $1.6
trillion per year. Nearly a third of the chemicals
produced are exported from their country of origin,
making up some 9 per cent of all internationally
traded goods (Chemical Manufacturer's Association (CMA), 1998). Hence the chemical industry is
profoundly affected by any changes in the domestic
and international regulatory frameworks concerning chemical production and trade and mobilizes
itself in various forms to influence the political
process. All developed countries have long-standing
national associations of chemical companies, such
as the US Chemical Manufacturers Association
(CMA), but, increasingly, such bodies have co-
ordinated their efforts on the international stage to
protect the interests of the industry in the face of
increasing global regulation.

The oldest international interest group representing the chemical industry is the International Union of Pure and Applied Chemistry (IUPAC), an association of national professional bodies dedicated to the advancement of chemical science. IUPAC has enjoyed 'specialized consultative' status with the Food and Agricultural Organization (FAO) since 1985 and regularly provides technical assistance to the International Programme of Chemical Safety, the focus of UN policy in this area, co-ordinated jointly by the FAO, **World Health Organization** and International Labour Organization.

More overtly political than IUPAC is the International Council of Chemical Associations (ICCA), an association representing 80 per cent of the world's chemical manufacturers. This was set up in 1987 to present the view of the industry at international organizations dealing with chemical trade and pollution. ICCA was created specifically for lobbying purposes and IUPAC's role now is primarily technical, aiming to influence the **epistemic communities** on chemical safety and pollution. ICCA is made up of both national associations and direct representatives of the larger chemical corporations. In effect, it co-ordinates the positions of longer standing regional groupings of national associations such as the European Chemical Industry Council (CEFIC). Other international lobby groups specialize in specific areas of the chemical industry, such as the Global Crop Protection Federation (GCPF), the representative of the **pesticide** industry.

The close links between the FAO and bodies representing the chemical industry have brought criticism from environmental NGOs (see **international non-governmental organizations**). An Industry Co-Operation Programme initiated in the early 1970s, which organized seminars in developing countries on the merits of chemical **technology** in promoting economic **development**, was wound up in the face of criticism of FAO involvement.

A watershed year for the chemical industry was 1984, when the **Bhopal disaster** heralded moves to tighten rules governing the trade in hazardous chemicals. The chemical industry has tried to respond to greater public concern over environmental pollution and industrial safety by co-

operating more in international environmental policy-making. GCPF, under its previous name GIFAP, did a 'U turn' and gave its support to the FAO/UNEP Prior Informed Consent (PIC) procedure controlling the trade in hazardous chemicals to **less developed countries** in the late 1980s. The ICCA have also lent support to PIC and the UNEP sponsored regime to eliminate the production of Persistent Organic Pollutants (POPs). The World Business Council for Sustainable Development, a coalition of MNC representatives including many chemical corporations, has lent its support to **Agenda 21** of UNCED, albeit on the condition that emergent international standards are uniform and scientifically based. Chapter 19 of Agenda 21, dealing with chemical pollution, prompted **United Nations Environment Programme** to sponsor a 'Code of Ethics on the International Trade in Chemicals' in 1994. ICCA and other bodies representing chemical companies signed up to this and produced the 'Responsible Care Initiative', a voluntary commitment to reduce pollution.

In line with the 'greening' of chemical companies in the 1980s and 1990s, the chemical lobby groups worked hard to present a better image of the industry and reached the conclusion that supporting the development of international regimes on chemical safety was the best way of achieving this. Being proactive in the development of international regimes on the environment has also come to be seen as a means of ensuring that the regulatory framework that emerges at least creates a level playing field for the trade in chemicals. The international harmonization of trade standards may impose some costs on the chemical industry but is preferable to radical domestic legislation such as the banning of certain chemical exports.

Reference

Chemical Manufacturers Association (CMA) (1998) *Statistical Handbook*, USA.

Further reading

Broadhurst, A. and Ledgerwood, G. (1998) 'Environmental Diplomacy of States, Corporations and Non-Governmental Organizations: the Worldwide Web of Influence', *International Relations* XIV,2: 1–20

Hough, P. (1998) *The Global Politics of Pesticides: Forging Consensus from Conflicting Interests*, London: Earthscan.

PETER HOUGH

Chernobyl

The radiation release accident at the Chernobyl Unit 4 RBMK-type nuclear reactor, about 130km north of Ukraine's capital city, Kiev, on 26 April 1986 killed 15,000 members of the clean-up teams, while another 30,000 people became significantly disabled during the 14-year aftermath to the end of the twentieth century, according to the Russian Deputy Prime Minister, Sergei Shoigu, in April 2000. At the time the Ukraine's Health Ministry said approximately 3.5 million people, more than a third of them children, had fallen ill as a result of the contamination, while the incidence of some cancers had reached 10 times the national average. The mass radiation exposure led to an outbreak of diseases of the nervous, blood and respiratory systems, with the rate of these diseases among children affected by the accident being 17 per cent higher than the national average. Meantime, the rate of thyroid cancer in 2000 remained 10 times higher than normal among Ukrainian children

Chernobyl is by some considerable degree the worst environmental and economic human-made disaster of the industrial age. The clean-up costs alone have amounted to over 8 times the Ukraine's entire annual GDP. The accident was truly international in its consequences, with virtually the entire continent of Europe affected to some degree. For example, in Britain, radiocaesium (137Cs) contamination in upland areas is predicted to last up to the year 2015. In Europe's lakes and foodstocks, radiocaesium has shown an unpredicted mobility leading to predictions of the need to monitor for at least a half century more (Smith, 2000: 141).

Altogether 135,000 people were evacuated from a 30km exclusion zone, 115,000 of whom were permanently resettled, with a further 80,000 outside the zone also relocated within five years (Gubanov, 1991:12). In all some six million people lived in contaminated zones in the Ukraine and Belarus, the two former Soviet states most affected by radioactive fallout and water. Between 600,000 to 800,000 *liquidators*, including press-ganged soldiers and prisoners, worked on the immediate control of the accident, and subsequent construction of a vast concrete sarcophagus to contain the stricken reactor. (Imanaka, 1998:1) Helicopters were used to drop over 5,000 tonnes of boron, dolomite, sand, clay and lead into the reactor core – exposed by the roof having been blown off – in the first two weeks of the accident aftermath (Gubanov, 1991:71).

There was also serious radiological damage done to tens of thousands of livestock and millions of acres of forest and soil used to grow the Ukraine's vast wheat harvest. There are still serious disputes over the cause and consequences of the accident. It is known that the plant engineers were trying an experiment to see whether they could use the so-called spinning reserve from the reactor turbines in close-down mode, in an emergency loss-of-power situation. They deliberately shut off the safety systems to test this, but succeeded in creating a run-away power surge, which some scientists say was an uncontrolled 'slow' nuclear explosion, followed by a hydrogen explosion (Patterson, 1986: 34–6).

Two reports from different United Nations agencies issued to mark the fourteenth anniversary of the accident demonstrate the continuing environmental heath implications. In one, the UN Secretary General acknowledged in a foreword that the exact number of victims may never be known, but that three million children need treatment and 'many will die prematurely'. Chernobyl's radioactive fallout remained a persistent blight. At least 100 times as much radiation was released by this accident as by the two atomic bombs dropped on Hiroshima and Nagasaki, said the booklet, published by the UN Office for the Co-ordination of Humanitarian Affairs. More than seven million people remained affected, with 50,000 additional cancers predicted, according to the **World Health Organization**. But a report issued by the United Nations Scientific Committee on the Effects of Atomic Radiation (UNSCEAR) asserted that there was no evidence of a major public health impact attributable to radiation exposure apart from a high level of thyroid cancers in children

The total cost of environmental, technical and economic restoration in the wake of the accident is literally incalculable. By the end of 1999, the **European Union** alone had invested over $150 million in technical aid to phase out Chernobyl's still operating reactors. A final decision to close the remaining three reactors at the site was made in early June 2000. Amongst the persistent long term victims outside former Soviet Union states are the Saami people of northern Scandinavia. Radioactivity uptake in their traditional foodstuff, the reindeer, was very high. But despite the Norwegian government raising the permitted 'tolerance level' 20 fold (to 6,000bq/kg), the Saami deemed it far too dangerous to eat (Bell, 1999: 410). Thus a whole traditional culture was put under permanent threat by this legacy of the world's worst accident.

See also: Russian nuclear power industry

References

Bell, S. (1999) 'Radioactive Reindeer: the Chernobyl Legacy', *The Ecologist*, 29(7): 410.

Gubanov, V.A. (1991) *The International Chernobyl Project*, Vienna: IAEA *Proceedings*.

Imanaka, T. (ed.) (1998) *Research Activities about the Radiological Consequences of the Chernobyl NPs Accident and Social Activities to Assist the Sufferers by the Accident*, Kyoto: KURRI Research Reactor Institute

Patterson, W. (1986) 'Chernobyl – The Official Story', *Bulletin of the Atomic Scientists*, November: 34–6.

Smith, J.T. *et al.* (2000) 'Chernobyl's legacy in food and water', *Nature*, 405,11 May:141

Further reading

Karaoglou,G. *et al.* (eds) (1996) *The Radioecological Consequences of the Chernobyl Accident*, Luxembourg: European Commission.

DAVID LOWRY

Chile

A country with around 15 million inhabitants and a territory of 292,300 square miles, stretching down the east coast of South America, Chile is encountering a broad variety of environmental problems. As a political issue, the environment has been firmly established in the 1990s with a range of governmental and non-governmental organizations dedicated to the solution of ecological problems.

Chile came to world attention in environmental circles when adverse health effects arising from the Antarctic ozone hole were reported in the early 1990s (see **ozone depletion**). While the ozone hole continues to be a problem for the most southern part of the country, Chile is facing a series of other environmental threats. In common with many other Third World countries, urban pollution is one major issue, particularly in the metropolitan region of the capital Santiago where 40 per cent of the country's population resides. In particular, **air pollution** is a major problem, and a policy of restricting vehicular access had to be introduced to curb car-related pollution.

Other environmental issues include industrial pollution and the location of major infrastructure projects which have led to a proliferation of environmental local protests. The most noteworthy case is a planned hydro-electric station which involves the damming of the Bio-Bio river. The Ralco project is particularly sensitive because the flooded area is part of the traditional homeland of the Pehuenche people, an indigenous population group that is protesting strongly against this plan (see **dams/hydroelectric power**).

The involvement of the interests of **indigenous peoples** is also of crucial importance in the protection of Chile's native forests. In the thinly populated south of the country, large areas have been taken over by logging companies. At issue in particular is the destruction of Chile's native forests. A coalition of Mapuche Indians and environmentalists is fighting for the preservation of these forests. Other major areas of environmental concern are agricultural pollution, in particular the use of **pesticides**, and the environmental impact of **mining**.

As in many other countries of the developing world, the first political initiatives for environmental protection were launched by members of environmental professions, such as biologists, physicians, and architects. Chile's first environmental group, the *Comité Nacional pro Defensa de la Fauna y Flora* (CODEFF – National Committee for the Defence of Fauna and Flora), was founded in 1968. CODEFF was and still is essentially concerned with nature protection issues. Other important non-governmental organizations are mainly research-based: the *Instituto de Ecología* (Institute of Ecology) was set up in 1974 by a medical doctor, Juan Grau. Dr Grau became Chile's most prominent environmental campaigner, frequently appearing on TV and other mass media and publishing a series of popular environmental books in the 1970s and 1980s. In 1979, the architect Guillermo Geisse founded the *Centro de Investigación y Planificación del Medio Ambiente* (CIPMA – Centre for Environmental Research and Planning), as a non-governmental organization devoted to inter-disciplinary environmental research (see **international non-governmental organizations**).

After the military coup of 1973, any political activity challenging the authority of the government was forbidden. Once the military regime had come to an end, following the referendum in 1988, a number of more politically orientated environmental groups were formed. Among them was the *Instituto de Ecología Política* (IEP – Institute of Political Ecology), formed by Manuel Baquedano who had become involved in green politics during his political exile in Belgium. A number of other organizations and groups were in turn set up, for example many organizations concerned with environmental education. Most of these organizations received funding from western Europe and North America for specific projects; they campaigned on a variety of environmental issues but were not membership organizations.

The other important foundation of the 1980s was the *Red Nacional de Acción Ecológica* (RENACE – National Network of Ecological Action), an umbrella organization of mainly local environmental groups. Its internal structure is democratic and non-hierarchical, with annual congresses

electing its executive committee and deciding about policy; its role is to provide resources for local groups and campaign on selected issues at national level. In 1990, **Greenpeace** decided to set up a branch in Chile as part of a broader international plan to sponsor the formation of Greenpeace branches in Latin America. How successful have Chilean environmental NGOs been in introducing environmental issues onto the political agenda? While there have been some notable successes on single-issue campaigns, the groups face a number of important constraints.

First, popular support for environmental groups in Chile is high but this does not translate into substantial activism or financial contributions. In a 1996 survey asking about the positive or negative influence of various social groups, ecological groups came top of all political and social institutions, with 90 per cent of the population ascribing a 'positive' influence to them (Mora y Araujo and Montoya, 1997: 310). Other environmental surveys have shown comparatively high degrees of environmental concern. By contrast, the number of Chileans who have joined environmental groups is very small. The largest national membership group, CODEFF, has just 3,700 members (CODEFF, 1998). Many of the most visible groups, such as the IEP, are not membership organizations and rely on financial support from abroad.

Second, there are few issues that have led to environmental mass mobilization. One such issue was the nuclear tests in the Pacific carried out by the French in the mid-1990s. Here, leading environmental groups acquired a very high profile, and a broad coalition of social and political forces was mobilized against these nuclear tests. But there has been no other issue that has impacted on public consciousness in a similar way.

Third, environmental activists and NGOs are divided on the political strategies to pursue. As in many other countries, there is a distinction between the less political nature conservationists/environmentalists and the more radical ecologists. In addition, in Chile attitudes to the dictatorship and to the policy of the new democratic government are playing an important role.

There is currently no Green Party in Chile, mainly due to the existence of a very restrictive system of party registration that imposes very high hurdles on the organization of a new party.

Soon after political parties were again allowed to organize in the late 1980s, a party *Los Verdes* (The Greens) was formed in Chile and registered as a political party in 1988. *Los Verdes* joined the main centre–left alliance of anti-Pinochet parties, but failed to gain parliamentary representation in 1989. *Los Verdes* merged with the Humanist Party in 1990, forming the *Alianza Humanista–Verde* (Humanist–Green Alliance). The party left the government alliance and contested the 1993 parliamentary elections on its own. Another party contesting the 1993 elections was the *Movimiento Ecologista* (Ecological Movement) founded shortly before the election. Both parties again failed to win representation, and subsequently merged under the name *Alianza Humanista–Verde* (Humanist–Green Alliance). The party changed its name to *Partido Humanista* (Humanist Party) in 1996 and took part in the 1997 parliamentary elections.

The second strand of green party politics in Chile is associated with the independent left that is critical of the policies of the centre–left government, dominated by the Christian Democrats and Socialists, and also finds little in common with the rather traditional Chilean Communist Party, the main left force outside the government bloc. After the return to **democracy** in the late 1980s, there was no social basis for a European-style green party. The major social movements of the 1980s had concentrated on civil rights, democracy and social justice issues, with environmental questions playing no role whatsoever. In 1993, the Chilean economist Manfred **Max-Neef** ran as an independent in the Presidential Election, supported by a range of ecological and minority rights groups as well as other political groups, such as the Christian Left, that had failed to reach party status. Max-Neef polled 5.6 per cent of the votes, a remarkable achievement.

Modern environmental policy in Chile started under the military dictatorship of General Pinochet. The lobbying of Dr Grau and his *Instituto de Ecología* contributed to a right of the citizen to live in an environment free of pollution to be enshrined in the new constitution that came into force in controversial circumstances in 1980. After the

return to democracy, hopes were high for some new initiatives on environment issues. It took until 1994 for a first comprehensive environmental law to be passed. The main task of the law was to establish 'environmental impact assessment' as a major policy tool.

References

CODEFF (Comite Nacional pro Defensa de la Fauna y Flora) (1998) *30 Años por la Naturaleza, por el Medió Ambiente, Por la Vida, 1968–1998*, Santiago: CODEFF.

Mora y Araujo, M. and Montoya, P. (1997) 'Los Actitudes de la Población Ante el Cambio Político y Económico en la Argentina y Chile', *Estudios Publicos*, 67 (Spring): 299–327.

Silva, E. (1997) 'Chile', in Jänicke, M. and Weidner, H. (eds) *National Environmental Policies: A Comparative Study of Capacity Building*, Berlin: Springer, pp. 213–35.

WOLFGANG RÜDIG

China

The territory of the People's Republic of China (PRC) extends from Central Asia (Xinjiang) to the East China Sea, and from the Amur River (Heilongjiang) in the north to tropical Yunnan bordering Myanmar. This huge land mass (about 9.5 million km^2 is almost the same area as the USA; in addition, PRC also claims most of the South China Sea islands) contains a wide variety of natural ecosystems including the Himalayas and Tibet's high plateau, deserts and arid grasslands of the north, boreal forests in the north-east, temperate mixed and subtropical forests and woodlands in eastern and southern provinces and tropical forests in the south-west.

China is the oldest continuous civilization, and its population has been always concentrated in the eastern third of the country: while the western interior is arid and largely inhospitable, monsoonal precipitation brings plenty of seasonal moisture to southern and eastern provinces. Virtually all cultivable land in these regions has been converted to agro-ecosystems whose intensive cultivation now supports the world's largest population which has grown from about 550 million people in 1949 to 1.25 billion people in 2000, and which may not stabilize before adding another 250 million before the middle of the twenty-first century.

Establishment of the PRC in 1949 led to three decades of fairly intensive, Stalinist-type (and hence very inefficient) **industrialization** of the country. Only the wide-ranging reforms initiated by Deng Xiaoping in the late 1970s after Mao Zedong's death began changing China into a modern economy. Between 1950 and 2000 China's gross domestic product (GDP) rose roughly 100-fold and its industrial output increased more than 80-fold. China is now the world's largest producer of coal and it ranks only behind the USA in its total consumption of all forms of primary commercial energy. Its area of irrigated farmland has tripled since 1950, and it is now the world's largest user of synthetic fertilizers and the largest producer of food grain whose harvest has nearly quadrupled between 1950 and 2000. Not surprisingly, these developments have caused extensive environmental pollution and worrying ecosystemic degradation.

Natural ecosystems

Even when defined liberally as all areas where at least 30 per cent of the ground is covered by tree canopies, forests cover only about 13 per cent of China's territory. Remaining undisturbed natural stands can be found in only small patches in Heilongjiang province in the north-east and in parts of the south-west (Sichuan, Yunnan, eastern Tibet). Traditionally high deforestation rates intensified after the establishment of the PRC. About 20 million hectares (Mha), or almost a quarter of the 1950 forest area, were lost by 1980. Better post-1980 afforestation has suceeded in reversing this decline (see **forest management**).

During the 1990s official statistics conveyed a message of expanding forest growth, as China's total wood increment surpassed the annual cut. Even if correct, these figures hide a much more sobering reality because no less than three-quarters of China's forests are young or middle-aged stands, while the growing stock ready for harvesting in mature forests amounts to less than one-fifth of all

standing timber, a total which could be cut in less than a decade. A conservative valuation of economic losses due to the mismanagement of China's forests adds up to an annual equivalent of up to 4 per cent of GDP. Eventual monetization of a number of elusive valuations – such as the forfeited recreation value of degraded or destroyed ecosystems and the loss of **biodiversity** could raise that rate substantially.

China's largely arid grasslands (about 400 Mha, mostly in Inner Mongolia and Xinjiang) have been seriously degraded by overgrazing, mineral extraction, and desertification. Both inland and coastal **wetlands** have been extensively converted to crop fields, a process reducing natural water storage in flood-prone areas and destroying some of the country's richest ecosystems. China is one of the world's five most important centres of plant and animal biodiversity (Indonesia is Asia's other major centre), but limited area of remaining undisturbed ecosystems, their often fragmented nature, and their continuing widespread abuse make the preservation of the country's genetic riches very difficult. Extraordinarily destructive, but widespread, demand for exotic foodstuffs is responsible for serious species loss even beyond China's borders as the country brings in animals and fish from abroad. Area protected by **national parks** and other reserves has been expanding but illegal poaching and tree cutting in these reserves is common.

Farmland

Official statistics put China's farmland at about 95 Mha during the last years of 1990s. This translates to a mere 0.08 ha/capita, about as low a rate as in **Bangladesh**, and only **Japan**, Taiwan and South Korea have lower per capita availabilities of farmland. Fortunately for China, the official claim greatly underestimates the real extent of arable land. Actual field surveys and studies using high-resolution satellite imagery agree that the PRC has at least 130, and more likely 140 Mha of farmland, more than 40 per cent above the official total, or about 0.11 ha/capita. Nationwide multicropping index (number of crops grown per yield in one field) has surpassed 1.5, and almost half of China's farmland is irrigated.

China's intensive food production actually claims about 160 Mha as increasing areas of orchards and ponds must be added to the total of arable land: PRC is now the world's leader in freshwater acquaculture, and a growing exporter of fruit. At the same time, it must be acknowledged that the largest amount of farmland omitted by official statistics is in hilly and mountainous interior provinces where the soil quality and average yields can never equal those typical of the coastal plains. Moreover, only a limited amount of uncultivated land can be converted to fields without further serious damage to remaining natural ecosystems. Consequently, China must reduce its currently rather high rate of farmland losses to urban and industrial uses (up to 1 Mha/year), and it must also minimize topsoil losses to wind and water erosion. During the 1990s excessive soil erosion affected nearly a third of China's farmland, and the country's average annual erosion rate is about 50 t/year, compared to less than 20 t/ha in the USA. In addition, high rates of inorganic fertilizer use have led to unwelcome declines of soil organic matter.

Water scarcity

Average volume of usable per capita runoff in China is about as large as in India but the mismatch between North China's limited water resources and the region's rising water demand has created a chronic supply crisis in half a dozen northern provinces. In the year 2000 water shortages amounted to an equivalent of almost 10 per cent of the country's total water demand. During the 1990s Huang He's lower-course volume has been repeatedly reduced to as little as 2/5 of its long-term mean, with the river's summer flow into the North China Sea ceasing repeatedly for periods of up to five months. Chronic shortages of northern runoff have led to excessive reliance on underground water, but overdrawing of aquifers is not limited to the north. One-third of China's nearly 700 major cities rely on ground water as their main source of supply, and about 30 cities experience severe overpumping. During the 1950s Beijing's water table in places was just 5m below the surface, but it has been sinking by as much as

2m/year, and many wells now draw water from depths of around 50m.

Serious water shortages have spread beyond cities: they now affect an area of North China larger than France. Supply is particularly restricted in Hebei and Shanxi provinces, as well is in large areas in Shandong and Henan. Some parts of the Hai He basin have seen the water table dropping over 100 m. And as many as 50 million people in North China's countryside do not have enough water even for basic daily use. Direct economic costs of water shortages include reductions in crop yields and industrial output, and damage to land and real estate caused by surface subsidence. Increased urban water treatment could greatly expand the available supply – but during the late 1990s only about 7 per cent of China's municipal waste water was treated.

Water pollution

Given such a low rate of water treatment it is not surprising that **water pollution** is China's most common environmental degradation. During the 1990s about 80 per cent of 900 major rivers were polluted to some degree, more than 1/5 to such an extent that it was impossible to use their water for irrigation. Half of monitored urban river sections in North China do not meet even the lowest quality standard. Some 4/5 of China's surface water in urban areas is contaminated, and drinking water meets the state quality standards in only six of China's 27 largest cities; ground water does not meet state standards in 23 of the 27 largest cities.

A growing share of waste water is generated by China's expanding cities but industries are still the leading source of water pollution. Pulp and papermaking are the worst industrial offenders, dumping directly some 60 per cent of all waste water, and treating to discharge standard only about 15 per cent of it. Mushrooming of small and mid-size factories outside large cities has carried increasing volumes of industrial water pollution into China's countryside. Nitrate water pollution from intensive fertilization is becoming much more prominent. The country is already the world's largest consumer of nitrogen fertilizers and their losses to the environment are particularly high in the case of rice cultivation. Cancers of digestive system are three to ten times more frequent in the areas with heavy water pollution than in unpolluted places; other effects include enlarged liver, anaemia, skin diseases, and higher incidence of congenital deformities. Water pollution also helps to make hepatitis and dysentery the two leading infectious diseases in China.

Air pollution

China's severe **air pollution** results from the country's traditionally high dependence on coal (it now supplies nearly 3/4 of China's commercial energy), from its inefficient combustion in households and in small industrial boilers, and from the recent rapid increases of automobile traffic. Long-term averages of China's urban concentrations of sulphur dioxide (SO_2) and particulate matter (PM) are commonly multiples of both the national and international health standards. Cleaner fuels and better PM emission controls introduced during the 1990s brought some notable improvements in a number of the worst affected cities – but a fundamental change in China's air pollution would require not only a substantial reduction in the share of coal in overall primary energy supply but also a sharp drop in the fuel's share of the residential and commercial market. There is no possibility that this could happen very rapidly.

Emissions of SO_2 are also the principal cause of China's spreading **acid rain**. While the abundance of airborne alkaline dust prevents acid deposition throughout the arid north, an increasing portion of the south now has acid precipitation as in the worst affected regions of Europe and North America. And a new problem has arisen since the early 1980s: levels of photochemical smog have been increasing, and areas affected by high ozone concentrations have been expanding.

Severe air pollution is a major reason for China's high incidence of respiratory diseases, ranging from seasonal infections and chronic bronchitis to lung cancer. Standardized mortality due to chronic obstructive pulmonary disease is five to six times higher in China than in the USA, and air pollution is responsible for up to 60 per cent of all urban cases nationwide. As elsewhere, spreading photochemical smog will aggravate more frequent asthmatic attacks. Direct economic impacts of polluted air include more rapid corrosion of metals and damage to forests in southern areas receiving highly acid precipitation, and decreased crop yields in periurban regions blanketed by rising levels of ozone.

Greenhouse gases

Carbon dioxide (CO_2), methane (CH_4) and nitrous oxide (N_2O) are the three principal greenhouse gases (GHG). Between 1950 and 1995 China's CO_2 emissions from **fossil fuels** and cement production rose about 40-fold, from 21 to 871 million tonnes (Mt) of carbon a year, and their share of the global flux rose from just 1.3 to almost 14 per cent, second only to the USA. China also leads the world in emissions of CH_4 (almost 20 per cent of the total, mainly from anaerobic fermentation of organic matter in rice fields, from livestock, landfills, and from coal mines) and N_2O (about a quarter of the total, mainly from denitrification of inorganic fertilizers). When taking into account different atmospheric residence times of GHG and their specific radiation-absorbing properties, China contributes roughly 15 per cent of the world's **global warming** potential (GWP), already not far behind the USA which generates about 18 per cent of the planet's GWP.

Should the USA meet its Kyoto Treaty target by reducing its 1990 CO_2 emissions by 7 per cent, the country would emit about 1.2 Gt C/year by the year 2008, less than the most likely Chinese emissions at that time. This early switch of ranking could have profound international, as well as domestic policy, implications. China has always maintained that GHG controls should be based on per capita emissions, and that they should also take into account historical rates of fossil fuel consumption. This means that even after the country had become the world's largest producer of GHG it might resist any international pressure to limit its emissions as its per capita GHG output would be still only a fraction of the affluent world's mean, and its cummulative consumption of fossil fuels would be still far behind the amounts used by Europe or the USA. On the other hand, substantially lower Chinese GHG emissions could come from reduced share of coal in primary energy supply and from more efficient energy conversion and less wasteful fertilization (see **ozone depletion**).

Environmental management

There is no doubt that China needs aggressive and farsighted **environmental management**. Conservative calculations put the economic burden of China's environmental pollution at no less than 5 per cent of the country's GDP in the mid-1990s, and possibly as high as 10 per cent. Even the lowest estimates would roughly halve the recent rate of China's GDP growth, and higher estimates would result either in no net creation of wealth or in its actual loss. Although these facts are known to the country's top leadership, environmental affairs are not high on any list of Chinese priorities. There should be no illusions about the depth of environmental commitment in a country so transfixed with short-term profit. Only when it is faced with acute crises does the government step in resolutely in order to maintain the cherished social stability – otherwise it tackles environmental problems inconsistently and half-heartedly.

PRC has a fairly complete set of essential domestic environmental laws and standards, and China is also a party to just about every important international environmental treaty. But the whole system of environmental regulation and protection is basically administrative rather than legal: liabilities are unclear, litigation is a minor part of the process, and party and local interests are commonly decisive. At the same time, the system is skewed toward punishment and coercion, rather than toward incentives and prevention. Enforcement of existing regulations is weak and prospects for prompt and equitable action remain very poor. Environmental protection bureaus rank low in the power hierarchy.

At the same time, the government pays more attention to the environment than was the norm in nearly all of today's rich countries at comparable stages of their development. *China's Trans-Century Green Project Plan* envisaged investing an equivalent of 1.3 per cent of annual GDP during the years 1996–2000, but the real rate was almost certainly

less than one per cent. Foreign capital invested in China's environmental protection amounted to $1.2 billion during the first half of the 1990s, and the World Bank's and the Asian Development Bank's environment-related loans have recently averaged about $800 million a year. But all of this is still highly inadequate in relation to the enormous task at hand.

Outlook

As in any rapidly modernizing economy, environmental concerns still rank far behind the worries about jobs, prices and housing – but expressions of environmental consciousness are becoming increasingly common. Public opinion surveys show that water and air pollution, noise, lack of green spaces, dirty public places, and **pesticide** residues in food dominate people's environmental concerns – while fewer than 10 per cent of respondents mentioned deforestation, loss of wildlife or desertification. Similarly, PRC's environmental ministry puts **water pollution**, water scarcity and urban **air pollution** at the top of the country's environmental priorities, followed by toxic wastes and soil erosion (see **hazardous and toxic waste management**). Acid precipitation is also seen as a high-priority challenge.

Local anti-pollution protests have been reported for many years – but groups organized to promote nature conservation and fight against pollution are still uncommon. The first citizens' environmental organization, Friends of Nature, was permitted to incorporate in 1994, and most groups now active at China's universities have been established since 1995. With the commitment to environmental protection shown by many western companies, and by the **World Bank** or the Asian Development Bank, a slow conversion to environmental responsibility is under way among the more far-sighted Chinese businessmen.

Given the nature of most of China's major environmental problems, the kind and distribution of the country's natural resource endowment, and the still limited capacity to deal concurrently with many pollution and degradation challenges, no fundamental across-the-board changes can be expected in respect of any of these concerns in the near future. Perhaps most notably, there is no possibility of a rapid decline of coal's dominance in China's overall primary energy supply during the next ten years, and hence of any substantial decline of PM and SO$_2$ emissions.

Per capita rates of renewable resource availability will be still falling, as will be many nationwide indicators of air and water quality and of the ecosystemic capacity to deliver critical environmental services. Water supply will be getting truly critical: unless major steps are taken to conserve and recycle water, the country may come very close to using all of its available runoff. Opportunities for many technical fixes are impressive – but their results may be still overwhelmed by the rapidly rising consumption. China's unfortunate policy of promoting private cars and building of highways while neglecting the development of rapid rail links and subways will have particularly undesirable environmental impacts (see **car industry**; **transportation**). This is why demand-side management should play a critical role in managing China's environmental impacts – but much more realistic prices for China's dwindling natural resources will have to come first.

Further reading

Edmonds, R.L. (1994) *Patterns of China's Lost Harmony*, London: Routledge.

Qu Geping and Li Jinchang (1994) *Population and the Environment in China*, Boulder, CO: Lynne Rienner Publishers.

Smil, V. (1983) *The Bad Earth*, Armonk, NY: M.E. Sharpe.

—— (1993) *China's Environmental Crisis*, Armonk, NY: M.E. Sharpe.

—— (1996) *Environmental Problems in China: Estimates of Economic Costs*, Honolulu: East–West Center.

World Bank (1997) *Clear Water, Blue Skies*, Washington, DC: The World Bank.

VACLAV SMIL

Chipko Andolan Movement

The Chipko Andolan Movement (*chipko* literally means 'to embrace') was a movement that challenged the destruction of environment in the Himalayan region, particularly in the Kumaon and Garhwal divisions. The continued deforestation resulted in much hardship to the people, particularly to women who bore the brunt of natural and social transformation. Voluntary organizations, and movements which had earlier campaigned against the use of alcohol joined hands to fight the destruction of forests and natural resources.

Their struggle was non-violent in nature and two prominent Gandhian activists Sunderlal Bahuguna and Chandi Prasad Bhatt mobilized the people in the region against deforestation (see **Gandhi**; **non-violent direct action**). Women joined the protests in large numbers and resisted the commercial logging operations. This resulted in the banning of all tree felling above 1000 metres in 1980. And this non-violent resistance inspired many such efforts. Women's groups are active in reforestation and in restoring ecological balance. Much has been written about the Chipko movement, from various perspectives.

K. RAVI SRINIVAS

CITES

The Convention on International Trade in Endangered Species of Wild Fauna and Flora (CITES) was adopted in March 1973 and came into effect in July 1975. It was amended again in June 1979. The Convention's Secretariat in Geneva is administered by the **United Nations Environment Programme**. The agreement's objective is to contribute to the protection of species which are placed in danger as a result of trade by regulating and, where necessary, prohibiting commercial trade in those species. This includes live and dead animal, bird, plant and tree species as well as parts thereof (such as skin, eggs, bone, seeds and bark). The appendices to the Convention list three categories of **endangered species** (including sub-species) and populations. Decisions on the listing of species are made by regular meetings of Parties to the Convention. Appendix I lists those species which the Parties determine are vulnerable to or endangered by trade. Appendix II species are those which might become threatened by large volumes of trade. This Appendix can also include species where it is difficult to distinguish between endangered and non-endangered sub-species. Listing can therefore help to prevent an endangered individual being passed off as a more common member of the species. The third Appendix covers species which are protected in the host or range country where listing invokes the assistance of the international community to maintain that protection through restricting trade.

The regulation of trade in listed species is supported by a system of permits. Permits are issued by a designated management authority within each state which is a party to the Convention. Commercial trade in Appendix I species is prohibited although limited trade is permitted for individual members of the species which were bred in captivity. Any non-commercial trade requires export and import permits. For species listed under Appendix II and III only a permit from the exporting country is required. The Convention does not cover species which might be endangered for reasons other than those related to trade. It also excludes scientific samples and specimens collected before the Convention came into effect although individual governments may enact legislation more stringent than the Convention. Coverage is extensive. As at March 2000, Appendix I alone included 821 species, 47 sub-species and 22 populations. Almost 29,000 species (many of them plants) are listed under Appendix II.

The Convention has been controversial and its success a matter of some debate. As with all international law, the provisions of the Convention apply only to those countries which are signatory parties. Parties have been slow to enact implementing legislation, and estimates suggest that up to 45 per cent of all CITES transactions go unreported to the Secretariat. Strategies such as smuggling, mislabelling and diversion through non-party countries are used to circumvent the provisions of the Convention. There are no agreed sanctions for non-compliance. Penalties are the province of individual governments. The Convention has also been under scrutiny over the use of trade bans as a species protection mechanism. Bans on already endangered species are seen as inadequate as a

means of preventing further loss of numbers. Others argue that trade bans take no account of disparity of population numbers in individual countries or of the need to generate income for conservation and sustainable management programmes where numbers are not threatened. CITES resolutions now recognize ranching and quota strategies to enhance sustainable resource management without undermining overall population numbers.

The most public debate in this regard has been over the Appendix I listing of the African elephant in October 1989 to prohibit the trade in ivory as well as other elephant products. In 1997, in response to lobbying from the relevant governments, elephant species in Botswana, Namibia and Zimbabwe were downlisted to Appendix II categories. Severe restrictions allowed trade only in a quota of stockpiled ivory and only to **Japan** with the provision that the income be used for conservation programmes. The South African elephant was downlisted in June 2000. Supporters of the ban argue that it drove down the price of ivory and slowed the decline in elephant population numbers in range states. Critics argue that the illegal trade increased and that poaching declined only temporarily but that income for monitoring and enforcement declined substantially which has, in the long term, undermined conservation programmes.

See also: Endangered Species Act; endangered species

Further reading

Dickson, B. (1999) 'The Precautionary Principle in CITES: A Critical Assessment', *Natural Resources Journal*, 39(2): 211–27.

Hepworth, R. (1998) 'The Independent Review of CITES', *Journal of International Wildlife Law and Policy*, 1(3): 412–32.

Ong, David M. (1998) 'The Convention on International Trade in Endangered Species (CITES 1973): Implications of recent developments in international and EC environmental law', *Journal of Environmental Law*, 10(2): 291–331.

LORRAINE ELLIOTT

Citizen's Clearinghouse for Hazardous Wastes

The Citizen's Clearinghouse for Hazardous Wastes (CCHW) is an organization located in Arlington, Virginia, USA that provides information to local citizens' groups that have identified toxic materials and/or wastes dumps in their communities. CCHW informs such grassroots groups about how to organize and convince local governments to take action.

Lois Marie **Gibbs** founded CCHW in 1981 after she and her neighbours organized to force New York state and federal officials to respond to a leaking toxic landfill called **Love Canal** in Niagara Falls, New York. The group was instrumental in the passage of amendments to the Comprehensive Environmental Response, Compensation and Liability Act that forces industry to identify toxic chemicals that are stored or disposed of to local authorities. CCHW publishes a quarterly magazine *Everyone's Backyard* to inform the public about hazardous waste problems.

LETTIE McSPADDEN

citizens' initiatives/referenda

A citizens' initiative is the process whereby a certain number of voters (usually a small percentage of the number of citizens who voted in the previous election) sign a petition to put an issue on the next ballot for the rest of the citizenry to vote on. These issue ballots are called propositions. This is different from the referendum process where elected legislators decide to let the citizens vote on an issue. In both processes, though, the citizens actually make the law by voting. Both these processes are in great usage around the world at all levels of government. Switzerland is currently the only country in the world to allow binding citizens initiatives at the national level (see **Swiss green parties**), but almost every European nation features referenda at the national level to help resolve issues of national importance. In the USA, there is no initiative or referendum at the national level, but 24 states allow for citizens' initiatives at the state level and many local governments provide for them as well.

But why is this kind of democracy better for the environment than purely representative democracy? There are two major, growing global crises at the start of the third millennium: a steep decline in legitimacy of representative democracies and the decreasing stability and sustainability of the global environment. These pressing problems are closely linked. In other words, the same forces behind the increasing credibility gap between citizens and their national, state, regional and local governments are the same forces behind the rapidly deteriorating **ecology** of this planet, i.e., the economic and political dominance of global corporatism (see **globalization**; **multinational and transnational corporations**).

The best way to curtail and perhaps reverse the corruption of representative **democracy** by these gigantic corporations is to expand direct democracy in the world, particularly, citizens' initiative and referendum. There are several reasons for this. First, the agendas of ordinary citizens will be significantly different than those of big corporations and their devoted servants in government. Moreover, it is more difficult for the huge corporations to convince large numbers of citizens to vote their way than to persuade, cajole or even bribe a few lawmakers and chief executives. Furthermore, many laws and administrative rules harmful to the environment are made in legislative committees and obscure administrative agencies without the citizenry noticing. When environmental issues enter public debate during an initiative and/or referendum campaign, they are much harder to hide.

Second, the evidence is mounting that when projects favoured by big business and representative government are hostile to the environment, they can be stopped or reversed through the citizens' initiative and/or referendum process. For example, big business and big government favoured nuclear energy in **Sweden** and Austria (see **Austrian Greens**). But, in part due to the **anti-nuclear movements** there, the politicians were afraid to build the plants without public approval. So, they put the proposition to a public vote by referendum in both countries and lost. Another example is that the American-created Japanese constitution gives the power of referendum only to local communities. Up until recent years, it was never used. In the late 1990s, though, it has been exercised a number of times to preserve local environments against the wishes of big companies in league with the central government in Tokyo, i.e., to oppose nuclear sites, toxic waste disposal, the building of a dam, etc. (See **Japan**; **Japanese nuclear power industry**.)

In the USA, the use of initiative and referendum is generally on the rise with many focused on preserving the environment. In 1998, for example, '173 cities and towns across America passed citizen-sponsored laws that improved parks, set aside large tracts of land for conservation, and protected a wide variety of farmlands, historic resources, biological habitats, etc'. (Becker and Slaton, 2000: 161). It is possible, of course, that a new populism or progressivism led by green parties in Europe, Asia, North America could take over governments in the future and put forth new policies to accomplish environmentally friendly goals. After all, the Green Party of Germany (*Die* **Grünen**), once it became part of the ruling coalition in 1998, helped implement a policy to eliminate nuclear energy in Germany over the next several decades. However, it is equally important to spread the use of initiative and referendum as an alternative and/or complement to future pro-environmental victories in representative elections. Direct democratic systems activate more citizens in the process of saving the environment and put even greater pressure on representative democracies to pass laws devoted to ecological **sustainability** and sanity.

See also: Bürgerinitiativen; business and the environment; democracy; globalization; liberalism/liberal democracy; nuclear energy/ nuclear waste management

Reference

Becker, T. and Slaton, C. (2000) *The Future of Teledemocracy*, Westport, CT: Praeger.

THEODORE L. BECKER

Citizens Party

In 1979, a small group of left of centre dissidents, inspired by Gar Alperovitz's ideas on economic **democracy** and Barry **Commoner**'s environmentalism, decided to form a new US political party. It would be a party of solutions for problems, such as the **energy crisis**, being ignored by the major parties. The Citizens Party, whose logo was a fir tree, was officially launched in April 1980 by delegates representing 3,500 members. Commoner became its presidential nominee, with American Indian activist and feminist LaDonna Harris as vice-presidential nominee. Its programme emphasized: economic democracy, phasing out nuclear power, **renewable energy**, reducing military spending, and action against racism and sexism. Commoner's goal was to win 5 per cent of the vote so that his party would qualify for retroactive federal funding. Due to the costs of winning ballot access in 29 states, the campaign was cash strapped, and largely ignored by the national media. Unfortunately Republican Congressman John Anderson ran as a socially liberal independent candidate, drawing votes that might have otherwise gone to Commoner. Leftist organizations steered clear of the Citizens Party, and most dissident Democrats ended up backing President Carter as the lesser of two evils in the campaign versus Republican Ronald **Reagan**. Commoner received only 0.27 per cent of the vote in November 1980.

However, the party remained alive (16,000 members in 1982), scoring some local electoral victories. New members moved it leftward and began to identify themselves as the US version of *Die* **Grünen** (German Greens). Feminists prevailed in the intra-party struggle with other factions. Commoner withdrew from the party (whose membership was 9,000 in 1984) and backed Reverend Jessie Jackson's 'Rainbow' candidacy for the Democratic presidential nomination. Sonia Johnson, a radical feminist, became the Citizens Party's 1984 presidential nominee. She won only 0.08 per cent of the vote, and the national office of the party closed (Lowe, 1995: 148–50). Some state and local parties survived a few more years.

Reference

Lowe, P. (1995) 'Red-Green US Style: The Rise and Demise of the Citizens Party, 1979–1984', in W. Rüdig (ed.) *Green Politics Three*, Edinburgh: Edinburgh University Press, pp. 112–53.

E. GENE FRANKLAND

civic science

Civic science is the term used to describe a less hierarchical, elitist and more open and participatory mode of science. Starting from a recognition that 'knowledge is power' and that in modern, industrial societies science is often the most powerful form of legitimation in politics, and particularly in the proposal and evaluation of technological interventions in the natural world, civic science represents a critical–reflective alternative to the dominant 'top-down' view of science in which a small scientific elite create and disseminate scientific knowledge which is then used by politicians and/or the public as the most important criterion for making decisions. Civic science, while not rejecting science, seeks to democratize it, and in so doing remove it from its hegemonic position by integrating other criteria (ethical, democratic, social and so on) which are equally important in making decisions. Scientific expertise *qua* civic science should be 'on tap, not on top'.

JOHN BARRY

civil society

The term civil society denotes a political, cultural economic and social space separate from both the nation-state and market. Civil society is the object of much of radical environmental politics as the site where most of the proposed changes that many environmentalists wish to see happen, and the political space from which resistance to the environmental and social problems caused by the nation-state and capitalist market take place (see **capitalism**). Green/environmental politics sees itself as rooted in, defending and empowering civil

society as a space for individual and collective freedom and autonomy from the colonizing effects of state and market. Civil society is centrally important from a green perspective as the place and mode of human social, economic and political interaction that best accords with green political and ethical prescriptions within a sustainable relation to the natural world. It is within the realm of civil society that most of the changes greens wish to see take place: from grassroots, community-based forms of economic activity (see **social economy, informal economic activity**), to active citizen participation and organization, and more localized and sustainable social–environmental interaction.

JOHN BARRY

class

The term 'class' refers to stratification into social groups sharing some common characteristics and often thinking and acting similarly. Sociological debates about class often start with two competing classical theories (and their modern derivations or reconstruction), those of Marx and Weber. Marx's approach rested on socio-economic classes, while Weber opened the way for wider criteria to be entertained.

Marx considered that capitalist society polarized into two-classes, defined in economic terms: the *bourgeoisie*, owning and controlling the means of production, and the *proletariat*, having only their labour to sell. The former own 'productive wealth' (i.e. are capable of generating additional income through investments), the means of production and the product of labour – so they appropriate the difference between the value of labour and that of the goods and services which labour produces. Marx's model saw social change proceeding from the *inherent* and *latent* conflict between bourgeois and proletariat. The competitive dynamic of **capitalism** resulted in concentration of economic (therefore political) power into ever-fewer hands, therefore the petty bourgeois (small business owners) were forced to swell the ranks of the proletariat. Capitalism's constant productivity drive concentrated the proletariat in factories, where, Marx thought, they would develop a collective revolutionary consciousness and direct it against their exploiters. This struggle would eventually liberate all people in a class-less, communist society.

Weber agreed that classes could be conceived as groups sharing similar positions and economic rewards in a market economy. He recognized four such groups (propertied, white collar, petty bourgeois and working class), reflecting different 'market capacities' (i.e. rewards obtained from selling their labour), and therefore differences in life chances. But he also considered that societies could be stratified through non-economic factors conferring social status (such as manners, education, family or racial origin) and/or political power (such as development of bureaucracies in state-dominated societies). Hence there were three stratification systems, economic, social and legal/political.

Marxists would consider these categories all reducible to economic power based on property ownership, and some commentators consider that *economic* classes constitute a defining feature of modern society, while non-economic status differences characterize pre-modern 'traditional' societies. The Marxist's conflictual perspective on class contrasts with the structural–functionalist view of some sociologists, which sees (many) different classes occupying the positions they do because this works to the overall best functioning of society as a whole. Society is therefore conceived as a plurality of groups all related in a system, and when one is alienated or disadvantaged the system adjusts and accommodates, to keep functioning and stable. In this view, society, like any natural system, remains robust and stable by adjustment, not by being forcibly impelled over new thresholds.

Today, certainly, many challenge Marxism's economically deterministic view of class, arguing that the development of 'middle' classes has complicated the picture, that the working classes are fast disappearing, and that historically a 'false consciousness', rather than a revolutionary class consciousness, developed amongst them – indeed it is now the middle-class **'new social movements'** who seem most likely agents of social change. Since the 1970s particularly, challenges arising from shrinking manufacturing industry, the insecurity

of labour, and physical reconstruction of working-class areas may have rendered the notion of a working-class movement redundant, while there have also been challenges to wealthy classes from rapid rises and falls in property and share prices. Furthermore, categories have become blurred, for instance between manual and non-manual labour and by expansion of the white collar service sector and a 'managerial' class. And some sociologists argue that class resides more now in our status as consumers, rather than our position within production processes.

Against such arguments, Marxists observe that ownership and *control* over the means of production has not in practice been widened and democratized by the spread of middle-class share ownership, that managers either are themselves bourgeois or that they invariably act in the bourgeoisie's interests, and that in western countries since the 1970s wealth distribution has become more, not less, polarized (theories of social mobility and trickle down have been found wanting). They might add that class conflict is being restructured by global modernization, and that an international capitalist class has privileged access to wealth and power over a growing world-proletariat: multinational private capital's interests being defended by the **World Bank**, **World Trade Organization**, International Monetary Fund (see **International Monetary Fund and neoliberalism**), international commodity exchanges, etc. Finally, they might stress that Marx's value lay in defining class not in the occupational terms commonly used (Britain's Office of Population, Censuses and Statistics uses a five-class categorization), but in terms of a deeper understanding of property relations, control and ownership.

DAVID PEPPER

Clean Air Act

The first law to bear the name 'Clean Air Act' was passed by the US Congress in 1963; there were additional laws passed in 1965 and 1967. What became known as 'the' Clean Air Act (CAA) was passed in 1970 as amendments to earlier laws; in reality, however, it represented a new departure.

The CAA of 1970 became the prototype for subsequent federal pollution laws, most notably the **Clean Water Act** of 1972. The goal of the CAA was to clean up the country's air by 1975. In order to accomplish such an ambitious goal, it embraced the 'pressing technology' approach: set national quality and emission standards, establish timetables for state and localities to comply, and penalize laggards.

Responding to public concern about **air pollution**, the Congress passed the CAA in 1970 with large bipartisan majorities, and President Nixon signed it. However, when it came up for revision in 1977, there were major battles between environmental and industrial interests in Congress. Ultimately a package of compromises maintained strict air quality and emission standards regarding six conventional air pollutants, but it also extended deadlines for compliance, for example, by auto manufacturers. The CAA's implementation was the joint responsibility of the federal government and the states, once the state implementation plan had been approved by the **Environmental Protection Agency** (EPA). Industries were critical of the CAA's provisions granting the EPA authority to determine technological controls for existing and new facilities, thus precluding more cost effective methods to comply with the standards.

. When the CAA came up for revision in 1981, the **Reagan** Administration was inclined to replace standards with recommendations and to eliminate federal sanctions. However, the Administration shelved its plan and supported the Dingell-Broyhill bill, which sought to lower the costs of pollution control for business by rolling back the CAA. Environmentalists were able to marshal enough support to defeat this so called 'dirty air' bill. Congress stayed 'gridlocked' over the revision of the CAA throughout the Reagan Presidency (1981–9). Although during the decade, public concerns about **acid rain** grew, the Administration with its allies in Congress blocked new legislation that would target acid rain producing emissions.

In the 1988 presidential campaign, George Bush declared his intention to be the 'environmental president'. In June 1989, he delivered on his promise to introduce a new clean air package (which focused on toxic air emissions, acid rain, and urban smog). Seventeen months later, the Senate and the House of Representatives passed by lopsided majorities the Clean Air Act of 1990, which turned out to be a tougher, more comprehensive, and costlier law than Bush ever had in mind. The new CAA was a complex piece of legislation more than 600 pages long. The thrust was to build on the existing regulatory infrastructure and to expand its scope into new problem areas, such as atmospheric ozone. Congress also included innovative provisions, most notably reflected in its plan for reducing acid rain. The CAA of 1990 caps sulphur dioxide emissions and sets up a market of **tradeable emission permits** for coal-burning power plants. These permits allow plants to emit legally a certain amount of sulphur dioxide. But if companies clean up their operations, they may sell those permits they do not need to others. Proponents see the scheme as providing economic incentives to address air pollution in a more cost effective manner, while opponents worry that pollution may not be reduced, just relocated.

In the early 1990s, the EPA fell behind in conducting studies and issuing regulations to carry out the new CAA. The states began missing their deadlines to implement the stages of its urban smog control. Nevertheless, EPA statistics indicated that most conventional air pollutant levels were declining despite a growing population and economy. However, there was mounting evidence that EPA 'healthy' levels for ground level ozone (smog) and fine particles (soot) were too permissive. Prompted by a CAA suit by the American Lung Association, the EPA proposed tougher standards for smog and soot. Despite an aggressive lobbying campaign by industrial lobbyists (predicting the loss of tens of thousands of jobs due to costly new regulations) and 30 state governors, the EPA enacted the rules. However, adverse rulings in the federal courts in 1999 put them on hold. In the final months of the Clinton Administration, the EPA moved to tighten other CAA regulations, such as diesel emissions from large trucks. It is likely that the new Bush Administration will revise or cancel them.

Further reading

Bryner, G.C. (1995) *Blue Skies, Green Politics: The Clean Air Act of 1990 and Its Implementation,*

Washington, DC: Congressional Quarterly Press.

E. GENE FRANKLAND

Clean Water Act

In 1972, the US Congress rewrote water pollution law by passing the Federal Water Pollution Control Act Amendments, which became known as the 'Clean Water Act' (CWA). The initiative had come from the Nixon Administration, which sought to impose federal effluent controls and authorize $4 billion in grants for sewage treatment plants. Inspired by the **Clean Air Act** of 1970, the Democratic-controlled Congress went far beyond the President's proposal in goals and funding; as a result, Nixon vetoed the bill. But Congress over-rode his veto.

The subject of the Clean Water Act was the country's surface waters (the Safe Drinking Water Act of 1974 was to address groundwater). The CWA sought the abatement of all significant **water pollution** ('zero discharge') by 1985, with the interim goal of having all navigable waters 'fishable and swimmable' by 1983. To accomplish these goals, the CWA authorized a national permit system for all municipal and industrial effluent dischargers with standards established by the **Environmental Protection Agency** (EPA). Furthermore, the lengthy and complex law gave the EPA the authority to specify the best available control technology and best practicable control technology to be used. Federal grants of $4.5 billion per year were authorized for four years; under the previous law, there had been $50 million per year. Implementation was shared with the states. The CWA was amended in 1977. More money was authorized by Congress for grants. Deadlines were extended for industrial dischargers and municipal treatment plants (only a third had met their deadlines). In 1981 there were amendments to readjust the funding formula so that federal grants would cover only 55 per cent (rather than the original 75 per cent) of the construction costs of sewage treatment plants (the states and localities were responsible for operating costs).

In the early 1980s, the CWA was due for re-authorization. The rewrite of the law was vetoed by President **Reagan** in 1986 and in 1987, the latter veto was overridden by the Congress. Reagan's rationale was the bill's price tag of over $20 billion. Yet the CWA of 1987 provided for a phasing out of grants and phasing in of loans for sewage treatment plants. It is also noteworthy for providing the first federal funds to combat 'nonpoint' pollution. Previous versions of the law had focused solely on 'point' pollution (end of the pipe), thus ignoring diffuse agricultural and urban runoff. Like its predecessors, the CAA of 1987 extended industrial and municipal compliance deadlines.

The law came up again for re-authorization in the mid-1990s. The Republican-controlled House passed a bill (HR 961) rolling back numerous provisions of the CWA. Much of the public controversy centred on the **wetlands** protection issue. **Property rights** activists have sought ways to blunt the impact of Section 404 which gives to the Army Corps of Engineers the authority to regulate the alteration of wetlands with a permit process. Thus, the bill's sponsors narrowed significantly the definition of a 'wetland'. The bill would also have abandoned the federal programme to control agricultural runoff; required the federal government to reimburse landowners for financial losses from a wetland designation preventing them from developing their land (**takings**); and eased federal requirements that industries pre-treat their discharges into the public sewers. The Republican-controlled Senate never acted on the bill, which President Clinton had already pledged to veto.

In 1999, Vice President **Gore** announced the Administration's Clean Water Action Plan, which in the absence of a revised and stricter law, sought via executive authority to strengthen and expand existing federal efforts, for example, in dealing with pollution caused by concentrated livestock feeding operations. Opponents have favoured providing the states with the 'incentives' and 'flexibility' to develop their own approaches to water pollution, which were themes echoed during the 2000 presidential campaign by George W. Bush. Environmentalists have less confidence in the administrative capability and political willpower of the states, facing well organized and financed agricultural and industrial lobbies, to enforce strict water quality standards.

Cleaning up US waters has proven a more difficult task than the sponsors of the CWA in 1972 could have anticipated. There have been local success stories, such as the Potomac River, which flows through the nation's capital; and the **Cuyahoga River** in Ohio has not caught fire again. However, 25 years after the passage of the Clean Water Act of 1972, the EPA's first comprehensive assessment of US watersheds found only 16 per cent to have good water quality. With a growing US population and economy, the struggle for water clean enough to be 'fishable and swimmable' will be ongoing in the twenty-first century.

Further reading

Adler, R.W., Landman, J.C. and Cameron, D.M. (1993) *The Clean Water Act 20 Years Later*, Washington, DC: Island Press.

E. GENE FRANKLAND

Climate Action Network

The Climate Action Network (CAN) is an international network of almost 300 non-governmental organizations (NGOs) working to promote government and individual action to limit human-induced climate change to levels that are ecologically viable while allowing for sustainable and equitable development (see **international non-governmental organizations**). Established in March 1989, CAN is now the recognized umbrella NGO at international climate change negotiations. The Network has been monitoring and co-ordinating interventions at negotiations convened by the UN **Framework Convention on Climate Change** and working on national, regional and global climate policies and measures. CAN has seven regional offices around the world. The Network produces three newsletters: *ECO*, published during negotiations; *Hotline*, published by CAN's US office; and *Hotspot*, published by the Europe office. The publications are available at the CAN website: URL: http://www.climatenetwork.org.

See also: civil society; civic science; ecological modernization; fossil fuels; Global Climate Coalition; Kyoto Conference/Protocol; renewable energy

PETER DORAN

cloning

Routinely performed by gardeners for centuries, cloning has become the centre of social, ethical and legal debate. *Klon*, from the Greek meaning twig, was first used to describe the results of gardeners removing a twig from one plant and growing another whole plant from this part. In 1963, the British biologist J.B.S. Haldane was one of the first to give the name 'cloning' to a set of experiments designed to create genetically identical amphibians from one adult. Such research in animals has developed several techniques resulting in genetically identical offspring from one adult. It is important to distinguish cloning from twinning where two identical offspring are produced by the separation of embryonic cells very early in development. In contrast, cloning techniques take one cell from an adult organism and attempt to produce an identical copy from this one cell. The difficulty with this technique is that the cells of adult organisms are already specialized to be one type of cell such as skin, liver or intestine. Producing all of the different types of cells in an organism from one type of cell has been the focus of most cloning research. One way researchers have solved this problem is to use cells that are not yet specialized. This technique was successful in the 1980s when researchers were able to clone sheep and cows from cells very early in embryonic development. This technique, called nuclear transplantation, was an intermediate step toward the most famous sheep clone of the twentieth century, Dolly. Because it is the nucleus that determines many characteristics of the offspring, a clone closely resembles the individual from whom the nucleus was taken.

On 5 July 1996, Dolly, the first sheep cloned from an adult sheep cell was born at the Roslin Institute in Roslin, Scotland. Ian Wilmut, an embryologist, is credited with the technique by which she was born. Dolly was created from an adult ewe udder cell that was frozen and starved of nutrients. Because of these unusual conditions, the nucleus of the ewe udder cell only maintained its most basic genetic functions. When the nucleus of the udder cell was placed into an egg whose nucleus had been removed, the udder nucleus and egg cell began to function as an unspecialized cell. It then replicated and differentiated into the different types of cells needed for an adult sheep.

Such research has been pursued for agricultural and economic reasons and is part of a revolution in **biotechnology**. Livestock that have been shown to produce more food, have fewer diseases or even produce biological commodities for human consumers could simply be cloned, thus preserving their economically valued characteristics. With the possibilities raised by genetic engineering, animals can be engineered to become biofactories. They could produce human proteins such as clotting factors in their milk and then be cloned to produce enough of them to make the process financially viable. Human cloning, banned in Britain, but not in most states of the USA or Australia, offers further therapeutic and medical options.

Such research is not without serious ethical and legal challenges. Opinion differs as to when human cloning would be technically possible, but it already exists as a theoretical possibility. Cloning individuals, tissues or organs on a human scale would involve the use of human embryos. Collecting discarded or donated embryos raises issues about the ownership of those embryos as well as their moral status. Radical critics, such as deep ecologists (see **deep ecology**), argue that this is another example of research supporting **anthropocentrism** while exploiting natural resources. Feminists also point out that these techniques rely on the resources of female animals and humans as well as women's biological labour (see **eco-feminism**). Ecologists worry that livestock clones raise ecological problems akin to those of monocropping in plant crops. Additionally, animal cloning raises moral issues as the creation of large numbers of animal clones may increase the likelihood of their mistreatment. One scenario includes breeding sheep with cystic fibrosis to provide a large supply

of research ready animals. Much of this research has been undertaken by private research laboratories who have plans to clone entire cell lines and claim patents on their use. This furthers discussion over whether life, including cells, cellular constituents and life processes can be patented and thus, sold.

See also: environmental ethics; genetic engineering, animals; genetic engineering, humans

Further reading

Caplan, A.L. (1985) 'Blood, Sweat, Tears and Profits: The Ethics of the Sale and Use of Patient-Derived Materials in Biomedicine', *Clinical Research*, 33(4): 448–51.

Kitcher, P. (1996) *The Lives to Come: The Genetic Revolution and Human Possibilities*, London: Penguin.

Tauer, C. (1997) 'Embryo Research and Public Policy: A Philosopher's Appraisal', *Journal of Medicine and Philosophy*, 22(5): 423–40.

JOAN LEACH

coastal zone management

Coastal zone managers work at the land–sea interface, straddling the social and natural sciences to meet multiple societal goals for coastal and marine areas. Coastal Zone Management (CZM) programmes are most often organized through federal or state governments, as in Sri Lanka and the USA, though they often integrate the interests (e.g. **biodiversity** conservation, education and research, **fisheries** and aquaculture, navigation, shoreline development, tourism, and water quality) of marine industries and non-governmental organizations, as well. 'Integrated' CZM programmes emphasize the involvement of local communities and unified, rather than sector-based, approaches. Full valuation of the goods and services provided by coastal ecosystems and the use of remote sensing and geographic information systems (GIS) to inform management are two of many areas under rapid development.

Further reading

Cicin-Sain, B. and Knecht, R.W. (1998) *Integrated Coastal and Ocean Management*, Washington, DC: Island Press.

HEATHER LESLIE

Cohn-Bendit, Daniel

b. 4 April 1945, Montauban, France

Politician

Daniel Cohn-Bendit (nicknamed Dany the Red for his red hair and his leftist political stance) emerged as a political figure in 1968 as the leader of the French students' movement. The same year the French authorities invoked his German passport to ban him from French territory for ten years. Active in the German counter-culture movement in the 1970s, he joined the German Greens in 1981 and was vice-mayor of Frankfurt between 1989 and 1997. A committed European, he was elected MEP for *Die Grünen* in 1994, then for **Les Verts** in 1999. His political come-back on the French political scene has been reluctantly accepted by the French Greens. Not only are his liberal ideas at odds ·with some of *Les Verts'* policies but his independence and flamboyance make him a character hard to control and predict.

FLORENCE FAUCHER

Commission on Sustainable Development

The United Nations Commission on Sustainable Development (UNCSD) is a functional commission of the Economic and Social Council (ECOSOC), itself a subsidiary organ of the UN General Assembly. It was established after the 1992 United Nations Conference on Environment and Development (UNCED) to receive national reports of the UN members on the implementation of **sustainable development** policies adopted in connection with the UNCED (see **Rio Conference 1992**). The CSD meets in New York for two to three weeks annually. Its work is organized in a rolling programme highlighting different sectional and cross sectional issues in different years. After initial optimism that the CSD might focus on and promote sustainable development measures across the UN system, the CSD has itself become routinized and near moribund within the un-reformed General Assembly structure.

Further reading

Mensah, C. (1996) 'The UN Commission on Sustainable Development', in J. Werksman, (ed.) *Greening International Insitutions*, London: Earthscan.

MARK IMBER

Common Agricultural Policy

The Common Agricultural Policy (CAP) is a structural policy of the **European Union** (EU). One of two policy areas unified at EU level (the other is the Common Fisheries Policy) in the 1957 Treaty of Rome, it is the largest single area of EU expenditure, taking almost half the EU budget. Article 59 of the Treaty defines the goals of the CAP: increased agricultural productivity through technical progress and efficiency; a fair standard of living and increased earnings for the agricultural community; market stabilization; supply stabilization; and reasonable prices for consumers. Policy instruments have included a varying mix of guaranteed prices; export subsidies; import tariffs and controls; and, increasingly, direct payments to producers.

The CAP has been blamed directly for many environmental problems in the EU, particularly eutrophication in lakes and rivers from over-application of nitrogenous fertilizers; pollution of groundwater from poor storage and use of slurries and farm wastes; and salinization along Mediterranean coasts where aquifers have been over-stretched. Indirect effects due to intensification and uneven agricultural development include: declining **biodiversity** (particularly songbirds, but also traditional breeds of domestic animals); poor conditions for animals in intensive production units; loss of traditional **landscapes**; increased soil erosion, both from larger fields in productive areas and from abandoned marginal landscapes. Finally, the CAP has been accused of damaging **less developed countries** through 'dumping': subsidized EU exports, particularly beef to West Africa, have undercut local food producers, leading to rural recession and import dependency.

Many of these problems can be attributed to **agribusiness**, rather than the CAP; EU agricultural sectors less subject to the CAP have equal if not greater environmental problems. The CAP could also be argued to have benefited the environment: despite favouring larger farms, there has been support for marginal farms producing attractive rural landscape, which would have vanished under free-trade conditions, e.g.: the 1975 Less Favoured Areas Directive (75/268). However the CAP has certainly encouraged overuse of chemical inputs, overstocking, surplus production of manure, and homogenization of agricultural ecosystems.

The CAP's environmentally destructive effects were not considered until the 1973 First Environmental Action Programme (EAP); even then its recommendations went unimplemented. The first EU Agri-Environmental Policy (AEP) was introduced in 1985 (Regulation 707/85). It allowed member states to designate Environmentally Sensitive Areas (ESAs) for national direct payments, compensating for subsidies lost, made to farmers to protect landscapes by reducing chemical usage or lowering livestock stocking rates. Regulation 707/85 was adjusted by Regulation 1760/87, which made ESA schemes eligible for 25 per cent CAP funding. However several countries did not implement them.

The 1986 Single European Act required that the environment be considered in all areas of policy. 1992 saw the 5th EAP target agriculture for environmental integration. CAP reform was under way, but the 'MacSharry Reforms' were motivated by concerns about overproduction, distribution of agricultural support, and General Agreement on Tariffs and Trade (GATT) negotiations, rather than environmental problems.

However, one of three 'accompanying measures' was Regulation 2078/92. This AEP provided 50–75 per cent EU funding for extensification; reduced chemical inputs; reduced stockage rates; agricul-

tural conservation practices; maintaining abandoned rural areas; access and leisure; and long-term ecological set-aside. The last was responding to criticisms of earlier voluntary short-term set-aside schemes to combat over-production, which either had no environmental benefit, or were damaging. The Regulation was to operate both within geographical zones, and horizontal regulatory frameworks, designated by member states. Results varied widely with **Denmark** and Austria favouring organic and environmental farming; the UK supporting low-input, but prioritizing existing low intensity agriculture over organic; Germany funding other forms of non-productive land management. Germany, Austria and Scandinavian countries have used 2078/92 more than **Belgium**, **Netherlands**, UK and Mediterranean nations (except Portugal). However, despite the benefits, AEPs have done little to combat agricultural pollution; aid has been targeted at existing extensive farming, rather than altering intensive farming practices.

The restructuring of the CAP under Agenda 2000, the EU's programme for eastward enlargement and coping with the requirements of the **World Trade Organization**, provides new opportunities: further movement from production subsidies to farm diversification and countryside management payments; cross-compliance between environmental and agricultural objectives; and the Rural Development Regulation, offering environmental benefits linked to broader, more radical socio-economic objectives. However, agriculture lags behind EU environmental policy; often CAP reforms are catching up with environmental Directives, particularly the Birds (79/409), Nitrates (91/676) and Habitats (92/43) Directives. Many members do not even comply with these: in 1999, eight were prosecuted in the European Court of Justice for non-compliance with 91/676.

See also: agriculture; environmental law and litigation

Further reading

Brouwer, F. and Lowe, P. (2000) *CAP Regimes and the European Countryside*, Wallingford: CABI Publishing.

Buller, H. *et al.* (2000) *Agri-Environmental Policy in the European Union*, Aldershot: Ashgate.

DAVID WOOD

common law/torts

Common law/torts is a concept in Anglo–American common law countries whereby any person who causes an injury to another's person or property must pay compensation. In addition to compensatory damages, it is also possible to obtain punitive damages designed to force the defendant to change his/her behaviour in order to avoid future suits.

Before regulatory environmental law was created, some individuals attempted to use this common law concept to force polluting industries to clean their effluents or emissions before discharging them into public waterways or the air. Using this common law of personal injury, individuals sued for damages they believed were owed them because polluted air or water from an external source had caused injury to their property. Common waterways that were used to convey industrial waste away from its source often damaged land, crops, animals and people downstream from the source. Downstream users hoped to convince the owners of such industries of the need to clean their effluents before releasing them in order to avoid multiple lawsuits.

Plaintiffs find it difficult to win such cases because of the need to prove that one particular source was the cause of their injury. Disease and injuries often have multiple causes, and it is difficult for judge or jury to single out a particular culprit. Even when such causation can be demonstrated, it is difficult to obtain a remedy. Compensation for the injury is the normal common-law remedy, but this does nothing to alleviate the condition if the nuisance is a continuing one. Industries may choose to simply pay recurring damages as an additional 'cost of doing business' until the plaintiffs become weary of repeated litigation.

Courts may issue injunctions against the operation of plants that are a continuing danger to the community. But it is rare that a judge will do so given the dependence of most communities on the tax base and employment opportunities of major manufacturers in their jurisdictions. One example of an unsuccessful attempt by a group of citizens to obtain damages for contaminated water in Woburn, Massachusetts and the resulting leukemia deaths of children is Jonathan Haar's film *A Civil Action* (1995). In that true story the law firm, which took the victims' case on contingency fees, went bankrupt in the process of attempting to obtain damages.

Reliance on common-law remedies to solve pollution problems has generally been replaced with regulatory laws that seek to prevent the damage before it occurs. However, there are some legal scholars who argue that the threat of multiple suits is sufficient to convince polluters to treat their emissions in order to avoid future lawsuits.

See also: environmental law and litigation

References

Findley, R. and Farber, D.A. (1991) *Cases and Materials on Environmental Law* St Paul, MN: West Publishing

Haar, J. (1995) *A Civil Action*, New York: Vintage Books

Stensvaag, J-M. (1999) *Materials on Environmental Law*, St Paul, MN: West Publishing.

LETTIE McSPADDEN

common pool property resources

Common pool property resources (CPPRs) are natural resources which can be utilized by more than one group of actors. **Property rights** provide a means of protection for property owners. These rights grant individuals a measure of protection against theft, vandalism, and abuse. Resources which are not protected by property rights fall victim to unregulated exploitation. These resources are common property, and as such are commonly abused.

CPPRs are mutually available and as such create serious management problems. In contrast to a single plot of land, for example, which may be owned by a sole proprietor, resources like air, water, and marine animals are not static and are therefore subject to exploitation by multiple states and organizations.

To illustrate, suppose that Countries A, B, and C all fish heavily in the South Pacific for tuna. If Country A annually takes 60 per cent of the tuna stock, the numbers of tuna will sharply decline and directly affect the fishing industries in Countries B and C. If Country B emits toxins into the atmosphere, air and water quality in Countries A and C may be adversely affected.

Since CPPRs are not technically owned, exclusion of access to these resources is nearly impossible. The establishment of institutions to limit common property extractions can be extremely difficult. Organizations which are exploiting the resource often have no interest in preservation. An organization that profits will rarely be convinced to enter into an agreement that severely limits its production scale without sanctions.

Although they are not property of any country in particular, many CPPRs temporarily exist within established sovereign geographic boundaries, a fact that adds to management problems. Rivers flow through multiple countries and eventually empty into oceans, and air masses move from continent to continent. Living CPPRs, such as anadromous Pacific Salmon and Steelhead, will inhabit oceans for several years before travelling hundreds of miles inland to spawn. Static CPPRs, such as **national parks**, often fall victim to competing interests. Developers, sportsmen, native peoples, and environmentalists all display conflicting intents towards such common property. As Hardin reminds us, 'we must soon cease to treat the parks as commons or they will be of no value to anyone' (1977: 27).

Steps are being taken to rectify the current problems surrounding CPPRs. Some countries have established exclusive economic zones around their borders to protect marine life that exists offshore. Property rights regimes have been developed to monitor the use and abuse of CPPRs, while international organizations such as the **European Union** have begun to regulate the exploitation of that continent's common resources.

Reference

Hardin, G. (1977) 'The Tragedy of the Commons', G. Hardin and J. Baden (eds) *Managing the Commons*, San Francisco: W.H. Freeman and Company.

Further reading

Barkin, J. and Shambaugh, G, (eds) (1999) *Anarchy and the Environment: The International Relations of Common Pool Resources*, Albany: SUNY Press.

Berkes, F. (1989) *Common Property Resources: Ecology and Community-Based Sustainable Development*, London: Belhaven Press.

MATTHEW P. TUNNO AND ZACHARY A. SMITH

Commoner, Barry

b. 28 May 1917, Brooklyn, New York, USA

Biologist, environmental activist

Barry Commoner, the son of a Russian immigrant, was born and raised in Brooklyn, New York. He was an honours graduate of Columbia University, and received his MA and Ph.D. from Harvard University in cellular biology. After the Second World War, he became a professor at Washington University in St Louis, Missouri, researching viruses and 'free radicals' in tissues. In the 1950s, alarmed by the failure of the US government to inform the public about the dangers of strontium 90 fallout from atomic bomb tests, Commoner co-founded the St Louis Committee for Nuclear Information (later the Committee for Environmental Information). The Committee began collecting some 150, 000 baby teeth and having them analysed for radioactivity. Ultimately the combined efforts of scientists and citizens brought about a change in the official US position on atomic fallout (paving the way for the 1963 treaty banning aboveground nuclear testing).

Commoner became one of the most prominent of US scientists expressing concerns about how byproducts of urban-industrial society were overloading natural cycles to the point of threatening human survival. In *Science and Survival* (1963) he combined scientific knowledge and moral sensibility. As early as 1965, Commoner was warning the public that 'scientific' **risk assessment** is laden with political values. In 1966, he founded the Center for the Biology of Natural Systems at Washington University, which later relocated to Queens College, City University of New York with its director, when he became Professor of Earth and Environmental Sciences there. Commoner sounded the alarm in numerous speeches, articles, and interviews about the pollution of the nation's air, water, and land resulting from overuse of detergents, **pesticides**, vinyl chloride, and other chemicals. Lewis Green, an air pollution expert, described Commoner as 'a Paul Revere waking the country to environmental dangers'. In 1971, Commoner's *The Closing Circle* became a bestseller, one of the classics of the modern environmental movement. The book helped to popularize the science of **ecology**, especially amongst the younger generation. In it Commoner sets forth his four laws of ecology: 'Everything is connected to everything else. Everything must go somewhere. **Nature** knows best. There is no such thing as a free lunch.' These laws have a conservative ring to them, but if taken seriously, the operational implications for society are radical.

Commoner's political views put him to the left of most American environmentalists in that he dared to speak about the 'social' control of technology. Commoner became a member of the committee which founded the **Citizens Party**, a coalition of environmentalists, various public-interest activists, and pacifists. In 1980 it nominated him as its first presidential candidate. The party got a late start, failed to draw support from left-wing organizations, and lost liberals to Jimmy Carter because of their '**Reagan**-phobia'. Commoner ended up receiving only 0.3 per cent of the vote. With the Citizens Party adrift in the mid-1980s, he transferred his support to Reverend Jesse Jackson's Democratic presidential candidacy.

Commoner continued to publish on the environmental crisis, e.g., *Making Peace with the Planet* (1990). The central theme running through his numerous writings is that inappropriate **technology** is the cause of the environmental crisis, and the cause of inappropriate technology is that corporate elites seek short-term private gains and ignore long-term social needs. Commoner has cited the example of trying to control **air pollution** from automobiles by putting catalytic converters on exhaust pipes rather than redesigning the engine in the 1970s so that it would produce little or no harmful emissions. Reviewing 20 years of environmental efforts in the USA, Commoner concluded that 'the lesson of both the few successes and the far more numerous failures is the same: Environmental pollution is a nearly incurable disease, but it can be prevented'. Thus he argued for sweeping technological redesign of productive processes. And the policy objective should not be societal acceptance of 'low' pollution as prosperity's trade-off, but its elimination. Commoner has pointed to the US's phasing out of leaded gasoline, **DDT**, **PCBs** as examples of successes in pollution prevention. In 1997 on the occasion of Commoner's eightieth birthday, an international symposium recognized his many contributions on a wide range of environmental issues.

References

Commoner, B. (1971) *The Closing Circle*, New York: Bantam Books.

—— (1990) *Making Peace with the Planet* New York: Pantheon Books.

—— (1992) 'The Failure of the Environmental Effort', *Current History* 91 (April): 176–81.

Kriebel, D. (2001) *Barry Commoner's Contribution to the Environmental Movement: Science and Social Action*, Amityville, NY: Baywood Publishing.

                                        E. GENE FRANKLAND

communism

Communism is a political theory featuring communal ownership of property, in particular of the means of production. Focusing on the community, commune or collective as the basic social, political and economic unit, it is relevant not just to socialism, with which it is particularly associated, but to anarchism and thereby to radical green ideology.

Marx, according to Bottomore (1985), used 'communism' to denote both a political movement and a social form. The political movement was that of the working class in capitalist society. In the early twentieth century some commentators began to contrast the previously synonymous terms 'socialism' and 'communism'. They gave the latter the sense of revolutionary action aiming at violent overthrow of capitalism, distinguishing it from 'socialism' as a more peaceful, pragmatic and incremental movement. And the meaning of communism was further changed, particularly by its opponents, during the Soviet Stalinist period, when to many in the West it became synonymous with the authoritarian regimes behind the 'Iron Curtain' – especially the Soviet 'Communist' Party. Many western socialists and communists today deny that these regimes ever were, or could be, communist because of their anti-democratic features.

As a form of society which the working class would bring into existence, Marx described communism only in very general terms, because he wanted to avoid creating utopian blueprints (such as those of Campanella, More, Cabet, Fourier or Owen). In these terms, communism is abolition both of private property and of human self-alienation: therefore it is the real appropriation of human nature through and for society – the return of 'man' as a really human being, rather than as the incompletely fulfilled individual of capitalist society.

The precondition for this future modern, or 'advanced', communism (as opposed to the primitive communism of non-literate tribal societies) would be the abolition of classes and of capitalism's division of labour and wage slavery. It would represent a genuine *community* – one where freedom is attained through association of producers (as distinct from the 'community' of capitalism, which is dominated by the interests of one class against all others, and is not freedom). These associations would constitute 'socialized humanity', who would regulate for themselves their interchange with nature, rationally and under common control 'instead of being ruled by it as by some blind power' (Marx's *Capital* III). There would therefore be no limit to the development of individual human potentialities, and of the productive forces of society (except perhaps the limits implied by the notion of 'rational' interchange with **nature**, which all of society might agree to observe). In

communism the differences between manual and intellectual labour, and between urban and rural life would disappear. Social relations would be regulated by the principle of 'from each according to ability, to each according to means', making exchange and money unnecessary.

This vision tends to suggest that spontaneous, co-operative fellowship is a natural state. Communism would encourage people to see society as qualitatively more than just the sum of its individual parts – a sort of secular, non-conservative, non-hierarchical version of *Gemeinschaft*, an organic community with a common life which absorbs individuals fully.

Socialists/communists often argue about the potential role of the state. In **capitalism** the state represents the interests of the bourgeois class, therefore in classless communist society the state would wither away, becoming unnecessary. However, some interpreters, notably Lenin, have argued that Marx distinguished between two stages of communism. The early one ('socialism' according to Lenin) would be transitional from capitalism, individuals still being paid for their labour and buying consumer goods, i.e. exchange persists. Not until the higher, classless, stage ('communism') would each contribute according to ability, taking from common stocks according to need. In this interpretation, the proletariat (led by a revolutionary 'vanguard' of activists and intellectuals) would first create 'socialism' by taking over the state, then use its power to establish communism, (classless, and therefore the vanguard must eventually abolish itself).

Anarchists, and some anti-'vanguardist' socialists, always sceptically regarded this dictatorship-of-the-proletariat model as inherently totalitarian, and the lesson of history in Stalinism, Chinese 'communism' and so forth appears to have vindicated them. Their preferred, non-statist revolutionary model might be the short-lived Paris commune of 1871. This involved federalism, decentralization, participatory **democracy** and social justice. Yet other socialists, such as André **Gorz**, may want the transition to post-industrial communism to be direct and without a 'socialist stage' – but they nonetheless see a localized state as necessary to enable and facilitate the planning of this society.

See also: anarchism/eco-anarchism; class; eco-socialism; Gorz, André; social ecology

Reference

Bottomore, T. (1985) *A Dictionary of Marxist Thought*, Oxford: Blackwell.

DAVID PEPPER

community-right-to-know laws

In the USA, community-right-to-know laws are statutes that establish the principle that communities where toxic materials are stored, used, and may be released into the environment have a right to be informed about such sites. Any industrial plant or other user of such materials must inform the public safety officials in municipalities, counties and other jurisdictions about the quantity and location of these materials, in order for safety officials to prepare for any emergency. Such laws also stipulate that when a plant has an accidental release of toxic materials into the air or water, public safety officials must be contacted immediately. These laws require that pollution control agencies categorize hazardous materials and prepare material safety data sheets for them. Users of these materials and public officials must keep an up-to-date inventory of such materials and have emergency response procedures in place.

LETTIE McSPADDEN

conservation biology

Conservation biology is a sub-discipline of biology that integrates knowledge from basic sciences (e.g., evolutionary biology, genetics, **ecology**) and applied sciences (e.g., **agriculture**, forestry, **wildlife management**, **fisheries** management) to understand the effects of human activities (e.g., land use change, exploitation, introduction of **exotic species**, pollution) on species, biological communities, and ecosystems. The primary goal of conservation biology is to prevent extinction of species as a means of maintaining the integrity of natural communities and ecosystems.

Further reading

Primack, R.B. (1995) *A Primer of Conservation Biology*, Sunderland, MA: Sinauer Associates Inc.

DAVID C. LeBLANC

conservation movement

The conservation movement was and is a political movement aimed at protecting and conserving natural resources. The movement derives its name from the term conservation, which can be defined as the management and protection of natural resources, including land, water, minerals, air, plants and animals, in order to prevent their pollution, damage, or destruction, and to ensure the availability of those resources in the future.

The conservation movement traces its origin to the USA in the mid-1800s as a response to concerns regarding the protection and preservation of natural resources as articulated by early writers, artists and poets, and exemplified by public reaction to the slaughter of bison in the American West. The conservation movement developed largely in the American West as a movement by those who crusaded to protect and preserve natural areas by severely restricting, if not eliminating, human contact with the natural areas they sought to protect. These early conservationists would now more properly be labelled preservationists.

The conservation movement, in the USA, was inspired by nature writers and artists such as George Catlin, ornithologist John James Audubon, writer George Perkins **Marsh**, and naturalist John **Muir**, the co-founder of the **Sierra Club**, who idealized the wilderness as pristine, emphasizing the importance of its natural beauty and a need for preservation. One of these early conservationists, George Catlin, proposed the creation of **national parks** that would allow both Native Americans and the wilderness to be preserved in their natural grandeur.

George Perkins Marsh, who published *Man and Nature* in 1864, brought public attention to environmental degradation and the impact of humans on the environment. Influenced by Marsh's work, President Theodore **Roosevelt** became an ardent proponent of resource conservation. During his two terms in office (1901–9) Roosevelt strongly supported and promoted policies aimed at the conservation and efficient use of natural resources. Conservation, however, meant something different to Roosevelt than it had to the earlier conservationists. Whereas the earlier conservationists sought to preserve natural areas in a state untouched by human influence, later conservationists viewed conservation as the managed use of natural resources to benefit humankind. Roosevelt gave free rein to those officials in his administration who promoted efficient resource development aimed at managing resources for human use. Gifford **Pinchot**, head of the US Department of Agriculture's Division of Forestry (after 1905, the Forest Service) from 1898 to 1910, exemplified this new conservationist approach. Pinchot was a strong advocate of a utilitarian and very anthropocentric approach to conservation, proposing that forests be developed and scientifically managed to promote a sustained yield for the use of mankind, rather than simply being preserved in their natural state (see **anthropocentrism**). In contrast to Muir and other preservationists, later conservationists like Pinchot did not believe that values and uses other than those associated with humans should be considered in the management of natural resources. These new conservationists and their resource policies dominated natural resource policy throughout most of the twentieth century.

Aldo **Leopold**, who also worked for the Forest Service, diverged from Pinchot's approach to forest management. Leopold leaned toward the preservationist approach articulated by John Muir. In *A Sand County Almanac*, published in 1949, Leopold argued that natural processes must be understood as a complex system that reacts to man's impact on it. Leopold's conception of a 'land ethic' is one of the earliest attempts to vocalize an ethics of the environment. Leopold called for humans to recognize the effect of human actions on the system, and to take responsibility for the health of the ecosystem.

In the year 2000, the conservation movement continues, encompassing a continuum of approaches to the environment. At one end are deep ecologists who, like preservationists, believe that the use and misuse of natural resources by humans has already gone too far, and propose a reduction in human population and return of wilderness areas to their natural states (see **deep ecology**; **population movement and control**). At the other end of the continuum is the **wise-use movement**, which emphasizes the **development** and use of resources for human consumption. Between these two extremes exists a diverse range of views regarding the balance that should be maintained between the human use of resources and the preservation of those resources.

See also: environmental management; environmental movements; sustainable development

Further reading

Hays, S.P. (1974) *Conservation and the Gospel of Efficiency: The Progressive Conservation Movement 1890–1920*, New York: Atheneum.

Leopold, A. (1966) *A Sand County Almanac*, New York: Oxford University Press.

Marsh, G.P. (1965) *Man and Nature*, Cambridge, MA: Belknap Press of Harvard University.

JANET HUNTER AND ZACHARY A. SMITH

consumerism

Consumerism has both economic and socio-cultural dimensions. It is sometimes claimed that consumption has become more important than production as industrial society has given way to a **post-industrial society**. The former was characterized by mass, assembly-line production in which the worker was just another substitutable element of the production process. Therefore, consumption was also geared to the mass rather than to the individual. The assumption that taste and desire were homogenous was captured by Henry Ford's quip: 'you can have any colour you want, so long as it's black'. However, in a post-industrial society production is said to take its lead from the individualistic preferences of sophisticated consumers. Marketing and advertising become more important and the service industries become dominant.

Therefore, consumerism is now thought to be an important source of individualized, post-collective identity in western nations. No longer simply referring to a set of desires, consumerism has itself become a need, a lifestyle, rather than a means of fulfilling other more basic needs. We do not consume in order to live but live in order to consume. The freedom to shop and the vast spectrum of goods on offer makes consumerism appear empowering. However, it can also be disempowering by leading to problems such as shopping addictions and credit card debt. It has also been blamed for the increasing commodification of society and of the self where everything and everyone is judged according to monetary norms.

For Marxists we live in an age of advanced capitalism where 'commodity fetishism' is stronger than ever: goods are fetishized as desirable by the very people whom consumer capitalism exploits in order to produce them. The belief in consumer sovereignty is just the latest form of 'false consciousness'. By contrast, some cultural conservatives acknowledge that ours is a society of post-industrial consumerism but maintain that this represents a dangerous erosion of elitist taste, educated opinion and social status. Another important thesis has been proposed by George Ritzer (1996) who identifies the 'McDonaldization of society'. Although consumers are now sovereign in some respects, in others they are deceived by the standardization and subtle controls of our Americanized 'fast food' culture.

However, there are those who welcome the sociocultural changes of the late twentieth century. According to **post-modernism** taste has become more democratic and heterogeneous. There is no single cultural logic but a multiplicity of cultures that are available for consumption anywhere and everywhere. Society becomes less hermetic and more diverse and cosmopolitan with the emergence of **globalization** and the shrinking of spatial and temporal distances (see Featherstone, 1990; 1991), culminating in the Internet where the very distinction between producers and consumers collapses into the 'prosumer'.

In addition, there are those who adopt a complex synthesis of these critiques. For instance, Baudrillard (1988) implies that homogeneity and heterogeneity are the twin faces of a cultural implosion where a 'hyperreality' of simulations takes over and consumerism is the means by which we play in our imaginations and memories with the wreckage of reality.

The debate about **green consumerism** often follows the contours of this debate and ties into the wider discussion about the extent to which consumerism can be ethical and responsible. Critics allege that consumerism is an ideology that individualizes society and so is largely irrelevant to the collective social action that is required to bring about radical economic and political change. Habits of personal consumption can be altered, but consumerism is inherently materialistic, competitive and short-termist. However, others argue that consumerism can be a useful tool of political and moral progress, e.g. the consumerist protests against South Africa's Apartheid in the 1970s and 1980s. Therefore, a green consumerism encourages people to take responsibility for their environment by recycling waste, checking labels on goods, holding supermarkets and multi-nationals to account and becoming more energy efficient.

This debate regarding ethical consumerism is not one between those who would and those who would not abandon consumption, as people need to consume in order to live; it is between those who believe that ethical consumption and consumerism go together and those who believe that in order to achieve the former we need to abandon the ideology of the latter. The arguments regarding green consumerism start from that point.

See also: capitalism; counter-culture; recycling; tourism, environmental impact of

References

Baudrillard, J. (1988) *Selected Writings*, ed. M. Poster, Cambridge: Cambridge University Press.

Ritzer, G. (1996) *The McDonaldization of Society*, California: Pine Forge Press, 2nd edn.

Featherstone, M. (ed.) (1990) *Global Culture*, London: Sage.

Featherstone, M. (1991) *Consumer Culture and Post-modernism*, London: Sage.

Further reading

Lee, M.J. (ed.) (1999) *The Consumer Society Reader*, Oxford: Blackwell.

TONY FITZPATRICK

co-operatives

The worker (or producer) co-operative is an organization that is owned and controlled by those working in it. Individual members own the organizational capital either collectively or through individual shares, and all members have the right to a share in any profit. Decisions are made democratically on a one member, one vote principle.

Co-operatives are commonly associated with the green principles of small-scale production, participatory **democracy** and equality, and they appear prominently in many models of a sustainable economy. Greens argue that co-operatives, unlike capitalist firms, will make business decisions – e.g. about methods of production or distribution – that seek to minimize damage to the environment and the local community.

See also: bioregionalism; counter-culture; anarchism/eco-anarchism; eco-socialism; Robertson, James

NEIL CARTER

coral reefs

The world's coral reef communities are experiencing increased stress from a combination of rising carbon dioxide levels, temperature increases, and the impacts of sedimentation, **pesticides**, overfishing, sewage and stormwater flows, ship groundings, construction activity, and recreational use. Scientists estimate that over 80 per cent of coral reefs in South East Asia are at risk from human disturbance, as are 70 per cent of all reefs outside the Pacific. The International Coral Reef Initiative of 1995 inaugurated a series of multilateral conservation efforts, but most action so far has been confined to the national or subnational level. Currently, there are more than 40 countries with coral reefs that lack marine preserves and regula-

tions to protect coral. Given that over half of the world's coral reefs lie within the political jurisdiction of just six countries – Australia, Fiji, **Indonesia**, Maldives, Papua New Guinea, and the **Philippines** – unilateral action by these states could make a critical difference. However, recent studies showing the deleterious effects of increased concentrations of carbon dioxide on reef calcification suggest that the threats to coral are truly global in nature. A sharp reduction in anthropogenic carbon emissions may be needed to ensure the survival of many coral ecosystems beyond the twenty-first century.

Further reading

Bryant, D. *et al.* (1998) *Reefs at Risk: A Map-Based Indicator of Threats to the World's Coral Reefs*, Washington, DC: World Resources Institute.

LAMONT C. HEMPEL

cost-benefit analysis

Cost-benefit analysis (CBA) is a collection of techniques which purport to obtain a monetary value for environmental and other untraded resources which are used up in industrial developments, thereby enabling the cost of these resources to be compared to the value of other economic benefits.

CBA was originally developed as a means of valuing industrial projects in developing nations, where market costs and values were regarded as distorted and inappropriate. Only later was it used to evaluate projects in industrial economies.

The logic of CBA is derived from welfare economics. According to this approach, it is always possible for those who gain from a change in the allocation of resources to overcompensate the losers. Unfortunately, environmental resources are not traded, and have no pecuniary valuation. They are often regarded as **externalities**, as resources which are used by but not owned or paid for by individuals, who obtain the benefit of the use of resources such as clean air and clean water, but pass the *social costs* of their use onto the rest of society, or indeed the rest of the world.

CBA is therefore employed in an attempt to obtain a monetary value for untraded environmental resources. It is often claimed that unless such a valuation is obtained, scarce environmental resources will be regarded as free, and will be squandered. Only by placing a monetary value on environmental social costs, it is maintained, will the value of the environment be considered. In addition, it is claimed that only by using the 'measuring rod of money' can the use of environmental resources be measured against other resources, or indeed one aspect of environmental protection be measured against another. Furthermore, monetary measures ('money votes') are regarded as superior to consultations by opinion poll, focus group or especially the ballot box, since it enables the degree of environmental concern to be expressed.

While the practice of CBA is fairly technical, the basic ideas are straightforward. CBA attempts to obtain the Total Economic Value of a proposed development. This has three components:

Total Economic Value = Use values + Option values + Existence values

Use Values   are a quantification of the direct use of resources by individuals.

Option values   are values derived from the satisfaction of the use of resources by others, or use in the future, or both.

Existence values   are a monetary measurement of the value of non-human rights.

There are two main methods for obtaining these values:

Shadow Pricing   Shadow Pricing attempts to find the value or cost of an untraded resource by pricing a traded resource which it is believed moves in parallel (e.g. house prices), or by valuing something which stems from the untraded environmental resource (e.g. lower travel time).

Surveys   The surveys used are called *contingent valuation* (CV) surveys. These are elaborate monetary value surveys which are related to the income of the respondents, and attempt to find out how much a respondent is willing to pay to preserve an environmental resource.

There are many critics of CBA. Some of these, including eco-socialists and Marxists (see **eco-socialism**), as well as those with a **deep ecology** or eco-centric philosophy, are critical of the idea of treating the environment as a resource or as a commodity (see **eco-centrism**; **eco-philosophy/ecosophy**). It has also been suggested that the idea of aggregating individual pecuniary valuations of such things as environmental degradation or the death and suffering of animals is inappropriate, since the damage is not being borne by the valuer. Sagoff (1988), arguing along similar lines, suggests that CBA in general, and Contingent Valuation in particular, commits a 'category error', in that it confuses questions about individual desires with ethical and political questions about right and wrong. Questions about the environment involve political judgements about what is best for the nation or even the world, rather than decisions about individual preferences. These sorts of questions, others have suggested, may be better dealt with in the public forum rather than private markets. This is why CV surveys have such a high non-response rate.

There are also critiques of the logic of CBA. The welfare economics models on which CBA is based assume small changes, whereas the risks that some CBAs are used to assess are enormous. Furthermore, in practice, CBAs have been open to bias, and have invariably followed the predisposition of their sponsors.

Nonetheless, CBAs are almost regarded as an *ante* to take part in any deliberation or public inquiry on environmental protection, since they do provide a single figure which aims to judge the net worth of proposed developments.

Reference

Sagoff, M. (1988) *The Economy of the Earth*, Cambridge: Cambridge University Press

Further reading

Jacobs, M. (1997) 'Environmental Valuation, Deliberative Democracy and Public Decision-Making Institutions' in Foster, J. (ed.) *Valuing Nature: Ethics, Economics and the Environment*, London: Routledge.

Pearce, D., Markandya, A. and Barbier, E. (1989) *Blueprint for a Green Economy*, London: Earthscan.

JON MULBERG

Council for the Protection of Rural England

This overview of the Council for the Protection of Rural England (CPRE), one of the UK's older and more venerable conservation organizations, contains data on its history, structure, income and membership profile, political style and future directions. Where appropriate, the Council has been compared and contrasted with cognate organizations. Launched in 1926, during the second phase of environmental mobilization in Britain, the CPRE contrasts with the **National Trust**, a cognate organization. In the inter-war period, the Trust was gradually developing a land portfolio with a predominance of specific sites of cultural and historic interest. By contrast, the CPRE was not ownership orientated, but instead dedicated to tackling (sub)urban sprawl and protecting the integrity, beauty and productivity of the countryside as a whole. However, both organizations invited grandees onto their governing bodies. The Duke of Westminster was president of the Trust, whilst the Earl of Crawford and Balcarres played the same role at CPRE, and Professor Patrick Abercrombie, of planning fame, became its first honorary secretary. Thus the Council was politically and socially conservative. Its sympathies were with the hereditary land-owning classes. This brought it into conflict with other contemporary environmental groups with which it otherwise had much in common. One may mention, for example, the federations that in 1935, became the **Ramblers Association** (RA). Consequently, although the CPRE was active in the formation of the RA, and at various points in its history has shared leaders and political goals (such as the establishment of national parks and extension of public planning controls), in the early days, the Council's cautious political style and social intimacy with the landowning aristocracy engendered distance and ill feeling between these two organizations.

Founded as a council of concerned individuals and other bodies, over time the CPRE has developed into a formal federation, consisting of a London based national office, 43 affiliated county branches and 200 local groups. In many rural areas these independent membership-based groups are established and influential participants in the local planning system. Indeed some of the constituent groups, such as the Sheffield and Peak Society, are older than the CPRE itself. However, by developing a local base with jurisdictions similar to those of local authorities, the CPRE has a strong foundation from which to influence planning outcomes. Internally democratic: individual members of the Council may participate in decision-making through their local groups. However in common with virtually all other British environmental groups, policy-making at national levels is the province of the organizational elite.

Income is complex. The principal sources of support are legacies, members' subscriptions, charitable trusts and government grants, public donations and responses to specific appeals. Mindful of competition for scarce resources and with a view to expansion, in 1989, the CPRE began to co-ordinate and build a direct individual membership nationally. In parallel a systematic attempt has been made to co-ordinate membership recruitment drives with political campaigns, often focusing on local issues. However, by contrast with the exponential growth of groups such as the **Royal Society for the Protection of Birds**, **World Wide Fund for Nature**, **Greenpeace** and **Friends of the Earth**, in the 1980s and 1990s, the CPRE's growth rate was slow, but comparatively steady.

Traditionally, the organization has favoured a consensual political style. This encompasses constructive dialogue with government, achieving progress in incremental steps, building pragmatic alliances and campaigning on an issue-by-issue basis. However, since the late 1970s, the preservation of landscape has been used increasingly as a mechanism or metaphor for campaigning on wider conservation and more topical environmental issues. For example, during the time of electricity privatization, CPRE lobbied collaboratively with groups such as WWF and FoE to raise awareness about the environmental protection arrangements for the newly privatized energy industry. In addition, as part of the British government's response to the 1992 Earth Summit (see **Rio Conference 1992**), CPRE has been actively involved in the governmental round table on **sustainable development**.

Ironically, by integrating social and economic issues into its twenty-first-century campaigns, the CPRE is mimicking the bold vision of the Victorian social and moral reformer movement. By collaborating with the Civic Trust on ways of regenerating towns and making them better places to live, by linking rural planning with urban issues through campaigns for brown field development, and by developing a more integrated and comprehensive vision, the further back the CPRE goes, the further forward it advances.

Further reading

Dwyer, J.C. and Hodge, I.D. (1996) *Countryside in Trust*, Chichester: John Wiley & Sons.

Rawcliffe, P. (1999) *Environmental Pressure Groups in Transition*, Manchester: Manchester University Press.

Shoard, M. (1997) *This Land is Our Land*, London: Gaia Books Limited.

PENELOPE LAW

Council on Environmental Quality

The US **National Environmental Policy Act** (NEPA) of 1969 created the Council on Environmental Quality (CEQ) within the Executive Office of the President. The CEQ has monitored the NEPA compliance of federal agencies. This has entailed developing standardized procedures for environmental impact statements (EISs). The Chair of the CEQ, who is appointed by the President and confirmed by the Senate, functions as the President's environmental policy adviser. It is the job of the CEQ to prepare the annual Environmental Quality Report, which in recent years it has done with the assistance of the **Environmental Protection Agency** (EPA).

In the early 1980s, President **Reagan** attempted to abolish the CEQ. Congress refused, so he cut most of its staff and ignored its members' advise. His successor, George Bush, promised to restore the CEQ's influence; however, his inner circle of advisors consisted of conservatives who favoured deregulating business. President Clinton sought to replace the CEQ with the Office of Environmental Policy as part of his plan to raise the EPA to cabinet status. Congressional conservatives sought to attach conditions to limit the regulatory authority of the elevated EPA. Thus, the plan came to nothing, and in 1994 the Office of Environmental Policy was folded into the CEQ by President Clinton.

Further reading

Vig, N.J. and Kraft, M.E. (2000) *Environmental Policy*, Washington, DC: Congressional Quarterly Press, 4th edn.

E. GENE FRANKLAND

counter-culture

Dominant ways of attaching meanings and values to social actions and personal characteristics in any society are potentially open to opposition from subordinated counter-cultures. Periods of rapid economic and technological change have been characterized by dominant instrumental cultures and expressive counter-cultures, such as the Dionysian cults of Classical Greece and the romantic movement of early modernity (Musgrove, 1974). Yet, 'the counter-culture' usually refers to the oppositional social networks and values of the late 1960s in the USA and western Europe, where **New Left** politics, Hippie subculture and the student movement intersected. Like the romantics, the 1960s counter-culture consisted largely of young, relatively affluent people in a time of expanding wealth and personal freedom. Their opposition to the dominant culture was not based on exclusion from power, wealth and status, but on the corrupting and stultifying effects of such power and status. The ideological critique of the power of the 'military-industrial complex', which linked together warfare, high **technology** and university education, took a political form in Anti-Vietnam War protest and evolved into the **new social movements** of the 1970s, the gay, feminist and **environmental movements**.

The expressive cultural critique repeated themes from earlier counter-cultures. In the nineteenth century, the Romantics rejected bourgeois puritanical values and favoured passion, creativity, imagination, physical pleasure, use of mind-altering drugs, poverty and loss of ego in identification with nature. In post-Second World War America, the Beats turned their backs on a conformist suburban America to search for an authentic lifestyle mixing Zen Buddhism, jazz, sex, drugs, poetry, hitch-hiking and nature. The Beats' contemporary form of Romanticism flowered into the 1960s counter-culture, with its hedonistic inclination to sex, drugs, particularly marihuana and acid (LSD) and rock music combined with eastern religious and **New Age** mysticism.

In spite of the currency of the Marxist concept of exploitation at the time, Max Weber's concept of the modern 'disenchantment of the world' by the relentless application of instrumental rationality to every aspect of life, provides a better indicator of the worldview of the counter-culture. Hence the importance of the expressive forms of protest, dispute and ways of life that the counter-culture embodied.

Universities became targets of protest, for their role in military research, as well as their undemocratic structures and also for their promotion of instrumental rationality against the expressive. 'The Underground', as the counter-culture media was known, was committed to freedom of expression, iconoclasticism and lack of deference towards 'the establishment', with Underground publications frequently clashing with obscenity laws. This was a period of rapidly developing cultural industries, such as music and fashion, which both promoted and absorbed counter-cultural influences.

The values of the counter-culture were characterized by a combination of individualism and communitarianism. Suspicion that the organizations of the Communist or Marxist Old Left shared with the capitalist Right, many of the worst disenchanting aspects of modernity (e.g. technophilia, bureaucratic rigidity, self denial) led to attempts to pursue new ways of living, leaving the institutions of modernity to wither (see also **communism**; **capitalism**). Individual lifestyle became a major form of political and cultural expression. The prototype for this strategy was resistance to conscription into the US Army during the Vietnam War. This withdrawal from mainstream institutions was extended from the military to careers and family structures, which were also abandoned, and replaced with utopian experiments in developing alternative lifestyles (see **utopia/ecotopia**). Communal living arrangements and self-sufficient farming appeared as symbolic of the counter-cultural rejection of the nuclear family and urban middle-class careers.

The moment of the counter-culture passed, but many of the counter-cultural ideas have developed and remained as elements of alternative lifestyles. For example, the interest in eastern philosophy and practice has blossomed into an alternative health sector, which provides many jobs as therapists and a wide range of services. Similarly while self-sufficiency and communes are little in evidence, organic food and farming is increasingly popular and a wide range of family types are now widely recognized.

Post-modernism suggests that there is no longer a single mainstream culture and certainly more than one alternative. Numerous social networks and practices embody alternative or counter-cultural values. The DIY culture of the 1990s, festivals and **anti-roads movement** protest sites is perhaps the closest recent relative of the 1960s counter-culture.

See also: New Age; Romanticism

Further reading

Kerouac, J. (1994) *The Dharma Bums*, London: Harper Collins.

Musgrove, F. (1974) *Ecstasy and Holiness: Counter Culture and the Open Society*, London: Methuen.

Reich, C. (1970) *The Greening of America*, London: Penguin.

Roszak, T. (1995) *The Making of a Counter Culture*, Berkeley: University of California Press.

DERRICK PURDUE

critical theory

Critical theory has its origins in the work of the Frankfurt School, and is associated particularly with such thinkers as Horkheimer, Adorno, Marcuse and Habermas. With intellectual roots that go back to Kant and Hegel, it represented a synthesis of theoretical insights from such thinkers as Marx, Weber and Nietzsche; these insights were applied to a wide range of studies of society and culture.

Although strongly influenced by Marx's critical social theory, especially his critique of ideology, the members of the Frankfurt School were more sceptical than orthodox Marxists about the revolutionary potential of the industrial proletariat in the mid-twentieth century or about the latent progressive tendencies of **capitalism**. Marxists tended to see the growth of industrial productive forces as a positive and potentially liberating phenomenon, the realization of whose promise was only held in check by the capitalist system of property ownership. The Frankfurt School thinkers considered it necessary to understand socio-historical reality in terms of determinations other than the economic. Hence one major area, neglected by Marx, which they developed was a critique not only of the economic sphere but also of culture. In their examination of culture, they utilized categories drawn from thinkers less buoyant than Marx about the emancipatory possibility of **progress**, to investigate the entwinement of myth and enlightenment, bringing into focus the subterranean history of Europe, revealing the dark underside of the **Enlightenment** heritage. They were thus also sensitive to respects in which Marx did not overcome the dominant ideology, as, for instance, in perpetuating a belief in economic growth and mastery of nature as progress, allowing the emancipation of people at the expense of dominated **nature**.

Hence, particularly relevant in the present context is how members of the Frankfurt School anticipated major ecological themes. In their critique of instrumental reason, and their attendant critique of enlightenment as domination, there was a common concern to oppose the instrumental forms of reason and action which prevail in modern societies regarding both relations between humans and relations between humans and nature. The role of critical theory was to anchor ethical criticism of prevailing human–human and human nature relations in determinate criticism of the actual social relations and cultural forms which sustain them. This sociologically grounded critique of the 'human domination of nature' was influential for those left-leaning green thinkers of the 1960s and 1970s who embraced a concern for non-human nature as a political cause. In a contrast which became very explicit with the publication of Murray **Bookchin**'s polemics against **deep ecology**, the project of **social ecology**, was claimed to offer a more robust and realistic guide for action than the abstract moralism of exhortations to 'us' (humans) to recognize 'our' oneness with nature, when the actual practices devastating ecological relations arise from and sustain relations of exploitation and domination between socially and economically distinct groups of people.

Nevertheless, there is a tension at the level of the basic aims of critical theory which bears on its ecological or environmental uptake too. On the one hand, as initially conceived, the normative purchase of critical theory essentially involved immanent critique: evaluating the practices and institutions of existing society in terms of their own professed values. Yet Horkheimer and Adorno (1973) could hardly sustain this approach in the face of societies whose values were stamped by a Hitler or Stalin. The alternative was to develop a more totalizing critique of the whole cultural formation itself; yet this approach appeals to values that cannot be located immanently. A similar tension affects contemporary ecological politics. If the view is taken that modern societies are radically flawed in their ecological values, then a totalizing critique could seem necessary; but the problem would then be in justifying its grounds and identifying a political constituency motivated to pursue it in practice. Conversely, if an immanent approach is taken, insufficiently radical steps might be taken to address ecological problems: in fact, the most recent debates about the relevance of critical theory to green politics have focused on the work of Jürgen Habermas (Hayward, 1995; 1998) whose theorization of discursive **democracy** has quite widespread appeal but is also taken to reveal the limits of immanent critique.

Still, if critical theory does not have all the answers for ecological politics, it has helped focus important questions about how the human relation to non-human nature can be understood as both material and socially constructed.

References

Hayward, T. (1995) *Ecological Thought: An Introduction*, Cambridge: Polity Press.
—— (1998) *Political Theory and Ecological Values*, Cambridge: Polity Press.
Horkheimer, M and Adorno, T (1973) *Dialectic of Enlightenment*, London: Allan Lane.

TIM HAYWARD

culture and the environment

Culture has been used in two different ways since the European **Enlightenment**: to refer to an achieved moral–intellectual status; and alternatively to describe the characteristic collective beliefs and practices of social groups. This ambiguity has been at the core of anthropologists' discussions about the influence of culture on human relations and environmental agency. For some, culture is about the all-embracing 'webs of significance' in which people live (Geertz, 1973), for others it is an abstraction, or epiphenomenon of deeper social realities.

It is often suggested that culture is what makes humans distinct from other species: human inter-action with the environment is unique due to shared technical knowledge, the communication of meanings and intentions, and the organizational complexity of social relationships. Culture is, though, further seen as what sets groups of humans apart from each other; culture shock being the experience of radical unfamiliarity with other learned ways of perceiving and being. Culture thus

combines notions of invention and convention (Wagner, 1975).

Characteristics of languages show how perceptions and understandings of the world can differ radically. Some languages offer elaborate vocabularies for environmental features which others do not distinguish. Concepts of time process may diverge significantly from the sequencing of past, present, and future. Recognition of diverse cultural worldviews, unhinged from nineteenth-century notions of evolution from the 'primitive' to the 'scientific', obviously presents cultural theory of the environment with a set of critical issues over relativism and universality. Whether as adaptive livelihood practice, or meaningful filter of symbolism, culture became in the twentieth century the key concept for talking about unities of collective difference, as opposed to the nineteenth century's use of race. This notion of culture entailed a patchwork view of the world as partitioned up into functionally coherent, discretely bounded entities. Within anthropology, 'cultural ecology' became a suggestive, if largely inconclusive, investigation into possible causal linkages between aspects of core techno-environmental features, for example of hunting and gathering or irrigated agriculture, and functional correspondences in the domains of domestic social life, political leadership, inter-tribal exchange or warfare, and symbolic representations (Ellen, 1982).

From the 1970s critiques of patchwork cultural coherence emerged with a growing understanding of how ethnic identities, cultural boundaries, and livelihood adaptations were deeply affected by colonial policies, and other historical processes contributing to 'the invention of tradition' and ethnic/racial essentialism in modernity. Previous interest in cultural holism sustained by stable rules and norms was replaced by investigation into cultural contradiction and conflict. Studies of gender inequalities in particular questioned the normative assumptions of a shared culture, and highlighted historical changes in gendered access to environmental resources by inheritance systems (Guyer, 1991; Agarwal, 1994).

By the 1980s anthropological studies of the environment were questioning the extent to which the idea of 'nature' itself was an appropriate term for cross-cultural analysis. In contrast to Levi-

Strauss's universalistic use of the nature/culture opposition for interpreting indigenous cosmologies, the western concept of nature was seen as too embedded in specific meanings of the non-human other, and to western society's self understanding, to be helpful for analysing how non-western peoples interact with and conceptualize their environments (MacCormack and Strathern, 1980).

In attempting to move beyond the modernist opposition between **nature** and culture, phenomenologically inspired approaches to ecological dwelling challenged both the idea of an inert biophysical environment separated off from people living in it, and the idea of culture as a cognitive model of meaning that mediates all environmental interaction (Ingold, 1992). These arguments echo elements of deep ecology's stance against the disenchanted perception of nature as mere resources, but biocentrism's celebration of de-socialized wilderness inversely reproduces, rather than transcends, the dualism of western anthropocentric thought (see **deep ecology**; **disenchantment of nature**; **eco-centrism**; **anthropocentrism**). Indigenous cosmologies demonstrate, alternatively, multiple ways in which people's notions of social interaction put them into meaningful exchange and communication with other natural species in a phenomenological unity (Viveiros de Castro, 1998; Descola, 1996; Rival, 1998).

Universalistic environmental conservation models based on the modernist separability of biophysical from socio-cultural considerations have resulted in enormous problems of implementation in the non-western world, encountering cultural incomprehension and resistance by communities forcibly alienated from their practices and cosmologies of environmental engagement (Grove, 1998; Stevens, 1997). Making explicit the cultural politics of environmentalism is both to disembed the issue of **biodiversity** from globally privileged cultural values (all be they not of a wholly shared variety), and to allow a debate on the politics of a peopled planet beyond the simplistic assumption of certain cultures having 'natural' propensities for sustainability (Milton, 1996). Culture is a concept for exploring the diversity of human-environmental experiences and meanings, not a programming mechanism to act in certain ways.

See also: environmental history; humanism and the environment; indigenous peoples; landscape; nature; noble savage, myth of

References

Agarwal, B. (1994) *A Field of One's Own: Gender and Land Rights in South Asia*, Cambridge: Cambridge University Press.

Descola, P. (1996) 'Constructing Natures: Symbolic Ecology and Social Practice', in Descola, P. and Palsson, N. (eds) *Nature and Society*, London: Routledge.

Ellen, R. (1982) *Environment, Subsistence and System: The Ecology of Small-Scale Social Formations*, Cambridge: Cambridge University Press.

Geertz, C. (1973) *The Interpretation of Cultures*, New York: Basic Books.

Grove, R. (1998) *Ecology, Climate and Empire: The Indian Legacy in Global Environmental History 1400–1940*, Oxford and Delhi: Oxford University Press.

Guyer, J. (1991) 'Female Farming in Anthropology and African History', in M. di Leonardo (ed.) *Gender at the Cross-roads of Knowledge*, Berkeley: University of California Press.

Ingold, T. (1992) 'Culture and the Perception of the Environment', in D. Parkin and E. Croll (eds) *Bush Base, Forest Farm: Culture, Environment and Development*, London: Routledge.

MacCormack, J. and Strathern, H. (1980) *Nature, Culture and Gender*, Cambridge: Cambridge University Press.

Milton, K. (1996) *Environmentalism and Cultural Theory*, London: Routledge.

Rival, L (ed) (1998) *The Social Life of Trees: Anthropological Perspectives on Tree Symbolism*, Oxford: Berg.

Stevens, S. (ed) (1997) *Conservation Through Cultural Survival: Indigenous Peoples and Protected Areas*, Washington: Island Press.

Viveiros de Castro, E. (1998) 'Cosmological Deixis and Amerindian Perspectivism', *Journal of the Royal Anthropological Institute*, 4: 469–88.

Wagner, R. (1975) *The Invention of Culture*, Englewood Cliffs: Prentice-Hall.

BEN CAMPBELL

Cuyahoga River

The Cuyahoga river is a 100-mile natural water-way located in north-east Ohio in the USA. The river begins its journey in Geauga County flowing south until it reaches the Cuyahoga Falls where it turns north and empties into Lake Erie. The Cuyahoga River gained national attention on 22 June 1969 when oil and debris floating on its surface caught fire. Prior to this blaze the river had caught fire on two other occasions, once in 1936 and again in 1952. After the 1969 blaze the river quickly became recognized as the river that 'oozes rather than flows' and in which 'a person will decay and not drown'. These events, however negative, helped to set the stage for the **Clean Water Act**, Great Lakes Water Quality Agreement, and the **Environmental Protection Agency**. Today, the river is no longer a fire hazard and has improved greatly.

Further reading

'Cleveland Alive' (22 February 2001) *Cuyahoga River* at
URL: http://www.chuh.org/CleveAlive/Water/Cuya%20riv.htm.

JON E. FITCH

D

Daly, Herman E.

b. USA

Economist

Herman Daly is one of the world's most influential champions of a steady-state economy. His many articles and books present an alternative paradigm to growth-centred mainstream economics (see **paradigms**). Arguing that mainstream economics is appropriate only when we are far from the physical limits imposed by a finite ecosystem, Daly has urged and participated in the creation of a more general theory of **development** that includes the 'close to the limits' case.

Currently Professor at the University of Maryland, School of Public Affairs, Daly was Senior Economist in the Environment Department of the World Bank from 1988 to 1994. He is co-founder of the journal *Ecological Economics*.

Further reading

Daly, H. (1973) *Toward A Steady State Economy*, San Francisco: WH Freeman.
—— (1991) *Steady State Economics*,Washington, DC: Island Press, 2nd edn.
—— (1996) *Beyond Growth: The Economics of Sustainable Development*, Boston: Beacon Press.

STANLEY R. KEIL

dams/hydroelectric power

Massive hydroelectric projects are an enduring symbol of humankind's hubris, a stark reminder of the arrogance, the dreams, and the passion for control of **nature** that mark the human species. Dams themselves have been with us for aeons. Ancient civilizations built irrigation schemes – tanks, bunds, small dams, and so on – relics of which remain to this day, as reminders of the engineering skills of the past. Yet, it is only in the twentieth century, with the development of the necessary technology, that we have been able to build dams of such size and complexity that they have fundamentally changed the face of the planet. Although hydroelectric projects are still seen by governments and international aid agencies as an essential part of national economic **development**, the devastating environmental and social consequences of these projects are now posing a potent political challenge to the dam-building industry.

The frenetic dam building of the twentieth century may be explained first in light of the allure of hydropower for countries bent upon massive **industrialization**. Hydropower is seen as one of the cheapest and cleanest sources of electricity – cheaper and cleaner by far than thermal power or nuclear power – although such a conclusion rests on firmly ignoring the environmental and social impacts of large dams. A second major attraction of large dams is their promise of irrigation: stored water would be available to bring arid and semi-arid lands under irrigation for the first time, dramatically increasing the capacity for food production. Thus, abundant supplies of electricity and food, the primary goals of countries, have been the major reasons for dam building. In addition, dams are also built for flood control and navigation purposes.

The International Commission on Large Dams defines a large dam as one measuring 15 metres or more from foundation to its crest. A major dam is one that is at least 150 metres high, or has a volume of at least 15 million cubic metres, a reservoir storage of at least 25 cubic kilometres, or electrical generation capacity of at least 1,000 megawatts. By 1995, over 300 dams had met these criteria. The leading builder of major dams is the USA, followed by the former Soviet Union, Canada, **Brazil**, and **Japan**. The dams with the largest capacity hydroplants include the Itaipu on the Brazil–Paraguay border, the Guri in Venezuela, the Sayano-Shusenk in Russia, and the Grand Coulee in the USA. The **Three Gorges project** in **China** will be the largest dam in the world, with a capacity of 18,200 megawatts, if completed. In addition to major dams, large and small dams have also proliferated, with the USA reportedly having 96,000 small dams and 5,500 large dams and China having 19,000 large dams.

National governments have been at the forefront of dam building activity. But, since 1945, international agencies such as the **World Bank** and the **United Nations Development Program**, as well as bi-lateral aid agencies such as the United States Agency for International Development and the British Overseas Development Administration have become major actors in fostering dam building in developing nations. The pace of dam building slowed in the 1990s with international agencies, especially the World Bank, under increasing pressure from environmental and **human rights** organizations. Fundamental questions are being asked about hydroelectric dam projects as it becomes increasingly evident that they have not delivered what has been promised.

Hydropower accounts for about 18 per cent of the world's electricity, with 24 countries depending on hydropower for over 90 per cent of their electricity supply. The cost of hydroelectricity is claimed to be low over the lifetime of a dam but the initial costs of building the hydroelectric systems (inclusive of the dam) are extremely high. The Itaipu dam, for instance, cost around $20 billion while the Three Gorges dam is estimated to cost on completion around $20–50 billion. Yet, the advantages of hydroelectricity over other sources of electricity have been put forward to justify hydroelectric projects, including the fact that no fuel is needed to run the hydroplant, there are few or no emissions into the atmosphere or wastes of any kind, and the dam and the generating plants have a long life. There is increasing evidence, however, that dams cost more than is estimated, supply much less electricity than promised, have a shorter life than expected, destroy riverine ecosystems, damage soil and often result in the concentration of land in the hands of the wealthy as smaller farmers become bankrupt. In addition, of course, there is the impact of dams on people who are displaced by the reservoir and canals.

Among the major environmental impacts of dams are the following: (a) salinization of soils resulting in loss of productive agricultural lands; (b) siltation of dams reducing their life; (c) fragmentation and destruction of riverine ecosystems; (d) reduction and frequent destruction of local **biodiversity** through loss of forests, wildlife habitats, and impacts on the river; (e) impact on water quality downstream; (f) impacts on coasts and estuaries; and (g) increase in some water-borne diseases such as malaria and schistosomiasis. The cumulative environmental effects of small dams too are significant. They can flood more land per unit of water stored than larger dams and, as in the case of India's Farraka Barrage on the Ganges, which is less than 15 metres high, can have devastating ecological consequences downstream.

Furthermore, large dams can trigger earthquakes, although this is disputed by the engineering community. The frequency of earthquakes can increase in areas of high seismic activity and dams can also cause earthquakes in areas previously assumed to be seismically inactive. Reservoir-induced seismicity is believed to be responsible for the earthquake that killed 180 people and injured thousands more, in 1967, near the 103-metre high Koyna dam, in **India**, and for the overtopping of Vaimont dam in Italy in 1963, which killed over 2,600 people. Perhaps the very worst dam disaster of all time took place in Henan province in central China in 1975, when, following a freak typhoon, the Banqiao dam burst and 500 million cubic metres of reservoir water drowned entire villages and cities. Although official statistics of the death toll remain few and contradictory, Human Rights Watch believes that 85,000 people were killed by the initial flood and a further 145,000 died in the ensuing epidemics and famine.

Equally significant are the social impacts of dams. Involuntary displacement and resettlement of people; the ensuing loss of cultural and social **sustainability**, which have gender-specific implications; and changes in economic systems whereby the subsistence economies of tribal people have to give way to monetized, market-driven systems are some of the most serious social consequences of large dam projects. The **Narmada Valley development programme** in India is expected to displace about 250,000 people when completed. The Kainji dam in Nigeria displaced 44,000 people and also had severe impacts on people downstream where both fish catches and agricultural production plummeted. The Sobradinho Dam in Brazil displaced 72,000 people directly, and the **Aswan Dam** in Egypt some 110,000 (about half of them in Sudan). The Garrison Dam in the USA flooded most of the productive land of the North Dakota reservation of the Three Affiliated Tribes and displaced 80 per cent of the population, who received no compensation. About 2.5 million people were forcibly displaced by World Bank projects alone for the years 1986–93. World Bank estimates state that between one and two million people are displaced by new dam construction each year. Although the World Bank has progressive, if not gender-sensitive, resettlement and rehabilitation policies in place, in practice, local people have systematically suffered greater impoverishment after displacement. Tribal people often do not hold legal title to the lands they have traditionally used and hence are rarely compensated for their loss of access to land, forest produce, and so on. Overall, indigenous and tribal people, often the most marginalized sections of society, make up a significant percentage of those being displaced by dams.

The environmental and social consequences of dams have resulted, since the 1980s, in the emergence of anti-dam movements worldwide. The movements comprise environmental, human rights and social activist groups, as well as displaced people, who have mobilized and lobbied with some success to make dam building more difficult. These anti-dam movements represent some of the most successful orchestration of protests at local, national and international levels. Such cross-national linkages are evident in movements such as the Narmada Bachao Andolan (Save the Narmada Movement), the struggle of the Cree Indians against the **James Bay Hydroelectric Project** in Canada, and the campaigns against the Katun Dam in Russia, and the Chico dams in the Philippines. More localized protests against dams go back much further. The 1913 construction of the **Hetch Hetchy dam** in Yosemite Valley in the USA despite the protests of preservationists had an enormous impact on the development of US environmentalism.

The challenge posed to hydroelectric projects is one that calls into question governments' and development agencies' commitment to sustainable development. If environmental and social sustainability must have priority in decision-making, then ultimately there may be no way of continuing with large-scale hydropower projects.

Further reading

Goldsmith, E. and Hildyard, N. (1984) *The Social and Environmental Effects of Large Dams*, Cornwall: Wadebridge Ecological Centre.

McCully, P. (1996) *Silenced Rivers: The Ecology and Politics of Large Dams*, London: Zed Books.

PRIYA A. KURIAN

Danube Circle

The Danube Circle (Duna Tor) is a Hungarian environmental movement founded in 1984 by the biologist Janos Vargha (see **environmental movements**). It organized opposition to Gabcikovo–Nagymaros, a joint Czechoslovak–Hungarian project to build two hydroelectric dams on the Danube river (see **dams/hydroelectric power**). Petitions and 30,000-strong demonstrations organized by the Danube Circle forced Hungary's last communist government to permanently halt construction of the Nagymaros dam on its territory in May 1989. In 1991–2 the Danube Circle unsuccessfully campaigned against the completion of the Gabcikovo dam on Czechoslovakian territory. It remained Hungary's largest environmental group in the 1990s, working on environmental quality and habitat preservation along the Danube river. In March 1998 it mobilized 10,000 demonstrators as part of a successful campaign against a new Slovak–Hungarian proposal to dam the Danube.

See also: East and Central European Greens

MARTIN HORAK

DDT

DDT (dichloro-diphenyl-trichloroethane) was one of the first and best-known examples of the class of broad-spectrum synthetic **pesticides** that dominated pest and disease control efforts after the Second World War. First synthesized in Switzerland in the 1930s, by the late 1940s DDT was regarded as a chemical miracle. It was inexpensive to manufacture and, unlike pre-war pesticides, essentially non-toxic to humans. It was easily applied, and thus aided in eradicating typhus and malaria throughout the world. DDT use soared in the 1950s, but its often indiscriminate use soon provoked concerns about its apparent effects on wildlife reproduction and, by extension, its accumulation in human tissues. In developed nations, such concerns led to the cessation of most uses of DDT by the late 1970s. However, it still enjoys some use in **less developed countries**.

Further reading

Dunlap, T. (1981) *DDT: Scientists, Citizens, and Public Policy*, Princeton, NJ: Princeton University Press.

CHRISTOPHER J. BOSSO

debt-for-nature swaps

The idea of cancelling some proportion of developing-country debt in return for environmental protection was first mooted in 1984 by Thomas Lovejoy, then Vice-President of the World Wildlife Fund (WWF) in the USA (see **World Wide Fund for Nature**). In a debt-for-nature swap (DFNS), a small part of a country's debt is purchased, with the agreement of the debtor country, from a public or private creditor. The purchaser is usually a non-governmental organization (NGO). In effect, the NGO becomes the creditor but agrees to forgive the debt in return for environmental or conservation programmes being undertaken by the debtor government in the debtor country. The debtor government pays for these programmes by issuing local currency or bonds either to the new creditor or to a designated local environment or conservation organization. The value of this 'swap' is usually more than the purchase price of the debt and is sometimes the full face value of the debt. Major NGOs involved in DFNS include Conservation International, the Nature Conservancy and the World Wildlife Fund. Individual governments have also cancelled debt owed to them in return for environmental programmes. Both the German and Swiss governments have established formal debt swap programmes of this kind.

The first debt-for-nature swap was undertaken in 1987 by Conservation International in an agreement with the Government of Bolivia. By the late 1990s, over 30 debtor countries had agreed to such swaps with NGOs and governments and over $1 billion had been generated for environment and conservation programmes. In 1990 the Paris Club of primarily OECD (Organization for Economic Co-Operation and Development) creditor countries gave effective approval to those DFNS which involved the rescheduling or conversion of bilateral debt (that is, debt owed to governments). In 1998, the US Congress passed legislation empowering the US administration to allocate up to $400 million to forgive debt in return for tropical forest conservation. The **United Nations Development Program** has also examined the use of such swaps to assist in funding National Desertification Funds.

Debt-for-nature swaps (sometimes now referred to as debt-for-environment swaps) were perceived to offer a win–win strategy: both debt relief and environment protection in situations where neither would otherwise have been possible. Repayment of the debt in local currency relieves the debtor country of having to draw on its foreign currency reserves. The NGO which purchases the debt acquires local currency usually greater than the value of the amount assigned to purchase the debt and the designated NGO within the debtor country gains access to funds and project experience.

In practice there have been a number of problems. Only those countries whose debts are available at a discount can benefit from such swaps. Many poorer countries, however, continue to service their debt and creditors therefore have no incentive to sell the debt at a discount. In situations where debt is available for purchase, debtor governments may not have sufficient financial resources available to fund the required environment or conservation programmes. The injection of local currency can also have an inflationary impact and there is no guarantee that such swaps will increase funding to environmental programmes. Debtor governments can simply cut funding to other environment programmes to fund the swap project. The amounts involved are small compared with the level of third-world indebtedness and swaps divert attention from the structural conditions of large-scale debt.

Concerns have also been raised about sovereignty in situations where the agreement involves restriction on use of a country's resources or land, or where it directs a government's decisions on funding. Criticisms from a group of South American countries in the early 1990s characterized DFNS as reaffirming the creditors' political and economic control over debtors. Eligibility requirements, such as those in the US legislation requiring governments to open their economies to international investment, can also restrict policy choices. International environmental organizations have been criticized for ignoring local communities in making decisions on the kinds of environmental programmes involved in swaps which they have funded. Indigenous organizations have been parti-

cularly critical of their exclusion from negotiations involving indigenous land.

Finally, the assessment of the contribution DFNS have made to environmental protection goals is mixed. In some instances, they have had considerable positive impact on local environmental outcomes but in others the areas designated for protection have been over run by loggers in search of profit and the landless in search of a sustenance livelihood.

Further reading

Jakobit, C. (1996) 'Nonstate Actors Leading the Way: Debt-for-Nature-Swaps' in Robert O. Keohane and Marc A. Levy (eds) *Institutions for Environmental Aid*, Cambridge, MA: MIT Press.

Lewis, A. (1999) 'The Evolving Process of Swapping Debt for Nature', *Colorado Journal of International Environmental Law*, 10 (2): 431–50.

Mahony, R. (1992) 'Debt-for-Nature Swaps: Who Really Benefits?', *The Ecologist*, 22(3): 97–103.

Wee, L.C.W. (1994) 'Debt-for-Nature Swaps: A Reassessment of their Significance in International Environmental Law', *Journal of Environmental Law*, 6(1): 57–72.

LORRAINE ELLIOTT

deep ecology

Deep ecology as a movement and a philosophical approach to environmental issues has exerted a remarkable influence on green political theory and practice since its origins over 20 years ago. While more of a particular ecocentric philosophical orientation to thinking about the environment and the relationship between the environment and humanity, than an environmental political movement, deep ecology is a shorthand term for a closely related set of ecocentric philosophical positions. Deep ecology has, by turns, inspired, infuriated, confused, hindered or aided the theory and practice of environmental politics and those wishing to understand it. While for Dobson, writing in 1989, 'There must be no doubt that Deep Ecology is indeed the Green Movement's philosophical basis' (1989: 41), for social ecologists, such as Murray **Bookchin**, deep ecology has been accused of political naiveté or fascist implications, profoundly harming the environmental cause. Although it would be going too far to suggest that deep ecology is the philosophical basis of the green movement, it is true to say that it does provide the normative basis of certain strands of green politics, such as radical ecological movements like **Earth First!** and **bioregionalism**.

The deep ecology movement can trace its roots to a seminal article written by the Norwegian philosopher and environmental activist, Arne **Naess** in 1973 entitled 'The Shallow and the Deep (Long-Range) Ecology Movement: A Summary', and he remains the founding father and leading thinker of deep ecology. In this short article Naess distinguishes between two fundamentally opposed wings of the emerging 'ecological movement'. For Naess, 'The Shallow Ecology movement', had the following main concerns, 'Fight against pollution and resource depletion. Central objective: the health and affluence of people in the developed countries' (1973: 95). For Naess, this dominant, mainstream shallow ecology movement views the environmental crisis as essentially a technical or instrumental problem, which can be solved by 'technical' means, such as less polluting technology or through better management of environmental resources.

Naess rejects this approach as not being 'deep' enough to diagnose the causes of the ecological crisis or to suggest lasting solutions. In contrast the 'Deep Ecology movement' is concerned with the following; '(1) rejection of the man-in-environment image in favour of the relational, total-field image; (2) biospherical egalitarianism – in principle; (3) principles of diversity and of symbiosis; (4) anti-class posture; (5) fight against pollution and resource depletion; (6) complexity not complication; (7) local autonomy and decentralization' (1973: 95–8).

It is from this distinction between 'shallow' and 'deep' ecology that we can trace many of the common approaches used to categorize green politics. For example, the 'deep/shallow' dichotomy 'maps' onto the following sets of binary or dualistic ways of describing environmental politics: 'ecologism/environmentalism'; 'fundi/realo';

'dark/light green'; 'radical/reformist' environmentalism. Thus deep ecology's importance is not simply confined to its place as part of the wider environmental movement, but more importantly, covers its central role in furnishing the dominant way in which the environmental movement and green politics has been categorized.

It is fair to say that deep ecology is predominantly a non-European stream of environmental politics, both in origin and orientation, being primarily based in North America, Australia and Scandinavia. Leading deep ecological theorists and activists include Warwick Fox, Bill Devall, George Sessions, Gary Snyder, John Seed, Joanna Macy, Delores LaChappell and Edward **Abbey**. As it developed, the principles of deep ecology evolved into the following eight point 'platform', which is accepted by almost all who call themselves deep ecologists:

1 the well-being and flourishing of non-human life has intrinsic value, independent of human usefulness;
2 richness and diversity of life contribute to the realization of these values and are values in themselves;
3 humans have no right to reduce this diversity except to satisfy vital needs;
4 the flourishing of human life and culture is compatible with a substantial decrease in the human population, while the flourishing of non-human life requires this decrease;
5 present human interference in the world is excessive, and the situation is worsening;
6 policies affecting basic economic, technological and ideological structures must change;
7 the ideological change is mainly that of appreciating *life quality* (dwelling in situations of inherent value) rather than adhering to an increasingly higher standard of living;
8 those who subscribe to the above have an obligation to implement the necessary changes.
(Devall and Sessions, 1985: 70)

The general goals of deep ecology can be stated as the preservation of **nature** 'wild and free' and to limit the human impact on nature as the way to achieve this. Breaking this down we can group deep ecology proposals under three broad head-ings; (a) wilderness preservation; (b) human population control; and (c) simple living (or 'walking lighter on the planet'). A further important principle is 'self realization' of all beings, human and non-human. The 'Center for Deep Ecology' describes deep ecology thus:

> Deep ecology encourages a fundamental shift in the way we experience nature and how we respond to the environmental crisis. Deep ecology rises from a belief in the essential value and interdependence of all forms of being. Supporters of deep ecology are committed to minimizing humanity's destructive interference with the rest of the natural world and to restoring the diversity and complexities of ecosystems and human communities. The deep ecology vision promotes practices to help change old patterns of thinking and acting. It reconciles us with the larger natural world that is our home.
>
> (Salmon, 1996: 1)

For deep ecology the root of the ecological crisis is anthropocentric 'industrialism', the culture, practices and institutions originating in western Europe and now the dominant 'worldview' and political-economic system on the planet. Since the problem is 'industrialism' in all its forms, solutions to the ecological crisis cannot be found in 'industrial' politics or moral theory. It is for this reason that deep ecology is equally critical of **capitalism** as it is of socialism, since both are simply different forms of industrialism. One can also see in this view the origins of the green slogan 'neither left nor right'.

One of the main distinguishing features of deep ecology as opposed to other branches of environmental philosophy, is its focus on consciousness and being, as opposed to establishing an 'environmental ethics' based on the intrinsic value of nature. This shift away from environmental ethics within deep ecology has been described by Sessions, who holds that, 'The search then, as I understand it, *is not for environmental ethics but ecological consciousness*' (in Fox, 1990: 225), or 'cosmological consciousness' (Fox, 1990: 255).

A central part in this shift from value theory and environmental ethics to wider issues concerning consciousness reflects deep ecology's contention that there is an 'ecological crisis' which is, at root, a crisis of human psychological self-understanding and culture. One of the reasons given as to why deep ecology is deeper than other green moral positions is that it claims to deal with the root causes of the ecological crisis rather than its effects. The root causes for deep ecology are found in the dominant western view of the self and a related anthropocentric culture which sees the world as dead, valueless and simply there for human enjoyment and consumption. From this ecocentric perspective the ecological crisis is first and foremost a crisis of culture and self. References to the need for a cultural 'paradigm shift', based on alternative world-views which affirm the unity of humans with and dependence upon nature, are part and parcel of the deep ecology claim that only a widespread change in consciousness will solve the ecological crisis.

Various other reasons can be found for this shift to questions concerning consciousness, identity and culture. For some deep ecologists the reason for this lack of attention to 'normal' ethical theorizing is that the crisis we face is too severe and deep. For Devall, 'Our ontological crisis is so severe that we cannot wait for the perfect intellectual theory to provide us with the answers. We need earth-bonding experiences' (1988: 57). Another reason for this lack of concern with environmental ethics is the non-academic nature of much of deep ecology writing and concerns (McLaughlin, 1994). For many, deep ecology is primarily activist-orientated as exhibited in the relationship between it and the radical environmentalist group **Earth First!**.

Deep ecology often comes across as a metaphysical theory, given its concerns with shifting cultural paradigms and tying its critique of anthropocentrism closely to the historical emergence of particular forms of rationality, knowledge and practices in the west. The latter refer generally to the change in human–nature relations as a result of the **Enlightenment**. This equation of modernity with **anthropocentrism** can be readily seen in deep ecology's historical account of the 'disenchantment of nature'; that is, the transformation of nature from a realm of meaningful normative significance, into a collection of resources for human instrumental use and exploitation. The historical shift to a mechanistic, reductionist, instrumentalist worldview is what deep ecology means by 'anthropocentrism'. Anthropocentrism thus refers to a complete metaphysical worldview, one deep ecologists claim as the root of the ecological crisis. This worldview is held to underpin all dominant moral theories and political ideologies, apart from the deep ecological one.

One way to understand deep ecology can be found in a seminal essay by Lynn **White** Jr on 'The Historical Roots of our Ecologic Crisis'. He concludes that, 'Since the roots of our trouble are so largely religious, the remedy must also be essentially religious, whether we call it that or not. We must rethink and re-feel our nature and destiny' (1967: 1207). This demand for a metaphysical 'paradigm-shift' is an enduring feature of deep ecology, which can be seen as a critical reaction to the 'disenchantment' of nature, and the 'dominant paradigm' or industrial-anthropocentric worldview which caused this disenchantment. The thrust of deep ecology follows the logic of White's argument suggesting that if the cause of the ecological crisis is to be found in the disenchantment of nature then the solution lies in its re-enchantment. The importance of this spiritual self-understanding within deep ecology is that this has been taken to excuse its lack of a political dimension. For example, according to Devall, 'The deep, long-range ecology movement . . . is only partly political. It is primarily a spiritual-religious movement' (1988: 160). Naess offers the fact that many deep ecologists find 'politics boring and distasteful' (1995: 261) as a possible reason for their lack of interest in the political implications of deep ecology.

One critique of deep ecology is that it goes beyond seeing the resolution of the ecological crisis as based on a shared *respect* for nature to a much stronger argument concerning the necessity for a shared *reverence* for nature. That deep ecology is more concerned with reverence than respect, can be seen in Mathews' statement that, 'When our culturally-endorsed cosmology represents the world as inert, blind, bereft of worth or purpose, indifferent to our attitudes towards it, *then our natural urge to celebrate Nature may be thwarted*' (1991:

162–3, emphasis added). This idea of a 'natural urge to celebrate Nature' is also tied up with deep ecology's diagnosis of the 'pathology' of the modern self which becomes 'ill' when such 'natural' urges are repressed. The deep ecology aim to re-enchant the world is understood as a return to a 'natural' harmony between humans and nature. Thus the re-enchantment of nature is at root concerned with overcoming the alienation of humans from nature, to overturn the dominant worldview which stresses the separation of humans from nature (see **disenchantment of nature**).

The solution to the 'environmental crisis' consists not in the formulation of 'environmental ethics' (understood as a system of moral 'oughts' coming from an environmentally informed value theory). Although acknowledged as having a role to play, the latter is regarded as inferior to encouraging ecocentric habits and dispositions so that 'beautiful' ecological actions follow 'naturally' as part of the process of self-realization. 'Ecological identification' is part of the 'maturing' of the self according to Naess (1989: 86). It is the 'immaturity' of the self and the type of ethics associated with that view of the self, which results in a dis-valuing of nature and a simultaneous underestimation of the individual. In treating nature disrespectfully we simply reveal our misunderstanding of what it means to be a 'mature' self.

McLaughlin (1994), in a chapter tellingly entitled 'Beyond Ethics to Deep Ecology', highlights this aspect of deep ecology. According to him,

> the social dependency of ethical theory is a serious problem for any attempt to develop a non-anthropocentric environmental ethic. If the issues posed by ecological crises go to the very roots of industrial society, *then it is unlikely that any ethical theory that is grounded in reflection on current social practice will penetrate deeply enough . . . Thus, the possibility of grounding ethical argument for any radical transformation of humanity's relations with the rest of nature requires going far beyond ordinary ethical discourse.*
>
> (1994: 169; emphasis added)

McLaughlin's claim that an immanent critique of anthropocentrism and its cultural manifestation 'will not penetrate deeply enough' is premised on a presumption that the only solution to the ecological crisis must be an ecocentric one. Alternatives, both from non-anthropocentric environmental ethics, and more importantly, from within anthropocentrism, are dismissed. However, the argument that ethical reflection is constrained by contemporary social practices can be, and has been criticized. That conventional ethical theory may be grounded in reflection on those social practices does not prove that the former is determined by the latter or that it cannot radically change practices. One has only to survey the recent history of moral and legal theory and practice to see the effect it has had on social practices from women's rights to the legal protection of some non-humans, such as certain species and categories of animals.

Norton in his plea for unity among environmentalists (principally between 'deep' and 'shallow' ecologists) demonstrates the positive contribution of science. According to him, 'Environmentalists' emerging consensus, it will turn out, is based more on scientific principles than on shared metaphysical and moral axioms' (1991: 92). He then goes on to point out that

> the attack on human arrogance, which was mounted as a response to anthropocentrism, was well motivated but badly directed. One need not posit interests contrary to human ones in order to recognize our finitude. If the target is arrogance, a scientifically informed contextualism that sees us as one animal species existing derivatively, even parasitically, as part of a larger, awesomely wonderful whole should cut us down to size.
>
> (1991: 237)

The metaphysical drift of much of deep ecology makes it very abstract since its concern is with finding a more or less determinate answer to the general metaphysical question as to the 'lasting truth' of the relationship between humanity and nature. For critics, deep ecology tends to have little to say about ethical guidance or actual interactions between human societies and their environments, or where they do it differs little from a reformed anthropocentrism.

Deep ecology's general frame of reference is the restoration of something that has been lost, a return to 'the true path' from which we have diverged. Aboriginal cultures are often regarded as exemplars of good ecological behaviour by deep ecologists. 'Wilderness experience' is regarded as a close approximation to these ancient and 'true' human ways of 'being in the world'. This can explain much about deep ecology. For one, it explains the stress placed on the direct experience of nature, rather than abstract reasoning about nature. Through the experience of nature we may relearn and recover our place in the natural order of things, rediscover the perennial rhythms of the earth, and once again be in harmony with the world.

However, one could suggest that it is the *arrogance* of humanism (Ehrenfeld, 1978), rather than humanism (anthropocentrism) itself that is, or ought to be, the proper object of the deep ecology critique, and should be a central orientating feature of green moral theory. Deep ecology remains as a powerful reminder of the dangers of crude anthropocentrism, and the basic idea that humans are not divorced from, or above the natural world, but fundamentally part of it.

See also: eco-centrism; environmental ethics; environmentalism and ecologism; green political theory; humanism and the environment; intrinsic value; Naess, Arne; voluntary simplicity

References and Further reading

Barry, J. (1999) *Rethinking Green Politics: Nature, Virtue and Progress*, London: Sage.

Devall, B. (1988) *Simple in Means, Rich in Ends: Practising Deep Ecology*, Salt Lake City, UT: Gibbs Smith.

Devall, B. and Sessions, G. (eds) (1985) *Deep Ecology: Living as if Nature Mattered*, Layton, UT: Peregrine & Smith.

Dobson, A. (1989) 'Deep Ecology', *Cogito* 3(1).

Ehrenfeld, D. (1978) *The Arrogance of Humanism*, Oxford: Oxford University Press.

Fox, W. (1990) *Toward a Transpersonal Ecology: Developing New Foundations for Environmentalism*, Boston: Shambhala Press.

McLaughlin, A. (1994) *Regarding Nature: Industrialism and Deep Ecology*, New York: State University of New York Press.

Mathews, F. (1991) *The Ecological Self*, London: Routledge.

Naess, A. (1973) 'The Shallow and the Deep, Long-Range Ecology Movement: A Summary', *Inquiry*, 16.

—— (1989) *Community, Ecology and Lifestyle*, Cambridge: Cambridge University Press.

—— (1995) 'Deep Ecology and Lifestyle' in G. Sessions (ed) *Deep Ecology for the Twenty-First Century*, Boston and London: Shambhala Press.

Norton, B. (1991) *Toward Unity Among Environmentalists*, Oxford: Oxford University Press.

Salmon, E. (1996) 'Towards an Ethic of Our Environments: A Course Correction for Deep Environmental Ethics' at

URL: http://www.mosquitonet.com/~esalmon/env/thesis/index.html.

White, L. (1967) 'The Historical Roots of Our Ecologic Crisis', *Science*, 155.

JOHN BARRY

democracy

Environmental politics is rather unique in that it encompasses both radical democratic and anti-democratic proposals, policies and schools of thought. The anti-democratic position holds that the root cause of the environmental crisis is to be found in the democratic organization of society in general and in particular the unregulated multiplication of wants and desires which the modern (liberal) democratic system is based upon and maintains. On this view, greater state authority, order and regulation are absolutely needed to deal with the various environmental problems facing modern societies. On the other hand, there are those who hold that the solution to environmental problems requires more not less democracy and suggest the democratization of the state, the cultivation of a robust and active sense of 'environmental' citizenship, more open, transparent modes of public policy-making and the extension of democratic norms to the economic sphere.

The anti-democratic position on environmental politics was first articulated in the early 1970s in the aftermath of the **Limits to Growth** report,

and was closely associated with thinkers such as William Ophuls, though elements of the authoritarian position can be found in the 1960s in the early work of Garret **Hardin** and his infamous (and mistaken) view of the environmental crisis as a 'tragedy of the commons'. Often closely identified as **doomsayers**, other 'ecoauthoritarians', sometimes also known as 'survivalists' (Eckersley, 1992), included Robert Heilbroner (1980), and elements of the deep ecology movement such as Edward **Abbey** in the USA and Rudolf **Bahro** in Germany (Barry, 2000).

A clear account of the ecology–authoritarian position, which also demonstrates its central political–ethical justification is the following statement from Ophuls in which he concludes that with the advent of the ecological crisis, interpreted as a return to scarcity (following 'the limits to growth' thesis), 'the golden age of individualism, liberty and democracy is all but over. In many important respects we shall be obliged to return to something resembling the pre-modern closed polity' (1977: 145). He interprets this, in terms of a (benign) technocratic dictatorship. The justification of this ecologically motivated anti-democratic stance is basically the traditional argument of 'the ship of state' requiring the best pilots, and the dangers of 'rule by the ignorant' (i.e. democratic rule) when faced with such a complex and complicated issue as social-environmental dilemmas. At root, the anti-democratic environmental argument boils down to the idea that:

- democracies in modern liberal democratic states are really about governments making sure of the 'economic goodies' allowing greater and greater levels of personal consumption and income accumulation (thus, liberal democracies are systematically and structurally 'locked into' an 'environmentally destructive cycle' meaning they are unable and unwilling to impose limits on consumption and human impact on the environment); and
- to identify, cope and/or solve environmental problems are technical matters of expertise, best left to those with the requisite knowledge – rule by an expert few is to be preferred to rule by the ignorant many. Democracy is at best superfluous and at worse a hindrance in times of crisis, when

decisions (tough and often unpopular decisions) have to be made for the sake of survival.

Those who reject this anti-democratic view, and instead propose that the environmental problems we face call for more not less democracy, base their critique of the anti-democratic argument on the basis that:

(a) Environmental problems are not 'technical' problems and thus best left up to some group of scientific experts, but rather are at root political-ethical matters of 'right and wrong' not just matters of 'cost and benefit'. As moral matters these lend themselves to democratic (and indeed deliberative democratic) decision-making (Barry, 1999).

(b) The effective solution to environmental problems requires that people are persuaded (rather than forced) to change their lifestyles, that is, if people are convinced of the normative rightness of the environmental course of action, this is more likely to result in effective environmental action than if people are forced to obey some set of environmental laws in the making of which they had no say.

(c) Democracies promote the free flow of information, encourage debate and alternative views, all of which are absolutely central to finding solutions and debating responses to various environmental problems. Democracy is the best mode of political decision-making under conditions of uncertainty and complexity.

(d) The extension of democratic accountability to the 'sub-politics' of scientific and technological innovation is suggested by many as the only effective way of preventing the development and use of environmentally harmful, risky and ethically questionable forms of technological control over the environment (such as **biotechnology**).

(e) The establishment and maintenance of democratic norms and institutions are central aspects of **sustainable development**, as a normative and practical socio-economic aim of societies.

(f) While democracy is necessarily 'of the people and by the people' it need not necessarily be limited to 'for the people', in that democratic systems can allow for the representation and protection of non-human beings, and future generations (Eckersley, 1996).

(g) Finally, democratic politics allows those groups, organizations and individuals who feel strongly about environmental matters to lobby government, publicize and try to educate and persuade the public of their aims. In this way, democracy can be regarded as a 'mode of social learning' through which people become more knowledgeable and educated through public, political debate and argument.

It is clear that while neither democratic or anti-democratic modes of political organization can *guarantee* the avoidance of ecological damage, it is clear that the practical dangers and the normative failings associated with the anti-democratic position mean that the resolution of environmental problems must go with rather than against the grain of democracy and the processes of democratization. At the end of the day, we must ask ourselves if it is worth sustaining a non-democratic society, and whether, as the anthropocentric-democratic environmental position holds, the environmental crisis threatens the survival of society as we know it.

See also: environmental ethics; liberalism/liberal democracy; Limits to Growth; risk society

References

Barry, J. (1999) *Rethinking Green Politics: Nature, Virtue and Progress*, London: Sage.

—— (2000) 'Rudolf Bahro', in Plamer, J (ed.) *50 Key Environmental Thinkers*, London: Routledge.

Eckersley, R. (1996) 'Greening Liberal Democracy: The Rights Discourse Revisited', in B. Doherty and M. de Geus (eds) *Democracy and Green Political Theory: Sustainability, Rights and Citizenship*, London: Routledge.

Heilbroner, R. (1980) *An Inquiry into the Human Prospect*, New York: Norton, 2nd edn.

Ophuls, W. (1977) *Ecology and the Politics of Scarcity*, San Francisco: W.H. Freeman.

JOHN BARRY

Denmark

In Denmark environmental protection has been an important priority area in both official governmental policy-making, and in the overall political culture, since the early 1970s. Even without an influential green party, the so-called 'green majority' in the parliament has kept environmental issues high on the national political agenda. An environmental ministry was established as early as 1971, and, in the 1990s Denmark has been one of the more active countries in Europe in supporting programmes in **sustainable development.** In particular, the state efforts to encourage 'cleaner technologies' in industry have been ambitious and substantially funded. The Danish environmental movement has been particularly successful in relation to energy issues, where a strong popular opposition in the 1970s led to the curtailment of government plans to develop nuclear energy, and encouraged the emergence of a wind-power industry that is one of the largest in the world.

ANDREW JAMISON

Department of the Environment, Transport and the Regions

The Department of the Environment, Transport and the Regions (DETR) was established in the wake of the Labour Party victory in the UK General Election in 1997 with the merger of the former Departments of the Environment and Transport. According to the Department, 'The aim of the DETR is to improve the quality of life by promoting **sustainable development** at home and abroad, fostering economic prosperity and supporting local **democracy**.' In principle the combination of environment and transport departments and their integration with a strategy to create regional development agencies bodes well for sustainable development. Out of five policy priorities, two are directly related to environmental concerns: 'Giving practical effect to sustainable development, and promoting this across the work of government'; and 'Implementing the climate change commitments made at Kyoto'. A further

priority, 'Implementing the Government's white paper *New Deal for Transport*', is equally pertinent as it is an attempt to create an integrated transport policy that reduces the need to use motor vehicles.

Within the DETR it is the Environment Protection Strategy Directorate which is responsible for the Greening Government Programme, has policy and financial oversight of the **Environment Agency**, and sponsors the UK Round Table on Sustainable Development, the Government Panel on Sustainable Development (both created by the previous Conservative administration) and the Royal Commission on Environmental Pollution (see **sustainable development**).

The UK was the first liberal democracy to create a cabinet-level department of the environment in 1970 (see **liberalism/liberal democracy**). However, it has never simply focused on environmental protection and thus environmental issues are not always at the top of its policy agenda. Even before the creation of the DETR, the previous Department of the Environment had responsibility for issues beyond a limited environment focus, including planning and regional development, local government, housing and urban regeneration. Although setting the policy framework for pollution control, day-to-day activities are carried out by a semi-autonomous Environment Agency (see **British regulatory agencies**).

Co-ordination of environmental issues is made more difficult because a number of other departments have responsibility for issues that clearly impinge on the environment. For example, the responsibility for most agri-environmental policy lies with the Ministry of Agriculture Food and Fisheries, energy policy with the Department for Trade and Industry, and the Treasury has overall responsibility for macro-economic policy and thus for the introduction of environmental taxation systems. Whereas environmental pressure groups have gradually found a niche within the policy networks surrounding the DETR, they are typically peripheral actors when it comes to these other departments.

In May 1999 after a large-scale consultation process (both inside and outside Whitehall) led by the DETR, the Labour Government published

A Better Quality of Life: A Strategy for Sustainable Development for the United Kingdom. The strategy has been criticized for avoiding difficult targets and objectives, although it has been praised for introducing a series of headline indicators for 'measuring' progress towards sustainable development. These economic, social and environmental indicators are to be published annually (see **green accounting**). The strategy also promises to bring together the work of the Panel and Roundtable to create a Commission on Sustainable Development and to make important internal changes within Whitehall. The ineffective system of Green Ministers, first introduced in 1990, is to be revitalized and a Cabinet Committee on the Environment (chaired by the Secretary of State for the Environment Transport and the Regions) and the House of Commons Environmental Audit Committee have been established.

In principle, the DETR can be seen as a force for integration, bringing together environmental, transport and local and regional democratic and development responsibilities. However, in practice the first 18 months have shown that it is difficult to co-ordinate such a large department and it is far from clear that environmental concerns are prioritized in its work. Like most liberal democracies, the DETR is promoting a vision of sustainable development and environmental protection that bears all the hallmarks of **ecological modernization** – the key objectives of its strategy for sustainable development include the 'effective protection of the environment' and 'prudent use of natural resources', alongside the 'maintenance of high and stable levels of economic growth and employment'.

In June 2001, following the election of New Labour, the DETR was restructured into the Department of Environment, Food and Rural Affairs (DEFRA).

Reference

Department of the Environment, Transport and the Regions (1999) *A Better Quality of Life: A Strategy for Sustainable Development for the UK,* London: HMSO, Cm.4345. Also available on the DETR website.

Further reading

Carter, N. and Lowe, P. (1998) 'Britain: Coming to Terms with Sustainable Development', in K. Hanf and A. Jansen *Governance and Environmental Quality: Environmental Politics, Policy and Administration in Western Europe,* Harlow: Addison Wesley Longman.

Connelly, J. and Smith, G. (1999) *Politics and the Environment: From Theory to Practice,* London: Routledge, pp.262–70.

DETR website at URL: http://www. detr.gov.uk containing an introduction to the department, policy documents, and other information and links.

Voisey, H. and O'Riordan, T. (1997) 'Governing Institutions for Sustainable Development: The United Kingdom's National Level Approach', *Environmental Politics,* 6(1):24–53.

GRAHAM SMITH

Department of the Interior

The US Department of the Interior (DOI) was established on 3 March 1849 to take charge of the USA's internal development and the welfare of its people. Prior to the creation of the DOI, domestic matters were apportioned by Congress among the existing departments: the Department of State, the Department of the Treasury, and the Department of War. At the time of its creation, the DOI was responsible for such diverse functions as the oversight of the District of Columbia's jail and the settlement of freed slaves in Haiti. The Department has since developed into the USA's primary conservation agency with the responsibility for providing, preserving, and managing the nation's public lands. The DOI's mission is to manage these vast natural resources in a scientific and environmentally sound manner.

The DOI has approximately 72,000 employees within its numerous bureaus, departments, and offices. The Bureau of Land Management (established 1946) is responsible for sustaining and improving the health and productivity of public lands. The Bureau of Indian Affairs (established 1849) serves to carry out the trust responsibilities of the US Government with respect to American

Indians and Alaskan Natives. The Bureau of Reclamation (established 1902) is responsible for the management, development, and protection of the nation's waterways and their related resources. The US Fish and Wildlife Service (established 1940) works to protect and to conserve America's diverse wildlife including its threatened and **endangered species**. The National Park Service (established 1916) promotes and regulates the **National Parks**. The US Geological Survey (established 1879) is an independent fact-finding agency that is responsible for locating, analysing, and monitoring the conditions of the Nation's natural resources. The Mineral Management Service (established 1982) is responsible for the management of all offshore public holdings and the resources located within those holdings. The Office of Surface Mining (established 1977) oversees the **mining** and reclamation of all coal depositories and abandoned mines. The DOI is also administratively responsible for the development of federal policies regarding overseas dependencies, such as the US Virgin Islands, as well as the implementation of federal programmes in freely associated states, such as the Republic of the Marshall Islands. The fiscal year 2000 budget for the DOI was over $8 billion, significantly larger than that of the **Environmental Protection Agency**.

The Secretary for the DOI is responsible for approximately 1/3 of all the lands in the USA; as a result the individual who fills this position is often surrounded by political controversy. The most controversial past Secretary was James **Watt**, who was appointed in 1981 by President Ronald **Reagan**. Previously the head of the Mountain States Legal Foundation, a conservative pro-development group litigating to limit environmental regulations, he was labelled as an anti-environmentalist. While serving as Secretary, Watt openly favoured development over conservation, cut funding for the protection of endangered species, and referred to those involved in the environmental movement as 'communists' and 'Nazis'. National environmental groups soon were petitioning for Watt's removal from office and collected 1.1 million signatures in support of this action. After a series of public relations gaffes, Watt resigned as DOI Secretary in 1983.

The Administration of George Bush (1989–93) did little to change the federal land-use policies of the Reagan Administration. Bush appointed Manuel Lujan, Jr, a retired Republican congressman from New Mexico as DOI Secretary. During his term Lujan made no departures from previous Republican pro-development policies.

Under President Bill Clinton the DOI fell under the watch of former Arizona governor Bruce Babbitt, who had recently served as the President of the League of Conservation Voters. While serving as DOI Secretary, Babbitt sought to take a more balanced and environmentally friendly approach to western land-use policies than under the Reagan and Bush Administrations. In January 2001, Gale A. Norton became the first woman to head the DOI in its 152 year history. Conservative Republican Norton was appointed by President George W. Bush and confirmed by the Senate, despite vocal opposition from national environmental groups. Prior to her appointment, Norton had served as Attorney General for the state of Colorado and as a senior attorney for the Mountain States Legal Foundation. In the latter position Norton had worked closely with Watt and, as a result, has been described as 'James Watt in a skirt' (Kendall, 2001).

References

Kendall, D. (4 March 2001) 'Common Dreams News Center', *Gale Norton Is No James Watt; She's Even Worse* at
    URL: http://www.commondreams.org/views01/0109–07.htm.
Kriz, M. (1993) 'Grounds Keepers', *National Journal*, 25: 1534–7.
US Government (20 February 2001) 'US Department of the Interior', *About DOI and Bureaus*, at
    URL: Wysiwyg://52/http://www.doi.gov/indexj.html.

JON E. FITCH

development

Until recently, analysts assumed that there is a trade-off between development and environmental protection. From this perspective, everything from

urbanization to population growth puts new and often unmeetable demands on an already stretched ecosystem. Especially since the UN Conference on the Environment and Development in 1992 in Rio de Janeiro, we have been exploring ways in which the two can go hand in hand, most notably through policies promoting sustainable development (see **Rio Conference 1992**). Although academics have been studying it for more than half a century, there is no agreement on what development itself means. Most definitions of the term stress such features as urbanization, industrial development, higher standards of living, improved health care, a greater role in the global economy, and so on. Most lists of developing countries include all of Latin America, Africa, and most of Asia.

It is easy to see why observers believed in the trade-off in the following examples. The population in the world's poorest countries is growing more than three times as fast as in the richest ones. In **Nigeria** where the growth rate is nearly three per cent, the country's total population will double in less than 25 years. Egypt, which remains heavily dependent on the Nile River, adds a million people to its population every year. Put simply, population growth adds to the demand for food, housing, and other goods which, in turn, often have severe environmental consequences. The urban population in the Third World is growing even faster. The downtown, business area of a city like Nairobi or Rio de Janeiro may look a lot like that of New York or London. However, most people live in shanty-towns that do not even warrant being called slums. They live in shacks that do not have electricity, heat, or running water. Neighbourhoods typically lack proper sewerage facilities so that waste water becomes a breeding ground for diseases of all sorts.

Poor people in the Third World often have to make personal choices that adversely affect the environment. For instance, peasants in the Brazilian rainforests feel they have to cut down and burn trees in order to farm the land and feed their families. In so doing, not only do they add to the supply of greenhouse gases that contribute to **global warming**, but they worsen the problem of soil erosion since rainforest land is, in fact, not very fertile. What **industrialization** there has been has also had environmental consequences.

Thus, many 'first world' companies have exported their environmentally risky operations to the Third World. Most famous in this respect was the December 1984 gas leak at the Union Carbide factory in Bhopal, India (see **Bhopal disaster**). Within two weeks, more than 2,500 people were killed, and another 10,000 have died in the sixteen years since the accident. Bhopal was unusual only in the scale of the disaster. Third World countries normally have less restrictive environmental laws than are found in western Europe or North America. Furthermore, given their poverty, many such countries are willing to accept highly polluting enterprises for the simple reason that they provide employment. Thus, by 1990, Mexico had about 1,500 *maquiladora* factories dotting its border with the USA. Their workers assembled a range of goods including dolls and automobiles for export. Research has shown that local environmental conditions have deteriorated and the rate of diseases with environmental causes has rocketed.

There is reason to believe that environmental conditions could worsen in the foreseeable future given the now all but total shift to structural adjustment as the world's leading development strategy (see **structural adjustment programmes**). Put simply, the international financial community has pressured Third World and former communist governments to adopt policies that will integrate their countries as quickly as possible into the global capitalist market. These include privatizing industry, reducing government expenditure, cutting debt, and limiting economic regulations, including those regarding the environment. Also, the accumulation of wealth typically leads to increased consumption which, in turn, has environmental consequences. To see that, consider a simple question: what will happen to the environment as more than a billion Chinese get what the Japanese call the 'new three sacred treasures', a colour television, automobile, and air conditioning.

Finally, note that many of these problems overlap. To cite but the most obvious example, population growth is higher than average in most countries with significant **rainforests**, which means that deforestation is likely to occur at an ever faster rate in those regions that can afford it least. We should not, however, assume that the world's major environmental problems lie in the Third World. In fact, the industrialized countries are responsible for the lion's share of the world's environmental problems, including everything from solid-waste management to the production of greenhouse gases and the destruction of the ozone layer (see **ozone depletion**). In 1994, the USA poured nearly a billion tons of carbon dioxide into the atmosphere. By contrast, Brazil only produced a little over 300 million tons or well under 10 per cent of the US total.

It is no longer clear that there is a one-to-one relationship between development and environmental decay. No one denies that these environmental threats exist. However, there are alternatives looming on the world's political horizon, three of which are worth mentioning. The most obvious but perhaps least important of them is the growth of what some have labelled environmental resistance movements. Overall, the **environmental movement** in the West is probably not as strong as it was during its heyday in the 1970s and 1980s. In the Third World, however, such movements are growing, often in response to environmental threats and/or disasters. There is also some indirect evidence that environmental and other protesters have had an impact on some of the major international institutions. Despite the protests that shook Seattle and Washington DC in late 1999 and early 2000 respectively, the **World Bank** has been paying more attention to the environmental consequences of its development strategy since the early 1990s and now requires environmental impact statements for all its major projects. In 1999, 7 per cent of its lending went to projects aimed at improving the environment which made it the world's leading lender for such programmes.

Second is the work of the United Nations, other international organizations, and hundreds of NGOs which have not received the same publicity as the Bank or its critics. As has been the case on many other issues, the UN has played a major role in getting environmental issues onto the development agenda. The UN Environmental Programme today is one of the world's leading bodies supporting environmentally responsible development policies. The UN first discussed the environment seriously at the 1972 Conference on the Human Environment in Stockholm where the developing countries argued that the environment was a minor issue compared to their poverty. That began to change with the publication of *Our Common Future* (popularly known as the **Brundtland Commission**) in 1987. The most important event in this respect was the 1992 United Nations Conference on the Environment and Development in Rio de Janeiro which joined the two problems in the minds of many for the first time (see **Rio Conference 1992**). While many observers have been critical of the accomplishments at Rio and later summits, they did produce agreements to reduce greenhouse gas emissions and created the **Global Environment Facility** to help fund efforts to protect the ecosystem. Among the other international organizations, the **European Union** has taken the lead by tying environmental criteria to many of its grants to the Third World.

The central concept in this regard has been **sustainable development**. The idea was first put forward by E.F. Schumacher in the 1970s and became the centrepiece of the Brundtland Report and the agreements reached at Rio and subsequent meetings. Sustainable development calls for integrated strategies for economic growth that do not damage the world's supply of natural resources or the ecosystem. Since Rio, noticeable progress has been made in some areas, including population growth and food production. However, world leaders have barely made a dent in solving some of the most worrying environmental problems (especially the emission of greenhouse gases) or eroding the poverty in much of the Third World.

Finally, the most recent 'hot' development strategy may also have positive implications for the environment. Muhammad Yunus, a professor of economics at Chittagong University in Bangladesh, created the Grameen Bank in 1976. Grameen and other microcredit lenders offer very small loans. In **Bangladesh**, almost all of those loans go to women and average about $35. The women then form their own small businesses, for instance, making rattan stools. Well over 99 per cent of the loans are repaid giving the microcredit institutions more capital to generate more loans. Meanwhile the borrowers develop businesses and skills that allow them to pull themselves out of poverty. Microcredit institutions now exist in over 50 countries – including the USA – and Grameen itself has expanded to provide cell phone and internet service to villages which would otherwise be cut off from the electronic world. Given the size of the loans, it is hard to see how these microbusinesses could damage the environment

See also: appropriate technology; business and the environment; capitalism; ecological economics; environmental economics; ozone depletion; social economy, informal economic activity in; sustainable development; United Nations Environment Programme

Further reading

Cairncross, F. (1995) *Green, Inc*, London: Earthscan.

Durning, A. (1992) *How Much is Enough: The Consumer Society and the Future of the Earth*, New York: W.W. Norton.

World Commission on Environment and Development (1987) *Our Common Future*, New York: Oxford University Press.

Stone, R.D. (1992) *The Nature of Development*, New York: Knopf.

Virtual Library on Sustainable Development, at URL: http://www.ulb.ac.be/ceese/meta/sustvl.html.

CHARLES HAUSS

dioxins

The chemical usually referred to as dioxin is 2,4,7,8-tetrachlorodibenzo-p-dioxin (TCDD), the most toxic of the family of chlorinated dioxins. Dioxins can be produced as unintended byproducts of processes such as pesticide manufacture, bleaching of paper products, and incineration. TCDD's reputation as 'most toxic substance known to humankind' reflects its extreme toxicity in laboratory animals, and has guaranteed political controversy wherever dioxin has been detected, including the **Love Canal** toxic waste dump, a chemical plant explosion in Seveso Italy (see **Seveso disaster**), and dioxin-contaminated herbicides used during the Vietnam war. The extent of dioxin's toxicity to humans has long been con-

tested, however. In 1997 the International Agency for Research on Cancer declared TCDD to be a known human carcinogen. A draft review of dioxin released by the US **Environmental Protection Agency** in 2000 also expressed concern about the potential for reproductive, developmental, and immunological effects.

KATHRYN HARRISON

disenchantment of nature

'Disenchantment of nature' is a phrase used by and associated with ecological critics and writers to describe the way nature, particularly in the western world, has increasingly become ethically and spiritually empty. Historically, the term is related to Max Weber's claim that instrumental rationality (especially as exemplified by economics, science and technology) and the **Enlightenment** is incompatible with a view of nature as anything more than a collection of resources for human beings. In essence what the disenchantment of nature conveys is the sense that the natural world has changed from being a realm of *meaning* for humans to being a set of *means*, and that this is something which is not only to be regretted but also dangerous. It is particularly associated with **deep ecology**, **eco-centrism**, and **Romanticism**, and is often used in conjunction with or as the basis for arguments about the desirability or necessity of re-enchanting nature to create a more sustainable society.

JOHN BARRY

distributive justice

Distributive justice, or social justice as it is also known, is usually defined as being about the fair distribution of benefits and burdens in society. Much of the debate turns on the meaning of 'fairness', and it is worth pointing out that fairness does not necessarily mean 'equal shares': a fair society can be an unequal one if we believe that some people deserve more than others – because they work harder, for example.

The nature of 'benefits and burdens' varies too.

We might normally think of them in terms of money, prestige or the like. In recent times we have been made aware by the **environmental justice** movement that benefits and burdens can have an environmental component – a landfill site is an environmental burden, for example, while a clean beach is an environmental benefit. The environmental justice movement is organized around the observation that poor people live in poor environments – in other words, that environmental benefits and burdens are unfairly distributed in society.

The environmental agenda has given rise to another set of questions concerning the nature of the *bona fide* distributors and recipients of social justice. Paradigmatically, justice is predicated only of human beings, which is to say that only human beings can properly be regarded as distributors and recipients of justice. This is because, so supporters of this view say, only human beings possess the necessary qualities of sentience and rationality that can lead to a sense of justice in the first place, and because only human beings can act with reciprocity towards one another – a further condition for 'justice' to be predicated on the participating parties. All of these 'preconditions for justice' have led to fiery debate over whether the idea of justice to future generations of human beings, or **intergenerational justice**, makes any sense.

Inevitably, given the political potency of 'justice' as a rallying cry, environmentalists have called into question the 'rationality, sentience and reciprocity' preconditions for entry into the community of justice. They will accept that only human beings can properly be regarded as *distributors* of justice, for obvious reasons, but will wonder whether the community of *recipients* might not be widened to include at least some non-human animals and even perhaps the non-human natural world more broadly. Are factory-farmed animals victims of injustice? And if so, what about deforested trees?

One way to admit beings other than human beings to the community of justice is to ascribe to them rights, on the basis that justice is a matter of rights recognition (Feinberg, 1981). Then the question becomes one of whether we can ascribe rights to animals – and beyond (see **animal rights**). These debates nearly always involve

developing a list of characteristics for membership, and those who would deny animals the possession rights or membership of the community of justice will say that animals do not possess those characteristics. Supporters of the idea of rights or justice for animals, though, will employ the metaphor of the continuum rather than the boundary, and point to the 'limit cases' where some human beings, through illness or other incapacity, find themselves possessing fewer of the characteristics that would admit them to the community of justice than is 'normally' the case. If, despite this, we grant them justice, it would be 'speciesist' to deny it to similarly equipped non-human animals. Ted Benton (1993) adds a further criterion for determining whether non-human animals can be recipients of justice – whether our social and productive needs involve us in relations with animals. If they do – as in agriculture – then our relations with them can properly be regarded as relations of justice, and **factory farming** then becomes unjust as well as immoral.

Those who deny that justice can be predicated on the non-human world do not conclude that 'anything goes' as far as our relationship with it is concerned, but they argue that this relationship should be regulated by broader moral considerations, rather than by the more specific rules and conditions associated with justice. Thus one can oppose cruelty to animals, or deforestation, or species loss, without admitting animals, trees, or species other than the human one to the community of justice. If nothing else, the issues raised by environmentalists in connection with justice show that Michael Walzer was absolutely right when he wrote that, 'The community itself is a good – conceivably the most important good – that gets distributed' (Walzer, 1983: 29).

References

Benton, T. (1993) *Natural Relations*, London: Verso.

Feinberg, J. (1981) 'The Rights of Animals and Unborn Generations', in E. Partridge (ed.) *Responsibilites to Future Generations*, New York: Prometheus Books.

Walzer, M. (1983) *Spheres of Justice*, Oxford: Blackwell.

Further reading

Dobson, A. (1998) *Justice and the Environment*, Oxford: Oxford University Press.

Low, N.P. and Gleeson, B.J. (1998) *Justice, Society and Nature: An Exploration of Political Ecology*, London: Routledge.

Wenz, P.S. (1988) *Environmental Justice*, New York: State University of New York Press.

ANDREW DOBSON

doomsayers

'Doomsayers' is a general term applied to prophets of doom. More narrowly, it is a derogatory term applied to environmental scientists who warn of potential global catastrophe due to 'overshoot': exceeding ecological carrying capacity limits, human overpopulation, resource depletion, and related issues. Examples of classic doomsayer literature include the writings of Thomas **Malthus**, Rachel **Carson**, and Paul **Ehrlich**. The doomsayer label was given to the Club of Rome's report ***Limits to Growth*** and the *Report to the President (Carter) on the Year 2000*. Anti-environmental critics include individuals, such as the late Herman Kahn, and groups such as the so-called **wise-use movement**. Kahn, for example, argued that resource substitution and technological advances would continue to expand the global carrying capacity. Doomsayer status has also been given to atmospheric scientists and climatologists warning of **global warming** and to international bodies such as the International Panel on Climate Change.

See also: anti-environmentalism

Further reading

Ehrlich, P. and Ehrlich A. (1996) *Betrayal of Science and Reason*, Washington, DC: Island Press.

CHRISTOPHER B. JONES

Douglas, William O.

b. 16 October 1898, Maine, Minnesota, USA; d. 19 January 1980, Washington, DC

Supreme Court Justice and preservationist

William O. Douglas, a member of the US Supreme Court from 1938 to 1975, was one of his country's leading supporters of land and wildlife preservation in the post-Second World War era. A life-long hiker and camper, Douglas early in his career advocated a utilitarian view of conservation, but gradually came to espouse the preservationist philosophy most closely identified with John **Muir**. An author of several books on the preservation of wild places, Douglas became an internationally known spokesperson for wilderness values. He also wrote a number of Supreme Court opinions, most notably a dissent in ***Sierra Club v. Morton*** (1972), which were firmly on the side of nature.

Further reading

Douglas, W.O. (1972) *The Three Hundred Year War: A Chronicle of Ecological Disaster*, New York: Random House.

WARREN VANDER HILL

Dumont, René

b. 13 March 1904, Cambrai, France; d. 18 June 2001

Agronomist, politician

Through his research projects and lectures in **France** and all over the world (especially in Third World countries) since the 1930s he has developed a critical approach to the productivist model of **agriculture**. He gradually moved towards ecology, with a growing concern for sustainable management of natural resources, for demographic balances. A committed scientist, he militated in favour of human rights and social justice. Though a declared socialist, opposed to bureaucracy and in favour of self-management, he became one of the most faithful supporters of an autonomous political **ecology**. In 1974, he was the first ecologist candidate for a presidential election (1.34 per cent). Under the heading 'L'écologie ou la mort', his manifesto launched the movement for political ecology in France. Since then, he supported every green party's electoral campaign. He developed an unyielding analysis of liberal logics, giving priority to the defence of Third World countries.

BRUNO VILLALBA

Dust Bowl

The Dust Bowl is the common name for the environmental catastrophe of the 1920s and 1930s that launched North American environmental consciousness on a large scale. Farmers in the US Great Plains introduced iron-bladed ploughs and power equipment between 1910 and 1925. This new technology turned heavy sod soils that were not tillable with wooden ploughs and draught animals. Widespread exposure of tilled soils combined with low rainfall in the 1920s to cause extensive wind erosion, massive loss of topsoil and widespread displacement of the farming population. The connection between human and environmental tragedy became profoundly etched in the American mind. Songs and stories of the Dust Bowl era reinforce the idea that keeping small-scale farmers on the land is vital to environmentally sound agriculture. Ironically, the Dust Bowl has subsequently been analysed as a case of inadequate market-based incentives for conservation, implying that wide landholdings were partially responsible for the event.

Further reading

Steinbeck, J. (1972) *The Grapes of Wrath*, ed. and annotated by P. Lisca, New York: Viking Press.
Worster, D. (1979) *The Dust Bowl: The Southern Plains in the 1930s*, New York: Oxford University Press.

PAUL B. THOMPSON

Dutch National Environmental Policy Plan

In 1989, the first Dutch *National Environmental Policy Plan* (NMP 1) was issued. It was innovative because it contained the first fully integrated and strategic long term environmental plan in which the Dutch government formulated the main components of environmental policy: the strategy, goals and the measures to be taken in the 1990–4 period. The starting point of the NMP 1 was the **Brundtland** definition of **sustainable development**: a development that provides for the needs of the present generation without compromising the possibilities of future generations to provide for their needs.

In order to cope with environmental problems within the timespan of one generation (20–25 years), a comprehensive and integral approach on the basis of a long term strategy was seen as necessary. Three main premises were seen as essential to an **ecological modernization** of society: the closing of natural resource cycles, reduction of energy use and the stimulation of quality over quantity.

In order to realize these goals, special attention was given to the overall implementation process of environmental policy, the issuing of systematic measures in those fields where policy had been unsuccessful (e.g., waste disposal, **water pollution**, and dispersion of heavy metals), and future sustainable forms of production and consumption. The acknowledgement of the seriousness of environmental problems also forced the Dutch government to start systematic action on an international level: initiatives were taken on a European and world level.

The central ideas behind the NMP 1 were self-regulative behaviour by target groups (*doelgroepenbeleid*), internalization of ecological responsibilities (*verinnerlijking*), and the creation of new financial and social policy instruments. The government set the environmental goals, but trade and industry were held responsible for realizing the targets on the basis of self-regulation. Citizens, intermediary organizations (**civil society**) and local governments were assumed to take their own responsibilities with regard to the environment, to 'internalize' environmental values and principles and to act accordingly. A start was made by implementing the 'polluter pays principle'. Apart from issuing comparatively strict environmental laws and regulations, various financial incentives (**eco-taxes**) were introduced to promote environmentally friendly behaviour. A comprehensive action programme with a list of more than 200 action points completed these measures.

In 1990, the Dutch *National Environmental Policy Plan-plus* (NMP-plus) was published, containing a series of policy intensifications and an extension of the environmental action programme. In 1993, the second Dutch *National Environmental Policy Plan* (NMP 2) was launched, containing the strategy for environmental policy for the medium long range, 1995–8. It also proposed measures to implement **Agenda 21** and the decisions taken at the United Nations Conference on Environment and Development (see **Rio Conference 1992**). New and more stringent environmental goals were formulated, in particular in the field of climate change and acidification.

In 1998, the third Dutch *National Environmental Policy Plan* (NMP 3) was issued. Here, the focus was on the greenhouse effect and the consequences for environmental policy of the climate conference in Kyoto. Actual steps were taken to further improve energy efficiency in trade and industry, to reduce overall air, water, and land pollution, and to stimulate environmentally benign patterns of consumption and production.

The Dutch National Environmental Policy Plans led to a considerable improvement of air, water and land quality in the Netherlands. The dispersal of heavy metals, for example, has been drastically restricted, **air pollution** has been reduced, and energy efficiency has improved by more than 10 per cent over the last decade.

Despite these hopeful developments, the Dutch Institute of Public Health and Environmental Protection (RIVM) concluded in its National Environmental Outlooks that in the Netherlands numerous environmental problems are still underestimated, such as the distribution of dangerous substances, drought resulting from sinking groundwater and most of all CO_2 emissions. In addition, the RIVM confirmed that a large number of the effects of current Dutch environmental policy are nullified by unanticipated developments, such as economic growth, population growth and a general increase in energy use and mobility.

See also: ecological modernization; Netherlands, the; polluter pays principle; sustainable development

Further reading

Dutch Committee for Long-Term Environmental Policy, (1994) *The Environment: Towards a Sustainable Future*, London: Kluwer Academic Publishers.

Minister van VROM, (1989) *Nationaal Milieubeleidsplan 1*, Den Haag: SDU.

—— (1990) *Nationaal Milieubeleidsplan-plus*, Den Haag: SDU.

—— (1993) *Nationaal Milieubeleidsplan 2*, Den Haag: SDU.

—— (1998) *Nationaal Milieubeleidsplan 3*, Den Haag: SDU.

—— *Nota Milieu en Economie*, Den Haag: VROM.

Rijks Institute for Public Health and Environmental Hygiene (1989) *Concern for Tomorrow*, Bilthoven: RIVM.

MARIUS DE GEUS

E

Earth Day

The first Earth Day was observed in the USA on 22 April 1970 when many local and national environmental activists turned out on American college campuses to celebrate Mother Earth. It was the brainchild of Senator Gaylord Nelson of Wisconsin, who used the model of anti-war teach-ins that had gained popularity in the 1960s. Other politicians gave speeches and helped to gain media attention for the event. Out of this first Earth Day came Environmental Action, an organization dedicated to keeping alive the spirit of that day. Earth Day has been observed every year since 1970 by activists holding celebrations and demonstrations on most college campuses around the USA. As the movement grew, additional office holders have joined the festivities of the day by making speeches to demonstrate their concern for the environment. School children undertake such activities as cleaning up littered highways and streams and rivers and planting trees and native species of wildflowers.

LETTIE McSPADDEN

Earth First! (UK)

Earth First! (UK) is a loose network of direct-action activists inspired by **Earth First! (US)**. The network has been particularly active in the wider UK **anti-roads movements** and espouses a discourse combining elements of both **social ecology** and **deep ecology**. It has been strongly influenced by anarcho-communist ideas (Wall, 1999).

Earth First! (UK) was launched by two further-education students, Jake Burbridge and Jason Torrance in 1991. Disillusioned after involvement in the **Green Party UK** and **Greenpeace** they aimed to promote deep ecology ideas and direct action to protect the environment. Their first campaign targeted **rainforest** destruction and along with allies in the Green Student Network they occupied a number of timber yards. From 1992 to the late 1990s Earth First! was involved in campaigns to halt motorway construction at Twyford Down in Hampshire, Pollok in Glasgow, Newbury in Berkshire and other sites. The Earth First!'s Reclaim the Streets (RTS) campaign was used to create street parties where existing roads were occupied by activists. The largest street party in 1996 saw nearly 8,000 individuals fill a London motorway.

During the late 1990s, RTS which had become a separate body within the network promoted large anti-capitalist actions in co-operation with **Peoples' Global Action**, a worldwide alliance of grassroots environmental and social justice organizations. The J18 event in 1999 saw thousands of activists in the financial heart of London causing thousands of pounds worth of damage (Freedland, 1999). Earth First! and RTS activists also participated in action against the **World Trade Organization** agenda talks in Seattle in 1999. Earth First! and RTS have also used direct action to campaign against the arms trade, nuclear power and weapons, housing on greenfield sites and genetically modified crops (see **genetic engineering, crops**).

Earth First! has sought to build links with working-class movements from the onset. During the 1990s the network created joint campaigns with sacked Liverpool Dockers, health workers and underground train drivers. In 1997 a social justice protest was organized by union activists and RTS to coincide with the General Election. Earth First! (UK) has rejected the misanthropic approach of Edward **Abbey** and other early inspirers of its US equivalent, adopting a clear anti-capitalist analysis of ecological ills. Yet ideological debate has been of secondary importance to Earth First! (UK) which has emphasized its commitment to direct action and loose organizational structure. Its repertoires of direct action have been disruptive including mass non-violent civil disobedience and **monkey-wrenching** (physical sabotage). See also **non-violent direct action**.

Activists have jumped onto construction equipment, tunnelled underneath sites and built tree-top villages on planned motorway routes (Doherty, 1999). Earth First! has utilized music and the arts to build protests as part of a wider DIY movement which has linked in youth cultures based round vibrant forms of dance music. Earth First! is very loosely organized. It has no headquarters, officials or office. It does not produce policy statements and has no formal membership. Its only 'institutions' are a newsletter, the 'Action Update' that reports on protest events, a fascinating theoretical journal 'Do or Die!' and annual national gatherings that attract around 500 participants. Local Earth First! groups are best conceptualized as networks of local activists drawn from a range of local protest groups who mobilize against particular threats or events. The national network largely dissolved into the wider anti-roads movement of the 1990s and remains fragile. Earth First! has acted as a catalyst for an impressive mobilization of direct action and has radicalized British green politics through its articulations with environmental pressure groups and the Green Party. It has made creative links with a range of groups including youth cultures, residents' organizations and trade union militants.

Yet it is rather more a sensibility about what radical environmental politics is than an institution.

While Earth First! (UK) can be conceptualized as the modern prince of revolutionary green politics it resembles more the taste of salt in salt water than a vanguard party.

References

Doherty, B. (1999) 'Manufactured Vulnerability: Eco-Activist Tactics in Britain', *Mobilization*, 4(1): 75–89.

Freedland, J. (1999) 'The Theatre of Riot', *The Guardian*, 23 June: 15.

Wall, D. (1999) *Earth First! and the Anti-Roads Movement*, London: Routledge.

Further reading

Earth First! at URL: http.www.eco-action.org/efau.

Reclaim the Streets at URL: http://www.gn.apc.org/rts/.

DEREK WALL

Earth First! (US)

Earth First! is a non-governmental organization established in the USA in 1980 by disillusioned members of several more mainstream environmental groups. They believed that their old organizations were not effective because they were too willing to compromise with industry and government. The organizing principle of Earth First! is to remain on the radical edge of environmental issues to push other groups further toward **deep ecology**. Its members do not use traditional methods of influencing policy-makers through lobbying legislatures and suing in court. Rather, they have adopted direct action tactics labelled by their critics as **eco-terrorism**. For example, members have been arrested and accused of spiking logging roads and trees designated to be cut, damaging power lines, and sabotaging heavy equipment left at construction sites overnight.

Earth First! has no national headquarters; it consists of various informal groups around the USA who recognize no office holders or hierarchy. Each local group determines its own targets and its own tactics. It publishes a newsletter *Earth First!* sporadically, informing its adherents of various projects undertaken or completed by local chapters. Dave Foreman, a staffer in the Wilderness Society, helped to found it after the Carter Administration failed to accomplish its environmental goals. He argued that even when officers of mainstream organizations were included in the administration, they had little impact because they become co-opted and accustomed to their status and incomes. Foreman wrote a guide to **monkeywrenching** in 1985, but he left the organization in 1990 to start a new journal, *Wild Earth*, because he felt the group was losing its connection to its Deep Ecology roots and becoming too anthropocentric (see **anthropocentrism**).

Different chapters have become involved in such projects as protecting the grizzly bear, arguing for the destruction of Glen Canyon Dam, and protecting Harp Seal pups, whales, and other species from their hunters. Edward **Abbey**, Earth First!'s unofficial godfather, wrote several books in his lifetime in which he described the actions of fictional activist groups that may or may not have been loosely based on reality. Earth First! holds an annual rendezvous in summer where they discuss what tactics have been successful. They claim that they are more successful than they appear in the media, because industry hesitates to report their sabotage out of a desire to avoid giving them more publicity.

References

Foreman, D. (1985) *Ecodefense: A Field Guide to Monkeywrenching*, Tucson, AZ: Ned Ludd Books.

LETTIE McSPADDEN

East and Central Europe

Since the collapse of **communism** (1989), East and Central Europe (ECE) has undergone a complex process of political, economic and social transition. There is no simple one-to-one relationship between the end of communism, the transition process and improvements in ambient quality and environmental management. Transition differs between countries due to different experiences

under communism and diversity in cultural, religious and ethnic make up. The transition process in the Balkans is less stable than in the Visegrad countries, in terms of turnover rates of post-communist governments, public acceptance of change, strength of the communist successor parties and commitment to economic and political reforms. The wars in the former Yugoslavia have contributed to instability in the Balkan region.

Political reforms have enhanced **environmental management** capacity, particularly at the formal level. New environmental units within ministries, monitoring bodies and environmental agencies have been formed, often in response to the demands of international agencies. Environmental legislation has been strengthened (for example, the Bulgarian Environmental Protection Act (1991); the Hungarian national environmental framework law (1992)). Furthermore, reforms have given regional and local government a greater role in policy formulation and implementation. The participation of environmental interest groups in governmental-level environmental fora is leading to more openness and accountability. Democratization, in particular the consolidation of party politics, has opened new political arenas to environmentalists. However, substantive change remains slow. Policy implementation continues to suffer from bottlenecks. Many of the new environmental acts passed in the aftermath of the collapse of communism were poorly prepared and have subsequently required amendments. Lack of progress in reforming regional and local government in some countries, and insufficient expertise and resources in others, impedes more effective environmental governance. Green activists in positions of power in post-communist governments found their hands tied by pressing economic and political considerations and by the limitations of being in coalition governments. Despite the role played by the **environmental movement** in bringing an end to communism (especially in Bulgaria), environmental concerns are now channelled through professional NGOs (see **international non-governmental organizations**). However, participation by NGOs in the policy-making process remains limited.

Similarly, the environmental impact of economic restructuring is complex. On one hand, marketization is exposing domestic firms to the rigour of the market, forcing them to reduce energy and other resource use. Marketization also widens the range of policy tools available to governments. Privatization has forced many countries to clarify their laws and practices on environmental liability. It has led to the penetration of ecologically modernizing foreign firms, in turn contributing to the acceptance of environmental norms within domestic business practices. More generally, economic re-structuring has resulted in the collapse of industrial production, reducing the high pollution levels in the region. However, here there is a danger that future upturns in the economy will result in a return to the old environmentally damaging ways. On the other hand, economic reform is proving problematic. In many countries, such as Bulgaria, privatization has often been into the hands of the old *nomenclatura*, which have a history of eschewing environmental regulations. In addition, new sources of environmental pressures are emerging, including from increased consumerism, such as growth in private-car ownership. The emergence of a *nouveau riche* class, organized crime and the concentration of wealth into the hands of the old *nomenclatura* through privatization programmes has the potential to threaten the environmental gains won by transition.

Since 1989, many countries in the region have signed Association Agreements with the **European Union** (EU). Preparation for membership of the EU is now the key external factor shaping environmental policy in ECE. Association countries must adopt the *acquis communautaire* of the EU, ensure that policy is guided by the principle of **sustainable development** and meet certain EU norms and standards regarding the conduct, implementation and monitoring of policy. Association Agreements have released funding, through the Phare programme, to help with environmental clean up. The 'Environment for Europe' process, which resulted in the Environmental Action Programme for Central and Eastern Europe, provides the concrete framework for guiding national action and international assistance programmes on the environment in preparation for the EU's eastern enlargement.

Further reading

Baker, S. and Jehlika, P. (eds) (1998) *Dilemmas of Transition: The Environment, Democracy and Economic Reform in East Central Europe*, London: Frank Cass.

Carter, N. and Turnock, D. (eds) (1993) *Environmental Problems in Eastern Europe*, London: Routledge.

Henderson, K. (ed.) (1999) *Back to Europe: Central and Eastern Europe and the European Union*, London: University College London Press

Pickles J. and Smith, A. (eds) (1999) *Theorizing Transition: The Political Economy of Post-Communist Transformations*, London: Routledge.

SUSAN BAKER

East and Central European Greens

The environmental legacy of eastern Europe's communist regimes and their role in the anti-communist revolutions seemed to provide Greens with an opportunity for success. This early optimism was not realized due to the co-option of issues by major parties, their fractious organizations, and the voters' prioritization of material concerns. The Greens may yet emerge as national actors as these countries politically mature based on their continued local activism, but the apparent move to the right in much of eastern Europe may forestall this.

The Polish Party of Greens was the first one to emerge in eastern Europe in 1988. The party's membership and policies originate with the Polish Ecology Club, established in 1980, and Solidarity. The party's congress in June 1989 seemed to unify hundreds of environmental groups, but this apparent unity vanished after its dismal 1989 electoral showing and most members returned to the pre-existing groups. By 1990, the movement seemed destined to vanish when the then three green parties fragmented into over 140 organizations. This situation arose due to the parties' limited support base, their factionalism, and the misappropriation of the green label by 'fake' groups. Another factor was public political disaffection, which is now a general trait among eastern Europe's voters who seem to be 'party tourists' lacking in loyalty and knowledge (Olson, 1999:18–19).

In late 1990, the Greens' fortunes seemed to be improving after electing 120 local officials and unifying as the Polish Greens. This was the party's climax until 1997 when it re-entered the national scene as part of the Democratic Left Alliance. The Polish Greens' impact was twofold. First, the party highlighted environmental problems prompting the government to implement a variety of progressive policies including industrial anti-pollution standards, the preventive Green Lungs of Poland, and cleanup of the **Black Triangle** region. These advances have prompted the party to promote a broader policy agenda including gender equality, youth issues, and enhanced regulations. Second, the Greens have invigorated local activism due to their broad-based membership and salient issues. Such activism is exemplified by the creation of the Green Electoral Committee in Krakow to promote changes in municipal policies and public involvement.

The Hungarian Green Party, which was founded in 1989, drew impetus from the creation of the Blue **Danube Circle** (BDC) in the early 1980s by young professionals opposed to the Hungarian–Czechoslovakian Gabcikovo–Nagymaros dam. The BDC used publications and public gatherings to heighten awareness about the dam's ecological consequences. The continuous pressure from the BDC and other organizations led to the creation of the first East European Environment Ministry, the establishment of an Independent Ecological Centre, and withdrawal from the dam project.

The Greens' success in changing policy and public opinion failed to bring electoral success in the 1990s. Their political fortunes dissipated after the withdrawal from the dam project with the party failing to crack the one per cent threshold as it fragmented into fundamentalists and 'watermelons' (green-shaded communists). Similar to other East European Greens, the electoral threshold hindered the party's efforts as well as the greening of major parties like the Hungarian Democratic Forum. This transparent greenness seems to appease an electorate uninterested in environmental issues without the dam. Similar to Poland, the Hungarian Greens may yet emerge as a local political force, but their national fortunes seem limited.

The Czechoslovakian Green Party, founded in 1990, drew from a rich pool of environmental and progressive groups dating to the 1970s including the Brontosaurus Movement, the Slovak Union of Landscape and Nature Protectors, and Charter 77. This foundation inspired the rise of four green parties in November 1989 (Bohemia, Moravia–Silesia, Slovakia, and a Prague-based party created by the secret police). Despite their differences, the three regional parties united as the Green Circle within the anti-communist movement which resulted in their gaining parliamentary seats. The new organization continued its unifying efforts as well as publicizing the ecological devastation left by **communism**. These efforts contributed to the union of the three regional parties and other groups as the Czechoslovakian Greens prior to the 1990 elections. This meteoric rise was due to public support for green inclusion in the transition and widespread support for their issues.

The Czechoslovakian Greens were unable to translate their appeal and issues into electoral success. The Greens failed to gain seats in either the federal or Czech legislatures, but they did obtain six seats in the Slovak National Council. Their dismal showing was again due to the co-option of green issues by the major parties (especially the Civic Forum), factionalism, fears of communist infiltrators, and public interest in 'real' issues like the economy and the union's future. Although there were some notable local successes, the Greens sought to revive their fortunes through finding coalition partners. These efforts led to their obtaining over 900 local posts by mid-1991.

The rapid, post-revolution deterioration of Czech–Slovak relations affected the Greens. In federal and Czech politics, the coalition drive (e.g., the 1991–2 Liberal and Social Union) garnered representation for them in both legislatures after the 1992 elections. The Slovak Green Party eschewed coalitions, but still gained similar electoral totals of around six per cent. Since the 1993 division of the country the Czech Greens have vanished from the national scene with electoral results barely at one per cent. But the Greens continue to be active in local politics, especially in heavily polluted Bohemia. In Slovakia, the Greens have not improved their standing despite victories like the stoppage of the renewed Danube dam project. Their fate now rests with the Movement for a Democratic Slovakia coalition which they joined in 1994 as their local influence has declined.

The emergence of Bulgaria's Greens under-scores the delegitimizing role that environmental problems had on the communist regimes. The **Bulgarian Green Party** emerged from illegal anti-pollution protests around Ruse in 1988 and the group Ecoglasnost was created in 1989 to draw attention to environmental problems. Despite official repression, Ecoglasnost and its cause were used by reformers within the country to eventually bring down the regime. In late 1989, Ecoglasnost unified its efforts with other green groups including the Party of Green Masses and the Green Party of Bulgaria. Ecoglasnost retained its premier position in the movement directing the green efforts within the anti-communist Union of Democratic Forces (UDF) in the 1990 elections, which resulted in it gaining 19 seats and the Green Party 13 seats.

The green rise was short-lived as the UDF fractured, leading to their disappearance from parliament in 1991. Ecoglasnost's fortunes rapidly deteriorated and the Green Party assumed the mantle of the movement, which by now had little popular support outside pollution concerns. In the 1997 parliamentary elections, the party gained one seat sustaining its national presence. The Greens' early vigor seems to have faded with the distance from the revolution, but they retain some urban support especially in Sofia.

The Romanian Greens have a brief history due to the repressive Ceaucescu regime though environ-mental concerns were publicized by the Democratic Action Movement in the 1980s. The Greens failed to coalesce until after Ceaucescu's execution when the Romanian Ecological Party (REP), the Ecologi-cal Humanist Party, and the Romanian Ecological Movement (REM) were formed. REM was a front for the new regime's efforts to co-opt the environ-mental cause, which also included the creation of an Environment Ministry. The 1990 elections did heighten public awareness about the country's environmental woes especially the Danube's pollu-tion. The elections also brought the REM 12 seats in the lower house and 3 seats in the senate plus the Environment Minister. The eclipsed REP won eight seats in the lower house as part of the short-lived Democratic Convention of Romania.

In December 1990, the two green parties joined with others in the National Convention for the Establishment of Reform and Democracy to oppose the government. This coalition collapsed in January 1992 prior to elections, which cost both parties their national representation and left the REM with modest local representation. This decline continued through the 1996 elections though again green causes, such as the Danube restoration programme, were utilized by the main parties to win votes.

Green parties and movements have appeared elsewhere in eastern Europe, but with overall minimal impact. Strife-ridden Albania has a public disgusted with politics, which has prevented the Green Party of Albania from moving beyond its paper founding. Albania's economic deterioration and inclusion in the post-Yugoslav conflicts pre-clude positive developments for the foreseeable future. Prior to its collapse, Yugoslavia was the site of numerous green organizations including the Association of Croatian Greens, Green Action Zagreb, the Belgrade Ecological Movement, and the Greens of Sarajevo. The resulting nationalistic violence undermined support for the Greens except in Slovenia. Greens in Croatia and Serbia may yet re-emerge, but they barely register as potential actors in Montenegro, Bosnia/Herzego-vina, and Macedonia.

The 1989 creation of the Greens of Slovenia, which later merged into the Green Party of Slovenia, represented the fruition of 1960s envir-onmental activism. This popular environmental awareness provided fertile ground for numerous green groups to form especially around Ljubljana. In December 1989, the Greens joined the United Democratic Opposition of Slovenia, which success-fully ran in the 1990 elections. For their efforts, the Greens received eight parliamentary seats and three ministerial posts. The party's environmental concerns continued to resonate with the public, but its fortunes faded as the people prioritized economic development and European integration.

By 1994, the Greens had slipped to two seats and no ministerial posts, and, by 1995, the party had begun to fragment with the emergence of the radical Green Alternative. The Greens have retained their environmental connections and local political visibility, but their primary role seems to be that of environmental conscience.

Reference

Olson, D. (1999) 'New Wine in Old Institutions: Parliaments in Post-communist Democracies', *Problems of Post-Communism* 46(1):15–23.

Further reading

Cole, D. (1998) *Instituting Environmental Protection: From Red to Green in Poland*, New York: St Martin's Press.

Frankland, E. (1995) 'Green Revolutions?: The Role of Green Parties in Eastern Europe's Transition, 1989–1994', *East European Quarterly* 29(3) :315–45.

Gobethner, S. (1997) 'Free Elections and Political Parties in Transition to Democracy in Central and Eastern Europe', *International Political Science Review* 18(4):381–99.

Ramet, S. (1991) *Social Currents in Eastern Europe: The Sources and Meaning of the Great Transformation*, Durham, NC: Duke University Press.

ERICH G. FRANKLAND

East and Central European nuclear power industry

Nuclear industry in central and eastern Europe started developing under specific political, economic and technological premises. The countries of that region – GDR (East Germany), Poland, Czechoslovakia, Hungary, Romania and Bulgaria had been part of the Soviet-dominated bloc since the end of the Second World War. The Baltic countries – Lithuania, Latvia, and Estonia – had been incorporated into the USSR.

Therefore nuclear industry emerged as part of a centralized planned economy. The build-up of nuclear power stations was subordinated to Communist Party led 5-year-planning, and, the nuclear power industry took the form of state-owned enterprises under administrative control of both the ruling party and the government.

The nuclear industry in east–central and eastern Europe was based almost entirely on Soviet reactor technology. It depended on fuel supply initially from the USSR, and after 1991 from the **Russian Federation**. While the development of nuclear power in the former Soviet Union always served both military and industrial purposes, the build-up of nuclear power stations in the central east European countries was restricted to civilian usage only. According to the Non-Proliferation Treaty, none of the Soviet dominated central east European nations ever acquired any nuclear warhead capacity.

The implementation of civilian nuclear power in central and eastern Europe was part of an ambitious, long-term **nuclear energy** programme agreed within the Soviet-led economic zone of COMECON. To reach this goal a joint reactor building industry with high degrees of specialization for parts and components had to be created resulting in a conveyer-line production of pressurized water reactors on the Volgodonsk plant model. Because of the intrinsic shortcomings of centralized planned economies of the Soviet block these over-ambitious dreams failed to materialize.

Nevertheless in east–central Europe a certain number of nuclear power stations came under construction. They were based on Russian PWR (Pressurized Water Reactors); most of the stations were equipped with the type WWER-440 MW. Some of them had been commissioned during the 1970s and 1980s: 'Kozloduj' in Bulgaria; 'Paks' in Hungary; 'Bohunice' and 'Dukovany' in Czechoslovakia; 'Rheinsberg' and 'Lubmin' in east Germany. In Lithuania the huge nuclear power complex at Ignalina, based on two 1500 MW reactors of the RBMK (Chernobyl)-type became operational in 1985. The production of electricity by nuclear power ranged from 10 per cent in east Germany to 50 per cent in Lithuania. Poland and Romania planned nuclear stations as well, although they continued to rely heavily on national coal, oil and natural gas resources.

The accident at **Chernobyl** in April 1986

tragically revealed two essential safety features lacking in Soviet nuclear technology: concrete-built containment and reliable control equipment. In eastern Europe – under Perestroika and Glasnost – this experience of nuclear risk triggered heated anti-nuclear debates and stirred up public distrust at using Soviet nuclear power – most notably in Lithuania.

The collapse of **communism** in east–central Europe in 1989/90 led to new political realities and economic structures. Consequently, plans introducing nuclear industry in Poland and expanding it in east Germany were abandoned. Czechoslovakia halted construction of the 'Temelin' Soviet-designed reactor blocks, whereas Romania completed its 'Cernovoda' nuclear power station based on Canadian technology.

During the 1990s the central and eastern European countries underwent economic reform, accompanied by a decline in gross national product. This in turn led to a reduced need for power generation by nuclear reactors. At the same time substantial western technical aid was given to improve the safety of the existing nuclear power plants

Nuclear energy in east–central Europe seems to retain its economic significance especially for exporting electricity to western Europe and for substituting lignite burning. The disparity between nuclear safety standards accepted in western societies and in the countries of central–east Europe remain unresolved. This is clearly marked by the example of nuclear power in east Germany after unification.

The Soviet nuclear reactors (WWER-440) being used in the former German Democratic Republic were shut down in accordance with nuclear safety standards legislated by the Federal Republic of Germany. This notwithstanding, the same type of Soviet built PWRs – albeit with some modifications and enhancements – are still operational in central and eastern Europe – from the Czech Republic to Bulgaria. Even more problematic is the Lithuanian situation with the Ignalina power plant running two inherently unsafe Chernobyl-type RBMK-reactors.

The envisaged enlargement of the **European Union** by granting central and east European countries status of full EU membership scheduled for 2002/3 undoubtedly makes the question of further enhancing nuclear power safety in the east–Central European countries a salient and a pressing one.

GERT-RÜDIGER WEGMARSHAUS

East Asia

The countries and bio-regions of East Asia are amongst the most ecologically diverse on earth, yet they are also amongst the most threatened by economic **development**, rising living standards in many areas, and ongoing population growth, particularly in South East Asia. The region is also characterized by a diversity of political and economic systems and nascent international regimes that complicate international co-operation for environmental protection.

East Asia can be defined as Greater **China** (mainland China, Hong Kong and Taiwan) and the adjacent countries to its east and south-east, including North and South Korea, **Japan**, Vietnam, Cambodia, Thailand, Laos, Myanmar (Burma), Malaysia, Singapore, Brunei, and **Indonesia**. Sometimes Russia and some countries of Oceania are included under this rubric. This region is now frequently referred to as Pacific Asia or Asia Pacific, although the latter term can include Pacific Rim countries.

The countries of East Asia vary greatly in their levels of economic development and environmental health. The most economically developed countries and regions – Japan, South Korea, Taiwan, Hong Kong, and Singapore – have resources to deal with their own environmental problems and those of other countries in the region. But others – Mainland China and most countries in South East Asia – have limited resources and seek international assistance to help them with sustainable development.

Much of the region (outside the most developed countries) suffers from significant environmental problems: high population growth, combined in many areas with increasing consumption and pollution; over-cultivation of land, soil erosion, desertification, and deforestation; pollution of rivers and regional seas; destruction of coastal and reef habitats; shortages of fresh water; loss of species due to deforestation and destruction of habitat; declining fish catches due to over-fishing and pollution; local, national and regional **air pollution**, including transboundary movements of pollutants and **acid rain**; increasing emission of greenhouse gases (albeit in most developing countries of the region at per capita levels far below those of the economically developed countries); and rapid **urbanization** and associated environmental damage.

Several countries are noteworthy for their importance in international environmental politics in East Asia. Japan, the second largest economy in the world, enjoys some of the highest standards of living anywhere. It still has polluting industries, manifested in ongoing **water pollution**. Its domestic environmental movement is relatively weak – at least compared to the countries of North America and western Europe, although environmental regulations have drastically reduced pollution. Japan also suffers from pollution of surrounding seas and from acid rain originating particularly in China. The latter problem has pushed Japan to increase its international assistance for **sustainable development**, particularly for energy efficiency in China. Japan is among the countries most adamant in pushing for renewal of commercial **whaling**, and its demand for raw wood in South East Asia and increasingly in other areas (South America and Siberia) has gained it a dubious reputation in the area of international environmental politics (see **South East Asian environmental politics**). Like other developed countries and regions, its high levels of consumption contribute to environmental damage farther afield.

Greater China – mainland China, the Special Administrative Regions of Hong Kong and Macao, and Taiwan – is characterized by environmental and developmental diversity. China is the largest country in East Asia and the most populous country in the world. It ranges from densely populated, highly developed – and heavily polluted – areas in the south-east, to rural areas that are noteworthy for stress from decades of intense cultivation. Environmental damage is widespread

and growing worse in most areas. The government is increasingly aware and taking initiatives to reverse this trend, but the focus on economic growth and the sometimes incommensurable goals of the national government, local governments, industries, and the military, mean that policy-making and implementation of environmental regulations are extremely difficult to achieve. Soon China will be the largest emitter of greenhouse gases; hence its path toward economic development is not merely a matter of national concern. In international environmental negotiations, China has sought to increase the level of financial assistance from north to south for sustainable development. While much of mainland China is poor and high population is not associated with high levels of personal consumption, this cannot be said of Hong Kong and Taiwan, which draw resources from the region and have high levels of per capita consumption and pollution (particularly when compared to the rest of China). The Hong Kong region's government, for its part, is aware of the impact of these factors on lifestyle and the marketability of Hong Kong as a place to do business and as a tourist destination. Hence it is making efforts to address environmental problems; the same is also slowly occurring in Taiwan.

Further reading

Dupont, A. (1998) *The Environment and Security in Pacific Asia*, Oxford: Oxford University Press.
Hirsch, P. and Warren, C. (1998) *The Politics of Environment in Southeast Asia*, London: Routledge.
United Nations Environment Programme (1999) *Global Environment Outlook*, London: Earthscan.

PAUL G. HARRIS

eco-centrism

Eco-centrism, which literally means an 'ecology-centred' environmental worldview, is typically contrasted with **anthropocentrism**. However, the term eco-centrism was first introduced into the environmental debate by Timothy O'Riordan (1981: 1) in contradistinction to technocentrism, which is a more encompassing and informative term than anthropocentrism. Understood in these terms, both eco-centrism and technocentrism are ideal types, representing the opposing ends of a broad spectrum of environmental beliefs. Whereas ecocentric environmentalists regard the non-human world as not only instrumentally valuable but also valuable for its own sake, those of a technocentric persuasion hold to an anthropo-centric and technologically optimistic worldview that regards **nature** as merely raw material to be transformed for human betterment. Whereas ecocentric environmentalists believe that there are both physical and social limits to economic growth and insist that the complexities of ecosystems and the limits to human understanding are such as to warrant a cautious approach to environmental and **technology** impact assessment, technocentric environmentalists are highly sceptical towards the idea that there are **limits to growth** and place their faith in human techno-logical ingenuity to solve any ecological problems human society may encounter. Finally, ecocentric environmentalists adhere to a **development** philosophy that seeks to minimize the material/energy throughput in the economy to ensure that it operates comfortably within the carrying capacity of ecosystems whereas technocentric environmentalists are concerned to maximize economic output and believe that most, if not all, natural resources are substitutable. Understood in these terms, eco-centrism provides the eco-philosophical underpinnings of the political ideology of ecologism (see **eco-philosophy/ecoso-phy**; **environmentalism and ecologism**).

In the more general eco-philosophical debates, eco-centrism serves as a broad, generic term that encompasses a variety of controversial philosophies at the radical end of the environmental spectrum, including **deep ecology**, **Leopold**'s land ethic and some expressions of **eco-feminism**. Despite many significant differences between these radical philosophies, they are united in their rejection of a purely instrumental posture towards the non-human world, their celebration and promotion of ecological and cultural diversity and their rejection of any essential hierarchy of value among the Earth's diverse life-forms and entities. However, not all of these ecocentric approaches employ the

language of **intrinsic value**. For example, some deep ecologists (or 'transpersonal ecologists') prefer to focus on the cultivation of a sense of human self-hood that includes the widest forms of identifica-tion with the non-human world. Many eco-feminists, drawing on both post-structural and post-colonial theory, prefer to argue the case for the recognition and respect for differently situated others, both human and non-human.

Eco-centrism (along with other non-anthropo-centric environmental philosophies) has attracted a variety of criticisms. The three most common criticisms are that eco-centrism is impossible/nonsensical; too vague/impracticable; and/or po-tentially misanthropic.

The first objection typically proceeds from a social constructionist perspective: that since hu-mans cannot avoid interpreting the world from a human vantage point then humans cannot avoid being human centred. However, while ecocentric environmentalists readily concede this truism, they typically argue that it does not follow that humans are the only beings that matter from a moral point of view or that humans are incapable of valuing non-human nature for its own sake.

The second common criticism of eco-centrism is that its rejection of any essential hierarchy of value among human and non-human beings makes it vague and difficult to apply in practical environ-mental conflicts. The most common response to this criticism by ecocentric theorists is to argue that while all beings matter, not all of their needs necessarily matter to the same degree when judged relative to others in changing circumstances. That is, in conflict situations, the more basic and essential needs (whether belonging to humans or non-humans) should be fulfilled before the more trivial, non-essential needs are met.

The third criticism is that eco-centrism is always in danger of being misanthropic. This criticism has some force if eco-centrism is understood in a restrictive sense to mean concern only for the flourishing of non-human nature. However, if eco-centrism is understood as a concern for the mutual flourishing of human and non-human nature, then the criticism becomes harder to sustain. None-theless, **animal rights** theorists have argued that Leopold's land ethic is potentially fascist, while social ecologists such as Murray **Bookchin** have argued that deep ecology is potentially misanthropic, at least in those circumstances when the needs of non-humans are favoured over those of humans in practical conflicts. In reply, ecocentric theorists argue that this criticism conflates non-anthropocentrism with misanthropy.

Eco-centrism is mostly used interchangeably with the term biocentrism, although some authors regard eco-centrism as a technically more comprehensive term on the ground that biocentrism is necessarily confined to all biological organisms whereas eco-centrism encompasses all of the inextricably connected parts of ecosystems, both living and nonliving.

See also: animal rights; anthropocentrism; deep ecology; eco-philosophy/ecosophy; environmental ethics; green political theory; Naess, Arne

References

O'Riordan, T. (1981) *Environmentalism*, London: Pion, 2nd edn.

Further reading

Eckersley, R. (1992) *Environmentalism and Political Theory: Toward an Ecocentric Approach*, Albany, NY: State University of New York Press; London: UCL Press.

ROBYN ECKERSLEY

eco-feminism

Eco-feminism is not strictly a movement as it has no organization or structure, but it is a framework of ideas that has encouraged or reflected widespread activism around women and the environment. Since its origins in the mid-1970s eco-feminism has also entered academia as a theoretical/philosophical perspective. Eco-feminism emerged alongside radical feminism and seemed to emerge spontaneously in several parts of the world, from France, Germany, **Finland** and the USA, to **Japan**, Venezuela and Australia. Its name is generally credited to the French feminist Françoise d'Eaubonne. The roots of eco-feminism

lie in radical feminism, feminist spirituality, the **peace movement** and grassroots environmental struggles led by women. From radical feminism it draws a critique of patriarchy, from feminist spirituality the notion of a Female spirit and the importance of pre-God or non-God spiritualities. Many of its early adherents were involved in the peace movement and inspiration for the movement was drawn from womens' struggles around environmental issues such as the Chipko tree-huggers of the Himalayas. Not all eco-feminists embrace all of these elements; in particular those influenced by Marxism/socialism or anarchism reject the radical/spiritual elements. It would also not be right to assume that all or even most women who are involved in grassroots struggles and global campaigns around the environment would see themselves as eco-feminists.

Within the USA the new grassroots environmental organizations and the early proponents of eco-feminism were brought together in 1980 for a conference 'Women and Life on Earth: A Conference on Eco-feminism in the Eighties' held in Amherst, Massachusetts. One of the organizers was Ynestra King, a social eco-feminist linked to eco-anarchism (see **anarchism/eco-anarchism**). A number of issues drove the movement in the early 1980s such as the nuclear near-crisis at Three Mile Island in 1979 (see **Three Mile Island accident**), toxic waste contamination at **Love Canal**, New York State and the siting of cruise missiles in Europe, as well as the growing awareness of the social and environmental impact of **development** on rural environments and poorer communities. The latter had been highlighted by campaigns in the 1970s led by women such as the **Chipko Andolan Movement** against commercial logging in the Himalayas and the Kenyan Green Belt tree-planting movement.

The conference at Amherst led to the Women's Pentagon Actions in November 1980 and 1981 when women surrounded the Pentagon peacefully for two days on each occasion. A 'Statement of Unity' was issued that declared, 'We are gathering at the Pentagon on November 16th because we fear for our lives. We fear for the life of this planet, our Earth, and the life of the children who are our human future.' This stance was echoed across Europe including Britain where women, and some men, marched from Cardiff to the cruise missile base at Greenham Common under the banner 'Women for Life on Earth Peace March 1981'. The establishment of an (eventually) women-only Peace Camp at Greenham Common served to emphasize the centrality of women to planetary survival. This was also the message of eco-feminism.

Those who formulated the ideas of eco-feminism were a mixture of academics, activists, writers and poets. The last in particular, wrote in ways that seemed to critics to be romantic or essentialist. For this reason much early eco-feminism was rejected by mainstream feminism as being reactionary, encouraging a cult of the Goddess or Mother Earth that seemed to push women back into an elemental association with motherhood and Nature that they were trying to escape. There is some justification in this critique as the core assertion of eco-feminism is that there is a link between women and 'nature'. **Nature** here is sometimes seen as the natural environment, for example women protecting trees or campaigning for access to clean water, and sometimes as something more supernatural, Mother Earth. The link between women and nature also ranges from an elemental association between Woman and Nature to the view that women and the natural environment have both been treated badly by male-dominated socio-economic systems: **capitalism**, science, **technology** and militarism (see **militarism and the environment**). Despite differences in analysis and emphasis, eco-feminists are united in the need for all feminists to make the link between the subordination of women and the destruction of the environment.

While white feminists from the North have dominated most of the published work on eco-feminism, much of the dynamism of the movement has been in the struggle of women against the development process in the South. Women in communities around the globe have made links between the destruction of the environment and the impoverishment of women. South groups critical of western-style development such as DAWN (Development Alternatives with Women for a New Era), and campaigners such as Vandana **Shiva** have challenged the global agenda on **industrialization** and the global market. They

have argued that the position for women and the environment under development and **globalization** has got worse rather than better. **Biotechnology**, **genetic engineering** and patenting have been particular objects of recent campaigns. Women's voices on the environment were eventually brought to global notice at the Rio Earth Summit in 1992 (see **Rio Conference 1992**). In making their critique of development women are also making links with other oppressions and mechanisms of exploitation such as racism, sex/sexuality, imperialism and fundamentalism.

Within eco-feminism there are a range of explanations for the origins of the ecologically destructive imbalance between the sexes. Those who draw on feminist spirituality see patriarchy as arising with the 'Sky God' religions that obliterated more ecologically sensitive deities based on female images and/or the pagan religions of indigenous peoples. The sky god is seen as representing both male domination over women and the control of humanity over nature, particularly in Judaeo-Christianity (see **religions and the environment**). Evidence for these changes is found in the allegedly more ecologically benign attitudes of original peoples and the existence of archaeological evidence for the pre-historic worship of female deities. While celebration of female bodies is often central to this approach and sometimes seems to declare the superiority of the Female, men are encouraged to join women in rejecting the Sky God for the Goddess and/or female spirituality. The solution to ecological destruction is an earth-based spirituality that celebrates the Earth and its mysteries.

Eco-feminists from a philosophical background see the woman–nature connection as representing the hierarchical dualisms of western philosophy. They see a logic of domination in western thought that can be traced back to the Greeks but is particularly exemplified in the work of Descartes. This logic has set Soul/Mind over Body, Reason over Emotion, Science over Folk Wisdom, Culture/Society over Nature and Male over Female. Women have been associated in western culture with nature and the body. Patriarchal assumptions about the superiority of science, technology and reason have led to the ecological destructiveness of western societies. The dualism in western thought is seen as particularly represented in its science. The idea of a malleable, dead nature in Newtonian mechanics is seen as destroying a more organic approach to the natural world as alive and vibrant, which many would argue characterized societies before the Scientific Revolution. The solution to dualism is to critique and transcend it. Eco-feminists from this perspective tend to call for a new philosophical position based on 'partnership ethics' or an 'ethic of care'. Sometimes this is seen as an ethic particularly associated with women, sometimes as an ethic both men and women can espouse.

Those who come from the social sciences or from a radical (anarchist/socialist) political background tend to focus on social inequality. Social eco-feminism, which emerged in the USA, stresses the centrality of social divisions based on sex and gender inequality in creating ecologically destructive societies. The origin of social eco-feminism was in eco-anarchism, which saw hierarchy in human society as the real problem. Hierarchy was not limited to gender and therefore the problems of human exploitation of nature could not just be set at the door of patriarchy. Eco-feminists who emerged from a Marxist/socialist background, mainly in Europe and Australia, have focused more on economic inequalities and the sexual division of labour. They have tended to take a materialist perspective that explores the importance of gender in the dynamics between human economies and the natural environment. In particular they have pointed to women's unpaid work around the body and in subsistence economies. Their solution is the recognition and prioritization of the daily work of provisioning, often done by women, rather than the emphasis on production for profit in capitalist markets or the production of military hardware.

Although eco-feminist writings are slowly moving into the academic mainstream, they still suffer from the early accusations of being essentialist and romantic. To avoid these associations, some writers prefer to use other concepts such as ecological feminism (Karen Warren) or feminist environmentalism (Bina Agarwal). Eco-feminism is by no means a unified framework of ideas, but it could be argued that its assertion that the socio-economic structures that are threatening the destruction of the natural environment of the planet are also those that exploit and subordinate women demands serious consideration.

References

Mellor, M. (1997) *Feminism and Ecology*, Cambridge: Polity; New York: New York University Press.

Salleh, A. (1997) *Eco-feminism as Politics*, London: Zed Press; New York: St Martin's Press.

Sturgeon, N. (1997) *Ecofeminist Natures*, London: Routledge.

Warren, K. (ed.) (1997) *Eco-feminism*, Bloomington: Indiana University Press.

MARY MELLOR

eco-philosophy/ecosophy

Both eco-philosophy and ecosophy, as terms, were first used by Arne **Naess** in 1972 in a paper, 'The Shallow and the Deep, Long-Range Ecology Movements: A Summary', that was published in 1973 and became foundational for **deep ecology**. Though his initial usage of the terms was roughly synonymous, Naess has subsequently distinguished the two and more distinctively employed the latter, with the result that the term eco-philosophy has become more ambiguous and less overtly associated with Naess's brand of deep ecology. Thus whilst Naess originally defined an ecosophy as 'a philosophy of ecological harmony or equilibrium' (Naess, 1973: 100), he later defined an eco-philosophy as the study of problems common to ecology and philosophy, such as the role of humanity on the Earth, approached via a holistic perspective (Naess, 1990). The term has also been used either to indicate a philosophy which is life-orientated rather than language-orientated (Skolimowski, 1981) or as a shorthand label to denote the philosophical fields of **environmental ethics** and environmental values more broadly. The latter two senses merge significantly in terms of the history of contemporary environmental thought, in that Skolimowski's self-conscious definition of eco-philosophy in terms of organic nature correlates to the rise of environmental ethics as a distinct philosophical field since the early 1970s; western philosophical reflections on **nature** *per se* extend back to classical Greece, but environmental ethics, the combination of applied philosophy with such elements as historical critique, **intrinsic value** theory, metaphysical holism and the examination of non-western philosophical systems in a manner which foregrounds concern for non-human nature, may be traced to this time.

Eco-philosophy may accordingly be taken either as being a particular holistic philosophical scheme geared to ecological balance or as being a broader label for the areas of enquiry covered by philosophy of the natural environment. In the broader case, it is used to indicate philosophies geared to eventual radical change in the human relationship to the natural world; as such, the resources of eco-philosophy are the habitual underpinning of **green political theory** and may incorporate suitable perspectives from **anthropocentrism** or humanism (see **humanism and the environment**). Some schemes, such as **Leopold**'s land ethic or pragmatist accounts of environmental value, tend in any case to sit awkwardly in relation to any simple division of anthropocentric from non-anthropocentric ethics. Thus not only specifically ethical and political issues, but issues of natural aesthetics, metaphysics, philosophy of science and the history of ideas may come under the banner of eco-philosophy. Naess's strong impact, however, means that the term often carries holist implications for philosophical approaches.

Ecosophy, by contrast, was coined by Naess from the Greek *oikos* (household) and *sophia* (wisdom), intending to capture the idea both of Earth as home and of the personal dimension of a philosophical worldview inspired by **ecology**. Accordingly, it has characteristically been used by deep ecologists in the sense of a personal ecological philosophy, and in this respect there may be a plurality of ecosophies but the term is not deployed as a collective label. In Naess' view an ecosophy will incorporate numerous interconnected philosophical components, not all of which are necessarily fully articulated, but which may ideally add up to a total view; his own variant, Ecosophy T, centres on the core goal of self-realization, whereby the self expands outward through identification with

nature to become the Self, at which point unnecessary suppression and exploitation will cease since recognition will exist that such behaviour is ultimately Self-harm. Such deep ecology ecosophies habitually attribute intrinsic value to nature and sometimes biospheric egalitarianism, but have been criticized for their apparent subjectivism, obscurantism and possible egoism.

References

Naess, A. (1973) 'The Shallow and the Deep, Long-Range Ecology Movements: A Summary', *Inquiry*, 16.

—— (1990) *Ecology, Community and Lifestyle*, trans. D. Rothenberg, Cambridge: Cambridge University Press.

Skolimowski, H. (1981) *Eco-Philosophy: Designing New Tactics for Living*, London: Marion Boyars.

Further reading

Callicott, J.B. (1989) *In Defence of the Land Ethic: Essays in Environmental Philosophy*, Albany: State University of New York Press.

Devall, B. and Sessions, G. (1985) *Deep Ecology: Living as if Nature Mattered*, Salt Lake City: Peregrine Smith Books.

Fox, W. (1986) *Toward a Transpersonal Ecology: Developing New Foundations for Environmentalism*, Tasmania: University of Tasmania Press.

Light, A. and Katz, E. (eds) (1996) *Environmental Pragmatism*, London: Routledge.

Plumwood, V. (1995) 'Nature, Self and Gender: Feminism, Environmental Philosophy, and the Critique of Rationalism', in R. Elliot (ed.) *Environmental Ethics*, London: Oxford University Press.

Witoszek, N. and Brennan, A. (1999) *Philosophical Dialogues: Arne Naess and the Progress of Eco-philosophy*, Lanham: Rowman & Littlefield.

PIERS H.G. STEPHENS

eco-socialism

Eco-socialism is a form of radical environmentalism. Its central argument is that **capitalism** is the major cause of contemporary global environmental problems, and that only in a socialist society can we discover a relationship with **nature** that is sustainable but not regressive in terms of human development.

Eco-socialism applies humanistic socialist (rather than state totalitarian 'socialist') analysis and prescriptions to environmentalism: it also modifies traditional socialism to take account of environmental issues and perspectives. Eco-socialists' critical analysis of history, social change and economics draws particularly on Marx's (early) writings, and may be heavily influenced by interpretations of Marx in the political and utopian writings of William Morris. Its prescriptions often revive utopian socialist traditions of decentralization, communalism, direct economic **democracy**, common ownership of the means of production and production for need, not profit. Hence the 'brand' of socialism represented is close to anarchist-communism, although there are some major differences between eco-anarchists and -socialists concerning analysis and strategies (see **anarchism/eco-anarchism**).

Eco-socialism's historical materialism locates the causes of contemporary environmental abuse specifically in the workings of the economic mode of production known as **capitalism**, and institutions and world views necessary to its continuation. In particular it focuses on capitalism's *inherent* tendency towards overproduction, and its expansionary dynamic, as fundamentally inimical to strong environmental **sustainability** because of the tension which these forces produce between (a) the demands of constant economic growth in order to expand capital and (b) the limits of the demands which societies wish to place on Earth's carrying capacity. Eco-socialists, therefore, identify an *ecological contradiction* in capitalism. Impelled by the need, in ever-intensifying competition, for constant productivity gains, business and industry are fundamentally unwilling to internalize environmental and social production costs – yet in seeking to avoid them they undermine the natural and human resources on which production ultimately depends. In practice it is difficult for capital to take the long-term perspective on society–environment relationships which **sustainable development** implies.

Eco-socialists maintain that because such tensions inhere within capitalism, attempts (especially in globally modernizing society where capital is increasingly footloose) to mitigate them by state spending, legislation or appeal to logic or ethics are ultimately futile. The corollary is that to end environmentally unsustainable development capitalism itself must be abolished and replaced by socialism. In socialism, it is argued, people can end the alienation from nature and from each other resulting from commoditization and capitalization of human labour and the physical environment under capitalism, yet development in pursuit of **Enlightenment** goals can continue. Socialism would allow production, along with distribution, to be rationally, ecologically and humanely planned rather than determined by markets. Planning might be done by an enabling state (rather than one which, as now, chiefly reflects bourgeois interests), or, in more anarchistic socialist visions, this function might fall to bodies representing federation of local communities and regions.

In socialism's inclusive, discursive, decentralized democracy, with community ownership of the means of production, **development** decisions could be determined by political debate rather than being the outcome of interplay between capital-owning vested interests. Such decisions would very likely favour genuine majority interests, and these would not include the irrationalities of environmental degradation, waste or handing on an impoverished world to future generations. Socialist communities would probably want to steward, protect and wisely manage their relationships with nature, for the benefit of all their members.

But **stewardship** would not imply the degree of nature preservation and 'living lightly on the earth' that some other radical environmentalists (e.g. **deep ecology**) demand. For eco-socialist society would express our real relationship to nature – neither separation and superiority, as contemporary capitalism presupposes, nor mere equality, as **eco-centrism** believes. Rather, society and nature are dialectically related, so each is a manifestation of the other, whilst humans are nature's highest expression. It is accepted that nature is socially produced, and that what humans do is natural.

Hence the reasons for protecting and using nature sustainably in socialist society are to do with utilitarianism, rationalism and **humanism**, rather than any romantic, quasi-mystical beliefs about it. Neither are socialists inclined to accept simplistic environmental determinist arguments about absolute limits to growth, finite resources or 'overpopulation' (see *Limits to Growth*). Marxism's materialist analysis requires a historical perspective on these issues, recognizing that questions of what constitutes resources or a sustainable population size are conditioned by, and cannot be seen apart from, the mode of production of a given time, and the relationships between people and nature that correspond to it.

DAVID PEPPER

eco-taxes

Eco-taxes are one of the members of the family of environmental policy instruments known as economic instruments, the defining characteristic of which is that they give direct financial incentives for reduced environmental impacts. Other environmental economic instruments include subsidies, emissions trading and deposit–refund schemes, performance bonds and liability regimes. Eco-taxes, or environmental taxes and charges, are charges levied by the government, or by a public agency, on an emission, or the use of a resource or a product, which is associated with environmental damage.

The fundamental rationale for eco-taxes is that they internalize environmental **externalities** and thereby implement the **polluter pays principle**. By making those activities which cause environmental damage more expensive they may be expected to reduce them and the associated damage. They also give incentives for the development of different products and processes which serve the same purposes but with a lower environmental impact.

Environmental economists tend to favour economic instruments over other environmental policy instruments (for example regulation or negotiated agreements) because, if appropriately applied, they are likely to achieve environmental improvements

at lower cost. They achieve this by equalizing the marginal cost of emission reduction, or other environmental improvements, between polluters or other affected parties. They also give incentives for continuous environmental improvement, because any improvement reduces their tax bill, unlike regulations or agreements, which give no incentives to exceed specified standards or targets.

Eco-taxes may be classified according to their main purpose:

- *Incentive taxes* are principally intended to change behaviour and reduce the environmental impact towards which they are directed.
- *Environmental charges* are principally intended to raise the revenues necessary to cover the costs of the public bodies which monitor and regulate the targeted impact, and, perhaps, for reducing those impacts (for example, **water pollution** charges may pay for the regulation, monitoring and improvement of water quality in rivers).
- *Revenue-raising taxes* are principally intended to raise revenues for the government.

Clearly any particular tax or charge may serve each of these purposes to some extent, but its principal purpose will be the main determinant of the level at which it is set, and achievement of one purpose may make no contribution to another (for example, cost-covering charges may not be high enough to change behaviour; taxes which succeed in changing behaviour may not yield the revenues which were originally envisaged from them).

Historically, tax systems have relied on labour taxes (for example employers' payroll taxes or employees' income taxes) for the majority of their revenue, thereby making employment more expensive than it would otherwise be and, perhaps, reducing employment. Combined with perceptions of excessive levels of environmental damage, this has led to proposals for environmental tax reform (ETR, also called eco-tax reform), whereby eco-taxes would be systematically increased and other taxes, especially labour taxes, lowered in compensation. It is hoped that this revenue-neutral change in the structure of the tax system would simultaneously lead to reductions in environmental damage and increases in employment – a so-called double dividend.

ETR is only one way of 'recycling' the revenues from eco-taxes. Other ways include making funds available for purposes which would increase the environmental effectiveness of the tax (for example, for investment in pollution abatement); or for compensating those who are worse off because of the tax, especially when they are poor people who are disproportionately affected by it, or environmentally intensive economic sectors which might suffer a loss of competitiveness.

Eco-taxes have been the subject of intensive modelling over the last ten years, particularly to gain insights into their possible economic impacts. While the results of such exercises inevitably depend on the detailed specification of the models used, there is wide, though by no means universal, agreement that there is no reason to suppose that a revenue-neutral ETR would have negative macro-economic effects, and it could have a small but not insignificant positive effect on employment.

Given these perceived benefits it is perhaps not surprising that the implementation of eco-taxes, especially but not only in European countries, has accelerated in recent years. Since 1989, the year of the first review of economic instruments by the Organization for Economic Co-operation and Development (OECD 1989), which revealed that the scale of implementation of economic instruments in OECD countries was very limited, eco-taxes have been introduced in respect of a very wide range of environmental impacts, taxing both the impacts themselves and the products that are responsible for them. Examples include taxes on:

- Emissions to air, including carbon dioxide, sulphur dioxide and nitrogen oxides, in Denmark (DK), Finland (SK), Italy (I), the Netherlands (NL) and Sweden (S).
- **Fossil fuels**, including especially motor vehicles, in practically all OECD countries.
- Motor vehicles, in practically all OECD countries.
- Emissions to water, in France (F), Germany (D), DK and NL.
- Water supply, in D and NL.
- Disposal of solid wastes, in DK, I, NL and the UK.
- Aircraft noise, in many European countries.
- Other product taxes, including batteries, **pes-**

ticides, fertilizers and disposables, especially in Belgium (B).
- Traffic congestion, in Norway (N).

ETRs on some scale have been or were to be introduced in D, DK, I, N, NL and UK.

Evaluating the effectiveness of environmental taxes is no easy matter, because of uncertainty about what the environmental situation would have been in their absence ('the baseline'). However, a number of assessments of experience of eco-taxes in the 1990s suggest that they do have the positive environmental effects anticipated. However, notwithstanding their advantages over other policy instruments, they are difficult to introduce both because of the general unpopularity of taxes and because of concerted opposition to them by business interests in those environmentally intensive sectors which would be most affected by them. The result is that eco-taxes are now often introduced as parts of complex policy 'packages', which also include regulations and negotiated agreements, and full or partial exemptions from the taxes for the economic sectors most affected by them. While these exemptions may sometimes be justified as transitional measures during the period of economic adjustment, they both undermine the efficiency of the eco-taxes and make the overall environmental improvement more expensive than it would otherwise have been. Political pressures mean that such 'packages' are, however, likely to be the predominant means of introducing eco-taxes in the future.

Reference

Organization for Economic Co-operation and Development (1989) *Economic Instruments for Environmental Protection*, Paris: OECD, pp. 27–30.

Further reading

Ekins, P. (1999) 'European Environmental Taxes and Charges: Recent Experiences, Issues and Trends', *Ecological Economics*, 31: 39–62.

Ekins, P. and Speck, S. (1999) 'Competitiveness and Exemptions from Environmental Taxes in Europe', *Environmental and Resource Economics*, 13(4): 369–95.

—— (1999) *Database on Environmental Taxes in the European Union Member States, Plus Norway and Switzerland; Evaluation of Environmental Effects of Environmental Taxes*, Luxembourg: European Communities, Office for Official Publications of the European Communities.

Organization for Economic Co-operation and Development (1994) *Implementation Strategies for Environmental Taxes*, Paris: OECD.

—— (1996) *Evaluating Economic Instruments for Environmental Policy*, Paris: OECD.

—— (1997) *Evaluating Economic Instruments for Environmental Policy*, Paris: OECD.

PAUL EKINS

eco-terrorism

Eco-terrorism is a tactic adopted by radical contemporary environmentalists who believe that the approach of mainstream environmentalists is ineffective. Eco-terrorists argue that the destruction of the Earth brought about by industry and **development** is a violent infringement upon a natural state of affairs, and as such calls for violent retaliation. Eco-terrorists advocate the intentional destruction of instruments and machinery that they believe are detrimental to the natural world, such as bulldozers, cranes, and **whaling** vessels. Eco-terrorist activity may also include the forceful emancipation of caged animals from laboratories and zoos.

The theoretical basis for eco-terrorism can be traced to thinkers as diverse as Aldo **Leopold** and Edward **Abbey**, while eco-terrorist activity has been compared with that of the **Luddites**. Organizations such as the Animal Liberation Front actively embrace the tactics of eco-terrorism, while **Earth First!** publicly announces the need for direct and radical environmental action.

See also: animal rights

Further reading

Scarce, R. (1990) *Eco-Warriors: Understanding the Radical Environmental Movement*, Chicago: Noble Press.

MATTHEW P. TUNNO AND ZACHARY A. SMITH

eco-tourism

Nature tourism is a chance to maintain at least some ecosystem diversity for the future using eco-tourism as the tool. Ecotourism involves exposing the natural amenities of an area to minimal economic **development**, and limiting visitors. Locals can be attracted to this form of minimum environmental impact because they receive profits from leaving the sites in a more natural state. The complexities of eco-tourism appreciate that it is based on a fragile foundation, and that left unregulated, unplanned and unmanaged, natural areas could be destroyed by over-crowding and habitat destruction. To develop successful nature tourism, areas need to concern themselves with planning and management of eco-tourism locations as well as analysis of the costs and benefits of nature tourism. Planning, marketing and management of nature tourism are part of the structure necessary for a successful eco-tourism project. This represents a chance to save some selected natural areas. It should not be approached naively. Also, eco-tourism is not necessarily a way to preserve key natural areas in pristine form.

See also: tourism, environmental impact of

Further reading

Wearing, S. and Neil, J, (1999) *Ecotourism: Impacts, Potentials and Possibilities*, Oxford: Butterworth-Heinemann.

THOMAS LOWE

Ecolo

Ecolo is the Belgian French-speaking Green Party. Along with its Flemish-speaking counterpart *Agalev*, it has become one of the most institutionalized and successful green parties worldwide.

The creation process can be traced back to 1973 when Paul **Lannoye** created the progressive political movement *Démocratie Nouvelle*, which presented a list at the 1974 legislative elections, and again with several other movements at the 1976 local elections. In parallel, a Belgian section of **Friends of the Earth** was created in 1976 by several future 'founding fathers' of *Ecolo*. Eventually, after some further electoral attempts at the 1977 and 1978 legislative elections, the first breakthrough occurred at the 1979 European elections, when the list *Europe-Ecologie* gathered 5.1 per cent of the French-speaking vote.

This success acted as a catalyst, and *Ecolo* was formally founded in March 1980. At the 1981 legislative elections, it obtained 5.9 per cent and six parliamentary seats, the first ever *collective* parliamentary presence of Greens at the national level. Consequently, the party experienced a quite quick process of professionalization and institutionalization. Following the 1982 local elections, the Greens gained access to executive power for the first time in the city of Liège, and also obtained a first MEP seat in 1984.

At the 1985 and 1987 legislative elections, *Ecolo* consolidated its parliamentary presence, but made little headway. By then, the party was hampered by a bitter internal conflict between a 'reformist' majority and a more 'radical' and more clearly left-wing minority (similar in some respects with the *Fundis/Realos* cleavage in Germany). Eventually, most radicals left the party in 1986.

The party achieved a major breakthrough at the 1989 European elections (16.6 per cent, 2 seats) and the 1991 legislative elections (13.5 per cent, 16 seats). In addition, a reform in the public financing of parties was largely beneficial to the Greens. Hence, *Ecolo* became politically more influential, and its organization increased in size and professionalized even further.

The next few years were more difficult. The party had difficulties coping with its increasing size and, more importantly, suffered a major political defeat in connection with the **eco-taxes** after 1992–3 (see **Agalev**). Hence, *Ecolo* experienced its first electoral setbacks, both in terms of percentage and seats, at the 1994 European and 1995 legislative elections. This spurred a second phase of intra-party conflict between a more 'social' and a more 'environmentalist' wing. Eventually, a satisfactory synthesis was reached in early 1996. A process of ideological renewal and a broadening of the party's activist base and relays towards various social movements was also launched: the *Etats généraux de l'écologie politique*. From 1996 onwards, the country was also shaken by a whole series of

financial–political scandals, the 'Dutroux affair' (a paedophile and murderer) and the emergence of the 'white' citizens' movement, and several other political affairs and crises –including the **dioxin** scandal right before the 1999 elections. *Ecolo* was able to capitalize on all these events and to obtain an unprecedented success at the June 1999 general (18.9 per cent; a total of 45 parliamentary seats at the federal and regional levels) and European (22.7 per cent, 3 seats) elections, thus becoming the third party in French-speaking Belgium.

From July 1999 onwards, *Ecolo* has joined a 'rainbow coalition' with Liberals and Socialists, both at the federal and regional levels (with *Agalev* at the federal level). Altogether, it has obtained 7 governmental positions covering a broad range of portfolios (mainly transportation, energy, social affairs and education). This further stage of development generates a lot of challenges, in terms of internal organization, strategy and effective policy impact. The presence of green ministers has been marked by quite a few striking initiatives and subsequent controversies, e.g. about **nuclear energy** and **'quality of life'** issues (noise reduction around airports, country planning), but also regarding education and immigration policies.

Further reading

Delwit, P. (1999) 'Les défis du "plus grand" des partis verts en Europe', in P. Delwit and J-M. De Waele (eds) *Les partis verts en Europe*, Brussels: Editions Complexe.

Delwit, P. and De Waele, J-M. (1996) *Ecolo. Les Verts en politique*, Brussels: De Boeck Université.

Hooghe, M. and Rihoux, B. (2000) 'The Green Breakthrough in the Belgian General Elections of June 1999', *Environmental Politics* 9(3): 129–36.

Kitschelt, H. and Hellemans, S. (1990) *Beyond the European Left. Ideology and Political Action in the Belgian Ecology Parties*, Durham, NC and London: Duke University Press.

Rihoux, B. (2000) 'Ecotaxes on the Belgian Agenda, 1992–5 and Beyond. Environment and Economy at the Heart of the Power Struggle', in S. Young (ed.) *The Emergence of Environmental Modernisation*, London: Routledge.

BENOÎT RIHOUX

ecological debt

Around 1990, groups such as the *Instituto de Ecologia Politica* in Chile defined ecological debt as a payment due from North to South on account of ecologically unequal exchange, and on account of the use of environmental space by the rich economies. They asked 'who owes whom?'. In 1999 **Friends of the Earth** International started an ecological debt campaign as a complement to the Jubilee 2000 platform for the non-payment of the external debt of poor countries. Prices of commodity exports do not include local damages, such as sulphur dioxide from copper production. Also, the knowledge about genetic resources, and the genetic resources themselves, have been exported gratis (**biopiracy/bioprospecting**). Moreover, the rich economies have *de facto* appropriated the carbon sinks, and there is also some traffic of toxic waste from North to South (see **hazardous and toxic waste management**). Money values of some items of the ecological debt have been calculated by economists (Jyoti Parikh), also by Christian Aid. Other authors use ecological debt not so much in a North/South context as in an intergenerational context (see **intergenerational justice**).

JOAN MARTINEZ-ALIER

ecological economics

Ecological economics is a newly emerging discipline, which seeks to integrate a variety of approaches and understandings of human–nature interactions, to better conceptualize environmental problems and to allow improved policy analysis. It draws upon a range of established disciplines, including: economics, biology and **ecology**, physical science, and philosophy.

Ecological economics differs from the longer-established **environmental economics**, in that the latter draws almost exclusively on neoclassical economics, with its focus on rational individuals functioning in markets. This approach sees environmental problems as being caused by market failure through the existence of **externalities**. In environmental economics, there is also a tendency to concentrate on formal mathematical modelling. In contrast, ecological economics is pluralist in its approach, drawing on ideas from a range of disciplines. It explicitly rejects the focus on the 'rational individual', instead stressing the role of ethical principles in determining human action. There is a tendency towards verbal reasoning, often because it is felt that the environmental problems being addressed are not amenable to representation in mathematical form. For example, in environmental economics the **global warming** literature involves the practice of 'valuing' the environmental costs to society of climate change, and of seeking optimal strategies to deal with the problem (e.g. carbon taxes). In contrast, the ecological economics literature tends to stress the ethical and social dimensions of climate change, urging precautionary measures.

Instead of employing the usual analytical tools of economics, such as marginal analysis and optimization theory, ecological economics tends to use approaches which focus on economic structures, and how such structures interact with, and are affected by, the rest of nature. An example of such a technique is input–output analysis, which has also been generalized to studying the internal structures of ecosystems. A related aspect of ecological economics is its interest in the role of national accounts as a tool for environmental management, especially by the extension of the standard accounts to include 'satellite accounts', including quantitative information on the environmental consequences of various economic activities. There is even an attempt to recast the standard measure of gross domestic product, to take account of the (unpriced) contributions of nature to economic production (e.g. natural pollution degradation), though this approach is not without its critics.

Biological and ecological ideas are embodied in ecological economics in three ways. First, it is explicitly recognized that human activity is not independent of the rest of **nature**, but draws upon it, including upon biological systems. Second, ideas from ecosystem analysis, such as ecosystem stability and resilience, are being transferred to the analysis of systems that include economic activity, as a means of giving the concepts of **sustainability** and **sustainable development** some empirical and modelling foundations. Third, biological notions of evolution are being generalized to examine how the evolution of human–nature interactions limits the predictability of this dynamic system.

The influence of physical science in ecological economics is largely through the concept of **entropy**, as embodied in the Second Law of Thermodynamics. This is used mainly to stress the necessary and unavoidable relationship between economic activity and environmental degradation, through resource use and the production of polluting wastes. As in the case of the drawings from biological science, the use of the entropy principle is mainly heuristic, especially in seeking to demonstrate that any economic system must stress natural systems, and may produce significant and even irreversible damage.

The role of philosophy in ecological economics is twofold. First, **environmental ethics** offers an alternative to the assumption of conventional economics, that humans are solely self-interested, seeing future generations as irrelevant and other species as being of only instrumental value. Instead, environmental ethics allows a much richer range of concerns to be included in conceptual and policy analyses, including assessments of the 'rights' of future generations (see **intergenerational justice**), and the 'moral worth' of other species. The second contribution of philosophy to ecological economics is through epistemology (theory and knowledge). Clearly, policy analysis of human–nature interactions depends on knowledge of these systems, and the use of this knowledge to make predictions of the world both with and without policy interventions. Modern work in the foundations of language and mathematics, as well as the recent emergence of 'chaos theory', cast doubts on the degree to which we can predict many human–nature interactions, with strong implications for policy formulation.

Further reading

Costanza, R. (ed.) (1991) *Ecological Economics: The Science and Management of Sustainability*, New York: Columbia University Press.
Ecological Economics (1989–) Amsterdam: Elsevier. (Journal).

Faber, M., Manstetten, R. and Proops, J. (1996) *Ecological Economics: Concepts and Methods*, Cheltenham: Edward Elgar.

JOHN PROOPS

ecological footprint

This term is used in one of two ways in discussing **sustainability**, **sustainable development** and **green political theory**. Loosely used, it denotes the broad environmental impact of resource use by given human individuals or communities, where the needs involved may be regarded as either absolute (biologically given) or relative (mediated by social practices). Its more precise sense denotes a form of measurement whereby evaluation may be made of the sustainability of lifestyles; this operates by translating types of human consumption into the quantitatively measured areas of productive land needed to sustain this activity. Though several forms of ecological footprint accounting are available, the primary use of the measurement is to calculate the ecological resources needed to support an individual, community or region, and thus evaluate the sustainability of the relevant local practices involved.

Further reading

Wackernagel, M. and Rees, W. (1999) *Our Ecological Footprint*, Philadelphia: New Society Publishers.

PIERS H.G. STEPHENS

ecological modernization

During the 1970s, reports such as *Limits to Growth* and *Blueprint for Survival* and the works of leading environmental writers such as Paul **Ehrlich** and E.F Schumacher were predicated on an irresolvable antagonism between environmental protection and economic growth. They proclaimed the need for zero population growth, reduced global resource use and a deindustrialization of the developed world (see **Zero Population Growth**). These survivalist claims and ensuing conflicts over the preservation of nature-led industry groups, national governments and international agencies to articulate an alternative view in response. Promoters of ecological modernization claim that this reaction, first perceived in the 1980s, now represents a widespread cultural shift with identifiable features most evident in industrialized economies and some developing countries.

The term 'ecological modernization' (EM) was coined by Joseph Huber in the early 1980s. It has since gained popularity among European sociologists, political scientists and policy analysts and has been used, with considerable flexibility and some ambiguity, to describe and conceptualize changes in political, industrial and consumer behaviour in relation to the environment. In general, these changes have been understood as defining a new link between ecological and economic well-being, with environmental protection providing an essential precondition for and potential benefit to sustainable economic growth. Despite the range of interpretations, four broadly related uses of the term can be identified. These move from a narrowly instrumental and Euro-centric understanding of industrial eco-efficiency through to a radical, reflexive and global transformation of social relations based on a pre-eminent recognition of ecological limits and the 'rights of nature'. In this sense, the many uses of EM can be judged 'weak' or 'strong' depending on where they rest in this continuum (Christoff, 2000).

First, it has been used to characterize 'trends towards eco-efficiency'. The ecological refinement of industrial production depends on innovation to minimize resource use. It also promotes a shift from remedial technologies and processes that reduce the environmental impact of waste and pollution ('end-of-pipe' solutions), to precautionary measures – innovations integral to the production process that are aimed at eliminating or minimizing pollution and waste at source: the push for clean production is a feature of all definitions of ecological modernization. This use of EM has been extended to encompass environmentally beneficial actions at each stage of the interlinked processes of production and consumption. The activities of primary producers such as farmers or timber harvesters are guided by the green demands of processors and consumers;

manufacturers – for instance, in the chemical or motor vehicle industries – are increasingly influenced by local community pressure and the environmental demands of downstream users of their products; food retailers responding to green consumer demand in turn influence their growers, suppliers and packagers; individual investors, equity funds and services such as banks and insurance companies have become increasingly environmentally risk averse in their financial dealings. Consequently ecological modernization can be taken to encompass a wide span of environmentally beneficial economic activities including resource replacement in production, the transformation of manufacturing technologies and processes, **life cycle assessment** and product redesign, **recycling**, and environmentally informed consumer choice. Research by Amory and Hunter **Lovins** at the Rocky Mountains Institute and by the **Wuppertal Institute** confirms the benefits to be gained from such a trajectory. Janicke (1985) also considers that ecological modernization could still entail structural economic transformation – a 'partial deindustrialization' through the dismantling of those technical systems and economic sectors that were ecologically incompatible.

Second, Hajer (1995) uses ecological modernization to name the new *narrative* of environmental change that was articulated in national and international spheres during the early 1980s. For instance, in 1982 the Organization for Economic Co-Operation and Development (OECD) held a conference on environment and economics, which attempted to reformulate the relationship between these entities, suggesting that governments and markets could facilitate growth that was environmentally benign. Similarly, in 1987 the **Brundtland Commission**'s report, *Our Common Future*, articulated a discourse of sustainable development that emphasized the compatibility and desirabilty of economic growth with the achievement of ecological balance and **distributive justice**. Meanwhile the **European Union** mandated codes that required attention for certain industries to limit the environmental impacts of productive processes and individual governments, predominantly within Europe, and engaged in institutional innovations for mediating environmental conflict, further regulating pollution, and effecting more efficient resource use planning. As a result, in the 1980s and 1990s, governments, proponents of industry and some environmentalists constituted new storylines of EM to claim that the conflict-ridden relationship between environmental protection and economic growth could be reconciled and made synergistic. Simultaneously, this reformist narrative enabled national and transnational institutions of liberal democracy and capitalism to reclaim the initiative in the environmental debate, to manage radical political challenge and dissent, and represent themselves as sufficient for the resolution of local, regional and global environmental crisis. Mol (1995) suggests that such EM evidences the capacity for the institutions of **capitalism** to renovate themselves and successfully meet the physical and political environmental challenge.

Third, certain more wide-ranging, reflexive and ecologically sensitive *practices* in the state, **civil society** and the private sphere, are also considered by Weale (1992), Hajer and others to be evidence of a process of ecological modernization which could produce a radical redefinition of ecological governance and social action. The growing gap between environmental standards and regulations proclaimed in the 1970s and actual performance as defined by trends in environmental quality led analysts to proclaim the existence of an environmental policy implementation deficit. In addition, during the 1980s, neoliberal critiques of the state increased in influence throughout the Anglo-American world. Finally, the lack of integration between economic and social policies on the one hand, and environmental policies on the other, became an increasingly obvious source of environmental policy failure. Together these effects encouraged new attempts to integrate environmental and economic policy. While some governments employed strategies or 'green plans' for economic and social change involving both the public and private sectors, others legislated, regulated, or created supervisory agencies, to integrate environmental principles into policy-making across the public sector. Overall, there was a tendency towards policy integration and 'institutional reflexivity' incorporating environ-

mental values and concerns, a reduction of the emphasis – predominant in the 1970s – on direct regulation by environmental agencies, and greater reliance on market-based instruments, public education and negotiated partnerships with industry to improve environmental outcomes.

In addition, significant shifts in public environmental awareness and the rise of national and transnational environmental NGOs and national green parties provided spaces both in civil society and in the political sphere for the articulation of new environmental practices. These groups pressed for the formal recognition of environmental demands by previously impervious national and international institutions. In response, most OECD governments institutionalized limited public participation in environmental policy development. The representation of environmental interests in public decision-making and, in particular, the use of corporatist arrangements to include industrial and environmental concerns and their representatives in policy development and implementation, have been proposed as key features of a broad, culturally embedded ecological modernization.

These three uses of EM describe changes in social practice. EM has also been used to describe changes in the theoretical interpretation of society–environment interactions. Mol and Sonnenfeld (2000) suggest that recent writings on ecological modernization may constitute a new theory of social change. This is the least convincing of its uses: current theoretical writings on ecological modernization seem to offer no new coherent or partial contribution to political-economic or sociological interpretations of issues of agency or structure, or the economic or normative transformations of society.

Critics of the concept claim that it requires further critical development. They suggest that the narrow, instrumental and radical, ecologically driven uses of EM are contradictory. For instance, they suggest that some of its proponents fail adequately to differentiate between profit-seeking technological innovation which is incidentally environmentally beneficial and ecologically inspired technological change. Consequently, much ecological preservation remains beyond the scope of a narrowly instrumental EM. Similarly, EM tends to be considered at the level of the individual enterprise, sector or (European) nation-state, with little transnational analysis of environmental gains or losses. Yet the displacement of environmentally damaging production to newly industrialized countries and increasing global resource consumption undermine claims for accelerating EM in a global context. Separately, the discourse of EM may merely offer a sophisticated language for political crisis management, limiting the radical environmental challenges to capitalism through superficial changes to the rhetorics of state and industry practice while proposing a green-tinged model of western style industrial development as a global template for change. Lastly, it is suggested that the normative distinctions between different types of ecological modernization are often left unrecognized.

See also: ecological economics; environmental economics; free market environmentalism; progress; sustainable development; technology

References

Christoff, P. (2000) 'Ecological Modernisation, Ecological Modernities', in Young, S.C. (ed) *The Emergence of Ecological Modernisation: Integrating the Environment and the Economy?*, London and New York: Routledge.

Hajer, M.A. (1995) *The Politics of Environmental Discourse*, Melbourne, Oxford and New York: Oxford University Press.

Jänicke, M. (1985) *Preventative Environmental Policy as Ecological Modernization and Structural Policy*, Berlin: Berlin Science Centre.

Mol, A.P.J. (1995) *The Refinement of Production: Ecological Modernization Theory and the Chemical Industry*, Den Haag: CIP-Data Koninklijke Bibliotheek.

Mol, A.P.J. and Sonnenfeld, D.A. (2000) 'Introduction', in Mol, A.P.J. and Sonnenfeld, D.A. (eds) *Ecological Modernisation around the World: Perspectives and Critical Debates*, Environmental Politics, Special Issue vol. 9 (1), Spring.

Weale, A. (1992) *The New Politics of Pollution*, Manchester and New York: Manchester University Press.

Young, S.C. (ed.) (2000) *The Emergence of Ecological Modernisation: Integrating the Environment and the Economy?*, London and New York: Routledge.

PETER CHRISTOFF

ecology

The term 'ecology' was coined in 1866 by the German naturalist Ernst Haeckel, broadly denoting 'the science of the relations of living organisms to the external world, their habitat, customs, energies, parasites, etc' (Haeckel, 1905: 80). Drawing on the Greek *oikos* (household), from which the word 'economy' is also derived, Haeckel wanted the term to delineate a specific area of biology at a time when the impacts of Darwinism in science were yielding increased specialization and an explosion of new data and theory. However, by emphasizing the centrality of organic relationships the term also looked back to earlier ideas of the 'economy of nature' as a system that functioned as a unified whole; indeed, the older phrase was only displaced by Haeckel's term ecology at the end of the nineteenth century, and the extent to which scientific ecology can be distinguished from holist and organicist philosophy remains moot today.

Of such earlier thinkers, the geographer Alexander von Humboldt (1767–1835) probably made the most enduring impact on what was to become ecological science with his idea of a 'formation', a pattern of vegetation type (e.g. deciduous forest) that would predominate in a particular place due to local climate, and it was this notion that provided the toehold from which the first researchers were able to launch scientific ecology proper, the most important of them being the Danish plant geographer Eugenius Warming. In his work *Plantesamfund* (1895), later translated as *The Oecology of Plants*, he analysed the process of adjustment to habitat and added an examination of the organisms' communal life which highlighted their collective interdependence; moreover, he examined the dynamics of this, producing the first full-blown analysis of ecological succession, the processes by which one formation may be transformed into another. Moreover, Warming argued, the natural succession process has a direction, moving towards the most stable, diverse and self-perpetuating system possible within the habitat.

The political implications of these findings included the undermining of the Victorian individualist idea that nature was an arena of brutal all-out competition, for the clear message of Warming's findings was that hardly any species can prosper without assistance from others, whilst the implicit equation of stability with maximized diversity in an optimal community was later to inspire a number of thinkers in eco-anarchism (see **anarchism/eco-anarchism**). The dynamic emphasis on succession in Warming's system, meanwhile, proved the main focus for the next generation of ecologists, most prominently including Frederic E. Clements, Charles Elton and A.G. Tansley.

Clements argued that the succession process developed in a set of stages he called a sere, and at the level of both organism and community each sere contained within itself the conditions for its own replacement, thus meaning that nature was in constant process towards optimal local stability in an implicitly teleological process. The broad picture that resulted was one in which a pattern of climactically differentiated zones exists across the globe, with each formation of vegetation within the zone operating like an organism to develop towards the optimal stability of a so-called climax community. This global focus, however, became more locally orientated as a result of the rise of the New Ecology from the mid-1920s; the luminaries of this, including Elton and Tansley, aimed their attention instead at the organizational structure of particular ecological groupings, introducing the ideas of an ecological niche and, most vitally, that of an ecosystem. Elton developed the idea of the niche in economic fashion: the most significant element was the role played by any given organism in the local food chain, with those on the lower rungs needing and tending to reproduce more rapidly than their predators in order for stability to be maintained, and thus the New Ecology synthesized with Darwinian principles of competition. Further synthesis, meanwhile, was made possible by the development of the concept of an ecosystem. The term was coined by Tansley in 1935, partly so as to abandon the organicist implications of Clements's terminology of commu-

nity. Instead, Tansley proposed, the whole of a given grouping should be regarded as a physical system, incorporating both organisms and the inorganic energy flow, thus meaning that systems could be analysed, as they are today, in terms of energy flow and **entropy** and a new quantitative emphasis brought to bear in ecological analysis.

Politically, ecology is often used to support values of diversity (despite discrediting of the diversity/stability equation), interdependence, **sustainability** and non-hierarchy, and is closely linked to **deep ecology**, **social ecology** and the land ethic.

Reference

Haeckel, E. (1905) *The Wonders of Life: A Popular Study of Biological Philosophy*, London: Watts.

Further reading

Merchant, C. (ed.) (1994) *Ecology*, New Jersey: Humanities Press.

Worster, D. (1987) *Nature's Economy: A History of Ecological Ideas*, Cambridge: Cambridge University Press.

PIERS H.G. STEPHENS

education, environmental

The environmental education movement around the globe has evolved over many years with greatly increased activity and debate during the last two decades of the twentieth century.

The policy of involving government representatives in environmental education debate came to fruition in a milestone event held in Tbilisi, Georgia, USSR, in 1977. This was the UNESCO First Inter-Governmental Conference on Environmental Education, attended by official government delegations of 66 UNESCO member states together with representatives of numerous non-governmental organizations (NGOs). Its Final Report contains a Declaration, which established a framework for an international consensus, which has been the seminal influence on the development of environmental education policies around the world. Three core goals are central to this framework, *viz.* the fostering of clear awareness of, and concern about, economic, social, political and ecological inter-dependence in urban and rural areas; providing every person with opportunities to acquire the knowledge, values, attitudes, commitment and skills needed to protect and improve the environment; and the creation of new patterns of behaviour of individuals, groups and society as a whole towards the environment (UNESCO, 1977).

In the two decades that followed, individual countries and international organizations worked on the refinement and development of common goals, strategies and priorities for environmental education; a field characterized by tensions and paradox. Few would doubt the urgency and importance of learning to live in sustainable ways so that future generations may not only meet their own needs, but also enjoy life on our planet. Yet environmental education holds nowhere near the priority position in formal education programmes in many countries that this scenario suggests should be the case. It seems that it constantly has to 'engage in battle' with the demands of education in general rather than be a core element of it.

Environmental education has the task of addressing an extremely wide-ranging and bewildering array of content. This is a dynamic, ever-changing content, characterized by complex inter-relationships, priority problem causes, impacts and solutions. The knowledge base of environmental education is made all the more difficult to comprehend because the human race often simply cannot understand environmental issues or their potential resolutions in any definitive or permanent sense. It is a highly value-laden content, and one person's solution may be another's catastrophe. It is a content that incorporates aesthetic, spiritual, social, political and economic dimensions alongside (not separate from) the purely scientific. Furthermore, it is a content that does not and should not focus solely on environmental disasters and negative issues. Environmental education is not simply about 'saving the whale' or indeed 'saving the world'. It is equally about the development of an appreciation of the wonders and beauty of the world, and of a sense of *wanting* to save it – in short,

the development of ecological thinking or of **environmental ethics**.

Environmental education is about 'empowerment' and developing a sense of 'ownership', improving the capacity for people to address environment and development issues in their communities. It is about touching people's beliefs and attitudes so that they *want* to live sustainably, providing sufficient information to support these beliefs, and to translate attitudes and values into action. Of course this process includes formal teaching, but it also encompasses another dimension – that which may be placed at the 'core' of a teaching and learning model – the dimension of 'informal' education sources. These include communication and information that results from living and interacting in a particular community, the media, and 'events' in one's life and in the wider world. Environmental education depends upon the totality of an individual's experiences relating to the world – of which formal education is but a small part.

Progress in establishing environmental education, or 'education for **sustainability**' at a global level is uneven. In developed nations, it tends to be far more institutionalized, with much stronger support from governments. Education and communication tend to be separated, with formal environmental education being seen as the task of schools, colleges and universities and 'informal' environmental education being left to chance in the hands of the media and NGOs (see **mass media and the environment**; **international non-governmental organizations**). In the developing world on the other hand, the existence of structured, comprehensive programmes of formal environmental teaching and learning is still quite rare. Where such programmes exist, they are relatively new. Here, more attention is given to informal education via the media and local community projects often supported by a government. The world's *most* successful programmes in the twenty-first century will surely be those in which the formal and informal elements of education for **sustainability** are developed and supported alongside each other.

See also: environmental ethics; sustainable development

Reference

UNESCO (1977) *First Intergovernmental Conference on Environmental Education, Final Report*, Tbilisi, USSR and Paris: UNESCO.

Further reading

European Commission (2000) *Environmental Education and Training in Europe*, Brussels, May 1999, Conference Proceedings.

Holdgate, M. (1996) *From Care to Action*, London: IUCN/Earthscan.

Palmer, J.A. (1998) *Environmental Education in the Twenty-First Century*, London: Routledge

Palmer, J.A., Goldstein, W. and Curnow, A. (eds) (1996) *Towards Better Planning of Education to Care for the Earth*, Gland, Switzerland: IUCN.

JOY A. PALMER

Ehrlich, Paul

b. 1932, Kansas, USA

Ecologist

Paul Ehrlich is the Bing Professor of Population Studies at Stanford University. He has written extensively on human ecology since his early book, *The Population Bomb*. He argues that projected human population growth will soon reduce the carrying capacity of the earth if the trend goes unabated. Consequently he advocates family planning and reduced population growth worldwide in order to obtain a sustainable eco-system. In 1968, together with other eminent scientists such as Linus Pauling and Garrett **Hardin**, he helped found **Zero Population Growth**, an international organization dedicated to controlling population growth. He continues to serve as its honorary president.

LETTIE McSPADDEN

Emerson, Ralph Waldo

b. 25 May 1803, Boston, Massachusetts, USA; d. 27 April 1882, Concord

Essayist, poet

Born into a Unitarian family, Ralph Waldo Emerson abandoned a formal religious career due to doctrinal doubts, and stands with **Thoreau** as a representative of the philosophico-literary school of thought known as transcendentalism. Emerson was drawn in this direction partly through his European trip of 1832–3, which featured meetings in England with Coleridge, Wordsworth and other representatives of **Romanticism**. Emerson's transcendentalism, most fully represented in his 1836 book *Nature*, involved an emphasis on the unity of nature, science and spirituality, in which transcendent spiritual elements are revealed to us through the beauties of external nature and attentive sensory life, thus meaning that divinity can be seen as immanent in all things; these ideas have notably influenced green thought, especially in the USA.

Further reading

Richardson, R.D. (1995) *Emerson: The Mind on Fire*, London: University of California Press.

PIERS H.G. STEPHENS

enclosure

Historically, enclosure refers to the process whereby areas of common land in sixteenth- and seventeenth-century Britain were hedged in, ending traditional common rights of access for the poor to gain the means of subsistence, a process central to the rise of **capitalism** in early modernity. These enclosures were opposed by the radical Levellers on the Parliamentary side in the English Civil War (1642–9), but were allowed by Cromwell and intellectually supported by the philosophers Francis Bacon and John Locke, who defended enclosure as effective in maximizing economic productivity. Enclosure, and the trumping of common by private property thus represented, remains a key environmental issue today, with the debate over the tragedy of the commons highlighting questions about which land-use arrangements are most effective in attaining **sustainability**.

Further reading

Hill, C. (1996) *Liberty Against the Law: Some Seventeenth Century Controversies*, London: Penguin.

PIERS H.G. STEPHENS

endangered species

Extinction occurs where there are no longer any living specimens of a particular species anywhere in the world. But a species is in danger of extinction (i.e. an 'endangered species') well in advance of actual extinction. As numbers decline and habitats disappear the risk of extinction increases. There are several different measures of endangerment, or risk of extinction. The classification used by the International Union for Conservation of Nature and Natural Resources (IUCN: see **World Conservation Union**) takes account of the rate of decline, the area of distribution, the absolute population size and combinations of these factors. Threatened species are further assessed by reference to the risk of extinction – three categories of threat are used, i.e. critically endangered, endangered and vulnerable. In the IUCN Red List of Threatened Animals (Baillie, 1996: 24) were identified 5,205 animal species that were threatened with extinction in 1996. This number is likely to be a gross underestimate because not all known animal species were evaluated. However, all known mammals were assessed and 25 per cent were classified as threatened. A further cause of underestimation is that not all species have been classified. Estimates for the total number of species occurring on the Earth range from 2 million to 100 million, but only about 1.4 million of these have been fully catalogued.

Extinctions occur naturally as organisms respond to changing ecosystems. Darwin's theory of evolution explains how some species die out because newly evolved and better-adapted species compete successfully for the same niche. These 'background extinctions' occur at a rate of approximately one species every four years. 'Mass extinctions', on the other hand, are events where extensive species loss occurs on a global scale. Scientists have identified five mass extinctions, the most recent being the Cretaceous Extinction which occurred 65 million years ago. In that extinction, most famous for the extinction of dinosaurs, 85 per cent of all species became extinct. Current extinctions are estimated at between 20,000 and 35,000 species annually (or 4 species every hour). These rates are comparable to those of mass extinctions.

What distinguishes present-day extinctions from those mass extinctions that occurred in the past is that today's extinctions are occurring mainly as a result of human activity, whereas previous mass extinctions were due to natural causes, such as the onset of an ice age or the effects of a meteorite collision.

The main causes of extinction are:

Over-exploitation: over-harvesting of animals or plants makes it harder for the remaining specimens to reproduce in sufficient numbers to maintain population numbers.

Destruction and fragmentation of habitats: plants and animals are suited to particular habitats, some of which are very localized. As habitats are altered, largely by human actions (e.g. **urbanization**, construction of infrastructure and wars), the space available to, and suitable for, particular species of plants and animals decreases. Habitat fragmentation isolates plant and animal communities. The potential for dispersal and colonization may be reduced, reproduction rates may fall if mates are not available and the genetic diversity of the remaining population may decline, all of which increase the risk of localized extinction. The island bio-geography model (Macarthur, 1967), which has also been applied to 'islands' of natural habitat in an altered landscape, estimates that a reduction of the habitat area by 90 per cent results in a loss of 50 per cent of the species previously found in that habitat. When the habitat loss reaches 99 per cent only 25 per cent of the organisms survive.

Introduction of non-native species to new habitats: where non-indigenous species are introduced into an ecosystem this can upset the balance between organisms and lead to massive changes in the immediate environment. For example, approximately two-thirds of the haplchromine cichlids that used to inhabit Lake Victoria became extinct following the introduction of the Nile Perch, a non-native species. The extinctions were due to a combination of related factors – predation by Nile Perch, especially of species that consumed algae, leading to algal blooms, oxygen depletion and eutrophication affecting the habitat of the remaining fish.

Side-effects of human activities: the outputs of industries, farming and modern living can be hazardous to environments and to particular species. For example, in the early 1960s the bald eagle was at risk of extinction. A combination of factors, including over-hunting, loss of habitat and the use of **pesticides**, had reduced the known population in the USA to just 417 nesting pairs. Farmers were applying pesticides, such as **DDT**, to their crops. These pesticides were being washed into waterways and contaminating fish which were then eaten by the bald eagles. This led to an accumulation of DDT in the bodies of the bald eagles and was a direct causal factor in the thinning of eggshells. The shells were so thin that the eggs broke before hatching. As a result of the banning of pesticides like DDT and habitat protection the population of bald eagles has increased more than ten-fold.

Recognition of the current rates of species loss has led the international community, national governments, non-governmental organizations and communities to take action to reduce the exploitation of endangered species and to protect their habitats. Internationally, attempts have been made to limit the trafficking of endangered species through the **CITES** agreement. However, as with many international agreements, enforcement is complicated due to expense and technical difficulties. The Convention on Biological Diversity, which came into force in December 1993, is also intended to protect endangered species and habitats. The Convention supports the conservation of biodiversity, the sustainable use of biological resources and

the fair and equitable sharing of benefits derived from biological diversity (particularly in respect of the potential, but as yet unidentified, beneficial attributes of organisms occurring in developing countries). Other international agreements that protect habitats or species include the Ramsar Convention on Wetlands, the Convention on Conservation of Migratory Species of Wild Animals (or the Bonn Convention) and various conventions dealing with **whaling** and other **fisheries** conservation. Ratification of these international treaties is voluntary and, in general, their enforcement is dependent on signatory countries enacting appropriate laws at the national level and then enforcing them. Thus, international and public pressure is important in persuading countries to enforce the terms of these treaties. Non-governmental organizations (e.g. **Sierra Club**; **World Wide Fund for Nature**) are active in raising public awareness of issues relating to endangered species and in canvassing governments to take action to prevent irreversible depletion of **biodiversity**.

National governments follow a combination of strategies in order to promote the conservation of biodiversity generally, and more specifically of endangered species and their habitats. Legislation (e.g. the **Endangered Species Act**), economic incentives or disincentives, education and protected areas are the main components of national conservation strategies. Typical economic incentives involve the payment of grants to retain existing habitats or to rehabilitate them, whereas economic disincentives will usually take the form of taxes on environmentally damaging practices, such as waste disposal, pesticide use and fuel use. In addition, fines are often imposed when legislative restrictions are breached (for example, discharge of untreated effluents into waterways).

Protected areas (nature reserves and **national parks**) are areas set aside for the conservation of natural habitats and the animals that occur in them. Where there is pressure on land resources local communities may object to the fencing off of large tracts of land as national parks. Resentment is also possible where protected animals damage farmland, livestock and crops in areas adjacent to the parks. In Africa, attempts have been made to assist conservation at the local level by giving communities control over the endangered wildlife that occurs on communal lands near national parks. One of the best-known efforts to involve local communities in the conservation of wildlife is the CAMPFIRE (Communal Areas Management Programme for Indigenous Resources) project in Zimbabwe. CAMPFIRE addresses both over-exploitation and loss of habitat. The aim of the programme is to provide alternative livelihood sources for local communities by investing the preservation of both habitats and species with an economic value. **Ecotourism** and controlled trophy hunting are some of the mechanisms used by local communities involved in the programme to generate income. Since the wildlife, and its natural habitat, has a tangible value for the local communities they become actively involved in conservation.

References

Baillie, J. and Groombridge, B. (eds) (*c*.1996) *1996 IUCN Red List of Threatened Animals*, Gland, Switzerland: IUCN.

Macarthur, R.H. and Wilson, E.O. (1967) *The Theory of Island Biogeography*, Princeton: Princeton University Press.

Further reading

CAMPFIRE programme website at
    URL: http://www.campfire-zimbabwe.org/.

Glowka, L., Burhenne-Guilmin, F. and Synge, H. (1994) *A Guide to the Convention on Biological Diversity*, Gland, Switzerland: IUCN/The World Conservation Union.

International Union for Conservation of Nature and Natural Resources – The World Conservation Union website at
    URL: http://www.iucn.org/.

Primack, R.B. (1998) *Essentials of Conservation Biology, Second Edition*, Sunderland, MA: Sinauer Associates Inc.

Sutherland, W.J. (ed) (1998) *Conservation Science and Action*, Oxford: Blackwell Science Ltd.

World Conservation and Monitoring Centre website at

URL: http://www.wcmc.org.uk/.

NIAMH MURNAGHAN

Endangered Species Act

In the USA, although federal wildlife laws go back to the late nineteenth century, the first law actually to focus on **endangered species** was the Endangered Species Preservation Act of 1966. It empowered the Secretary of Interior to identify native 'species threatened with extinction' and to protect their habitat through land acquisition. All federal agencies were to protect such species in so far as 'practicable' and consistent with their primary purposes. Also the law did not prohibit the 'taking' of these species by private persons. A second law, the Endangered Species Conservation Act of 1969 extended protection to international wildlife, including also invertebrates.

Responding to concerns about the limits of the previous laws, the Congress passed with an overwhelming majority a new comprehensive law, the Endangered Species Act (ESA) of 1973, which Jay Hair of the **National Wildlife Federation** has described as the 'crown jewel' of US environmental law. It mandates that all federal agencies seek to conserve not only species endangered with extinction, but also those so threatened that they are likely to become endangered. It authorizes actions by the US Fish and Wildlife Service (FWS) (Interior) and the National Marine Fishery Service (NMFS) (Commerce) beyond habitat protection. All '**takings**' of endangered and threatened species on public or private lands are prohibited. The ESA's language is sweeping, in contrast to the 1966 law, protecting any living creature of 'esthetic, ecological, educational, recreational, and scientific value to the nation and its people'. Determination of endangered or threatened status by the FWS is to be done on biological grounds without consideration of economic costs. After listing, the government, with public participation, is to draw up a species recovery plan; only at this stage are economic costs considered.

In the 1970s and 1980s, the preservationist values of the ESA translated into thousands of potential conflicts with the economic values reflected in developmental projects. With rare exceptions, these were settled out of court. The first dispute that made it all the way to the US Supreme Court, the **snail darter case** (*TVA v. Hill*) in 1978, resulted in a decision reinforcing the preservationist values. The judges read the law (in their words: 'the most comprehensive legislation for the preservation of endangered species ever enacted by any nation') literally and concluded that they had no choice but to stop the $120 million Tellico dam project. Out of the controversy, however, came amendments to institute the 'God Committee', a cabinet-level review committee (which has rarely met) to grant ESA exemptions in special circumstances. (In 1992, it did vote to open up 1,700 acres of federal forests that had previously been designated as critical, spotted owl habitat. See **spotted owl controversy**.) In 1982, Congress amended the ESA to authorize 'incidental takings permits' if these were offset by property owners' habitat conservation plans to provide compensating protection for endangered species elsewhere.

Despite Interior Department statistics showing that since 1987 less than 0.06 per cent of developmental projects have been stopped, 'the ESA has become a lighting rod for anti-environmental rhetoric' (Kraft, 2001) from the **wise-use movement**. However, one such 'wise-use' group was dealt a setback by the US Supreme Court in *Babbitt v. Sweet Home* (1995). The court ruled that modification of the critical habitat of endangered species by private property owners constituted a 'taking' forbidden by the ESA and that the clear intent of the Congress in the ESA and its 1982 amendments was comprehensive protection. Subsequently, there have been efforts in the Republican-controlled Congress (thus far unsuccessful) to redefine 'taking' as well as to de-emphasize species recovery plans, require compensation for property owners who are prevented from using their land, and make it harder to list species for protection. The Clinton Administration responded to Congressional complaints by making the implementation of the ESA more sensitive to the needs of property owners. For example, it encouraged the negotiation of habitat conservation plans, which

guarantee 'no surprises', meaning that the government, even in face of new scientific evidence, cannot impose future restrictions on the use of the land.

There has also been criticism of the government's handling of endangered species from environmentalists in recent years. The Congress has failed to provide the funding to speed up the process of listing species and developing recovery plans. The total amount of money appropriated for the efforts of the FWS and NMFS in protecting endangered and threatened species in recent fiscal years has been roughly equivalent to the money required to build a couple of miles of urban interstate highway. In February 2000, the total number of US species on the endangered or threatened lists came to 1,222 (with hundreds of others still pending), but only 923 of the listed species had recovery plans. Beyond media reports about the recovery of 'charismatic' species like the bald eagle and the peregrine falcon, statistics have indicated that very few species have been de-listed due to recovery. Environmentalists would like to see the ESA not only better funded, but also more orientated to the preservation of endangered ecosystems (Pacific North-west old growth forests) rather than individual species (northern Spotted Owls).

In recent decades, studies have attempted to inventory US native species. For example, The **Nature Conservancy**'s study found that to some extent one-third of the country's species are imperilled. With US population and economic growth showing no signs of abating, the clash between preservation and **development** will continue to be reflected in efforts to reform the ESA.

Reference

Kraft, M.E. (2001) *Environmental Policy and Politics*, New York: Addison Wesley Longman, 2nd edn.

Further reading

URL: http://www.endangered.fws.gov.

E. GENE FRANKLAND

energy conservation

Although the term energy conservation is very common in both general and technical usage, it is a misnomer: according to the first law of thermodynamics energy is always conserved – but its usefulness decreases (i.e. its **entropy** increases) with conversions. The term rational use of energy is preferable. As so many energy conversions remain inefficient the scope for better use of fuels and electricity is enormous; reduced environmental impacts are its welcome corollary. Effects of such measures can be stunning on a sectoral scale: replacing incandescent light bulbs by fluorescent lights will more than halve the original use of electricity in lighting. The situation is different on a national scale where no single action, even if it transforms a sector using a relatively large share of total energy (be it household heating or ferrous metallurgy), can save more than a few per cent of a country's aggregate use. But, as shown by many national trends of energy use, a combination of such approaches can bring major and lasting gains.

Further reading

Schipper, L. and Meyers, S. (eds) (1992) *Energy Efficiency and Human Activity*, Cambridge: Cambridge University Press.

VACLAV SMIL

energy crisis

The energy crisis refers to a period of global economic disruption created by two sudden increases in crude oil prices. The Organization of Petroleum Exporting Countries (OPEC) used the rising global demand to quintuple its posted price of crude oil from just over $2/barrel in early 1973 to $11/barrel by the spring of 1974. The second wave of price increases accompanied the collapse of the Iranian monarchy: during 1979–80 prices rose to almost $40/barrel. These increases were misinterpreted as harbingers of a rapid decline of petroleum resources, and they led to predictions of OPEC being a dominant global economic and political force for generations to come. But the organization overplayed its hand: high prices led to high inflation, to a global economic slowdown – and eventually to substantial discoveries of crude oil outside OPEC, and to more efficient use, and to substitutions, of the fuel. As a result, in 1985 crude oil prices collapsed to less than $15/barrel, and they have remained mostly between $15–25/barrel ever since.

Further reading

Skeet, I. (1988) *OPEC: Twenty-Five Years of Prices and Politics*, New York: Cambridge University Press.

VACLAV SMIL

Enlightenment

In its everyday sense, to be 'enlightened' means to become aware of something about which one was previously in the dark; in certain, particularly eastern, cultural traditions, the idea of enlightenment refers to a more momentous kind of spiritual awakening or realization. In modern western culture, though, the idea also has different associations originating in the eighteenth-century 'Age of Enlightenment'. In that period of indisputable advances in human knowledge, enlightenment was understood as emancipation from the fetters of prejudice, superstition and arbitrary authority which had hitherto bound humanity in subjection and darkness. These advances could be exaggerated, however, to suggest humanity was coming to master its own destiny and even the forces of **nature**; and this arrogant and 'Promethean' aspect of the Enlightenment has been taken by many ecological critics to underlie our ecological problems. However, the enduring legacy of the Enlightenment as the critical deployment of reason, even against the claims of reason itself, arguably remains of crucial value to the practice of ecological criticism itself.

TIM HAYWARD

entropy

The entropy concept has its roots firmly in nineteenth-century physics, but since Georgescu-Roegens's work (1971), it has become an essential element in the emerging discipline of **ecological economics**. The entropy principle derives from the Second Law of Thermodynamics: Isolated systems (i.e. those allowing no inflow or outflow of matter or energy) tend towards a state of maximum 'mixed-upness'. For example, heat flows, of itself, from hot bodies to cold ones, thus 'mixing-up' the overall energy of the system. The formal term for this 'mixed-upness' is *entropy*, and the entropy principle states that systems which are isolated will always increase in entropy. The economic and social consequences of the entropy principle are that we should expect productive systems always to be self-destructive, using up low entropy raw materials and producing high entropy (potentially polluting) wastes.

References

Georgescu-Roegen, N. (1971) *The Entropy Law and the Economic Process*, Cambridge, MA: Harvard University Press.

JOHN PROOPS

Environment Agency

The Environment Agency is the government department responsible for many – but not all – environmental matters in England and Wales. It was founded in 1996 out of an amalgamation of separate agencies responsible for industrial pollution control, water and **fisheries** protection, and waste regulation. Rather than creating a new administrative agency for the whole of the United Kingdom, however, the administration of prime minister John Major opted to set up the Environment Agency for England and Wales, and a separate Scottish Environmental Protection Agency (SEPA). While its creation represented an attempt by the British government to add some coherence to the administrative structure of **British environmental law and policy**, it fell far short of bringing together the diverse interests of local government and national administrative institutions.

With a budget in 1999–2000 of £620 million (nearly $1 billion), and a staff of about 10,300, the Environment Agency is the largest body of its kind in the **European Union**. It is based around a decentralized system of organization, with seven regional offices and a separate Environment Agency Wales. Its 15 board members are appointed by the secretaries for the Environment and Wales, and by the Minister of Agriculture, Fisheries and Food. The Agency is responsible for policy in areas such as air and water quality, waste management, flood defence, and the management of fisheries. It is also responsible for overseeing the application of key European Union laws on the environment, including those dealing with integrated pollution control, water quality, dangerous substances, waste, and urban waste water treatment. However, it does not deal with **air pollution** from vehicles, noise issues, or planning permission, all of which are dealt with by local government authorities. The Agency is described by the British government as a 'non-departmental public body', and comes under the overall aegis of the **Department of the Environment, Transport and the Regions**, which was created out of a merger of pre-existing government departments by the Blair administration in 1997.

The Agency was early subject to considerable criticism, mainly from environmental interest groups, which argue that it has not been sufficiently open about its work. While it has clearly been very active, it has not always been willing to release the minutes of its Board meetings, or to fit in with the trend toward greater openness in the work of government in Britain. This has made it difficult to be sure about the progress it has made in meeting its objectives; these have included ensuring compliance with the requirements of environmental law, reducing the use of private transport, reducing water consumption, quantifying waste streams, reducing carbon dioxide emissions, improving the quality of bathing and fishing waters, and reducing incidents of **water pollution**.

See also: British environmental law and policy;

British regulatory agencies; Inspectorate of Pollution

JOHN McCORMICK

Environmental Defense Fund

The roots of the Environmental Defense Fund (EDF) go back to the gathering of local conservationists and scientists on Long Island, New York. The group (known as the Brookhaven Town Natural Resources Coalition) mobilized to halt the widespread spraying of **DDT**. Following their local victory in 1967, they incorporated as a non-profit organization and soon went national. With legal actions and scientific studies, they fought against lead additives, the supersonic transport jet, and especially **pesticides**. In 1980 the EDF had about 40,000 members. In 2000 it had over 300,000 (and a budget of over $28 million). Mainstream EDF sees itself as having 'linked science, economics, and law to create innovative, equitable, and cost-effective solutions to the most urgent environmental problems'. The EDF has a long history of seeking out corporate partners, such as McDonald's, BP Amoco, and United Parcel Service. Since the 1980s, the EDF has been a leading advocate of economic incentives rather than regulations to solve environmental problems, such as **acid rain**, **global warming**, and **endangered species**. In 2000 the EDF shortened its official name to Environmental Defense.

Reference

URL: http://www.environmentaldefense.org.

E. GENE FRANKLAND

environmental economics

Environmental economics is a sub-discipline of economics which analyses both why some economic decisions result in pollution problems and how policies can be designed to ameliorate pollution. Much of the work in environmental economics studies the application and performance of incentive-based regulatory practices, such as pollution tax systems or pollution allowance markets (see **eco-taxes** and **tradeable emission permits**). It also focuses on the political economy of environmental policy.

Environmental economics separates itself from 'natural resource' economics which focuses on methods to achieve efficient usage of renewable and non-renewable resources over time (see **non-renewable resources**; **renewable energy**). Natural resource economics has spawned a huge literature on the management of **fisheries**, forests, minerals, energy resources, extinction of species, etc. While these certainly have an environmental component, environmental economics generally restricts itself to the issues of regulating polluting activities and the valuation of environmental amenities.

Economists see most pollution as the result of a market failure. In particular, pollution was seen as the consequence of an absence of prices for certain scarce environmental resources such as clean air and clean water. In 1920 Alfred Pigou suggested that the solution to the problem was to introduce surrogate prices in the form of 'effluent fees' (Pigouvian taxes) for these resources. The failure of policy-makers to incorporate even minimal use of such prices in the environmental legislation of the 1960s combined with the unexpectedly high costs of the command and control programmes then enacted and the political resistence to price-based policies spurred the development of environmental economics as a separate sub-discipline in the late 1960s. While pure research has been an important part of the discipline, much of the work done has been motivated by its policy potential.

Study of the robustness of the Pigouvian tax approach (and equivalent prescriptions using subsidies or marketable permits) has dominated one thread of environmental economics. This thread has examined the impact of defensive activities on the part of victims, monopoly power, uncertainty regarding benefits and costs of pollution control, and difficulties in measurement of and enforcement of pollution levels on the efficiency of environmental policy. One result of this thread of environmental economics is mounting evidence that despite the compromises and imperfections inherent in the design of incentive-based pollution control policies that make it very difficult to achieve the least cost solution to a pollution problem, it appears that substantial saving can be achieved by designing policies with economic incentives.

Mainstream environmental economics which has concentrated on the use of governmental power to regulate the environment has been under continuous attack from the followers of Ronald Coase (1960). The Coasian argument is that, in the absence of transaction costs and strategic behaviour, the distortions associated with **externalities** will be resolved efficiently either through voluntary bargains struck among the interested parties or through litigation. This is true regardless of the initial assignment of liability for environmental damage. While the mainstream has rejected the feasibility of the Coasian solution, this critique has spawned an important literature on the importance of **property rights** and liability laws in improving environmental quality.

A second thread of environmental economics has focused on the problem of measuring the benefits and costs of environmental policies. Most of the attention has focused on the measuring benefits. The concern arises because environmental policies create 'goods' such as clean air and clean water that are not sold in markets and thus have no readily observable prices. Techniques for measuring these values fall into two general classes. These are: indirect market methods which attempt to infer the value people place on environmental goods from actual choices such as where to live or how far to travel for recreation experiences; and direct questioning approaches (known as contingent valuation methods), which ask people to make choices between environmental goods and other goods in a survey context. In addition to the theoretical research a significant accumulation of empirical work exists for health, recreation, visibility, and ecological benefits (particularly in **agriculture**). In the USA, after Executive Order 12291, **cost-benefit analysis** became an accepted part of policy design.

Reference

Coase, R. (1960) 'The Problem of Social Cost', *Journal of Law and Economics*, 3, Oct: 1–44.

Further reading

Baumol, W. and Oates, W. (1988) *The Theory of Environmental Policy*, Cambridge: Cambridge University Press, 2nd edn.

Cropper, M.L. and Oates, W. (1992) 'Environmental Economics: A Survey', *Journal of Economic Literature*, 20(2): 675–740.

Freeman, A.M. III (1993) *The Measurement of Environmental and Resource Values*, Washington, DC: Resources for the Future.

Hahn, B. (1989) 'Economic Prescriptions for Environmental Problems: How the Patient Followed the Doctor's Orders', *Journal of Economic Perspectives* 3: 95–114.

STANLEY R. KEIL

environmental ethics

Substantial evidence exists that continuing release of greenhouse gasses (GHGs) into the atmosphere will have grave consequences for the long-term health of the earth's environment and its human inhabitants. In its most recent assessment of the climate change issue, the Intergovernmental Panel on Climate Change (IPCC) concluded that human activity has had a discernible influence on climatic variables, such as temperature, sea levels, and the frequency of extreme weather events (see **Framework Convention on Climate Change**). Concerns about the harmful impacts of climate change, both for humans and non-humans, have led to mounting pressure on governments to secure binding agreements on the reduction of greenhouse gas emissions.

The motivating conviction behind much of the **environmental movement** seems straightforwardly to be that more must be done to limit the damage of human-originating activities on the global environment. However, the generality of this proposition leaves a number of questions unanswered. To what extent should members of the present generation sacrifice their well-being to secure a decent environment for their successors? How should the costs and benefits of human enterprises which bring about global environmental change (such as climate change) be distributed

(a) across time and (b) across space? Do animals, or environmental objects, or the biosphere itself, possess value (or moral standing) independently of the value they have to human beings? How should we go about balancing the activities of industrial and commercial activities with environmental preservation when they conflict? It seems that we must appeal to an environmental ethic, that is a normative framework for thinking about environmental issues, in order to answer these troubling questions. There are, of course, a multitude of environmental ethics that compete for our attention, and these will not only differ at the level of the principles they endorse, they will also tend to favour quite different public policies. In what follows, three of these ethics will be outlined and applied to the issue of global climate change. These are **anthropocentrism**, zoocentrism, and **ecocentrism**.

Anthropocentric theories are those which attribute value only to states of human beings. One prominent example is the 'green theory of value' proposed by Robert Goodin (1992). According to this view, the value of the natural world can be traced only to its value to human beings and the role it plays in their lives. A similarly anthropocentric stance on the value of the natural environment is endorsed by the World Commission on Environment and Development's (1987) influential report *Our Common Future* which maintained that securing, and enhancing, human well-being should be the ultimate goal of environment and development policies. Anthropocentric views are not necessarily committed to the view that only human beings are morally considerable (in the broadest sense of the term). Rather they hold that only human beings possess ultimate value. According to a useful typology introduced by Raz (1986), something is of ultimate value if its value does not derive from the way it contributes to something else; something is of instrumental value if its value is derived from the consequences it is likely to have, or be used to produce; and something is intrinsically valuable if it is constitutive of a valuable form of life. As such, that something is intrinsically valuable is a necessary but not a sufficient condition of that thing being of ultimate value. Anthropocentric environmental ethics can make

room for the idea that non-humans possess intrinsic value. However, human beings, on this view, are of ultimate value – indeed individual human beings are the only entities which are 'ultimately' valuable. In other words, everything else that has non-ultimate (i.e. intrinsic or instrumental) value must derive this from the way it relates, and contributes, to the well-being of individual human beings. The value of environmental preservation can at best be intrinsic for anthropocentric ethics, rather than instrumental, because of the way in which policies of environmental preservation provide one set of logically necessary conditions for individuals to enjoy environmental goods, such as clean air, beautiful scenery and so forth, and the options they give rise to. Returning to our example of climate change, the idea here is that we must reduce greenhouse gas emissions because of the possible, or likely, negative impacts climate change will have on particular present and future human beings – as well as on environmental goods which are constitutive of the well-being of human beings. The value of the natural environment is not necessarily instrumental as it is a necessary condition of human beings securing, and enhancing, their well-being – it is an essential context, for example, for people to have a meaningful array of options to choose between.

The version of anthropocentrism outlined above endorses the more or less liberal assumption that at least part of the story of environmental ethics concerns the extent to which acts and social policies promote human freedom. Whereas all of the above theories are united by the spirit of **humanism** – they presuppose that the goodness or badness of all acts and social policies derives ultimately from their contribution to human life and its quality – zoocentric theories go one step further in attributing value to states of all sentient creatures, including human beings. Note that this ethic goes far beyond the claim that non-humans possess intrinsic value, in the sense outlined above. Consider Raz's (1986) observation in *The Morality of Freedom* that some people lead a richer and better life because they own, and have a deep attachment to, a family pet. The value of the relationship between the person and their pet, here, is apparently of intrinsic value: it possesses value in virtue of being a constitutive part of a valuable form of life, as he puts it. As a result, the existence of the pet itself is intrinsically valuable as well, for its existence is a necessary condition of the relationship. However, the existence of the pet – for Raz, as for all anthropocentrics – cannot be ultimately valuable, for any value the pet has ultimately comes from the way in which it contributes to its owner's (or another person's) well-being. The key idea behind zoocentric ethics, however, is precisely that it is indefensible not to broaden the class of bearers of ultimate value to encompass many (if not all) non-human animals. Zoocentric ethics views the anthropocentric move of restricting the concerns of **environmental justice** to the well-being of human beings as being a sort of 'human chauvinism' which ignores the fact that species membership is a morally irrelevant difference between individuals. According to Peter **Singer** (1993), for example, if we are committed to the fundamental principle that each human being's interests must be treated with equal concern and respect, we are also committed to accepting this principle of equality as the moral basis for relations with other species. Proponents of the zoocentric view do not have to view human and non-human interests as being equally important. Nor do they have to view all non-humans as having moral standing. Nevertheless, the zoocentric approach to environmental change is to weigh up the impact of climatic change, for example, on all animal life. Insofar as global climate change seems likely to affect animal life even more adversely than human life, zoocentric ethics would appear to generate far-reaching objections to human activities which exacerbate climate change, even if it could be shown that in the long-run these activities brought about a net beneficial effect on human well-being. Some obvious difficulties are raised here concerning the balancing of human and non-human animal interests when they look likely to conflict.

Finally, ecocentric theories reject the idea that the natural environment is only valuable to the extent that it provides a context for the flourishing of humans or other sentient creatures. In contrast, this mode of thought presupposes that components of the natural world such as plant life, and possibly the biotic community as a whole, possess value independently of humans or animals. As such, **eco-centrism** has two main variants – both of which lead to far deeper, and more powerful, environmental ethics than those considered above. According to the first, all other things being equal it is wrong to despoil or destroy any living thing. The idea is that the sphere of ultimate value should be extended beyond the animal world to include animate things such as plants, trees, and so forth. According to the second, all other things being equal it is wrong to despoil or destroy natural objects. The idea is that the sphere of ultimate value should be extended beyond the animal world to include inanimate – but naturally occurring – objects such as mountains, streams, rocks and so forth. According to the second, while it is not in itself wrong to despoil individual natural objects (or indeed, any individual living thing) it is wrong to destroy, or to endanger the flourishing of, the biosphere as a whole. The idea is that the survival and flourishing of individual specimens of species, or the species themselves, is rarely a necessary condition of the survival and flourishing of the biotic system itself and thus should not be the object of our environmental concerns. To the extent that environmental changes, such as climate change, endanger the survival of the whole biosphere then these changes should be prevented. Eco-centrism has proved to be the most controversial, and the most powerful basis for the concerns of environmentalists. Indeed, some think that some version of eco-centrism is the only view of those discussed above that deserves to be called an environmental ethic at all.

See also: distributive justice; global warming; intrinsic value; sustainable development

References

Goodin, R. (1992) *Green Political Theory*, Cambridge: Polity.

Raz, J. (1986) *The Morality of Freedom*, Oxford: Oxford University Press.

Singer, P. (1993) *Practical Ethics*, Cambridge: Cambridge University Press.

World Commission on Environment and Development (1987) *Our Common Future*, Oxford: Oxford University Press.

Further reading

Elliot, R. (ed.) (1995) *Environmental Ethics*, Oxford: Oxford University Press.

Routley, R. and Routley, V. (1995) 'Against the Inevitability of Human Chauvinism', in Robert Elliot (ed.) *Environmental Ethics*, Oxford: Oxford University Press.

Taylor, P. (1986) *Respect for Nature*, New Jersey: Princeton University Press.

ED PAGE

environmental history

Environmental history, more popularly known as green history, focuses on the history of the environment and the history of environmentalism. One of its founding fathers, Donald Worster, has defined it as the interdisciplinary study of the relations of culture, **technology** and **nature** through time (Worster, 1993: viii). Its basic premise is that human activity takes place within a larger, more natural history and its objective is to reveal the various relationships over time between humans and the rest of nature (Coates, 1996:15). Or as Worster has said, its essential purpose is to put nature back into historical studies, or, defined more elaborately, to explore the ways in which the biophysical world has influenced the course of human history and the ways in which people have thought about and tried to transform their surroundings (Worster, 1993: 20). Another early pioneer, William Cronon, has defined environmental history as history which extends it boundaries beyond human institutions – economies, **class** and gender systems, political organizations, cultural rituals – to the natural ecosystems which provide the context for those institutions (Cronon, 1983: vii).

Environmental history has only become a distinct field of study in the last 25 years; before that it was considered part of historical geography or human ecology. As a distinct discipline it first emerged in the USA, with the founding in 1975 of the American Society for Environmental History and its journal *Environmental Review* in 1976 (re-named *Environmental History Review* in 1989).

North American historians have long had a deep interest in resource issues, particularly forestry, land and water, and Samuel Hays's book, *Conservation and the Gospel of Efficiency*, a history of the early nineteenth-century **conservation movement** (first published in 1959) was a landmark publication. Wilderness is another particular American concern, and Roderick Nash in his influential book, *Wilderness and the American Mind*, first published in 1967 gave an intellectual history of this cultural concept.

Until the early 1990s environmental history was dominated by American concerns. To redress this balance the English journal *Environment and History* was founded in 1995 and it has since given space to covering the environmental history of Africa, Asia and Australia, particularly the influence of colonialism and imperialism.

Originally the historian's viewpoint was from that of the white, Anglo-Saxon male, but this is rapidly changing under the impact of multiculturalism and gender; see for example eco-feminist author Carolyn Merchant. The impact of the **environmental justice** movement is being felt, and environmental history is increasingly merging with social and labour history.

The second prong of environmental history, the history of environmentalism or of **environmental movements**, is not as well developed. Generally the histories written of environmental groups like **Friends of the Earth** and **Greenpeace** are written either by activists or their supporters. There are few critical and original works. Those that are, like Anna Bramwell's *Ecology in the Twentieth Century* (1989) have proved controversial, while others like Meredith Veldman's, *Fantasy, the Bomb and the Greening of Britain* (1994) or Martin Holdgate's *The Green Web* (1999) attract little attention.

Environmental history, labelled green history, is popular when the 'lessons from history' (on soil erosion, deforestations, pollution etc.) are used to support green activism. Hence the success of Clive Ponting's *Green History of the World* (1991) which is a successor to earlier works like *Soil and Civilization* by Edward Hyams (1952).

Environmental history is part of the battle-ground between environmentalists and their critics. To the former it seeks to explain the landscapes and issues of today and their evolving and dynamic nature. The hope is that it will contribute to the sustainability debate by informing us of natural limits. To the latter it informs us of the environment's ability to recover from manmade damage, and our mistaken concepts of 'natural' **landscape**. Thus it is an essential part of environmental politics.

References

Coates, P. (1996) 'Clio's New Greenhouse', *History Today*, August.

Cronon, W. (1983) *Changes in the Land: Indians, Colonists and the Ecology of New England*, New York: Hill and Wang.

Worster, D. (1993) *The Wealth of Nature: Environmental History and the Ecological Imagination*, Oxford: Oxford University Press.

Further reading

Beinart, W. and Coates, P. (1995) *Environmental History: The Taming of Nature in the USA and South Africa*, London: Routledge.

Grove, R. (1995) *Green Imperialism: Colonial Expansion, Tropical Island Edens and the Origins of Environmentalism 1600–1860*, Cambridge: Cambridge University Press.

Miller, C. and Rotham, H. (eds) (1997) *Out of the Woods: Essays in Environmental History*, Pittsburgh: Pittsburgh Press.

Wall, D. (1994) *Green History: A Reader in Environmental Literature Philosophy and Politics*, London: Routledge.

HORACE HERRING

environmental justice

Gathering momentum in the 1980s, the movement for environmental justice grew in the USA out of civil rights struggles over the siting of toxic and hazardous industries. In that country charges of 'environmental racism' resonated with a history of racial and ethnic politics and a historic concern with the ethic of rights. Contemporaneously there developed a lively – and sometimes intersecting – international academic discourse of environmental justice that explores the human consequences of environmental ethics. The justice of environmentalism was brought to the foreground of the international political agenda at the United Nations Conference on Environment and Development in 1992, the 'Earth Summit' (see **Rio Conference 1992**). Sustainable development is both about justice between the present and future generations and justice between rich and poor nations. Although environmental justice mostly refers to the distributional fairness of the human impact upon local environments, the most difficult philosophical question concerns the ethical relationship between humans and the rest of the natural world.

In the USA the debate about environmental justice had its origins in the grassroots struggles of local communities during the 1970s against 'environmental racism'. These struggles, involving both local communities of colour (African American, Latino and Native American) and various progressive groupings (notably churches and civil rights organizations), sought to oppose the racially discriminatory distribution of hazardous wastes and polluting industries in the USA. Importantly, this grassroots campaign emerged outside, even at times in opposition to, the mainstream of the environmental movement in the USA, which was accused of failing to identify and oppose the disproportionate burden of toxic contamination on minority communities.

A seminal moment in the environmental racism campaign was provided in 1982 by the vigorous protests against the siting of a PCB landfill in a black community within Warren County, North Carolina (see **PCBs**). This action saw prominent national civil rights leaders uniting with the local community in a campaign of civil disobedience reminiscent of the racial justice struggles of the 1960s. Following this, a series of government, community and social scientific analyses on toxic waste patterns demonstrated that race was the central determining factor in the distribution of chemical hazard exposure in the USA. By the early

1990s, several thousand groups had emerged to oppose inequitable distributions of land uses which threatened the environmental health of local communities.

In 1991, a First National People of Color Environmental Leadership Summit in Washington, DC adopted 17 principles of environmental justice which extend the movement's focus on race to include other concerns, such as **class** and non-human species. This broadening of political purpose has also extended the social and institutional reach of the environmental justice movement, which has shifted from grassroots activity to the centres of corporate and government power. In 1992, the US **Environmental Protection Agency** established an Office of Environmental Equity and published a report on the national distribution of ecological risks. Two years later President Clinton signed Executive Order 12898, which required that every federal agency consider the effects of its own policies and programmes on the health and environmental well-being of minority communities.

The environmental justice movement gave new life to the idea of justice as a social ethic. The argument is that it is unfair for the risks and costs of production to be loaded on to the living environments of some people, while others enjoy the benefits but avoid the costs. The linking of 'social justice' and 'environment' opened environmentalism to increased reflection on the social consequences and conditions of its own ethics. At the same time it made possible a powerful political and discursive coalition between two congeries of politically mobilized groups: social reformers and environmentalists.

Bringing justice back into academic discussion, however, faced three serious obstacles. First, the neoliberal consensus of the political Right which had come to dominate political thought in the last quarter of the twentieth century tended to regard talk about social justice as 'nonsense on stilts' providing a rhetoric for undeserving pressure groups to demand special privileges from the state. Second, while justice must of necessity appeal to universal principles, the post-modernist consensus which had absorbed many of the liberal Left viewed universal ethics with profound scepticism

and distrust. So the political Right which believed in the universal principles of utilitarianism and the market tended to be reinforced by a political Left which did not believe in principles at all and thus had none to offer to effect change – except 'diversity' which was precisely the purpose of the market. Third, if the main ethical concerns of environmentalists were to be addressed, environmental justice had to embrace the relationship between humans and non-human creatures of nature (see **environmental ethics**).

These obstacles provided challenges to be overcome, and in fact the more innovative theorists of the period were already struggling with them. Environmental justice provided a rubric. Some (such as Peter Wenz following in the steps of John Rawls) ignored the neoliberal and post-modern threat and based their ethic on compelling intuitive understandings – in Wenz's case of diminishing obligation with social distance from oneself. Others such as Iris Marion Young embraced **post-modernism** but focused upon injustice. David Harvey tackled post-modernism, neoliberalism and environmentalism all at once from a Marxist perspective. Arran Gare found that poststructuralists were prevented by the structure of their philosophy from conceiving of both the reality of global environmental crisis and the means of overcoming it. Robyn Eckersley addressed the compatibility with liberal democracy of rights and representation of the non-human. These new currents of thought were confluent to some degree with philosophical perspectives of longer standing on justice to animals advanced by Peter **Singer** and Tom Regan, the social causes of environmental injustice rooted in human society portrayed by Murray **Bookchin**, and philosophies which comprehensively embraced an ecocentric perspective argued, for example, by Val Plumwood and Freya Mathews.

Along with the 'ethic of care' environmental justice has become a major conceptual building block of environmental politics. Its importance led Dobson (1998: 244) to conclude that 'no theory of justice can henceforth be regarded as complete if it does not take into account the possibility of extending the community of justice beyond the realm of present generation human beings'. Justice is about distribution. The most difficult question of environmental justice is the distribution of care, however conceived, between humans and non-human parts of nature. This is not just a matter of agreeing where a line is situated between those who count for moral purposes and those who do not. Dobson rightly points out that social reformers who place humans at the centre of their care do not have the same practical concerns and emotional commitments as environmentalists who place nature as a whole in that position. Nevertheless there are ways in which the two concerns may in practice converge. They may, for example converge on the need to protect species – from an ecocentric perspective because of the **intrinsic value** of species, from an anthropocentric perspective because of the instrumental value of species to future generations of humans (see **ecocentrism**; **anthropocentrism**; **intergenerational justice**). They may also converge on the need for new political institutions within which these and other questions of justice may be debated and decided.

The question of environmental justice has an international dimension that is increasingly the subject of political struggle and theoretical debate (Low and Gleeson, 1998). The uneven development of environmental regulation at the national scale poses new political–ethical problems. In the USA, for example, strict environmental regulations are increasingly cited by firms as a reason for their flight to more 'business friendly' countries, such as **Mexico** (Pulido, 1994). In many cases, the profits from industrial plants, as well as their products, are largely exported to the country of the operating firm. The developing nation that hosts the facility retains a small quantum of wage and land rent income, but incurs input expenditure as well as the environmental and social risks which attach to the hazardous industry (see **less developed countries**). Risk is also redistributed through the international trade in toxic waste, usually from wealthy, industrialized countries to developing nations that may be prepared to sacrifice the safety of their environments and peoples in exchange for monetary compensation (see **hazardous and toxic waste management**).

The question of justice also goes to the heart of new institutional relationships that are emerging to regulate the global environment. It has become clear that **sustainable development** involves conflict of interest: among different industries and those who depend on them, between developed and developing nations, between the interests of present and future generations. These conflicts demand *just* solutions and these solutions in turn require new global institutions and concomitant institutional change at national and local levels.

References

Dobson, A. (1998) *Justice and the Environment*, Oxford: Oxford University Press.

Low, N.P. and Gleeson, B.J. (1998) *Justice, Society and Nature: an exploration of political ecology*, London: Routledge.

Pulido, L. (1994) 'Restructuring and the Contraction and Expansion of Environmental Rights in the United States', *Environment and Planning A*, 26: 915–36.

Further reading

Bullard, R. (1990) *Dumping in Dixie*, Boulder, CO: Westview Press.

Harvey, D. (1996) *Justice, Nature and the Geography of Difference*, Oxford: Blackwell.

Plumwood, V. (1993) *Feminism and the Mastery of Nature*, London: Routledge.

Wenz, P.S. (1988) *Environmental Justice*, New York: State University of New York Press.

NICHOLAS LOW AND BRENDAN GLEESON

environmental law and litigation

Environmental law and litigation in the USA developed rapidly in the last three decades of the twentieth century, becoming a significant specialty in most law schools and generating many new specialized law journals. It covers all the statute law that has been passed on such subjects as water and air pollution, natural resource conservation, hazardous materials exposure of humans, and disposal of solid wastes, as well as all the regulations generated under these laws by the agencies responsible for administering them (see **hazardous and toxic waste management**). Rarely do opposing stakeholders interpret these laws in the same manner, and most of these disagreements are brought to court for interpretation and resolution. Hence, most contentious issues regarding the environment have been aired in court in the USA and in many countries in Europe as well.

Environmental groups in the 1970s were instrumental in getting environmental laws passed and amended. Sceptical of administrators' enthusiasm for enforcing these laws, they remained vigilant in order to see them faithfully executed. Using language in many of the laws that provide for 'citizen complaints', they have taken their cause to the courts when they felt that the government was not strictly enforcing the laws. In addition, environmental groups do not hesitate to sue government agencies themselves whenever the groups believe those agencies themselves are violating environmental legislation and failing to properly conserve the natural resources of the nation. One law that has been especially useful in this regard is the **National Environmental Policy Act** (US). This law requires government agencies to predict the impact planned programmes and projects will have on the physical environment. It took a number of court actions in the 1970s to convince administrative agencies of the need to write environmental impact statements. Law suits critiquing the contents of such statements have been less successful in getting projects modified.

Environmental groups are not the only ones to litigate under environmental laws. Government agencies, especially the **Environmental Protection Agency** (EPA), take violators of pollution control laws to court whenever administrative actions fail to obtain the desired result. Under the Clean Air and Clean Water Acts (US) it is possible to prosecute polluters for criminal offences when it can be shown that the offence was deliberate. Thus, these cases may result in both fines and jail terms.

Industries and trade associations became the most active initiator of environmental law suits in the 1990s. They challenge nearly all of the regulations promulgated by EPA in court, after making comments about them in the formulation stage. Often businesses will challenge even the constitutionality of the laws themselves. One of the most litigated areas of the law concerns the identification of responsible parties who must reimburse EPA for the cleanup of abandoned toxic waste dumps. When EPA identifies the companies it believes are responsible for the pollution, those companies will often initiate their own investigation to identify additional responsible parties and sue them to recover some of the costs. Suits over **Superfund** sites have become so common that often the total legal expenses outweigh the actual costs of cleaning up a site.

In addition to litigation designed to get courts to interpret and enforce the statute laws, some people who consider themselves injured by pollution continue to sue under the **common law** of torts to recover damages for those injuries. Generally speaking these suits are less successful than those founded in statute law.

See also: air pollution; Clean Air Act; Clean Water Act; common law/torts; property rights; water pollution

Further reading

Findley, R.W. and Farber, D.A. (1991) *Cases and Materials on Environmental Law,* St Paul, MN: West Publishing, 3rd edn.

Kubasek, N. and Silverman, G.S. (2000) *Environmental Law,* Upper Saddle River, NJ: Prentice Hall, 3rd edn.

Stensvaag, J.-M. (1999) *Materials on Environmental Law,* St Paul, MN: West Publishing.

Wenner, L. (1983) *The Environmental Decade in Court,* Bloomington, IN: Indiana University Press.

LETTIE McSPADDEN

environmental management

Environmental management is human intervention in the natural environment to retain or enhance some beneficial attribute, or remove or mitigate a harmful one. Environmental management, in contrast to planning or control, assumes positive and sustained action, and entails a blend of physical, economic, regulatory, advisory and educational remedies. Its aims include: safeguarding and maintaining the qualities and processes of valued **landscapes** and wildlife habitats; reducing and eliminating pollution and its wider effects; reducing the severity and impact of natural hazards; and maintaining the productiveness, integrity and amenity of natural resources. Environmental management is part technical and part political: whilst sound decision-making and robust science underpin specific interventions, solutions need to be negotiated between and jointly implemented by stakeholders within a wider political economy. Environmental management is related to **sustainable development**, as it requires long-term **stewardship** of natural assets.

PAUL SELMAN

environmental movements

Environmental movements are loose, non-institutionalized networks of informal interactions that may include, as well as individuals and groups who have no organizational affiliation, organizations of varying degrees of formality (including even political parties, especially green parties), and are engaged in collective action motivated by shared concern about environmental issues. The forms and intensity of action and the degree of integration of networks vary, but environmental movements are identical neither with organizations nor with episodes of protest. It is only when organizations (and other actors) are networked and engaged in collective action, whether or not it involves protest, that an environmental movement exists (see Diani, 1995: 5).

Such linkages are not always readily visible. Where environmental movements are well established, the balance of their actions has shifted from highly visible protest to less visible lobbying and 'constructive engagement' with governments and corporations. Also invisible are many 'subterranean' linkages among individuals, groups and organizations.

Conventionally, it has been assumed that 'success' for a social movement means its institutionalization, usually as a political party. However, Eyerman and Jamison (1991) argue that a movement exists only in the relatively brief liminal period when a new, autonomous public space is created. The identity of the environmental movement dissolves as its organization fragments and its 'movement intellectuals' become established in university departments of environmental studies, the environmental departments of industrial organizations, law and journalism, professionalized campaigning organizations such as **Greenpeace**, and political parties, including green parties. From this perspective, movements are by definition transient, and the notion of the institutionalization of the environmental movement is a contradiction in terms.

Recent history, however, suggests that environmental movements may have squared the circle. Whether measured by size, income, degree of formality of organizations, number and professionalization of employees, or frequency and kind of interaction with established institutional actors, environmental movement organizations (EMOs) in most industrialized countries are now relatively highly institutionalized. Yet such institutionalization has not necessarily entailed the deradicalization of the movement or a loss of shared identity.

In Britain, for example, during the 1990s EMOs grew in numbers and size as well as increased access and influence, but reported environmental protest also increased and became more confrontational. Although the rise of new, more radical groups such as **Earth First!** can be traced to dissatisfaction with the apparent moderation of more established organizations such as **Friends of the Earth** (FoE) and Greenpeace, shared identity survived. Even the radical 'disorganizations' most committed to direct action are connected by networks of advice and support to more established organizations. The sense of identity among the constituent parts of the movement has not dissolved with institutionalization and the reactions against it, but has instead grown as groups have come to practice a division of labours and have realized that there is much to be gained by co-operation.

The British experience shows that it is possible for an environmental movement to maintain many of the characteristics of a movement *in statu nascendi* whilst taking advantage of the opportunities presented by a measure of institutionalization. Whilst some writers have referred to the 'self-limiting radicalism' of green parties, it is no less important to recognize the 'self-limiting institutionalization' of environmental movements.

Their survival and their resistance to the deradicalizing effects of institutionalization has distinguished environmental movements from other **new social movements**. Because pressing environmental problems are part of the chronic condition of an industrialized world, western environmental movements, although by no means universally anti-capitalist, are recurrently influenced by the critical analyses of their radically anti-capitalist constituents, as recent campaigns against genetically modified organisms and anti-roads protests have shown.

Environmental movements are typically broad networks linking ideologically and thematically diverse constituents. Distinctions among traditional conservationism, modern environmentalism and political ecology do not reliably differentiate EMOs, their members and supporters. As Dalton (1994) discovered, by the mid-1980s the differences among the strategies, tactics and styles of action of European EMOs were, despite their original ideological differences, surprisingly muted. A process of convergence was under way within the broad environmental movement, and if EMOs such as FoE and Greenpeace were learning the etiquette necessary to smooth dealings with the powerful, so more traditional conservationist organizations were becoming more ecological in their worldviews and more radical in their tactics.

The character of environmental movements varies from one country to another according to material differences in their environments. Thus in the USA, Canada, Australasia and the Nordic countries, wilderness issues have often been more salient than pollution issues. In western Europe, where the romantic myth of unspoilt nature has had to come to terms with the fact that the physical environment is largely a human product, the concern to protect **landscapes** is more readily combined with concerns about the consequences of environmental degradation for people. Perhaps because it is in northern Europe that the experience of industrialism is longest and there is greater recognition of human interdependence as well as responsibility for the state of the environment, it is there that awareness of global environmental issues is most developed and most central to the agenda of environmental movements.

In the most recently industrialized parts of southern Europe and in the countries of central and eastern Europe ravaged by rapid **industrialization** under **communism**, environmental concern is more often a matter of personal complaint than global environmental consciousness. As a result, environmentalist action there usually takes the form of intense local campaigns; national EMOs are relatively weak. Environmental movements are often credited with a major role in the popular mobilizations against Communist regimes, but their subsequent weakness in eastern Europe suggests that green was often adopted as protective camouflage by anti-regime activists who subsequently turned to more mainstream political roles, or that the political and economic urgencies of post-transition states have sidelined environmental concerns.

In the Third World especially, environmental issues are bound up with those surrounding the distribution of social, economic and political power and resources. Struggles to protect the environment, although sometimes involving large numbers of people, rarely take the form of environmental movements. The lack of safeguards for democratic political activity or possibilities of judicial redress of grievances and the underdevelopment of **civil society** often defeat the efforts of some of the world's most impoverished people to defend their habitat. Success for their campaigns usually depends upon the support of western environmental or **human rights** organizations.

Third World environmental struggles are not unique in bundling claims for environmental protection with demands for social and economic justice, and often for substantive **democracy** as well. In the USA environmental demands have recently been conjoined with the critique of **class** and, especially, racial inequalities. Distrustful of the alleged elitism of established EMOs, the **environmental justice** movement takes the form of a loose network of local campaign groups.

The relationship of local environmental protests to environmental movements is problematic. Most are **NIMBY** in origin and usually do not centrally involve even the local branches of established EMOs. Only exceptionally do they grow into more general EMOs, but they nevertheless serve as sources of innovation and renewal within national environmental movements, by 'discovering' new environmental issues, initiating new generations of activists, and devising new tactics. A preference for deliberately informal networks rather than formal organization is characteristic of recent waves of environmental activism on both sides of the Atlantic.

National and local political cultures and material differences affect the forms, development and outcomes of environmental movements, as do differences among **political opportunity structures**. National EMOs are dependent for their resources and legitimacy upon national publics, and their dynamics and trajectories are shaped by locally and nationally idiosyncratic events and institutions. Consequently, the concertation of transnational environmental activism is difficult. Even within the best developed supra-national polity – the **European Union** – EMOs remain primarily national in their networks, collective action repertoires and thematic concerns, despite the EU's importance as the principal locus of environmental policy-making.

The absence of a developed global polity presents even greater obstacles to the formation of a global environmental movement. Although the advent of international agreements and agencies, not least those of the United Nations and the **World Bank**, has encouraged the development of transnational environmental non-governmental organizations, the latter are not mass participatory organizations and are rarely democratically accountable (see **international non-governmental organizations**). This lack of democratic accountability is unlikely to be merely temporary. However, if the prospects for an effective and genuinely democratic global environmental movement appear limited today, they are likely to

improve as better and cheaper means of communication make the global village ever better connected and as increasing access to higher education gives more people the personal skills and resources necessary to make common cause with their counterparts in other countries and regions.

See also: Earth First! (UK); Earth First! (US); East and Central European Greens; environmental justice; environmentalism of the poor; New Left; new politics; new social movements

References

Dalton, R.J. (1994) *The Green Rainbow: Environmental Groups in Western Europe*, New Haven and London: Yale University Press.

Diani, M. (1995) *Green Networks: A Structural Analysis of the Italian Environmental Movement*, Edinburgh: Edinburgh University Press.

Eyerman, R. and Jamison, A. (1991) *Social Movements: A Cognitive Approach*, Cambridge: Polity.

Further reading

Rootes, C. (1997) 'Environmental Movements and Green Parties in Western and Eastern Europe', in M. Redclift and G. Woodgate, (eds) *International Handbook of Environmental Sociology*, Cheltenham and Northampton, MA: Edward Elgar, pp. 319–48.

Rootes, C. (ed.) (1999) *Environmental Movements: Local, National and Global*, London and Portland, OR: Frank Cass.

Taylor, B. (ed.) (1995) *Ecological Resistance Movements: The Global Emergence of Radical and Popular Environmentalism*, Albany, NY: State University of New York Press.

Wapner, P. (1996) *Environmental Activism and World Civic Politics*, Albany, NY: State University of New York Press.

CHRIS ROOTES

environmental pragmatism

Environmental pragmatism is a contemporary environmental philosophical movement which builds on the rich tradition of American pragmatism, the chief pioneers of which were C.S. Peirce (1839–1914), William James (1842–1910) and John Dewey (1859–1952). As a philosophical movement, the classical pragmatists mounted a major challenge to **Enlightenment** epistemology, metaphysics and values. As radical empiricists, they rejected both abstract and absolutist philosophizing in favour of practical experience as the ultimate arbiter of truth. In particular, they emphasized the tentative and provisional character of knowledge, the self-corrective character of inquiry as an ongoing process, and the interpretation and validation of ideas, meaning and truth through their practical consequences. These themes, while commonplace today, were quite radical in their day in challenging the 'spectator' view of knowledge. For the pragmatists, what is true is that which is intersubjectively experienced as true, or able to withstand testing, by a community of inquirers. John Dewey, in particular, reinterpreted pragmatism as instrumentalism and interpreted truth as 'warranted assertability'.

As social constructionists, the classical pragmatists also rejected any notion of eternal essences. Humans were understood as active experimenters who constantly reorder their understanding of and orientation to the world as a result of their constructed and reconstructed experience *in* the world. Pragmatism proceeded on the basis of a relational ontology that rejected dualisms between self/world and thought/action. Socially and politically, the classical pragmatists were democrats and humanists who emphasized the importance of social learning through deliberation. For example, John Dewey believed that science advanced because it institutionalized criticism, and was therefore self-corrective. He also hoped that social change would be directed by intelligent and inclusive political deliberation.

Contemporary environmental pragmatists have sought to build upon these classical pragmatist insights by offering a practical approach to contemporary environmental problems and conflicts. In pursuing this project, environmental pragmatists seek to avoid methodological and theoretical dogmatism in order to remain sensitive to the fact of moral pluralism. They are critical of 'armchair philosophy' and emphasize the point that the practical resolution of problems does not necessarily require agreement on fundamental values since it is possible for people to agree on the same course of action for different religious and philosophical reasons. Here environmental pragmatists argue that achieving such an agreement requires not an 'applied philosophy' but rather a 'practical philosophy'. Whereas applied philosophy seeks to deduce policies from general principles that are determined in the abstract, in advance of practical problems, practical philosophy seeks a reconciliation of real world moral pluralism by developing principles and strategies in the context of specific practical problems. Deliberation, creative conflict mediation and social learning thus replace any quest for ethical perfection.

Environmental pragmatists are critical of monistic environmental philosophies which seek to reduce environmental values and practical policies to one ultimate moral principle or set of principles. This includes non-anthropocentric holism as well as those approaches which seek to construct an environmental philosophy on the basis of a defence of the **intrinsic value** of **nature**. For *some* environmental pragmatists, the human perspective is the only thing we know as humans and therefore the human perspective becomes the measure of all things by default (Parker, 1995: 33). However, 'methodological environmental pragmatists' (such as Andrew Light and Eric Katz) are more agnostic about the sources of value and are prepared to extend pluralism to encompass non-anthropocentric intuitions about value. For the committed Deweyians, however, it is meaningless to talk about the value of something in the absence of a human valuer, although this need not rule out the valuing of non-human entities by human subjects. Pragmatists also reject the ends–means distinction along with the notion of any fixed and final end. From this perspective, it makes no sense to say that an entity is intrinsically valuable in the sense that its value is self-sufficient, abstracted from its relations with other entities. Aside from the ongoing problem of providing a plausible account and justification of intrinsic value, the project of tracing all instrumental values back to some intrinsically valuable entity is always problematic because it involves tracing values back to some single, ultimate value – a project that is incompatible with moral pluralism (Weston, 1996: 289). Values are web-like, interrelated and specific to particular human/environment contexts and cannot be meaningfully defended outside such real world evaluations and choices where different clusters of values must always be related to each other.

Many of the central claims of environmental pragmatism have been contested, particularly by those who have been accused of moral monism. For example, J. Baird Callicott has mounted a spirited defence of moral monism, arguing that consistency or noncontradiction is 'the very foundation of critical judgment' (1995: 25) and that moral pluralism 'implies metaphysical musical chairs' (1990: 115). More generally, the pragmatists' embrace of moral pluralism carries with it the danger of lapsing into indecisive relativism. The refusal to privilege any substantive environmental values also carries ambiguous political implications. While environmental pragmatists embrace Dewey's emphasis on the need for institutionalized criticism, their focus on practical problem solving combined with a notable absence of any critical substantive ethic of environmental justice may lend just as much support to the development of practical policies of appeasement and interest accommodation as it does radical reform on behalf of marginalized others, whether human or non-human. In this respect, environmental pragmatists may be seen as *environmental* mediators rather than **environmental justice** advocates.

References

Callicott, J.B. (1990) 'The Case Against Moral Pluralism', *Environmental Ethics* 12(2): 999–1124.

—— (1995) 'Environmental Philosophy is Environmental Activism: The Most Radical and Effective Kind' in D.E. Marrietta Jr and L. Embree (eds) *Environmental Philosophy and Environmental Activism*, Lanham, MD: Rowman and Littlefield.

Parker, K. (1996) 'Pragmatism and Environmental Thought' in A. Light and E. Katz (eds) *Environmental Pragmatism*, London: Routledge.

Weston, A. (1996) 'Beyond Intrinsic Value: Pragmatism in Environmental Ethics', in A. Light and E. Katz (eds) *Environmental Pragmatism*, London: Routledge.

ROBYN ECKERSLEY

Environmental Protection Agency

Responding to surging public concerns, President Richard Nixon in 1970 by executive order created the Environmental Protection Agency (EPA) to coordinate the federal government's response to pollution. The EPA came into existence as a regulatory agency whose head administrator answers directly to the President; hence, it is not an independent regulatory agency like the Federal Communications Commission. It brought together 6,000 employees from 15 federal programmes. On day one, the EPA ranked as the federal government's largest regulatory agency. Thirty years later it has about 18, 000 employees, more than four of the executive departments of the federal government; its expenditures in fiscal year 2000 amounted to more than $7.2 billion. The EPA has developed as a decentralized organization, with some two-thirds of its staff based outside Washington, DC. Its ten regional offices work closely with the states' environmental agencies in the implementation of EPA regulations.

The EPA received heavy statutory responsibilities in the early 1970s. Environmental policy underwent non-incremental change as the Congress passed major amendments to clean air and water laws (see **Clean Air Act**; **Clean Water Act**). In the second half of the 1970s, the EPA received new mandates to deal with toxic substances and hazardous wastes. Congress departed from the traditional approach, which had left the states basically in charge of pollution control, by deciding ambitious national goals for environmental quality. It gave the EPA the authority to determine quality standards, set emission (effluent) levels, approve state implementation plans, and penalize states that missed deadlines. The EPA also received the power to specify what technologies were to be used by industries to meet the standards. While the Congress had set non-incremental goals for cleaning up the country's air and water, it provided the EPA with only incremental funding to do its job. As a result, the EPA began to waffle on enforcement. Soon political pressures resulted in continual extension of deadlines. The EPA also found itself in a crossfire of litigation with environmentalists charging it with being too lax and the industrialists, with being too tough. (William **Ruckelshaus**, EPA Administrator, observed in 1985 that 80 per cent of EPA decisions had been challenged in the courts.) In the late 1970s, the EPA during the Carter Administration began to institute reforms to increase cost effectiveness.

However, the great divide in the EPA's history came during first **Reagan** Administration. EPA Administrator Anne Gorsuch **Burford** (1981–3), sought reductions in the EPA budget of 25–30 per cent, de-emphasized enforcement of regulations, and sought to return responsibilities (without additional federal funding) for pollution control to the states. Ultimately Burford was cited for 'contempt of Congress' over her refusal to provide information on the federal programme regarding the cleanup of hazardous wastes, and she resigned. She was followed by a series of moderate Republican Administrators who sought both to be sensitive to business complaints about inflexibility and to make advances in environmental quality, such as the Clean Air Amendments of 1990. The EPA since the mid-1980s has embraced **risk assessment** in making more effective regulatory decisions.

National evidence indicated in the mid-1990s that progress had been made in cleaning up the air, and in some places the water as well (the data regarding hazardous wastes were less encouraging). But the EPA was subjected to increasing criticism from academic experts and practitioners regarding its ('command and control') **regulatory approaches**, unrealistic deadlines, lack of cross-media strategies, and the absence of a comprehensive pollution law. Congressional Republicans and state governors from both parties joined the chorus of criticism. Rather than see the EPA legislatively undermined, the Clinton Administration proceeded to 'reinvent' the agency using executive authority. Its Common Sense Initiative sought at the industrial level to encourage stakeholder committees to develop consensual plans addressing cross-media pollution and avoiding litigation. At the firm level, the EPA encouraged creative environmental management strategies under Project XL. The EPA entered into Performance Partnerships with the states in which priorities would be jointly set and then implemented by the states with considerable discretion, while the EPA provided Partnership Grants. It is too early to assess the success of this non-headline grabbing 'reinvention'. Clearly the Republican leadership in Congress has continued to maintain a belligerent orientation toward the EPA.

Despite the protests of business lobbyists and state governors, the Clinton EPA in the late 1990s decided to tighten the air pollution regulations for ground level ozone and soot. Court challenges have prevented their implementation. With the election of President George W. Bush it is unlikely that there will be such major initiatives by the EPA during 2001–5. During his campaign, Bush favoured turning environmental responsibilities back to the states and relying on voluntary compliance from industry to clean up the environment.

Further reading

Rosenbaum, W.A. (2000) 'Escaping the 'Battered Agency Syndrome': EPA's Gamble with Regulatory Reinvention', in N.J. Vig and M.E. Kraft, *Environmental Policy*, Washington, DC: Congressional Quarterly Press, 4th edn.

E. GENE FRANKLAND

environmental refugees

Environmental refugees are people forced to leave their traditional habitat, temporarily or permanently, because its carrying capacity for humans is exhausted as a result of marked environmental disruption. The concept was introduced in 1985 by the **United Nations Environment Programme**. Environmental refugees are displaced persons, either in their own country or beyond, often perceived as a threat to the host society's identity and social cohesion. Such perceptions may even lead to conflicts superficially seen as caused by ethnic tensions while the underlying cause is competition over scarce natural resources, such as water. Ultimately the problem of environmental refugees is intrinsically linked to the wider issues of **environmental security** and **sustainable development**.

Environmental refugees have no official status and are even less acknowledged than similarly officially unrecognized internal political refugees and economic refugees. However, these groups of refugees overlap and collectively outnumber the only recognized and protected group, namely international political refugees. Even by conservative estimates environmental refugees in particular are on the increase as more areas become ecologically vulnerable. It is generally accepted that environmental refugees are a dramatically worsening international problem which requires urgent policy and law responses.

Environmental refugees are not a new phenomenon. What is new is the magnitude and frequency of the phenomenon. This is a result of globally deteriorating environmental conditions, such as desertification, deforestation, soil erosion, drought, water shortages etc., caused by the interconnected and cumulative impact of natural and anthropogenic factors: volcanic eruptions, earthquakes, global climate change bringing extreme weather conditions, **global warming** and the prospect of rising sea levels; consumption of scarce natural resources by the developed states disproportionate to their declining population; population growth in the developing world increasing demands on natural resources thus creating a vicious circle of extreme poverty and further ecological pressures. These factors may also be exacerbated by failed **development** policies whereby increasing numbers of people are being marginalized within physically, socially, politically and economically impoverished environments. Unsurprisingly environmental refugees are located mainly in **sub-Saharan Africa**, the Indian sub-continent, **China**, **Mexico** and Latin America.

Given the gravity of the problem of environmental refugees, the international community needs to recognize formally that they are not a peripheral issue but represent an environmental, social, eco-

nomic and political crisis at global level. The global nature of the crisis requires urgent action under international law in order to regulate two key issues, the legal definition and rights of environmental refugees. The definition of who is a refugee must be widened and made more inclusive. The 1951 Geneva Refugee Convention operates a narrow and exclusive definition: a refugee is a person living outside the country of his/her nationality because of a well-founded fear of persecution on specified grounds. States apply this definition with notorious narrow-mindedness. As a result, the numbers of legally recognized refugees are seriously underestimated while the numbers of environmental, internal and economic refugees are unaccounted for. However, these refugees are as likely to face serious jeopardy as the recognized refugees having access to the protection and limited resources of the UN High Commissioner for Refugees. Environmental refugees come under the UN Disaster Relief Co-ordinator who has even less resources.

Widening the legal definition of refugee must be coupled with clearly stated legal rights. At present refugees have no legal right to asylum under international law. States, although they cannot turn refugees away, are not obliged to grant them asylum or any other rights. They may do so at their discretion. As a result state practice varies making refugee rights a matter of luck.

Improving the definition and legal rights of refugees is essentially a reactive response. Proactive policies are of critical importance. For instance, addressing the root causes creating environmental refugees means that developed states must remove crippling foreign debt and target foreign aid to relieve economic and political insecurity in the countries most at risk. Above all it means promoting sustainable development in order to provide people with adequate resources to live in their homelands free of destitution in all its forms. Ultimately environmental refugees are an indicator of the capacity of the international community to provide global environmental security based on political stability and social justice.

Further reading

El-Hinnawi, E.(1985) *Environmental Refugees*, Nairobi, Kenya: United Nations Environmental Programme.

Myers, N. and Kent, J. (1995) *Environmental Exodus: An Emergent Crisis in the Global Arena*, Washington, DC: Climate Institute.

Westing, A.H. (1992) 'Environmental Refugees: A Growing Category of Displaced Persons', *Environmental Conservation* 19(3): 201–7.

Woehicke, M. (1992) 'Environmental Refugees', *Aussen Politik* 43(3): 287–96.

ANNA SYNGELLAKIS

environmental research and development

Programmes for scientific research and technological development, often abbreviated as 'R&D', have been an important component of environmental policy, at least since the 1960s. Before then, environmental R&D was usually conducted under another rubric, or as part of another research or development activity. It was in the 1960s, as part of the broader institutionalization of environmental protection in the form of new state authorities and university departments that a particular policy sector for environmental R&D was established in many countries.

There are three main types of environmental R&D programmes: 1) basic research, which is usually supported by governmental or intergovernmental research councils; 2) applied, or regulatory, research, which is usually supported by environmental ministries or agencies; and 3) technological development, which tends to be supported primarily by industrial firms and corporate foundations.

Basic research programmes typically explore the underlying natural processes that are involved in, or influenced by, particular environmental problems, such as pollution or waste, and they are usually carried out by researchers in such natural sciences as hydrology, physical geography, geology, physiology, biochemistry and **ecology**. Applied research is often of a more technical, or instrumental character. Monitoring research is used to measure the effects of the control procedures that are applied by environmental authorities, while regulatory research, involving survey investigations

of the variables that are affected by environmental problems, is often used to provide a basis for modifying or imposing stricter pollution controls or emission standards. Technological development is carried out in a vast range of different areas, in an overall effort to provide particular techniques for controlling pollutants and other forms of waste emission, as well as alleviating other environmental hazards.

The diversity of environmental problems and the resulting need for knowledge from a number of different fields of investigation has meant that environmental R&D programmes have often required special administrative efforts by national governments and other funding agencies. Environmental R&D programmes are thus a case in which the 'internal' steering mechanisms of the scientific community have not been adequate. In many countries, special councils for environmental R&D have been established, often as part of environmental ministries, or agencies.

Since the 1960s, environmental R&D has gradually shifted its focus in many countries from pollution control and so-called 'end-of-pipe' techniques to more comprehensive and proactive approaches, such as pollution prevention, cleaner technology and industrial ecology. The general ambition has also shifted from developing technological 'fixes' to specific environmental problems to integrating environmental considerations into other scientific and engineering fields, as well as into other productive activities.

The thematic orientation of environmental R&D programmes has also shifted over the past 30 years. In the 1960s, research was primarily dealing with air, water and soil pollution (see **air pollution**; **water pollution**); while in the 1970s, **energy conservation** and **renewable energy** became important areas of research and development in many countries. By the mid-1980s, the global environmental issues of climate change and **biodiversity** had become increasingly significant. And in the 1990s, many countries have supported programmes in **sustainable development** and environmentally friendly production.

In terms of the scientific fields that have been involved in environmental research and development programmes, there has been a steady expansion over the years. Before the 1960s, it was primarily researchers in the areas of environmental and chemical engineering and such biological subfields as population ecology, zoology, ornithology, and plant geography who were active in environmental R&D. The large projects in systems ecology, that were conducted in the International Biological Program (IBP) in the 1960s, stimulated an environmental interest in many other fields of natural science and technology, such as computer science, biochemistry, geology, oceanography, and atmospheric science. Resource and energy economists became ever more active participants in environmental R&D programmes in the 1970s, while participation of other social scientists, from, e.g. political science, sociology, anthropology, psychology and history, has tended to be more limited.

In recent years, while funding for environmental R&D has diminished in many individual countries, major efforts in environmental R&D have been supported by the **European Union**, especially through its programmes in climate and environment. The EU was among the first bodies to provide substantial funding for environmental social science.

Environmental research and development programmes are typically organized around multi-disciplinary teams, or research groups, and, in recent years, there has been emphasis on strengthening the formation of networks between public and private sector organizations, and between universities and industrial firms. In general, the orientation of environmental research and development programmes has broadened to include ever more topics of investigation and ever more areas of economic **development**. The special problems of environment and development, in so-called developing countries, are a particular programme area in several European countries.

ANDREW JAMISON

environmental security

Security has traditionally been understood in state-centric and territorially defined terms, concerned with intentional physical (mainly military) threats

to the integrity and independence of the sovereign state. However, by the late 1980s, a broader view of what security is and of how one can try to achieve it – first expressed in the notions of 'extended' and 'common' security – began to be articulated in the foreign policy pronouncements of many western states on 'soft' or non-traditional security issues and goals. The environment has featured to varying degrees in the accompanying academic debates about the desirability of re-conceptualizing security and over precisely what is to be secured, against what threats, by whom, and how. It is in this context that the concept of environmental security continues to evolve. While some analyses are concerned almost exclusively with the possible contribution of environmental stress to the outbreak of violent conflict within and between states, others see environmental security as shifting the focus from state security to societal and individual well-being. More radically, others advocate the notion of 'ecological' security – security *for* the environment (of which humankind is a part) – seeing environmental security as essentially concerned with securing states and the interstate system *against* threats *from* the environment.

See also: militarism and the environment

DAVID SCRIVENER

environmentalism and ecologism

The terms environmentalism and ecologism have come to signify different approaches to the theory and practice of contemporary environmental politics. Neither the meaning nor the usefulness of the terms is universally agreed or endorsed, but the general lines are clear: 'ecologism' refers to radical forms of green politics, while 'environmentalism' is reserved for reformist approaches to sustainability. But what do 'radical' and 'reformist' mean in this context? The distinction has ethical, political, social, economic and strategic dimensions.

At the ethical level the disagreements have to do with how human beings should relate to the non-human natural world. Political ecologists (to use the term that denotes those who subscribe to ecologism) believe that the ecological crisis – as they regard it – is caused in part by inappropriate attitudes towards the non-human natural world. This attitude is described as 'instrumental' or, more technically, 'anthropocentric' (see **anthropocentrism**). According to the instrumental view, the non-human natural world has value only insofar as it is useful to human beings. Political ecologists argue that the criterion of 'usefulness' is insufficient for the broad-based defence of the non-human natural world that they would like to see, since those parts of nature that are regarded as being of no use for human welfare will not be protected. Similarly, political ecologists suggest that the 'usefulness' approach is a symptom of an attitude of mind that is more likely to lead to nature's despoliation than to its defence. This, they argue, is because privileging 'use' over 'defence' will inevitably lead to more using than defending, and while the two are not necessarily incompatible, the utilitarian mind will feel disinclined to search for compatibility.

Environmentalists counter that 'usefulness' can take many forms, and that a broad understanding of it can lead to the kind of widespread defence of the natural world that political ecologists argue for. If, for example, we regard nature as 'useful' for the aesthetic enjoyment it can provide, then bits of nature that we might not have regarded as useful from a material point of view suddenly become so. And if we add to this a 'precautionary' approach to usefulness, which is to say that we err on the side of caution before destroying a habitat, for example, then 'usefulness to humans' can underpin a much broader defence of the non-human natural world than political ecologists usually suggest (see **precautionary principle**).

This debate maps onto another common distinction in environmental political theory between 'deep' and 'shallow' ecology (see **deep ecology**). According to deep ecologists the non-human natural world has **intrinsic value** – that is, it has value irrespective of its usefulness to human beings. 'Shallow' ecology, on the other hand, is usually defined in terms of a defence of nature for its contribution to human welfare. Political ecologists find inspiration in deep ecology,

while for environmentalists shallow ecology does all the intellectual work required. Ecologism is radical in ethical terms, then, because it argues for an end to the belief that human beings are the measure of all value. This contrasts with the reformist view of environmentalists that ethical defences of the non-human natural world can be mounted from within a framework of human self-interest.

The radical/reformist distinction carries over into the realm of politics and society, where political ecologists and environmentalists often have different views as to what the 'sustainable society' would look like. The former suggest that sustainability presupposes wholesale changes in the organization of society while the environmentalist position is that sustainability is compatible with a broad range of societal types with which we are already familiar. The defining feature of the radical view is 'ecological decentralization'. Decentralization in itself, as political programme, is not of course specific to ecologism, but political ecologists offer ecological reasons for it. They argue that sustainability is more likely in a decentralized society for two reasons. First, because the distance between production and consumption is reduced, thereby reducing the ecological transaction costs involved in trading and transporting goods across the world; and second, because political ecologists believe that a 'sense of place' can encourage an awareness of the limits as well as the potentialities of a locality.

For this latter reason, the decentralization supported by political ecologists has an ecological, or ecosystem, dimension. That is to say that the boundaries of the polity should be dictated at least in part by ecosystem considerations, as well as political, social and economic ones. This is one aspect of the 'ecological rationality' that political ecologists believe should be added to the economic and scientific rationalities that are dominant in the modern world. Perhaps the most thoroughgoing form of ecological decentralization is **bioregionalism**, according to which political boundaries should be determined completely by ecological considerations, with patterns of production and consumption within the polity entirely dependent upon the resources available in the relevant 'bioregion'. By no means all political ecologists are bioregionalists, but most of them will agree that sustainability has a powerful local dimension.

Environmentalists will agree, but they add that the problems of unsustainability need addressing at a variety of levels beyond the local one. They will point, for example, to the way in which pollution crosses local, regional and national boundaries, and will conclude that the importance of the international dimension of **sustainability** policy is underestimated by ecologism.

The earlier reference to 'limits' marks another fault line between the ecological and environmental world views. Political ecologists regard the conclusions in the *Limits to Growth* report as central to their position. The report comes to the conclusion that the problems of environmental sustainability cannot be solved by 'technological fixes', and that there are fundamental and untranscendable limits to growth due to the finitude both of raw materials for production and of the sinks which can comfortably contain the wastes from the production process. Political ecologists believe that radical changes in the way society is organized and the ways in which people think and behave, rather than improved **technology** alone, are the key to sustainable living. For political ecologists, limits to growth imply limits to consumption, and they will often talk of a society of 'enough' rather than of 'more and more'. Environmentalists, on the other hand, will point to the way in which resource scarcity has most often led to the development of substitutes, and will conclude that scarcity is not absolute, but is relative to conditions of political, economic, and technical development. While political ecologists argue for doing less with less, then, environmentalists seek to do more with less.

Ecologism and environmentalism differ in terms of political strategy over the value of operating within the framework of 'parliamentary' politics. Environmentalists will suggest that their objectives can be met by working within a liberal democratic framework (see **liberalism/liberal democracy**), and will often be found in political parties (not necessarily green ones) and in pressure groups dedicated to lobbying governments for environmental change. Political ecologists feel that their radical objectives are unachievable in this kind of

way, and will adopt a range of 'extra-parliamentary' strategies, ranging from **intentional communities** where the deep-green society is prefigured on a small scale, to direct action, where opposition to unsustainable practices is taken to the streets and the fields (see **non-violent direct action**).

Those who believe that ecologism exists in distinction from environmentalism are also likely to argue that it – ecologism – is a modern political ideology in the same sense in which socialism, liberalism and conservatism are also political ideologies. On this view, ecologism has all the structural characteristics of an ideology – an orientating description of the present political, social and economic world, a prescription for a different one, and a strategy for getting from the first to the second. Moreover, this programme is distinct from those of all other political ideologies in such a way that it cannot be mixed with them. Environmentalism, on the other hand, is not 'ideological' in this sense. Environmentalists can be found in all political parties in a way in which political ecologists cannot.

The organizing contrast of this entry between ecologism and environmentalism has been the subject of recent criticism. There are those (for example, Norton, 1991 and Barry, 1999) who argue that ecologism and environmentalism converge at all the points that really matter. They suggest, for example, that the distinction between anthropocentric and ecocentric ethics is overdrawn, since a thoroughgoing concern for the welfare of future generations of human beings (an anthropocentric concern, note) involves sustaining current levels of **biodiversity** in order to provide future generations with the same opportunities as the present one (see **intergenerational justice**).

The debate between ecologism and environmentalism is very much a 'developed world' phenomenon. The ethical, political and strategic differences that separate them have developed in a quite specific context, and it is probably fair to say that these have little purchase beyond societies that would characterize themselves as 'liberal democratic'. There is every sign, however, that in such societies the debate between them over the nature of sustainability and the best way to achieve it will run and run.

References

Barry, J. (1999) *Rethinking Green Politics: Nature, Virtue and Progress*, London: Sage.

Norton, B. (1991) *Toward Unity Among Environmentalists*, Oxford: Oxford University Press.

Further reading

Dobson, A. (2000) *Green Political Thought*, London: Routledge, 3rd edn.

Eckersley, R. (1992) *Environmentalism and Political Theory*, London: UCL Press.

Goodin, R. (1990) *Green Political Theory*, Cambridge: Polity Press.

Smith, M. (1998) *Ecologism*, Milton Keynes: Open University Press.

ANDREW DOBSON

environmentalism of the poor

The **Brundtland Commission** report emphasized environmental damages caused by poverty. There is a contrary view, called the environmentalism of the poor, first proposed in the late 1980s to explain conflicts in which poor people defend the environment (in rural situations, but also in cities) against the State or the Market. Well-known instances are the **Chipko Andolan Movement** in the Himalayas, the Chico **Mendes** fight in **Amazonia**, and the struggles by the Ogoni and other groups in the Niger Delta against the damage from oil extraction by Shell (see also **Ogoni People**). Also, the complaints against eucalyptus in Thailand and elsewhere: plantations are not forests. Or the movements of those ousted from dams, as in the Narmada struggle led by Medha Patkar (see **dams/hydroelectric power**; **Narmada Valley development programme**). Or some new peasant movements in the 1990s, a sort of ecological narodnism against seed multinationals and **biopiracy/bioprospecting**. There are also historical instances. The Rio Tinto company mined and smelted copper for export in Andalusia in the 1880s. A lot of sulphur dioxide was produced. Both miners and peasants complained. On 4 February 1888, the Army attacked a demonstration in the village of Rio Tinto itself, and a number of people were killed. Another **mining** conflict: Tanaka Shozo, a peasant who became a member of the Diet, became well known around 1900 in Japan for his opposition, together with thousands of peasants, to pollution of the Watarase river from the Ashio copper mine. The words **ecology** and environment were not used politically at the time. Until recently, the actors of such conflicts rarely saw themselves as environmentalists. Their concern is with livelihood. Consider the following statement from a woman from Muisne on the coast of Ecuador in March 1999, defending the **mangroves** against the shrimp industry: 'they want to humiliate us because we are black, because we are poor, but one does not choose the race into which one is born nor does one choose not to have anything to eat, nor to be ill. But I am proud of my race and of being conchera [shell collector]... Now we are struggling for something which is ours, our ecosystem, not because we are professional ecologists but because we must remain alive, because if the mangroves disappear... we shall no longer be part of the history of Muisne.'

The environmentalism of the poor is often expressed in the language of legally established old community **property rights**. At other times, new communal rights are claimed. Thus, local fishermen in the middle Amazon river invent new communal rights against outside industrial fishing boats, in a conflict similar to that in Kerala in **India** between artisanal fishermen (who assert community rights, and claim that the sea is sacred), and industrial trawlers (see **fisheries**).

The environmentalism of the poor does not belong to either of the two main currents of environmentalism. First, the 'cult of wilderness', after John **Muir**, the defence of immaculate **Nature** without people, a rearguard action in order to preserve some pristine natural spaces outside the domain of the market and economic growth. From the 1970s, the increased appreciation for wilderness has been explained by the assumed cultural shift towards post-materialist values. Authors who propose the notion of an environmentalism of the poor argue against the post-materialist thesis (see **Ingelhart, Ronald**).

The second main current of environmentalism is **ecological modernization**. It could also be called the 'gospel of eco-efficiency', in the tradition of the Progressive Conservation Movement in the USA at the time of Gifford **Pinchot**. Nowadays, through research in industrial ecology and by applying environmental policies, it is believed (by **Lovins** and the **Wuppertal Institute**) that in the rich countries the material and energy inputs could decrease by a factor of 4, maintaining the present degree of welfare of the population. However, for the time being, economic and population growth imply in fact more energy and material inputs, and also more waste – if not proportionately at least in absolute terms. Hence increasing ecological distribution conflicts in the world. The environmentalism of the poor is outside the two main currents of environmentalism. It is a third current, born of the conflicts between economy and environment, which especially damage poor people. Women often become the main actors of such conflicts. It is close to the **environmental justice** movement in the USA, which fights against toxic waste in areas of African–American or Hispanic population. In the USA, environmental justice is a movement in favour of so-called minorities, while the environmentalism of the poor is potentially a movement of the majority of the world at large.

Further reading

Gadgil M. and Guha, R. (1995) *Ecology and Equity: The Use and Abuse of Nature in Contemporary India*, London and New York: Routledge.

Guha, R. and Martinez-Alier, J. (1997) *Varieties of Environmentalism. Essays North and South*, London: Earthscan.

Peet, R. and Watts, M. (eds) (1996) *Liberation Ecologies: Environment, Development, Social Movement*, London and New York: Routledge.

JOAN MARTINEZ-ALIER

epistemic communities

Epistemic communities is a term developed in international environmental politics by Peter Haas, originally in his analysis of the Mediterranean

Action Plan (Haas, 1990). The epistemic communities model is concerned to show the ways in which international environmental regimes are driven by knowledge-based actors (rather than for example by power-driven states), but without simplistic assumptions such as the common one concerning the importance of scientific consensus. Epistemic communities refers to those communities of scientists who share perceptions of a particular problem, and act at both national and international levels to forge international regimes on that problem. The term attempts to account for the ways in which some experts can get themselves to be regarded as the legitimate providers of knowledge to policy-makers.

References

Haas, P.M. (1990) *Saving the Mediterranean: The Politics of International Environmental Co-Operation*, New York: Columbia University Press.

MATTHEW PATERSON

European Environment Agency

A specialized agency within the **European Union**, the European Environment Agency (EEA) was created in 1990, and began work in 1993. Headquartered in Copenhagen, it had about 70 staff in 1999 and a budget of nearly 17 million euros ($16.2 million). Its membership is made up of the 15 members of the EU, joined by Iceland, Liechtenstein and Norway. The EEA does not make or implement policy, but instead collects, analyses and distills information from other sources. It makes that information available to EU institutions and member governments, promotes comparable data-gathering systems among its members, identifies new ideas for European environmental legislation, draws up triennial reports on the state of the European environment, liaises with national, regional, and international agencies, and co-ordinates the European Environment Information and Observation Network (EIONET), a network of national organizations that help retrieve information for the EEA, and identify issues that need to be addressed.

Further reading

Wynne, B. and Waterton, C. (1998) 'Public Information on the Environment: The Role of the European Environment Agency', in P. Lowe and S. Ward (eds) *British Environmental Policy and Europe*, Basingstoke: Macmillan.

JOHN McCORMICK

European Environmental Bureau

The European Environmental Bureau (EEB) is an umbrella organization whose membership includes 135 non-governmental organizations (NGOs) that are particularly concerned with environmental protection from 24 countries. However, only NGOs from the member (and official candidate) states of the **European Union** and European Economic Area, are granted voting rights. The EEB, whose Brussels office was set up in 1974 with the help of the European Commission, has consultative status not only with it, but also with the European Parliament, the Economic and Social Committee of the EU, and the Council of Europe. The EEB has no special relationship with the Green Group within the European Parliament. In fact, Green MEPs have tended to see it as being too close to the Commission and too willing to compromise (Bomberg, 1998).

The EEB's mission is 'to promote environmental policies and sustainable policies on the European Union level'. In doing this it has co-ordinated efforts with other environmental lobbies in Brussels, especially with the **World Wide Fund for Nature**, which has concentrated more on structural funds while the EEB has concentrated more on pollution issues. Its lobbying in recent years has focused on such issues as: strengthening the waste incineration directive, imposing a strict liability regime for environmental damage, and tightening the standards on airport noise levels.

References

Bomberg, E. (1998) *Green Parties and Politics in the European Union*, London: Routledge.

European Environmental Bureau website at URL: http://www.eeb.org/about/mission.htm.

E. GENE FRANKLAND

European Federation of Green Parties

The European Federation of Green Parties (EFGP) is the transnational party federation of the green political parties in Europe. At the end of 1999 the EFGP had 31 member and three observer parties, coming from all over Europe. It is the only European party federation where parties from non-EU-states have the same rights as parties coming from inside the EU.

The first permanent organization for the transnational co-operation of green parties, the Co-ordination of Green and Radical Parties in Europe, was founded at the end of 1980. In 1983 it was replaced by an organization containing only green parties, the European Green Co-ordination (EGC). In summer 1993 the EGC adopted a new basic declaration and new statutes and transformed itself into the European Federation of Green Parties (EFGP).

Since then the EFGP has especially concentrated on the support of small green parties in Europe, the elaboration of common platforms for the European elections and the extension of contacts with green parties from other continents (Dietz, 1999).

Although there has been a remarkable increase in the degree of interaction between 1979 and 1999, the establishment of the EFGP was not connected with a real transfer of national party sovereignty. Consequently, it is not yet possible to regard the EFGP as a real European party (Dietz, 2000).

The highest political body of the EFGP is the so-called Congress. It meets at least once every three years and decides on the policy formulation of the EFGP and on changes of the statutes. The board, called Council, meets at least once a year and is especially responsible for the co-ordination of initiatives and activities in line with the programme and the general policy of the Federation. The managing board, the Committee, is elected by the

Council for a period of three years and is responsible for the permanent political representation of the Federation and the execution of the Council's decisions. It usually meets four times a year.

Both the Council and the Congress are composed according to a principle of restricted proportionality. Bigger parties have more delegates and votes than smaller parties. Decisions in the EFGP bodies are either taken by qualified or simple majority.

The EFGP shows some organizational features that have been typical for almost all green parties since the 1980s: At least 40 or 50 per cent of the council and congress delegates and of the committee members must be female. Moreover, there is an unofficial agreement, accepted by all member parties since the beginning of the 1980s, that no member of the **Green Group in the European Parliament** (GGEP) can become a member of the Committee. As far as rotation is concerned, each member of the committee is elected in function by the Council for three years and no member may be elected for more than two terms consecutively.

As **new politics** parties, the Greens have always put a strong emphasis on questions of the environment, the Third World, **nuclear energy**, decentralization, genetic engineering, women's liberation, peace and disarmament and **human rights**. Consequently, all these topics have been dealt with in the four platforms of the EFGP (EGC) for the European elections since 1984. Since the 1994 platform the EFGP has also put forward concrete requirements concerning the enlargement and the institutional architecture of the EU, especially the extension of the European Parliament's powers. This platform represents the irreversible commitment of the majority of the EFGP member parties to a pan-European integration in the framework of the **European Union** and to a reform of the EU from within.

In spite of some problems in the beginning, the co-operation between the EFGP and the Green Group in the European Parliament can be described as a very construcitve and efficient one since then. They have elaborated common platforms for the European elections and have

organized several seminars on ecological and economic questions. There has been no political accountability of the green groups in the European Parliament to the EFGP, however.

Although the EFGP has elaborated platforms for the European elections and common statements on several topics, it has not yet been perceived as an important actor in the political system of the EU. Efficiently structured political co-operation processes on the European level and transmissional functions in the political system of the EU are still focused on the GGEP.

References

Dietz, T. (1999) 'Der "Club" der Internationalen – Die Grünen ante portas', *Zeitschrift für Parlamentsfragen*, (2): 433–47.
—— (2000) 'Similar but Different? – The European Greens Compared to the Other Transnational Party Federations in Europe', *Party Politics*, 6(2): 199–210.

Further reading

Dietz, T. (1997) *Die grenzüberschreitende Interaktion grüner Parteien in Europa*, Opladen: Westdeutscher Verlag.
Hix, S. and Lord, C. (1997) *Political Parties in the European Union*, New York: St Martin's Press.

THOMAS M. DIETZ

European Union

Although it began life in the 1950s as a limited experiment in regional economic integration, the European Union (EU) has since become involved in a wide variety of policy issues related to the overall goal of building a single European market. Among these issues is the environment. Early European initiatives on environment protection were driven mainly by the need to remove barriers to free trade, among which were different environmental standards within the member states of the EU. Recent activity has been more proactive, the EU is now involved in developing a more strategic approach to environmental issues, and it is now true to say that environmental policy in the member states of the EU is made more as a result of joint EU initiatives than as a result of activities within the individual states. Furthermore, several countries which lacked environmental policies before joining the EU – notably **Greece** and Portugal – have since developed national bodies of law mainly as a result of the requirements of EU law. Finally, there has been spillover into **East and Central Europe** as countries such as Poland, Hungary and the Czech Republic prepare for membership of the EU.

EU environmental policy is based on general principles contained within the treaties agreed among the member states of the EU. While there was no mention of the environment in the founding treaties of Paris (1951) and Rome (1957), the environment became a formal policy responsibility of the EU with the 1986 Single European Act, and its objectives were subsequently clarified with the treaties of Maastricht (1991) and Amsterdam (1997). The environment is now one of the primary policy interests of the EU, and is one of the only four policy areas that must be considered in the development of all EU policy (the others being consumer protection, culture and health). The European Commission (the executive-bureaucratic arm of the EU) develops proposals for environmental laws and policies, which must be approved by the European Parliament and the governments of the member states working through the Council of Ministers, and are then implemented by appropriate authorities in the member states with the encouragement of the Commission.

EU environmental policy is based on more than a dozen key principles, including the following:

The polluter pays principle The costs of preventing or making good on environmental damage must not be passed on to the taxpayer or the consumer, and must not be covered by public funds. Instead, the entity responsible for actually or potentially damaging the environment must meet the costs of repair or of avoiding damage.

The prevention principle This encourages the EU to initiate action in such a way as to protect the environment by preventing problems emerging.

The proximity principle This argues that en-

vironmental damage should be rectified at source rather than further down the line, for example by setting emissions standards rather than air or water quality standards, or by requiring that the producers of hazardous material dispose of it nearby rather than shipping it further afield.

The subsidiarity principle This argues that in policy areas which do not fall within the exclusive competence of the EU, it should take action only where it makes more sense for the EU to respond than for the member states. While transboundary environmental problems and matters related to shared resources and trade are arguably better resolved at the EU level, it is debatable in many other areas which level is more effective.

The proportionality principle The EU is not expected to go beyond the actions necessary to achieve the objectives of the treaties. In other words, the obligations of EU law must be reasonably related to the objectives sought, and the EU must leave the member states with as much freedom of movement as possible.

The precautionary principle This implies that the EU should take action even if there is a suspicion that an activity may cause environmental harm, rather than wait until the scientific evidence is clear.

The safeguard principle Member states of the EU are allowed provisionally to adopt stronger local standards than those outlined in EU law provided that they were for 'non-economic environmental reasons', and are subject to EU inspection.

The EU has agreed to a series of five Environmental Action Programmes (1973–6, 1977–81, 1982–6, 1987–92, and 1993–2000) and is working on a sixth. It has adopted more than 800 pieces of law on a wide variety of environmental issues, has developed programmes aimed at providing finance for environmental management projects, and in 1990 created a **European Environment Agency** to collect and process data on the state of the European environment. The emergence of the EU as an economic superpower has also meant that it is now a significant actor in international negotiations on environmental issues, and it has played a leading role – for example – in discussions at the 1990 World Climate Conference, the 1992 United Nations Conference on Environment and Development (see **Rio Conference 1992**), and meetings among parties to the Climate Change Convention.

The focus of EU environmental policy has been in five key areas. Water quality is the focus of the biggest body of EU law, and addresses issues as varied as the discharge of dangerous substances, the quality of drinking and bathing water, and urban waste water treatment. In the late 1990s, the EU was working on an integrated approach to water quality management aimed at protecting surface water, groundwater, estuaries and coastal waters, and encouraging member states to co-operate by using management based around river basins rather than administrative or political units.

Waste management policy is aimed at reducing the amount of waste produced, encouraging the re-use or **recycling** of waste, improving controls on waste disposal, and controlling the export of wastes across national borders. The latter has been a particularly controversial issue, revolving around the question of whether or not wastes are 'goods' that should be allowed to be traded, or whether member states should become self-sufficient in waste disposal facilities.

EU policy on air quality has used multiple different methods – including air quality standards, emission limit values, and reductions by manufacturers in the production of pollutants – and has focused on controlling vehicle emissions, lead in fuel, emissions from industrial plants, protection of the ozone layer, and climate change. European laws have been adopted on the sulphur and lead content of fuels, limits have been set for sulphur dioxide, particulates, and nitrogen dioxide, controls have been placed on the production of chlorofluorocarbons and other ozone-depleting substances, and the EU has been active in international negotiations on the reduction of greenhouse gases (see **ozone depletion**).

Among the most productive areas of EU environmental policy has been the control of acid pollution (see **acid rain**). A 1988 law on emissions from large combustion plants involved the member states in negotiations which led to agreement on different levels of pollution reduction (and allowed poorer states to increase their emissions), and helped the EU as a whole to reduce its sulphur dioxide emissions.

Under the auspices of the Common Fisheries Policy, a substantial body of law has been agreed aimed at managing and conserving fisheries, using a permit system, establishing protected areas where fishing is restricted or banned, using technical measures such as controls on the mesh size of nets and minimum sizes or weights for fish that are landed, and the fixing of total allowable catches (see **fisheries**).

The control of dangerous chemicals and other substances has been at the heart of another substantial body of law, aimed at the control of existing chemicals, all new chemicals placed on the market after 1981, **pesticides** and their residues in foodstuffs, and limits on trade in dangerous chemicals. Following several headline-making industrial accidents, a 1982 law encouraged safety features to be built into chemical factories at the design stage.

The EU example has implications for other exercises in regional integration, such as the North American Free Trade Agreement (**NAFTA**) and the Association of South East Asian Nations (ASEAN). Regional integration has several advantages over conventional international co-operation: most notably, multiple countries may be less resistant to agreeing action if they feel they are involved in a joint endeavour with shared costs and benefits, and member states with more progressive national environmental policies can set a pace which can encourage member states with a less progressive approach to keep up in the interests of enjoying the benefits of free trade. Furthermore, the case of the EU suggests that regional integration allows a shift of resources and knowledge that can help poorer or less progressive states deal with the problems posed by the burden of tightening environmental controls.

See also: European Environment Agency; European Environmental Bureau; European Federation of Green Parties

Further reading

Baker, R. (ed.) (1997) *Environmental Law and Policy in the European Union and the United States*, Westport, CT: Praeger

McCormick, J. (2001) *Environmental Policy in the European Union*, Basingstoke: Macmillan

Zito, A. (2000) *Creating Environmental Policy in the European Union*, Basingstoke: Macmillan.

JOHN McCORMICK

Everglades

Called 'a river of grass' (Douglas, 1947), Florida's Everglades is a 150-mile-long, 50-mile-wide **wetland** that declines in elevation by 20 feet across 11,000 square miles between Lake Okeechobee and Florida Bay. This mosaic of ponds, sloughs, sawgrass marshes, hardwood hammocks, and forested uplands drains to mangrove swamps, creating one of North America's most biodiverse habitats, regarded by the **National Audubon Society** as America's most endangered ecosystem (see **mangroves**). Following the devastating 1947 flood, the Army Corps of Engineers built flood control levees and irrigation canals to provide municipal water and recreational opportunities, preserve fish and wildlife, and (lastly) supply water to the newly designated Everglades National Park. Rapid **urbanization** and intensive **agriculture** increased pollutants flowing into the Everglades (notably phosphates), prompting fishery declines in Florida Bay. By 1993, declining habitat, **biodiversity** and water quality system-wide led to implementation of an ecosystem approach to resource management. Federal restoration funding initiatives steadily increased, exceeding $293 million in 2000, making the Everglades the world's largest ecosystem restoration effort ever attempted.

Reference

Douglas, M.S. (1947) *The Everglades: River of Grass*, Sarasota, FL: Pineapple Press, 1997.

JAMES EFLIN

exotic species

An exotic species is one that has been introduced to a geographic region and a biological community wherein it never before existed. Such introductions are often due to purposeful or inadvertent transport of species by humans from one continent or island to another. Because exotic species and native species have no prior evolutionary history, exotic predators and diseases can cause population decline and even extinction of native species that lack evolved defences (e.g., smallpox effect on native American populations, effect of pigs on Pacific island bird populations). Exotic species may have no natural enemies in their new environment, and may out-compete similar native species that are limited by natural enemies (e.g., kudzu introduced to the USA). Exotic species may eliminate native species, disrupting ecological relationships (e.g. food webs) and altering natural communities and ecosystems.

DAVID C. LeBLANC

externalities

The notion of the externality is central to **environmental economics** and the analysis of pollution. An externality is any effect which is not mediated through a market (Pearce and Turner, 1990). A classic example of an externality in environmental thought is the public good (e.g. pleasant views) or public bad (e.g. **air pollution**). A public good/bad has two properties: it is non-rival in consumption (e.g. nice views but not shoes) and it is also non-excludable (so has **property rights**). If an externality exists, through a public good/bad, then one can no longer rely on free exchange through markets to generate economic efficiency. Instead, there is a clearly defined role for government, both to decide on the appropriate level of provision of the public good (e.g. **landscape** protection) and to provide it.

Reference

Pearce, D.W. and R.K. Turner (1990) *Economics of*

Natural Resources and the Environment, London: Harvester Wheatsheaf.

JOHN PROOPS

Exxon Valdez oil spill

In March 1989, the Exxon Valdez, one of the oil tankers in the Exxon fleet, ran aground on a granite reef, spilling eleven million gallons of oil into Prince William Sound off the coast of Alaska. For weeks the coast guard and the Exxon Corporation attempted to contain the oil that swept over 1,000 miles of beaches and breeding grounds for hundreds of species of sea birds, mammals, and fish. In an attempt to mollify local fishermen whose fishing season had been abruptly terminated, Exxon paid many of them to use their boats to try to contain the oil and to use high pressure hoses on the sticky crude oil that washed onto the rocky shore.

The corporation claimed to have spent $2.3 billion on its clean-up operations and contested a federal jury's award of $5.3 billion in damages. The company claimed that all residue had been removed by 1992. However, ecologists employed by the fishing industry and environmental groups argue that the fragile ecosystem of formerly pristine Prince William Sound may never recover.

LETTIE McSPADDEN

factory farming

Factory farming is the dominant method of 'food' animal production used by **agribusiness** in developed nations around the globe. Factory farms are an outgrowth of the development of assembly lines in commercial industry and the development of antibiotics in the pharmaceutical industry. Before the development of factory farms, most animals raised for food were free to roam outdoors on small farms. The lives of the animals were relatively peaceful, until they were slaughtered and their body parts sold at local markets. The environmental impact of small farming was minimal. Today, agribusiness giants, using vast amounts of antibiotics, growth hormones, energy, plant food, and water raise animals indoors, monitoring their every move so as to produce the most meat for the lowest price. But there are hidden (and not so hidden) costs, to the environment, to the animals, and to public health.

The costs to the environment

Factory farms are massive operations. In a typical broiler chicken factory, 20,000–30,000 chickens are crowded together inside one building. Pig production typically involves keeping over 10,000 pigs completely indoors. With over 8 billion animals raised and killed for food every year in the USA alone, there is also a massive amount of waste. In the USA, 1.4 billion tons of animal manure are generated every year; approximately 130 times more than the amount of human waste produced annually. The waste from intensive rearing of animals seeps into the ground and pollutes aquifers or runs off into waterways. Factory farms have now replaced industry as the largest polluters of America's rivers and streams. In addition, intensive animal production is a major factor in deforestation, **air pollution**, and poses a drain on important natural resources, particularly water and energy.

The costs to the animals

Billions of animals are forced to endure manipulation, confinement, mutilation, terror, boredom, and a host of physical and psychological injuries before they are ultimately slaughtered. Broiler chickens are selectively bred and genetically altered to produce bigger thighs and breasts. This breeding creates birds so heavy that their bodies cannot support their own weight. Sows spend their lives in small crates on concrete- or metal-slatted floors where they eat, sleep, excrete, give birth, and nurse their piglets in the same small space. Veal calves are also kept in small wooden crates which prevent movement so as to keep their flesh tender. They are fed a diet deficient in iron to keep their flesh pale and are often chained by the neck to prevent them from licking rusted metal bars which would provide iron. Laying hens are crowded together, with between five and eight birds crammed into 'battery cages' that are only 14 square inches in size. They cannot nest, spread their wings, or scratch. Dairy cows in factory farms are kept in a cycle of constant pregnancy and lactation. Today in the USA there are fewer cows producing more milk. These cows are injected with Bovine Growth Hormone which increases their milk production but causes them to metabolize their own body mass. Animals on factory farms are not seen as individuals, with their own lives to lead, but rather as food-machines.

The cost to public health

The people who live next to factory farms and those who work in them also suffer. Those who live nearby suffer from immediate air, water, and noise pollution and also suffer from the stress associated with such exposure. Workers in factory farms, slaughterhouses, and meat-packing plants suffer more on-the-job injuries than any other industry. The line speeds at poultry processing plants are so fast that many workers are forced to perform repetitive motions that result in various painful and disabling disorders. As many as nine out of ten workers in pig confinement buildings suffer health problems from exposure to carbon monoxide at levels of two or three times those permitted by law.

Factory-farmed food also costs those who consume it. The way animals are raised and slaughtered has been associated with the doubling incidence of salmonellosis, has been linked to the spread of **mad-cow disease/BSE**, and has contributed to the growing problem with anti-biotic-resistant bacterial infections. This is all in addition to heart disease and stroke associated with diets high in animal products. Recently, environmentalists, small farmers, animal welfare activists, labour advocates and those concerned about public health have joined forces with politicians to raise awareness about the dangers of factory farming.

See also: agriculture; animal rights; food quality, politics of; health and the environment

Further reading

US Senate Committee on Agriculture, Nutrition, and Forestry. Report Compiled by the Minority Staff for Senator Tom Harkin (December, 1997) 'Animal Waste Pollution in America: An Emerging National Problem. Environmental Risks of Livestock & Poultry Production'.

LORI GRUEN

famines

Famines are periods of severe and protracted shortages of food causing both excessive mortality of the most vulnerable members of the affected population and postponed births. Their causes can be purely natural (most commonly prolonged droughts) but often famines are man-made. Mao Zedong's delusionary Great Leap Forward and the refusal of the ruling party to acknowledge the crisis and to seek foreign help were responsible for the most devastating famine in human history during which at least 30 million people died in **China** between 1959–61. Historical record shows that most modern famines could have been rapidly ended (or prevented) if the rulers had been willing to act. Amartya Sen's thesis about the critical link between political alienation of the governors from the governed explains the lack of such timely action: a famine's toll is not borne by the people making decisions as the rulers never starve. Accountability of democratic governments is the best means to prevent, or rapidly resolve a famine.

Further reading

Dreze, J. and Sen, A. (1997) *The Amartya Sen and Jean Dreze Omnibus: Comprising Poverty and Famines, Hunger and Public Affairs, and India*, Oxford: Oxford University Press.

VACLAV SMIL

Federación de Partidos Verdes de las Américas

The *Federación de Partidos Verdes de las Américas* (FPVA) is the co-ordinating body for green parties in the American hemisphere. Member parties retain autonomy, utilizing the *Federación* to address regional issues, further the development of green parties in the hemisphere, and provide representation in global initiatives. Founded in Ihla Bela, Brasil in March 1998, FPVA grew from the 1991 CanAMex alliance of Canadian, US and Mexican parties, formed against the North American Free Trade Agreement (**NAFTA**). FPVA's founding parties – Mexico, Brazil, Venezuela, Canada, Uruguay, and the USA – have since been joined by Ecuador, Peru, and Colombia. FPVA is allied with the **European Federation of Green Parties** (EFGP) and the Federation of African green parties (see **African Green Parties, Federation of**). FPVA offices in Mexico City are staffed by the *Partido Verde Ecologista de Mexico* (PVEM). A General Assembly meets every two years to set policy and an Executive Council meets more frequently. Spanish is FPVA's working language. See *http://www.fpva.org.mx/* for current information.

TONY AFFIGNE

federalism and decentralization

The cross-boundary nature of many environmental problems raises fundamental questions as to how environmental governance duties should be distributed among subnational, national, regional, and international entities. Many western governments, including those of Australia, Canada, Germany, and the USA, formally divide authority between subnational and national government authorities in most areas of environmental protection. In addition, neighbouring nations, such as those of western Europe, have worked to establish a more common and co-operative set of regulatory programmes across national boundaries in recent years.

Much recent scholarship endorses efforts to devolve environmental policy decisions to the most localized level possible. Proponents of this approach emphasize the desirability of giving local governments direct input in tailoring remedies to immediate environmental challenges, as opposed to the imposition of one particular policy approach upon all jurisdictions. Many contend that there is a sufficiently broad base of public support for environmental protection in most nations to assure strong commitment to locally designed policy initiatives. In systems with a formal balance of power between national and subnational jurisdictions, this can lead to various delegations of authority and transfer of resources to pursue environmental protection goals.

Other analysts contend that excessive decentralization creates a perverse incentive for particular jurisdictions to 'export' their problems elsewhere.

These strategies may range from the formal shipment of wastes to other locations to a limited interest in reducing air and water pollution as long as prevailing plumes or currents are likely to move the contamination to other areas. Such analysts contend that some degree of centralized control over jurisdictions remains necessary, particularly in those instances of environmental policy that cannot easily be contained within the boundaries of a particular jurisdiction.

The debate over federalism and decentralization also addresses the nature of relations between national and subnational governments in formulating and implementing environmental policy. Under 'co-operative federalism', subnational units are given considerable latitude in programme implementation and encouraged to pursue innovative approaches. In these instances, the role of the national government is largely confined to funding and technical assistance. This was the prevailing approach to environmental policy in many federal nations, including the USA, until the 1970s.

In contrast, under more 'centralized federalism' or 'coercive federalism', the national government assumes a much more active role in defining key policy goals and the regulatory tools that are to be utilized. National governments often depend on subnational units for implementation and provide them with supportive resources, but strive to establish a uniform framework for addressing environmental problems. This became an increasingly common approach to environmental policy in the USA and other federal governments in more recent decades. However, in the late 1990s, many of these governments began to experiment with methods to share power more formally between national and subnational jurisdictions, perhaps moving toward a model somewhere between the extremes of co-operative and coercive federalism.

Further reading

Harrison, K. (1996) *Passing the Buck: Federalism and Canadian Environmental Policy*, Vancouver: University of British Columbia Press.

Holland, K.M., Morton, F.L., and Galligan, B. (eds) (1996) *Federalism and the Environment: Environ-*

mental Policymaking in Australia, Canada, and the United States, Westport, CT: Greenwood.

Lowry, W. (1997) *The Dimensions of Federalism: State Governments and Pollution Control Policies*, Durham, NC: Duke University Press, revised edn.

Rabe, B. (2000) 'Power to the States: The Promise and Pitfalls of Decentralization', in N. Vig and M. Kraft (eds) *Environmental Policy: New Directions for the Twenty-First Century*, Washington, DC: Congressional Quarterly.

Scheberle, D. (1998) *Trust and the Politics of Implementation: Federalism and Environmental Policy*, Washington, DC: Georgetown University Press.

BARRY G. RABE

Finland

The European Year of Nature Conservation, 1970, triggered modern environmental policy in Finland; until then, environmental matters were spread among specific governmental organizations. In 1970, an Environmental Protection Committee was established to prepare an outline for environmental administration. The issue was hotly debated until a political compromise was finally reached: the central administration was divided into two parts, located within the Ministry of the Interior and the Ministry of Agriculture and Forestry (1973). The former was traditionally dominated by the Social Democratic Party, and the latter by the Centre Party (formerly an agrarian party). It took another decade before the environmental administration was unified into a Ministry of the Environment (1983).

These difficulties reflect peculiarities of the social and political power constellation which had developed in Finland during the preceding century. The **industrialization** of the country relied heavily on forest industries. Finland's vast forests acquired economic value, and forest owners – mostly farmers – and their corporatist associations gained a prominent position in the country's economic and political life. The construction of appropriate infrastructure for the **transportation** of timber – railways, roads and waterways – was a central national project. With the convergence of the interests of private landholders, forest indus-

tries, and the state administration, Finland became what has been called a 'forest sector society'.

This brought about a cultural climate emphasizing the importance of private property, and a corporatist political culture in which everything of consequence was planned and executed in close co-operation with the main industries. Everything perceived as harmful for the forest sector, for instance nature conservation, provoked suspicion. The first conservation programmes were discussed in parliament in the 1920s, but the opposition of the forest sector power bloc postponed the establishment of the first National Parks until 1938. The network of **national parks** was enlarged in the mid-1950s and again in the mid-1970s, but each time accompanied by intense political controversy.

Specific governmental bodies had, of course, practised their 'policies of the environment' for a considerable time. For instance, the construction and management of waterways had a separate administrative structure until 1986. Pollution interdict was added in the Water Law in 1960, well in advance of the origin of governmental environmental policy.

Another characteristic time-lag occurred with Environmental Impact Assessment (EIA) legislation. The first suggestions as to the need of an EIA system date back to the late 1970s; however, the passing of an IEA act in the parliament was delayed until 1994. Turf disputes between the environmental administration and traditional management sectors have occurred everywhere, but they have probably been particularly conspicuous and harmful in Finland.

The first task of the new environmental administration was to prepare legislation in basic fields of pollution prevention – except for waters, already covered by separate legislation. The basic tools adopted were pollution permits, connected with a notification duty. New legislation from the period 1978–89 included a waste disposal act, an air protection act, a soil materials act, a noise abatement act, and a chemicals act. Regional and local administrative bodies in charge of the environment were built up in the mid-1980s.

However, this new legislation was fragmented and included, for instance, several different systems of environmental permits. The preparation of an integrated legislation required another period of disputes until a new Environmental Protection Act was passed in 1999. A decisive impact on this process came from the EU which Finland joined as a full member in 1995. Harmonization with EU standards has brought about changes in specific environmental laws as well.

In international environmental politics Finland has had a low profile. This is often explained by its specific relationship with the Soviet Union, but the domestic political stalemate played its role as well. The protection of the **Baltic Sea** is an area where Finland took an initiative in the early 1970s, and the Baltic Marine Environment Protection Commission (Helsinki Commission) was founded in 1974.

Environmental research was originally located in specific institutes affiliated with corresponding policy sectors such as forestry, **agriculture**, water management, and so on, but in the mid-1990s, the Finnish Environmental Institute was established with the Ministry of the Environment to co-ordinate environmental research.

Further reading

Hermanson, A.-S. and Joas, M. (1996) 'Finland', in P.M. Christiansen (ed.) *Governing the Environment: Politics, Policies, and Organization in the Nordic Countries*, Copenhagen: Nordic Council of Ministers.

Jokinen, P. (2000) 'Europeanisation and Ecological Modernisation: Agri-Environmental Policy and Practices in Finland', *Environmental Politics*, 9: 138–67.

Sairinen, R. (2000) *Regulatory Reform of Finnish Environmental Policy*, Helsinki: Helsinki University of Technology.

YRJÖ HAILA

Finnish Green Party

Environmentalists emerged as a political force in Finland in the early 1980s. The first two parliament members were elected from a green list in 1983. The Finnish Greens resisted formal political organization until the late 1980s when, in fact, two parties were established and existed for a while side by side, by and large. The 'fundamentalist' wing proved short-lived, and the electoral politics has been unified within one party, the Green League. The proportion of the public vote has stabilized at 5–7 per cent. The Green League has participated in the government with the portfolio of the Ministry of the Environment since 1995. The most important non-governmental organization in environmental conservation is the Finnish Nature Conservation League which originated as a mainly academic society in the late 1930s but acquired a broad membership and a network of local chapters in the early 1970s.

YRJÖ HAILA

Fischer, Joschka

b. 12 April 1948, Gerabronn, Germany

Politician

Joschka Fischer emerged in the 1990s as the most influential member of the German Greens (*Bündnis 90/Die **Grünen***). During 1994–8, he was the co-speaker of their *Bundestag* group. In October 1998, he became the foreign minister (and vice-chancellor) of the first Social Democratic (SPD)–Green federal government.

Joschka was born Joseph Martin Fischer in 1948, the son of a Hungarian-German butcher. He left school at seventeen, backpacked around the world, and drifted between jobs as a taxi driver, factory worker, and book seller. Breaking with his family's conservative values, he became part of the radical subculture of house occupiers and street fighters. Fischer joined 'Revolutionary Struggle', which idealized spontaneous direct action. In the mid-1970s, the Frankfurt *'Sponti'* group dissolved.

Fischer played no role in the launching of the Greens (1979–80). In 1982, recognizing the electoral opportunities for radical-reformist forces, he joined the party. His Frankfurt base of support translated into a promising list position for the March 1983 federal election; thus, Fischer was among the first greens elected to the *Bundestag*. He served as their parliamentary manager (1983–4), and became one of the green stars in parliamentary debates.

Since 1982, the SPD had ruled Hesse as a

minority government. Fischer favoured a toleration agreement with the SPD and attacked advocates of fundamental opposition (*Fundis*) for preferring ideological proclamations over practical initiatives. *Realos* (realists) prevailed, and the Hesse Greens were to shift from opposition to coalition with the SPD. In December 1985 Fischer – dressed in jeans and Nike shoes – took the oath as the Hesse Minister for Environment, the first green minister in any country. He served until February 1987 when the coalition collapsed over nuclear policy differences.

Although the Greens' votes increased in the 1987 Hesse election, the SPD's decreased; thus, a majority left of centre no longer existed. Fischer took over as the Greens' parliamentary chairman in Hesse. He continued to lead *Realos* in the factional struggles over the national development of the Greens. His goal was a normalized party that competes for a broad electoral base and bargains with other parties.

In the aftermath of the (West) Greens' defeat in the December 1990 *Bundestag* election, Fischer and Antje Vollmer proposed structural reforms, which were largely adopted by the federal conference in April 1991, precipitating the departure of the last prominent *Fundis*. In the January 1991 Hesse election, the Greens ran a successful campaign that presented them as competent reformers and showcased Fischer. For the second time (1991–4), he became Hesse Environmental Minister in an SPD/Green government.

Fischer worked to have the federal party adopt a Red–Green strategy. In October 1994, the Greens were returned to the *Bundestag* as its third largest group; however, Chancellor Kohl's centre-right government retained its majority. Green MPs elected Fischer as co-speaker and re-elected him in 1996. Although the Green Party had its own co-speakers, the media treated Fischer as *de facto* party chair.

Fischer has pushed the Greens, whose founding principles included non-violence, toward a foreign policy that allows for the exceptional use of military force in the defence of **human rights**. Despite anti-NATO provisions of green programmes, he accepted NATO's eastern expansion, provoking protests from the party's left wing. Also Fischer has

maintained that **ecology** and **capitalism** are compatible. He has advocated a regime of **eco-taxes**. He has presented the Greens as reformers whose competence extends to preserving Germany's social market economy from neoliberal forces loosened by **globalization**. His colleagues have credited the self-educated Fischer with being 'the' generalist able to address a wide range of policy areas.

Fischer's intra-party critics have seen him as being so ambitious for ministerial office that he would compromise everything the party stands for. As foreign minister, Fischer backed NATO's air war against Serbia to force a political solution in Kosovo, provoking grassroots opposition in a party born as the arm of the eco-peace movement. In 1978 Fischer wrote, 'The old equation is still valid: only those who have power can make changes; but, those who have power, will also be possessed by it'. The former *Sponti* and the Greens have come a long way. Whether this equation holds, when they share national power, is a question of world-wide relevance to those committed to the transformation of industrial society.

Select bibliography

Fischer, J. (1978) 'Warum eigentlich nicht?' in *Von grüner Kraft und Herrlichkeit*, Reinbek: Rowohlt, 1984.

Further reading

The Economist (1999) 'Charlemagne: Joschka Fischer, a Sterner Shade of Green', 15 May.
Patterson, T. (1995) 'The Green Who Pruned the More Radical Shoots', *The European*, 3–9 August.

E. GENE FRANKLAND

fisheries

The main problem of fisheries is that it has been regarded a common (open access) resource, which is free to be utilized by anybody. Further, for a long time the ocean fish stock was recognized as one of the great renewable resources of the planet, and practically inexhaustible. Fishing is one of the oldest forms of hunting and the last one with any major importance in global terms. On average the nutritional contribution from fish accounts for one-sixth of human total intake of animal protein.

Until the 1940s, the total annual figure for the global fish catch increased slowly. Commercial fishing was still a largely random operation, pursued with tiny units. Since then, the fishing fleets of most countries have changed dramatically and today consist of powerful trawlers with refrigerated holds, which allow the vessels to stay out for longer periods and reach more distant fishing sites. Modern technologies also enable the boats to locate shoals with great precision.

The total catch per year doubled twice between 1950 and 1983. Since then, however, the average annual rate of increase has dropped. From 1990 to 1997, the total fish production increased from 99 to 122 million tonnes per year. Most of the increase originated from fish farming (aquaculture).

The modern commercial fishing has resulted in growth and recruitment overfishing, declining catches, destruction of fish stocks and over capitalization. Approximately 44 per cent of the main fish stocks are fully exploited (in 1998), about 16 per cent of the stock are overfished, and another 6 per cent appear to be depleted. The use of bottom trawls, dredges and suction fishing has not only caused over-fishing, but has had negative impacts on the aquatic **biodiversity** in general.

The twentieth-century international fisheries management can, roughly, be divided into two eras: pre- and post-1976's widespread adoption of the 200-nautical-mile exclusive economic zone (EEZ). Before 1976, international law restricted coastal state jurisdiction to a narrow band of water (usually three nautical miles). Within that area, a coastal state could regulate the fishing as it wished. Outside that area, however, everybody had the right to carry on fishing, which not only caused an uncontrolled over fishing in international waters, but also many international conflicts in the 1960s and 1970s. One example is the 'Cod War' between Iceland and the UK in 1972. In order to control a larger part of the international waters, the economic zones were extended. Today, about 90 per cent of the world's catches are based on fishery resources within national waters. That does not guarantee a recovery of the fish stocks, but provides an opportunity for national fishery policy to be successful.

According to many economists, the main problem of fisheries cannot be solved with traditional management measures. EEZs only transform the open access character of ocean fisheries to a national issue. Any effective solution to the fishery problem therefore ought to depart from the idea of **property rights**. Especially two main management approaches have been suggested: common property resource management (CPR: see **common pool property resources**) and individual transferable quotas (ITQ), which follows the logic behind **tradable emission permits**. ITQ management aims at limiting the number of fishing units by deciding a share of the total allowable catch in respect to each unit, and also at allowing the sale or lease of the right to quotas. Such a system creates incentives for a voluntarily reduction of excess capital by the vessel owner, and with well informed fishing authorities the catch can be sustainable. Most ITQ schemes have been implemented in developed countries.

An alternative way of bringing order into the marine eco-system, while at the same time providing society with enough resources is to expand aquaculture, which already today accounts for about 20 per cent of the world's total fish production and has a great future potential. Some types of aquaculture are, however, associated with environmental damage, which must be solved in order to offer an environmentally efficient alternative to traditional fisheries. Some of this potential is to be found in **biotechnology**.

See also: coastal zone management; International Convention on the Law of the Sea

Further reading

Eggert, H. (1999) 'Towards An Integrated Sustainable Management of Fisheries' *Environmental Economics Unit*, 5, Department of Economics, Gothenburg University

FAO (1998) *The State of the World Fisheries and Aquaculture 1998*, Rome: FAO.

FAO Fisheries Department website at
    URL: http://www.fao.org/fi/default.asp.

Jones, G. and Hollies, G. (1997) *Resources, Society and Environmental Management*, London: PCP.

Peterson, M.J. (1993) 'International Fisheries Management' in P.M. Haas, R.O. Keohane, and M.A. Levy (eds) *Institutions for the Earth: Sources of Effective International Environmental Protection*, Cambridge, MA: MIT Press.

SVERKER CARLSSON

food quality, politics of

Increased public concern about the quality of food has been generated by a series of food scares including those over **mad cow disease/BSE**, salmonella in eggs, and E. coli. Political debates about food quality centre on **regulatory approaches** and structures connected to the role of **policy networks**, and also on the impact of the processes of **industrialization** and **globalization**.

Food quality and safety issues provided the political justification for some of the earliest intervention in trade and markets by public authorities. The concern to safeguard public order and health, and to ensure free and fair trade, provided the impetus for the regulation of food standards, particularly from the mid-nineteenth century onwards. In the UK, a variety of legislation was introduced to ensure the provision of safe food to the public, to combat fraud such as adulteration, to prevent plant and animal disease, and to persuade producers to adopt modern marketing practices. The highpoint of state regulation of the food sector in both production and distribution came during the Second World War, but after the war a general *laissez-faire* approach to food policy was resumed although the state continued to subsidize food production. Smith argues that food policy in the UK was depoliticized between the 1950s and the late 1980s, and was also 'constrained by a consensus' that restricted the role of government to 'facilitating the best quality and choice of food at a reasonable price'. Nutrition and food safety were 'seen as technical matters and discussion of food policy and the views of consumers were largely excluded from the political agenda', which was dominated by a closed agricultural policy community (1991: 235).

Quality was also influenced by concerns for increased agricultural efficiency and improved prices for farmers, as enshrined for example in the basic aims of the **Common Agricultural Policy**. Indeed for much of the twentieth century, food policy was driven by considerations of quantity rather than quality in order to deal with food shortages. This was intertwined with the influence of dominant policy networks such as those in which farmers and state agencies had a common interest in promoting intensive productionist agriculture, for example through the application of chemical inputs and new technologies. In many countries the primary administrative responsibility for food regulation lay not with a food or health agency concerned with safety, quality, and the interests of consumers but with an agricultural ministry linked closely to dominant agricultural interest groups (see **agribusiness**). It was really only when food shortages were replaced by food surpluses, combined with the scares about food standards, that issues of quality and safety assumed greater importance and prompted policy action. For example, as a precursor to the creation of an independent European Food Authority, the **European Union** reorganized its administrative and regulatory systems to concentrate food quality and safety functions in a directorate for health and consumer protection rather than those for industry and agriculture. The opening up of the policy process to a wider range of interests is also evident at the national level, such as in the creation of the UK Food Standards Agency in April 2000 to protect public health and the interests of consumers.

Another difficulty is that there is disagreement about what 'quality food' is – it can be variously described as appealing, tasty, nutritious, healthy, natural, safe, and produced according to some well-defined set of standards such as quality assurance schemes. Industrialization and globalization have also contributed to the emergence of standardized food production and consumption practices, although there is some evidence of a re-emphasis on variation and diversity. Global standards enshrine the 'concerns of industrial transnationals and have rendered quality into a narrow set of efficiency and cost concerns' (Murdoch and Miele, 1999: 470). Alternatively, standards grounded in **nature** prioritize factors such as nutrition, health and environmental **sustainability** rather than efficiency and price. For advocates of **organic farming**, 'natural' production practices that shun **factory farming** and avoid the use of **pesticides** produce food of higher standards and quality to that produced by the agro-food system and **agribusiness**. In this way 'natural' food is deemed to be of higher quality than that produced through industrial global processes.

See also: agriculture; multinational and transnational corporations; nature; policy networks

Further reading

Murdoch, J. and Miele, M. (1999) '"Back to Nature": Changing "Worlds of Production" in the Food Sector', *Sociologia Ruralis* 39 (4).

Smith, M.J. (1991) 'From Policy Community to Issue Network: Salmonella in Eggs and the New Politics of Food', *Public Administration* 69 (summer).

ALAN GREER

Foreman, Dave

b. 18 October 1946, Albuquerque, New Mexico, USA

Environmental activist

Dave Foreman was a key figure in the organization of **Earth First!** in the early 1980s. A one-time staff member at the Wilderness Society, Foreman resigned greatly displeased with the establishment orientation of the **environmental movement**. For him and fellow Earth First! members, demonstrations and confrontation were the order of the day. When possible, Foreman and his associates worked legally, but they also advocated the use of civil disobedience and outright violence when necessary. Guided by Edward **Abbey**'s novel *The Monkey Wrench Gang*, Earth First! became best known for acts of ecological sabotage as it sought

to defend the 'rights' of trees, rivers, mountains, meadows, and flowers. Following a demonstration at Glen Canyon Dam in 1981, the Foreman-led group's membership grew to 10,000. However, by the early 1990s, the organization had factionalized and Foreman and his supporters left, concerned about the growing establishment views of some in the group as well as differences in style and political outlook. Since then, Foreman has continued to lecture and write about protection of the wilderness.

See also: eco-terrorism; monkey-wrenching

WARREN VANDER HILL

forest management

The management of forest resources has been part of human development for millennia. However, much of the world's original forest cover has now been lost, with the rate of loss accelerating rapidly since the 1950s. The challenge of managing areas of natural forest so that they continue to exist as forests, rather than being cleared for conversion to other uses, has made forest management an international political issue. Controversy surrounds how best to manage remaining natural forests because, although forests are considered by all forested countries to be a sovereign issue, two new concepts have been introduced to the debate since the 1980s: forests as global commons; and multiple-use forest management which is inclusive of all stakeholders.

The 1980s were the start of a period of great change in the discourse on forest management. What had for decades been the preserve of foresters, with technical training in silvicultural techniques, who worked within national economic development policies to produce sustained timber yields, became one of the most contentious global environmental issues. This was in large part as a result of increased public awareness in the developed countries about tropical rainforest destruction, especially in **Amazonia**. The sight of the Amazon rainforest burning from space in 1987 was one of the defining moments in making **rainforests** a global issue.

Increased public awareness of the extent of tropical rainforest destruction coincided with increased knowledge about the ecological functions of forests in regulating hydrological cycles and soil stabilization, the significance of **biodiversity** and concerns about **global warming**. As a result, conservation of tropical rainforests was placed on the international agenda as a global imperative. International environmental groups helped to keep the momentum going, for example with tropical timber boycott campaigns in the 1980s and early 1990s.

Two international initiatives were established in the mid-1980s with the aim of combating tropical deforestation through top-down conservationist and management approaches. The Tropical Forestry Action Plan was conceived by the World Bank, **UN Development Program**, UN Food and Agriculture Programme and the **World Resources Institute** to halt tropical deforestation by channelling donor funds into forest-based industrial development and conservation through National Forestry Action Plans. The International Tropical Timber Organization was the first trade body with conservation as an explicit goal. Both initiatives attracted criticism for, *inter alia*, failing to recognize the links between industrial forestry and deforestation. The 1980s also saw increased international interest in the protection of biodiversity through forest reserves which have a core area where human activities are not permitted. These high priority conservation areas are supposed to be protected by surrounding buffer zones where limited activities are allowed subject to overall management plans. This approach has been promoted by international environmental groups such as World Wildlife Fund (WWF: see **World Wide Fund for Nature**) and International Union for Conservation of Nature and Natural Resources (IUCN: see **World Conservation Union**).

The mainstream approach to forest management of sustained timber production with attempts to integrate conservation areas to protect biodiversity was challenged in the late 1980s and 1990s on a number of competing fronts, in particular: tropical forested countries' resistance to the North's attempts to treat rainforests as global commons; environmental NGOs' hostile attentions towards the tropical timber trade; campaigners' criticisms

of top-down approaches which excluded forest peoples from participation in forest management decision-making. All of these challenges shaped the forest management debate in the 1990s.

At the **Rio Conference 1992**, forests were one of the most controversial issues and polarized the North and the South. Whilst northern countries favoured the establishment of a Global Forest Convention, southern countries were opposed to such an institution, arguing that it undermined national sovereignty over forest resources. Thus, the only commitments towards forest management which could be agreed at United Nations Conference on Environment and Development (UNCED) were a non-binding set of Forest Principles. These enshrined the concept of national sovereignty over forest resources, in the face of increased pressure to treat tropical rainforests as global commons. Post-UNCED, international initiatives have continued under the auspices of the UN **Commission on Sustainable Development**. Critics argue that these processes are nothing more than 'talking shops' and that little concrete action towards halting deforestation has resulted.

The **North/South divide** which became an increasing feature of international forest politics in the late 1980s and early 1990s led to the focus of attention on deforestation broadening out from tropical forests to include temperate and boreal forests. These forests lie predominantly in the developed North and eastern Europe and are also under threat from large-scale deforestation. In British Columbia, Canada, environmental campaigns for the protection of old-growth temperate rainforests spear-headed the growth in awareness of these issues, with British Columbia being labelled the 'Brazil of the North' by environmentalists. Large-scale clear-cutting, where all vegetation is removed leaving a denuded landscape, is the logging technique utilized by logging companies in British Columbia. With its high visual impact and ecological destructiveness, clear-cut logging became a focus for environmental campaigners who increasingly worked with indigenous First Nations groups to lobby for a changing approach to forest management policies in British Columbia, with some success.

Identifying the causes of deforestation has proved to be as contentious as other aspects of forest management. Controversy over the distinction between causes of deforestation and agents of deforestation has been bitter. Whilst agricultural encroachment is accepted as one of the major causes of deforestation, there is heated debate over the role of peasant farmers and shifting cultivators in this. Many argue that to blame the rural poor for deforestation is to ignore the inequitable policies which drive them into the forests, for example the transmigration policies in **Brazil** and **Indonesia** funded by the **World Bank**, and insecurity of land tenure. Also, local agricultural systems such as shifting cultivation have proved sustainable over long time frames but fallow periods are often shortened due to increasing pressures on surrounding land.

Critics of top-down approaches to forest management contend that forests should not be viewed as empty wildernesses to be managed for industrial forestry and conservation, both of which exclude or deny forest-dependent peoples' traditional activities and the multiple uses of forests. They argue that local peoples' rights, especially **indigenous peoples**, should be recognized and that access to non-timber forest products for subsistence livelihoods, food, building materials and medicines should be protected. Calls for forest-dependent peoples to participate in forest management decision-making have led to the language of participation and inclusion of all stakeholders to be increasingly used at the international level.

Forest degradation, where the ecological quality of the forest is reduced rather than total loss of forest cover, has usually been associated with unsustainable harvesting techniques. However, increasingly the timber industry is being identified as the greatest threat to forests, especially remaining large natural forests. For example, loggers open up previously inaccessible areas by putting large networks of roads into the forests, thus attracting people to areas where there is little or no infrastructure to support them, leading to over-exploitation of resources. The independent certification of timber from sustainable sources is seen as one way of encouraging changing practices within the forestry sector through consumer-led demands, although its credibility is marred by the proliferation of certification schemes with varying degrees of stringency according to the level of industry involvement in designing them. In addition, certification schemes fail to address many of the criticisms levelled at mainstream forest management, such as the role of industrial timber production in undermining local peoples' traditional rights to and uses of non-timber forest products and the lack of meaningful participation by local people in forest management decision-making.

Further reading

Humphreys, D. (1996) *Forest Politics: The Evolution of International Co-operation*, London: Earthscan.

Verolme, H.J.H. and Moussa, J. (1999) *Addressing the Underlying Causes of Deforestation and Forest Degradation – Case Studies, Analysis and Policy Recommendations*, Washington DC: Biodiversity Action Network.

PAULA VANDERGERT

Forum for the Future

Forum for the Future was founded in February 1996 by three former leaders of the UK Green Party: Jonathon Porritt, Sara **Parkin**, and Paul Ekins. Its purpose is 'to accelerate the building of a sustainable way of life by taking a positive, solutions orientated approach to today's environmental challenges'. The co-founders envisaged a new type of environmental organization that does not compete with existing organizations, rather that adds a new dimension by working with key decision-makers and opinion leaders in the private and public sectors. In contrast to the earlier waves of environmentalism, the movement groups of the 1960–80s and the Green Party activists of the 1970–90s, the Forum has actively sought corporate partners. The Forum's view is that: 'the environment agenda' is no longer the exclusive property of environmentalists; the time is ripe to move from raising awareness to providing solutions; and issues of ecology, society, and economics overlap in the pursuit of **sustainability**. The Forum's core staff of 60 are involved with education, research, advocacy, and consultancy aimed at greening the practices of business and government.

Further reading

Forum for the Future, *Green Futures* (bimonthly magazine) ISSN 1366–4417.

E. GENE FRANKLAND

fossil fuels

Collective term for peats, coals and hydrocarbons (crude oils and natural gases), fuels formed in the uppermost strata of the Earth's crust by slow transformation of biomass. The oldest coals date back to about 500 million years ago, while many peats are less than 10,000 years old. Bituminous coals, which dominate the world market, contain typically 20–22 megajoules of energy per kilogram (MJ/kg), about 10 per cent of incombustible ash, and 1–2 per cent sulphur. Energy content of crude oils is about 42 MJ/kg, but there are substantial differences as to the fractions of light and heavy hydrocarbons and the content of sulphur. The simplest natural gas is pure methane, containing 35 MJ/m^3; other gases are a mixture of methane and heavier hydrocarbons. Fossil fuels now provide about 90 per cent of the world's primary commercial energy (the rest comes from hydro, nuclear, wind and geothermal electricity), and their combustion is the largest anthropogenic source of **air pollution**.

Further reading

Smil, V. (1991) *General Energetics*, New York: John Wiley.

VACLAV SMIL

Framework Convention on Climate Change

The United Nations Framework Convention on Climate Change (FCCC) is the key international legal instrument negotiated by states to regulate **global warming**. It was one of the major outcomes of United Nations Conference on Economic Development (UNCED) in June 1992 (see **Rio Conference 1992**). It was negotiated during the eighteen months preceding UNCED – an extremely short negotiating time for such a complex issue around which there were still many scientific uncertainties.

Negotiations for the FCCC were precipitated by the first report of the Intergovernmental Panel on Climate Change (IPCC) which was published in November 1990. This report stated the prevailing scientific consensus among climate scientists, that should existing trends emissions of the main greenhouse gases continue, some measure of global warming was inevitable. This was strong enough a conclusion to lead to international negotiations which resulted in the FCCC.

The FCCC contains a wide-ranging set of measures to deal with the problem of global warming. Of particular note are the following four.

- Article 2 states a clear objective for the Convention, which is to 'achieve … stabilization of greenhouse gas concentrations in the atmosphere at a level that would prevent dangerous anthropogenic interference with the climate system'. This sets a clear context within which all other articles in the FCCC and developments following the Convention's signature can be evaluated.
- Article 4 deals with the commitments states undertook in order to control greenhouse gases. All states undertook to establish inventories of greenhouse gas emissions, formulate national plans to mitigate such emissions, and communicate to the FCCC's secretariat their implementation of these commitments. In addition, industrialized country parties undertook to take measures which were aimed at stabilizing carbon dioxide emissions (article 4.2). The wording of this commitment is notoriously ambiguous and a wide range of interpretations were put on it. Very few states met this objective in the timescale outlined.
- Various articles deal with the need to transfer finance and **technology** from industrialized countries to developing countries to enable the latter to develop while limiting their greenhouse gas emissions. Article 4.3 develops this obliga-

tion most clearly. Other parts of article 4 elaborate on how the special situations of particular categories of developing countries should be taken into account in the implementation of the general commitments. Article 11 establishes a financial mechanism through which financial transfers should be organized.

• Finally, the FCCC sets up a number of institutions which were designed to help states co-operate over global warming in the future. In addition to a Conference of the Parties (COP), a Secretariat and the Financial Mechanism, these were principally a Subsidiary Body for Scientific and Technological Advice (SBSTA, Article 9), and a Subsidiary Body for Implementation (SBI, Article 10). The former is a mechanism to connect the FCCC to the work of the IPCC, to provide states with up-to-date scientific opinion on global warming. The SBI is the body which deals with the various reports governments are required to submit under the Convention.

The main developments of the FCCC have been at COPs in Berlin (1995) and Kyoto (1997). The first COP, held in Berlin shortly after the Convention came into force, reflected in particular debates concerning the adequacy of the commitments contained in Article 4.2. Most states agreed they were not adequate, but there was insufficient agreement about how to tighten up these commitments. Instead, states agreed the 'Berlin Mandate', which mandated states to negotiate to tighten up these commitments by the third COP, in 1997.

In the meantime, the IPCC produced its Second Assessment Report, which stated that the IPCC scientists now believed that the best explanation for the global warming already observed was in fact greenhouse gas emissions. This much stronger conclusion than the 1990 one helped to strengthen the impetus for stronger controls.

These controls were agreed at the Kyoto Conference in 1997 (see **Kyoto Conference/ Protocol**). Industrialized countries agreed for the first time to reductions in their carbon dioxide emissions, by varying amounts. In addition, Kyoto created mechanisms for introducing a **tradeable emission permits** system (established two years later) for carbon dioxide emissions, and a mechan-

ism for facilitating the transfer of technology to developing countries.

See also: global Climate Coalition; global warming; tradeable emission permits

Further reading

Bodansky, D. (1993) 'The United Nations Framework Convention on Climate Change: A Commentary', *Yale Journal of International Law,* 18(2): 451–558.

Grubb, M., Vrolijk, C. and Brack, D. (1999) *The Kyoto Protocol: A Guide and Assessment*, London: Earthscan.

Paterson, M. (1996) *Global Warming and Global Politics*, London: Routledge.

United Nations (1992) *Framework Convention on Climate Change*, New York: United Nations.

MATTHEW PATERSON

France

In France the first environmental protection movements were born in intellectual elite circles at the close of the nineteenth century. The issue was to defend certain remarkable natural sites against the early consequences of **industrialization**. In the inter-war period and even more so following the Second World War, nature scientists – zoologists, naturalists – continued the work of the former movements, denouncing the disappearance of certain living species, the deterioration of natural areas and the risk of natural resource depletion. These movements spread from a small intellectual and professional elite to a broader public at the end of the 1960s. At that time, the first major technological accidents received wide media coverage: in 1967, the tanker *Torrey-Canyon* ran aground on the Brittany coast, causing considerable damage to the local flora and fauna. In intellectual spheres, the publication of the famous Club of Rome report *Limits to Growth* in 1972 on the slowing of economic growth popularized the theme of natural resource depletion and sparked a real debate in the political sphere and the media.

In the 1970s, the **anti-nuclear movement** managed to organize a few mass protests, yet did not alter majority public opinion. In 1974, the first ecology party candidate ran for presidential election. From that time on, the Greens have been present, with varying success, in all national and local elections. Parallel to these movements, environmental issues gradually became integrated into state structures. The first major law governing risk from industrial pollution was passed in France in 1810: it was a series of measures regulating the activity of potentially dangerous industrial sites. The law instituting the creation of **national parks** was passed in 1960. In the mid-1960s as well, important provisions regarding the management of water resources were adopted. In addition to this legislation, the need to treat environmental issues on a more global level led the political authorities to create a dedicated ministerial structure: the Ministry of Nature and the Environment was set up in January 1971. At the start it was endowed with rather meagre budgetary resources, and its sphere of action was limited by comparison with more powerful ministries. During the 30 years that followed this initiative, the Environmental Ministry went through alternate phases of effacement and relative growth depending on changes in government and policy. At times it was grouped with other ministerial activities (for instance the Culture Ministry), at others it regained its autonomy. Under some governments it was degraded from 'ministry' to a mere state secretariat. But in all cases, the budget allocated to it remained fairly small, always smaller, to give an idea of scale, than that of the Culture Ministry.

It is generally agreed that in France, public sensitivity to environmental matters is less keen than in some northern European countries such as Germany. In light of recent events, this observation perhaps ought to be reviewed. In the early 1990s, the ecological movement, although divided into rival organizations, did fairly well at the polls. In the 1997 legislative elections, the Greens made an agreement with the Socialist Party (see **Verts, les**). The text pledged in particular that the Super Phoenix fast breeder reactor would be shut down permanently and there would be a freeze on orders for new nuclear reactors. In Lionel Jospin's government, the leader of the Greens, Dominique **Voynet**, was awarded the post of Environment Minister. To what extent has participation of the ecologists in government influenced France's environmental policies? It would seem that in a number of crises involving environmental and health risks (GMOs, importation of British beef), government leaders have demonstrated newfound firmness and regularly evoked 'the principle of caution' to justify the stands they have taken. It is true, however, that at the same time the powerful hunters' lobby has managed in part to thwart adoption in France of **European Union** directives regarding regulations on hunting migratory birds. Is France still Europe's slow learner with respect to environmental matters? It is hard to say for the moment: definite choices with regard to nuclear waste treatment and the possible replacement of existing nuclear power plants will be made in five to ten years (see **French nuclear power industry**). This is consequently after the next presidential and legislative elections scheduled for 2002.

DANIEL BOY

Franklin Dam

The battle to save the Franklin River, in the World Heritage wilderness area of south-western Tasmania, has been the most controversial environmental dispute in Australia to date and marks a critical turn in Australian environmental politics towards the national sphere. The Tasmanian Hydro-Electric Commission's Gordon-below-Franklin dam proposal was approved by the Tasmanian Parliament in 1979. In response and enlightened by the loss of Lake Pedder in 1974, major national groups such as the Tasmanian Wilderness Society and the Australian Conservation Foundation mobilized public opposition nationwide. Following a failed State referendum in 1981 and election of a conservative State government in 1982, they organized an effective protest blockade at the dam site. Then in March 1983 they intervened in national elections for the first time, helping a supportive Australian Labour national government to power. This government's first initiative was the World Heritage Act, which gave it power to declare the dam illegal. In July 1983 the High Court of

Australia upheld the constitutional validity of national laws based on international environmental treaties to overrule the States' autonomy within Australia's federal system.

PETER CHRISTOFF

free-market environmentalism

Free-market environmentalism is an approach to resource **stewardship** and protection of the natural environment by use of economic self-interest, private **property rights**, and traditions of **common law**. The **Nature Conservancy** (US) and **tradeable emissions permits** are examples. Free-market environmentalism arose from **environmental economics**. It rejects both regulatory and common pool resource management approaches as ecologically ineffective, economically inefficient, and destructive of human liberty (see **regulatory approaches**). In particular, government **land use regulation** is seen as necessarily creating a tragedy of the commons leading to resource waste, disincentives to control pollution, and increased threats to protected wildlife and ecosystems. It is often mistakenly seen as a form of **anti-environmentalism** as it rejects government planning, ownership, and regulation of resources and the environment as totalitarian.

See also: capitalism; environmental management; wise-use movement

Further reading

Anderson, T, and Leal, D. (1991) *Free Market Environmentalism*, San Francisco: Pacific Research Institute.

PAUL CHANDLER

French nuclear power industry

The first decisions regarding nuclear power equipment policy were made in France after the end of the Second World War. A high commissioner for atomic energy was created in October 1945, and construction began on the first industrial reactor in 1956. Over the next ten years, six nuclear power plants were built, using the French technique of natural uranium graphite gas. In the late 1960s, the French option was cancelled because of the small number of plants built throughout the world. As a result, France adopted the method patented by the American firm Westinghouse that uses enriched uranium to power the plants. In the early 1970s Georges Pompidou's government launched a construction programme of six new nuclear plants using this method.

In April 1974, arguing that the oil crisis was likely to increase the cost of France's energy dependence, Messmer's government ratified a programme to equip France in the following ten years with nuclear power stations producing a total of 40,000 megawatts, making France the world's second largest producer of electricity, behind the USA. In 1990, when this programme was completed, three-quarters of the electricity in France was produced by nuclear power. The creation and development of the French nuclear-generated electricity programme was facilitated by the strong cohesion of the nuclear production process under the auspices of the State. This very 'Cartesian' system is based on an extremely solid and efficient institutional model: the CEA (*Commission d'Energie Atomique*) and EDF (*Electricité de France*).

These two major and often rival powers, both of which benefit from a relative independence with regard to the State, were able to justify nuclear development and all electric power to the political authorities and thereby carry out resolute policies in favour of them. During the oil crisis the issue of energy independence was obviously the decisive argument. The homogeneity of engineer training – most of which took place at the prestigious Polytechnique engineering school and provided the ranks of civil nuclear power – also largely helped to implement these programmes. Construction of power stations was undertaken by organizing collaboration with powerful industrial groups: Empain Schneider, the CGE (*Compagnie Générale des Eaux*). Lastly, the entire fuel production cycle was awarded to a private company, the COGEMA. In the face of this typically French highly centralized industrial organization, neither parliamentary representation nor extra-parliamentary protest was able to weigh very heavily in decisions. In general, there was little political divergence. For a long time both the right and the left felt, as did the majority of public opinion, that development of civil nuclear energy was the normal road for industrial **development** and especially that national energy production guaranteed France's independence with regard to other energy sources (see **public opinion and the environment**). When the nuclear energy programme reached industrial proportions, the only criticism from the left-wing opposition had to do with the need to keep French nuclear power a national affair managed strictly by the State. For this reason, the left criticized the decision to abandon the French option of graphite-gas in favour of the coolant method developed by the American firm Westinghouse. But the Socialist Party and especially the Communist Party did not question the underlying principle for opting for nuclear power. Strong on-site protests coming from the ecology movement in the early 1970s never managed to shift public opinion away from civil **nuclear energy**.

To complete the logic of the nuclear production cycle, EDF engineers orientated the production process toward the fast-breeder technology: the development of Phoenix, and later Super-Phoenix, nuclear power plants that used the plutonium from classic reactors theoretically provided a way of closing the nuclear loop. But fast breeder reactors are extremely costly, complex systems that are delicate to operate due to the use of liquid sodium in the cooling process. The construction of Super-Phoenix in south-east France sparked the only demonstration that resulted in the death of a protestor during clashes with the police in 1977. The reactor never functioned properly, encountering successive incidents and breakdowns. In 1997, the government alliance between the Greens (les Verts) and the Socialist Party included a promise to shut down the operation of Super-Phoenix permanently. The decision to halt its operation was made in 1998.

Today, the replacement of nuclear power plants remains an open question. Agreements between EDF and the German firm Siemens have opened industrial horizons. But given the increased sensitivity of French public opinion regarding environmental topics, the authorities seem to have deferred making a political decision.

DANIEL BOY

Friends of the Earth

Friends of the Earth (FoE) was founded in 1969 by David **Brower**, who had been the executive director of the **Sierra Club**, 1952–69. During Brower's leadership, the Sierra Club's membership had increased ten fold, but he had grown impatient with the more moderate views of its board. He resigned and formed the FoE as a leaner, more active organization (7,000 members in 1970) with a less compromising, more confrontational approach to environmental protection. FoE was to take on issues generally ignored by conservationists, such as: nuclear power, population control, industrial pollution, and urban **quality of life**. Furthermore, in the early 1970s, Brower began to encourage the formation of FoE groups around the world. In 2001, FoE International had affiliates in 69 countries.

In the early years, FoE mirrored the aggressiveness of Brower, whose views put him to the left of many US environmentalists (for example, he was pro-nuclear weapon freeze). Eventually Brower fell out with the FoE board, which viewed him as too dictatorial and unwilling to cut staff for budgetary reasons. In 1986, Brower resigned and focused on Earth Island Institute, which he had founded in 1982 to promote conservation projects internationally. In 1990, FoE membership was relatively small (9,000) compared to that of the **Environmental Defense Fund** and the **Natural Resources Defense Council**, both of which were launched about the same time. Following its merger with the Oceanic Society, FoE's membership surged to 35,000 in the mid-1990s, but then declined to 12,000 in 1998.

Friends of the Earth portrays itself as 'dedicated to protecting the planet from environmental degradation; preserving biological, cultural and ethnic diversity of the planet; and empowering citizens to have an influential voice in decisions affecting the quality of their environment – and their lives'. In contrast to large mainstream groups,

FoE makes explicit the 'empowerment' theme. Another long running theme has been encouraging greater 'corporate accountability'. Especially noteworthy in recent years has been FoE's Green Scissors Campaign to spotlight how governmental subsidies (in 2001 estimated as $55 billion) for corporations squander US fiscal and environmental resources.

Les Amis de la Terre was formed in 1970 as the first European affiliate of FoE. Its activists played a noteworthy role in the formation of green parties in France during the 1970s. Soon British and Swedish FoE groups were also formed, to be followed by groups in fifteen additional western European countries. These groups in the 1970s tended to engage in **non-violent direct actions** that attracted media attention to issues such as pollution, energy, and **transportation**. Extra-parliamentary protest tactics drew members from student groups and middle-class citizen initiatives. However, by the 1990s, West European FoE groups had become more professionalized, technically competent, and reformist (Bomberg, 1998). With the end of the Cold War and the collapse of the Soviet Union, FoE groups emerged in eleven Central and Eastern European countries. FoE groups from Africa, the Middle East, Asia, the Americas, Australia, and New Zealand completed the 2001 list. While a few FoE groups may be little more than letterhead organizations, a number of them have been more active and influential than FoE (US).

A prime example is the Friends of the Earth, UK, which claims 250 local groups in England, Wales, and Northern Ireland (the Scottish FoE is autonomous). *The Guardian* in 1997 described it as 'the UK's most effective environmental group', which is not something that any major US newspaper would have said in the late 1990s about FoE (US). Also following the late 1980s surge of British environmentalism, FoE (UK) counted a membership of 120,000, far beyond that of its American counterpart. In the early 1990s its membership slipped, forcing cuts in a staff that had grown by 900 per cent in the second half of the 1980s (Garner, 1996).

During the late 1980s, FoE (UK), with Jonathon Porritt as its executive director, shifted from 'campaigning and working *against* industry to

working increasingly *with* industry' (McCormick, 1991). Over time, FoE has focused less on demonstrations (though they still occur) and more on providing technical information toward 'positive solutions'. Its website quotes the head of the Inspectorate for Pollution as saying, 'Technical dialogue is often better from the Friends of the Earth than from industry'. It also takes credit for saving numerous wildlife havens, protecting **endangered species**, halting unnecessary roads, blocking nuclear waste dumping, and achieving 'the passage of five Acts of Parliament' since 1971.

There has also been a regional co-ordination unit of Friends of the Earth International for Europe, separate from the **European Environmental Bureau** (EEB), which is a lobbying arm of environmental non-governmental organizations in Brussels. An example of FoE Europe's activities is its campaign launched in March 2000 to safeguard people from genetically modified food.

References

Bomberg, E. (1998) *Green Parties and Politics in the European Union*, London: Routledge.

Friends of the Earth's Magazine (winter 2001) *Earth Focus*, 30(4), Washington, DC.

Garner, R. (1996) *Environmental Politics*, London: Prentice Hall.

McCormick, J. (1991) *British Politics and the Environment*, London: Earthscan.

URL: http://www.foe.org.

URL: http://www.foe.co.uk.

E. GENE FRANKLAND

future studies

This twentieth-century movement has been variously called futuristics, futurology, futurism, prognostics, futuribles, and many other names – the study of alternative societies or visions ten to 50 or more years in the future. One thread might be called futurism: a future-orientated expression of modernism in art, architecture, and design; visionary future societies; and, popular literature about the future, such as Alvin Toffler's *Future Shock* (1970) and John Naisbitt's *Megatrends* (1982). Another thread, future(s) studies (FS) is an emerging scientific/academic field embodied in government planning offices, public and private sector think-tanks; a broad literature; post-secondary academic programmes; and professional organizations.

Futurism's historical roots lay in divination and religious prophetic beliefs, utopian literature, and early science fiction (see **utopia/ecotopia**). Twentieth-century roots extend to: national and military planning, nation building, think tanks, the *Limits to Growth* and the Club of Rome, regional and local government Year 2000 initiatives, policy studies and evaluation research, **technology assessment**, and the rise of the modern futures studies movement (Bell, 1997: 1–60).

Environmental roots of the FS movement are tied to **critical theory** analysis of patriarchy, **capitalism** and **industrialization**. Conversely, other elements within the movement have been anti-environmental and technocratic (see **anti-environmentalism**). A good example of the relationship between futuristics and environmental concerns is the Club of Rome (CoR) sponsorship of *Limits to Growth*. Fundamental to any contemporary understanding of the roots of FS is the contribution of the CoR of the concept of the 'global problematique' – the litany of looming environmental disasters: overpopulation, depletion of **non-renewable resources**, desertification, **ozone depletion** and CFCs, destruction of **biodiversity**, and **global warming**. From Rachel **Carson** to James Lovelock's **Gaia hypothesis**, environmental critiques have informed the FS movement. Furthermore, the success of green parties have provided an alternative image of the future in opposition to the dominant industrial **paradigm**.

Somewhat different influences have come out of the European and North American strands of futurism. European influences are more philosophical and ideological in nature and include: Marxism and Neo-Marxism, critical theory, and central state planning. The former two influences reflect a critical ideological edge in FS that questions the fundamental assumptions of industrialization and modernity, while the later influence embraces industrialization and the idea of **progress**. The North American strain in contrast is more pragmatic and technological in orientation.

FS also draws inspiration from alternative futures reflected in the anti-colonial and Civil Rights movements, women's rights, environmental, aboriginal rights, **human rights**, peace and justice movements, and non-western cultures. Thus, the global FS movement has strong leanings toward critical futurism (Jones, 1992).

Assumptions of FS include an expanded time frame (10–50 years or more), interdependence and holism, the possibility of better societies, the unidirectionality of time, the unpredictability of the future (contrary to popular media coverage), and an open (or alternative) futures (Bell, 1997: 115–57). Key for many futurists is the idea of plural futures, the idea that there is no one single future, but rather many possible alternative futures. Futurists use a variety of qualitative and quantitative methods from many fields including: time series extrapolation, cohort analysis, survey research, technology assessment, trend and emerging issues analysis, the Delphi method (which may include cross-impact analysis), simulation and computer modelling, gaming, and scenario building (Bell, 1997: 241–97). Other futures practices are more socially active, what Bell calls 'participatory futures praxis', range from experiments in electronic **democracy**, proactive futures workshops, social experiments, and ethnographic futures research.

Over the last two decades, hundreds of courses on the future and futures studies have been taught across the world and several university graduate programmes in futures studies exist in North America and Europe. Scores of local, regional, and nation futures studies professional organizations have formed. Examples of international professional organizations include the mass-membership World Future Society based in Washington, DC and the internationally orientated World Futures Studies Federation (whose secretariat has rotated from major cities across the globe – currently Bacolod City, Philippines).

See also: critical theory; doomsayers; Limits to Growth; technology; utopia/ecotopia

References

Bell, W. (1997) *Foundations of Futures Studies*, New Brunswick, NJ: Transaction Publishers.

Jones, C. (1992) 'The Manoa School of Futures Studies', *Futures Research Quarterly*, 8(4): 19–25.

Further reading

Masini, E. (1993) *Why Futures Studies?*, London: Grey Seal.

Slaughter, R. (1996) *The Knowledge Base of Futures Studies*, vols 1–3, Hawthorn, Victoria, Australia: DDM Media.

CHRISTOPHER B. JONES

G

Gahrton, Per

b. 1943, Hörby, Sweden

Politician

Per Gahrton, a well-known Swedish public debater, writer and politician, began his career as chairman of the youth organization of the liberal party (*folkpartiet*), from 1969–71, and served as a member of parliament for the liberal party from 1976–9. He wrote a doctoral dissertation in sociology in 1983, based on his experiences in the parliament. He has been a prolific journalist and campaigner for **human rights**, and has written many books and articles about the Middle East conflict, the **European Union**, as well as environmental issues. In 1981, he took the initiative to start a Swedish green party (***Miljöpartiet de Gröna***) and served as spokesperson for the party in 1984–5, and member of parliament from 1988–91, and again in 1994–5. Gahrton was elected to the European parliament for the Green Party in 1995, receiving the most votes of any candidate in Sweden, and was re-elected in 1998.

ANDREW JAMISON

Gaia hypothesis

James E. Lovelock's hypothesis aims to account for the fact that the physical conditions necessary for life on Earth, such as a specific temperature range, have always been maintained in existence in spite of potentially disruptive events such as large changes in the Sun's temperature.

The hypothesis is that the Earth's biota, biosphere and non-organic elements (atmosphere, water and rocks) form an evolving, non-conscious, living system which Lovelock dubbed 'Gaia'. Gaia is thus regarded as a superorganism with the property of self-regulation (homeostasis). The latter property comprises various feedback mechanisms which maintain within Gaia the conditions necessary for particular organisms to survive. Such organisms often play an unconscious part in the operation of these feedback mechanisms by acting in such a way as to change their environment.

Further reading

Lovelock, J.E. (1982) *Gaia: A New Look at Life on Earth*, Oxford: Oxford University Press.

BRIAN BAXTER

Gandhi, Mohandas Karamchand

b. 2 October 1869, Porbandar, India;
d. 30 January 1948, New Delhi

Political leader, philosopher

Mohandas Karamchand Gandhi, widely called the Mahatma ('great soul') is regarded as the father of independent **India**. Gandhi was educated in Great Britain and practised law in South Africa for more than 20 years, where he also organized resistance against racial discrimination. He returned to India in 1914. In 1917 he launched a non-violent campaign for the rights of indigo planters in Champran. It was a turning point in the freedom struggle. Gandhi mobilized people against the British government on various occasions but always insisted that the struggle had to be peaceful.

Under his leadership and direction the freedom movement took a distinctive turn. He was to go on fast many times. In 1942 the Quit India movement was launched. Although the British were willing to grant independence, they wanted the division of India into two nations. Gandhi opposed such a division and when violence broke out amidst the division he appealed for peace and harmony and visited the strife-torn areas. On 30 January 1948 he was shot dead by Nathuram Godse, a Hindu fundamentalist, at a prayer meeting.

The works and lives of Leo Tolstoy, John Ruskin, Henry David **Thoreau** and traditional Hindu thought greatly influenced Gandhi. He advocated *ahimsa* (non-violence), *satyagraha* (passive resistance), *aparigraha* (non-possession) and was a critic of a western civilization based on indiscriminate **industrialization** and greed. He tried to practise what he preached and had a simple lifestyle. His basic philosophy is expounded in *Hind Swaraj*, in which he provides a radical critique of western civilization and advocates an alternative model. Gandhi regarded all religions as equal and warned against politics without spirituality. His views on machinery, **development** and village-centred economy were not acceptable to many including Jawaharlal Nehru and B.R. Ambedkar. Ambedkar and others regarded his views as too conservative. Ambedkar and E.V. Ramasamy Naicker pointed out that for the untouchables and downtrodden of India there is little of benefit in Gandhi's philosophy since he was against radical transformation of Hindu society. Nehru was more influenced by Fabian socialists and the Russian model and regarded industrialization as an essential strategy for national development.

Gandhi warned against consumerist culture and the craze for material affluence (see **consumerism**). He differentiated between needs and wants and for him the needs of others were to be given priority over one's own wants. It is no wonder that his ideas have had greater influence in green politics and in **deep ecology** (see also **green**

political theory). Gandhi opposed the use of science and **technology** for the mindless exploitation of natural resources and the fulfilment of the material needs of the few. He favoured an education system that did not privilege the intellect over the manual crafts and skills and believed in principles of natural health cures. His followers tried to develop his principles and set up various institutions based on Gandhian principles and practices. Gandhi's ideas have inspired thinkers like J.C. Kumarappa to develop an alternative perspective to the dominant model of development. But such ideas were marginalized in post-1947 India: although many thought Gandhi a great man deserving of admiration and respect, they also thought his ideas anachronistic.

His use of non-violence as a political tool and passive resistance as a strategy have influenced **environmental movements** and greens. In these days when **sustainable development** is a fashionable slogan, Gandhi may sound more relevant than ever before. But only a critical and contextual examination of his life, times and ideas will give us more insights than merely portraying him as an apostle of green development. The political and moral philosophy of Gandhi was deeply influenced by indigenous religious traditions of India, particularly *Vaishnava* philosophy, American radical **democracy** and anti-industrialism. In his utopia it was the self-sufficient village or community that would form the core of society (see **utopia/ecotopia**). He abhorred structures of governance that centralized power and destroyed the creative capacity of the community. He favoured trusteeship as an alternative to concentration of wealth and capital in the hands of few. He promoted hand spinning and hand-spun Khadi over mill-made textiles and for him Charkha, the spinning wheel, was more than a technical device: it was a symbol of resistance and self-reliance.

His life, ideas and experiments will continue to inspire generations to come and each generation may interpret and apply his ideas as it deems fit, in the given contexts.

Further reading

Drengson, A. (1999) 'Eco-philosophy, Ecosophy

and The Deep Ecology Movement: An Overview', at URL: http://www.deep-ecology.org.

Gandhi, M.K. (1929) *Hind Swaraj*, Ahemadabad: Navjivan Publishing House.

Murti, V.V.R (1970) *Mahtama Gandhi :Essential Writings*, New Delhi: Gandhi Peace Foundation.

Sheth, P. (1999) 'The Eco-Gandhi and Ecological Movements', at URL: http://www.mkgandhi-sarvodaya.org.

K. RAVI SRINIVAS

Garzweiler controversy

Garzweiler is the site of a major brown coal (or lignite) open-cast mine in the German state of North-Rhine-Westphalia, located to the west of Cologne in a predominantly rural area. The lignite is used for electricity generation in large power stations constructed in the immediate vicinity of the mine. The integrated **mining** and power production operation is run by *Rheinbraun*, a subsidiary of the giant RWE utility.

Environmentalists are concerned about the environmental damage caused by open-cast lignite mining at local as well as global level. Lignite mining effectively destroys the entire **landscape**, including human settlements such as the Garzweiler village that gave the name to the site. While the resettlement of the people affected and reconstruction of the landscape are paid for by the operators, environmental critics point to lasting damage to the natural environment of the region and to the global impact on climate change of burning brown coal.

Lignite mining became politically controversial in 1995 when the regional government signalled its approval of a second giant open-cast lignite mine to open in 2006, Garzweiler II. Local people to be displaced protested against the plan, major environmental groups, such as the **BUND**, joined in. In the regional elections of 1995, the Green Party campaigned to stop Garzweiler II. As the Social Democratic Party (SPD) lost its parliamentary majority, it reluctantly looked to the German Greens, *Die **Grünen*** as a coalition partner. The fate of Garzweiler II became one of the major stumbling blocks in the coalition negotiations. Unable to reach an agreement on principle, the future of Garzweiler II was left open. The controversy came to a head in 1997 after the state Supreme Court rejected a case brought by the Greens against the Garzweiler II project which then cleared a major planning hurdle later in the year with the support of the SPD. The Greens convened a special delegate conference at Jüchen, near the Garzweiler II site, in January 1998 to decide whether to stay in the coalition with the SPD or not. After an emotional debate, the conference decided to stay in the coalition but asked state Environment Minister Bärbel Höhn (Greens) to use every remaining legal possibility to stop the plans. Höhn's efforts to block the project receiving its planning approval under water law provisions came unstuck, however, when in September 1998, state premier Wolfgang Clement (SPD) confronted Höhn with the choice of dropping her objections or leaving his government. This happened at a time when the federal Green Party was in negotiations with the SPD over the formation of a first national coalition government. Höhn backed down, and formally, the Garzweiler II project had cleared its final political hurdle.

For the Greens, the Garzweiler II controversy has been a painful experience, alienating the local population as well as many more radical Greens who were bitterly disappointed by the failure of the party to stand by its principles. The project continues to be pushed by the SPD, under pressure from unions in the state worried about further job losses in the mining sector. From the green point of view, the main hope is that the RWE utility will not pursue the Garzweiler II plans for economic reasons. The restructuring of German utility operations in the wake of the liberalization of the electricity market could make the project economically unattractive. Also, environmental groups are continuing their legal fight to stop Garzweiler II in the courts.

References

Hater, K. (2000) *Gesellschaftliches Lernen im politischen Prozess: Eine Fallstudie zum Diskurs über das Braunkohlentagebauvorhaben Garzweiler II*, Opladen: Leske & Budrich.

WOLFGANG RÜDIG

Génération Écologie

'Don't moan, act!' was the slogan of the political party *Génération Écologie* (GE), founded by Brice **Lalonde** on 11 May 1990 with the aim of forging an alliance between the centre parties, the Ecologists and the Socialist party in order to compete with the other green party *Les Verts* (see **Verts, les**). GE were successful in the 1992 regional election, matching their rival's score (around 7 per cent). After a strategic alliance with *Les Verts* in the 1993 parliamentary election (7.6 per cent), they were to radicalize their vision of a 'realistic ecology' able to reconcile **development** in a market economy with environmental protection. Moving away from *Les Verts* and the Socialists towards a Gaullist–Liberal Right, GE then experienced serious internal splits as well as a steady electoral decline: 1994 European election (2.01 per cent); 1995 Presidential election (no candidate); 1998 regional election (2 elected candidates). The remains of GE have now sided with the Liberals (Démocratie Libérale).

BRUNO VILLALBA

genetic engineering, animals

For centuries, if not millennia, techniques have been employed to alter the genetic characteristics of animals for many reasons. For example, canine breeds have been selectively combined and refined to conform to a culture's given aesthetics, altering their appearance, behaviour and temperament. Animals have also been bred for domestication in farming and to increase the value of, amongst other things, their meat, milk and fleeces.

Genetic engineering differs from these traditional methods of animal husbandry in some very important respects. First, genes from one organism can be extracted and recombined into that of another (using recombinant DNA technology or rDNA) without either organism having to be of the same species. Second, removing the requirement for species reproductive compatibility, new genetic combinations can be produced in a much more highly accelerated way than before. Since the late 1970s, rDNA has been used to produced animals that, for example, are able to secrete new drug compounds in their milk or which are able to express other characteristics usually found in unrelated species. The same period has been characterized by an ongoing and ferocious political debate over the risks, and **animal rights** implications of animal genetic engineering. Several key episodes have been at the centre of these debates.

In the late 1980s, the University of Harvard sought to patent a breed of laboratory mouse that had been genetically engineered to develop a human form of cancer. The 'oncomouse' was then sold to other research groups to be used to model the effectiveness of cancer treatments in humans. The oncomouse episode provoked concerns about **biotechnology** by raising questions about the welfare of genetically engineered animals and whether it was possible to patent life forms as humanly created inventions. Despite strong opposition from animal welfare and environmental groups, a US patent on oncomouse was granted in 1988 and the European Patent Office followed in 1992.

Another early landmark in the debate revolved around a series of experiments by US government laboratories at Beltsville to produce pigs with additional growth hormone genes. It was envisaged that the resulting animals would have a greater meat value than traditional breeds. Highlighting some of the uncertainties of the way genes interact within complex organic systems, the 'Beltsville Pigs' were grossly obese, suffered blindness, reproductive malfunctions and were unable to support themselves because of their weight. Illustrative of wider legal battles, the incident inspired a law suite by the American Humane Society against the US Department of Agriculture.

Probably the most high profile political test for mammalian genetic engineering was the disclosure by Edinburgh's Roslin Institute, in 1997, that it had cloned a sheep by 'nuclear transfer'. That is, the nucleus of a somatic udder cell was treated to 'forget' its specific cell function before being transplanted into an egg (ovum) from which the nucleus had been removed. Dolly, as she has come to be known, was claimed to be an exact clone of the ewe from which the somatic cell had been taken. Putting aside the controversy about the possible application of the technique in human reproduction, many organizations raised concerns about the welfare implications of this and other examples of animal genetic engineering. Because mammalian **cloning** and transgenics are highly experimental, large numbers of animals are often necessary to produce a small number of viable animals. Dolly was the 277th attempt at producing an adult ewe in this way and many previous attempts resulted in seriously deformed embryos and stillbirths. Also, it remains far from certain whether Roslin's claims to have produced a clone are correct since it has been demonstrated that Dolly also inherited DNA from the egg donor, and not the nuclear donor exclusively.

Animals, genetic engineering and the environment

Contemporary environmental debates about the genetic engineering of animals extend well beyond issues of adequate welfare standards. For instance, biotechnology relies heavily upon the use of viruses to move genes between animal species. Many applications in biotechnology proceed by 'splicing' genes into viruses which are then introduced to target cells and whole organisms. These 'viral vectors' find their way inside a cell, delivering the spliced gene into the DNA of the cell. The newly introduced DNA can then be reproduced as cells replicate and organisms reproduce.

This process itself raises certain environmental concerns. For instance, if viral vectors remain reproductively active, despite being engineered not to replicate, spliced DNA can be delivered beyond its intended target to other organisms. Another risk is that novel gene carrying viral vectors will combine with similar viruses producing potentially harmful strains of disease. There are also un- certainties around the way newly introduced genes will articulate with what others have described as the interlinked 'genomic ecosystem of plants and animals' producing potentially harmful combina- tions (Wheale, Schomberg and Glasner, 1998). Whilst many of these processes of genetic interac- tion occur naturally, biotechnology in animals increases their likelihood:

> the dynamic nature of genomes and their intimate relationship with viruses have impor-

tant implications for the risks of modern genetic engineering. The integration of viral vectors into the genome could trigger the mobilization, duplication and mutation of other parts of the genome, disrupting the expression of host cell genes [and] transforming the cells into cancer- ous cell lines.

> (Wheale, Schomberg and Glasner, 1998: 10).

The viral hazards of genetic engineering have also been the subject of international monitoring in respect to **xenotransplantation**. Regulatory agencies have been established to advise on whether the technology may create conditions for transspecies disease transfer. The problem largely rests on a conflict between the benefits to individual patients versus the risks to wider human and animal populations. Whilst patients can give their consent to a transspecies transplant, others may well be exposed to disease risks that, given the choice, they may be unwilling to take.

Political negotiations over the genetic engineer- ing of animals have also focused on the implications for **biodiversity**. For example, competitive pressures in the meat and dairy industries oblige producers to use large herds with as few genetic differences within the stock as possible. Whilst this standardization contributes to the efficiencies of **agribusiness**, animal herds with a high degree of genetic uniformity (whether because of traditional breeding techniques or genetic engineering and cloning) share a greater vulnerability to infectious disease. Controlling these risks is more difficult in less biodiverse populations of animals.

Perspectives in policy and ethics

The account above identifies some of the problems associated with the genetic engineering of animals that have been prevalent in environmental politics. However, it is also important to examine the underlying philosophical perspectives that guide policy in managing developments in mammalian biotechnology.

Most environmental policy approaches to reg- ulating the genetic engineering of animals for either agribusiness or medical research are based on a predominantly utilitarian view of other animals. That is, the more suffering an animal is likely to experience, the greater is the need to justify that suffering through potential benefit. This is broadly in keeping with a **cost–benefit analysis** for guiding policy whereby animal welfare is weighed against some possible or likely good. In this framework, animals have an instrumental value in that their purpose is defined in relation to human need. Versions of this outlook have largely prevailed within the institutional management of animal welfare policy.

By way of contrast to the instrumentalist welfare perspective, other frameworks operate on the basis that animals have **intrinsic value** and rights of their own which cannot be breached irrespective of expected benefits. Whereas in the previous perspective, the moral status of an animal would vary according to the dividends of genetic engineering, here an animal's moral status is fixed regardless of whether an experimental procedure will bring some greater good. Whilst this perspective has long characterized **animal rights** philosophy, some commentators argue that it is increasingly becoming a feature of the institutional policy management of genetic engineering, particularly in Europe (Verhoog, 1996). As Verhoog puts it, 'with this interpretation of intrinsic value it can be argued that the production of transgenic animals by crossing-species barriers violates the nature or integrity of the animals involved' (p. 250). And yet, the approach remains steeped in the difficulty of determining what criteria should be used to identify intrinsic value, whether it should be an animal's consciousness, its autonomy, its capacity to suffer, etc. Genetic engineering raises problems for adherents to the philosophy of intrinsic value for the very reason that it is capable of altering that which defines an animal's intrinsic value by, for example, removing the capacity for consciousness or suffering.

These two perspectives are far from being the only environmental policy preoccupations of governments seeking to manage the genetic engineering of animals. The way possible ecological and environmental harms are managed has itself been subject to changes of perspective. The emergence of the **precautionary principle**, for instance, places emphasis on anticipating potential risks where the chances of occurrence may be small but where the possible harm would be unacceptably large. Adherents to precautionary regulation have argued that it is not necessary to provide conclusive scientific evidence of actual risk to prohibit potentially harmful transgenic procedures; the mere theoretical possibility of the risk is sufficient. This perspective can be seen to have characterized a number of international regulatory positions, including to some extent that governing xenotransplantation.

See also: agribusiness; animal rights; biodiversity; biotechnology; cloning; genetic engineering, crops; precautionary principle

References

Verhoog, H. (1996) 'Genetic Modification of Animals: Should Science and Ethics be Integrated?', *The Monist*, 79: 247–63.

Wheale, P., von Schomberg, R. and Glasner, P. (eds) (1998) *The Social Management of Genetic Engineering*, Aldershot: Ashgate.

Further reading

Fox, M.W. (1999) *Beyond Evolution: The Genetically Altered Future of Plants, Animals, the Earth, and Humans*, New York: The Lyons Press.

Suzuki, D. and Knudtson, P. (1990) *Genethics : The Clash Between the New Genetics and Human Values*, Cambridge, MA: Harvard University Press.

NIK BROWN

genetic engineering, crops

The term genetic engineering became widespread in the 1970s, when recombinant DNA techniques were first developed to transfer genetic material across bacterial species. The techniques were aimed at engineering microbes to produce therapeutic agents or other valuable substances in contained facilities. The 1980s public debate focused on human health risks of such activity and its products. In response to public concerns, genetic 'engineering' was renamed 'manipulation', and even more euphemistically renamed as 'modification'.

Similar techniques were developed in order to transfer genetic material into plants. Since the late 1980s, various genetically modified (GM) crops have been tested in field trials. In the first-generation GM crops, the genetic inserts mainly conferred resistance to broad-spectrum herbicides and insect pests. Many such products entered commercial cultivation in the 1990s, especially in North America, **China** and Argentina.

From the very start, GM crops provoked a wide-ranging debate which indicates a legitimacy problem for agricultural **biotechnology**. According to supporters, it offers essential tools for environmentally friendly products, greater productivity and the means to increase food production, especially in the Third World; therefore society faces the risk of forgoing these benefits. According to critics, however, biotechnology will aggravate the problems of intensive **agriculture**, as well as imposing new hazards; therefore the technology poses the risk of precluding beneficial alternatives.

According to some proponents, genetic engineering is 'a natural science' which simply re-arranges a universal 'genetic code'. GM crops have been given 'in-built genetic information' which provides 'natural' defences against pests or other adverse conditions. In this way, the R&D diagnoses agricultural problems as genetic deficiencies which must be corrected. Some biotechnologists call this 'value-added genetics', i.e. the search for genes which can increase the commercial value of crops. This scenario recasts nature as a bioreactor whose efficiency must be enhanced for commodity production and exchange.

Likewise **biodiversity** has been recast. According to proponents, GM crops provide a greater variety of genetic combinations, which thereby increase biodiversity – redefined as laboratory simulations of nature. According to critics, GM crops threaten the diverse crop varieties which have been developed by farmers in the field; also, inadvertent gene flow could reduce the biodiversity of plant species in their centres of origin, mainly in countries of the South.

Patents are a related issue. By patenting the inserted genes of GM crops, companies can prohibit farmers from re-sowing seeds, charge royalties and even extend such controls to some traditional varieties. For advocates of greater patent rights, biopiracy means violations of those rights – essential for protecting the investment in 'biological inventions'. For opponents of such rights, 'biopiracy' means the patents themselves, which privatize mere discoveries and common resources (see **biopiracy/bioprospecting**).

Environmental development issues

GM crops have become linked to a wider debate over **sustainable development**; environmental risks have been linked to **development** issues about how best to manage plant resources. In that regard, the industry has adopted the language of 'high-input sustainable agriculture'. According to one company, their products mean more productive agriculture, more soil conservation, less insecticide use, less energy, better habitat protection. Such benefits are promised for all farmers, regardless of their economic circumstances.

According to some proponents, moreover, biotechnology will be essential for 'feeding the world'. In their scenario, greater world hunger may result from inadequate agricultural inputs and from population growing faster than food production. GM crops can solve the problem by increasing production, by resisting pests or tolerating inhospitable climates (dry or saline soils). In a more subtle version of this scenario, the fundamental problem is land degradation resulting from over-intensive or inefficient cultivation. As the solution, GM crops would increase productivity in environmentally benign ways, thus requiring less land.

According to critics, however, world hunger results mainly from unjust forms of land use and food distribution. In recent years, more and more land has been converted from staple food crops to cash crops – e.g., bulk commodities used as animal feed and/or specialty crops for export. GM varieties could accelerate the loss of staple food crops.

Moreover, critics attribute global agricultural problems to intensive monocultural methods which make crops more susceptible to pests and disease – and which may be aggravated by GM crops. As in the **green revolution**, 'high-yield' varieties have already displaced traditional crop varieties, while making farmers more dependent upon chemical-intensive methods and other purchased inputs. By analogy, multi-cropping methods previously protected farmers from pests and provided diverse nutrients such as vitamin A, but herbicide-tolerant crops may displace these benefits. Claims for **pesticide**-reduction have a different meaning in places where agrochemicals are little used anyway.

In **Mexico** maize yields have been increased by using green revolution-type 'modern varieties' with more purchased inputs, producing maize mainly for animal feed. This development has marginalized peasants who cultivate maize in crop rotations, which previously helped control pests. An estimated 2.5 million households still cultivate maize on small-scale, low-input, rain-fed farms. Their livelihoods are further threatened by cheap US imports, some of them higher-yield GM maize. This threat in turn increases the pressure on Mexican farmers to adopt intensive methods in order to compete in the market.

In the late 1990s opposition movements blocked GM crops in several Third World countries. Long before then, some Indian farmers' organizations had been campaigning against hybrid seeds as a threat to farmers' control over their livelihoods. They regarded Monsanto's GM insecticidal cotton as a further step towards privatizing seeds, and went on to organize 'cremations' of field trials. After the Brazilian government approved commercial cultivation of Monsanto's herbicide-tolerant GM soya, its use was partly blocked by a broad coalition. This included the landless movement, Sem Terras, which was already developing organic methods of cultivation on occupied land.

Risk regulation and trade

Under discussion since the mid-1990s, an international biosafety protocol was intended to govern transboundary shipments of 'living modified organisms' (LMOs). This was designed to guarantee 'advance informed agreement' via **risk-assessment** information for the importing country. When the Cartagena Protocol on Biosafety was finalized in 2000, it also included the **precautionary principle**. Member states may block the import of a GM product if they have reason to believe that it poses a risk; they may cite socio-economic reasons for doing so.

According to the Protocol, it is 'complementary' (rather than subordinate) to the 1994 **World Trade Organization** agreement, which requires member states to provide scientific evidence to justify any blockages on imports. The relation between the two treaties remains contentious. As a potential test case, Europe blocked some GM crops which had already gained commercial approval in the USA. In the late 1990s the US government characterized the blockages as 'non-tariff trade barriers'; this phrase implied that the real aim was to protect European products from economic competition or to accommodate public fears – rather than to protect human health or the environment.

In practice, responding to public protest, European regulation has indeed demanded more evidence of safety as a condition for allowing commercial use. For GM herbicide-tolerant crops, European critics raised the prospect that herbicide-tolerance genes would spread to weeds, thus jeopardizing future use of the herbicide, which may be regarded as relatively benign; debate also focused on the prospect that the broad-spectrum herbicides would harm wildlife habitats near agricultural fields. These issues hardly arose in the USA. For GM insecticidal maize, European critics raised the prospect of potential harm to non-target insects, as compared to conventional maize (which is not normally sprayed with chemical insecticides). Although scientists and NGOs raised this issue in the USA too, regulators there allowed commercial use to continue.

The US–EU trade conflict arises partly from different cultural meaning of agriculture. US farms are seen as analogous to factories, sharply demarcated from wilderness and nature conservation areas. Although European agriculture too uses chemical-intensive methods, it is widely regarded as an integral part of the environment, i.e., as an aesthetic **landscape**, a local heritage, a livelihood for artisanal peasants, and a wildlife habitat. As this example illustrates, different environmental values underlie regulatory conflicts – which cannot be resolved simply by scientific evidence.

Further reading

Chataway, J., Levidow, L. and Carr, S. (2000) 'Genetic Engineering of Development? Myths and Possibilities', in T. Allen and A. Thomas (eds) *Poverty and Development into the Twenty-First Century*, Oxford: Oxford University Press, pp.469–84.

de la Perrière, R. and Seuret, F. (2000) *Brave New Seeds: The Threat of GM Crops to Farmers*, London: Zed.

Food Ethics Council (1999) *Novel Foods: Beyond Nuffield*, Southwell: Food Ethics Council at URL: http://www.users.globalnet.co.uk/~foodeth.

Krimsky, S. and Wrubel, R. (1996) *Agricultural Biotechnology and the Environment: Science, Policy and Social Issues*, Chicago: University of Illinois Press.

Lappé, M. and Bailey, B. (1999) *Against the Grain: the Genetic Transformation of Global Agriculture*, London: Earthscan.

Levidow, L. and Carr, S. (eds) (2000) 'Precautionary Regulation: GM Crops in the European Union', special issue, *Journal of Risk Research* 3(3): 187–285;
URL: http://www.tandf.co.uk/journals/authors/r-authors/jrrspecialissue.html.

Shiva, V. and Moser, I. (eds) (1995) *Biopolitics: A Feminist and Ecological Reader on Biotechnology*, London: Zed.

LES LEVIDOW

genetic engineering, humans

Debates about the application of genetic engineering in humans have centred on three key areas. First, trials of gene transfer technologies (gene therapy) have been used to, for example, correct human genetic disorders and treat cancer. Second, mammalian **cloning** has generated widespread policy debate about the possible application of cloning in humans. Finally, genetic diagnostics has raised questions about society's changing acceptance of certain groups, especially with respect to disability. Each of these is considered below.

Gene transfer technologies or gene therapy involves genetically engineering a virus which can then infect target cells, introducing new genes in the process. The technique is a possible solution to diseases caused by the absence of genes that code for essential proteins (genetic deficiency disorders). Such disorders can result in serious pathologies and metabolic problems. However, far more research has concentrated on the use of human gene therapy to treat cancer. Here modified genetic inserts can either attack cancerous cells or attach markers to them so that toxic treatments target diseased cells rather than normal ones.

These potential benefits are also accompanied by questions of safety and efficacy. The viral vectors used to deliver genes are engineered not to continue replicating, but there are anxieties that viruses may mutate and thus reacquire replicability. In these circumstances, there is the risk that modified genes will be unintentionally delivered to other cells and whole organisms.

Another risk is that artificially introduced genetic traits may be inherited by a patient's offspring, making it difficult to restrict potential side effects to the patient alone. A major distinction in human genetic engineering is the difference between the body's somatic (non-reproductive) cells where gene transfer is legally permitted, and germ line (reproductive) cells in which gene transfer is legally prohibited. This distinction is supposed to confine genetic engineering to the consenting individual and prevent engineered genes being inherited by non-consenting unborn subjects. But there are concerns about the possibility of engineered genes accidentally entering the germ line from somatic cells.

Also, regulation prohibits non-medical genetic enhancements of humans, objecting to the engineering of human genetic elites who may, for instance, possess enhanced physical or cognitive attributes. The rationale behind this position is that such enhancements would be anti-meritocratic. That is, they would confer on an individual an unfair advantage from birth allowing them to excel in, for example, educational terms. The problem is that these opportunities would be physically denied other individuals who may strive to educational excellence with equal diligence but no chance of competing on a meritocratic basis.

The European Medical Research Council's 1988 measures illustrate other regulatory positions recommending that: a) gene therapy should be limited to interventions aimed at correcting disease or defects; b) that it should be limited to somatic cells; c) that research be aimed at the development of safe species and tissue-specific vectors for gene delivery.

Developments in the cloning of research and farm animals have also created heated international policy debates about the application of the technique to human reproduction. Regulation of the techniques distinguishes between human 'reproductive cloning' and 'therapeutic cloning'. Reproductive cloning can be defined as the application of the technique for the purpose of creating embryos that are allowed to continue developing to adulthood. In therapeutic cloning, a cloned embryo can be used for research into new treatments for a specified period after fertilization before being terminated. Whilst international sanctions against reproductive cloning have been put in place, an increasing number of countries allow therapeutic cloning for research.

Critics have argued that the definition of human genetic engineering should be broad enough to encompass developments in DNA diagnostics and testing since responses to tests (especially the termination of pregnancy) affect the composition of the human gene pool. In contrast to recent developments discussed above, this debate has preoccupied politics since the late nineteenth century. Key questions revolve around whether genetic diagnostics represent a new form of eugenics, refining the human gene pool by prohibiting groups defined as 'inferior' from reproducing. The problem is that society's definitions of genetic inferiority are subject to radical change. Concerns have been voiced, particularly from disability groups, that the eugenics policies that guided mid-twentieth-century fascism are now evident in the politics of contemporary DNA diagnostics.

See also: animal rights; biotechnology; cloning; genetic engineering, crops; genetic engineering, animals

Further reading

Fox, M.W (1999) *Beyond Evolution: The Genetically Altered Future of Plants, Animals, the Earth, and Humans*, New York: The Lyons Press.

Kolata, G.B. (1997) *Clone the Road to Dolly, and the Path Ahead*, London: Penguin Press.

Rapp, R. (1999) *Testing Women, Testing the Foetus: The Social Impact of Amniocentesis in America*, London: Routledge.

NIK BROWN

Georgescu-Roegen, Nicholas

b. 1906, Constanza, Romania; d.1994

Ecological economist

Nicholas Georgescu-Roegen was a Romanian-born ecological economist whose pioneering work in the area helped establish the discipline of **ecological economics**. He is particularly associated with integrating the ecologically significant concept of **entropy** into economic analysis, thereby establishing the ineliminable dependence of the human economy upon the natural world, its processes and inputs. This dependence he termed the 'metabolic flow' between society and **nature**. Central to his analysis was the distinction between solar energy income/flows (which are renewable) and terrestrial energy stock (which is finite). He argued that social evolution has in the past consisted of slow adaptations of our 'endosomatic organs' (heart, lungs, etc.), which run on solar energy. However, since the industrial revolution, social development has shifted to adaptations of our 'exosomatic organs' (technology, cars, airplanes, etc.), which depend on terrestrial low entropy, particularly carbon-based energy sources, such as oil, gas and coal. The unequal ownership of these external technological instruments and of the terrestrial stocks of fixed and scarce low entropy from which they are made, compared to the egalitarian distribution of ownership of endosomatic capital, is for him the root of social conflict in modern industrial societies.

JOHN BARRY

German Ministry of Environment

Founded in 1986, the German Federal Ministry of Environment, Nature Conservation and Nuclear

Safety (*Bundesministerium für Umwelt, Naturschutz und Reaktorsicherheit* (BMU)) has offices in both Bonn and Berlin.

Its responsibilities are far reaching. Under German federalism, environmental responsibilities exist at the level of the federal, state (*Länder*) and local governments. BMU is in charge of many environmental matters at the federal level; however, due to the cross-cutting nature of the subject matter, numerous environmental topics are handled by other ministries (e.g., **eco-taxes** by Finance and Economic Affairs; road tolls, speed limits by Transport, etc.). Most ministries have their own environmental protection division, but they are often reluctant to integrate environmental policy considerations and tend to exclude BMU from their decision-making.

At the end of 1999, BMU employed 880 full- and part-time staff. Its central task by its own definition is to further develop a legal framework to bring human life and in particular economic activities into harmony with the conservation of the natural basis of existence and to protect the population from health risks. Known for its predominantly command-and-control approach to regulation, it developed greater flexibility during the 1990s (see **German pollution control**).

The Ministry has a number of supporting organizations in scientific, technical and administrative areas. The UBA (*Umweltbundesamt* or Federal Environment Agency) was founded in 1974 and has a current staff of about 1,200; however it has little political autonomy and no regulatory function. It supports BMU in the policy areas of air, water, soil/chemicals, waste, noise, health, planning, research, information and documentation and environmental labelling. The Federal Agency for Radiation Protection (*Bundesamt für Strahlenschutz*), founded in 1989, has a current staff 680. It is active in reactor safety, transport of radioactive materials, nuclear waste disposal, and radiation protection. The Federal Agency for Nature Conservation (*Bundesamt für Naturschutz*), founded in 1994 with a current staff of 250 is responsible for **nature** and **landscape** conservation, **biodiversity**, man and biosphere-programme.

The BMU is also advised by a number of expert committees. The Council of Environmental Ex-

perts (*Sachverständigenrat für Umweltfragen*), founded in 1972, periodically formulates expertises on the environmental situation and recommends courses of action to all levels of government and to business. The Scientific Advisory Council on Global Environmental Change, created in 1992, responds to both BMU and the Federal Ministry of Research. The Reactor Safety Commission (created in 1958) and Radiation Protection Commission (created in 1974) since 1998/9 – minister Trittin – include scientists critical of nuclear power Scientific Advisory Council on Soil Protection (since 1999).

Despite its interaction with these numerous advisory bodies, the BMU is often undercut by more powerful ministries (e.g. Economic Affairs). In periods of national economic or fiscal problems (1975–80, 1990–8) **ecological modernization** was generally viewed as inhibiting economic growth and was consequently slowed down considerably. BMU's first clientele – environmental organizations – always remained at a critical distance. From the late 1980s onwards, business associations for **environmental management**, the pollution control (end of pipe) **technology** industry and, later on, clean technology industries became important allies.

Environmental policy as a national policy area was first created in 1969 by the incoming social democratic/liberal government of Willy Brandt. In that year and again in 1972, federal responsibilities for environmental problems were transferred to the Ministry of the Interior. Also in 1972, a revision of the constitution gave the federal government concurrent legislative powers on environmental protection matters; this means that the federal government is able to pre-empt the states in this area. The creation of the Federal Environment Agency in 1974 was part of the same reform movement.

During the recession of 1974/5, business and labour, the Economic Affairs minister and incoming chancellor Helmut Schmidt opposed BMU demands for environmental reform. This led to the rise of a powerful environmental movement, at first dominated by citizen action groups (*Bürgerinitiativen*) which strongly politicized environmental issues, often in opposition to government, business and labour. When the new conservative–liberal coalition took over in 1982, environmental affairs first remained with the Ministry of the Interior. In 1986, BMU was created and received additional environmental protection responsibilities from other ministries. The first incumbent of the new ministry, Walter Wallmann, was soon replaced by the more active Klaus Töpfer (1987–94). However, German unification in 1990 led to downplaying environmental reform in the name of economic growth and fiscal discipline. This approach continued under Angela Merkel (1994–8). In 1998, Jürgen **Trittin** became Green Party minister in the new social democratic/green coalition government. His chief concern: phasing out nuclear power and paving the way for **renewable energy**.

Further reading

BMU official site, Kennedy-Allee 5, D-53175 Bonn, URL: http://www.bmu.de.

Jänicke, M. and Weidner, H. (1997) 'Germany', in M. Jänicke and H. Weidner (eds) *National Environmental Policies: A Comparative Study of Capacity-Building*, Berlin: Springer.

Pehle, H. (1998) 'Germany: Domestic Obstacles to an International Forerunner', in M.S. Andersen and D. Liefferink (eds) *European Environmental Policy: The Pioneers*, Manchester: Manchester University Press.

VOLKMAR LAUBER

German nuclear power industry

The German nuclear power industry is really two *industries*. Both West and East Germany used nuclear power for 'civilian' purposes. The first commercial nuclear power stations in the West as well as the East became operational in 1966 (smaller 'research reactors' had operated from the early 1960s onwards). By the year 2000, 19 nuclear reactors were in operation – all in the West. They contributed over one third of the country's energy needs. However, compared to earlier expansion plans – including a 1957 East German proposal to erect 250 reactors in East Germany alone; and

West German predictions in the 1960s that *all* energy production would eventually be nuclear – the industry was relatively small. Despite continuous political support until 1998 – including several hundred billion Deutschmark in research money – the industry has been on the defensive since the 1980s. In the West, plans to build a reactor in the wealthy rural hamlet of Whyl (near Freiburg) and attempts to build a nuclear reprocessing facility at Wackersdorf (in Bavaria) created insurmountable public opposition. **Chernobyl**, whose radioactive clouds affected Germany directly and caused grave public concern, sealed the fate of these projects. After 1986, over 70 per cent of West Germans have continuously opposed nuclear power and the industry has had to shelve expansion plans. The pro-nuclear Kohl government of the day, tried to appease public concern through the creation of a **German Ministry of Environment** and Nuclear Safety. In the East, due to a lack of democratic representation, public pressure could not be effective directly. However, cancer clusters around nuclear installations were noticed by local residents, and anti-nuclear activities were a hallmark of the East German opposition movement in the late 1980s (Pflugbeil, 1995). Still: lack of money to invest was the main reason for the non-implementation of the East's expansion plans. When East Germany ceased to exist in 1990, the eastern reactors were closed immediately, both because they failed to meet western security standards (which were extended to the 'united' country) and because they were uneconomical.

Opposition to the nuclear industry was a hallmark of the German Greens, *Die **Grünen***, and contributed considerably to their popularity (Mittler, 1999). When they gained power at the federal level in 1998, therefore, it was expected that the nuclear industry would face a rapid phase out. Their coalition partners, the Social Democrats, had also – from 1986 onwards – pledged to abandon nuclear power 'as soon as practicable but at the latest within ten years of reaching power'. However, the deal that was signed between the German government and the nuclear industry in June 2000, read differently. The complicated document grants the nuclear industry the right to generate another 26 million kWh of electricity. This is equivalent to 32 years of continued nuclear power operation according to the industry; and to 35 years according to **Greenpeace** Germany. Either way, it is almost exactly as much **nuclear energy** as has been generated in (West) Germany from 1966 to 2000. Therefore, the amount of nuclear waste to be produced until 2032–5 will be another 7000 tons – the amount of nuclear waste produced (in the West) since 1966.

The issue of its wastes has been the Achilles heel of the industry. In the East, nuclear waste was often dumped in lakes causing grave crises in public health. The health statistics of the Wismut area, where uranium was mined and the resulting wastes dumped in the surrounding countryside, were a state secret. When they nonetheless were published underground and became known in the West, they were a considerable embarrassment. In the West, the opposition against Wackersdorf was followed by increased activism against nuclear waste transports. Nuclear waste transports to the prospective permanent storage facility at Gorleben (see **Gorleben controversy**), in particular became a focus of anti-nuclear activities in the mid-1990s. Further such transports will be necessary until 2035. Each one of them is likely to be a serious public relations and security problem for the industry.

The German nuclear power industry will possibly cease to exist by 2035 (though the deal signed in June 2000 is reversible). However, German engineering firms that sell nuclear installations, like Siemens, are likely to continue as nuclear providers. They are already investing heavily in ́emerging nuclear markeť such as eastern Europe and **China**.

See also: Grünen, Die; nuclear energy/nuclear waste management

References

Mittler, D. (1999) 'Eclipse of the German Greens', *The Ecologist* 29(8): 461–3.

Pflugbeil, S. (1995) 'Kernenergie in der DDR', in M. Ziesche (ed.) *Alles wird besser, nichts wird gut?*, Berlin: Aufbau.

DANIEL MITTLER

German pollution control

German environmental law traditionally refers to specific environmental media and is based on command-and-control policies: standards are established for specific public goods such as air and water and enforced by means of administrative and penal instruments. German environmental law is enacted by different levels of the federal state, this consists of federal law, state law and municipal law and presently is increasingly dominated by European law. Its history can be interpreted as a history of creating new federal competences: nuclear energy law 1959; waste law and emission control law (clean air and noise abatement) 1972; gene technology law 1993. Its breakthrough as an independent area of law in its present structure can be dated at the beginning of the 1970s under the governance of the first social democrat/ liberal coalition: emission control act 1974; integration of an environmental chapter in the criminal code 1980. In the course of German re-unification 1989/90 its application was extended to the new eastern states.

The act on the prevention of harmful effects on the environment caused by **air pollution**, noise, vibrations and similar phenomena (*Bundes-Immissionsschutzgesetz*) can be seen as the 'basic law' of German pollution control. According to its structure and regulatory technique it serves as a model for other environmental law. Installations such as factories, machines and other stationary and non-stationary facilities shall be constructed and operated in such a way that harmful effects on the environment are avoided or reduced to a minimum (arts 5, 21). These legal preconditions are further explained by administrative rules or regulations of the federal government. Traditionally emission standards are set up after experts from science and business are heard (*technische Anleitung Luft*; *technische Anleitung Lärm*). The construction and operation of installations which, on account of their nature or their operation are particularly likely to cause harmful effects on the environment, are subject to licensing (art. 4). It is fixed by decree which installations are concerned and whether licensing is subject to a formal procedure with public paticipation (art. 10) or simplified procedure (art. 19).

This command-and-control-approach also applies for the law concerning other environmental media. Water protection law (the federal water management act and the water acts of the states) take surface bodies of water as well as ground water into a regime of public management. The use of a body of water is dependent on a (revocable) permit. Under exceptional circumstances (mainly protection of investments) binding licences are granted. Beginning from 1976 the system of standards for admissible **water pollution** is supplemented by a discharge water fee calculated according to the quantity and nuisance of the sewage.

German waste law has been modified by the so-called Circulation Economy Act of 1994. The definition of waste has been clarified and the supervision of hazardous wastes has been strengthened. The transition from traditional waste-disposal law to waste-management law is characterized by a duty of producers and possessors of wastes to avoid and recycle them, combined with a corresponding responsibility of manufacturers of products. This regulatory system has to be put into concrete terms by administrative regulations. Thus the packaging regulation has established a so-called 'dual system' promoting a private recycling system in order to avoid duties to take back packaging material.

The Gene Technology Act of 1993 provides the constitutionally required base for installations and operations connected with genetically modified organisms. Those installations and operations are subject to licensing depending on different security levels. The standards for admission are fixed under participation of different expert commissions. On the basis of a broad consensus a nationwide Soil Protection Act was enacted in 1998, even if an explicit federal competence is missing. Subsidiary to other environmental laws harmful alterations of soil quality will be avoided and existing residual pollutions abated.

Since the beginning of the 1990s political priorities have been changed in Germany and the development of German environmental law has slowed. Thus at the moment the codification of environmental law in a unified Environmental Code has little chance of being realized. In this situation European law is the most important motor for further developments: the environmetal impact assessment directive and presently the integrated pollution control directive bring German environmental law on the way to a more integrated concept beyond single environmental media.

See also: environmental law and litigation; hazardous and toxic waste management; regulatory approaches

References

Rodi, M. (1996) 'Public Environmental Law in Germany', in: R. Seerden and M. Heldeweg (eds) *Comparative Environmental Law in Europe*, Antwerpen: Kluwer.

—— (2000) 'Country Report Germany', in H. Somsen (ed.) *Yearbook of European Environmental Law*, Oxford: Oxford University Press.

Further reading

Ministry for the Environment (ed.) (1998) *Environmental Code*, Draft, Berlin: BMW.

Schlemminger, H. and Wissel, H. (eds) (1996) *German Environmental Law for Practitioners, Series of Legislation in Translation 8*, The Hague/London/Boston: Kluwer Law International.

MICHAEL RODI

Gibbs, Lois Marie

b. 1961, New York, USA

Environmental activist

In 1978 Lois Gibbs discovered that her **Love Canal** housing estate in Niagara Falls, NY, USA, was built on top of 20,000 tons of toxic chemical dump. She galvanized her community to fight the contamination, gathering information on a range of health problems including birth defects, miscarriages and cancers. The campaign went to the White House and in 1980 President Carter issued an Emergency Declaration to relocate 900 families. In 1981 Gibbs set up the **Citizens' Clearinghouse for Hazardous Wastes** (CCHW), now the Center for Health, Environment and Justice, which advised thousands of local toxic waste campaigns. Gibbs is now an international campaigner on hazardous waste pollution and part of the growing grassroots **environmental justice** movement. With others she launched the Stop Dioxin Exposure Campaign which published *Dying from Dioxin* in 1995. She was awarded the Goldman Environment Prize in 1990 and has received an honorary PhD from the State University of New York.

MARY MELLOR

Global Climate Coalition

The Global Climate Coalition (GCC) is an organization of over 55 business trade associations and companies including the American Petroleum Institute, the US Chamber of Commerce, Du Pont, Dow, Exxon, Texaco, Chevron, Mobil and a number of car manufacturers (General Motors, Chrysler) and road construction companies. The coalition was established in 1989 and claims to be 'the leading business voice on climate change'. Until recently GCC has been described as 'the giants of the lobbying business'. Its confrontational approach to lobbying and the conservative nature of its position in the climate change debate, however, has served to alienate some of its traditional industry supporters including oil companies Shell and British Petroleum and the car company Ford (see **global warming**). Despite increasing consensus on the science of climate change, GCC has continued to question whether it is a problem at all. The coalition also funds and publishes studies that highlight the economic costs of action to address climate change and places emphasis instead upon the growing contribution of developing countries to the problem and the desirability of using carbon sinks and technological fixes to address the problem. GCC works with a number of governments seeking to stall further action on climate change, most notably within the international negotiations, the OPEC group.

PETER NEWELL

Global Environment Facility

The Global Environment Facility (GEF) was established (initially as a pilot programme) by the **World Bank**, the **United Nations Environment Programme** and the **United Nations Development Program** in 1991. The Facility provides grants and concessional funding to developing countries for projects which contribute to ameliorating the global consequences of loss of **biodiversity**, climate change, oceans pollution and **ozone depletion**. The World Bank manages the Trust Fund (the GEF's core fund) and administers the Secretariat. All three agencies have implementing responsibility for GEF projects which fit with their own mandates. The Facility was restructured in 1994 in response to concerns that it was undemocratic, lacked transparency and did not allow adequate representation for developing countries. Eighteen of the 32 members of the restructured Council must be recipient (that is developing) countries. GEF projects also require consultation with local communities and, where appropriate, involve non-governmental organizations in their implementation.

LORRAINE ELLIOTT

global environmental governance

Global environmental governance is the phrase usually adopted to describe the complement of multilateral environmental agreements (MEAs) and inter-governmental environmental bodies, the processes by which these agreements are negotiated and implemented, and the ways in which the institutions function. Demands for global governance for the environment arise from concerns that the usual state-centric, exclusive and hierarchical practices of international politics are inadequate to the task of overcoming the challenges of environmental degradation. For this reason, global environmental governance is required to be co-operative, collective and democratic. It is required to be co-operative and collective because independent or unilateral action by states or governments is ineffective in the face of transboundary and global environmental problems and inefficient in the face of shared or common environmental concerns. It is required to be democratic and participatory to take account of the competing interests of a variety of stakeholders ranging from business and corporate actors through local governments and scientific associations to **indigenous peoples**' organizations and environmental non-governmental organizations (see **international non-governmental organizations**).

Global environmental governance is also required to address the issues of inequity which characterize the global environmental agenda: those inequities exist between rich and poor countries, in terms of contribution to and impacts of environmental degradation, and between rich and poor peoples, including indigenous communities. The richest 20 per cent of the world's population consume approximately 80 per cent of the world's resources and produce about three-quarters of the world's waste and pollution. Finally, the fundamental test of global environmental governance is that environmental degradation and its social and economic consequences are overcome, or at least mitigated.

The United Nations has become the public face of global environmental governance through the major environmental summits (such as the 1972 **Stockholm Conference** and the **Rio Conference 1992**) and through its two major institutions dedicated to the environment and **sustainable development** – the **United Nations Environment Programme** and the **Commission on Sustainable Development**. The institutional dimension of global environmental governance has also come to include the **Global Environment Facility** and the **World Bank** and, with a more recent and controversial interest, the **World Trade Organization**. The number of multilateral environmental agreements, declarations of principle and plans of action continues to grow, providing evidence of some degree of co-operation among states and among other actors. **Agenda 21** pays particular attention to the importance of the 'independent sector', and non-governmental organizations, as well as corporate actors, have become more involved in dialogue with intergovernmental environmental bodies and conferences.

Environmental governance has also become marked by an increasingly sophisticated web of environmental principles. Some, such as the **precautionary principle**, the **polluter pays principle** and common but differentiated responsibilities, are intended primarily to elaborate more specific rights and obligations for states and to enact normative guidelines for regulatory mechanisms. Others, such as **intergenerational justice**, the common heritage of humankind and environmental rights, have the potential to widen the scope of those to whom obligations are owed in international law beyond states and beyond present generations. In theory, this incorporates a deeper ethic of justice in international law and articulates an ethic of **stewardship** rather than management for jurisdictions both within and beyond the borders of states. Sustainable development has been confirmed as the guiding principle for multilateral environmental agreements and for best practice and national and international level.

Some commentators welcome this increasing web of environmental agreements and principles, negotiating fora and formal environmental institutions as evidence that global environmental governance exists, that it is both qualitatively and quantitatively different from usual patterns of world politics, and that it is working. Others are more critical, suggesting that the definition of what counts as 'global' remains narrow, that co-operation exists more in the process of negotiating than in the process of agreeing to substantive environmental provisions, that democratization is partial, and that the overall state of the global environment continues to deteriorate. In this view, environmental treaties are often cautious (lowest common denominator) agreements with permissive sanctions and inadequate targets. Environmental institutions often lack formal competence and real powers. They are often poorly funded and have little political clout. A critical approach to global environmental governance notes also that there has been little real commitment to addressing issues of poverty, or the provision of adequate funding and technological assistance to poorer countries. In particular, this critical perspective laments the ways in which local interests and local voices, particularly but not exclusively from the developing world, have been marginalized from international debates about the environment. In this view, global environmental governance is not simply about policy choices but about politics and power.

See also: international environmental law

Further reading

Elliott, L. (1998) *The Global Politics of the Environment*, London: Macmillan, chapter 4.

Paterson, M. (1999) 'Interpreting Trends in Global Environmental Governance', *International Affairs*, 75 (4): 793–802.

Soroos, M.S. (1999) 'Global Institutions and the Environment: An Evolutionary Perspective' in N.J. Vig and R.S. Axelrod (eds) *The Global Environment: Institutions, Law and Policy*, Washington DC: CQ Press.

Wapner, P. (1997) 'Environmental Ethics and Global Governance: Engaging the International Liberal Tradition', *Global Governance*, 3 (2): 213–31.

Young, O.R. (ed.) (1997) *Global Governance: Drawing Insights from the Environmental Experience*, Cambridge, MA: The MIT Press.

LORRAINE ELLIOTT

global warming

Global warming has been one of the key environmental problems with which human societies have tried to deal from the late 1980s onwards. It is arguably one of only two genuinely global environmental problems (along with **ozone depletion** and CFCs), global in the sense that emissions anywhere have effects across the entire globe, and thus has helped to transform environmental politics into a properly global form of politics. It is also particularly important as (again, arguably) it has particularly deep consequences in terms of the social and political changes which dealing effectively with it require.

The scientific debate around global warming has been subject to much controversy. The body which is most widely regarded as authoritative in relation to the science of global warming is the Intergovernmental Panel on Climate Change (IPCC). This has produced two major reports, in 1990 and 1995, which are used officially as the basis for government and intergovernmental action on global warming. There is, however, a small but vocal group of scientists, 'greenhouse sceptics', who contest the IPCC's conclusions.

The IPCC concluded in 1990 that should existing trends in emissions of various gases by human societies continue, then some measure of global warming would occur. In 1995, it strengthened this conclusion by arguing that observed warming in the twentieth century was most likely to have been caused by anthropogenic emissions: 'the balance of evidence ... suggests a discernible human influence on global climate'. While sceptics have questioned the basis of this conclusion, the IPCC has been taken as the basis for political decision-making by most governments.

The most important gases involved in producing global warming are carbon dioxide (CO_2), methane (CH_4), chlorofluorocarbons (CFCs), and nitrous oxide (N_2O). There are a number of less important gases: in addition, water vapour is a very important greenhouse gas, but its atmospheric concentrations are not rising so it is not an important factor in global warming. These greenhouse gases allow radiation from the sun to reach the earth's surface but absorb the longer wavelength radiation re-emitted from the earth's surface. Thus they maintain the earth's surface temperature at a significantly higher level than it would be otherwise. The atmospheric concentrations of these gases are all rising, leading scientists to believe that warming may occur. At the same time, the observed mean temperature of the earth's surface has increased by 0.3–0.6°C in the twentieth century.

There are a number of impacts scientists anticipate such warming will have. The most clear is sea-level rise, since water expands as it warms, and this has particularly large consequences for the substantial portion of the world's population who live close to the sea, and for particular countries such as small island states (see **Alliance of Small Island States**), some of whom stand to disappear with a very modest rise in sea level. The migration of climatic zones and therefore the places where various plants – both agricultural and other (tree species, for example) – can grow, and where other species will thrive, is a particular concern. (Of particular worry are diseases and disease-bearing insects.) The possibility of increased frequency and severity of natural disasters, in particular wind-storms and flooding, is a worry, and one which many insurance companies argue is already occurring. The impacts in particular will have significant consequences for human societies across the globe.

There are various acknowledged uncertainties concerning the science of climate change. These range from, questions about the availability of certain types of data, the internal logic and construction of the computer models used to simulate global climate and make projections about global warming, to particular debates about whether certain feedback mechanisms (for example the changes in different types of cloud formation) will have a positive or negative effect on global warming. For some scientists, they call into question the whole viability of making claims about global warming. For most, however, they are simply questions which need to be answered to increase the precision with which they can make projections of the extent of warming.

The scientific debate has also been highly politicized. Fora like the IPCC are ultimately intergovernmental, so governments have had clear opportunities to make sure that their own position is reflected in IPCC documents. More generally, the sceptics have received a great deal of funding from large corporations (in particular coal, oil, and heavy industry) which stand to lose out as a result of measures to reduce CO_2 emissions and thus (**fossil fuel**) energy use. There have also been accusations by some sceptics and others that the IPCC scientists have made overly alarmist claims concerning global warming in order to receive more research funding and increase their international prestige (Boehmer-Christiansen, 1995).

Most of the political questions however have centred around measures to reduce CO_2 emissions. The focus has been on CO_2 because it is responsible for more global warming than the other gases (especially since CFCs now have been eliminated under treaties to deal with ozone depletion), and also because some of the other gases are byproducts of the fossil fuel combustion which is the main origin of CO_2 emissions. The main political focus is therefore on reducing emissions from coal, oil and natural gas.

Within countries, the central political questions governments have faced are the possible economic costs involved in reduction emissions and the capacity of certain lobby groups to prevent policies from emerging. In general, the US government in particular has argued that the economic costs of reducing emissions are very high, and the Bush administration regarded this as a reason for resisting commitments to reduce or even stabilize emissions. Governments particularly dependent on export fossil fuel exports as a source of revenue – in particular OPEC, but also increasingly Australia (a major coal exporter) – have also argued that the costs would be very high (Kassler and Paterson, 1997). European governments have not been so pessimistic about the costs of reducing emissions. Apart from clear political interests as in the case of OPEC, the differences in assumptions about the costs reflect technological confidence about the possibilities of pursuing energy efficiency at low cost, and the possibilities of switching to renewable sources of energy (see **renewable energy**). In the economic modelling exercises which produce the cost estimates of emissions abatement, this confidence in turn reflects an assumption about the operation of market economies – many models assume that actually existing markets invest in energy efficiency in the optimal manner, and therefore any policy intervention which increases the rate of such investment will necessarily reduce GDP. Other models do not make this assumption.

These economic costs of reducing emissions also are not evenly distributed. Various groups have therefore lobbied governments to prevent policies emerging to reduce emissions. In particular organized in groups like the **Global Climate Coalition**, companies involved in production of coal and oil in particular (gas has a lower rate of CO_2 emissions per unit of energy, so is a short-term winner from emissions-reduction policies), as well as large energy consuming industries, like the **car industry** or metals production, have lobbied governments hard, spent a great deal in advertising to influence public opinion, and funded sceptic scientists to cast doubt on the science of global warming, to defend their interests. In some countries, some consumer groups, for example pensioners and others who may be hit particularly badly by fuel-price rises, have also lobbied against such rises. These groups (in particular the corporate lobbies) have clearly been able to slow the pace of emissions abatement (for example they were key in preventing the emergence of carbon tax in the EU), and secure various special exemption clauses in measures to reduce emissions (such as the Climate Change Levy in the UK).

However, this position is undergoing change, which may undermine the capacity of the global climate coalition to continue to succeed. Some companies, notably oil companies (less threatened than coal companies, and also linked to gas as oil and gas fields are often together, and in some cases also to solar energy) have left the coalition, and taken a line less hostile to emissions reductions. Companies involved in energy efficiency or in renewable energy have also become politically active. Perhaps most importantly, insurance companies have begun to become active after realizing that they could already be suffering the impacts of climate change, from increased payouts to natural disasters.

Many of the deeper questions however become clear at the international level. Of course, in general, this makes it clear that global warming is a collective action problem of extreme proportions – no state can individually prevent global warming from occurring, or insulate itself against its effects. States have strong interests (assuming the costs of reducing emissions are high) in trying to make others act on emissions while they can free ride. On the other hand, there is good evidence that many states have taken leadership roles to try to overcome this collective action dynamic.

The deepest question internationally is the division between North and South (see **North/ South divide**). Southern governments argue that global warming is almost entirely caused by the North and that they thus have the primary responsibility for reducing emissions. On the other hand, some northern governments (particularly the US and since 1996 Australia), argue that even if they reduce their emissions, emissions in the developing world are rising rapidly, so the overall effect in mitigating global warming will be minimal. In the **Framework Convention on Climate Change** the South was able to make

sure its position was accepted, but increasingly, northern governments are questioning whether they can go on agreeing to reduce emissions without some sorts of obligations being undertaken by developing country governments.

The other aspect of North–South politics on global warming concerns financial and technology transfers from North to South (see **technology transfer**). All parties have agreed that if the South is to be able to take action to limit emissions, it has to be helped through finance and technology. Many debates at the international level have been about mechanisms to organize such transfers. The Kyoto Conference in 1997 created a Clean Development Mechanism which now acts to facilitate such developments (see **Kyoto Conference/ Protocol**). Other features of the negotiations, particularly 'Activities Implemented Jointly', also help in this regard. But conflicts over these questions persist.

The efforts of governments so far have been varied. In Kyoto, industrialized countries agreed to reduce their emissions collectively by 5.2 per cent over 1990 levels by between 2008 and 2012, but specific targets for each country varied. Many countries failed to meet their (unilaterally set) targets to stabilize their emissions by 2000. The general assessment of many observers is that while clearly more progress can be made on reducing emissions, negotiators in Kyoto struck a fairly hard bargain and held out against reluctant countries. Whether the agreement will ever be successfully implemented and then improved on remains to be seen.

On 26 March 2001 President George W. Bush withdrew the USA from the Kyoto Global Warming Treaty process.

See also: tradeable emission permits

References

Boehmer-Christiansen, S. (1995) 'Britain and the International Panel on Climate Change: The Impacts of Scientific Advice on Global Warming Part I: Integrated Policy Analysis and the global Dimension', *Environmental Politics*, 4(1): 1–18.

Kassler, P. and Paterson, M. (1997) *Energy Exporters and Climate Change Politics*, London: Royal Institute of International Affairs.

Further reading

Gelbspan, R. (1997) *The Heat is On: The High Stakes over Earth's Threatened Climate*, Reading, MA: Addison-Wesley.

Houghton, J. *et al.* (eds) (1995) *Climate Change 1995: The Science of Climate Change*, Cambridge: Cambridge University Press. [IPCC Second Assessment Report]

Leggett, J. (1999) *The Carbon War: Dispatches from the End of the Oil Century*, Harmondsworth: Penguin.

Paterson, M. (1996) *Global Warming and Global Politics*, London: Routledge.

MATTHEW PATERSON

globalization

The term 'globalization' is often taken as a byword for any activity which extends beyond sovereign borders in the economic, political social or cultural domain. The fluidity of the term has led to a debate about what really is new about globalization. It has been suggested for instance that there has merely been a deepening of the trend towards internationalization which has waxed and waned over the last century, rather than a quantifiable break with previous eras of economic integration. It is also often argued that the term globalization is misleading because it describes a trend which is largely confined to the relations between a small number of highly industrialized states and firms operating within the triad (East Asia, North America and Europe).

Whichever term we use, the major features of the contemporary global economy mean a number of things for the environment. First, there are the ecological impacts of globalization. It is clear that the internationalization of production, facilitated by technological change and reduced transport costs, has brought waste and pollution to new areas of the globe in a way which has spread the risks associated with environmental change. The export of toxic wastes to developing countries is an often cited example. Other concerns centre on the ecological impact of increasing levels of transport around the world, moving goods over longer distances, as well as that of increased production and the expansion of consumer markets. It is also argued that export-led growth patterns have encouraged unsustainable and environmentally damaging environmental practices such as increased **pesticides** use in boosting crop yields.

There is a fear that the imperatives of competing in the global market place force governments to prioritize economic objectives at the expense of environmental protection. Deregulation and liberalization are said to heighten pressures to lower environmental standards leading to the creation of 'pollution havens', a regulatory 'race to the bottom', where countries compete to lower standards in order to attract increasingly mobile capital. With annual turnovers that dwarf the GDPs of most developing countries, and the ability to make investments with enormous natural resource implications, as well as control of the technology and capital that is likely to be the vehicle for the implementation of many international environmental agreements, **multinational and transnational corporations** are central agents in the environmental debate. They have the potential both to exploit lower standards for profit as well as diffuse best practice though global operations along their supply chains bringing beneficial technologies to new areas of the world.

Ensuring that the liberalization of trade does not run counter to efforts to protect the environment is an increasingly salient international concern. The issue here is the primacy given to trade rules that may pose a threat to international environmental regimes that depend upon trade-discriminating measures for their effectiveness. Conversely, developing countries fear that environmental standards may be used as back-door protectionism to exclude their exports from western markets. The picture about the impact of trade liberalization on the environment is mixed. Whilst we have seen the proliferation of pollution havens (most visibly demonstrated by the *maquiladora* zone in Mexico as a result of the **NAFTA** agreement) trade liberalization has also encouraged the 'trading up' of standards as exporters seek access to lucrative western markets where environmental standards are higher.

At the heart of much concern about globalization is global finance. Perceived to be footloose and beyond the control of sovereign governments, the financial crises in Asia in 1997 served only to heighten anxiety about the negative social and **development** implications of short-term capital flows. The crisis also brought serious environmental implications in the countries of South East Asia. The economic turmoil it produced heightened water quality problems and in other areas such as **agriculture**, plantations, and **fisheries**, currency devaluation created powerful incentives to expand export-orientated production to earn foreign exchange. In other areas, most notably commercial timber and urban **air pollution**, it has created temporary respites and windows of opportunity for environmental reformers. One key lesson from the crisis was that economic stability is critical to the promotion of sustainable livelihoods and for ensuring that environmental reforms receive the necessary backing of government and business.

The globalization of economic activity increasingly provides the backdrop to efforts to promote **sustainable development**, encouraging particular patterns of resource use and constraining the use of policy instruments that regulate powerful market actors. Students of environmental policy will need to look more seriously than they have done to date at the relationship between globalization and environmental change in order to understand the possibilities and limitations of future environmental action.

See also: global environmental governance; International Monetary Fund and neoliberalism; NAFTA; sustainable development; World Trade Organization

Further reading

Hirst, P. and Thompson, G. (1996) *Globalization in Question*, London: Polity Press.

Hoogvelt, A. (1997) *Globalization and the Postcolonial World: The New Political Economy of Development*, London: MacMillan.

Newell, P. (1999) 'Globalization and the Environment: Exploring the Connections', *IDS Bulletin*, 30 (3), July.

Strange, S. (1998) 'Globalony?' *Review of International Political Economy*, 5 (4).

Waters, M. (1995) *Globalization*, London: Routledge.

PETER NEWELL

Goldsmith, Edward

b. 8 November 1928, Paris, France

Editor, campaigner, intellectual

Edward Goldsmith has long been a controversial figure in the British green movement. He first came to prominence in 1972 through his role in writing the half-million-selling Malthusian tract ***Blueprint for Survival***. In the mid-1980s he co-wrote a three-volume study, *The Social and Environmental Effects of Large Dams*. Most recently, he has sought to synthesize ecosystems **ecology**, Gaia and the Tao into a philosophical/spiritual theory entitled *The Way*. *The Way* is the path we must follow to safeguard Gaia and it could be read as an attempt to resurrect natural law theory. Goldsmith's principal vehicle over the past three decades has been *The Ecologist* magazine. He co-founded this project in 1969 and has only recently stood down from the editorship. He is presently director of the International Forum on Globalization based in San Francisco.

DAMIAN WHITE

Gore, Albert

b. 31 March 1948, Washington, DC, USA

Politician

Al Gore, Member of the US Congress and Vice President of the USA (1993–2001), is perhaps best known in environmental circles as the author of *Earth in the Balance*, published in 1992, a work which placed him firmly in the ranks of environmental pessimists. Influenced by the views of Rachel **Carson**, among others, as well as his own research in the late 1970s and early 1980s on strategic arms control, Gore quickly became the Clinton White House's major spokesperson on such issues as auto emissions, **global warming**, **ozone depletion**, species extinction, Third World 'green' issues, and **renewable energy**. Although individuals and groups friendly to the environment had more access to the White House during the Clinton years, critics believed that Gore too often followed the President's lead in basing environmental decisions on pubic opinion polls. In 2000, he was the Democratic party's presidential candidate, but lost to Republican George W. Bush in a close, disputed election which also involved Green Party candidate Ralph **Nader**.

Further reading

Gore, A. (1992) *Earth in the Balance: Ecology and The Human Spirit*, Boston: Houghton Mifflin.

WARREN VANDER HILL

Gorleben controversy

Gorleben is a small village in a rural, comparatively remote area of Lower Saxony in northern Germany. Since the late 1970s, Gorleben has been the focal point of radical anti-nuclear protest in Germany (see **anti-nuclear movements**). In 1977, Gorleben was identified as the site of a nuclear disposal centre, combining a plant for the reprocessing of spent nuclear fuel and a final depository for nuclear waste in the salt-rock formations in the area. Local opposition to these plans emerged in force, and the central importance of the plants for the future of Germany's nuclear programme made Gorleben a key focus of the national anti-nuclear movement. In 1979, opposition reached a peak when a major anti-nuclear demonstration coincided with news of the Harrisburg nuclear accident. The regional government refused permission to build the reprocessing plant, and the integrated waste disposal strategy centred on Gorleben thus had failed.

Plans to use Gorleben as a site for nuclear waste disposal were not abandoned, however. While investigations into the suitability of the salt formations for final disposal continued, Gorleben also became the site of an 'interim' nuclear waste disposal facility due to hold nuclear material until a final deposit site becomes operational. From its opening in 1983, transports of nuclear waste products to Gorleben became a focus of major protests. In the 1990s, protests against nuclear waste transports to Gorleben involved unprecedented levels of non-violent as well as violent actions, requiring massive police operations. After a safety scandal over nuclear radiation levels in the CASTOR containers used for these shipments, all nuclear transports were put on hold in 1998. The fate of the Gorleben site then became a major negotiating issue in the attempt by the SPD/Green government to reach an agreement with the electricity utilities for a planned phase-out of nuclear power production.

The final agreement reached in June 2000 provided for a temporary halt to the exploration of Gorleben as a final waste disposal site. A new process of identifying a suitable site was started, looking at a range of potential sites. At the same time, the investigation of the Gorleben site was suspended for at least three years. The interim storage facility at Gorleben will, however, continue to be used. There is the need for large quantities of German nuclear waste stored at the reprocessing plants at La Hague and Sellafield to be returned to Germany (see **Sellafield/Windscale**). Waste transports from La Hague to Gorleben are due to start in 2001. The local protest movement against Gorleben has remained one of the most active anti-nuclear groups in Germany since the 1970s, and it has also been a mainstay of the opposition to the Red–Green government's 'phasing out' policy. With regular transports of nuclear waste to Gorleben for many years to come, the village is likely to remain a major focus of German nuclear politics.

See also: German nuclear power industry

Further reading

Rüdig, R. (1990) *Anti-nuclear Movements: A World Survey of Protest Against Nuclear Energy*, Harlow: Longman.
Rüdig, W. (2000) 'Phasing Out Nuclear Power in Germany', *German Politics*, 9(3): 43–80.

WOLFGANG RÜDIG

Gorz, André

b. 1924, Austria

Philosopher, economist, social theorist

André Gorz is one of the most original and long-standing defenders of a post-industrial version of **eco-socialism**. Since the early 1970s, he has challenged orthodox Marxism by arguing that the industrial working class is no longer central to politics. Gorz sees the chief contradiction of contemporary **capitalism** as ecological degradation and the distribution and content of work. Progressives should argue for an ecologically self-limiting economy and not for the creation of more work but for 'liberation from work'. An eco-socialist programme should not be understood as a fundamental break from modern society but rather a society that extends the sphere of autonomous human activity and increases the possibilities for individual self-fulfilment. Influential in France, Gorz's work has also inspired recent discussions of **basic income** schemes.

Further reading

Gorz, A. (1994) *Capitalism, Socialism, Ecology*, London: Verso.

DAMIAN WHITE

Great Lakes International Joint Commission

The Great Lakes International Joint Commission (IJC) was created through the 1909 Boundary Waters Treaty signed by the federal governments of Canada and the USA and has retained considerable authority on all matters pertaining to water quality and quantity among water sources shared by the two nations. It addresses a wide range of cross-boundary water issues, although it has increasingly become focused upon matters concerning the Great Lakes Basin.

The IJC is led by a body of commissioners appointed by the Prime Minister of Canada and the President of the USA. These commissioners are empowered to conduct quasi-judicial hearings over proposals to alter the levels, flows, and integrity of Great Lakes boundary waters, and to monitor and co-ordinate various programmes implemented by the Commission's constituent members. The Commission regularly offers formal policy recommendations, although neither federal, state, nor provincial governments are legally required to implement them.

The Commission has traditionally focused on control of **water pollution** from major point sources. In more recent decades, however, it has increasingly addressed such issues as cross-media pollutant transfer, reduction of toxic releases to water from a much wider range of sources, and remedial 'action plans' for those areas within the Great Lakes Basin that suffer from the most severe environmental degradation. It has utilized a number of tools to attempt to influence policy, including a series of Great Lakes Water Quality Agreements.

BARRY G. RABE

Greece

Although environmental politics in Greece have been overshadowed by economic **development** concerns, their evolution during the last three decades attests to significant changes in the way various actors respond to the growth of environmental problems in the country.

Since the early 1960s, the Greek government promoted growth at the private and state producer levels, paying minimal attention to environmental concerns. After many attempts, the Greek Parliament did manage to pass an Environmental Policy Act and the government reached a compromise agreement with the Federation of Greek Industrialists in the 1980s (Kousis, 1994). During the 1990s, even though Greece signed Local **Agenda 21**, the country's first national report to the United Nations Conference on Economic Development (UNCED) clearly delineated that economic growth still remained its main priority, a position which Greece is determined to defend internationally, striving to achieve the economic prosperity of the other EU member states. This is reflected in

Greece's request to the EU Council of Ministers to be exempt from introducing a carbon tax.

Although Greece does not have a unique national plan for the environment, the Ministry of Environment, Physical Planning and Public Works has co-ordinated environmental policies aiming towards a marriage between **ecology** and **sustainable development**, environmental protection, international as well as NGO collaboration. Yet, departmental fragmentation and the absence of effective inter-ministerial co-ordination remain obstacles to implementing sustainable development strategies. Although some interest has come up in the unions' position on sustainable development, workers appear more concerned about their economic futures. Limited power over environmental matters has gradually been granted to municipalities and communities, which are still financially dependent on the central government. Some steps, such as ecolabelling and eco-management and audit schemes, are taken by businesses at a very slow but gradual pace (Fousekis and Lekakis, 1997). Overall, while Greece has succeeded in adopting many EU environmental directives, problems of implementation are quite evident.

During the past three decades the state has been challenged by a variety of environmental groups collaborating with local governments, citizens groups, the media, professional groups and the judiciary. As a result, the state has been more open to collaborations and readier to foresee public objections (Close, 1999).

The **environmental movement** in Greece has, in general, been considered weak by comparison to its counterparts in northern European countries, given the limited political opportunities under the military juntas, lower levels of **industrialization**, and limited resources. Nevertheless, there is increasing evidence on qualitative and quantitative changes in Greek environmental activism (Close, 1999; Kousis, 1999). The rich political culture of the left which developed intensely in the postwar period has been attributed to the growth of environmental activism.

Local resistance against environmentally damaging government-promoted industrial projects appeared even under the military dictatorship. After its fall, environmental activism witnessed significant increases. Local activists challenged the state, producers and other groups causing ecosystem damages (Kousis, 1999). In order to defend local ecosystems, they often resorted to more radical, yet non-violent actions, usually through informal, but not necessarily associational, structures, i.e. community based groups, such as residents, neighbours, and a wide variety of local associations.

During the 1980s, more than one hundred formal environmental organizations surfaced in various parts of the country, focusing on air, water and soil pollution as well as **quality of life** concerns (Kousis, 1994). By the second half of the 1990s, environment-related organizations numbered almost two hundred, including the Hellenic Society for the Protection of Nature, the Ornithological Society, the Union of Greek Ecologists, WWF-Greece, Greenpeace-Greece, Citizens against the Smog, and the Movement of Alternative Ecologists. The last organization, founded by 46 groups, succeeded as a green party, albeit for a short time, entering Parliament in the late 1980s.

Collaboration between informal environmental groups and organizations is not the norm. Some collaboration does occur between local environmental activists and agencies approached for assistance, as well as between large organizations and the related ministries. Nevertheless, in general, the challenged state and, more so the producers are hesitant in accepting the environmental protest demands.

Thus, contemporary environmental politics in Greece have been marked with a sprouting of environmental activism based at the local, national and international levels as well as with the effects of Europeanization.

See also: eco-taxes; environmental movements; European Union; Greenpeace; Rio Conference 1992; World Wide Fund for Nature

References

Close, D. (1999) 'Environmental Crisis in Greece and Recent Challenges to Centralized State Authority', *Journal of Modern Greek Studies* 17(2): 325–52.

Fousekis, P. and Lekakis, J.N. (1997) 'Greece's

Institutional Response to Sustainable Development' *Environmental Politics*, 6(1): 131–52.

Kousis, M. (1994) 'Environment and the State in the EU Periphery: The Case of Greece', in S. Baker, K. Milton and S. Yearley (eds) *Protecting the Periphery: Environmental Policy in Peripheral Regions of the European Union*, London: Frank Cass.

—— (1999) 'Sustaining Local Environmental Mobilizations: Groups, Actions and Claims in Southern Europe', *Environmental Politics* 8 (1): 172–98.

Further reading

Kousis, M. and K. Eder (2001) 'Introduction: EU Policy-Making, Local Action, and the Emergence of Institutions of Collective Action', in K. Eder and M. Kousis (eds) *Environmental Politics in Southern Europe: Actors, Institutions and Policies in a Europeanizing Society*, Dordrecht: Kluwer Academic Publishers.

Pridham, G., S. Verney and D. Konstadakopoulos (1995) 'Environmental Policy in Greece: Evolution, Structures and Process', *Environmental Politics*, 4(2): 244–70.

MARIA KOUSIS

green accounting

It is now often argued that society is steering with the wrong compass. Most decision-making processes are based on Gross Domestic Product (GDP), favouring economic options that generate its increase. GDP has long since been used as an indicator of economic performance, **progress**, and even welfare. Moreover, it is on the basis of GDP that countries are internationally 'ranked'.

However, the increasing salience of environmental issues since the end of the 1960s has led to growing controversy concerning the interpretation of GDP, in particular regarding a number of shortcomings, summarized as follows:

- The traditional System of National Accounts (SNA) focuses on flows only whilst ignoring stocks (environmental or cultural) and the problems generated by their depreciation.
- Negative **externalities**, such as environmental

pollution or crime, are not taken into account in the assessment of economic performance and progress.
- Distribution and inequality issues are not taken into account either.
- The SNA focuses on production processes that generate only monetary exchanges; therefore, services that do not involve monetary exchange (e.g. house work) are not considered to be contributive to economic welfare.

The rationale of research in 'green accounting' has been to correct these shortcomings.

Two general approaches have been developed. The first aims at constructing an 'adjusted' economic indicator by subtracting or adding what is not included in the calculation of GDP. Numerous methods have been developed to calculate a 'sustainable income', an 'aggregate adjusted indicator' or a 'Sustainable Social Net National Product'. They are all based on the idea that environmental resources can be seen as **'natural capital'** since they contribute to the production of goods and services. The strength of the first approach is that the depreciation of natural capital is viewed, as is the case for human-made capital, as detrimental to wealth and welfare. Hence, it is subtracted from GDP, and so are 'Defensive Expenditures', incurred to repair or prevent damages caused by environmental degradation (to our health, for instance). Perhaps the main weakness of viewing the environment as capital, however, is that, embroiled in the economic logic and jargon, it has lost its **intrinsic value** and dynamic dimension in the eyes of those who calculate 'green types of GDP'. Even worse, the calculation of a green GDP is based on the idea that the newly included figures must be expressed in monetary terms in order to be included in the equation. Consequently, in this first approach of 'green accounting', research efforts became centred on developing valuation methods to measure the importance of the environment in monetary terms, viewed as the only way of communicating with policy-makers. These methods animated much controversy, both from a technical and an ethical perspective and, in parallel, some countries' experience of environmental policy-making showed that policy-makers can use information that is not expressed in monetary terms. This resulted in giving more importance to the second type of research, focused on 'satellite accounts' in physical rather than monetary terms.

Satellite accounting has provided new ways of apprehending environmental valuation and policy-making. It focuses on describing ecosystem functioning, hence allowing us to identify better the impact of economic activities on the environment. This is the case for the two most famous and established systems of environmental resource accounts, the French Natural Patrimony Accounts, and the Norwegian Material Flow accounts. Satellite accounts can also focus on social information (as is the case in the Social Accounting Matrices). They are therefore expressed in physical terms, but linked to the standard SNA in order to show the interactions between the natural and the economic systems.

The System of Integrated Economic and Environmental Accounts (SEEA), developed by the United Nations, uses both the physical and monetary approaches and synthesizes various valuation methodologies into a flexible framework. At present, it is the only green accounting framework that carries any international authority.

The debate on green accounting forms part of the broader debate on indicators of sustainability, which is currently extremely popular since indicators are viewed as a first step towards realizing **sustainability**. Numerous 'partial' indicators have been developed. Some indicator frameworks have also been constructed that are more informative concerning the interdependencies between fundamental environmental, economic and social themes, and that reflect the holistic and systemic dimension of sustainability. A growing number of these frameworks are being developed into systems of green accounts (e.g. the Dutch National Accounting Matrix including Environmental Accounts). The European Commission has also developed frameworks of environmental indices to help the decision-making process shift towards policy tools that are more adequate to help in the operationalization of sustainability.

SANDRINE SIMON

green bans

Green bans were the withdrawal of labour by Australian construction workers from environmentally irresponsible projects between June 1971 and 1975. Initiated by the New South Wales branch of the Australian Builders Labourers' Federation, these pioneering industrial bans were enthusiastically supported by residents and conservationists. This green bans movement was led by the union's left-wing secretary, Jack Mundey, who coined 'green ban' in May 1973. Bans were imposed in other states and cities, but were most spectacular in Sydney, where they prevented five billion dollars' worth of development. Green bans resulted in Australia-wide improvements in environmental awareness, planning and legislation. The political designation 'green' originates in these bans because they inspired Petra **Kelly** to name her party The Greens (see **Grünen, Die**).

VERITY BURGMANN

green consumerism

Green consumerism refers to the attempt by environmentally concerned consumers, operating in the market system of **capitalism**, to use their ability to make choices about which products to buy in order to influence the economic activities of firms, with the aim of making them more environmentally responsible.

In the 1980s the intensification of interest in environmental matters, coupled with clear cases in which specific products were implicated in environmental destruction (see **ozone depletion**) gave rise to the first phase of green consumerism. In the UK best sellers such as *The Green Consumer Guide* (Elkington and Hailes, 1988) suggested ways in which consumers, in the course of their purchasing decisions, could strongly influence the production decisions of manufacturers. Consumers who refused to buy environmentally harmful products could, via their 'dollar votes', move economic activity in an ecologically beneficial direction. This approach could apparently circumvent problematic political processes and directly push corporations towards environmental responsibility. It also fitted well into an era (see **Reagan, Ronald**) when the importance of the role of the consumer in competitive markets was receiving enormous emphasis.

The result was an initial outpouring of self-styled green products as firms sought to exploit this new market opportunity. Repeated opinion poll evidence supported the commercial wisdom of this by suggesting that in affluent countries buyers would be willing to pay a premium for 'green' products. However, the economic recession of the early 1990s diminished environmental ardour among consumers, who reverted to their traditional 'value for money' concerns. The hope that green consumerism could provide a secure route to the greening of capitalism receded.

In any case, certain serious difficulties appeared inherent in green consumerism. Reliable information about the environmental impact of the processes of manufacture, use and disposal of products was not easily obtainable (see **life cycle assessment**). In this information vacuum scepticism quickly arose, with accusations that firms were '**greenwashing**' their products. Science, too, did not speak with a single or a consistent voice on the issue of what was the actual environmental impact of productive processes.

However, environmental concern had not disappeared and in the later 1990s firms such as Shell, during the **Brent Spar controversy**, and Monsanto, with respect to genetically modified food (see **biotechnology**), felt the power of adverse consumer reaction when people cast their 'dollar votes' against the companies' products. The attempted defence of the environmental soundness of the products and activities on the basis of appeals to scientific evidence was weakened by growing public disinclination to accept that scientific expertise could be entirely trusted. The **mad cow disease/BSE** crisis in the UK, and the perceived closeness of connection between scientific research and the commercial enterprises which often funded it, were two factors leading to this suspicion.

By the start of the twenty-first century green consumerism appeared to have undergone a subtle change, focusing more on the environmental credentials of corporations than on the problematic matter of assessing the environmental impact of particular products (Mackenzie, 2000). In an intensely competitive marketplace major firms increasingly took the view that the possession of a reputation for social responsibility can make the crucial difference in attracting consumers to the products of one firm rather than another. As a result manufacturing and retail companies have sought a reputation for environmental responsibility and transparency by suitable additions to their annual reports and the implementation of environmental impact assessments. In capital markets the growth of 'ethical investment' is a related phenomenon.

Detractors from green consumerism argue that at best it can only delay the capitalist-driven destruction of the Earth's biosphere, for it does not address what is seen as the fundamental problem, namely capitalism's necessary commitment to economic growth. However much we succeed in diminishing the adverse environmental impact of any given product over its entire lifetime, it cannot be reduced to zero. Inevitably, therefore, the aggregate impact of ever-increasing numbers of products will take its adverse environmental toll. On this view, only the abandonment of **consumerism** as a putative recipe for happiness will save the environment.

See also: business and the environment; ecological modernization; Inglehart, Ronald; McDonalds/'McLibel'; Nader, Ralph

References

Elkington, J. and Hailes, J. (1988) *The Green Consumer Guide*, London: Gollancz.

Mackenzie, D. (2000) 'You Can Still Shop to Save the World', *New Statesman*, 1 January.

Further reading

National Consumer Council (1996) *Green Claims: A Consumer Investigation into Marketing Claims about the Environment*, London: National Consumer Council.

BRIAN BAXTER

Green Group in the European Parliament

During the 1970s green political parties began to emerge in western European countries, although it was not until 1984 that representation in the European Parliament occurred. In 1984 *Die Grünen* argued that the European Greens should support the Green Progressive Accord (GPA) in the Netherlands, a federation of three left-wing parties including the Communists rather than the small ecology party *De Groenen*. This led to conflict with other European green parties. After the 1984 European elections *Die Grünen* established the Green Alternative European Link (GRAEL) which as well as other Greens included the Dutch GPA and two Italian Marxist MEPs. The GRAEL in turn was part of the larger Rainbow Group which allowed small parties to gain access to the parliament's facilities. In 1989 *Die Grünen* accepted a common programme with other green parties and success in elections allowed the creation of a new Green Group in the European Parliament which replaced the GRAEL. The 27 MEPs elected included a socialist from Denmark but were otherwise purely green. By June 1999, 33 Greens were elected, including for the first time two from the UK.

DEREK WALL

green parties, US

In the USA, despite the historic role of environmental and **new social movements**, green political parties have been slow to develop and relatively weak, compared to those in other parts of the world. In recent years, however, US Greens appear to have made progress. They emerged from the 2000 elections as the country's third-largest political formation, representing 2.88 million voters, and achieved legal status in 21 states and the federal district, a notable achievement in the restrictive US electoral system (for a list of the 21 states, see *http://www.greenparties.org*).

Ideologically, Greens in the USA fit a postmaterialist profile, comparable to green parties in other countries, blending economic populism with a programme of ecological **sustainability**, social justice and equality, participatory grassroots **democracy**, and non-violence (see **distributive justice**; **ecology**; **ecological economics**; **environmental justice**; **green political theory**; **sustainable development**).

Ralph **Nader**'s Green Party campaign for president in 2000, for example, was left-populist and anti-corporate, drawing on the same insurgent energy which fuelled earlier mass protests against the **World Trade Organization** in Seattle, and the International Monetary Fund in Washington, DC. Nader called for public control over private corporations, arguing that corporate power, free trade and **globalization** threaten living and working conditions, and natural environments, for people in the USA and elsewhere (see **global warming**; **multinational and transnational corporations**; **NAFTA**; **North/South divide**; **political action committees**; **World Bank**).

While minuscule compared to support for the Democratic and Republican parties which have dominated US politics since before the Civil War, the 2000 national vote for Nader and the Greens was nonetheless the third-highest for any minor party in the USA since 1924. Only the American Independent Party (George Wallace in 1968) and the Reform Party (Ross Perot in 1996) have been stronger among US voters. Among candidates of the US left, Nader's 2.74 per cent of the vote exceeded that for the period's most successful socialist candidate, Norman Thomas, whose campaign drew 2.2 per cent in 1932, or postwar progressive Henry Wallace, who polled 2.1 per cent in 1948. Independent presidential candidates John Anderson in 1980 and Ross Perot in 1992 earned more votes than Nader, but neither of these established lasting party structures.

US Greens, by contrast, had by the year 2000 built autonomous party organizations in a majority of the 50 states; developed future-orientated national and state party platforms; and established links with more powerful green parties and regional federations in other parts of the world (see *Federación de Partidos Verdes de las Américas*; **European Federation of Green Parties**; **African Green Parties, Federation of**; *Partido Verde Ecologista de Mexico*).

The emergence of political ecology in the US

In December 1968, three Apollo 8 astronauts from the USA orbited the Moon, sending to Earth new photographs of a solitary blue planet, images which forever altered our view of our planetary home and its fragile biosphere (see **whole earth photograph**; **Earth Day**). Around the world at the same time, **environmental movements** were gaining strength, as were new social movements for democratization, **human rights**, and demilitarization (see **anti-nuclear movements**; **counter-culture**; **militarism and the environment**; **peace movements**). During the 1970s these four strands of post-materialist politics found electoral expression in new ecology parties, especially in Europe and the Antipodes (see **Australian environmental groups**; **Values Party**; Die **Grünen**). In the USA, however, environmental and social movements remained outside electoral politics altogether, or were incorporated into the Democratic Party coalition. Independent ecology parties did not begin to appear in the USA until 1984 (the Maine Green Party), and the first of them to gain legal status (the Green Party of Alaska) was formed in 1990, after the **Exxon Valdez oil spill** disaster.

Ecology parties in a two-party system

Green parties in the USA developed within a strongly bipolar partisan structure which, dating to the 1840s, is the oldest of the world's party systems. Under US federalism, moreover, Greens faced a patchwork of local, state and national requirements governing party recognition and governance, the nomination and election of candidates, and campaign financing, all of which varied from state to state (see **federalism and decentralization**). This made co-ordination difficult, and forced party organizers to learn new laws for each new constituency they contested. Moreover, different ground rules often applied to third parties other than the dominant Republican and Democratic organizations.

The lack of significant public funding for parties in the USA, leaving them dependent on financial support from individuals, private corporations, NGOs, and labour unions, placed anti-corporate

ecology parties at a further disadvantage (see **labour/trade unions**). Finally, the absence of proportional representation, in a system of first-past-the-post, winner-take-all elections, provided few opportunities and many obstacles, for small parties like the Greens.

Significantly, none of the US Green parties were established by major environmental organizations, many of whose lobbying activities depended on relationships with incumbent Democratic and Republican policy-makers. US tax laws governing private organizations provided strong incentives for environmental activists to establish non-partisan NGOs which raise operating funds through tax-advantaged contributions and foundation grants instead of forming new political parties, which enjoy no such financial advantages (see **Environmental Defense Fund**; **Friends of the Earth**; **National Wildlife Federation**; **Natural Resources Defense Council**; **Nature Conservancy**; **Sierra Club**).

US Green politics, 1984–2000

Influenced, perhaps, by these constraints, the first national green organization, the Green Committees of Correspondence (GCOC), was formed in 1984 not as a political party, but as a direct action-orientated, non-governmental association. Organized around geographic bioregions, GCOC drew ideological inspiration both from the **social ecology** of Murray **Bookchin** and from a green ecological philosophy, incorporating **deep ecology**, feminism and green spirituality, often traced to the writings of Charlene **Spretnak** and Fritjof **Capra** (see **eco-centrism**; **eco-feminism**; **eco-philosophy/ecosophy**). Within both of these ideological groupings, however, support for building electorally orientated political parties to challenge Democrats and Republicans directly, had always been significant (see **New Left**; **new politics**).

A group of Bookchin adherents formed a Left Green Network in 1987. This faction gained control of the GCOC in 1991, renaming it The Greens/ Green Party USA and basing the reorganized groups structure on loosely federated green locals. G/GPUSA also restricted voting rights to dues-paying members, controlling the organization through a complicated system of weighted, super-majority voting at annual national gatherings. Ideologically, G/GPUSA's leadership advocated a socialist-municipalist social ecology, opposing deep ecology which they reviled on ideological grounds, and although holding the name Green Party USA working to limit the influence of increasingly active electoral green parties which, they reasoned, were more likely to buttress the state than to undermine it (see **capitalism**; **anarchism/eco-anarchism**; **eco-socialism**). Against this grouping developed an ideologically diverse alliance intent on finding a role for green policies and candidates in the nation's electoral politics. This party-building faction first appeared in 1990 as the Green Party Organizing Committee (GPOC) within GCOC, then in 1992 as the fully independent Green Politics Network (GPN), one of whose goals was creating a Confederation of Autonomous State Green Parties.

The distinction between political *Realos* and ecological *Fundis*, sometimes used to explain European Green factions, does not apply easily to the US case. Nor do simple left–right distinctions explain political conflicts between US Greens. From at least 1987 to 2000, the primary cleavage in US Green politics was less between political compromise on one hand and uncompromising ecological principle on the other, or radicalism and conservatism, than over the fundamental question of whether legally qualified green political parties should even exist. On one side was a small but strategically placed group of anarchist-inspired social ecologists and their allies, deeply sceptical of electoral politics and the people who engage in them; on the other, a larger alliance of green social democrats and progressive populists, deep ecologists, and their allies, determined to bring green electoral options to the US public. Despite these differences, on core issues of green philosophy and the urgency of threats to the world's people and environments, there had always been widespread agreement among US Greens. In 2000 this underlying consensus made possible US Greens' most successful effort to date, the presidential campaign of Ralph **Nader**.

Green parties in the US national election of 2000

In the USA electoral system voter registration, political parties, and the conduct of elections are state (not federal) responsibilities, and thus from 1992 to 1996, party activists concentrated on building state-level green organizations. At Middleburg, Virginia, ten days after the 1996 elections, delegates from parties in twelve states established the **Association of State Green Parties** (ASGP). The new federation expanded, and by June 2000 the original twelve parties had grown to 25. That month, ASGP hosted the Green Party national convention in Denver, Colorado, where delegates from 39 states nominated Ralph Nader and Winona LaDuke for President and Vice President, and approved a national platform. One of the world's best-known public figures, Nader was widely respected for his three decades of consumer, labour, and environmental advocacy (see **car industry**; **Clean Water Act**; **Clean Air Act**; **consumerism**; **environmental law**; **Environmental Protection Agency**). LaDuke was an economist, author, working mother, and environmental activist, familiar to progressives and American Indian communities, especially for her work on the White Earth Reservation in Minnesota, where she lived as a member of the Anishinaabeg Nation (see **indigenous peoples**). Nader and LaDuke had been the green candidates in 1996, appearing on ballots of 21 states and Washington, DC, but the earlier campaign was limited to fewer than half the states and spent, by official accounts, less than $5,000. That year Greens earned 685,128 votes, or 0.7 per cent of the national total. Things changed dramatically four years later, as Nader, LaDuke and the green parties launched a much more serious campaign, raising and spending a combined $8 million and challenging the major party candidates in every region of the country. Between March and June 2000, Nader visited all 50 states (a feat unmatched by either Bush or Gore), and qualified for the ballot in 44 (including the District of Columbia). In three states it was impossible to vote for the green ticket at all; in four others voters could manually write in the green candidates' names.

During the campaign Nader and the Greens co-operated more closely than in 1996, and Nader's staff surprised the nation with a series of massive Super Rallies where crowds of 10,000 to 15,000 supporters, the largest for any presidential candidate, filled sports arenas in Portland, Minneapolis, Seattle, Boston, Chicago, New York, Oakland, and Washington, DC. Nader groups became active on more than 900 college campuses, again outmanoeuvring the major parties. Despite its surprising strength, the campaign faced major obstacles. In the most important incident, the official Commission on Presidential Debates, controlled by the Democratic and Republican parties, refused to allow Nader a place in the only three nationally televised presidential debates. In fact, despite holding valid guest tickets, Nader was physically blocked from attending two of the debates, in Boston and St Louis, and threatened with arrest if he attempted even to sit in the audience. The final vote count showed Nader, LaDuke and the Greens with 2,882,807 votes, 2.74 per cent of 105 million votes cast. In eleven states Greens earned more than 5 per cent, and exit polls there found strong support for the Greens (exceeding 10 per cent) among liberals; youth 18–29 years old; and independents, who in 2000 comprised more than 27 per cent of the US electorate. In the five largest states, with the most electors at stake, Nader's vote totals were significant, especially in the very close 2000 election: California (3.8 per cent), New York (3.6 per cent), Illinois (2.2 per cent), Texas (2.1 per cent), and Florida (1.6 per cent).

Evaluating the 2000 election

Although they drew less than 3 per cent of the total national vote, Greens did offer a surprisingly strong challenge, appeared well-positioned to influence future national elections, and were continuing to grow at the local and state levels. Among 22 states with ballot-status green parties, states which collectively chose 262 presidential electors (270 were required for election), Greens earned 1.87 million votes, with an average 4.43 per cent of statewide totals. Almost 2/3 of all Nader/LaDuke votes were

in those 22 states, and in 7 with a combined 69 electoral votes the green vote share exceeded the difference between the winner and the loser. In Florida, for example, whose controversial election provided Bush with final victory, 97,488 Green Party votes easily exceeded Bush's 537-vote margin of victory. The green campaign surely influenced the election's outcome, but it is impossible to know how the election of 2000 might have been different without Nader's candidacy, as both Gore and Bush altered their electoral strategies to meet Nader's challenge. In addition, because of the country's restrictive voting system, final totals understate national support for the Greens. For example, nearly ten million people cast votes in seven states where Greens were not on the ballot, a combined electorate nearly equal to that of California, where Greens drew more than 400,000 votes. And in the three states where no Nader/LaDuke votes were counted at all, lived nearly one in five Native Americans, among whom LaDuke was very popular.

In the campaign's final weeks, prominent Democrats launched a bitter nationwide attack on Nader and the Greens, insisting that Nader voters would otherwise (and should) vote for Gore. Gore's narrow loss appeared to confirm their fears. It seems clear, however, that Republican Bush won not only because some voters who might have voted for Gore chose Nader instead, but also because Bush benefited from questionable voting procedures in Florida and elsewhere (including disenfranchisement of African American voters), a lack of enthusiasm for Gore among traditional Democratic constituencies, and most importantly, the 210-year old constitutional mechanism of the Electoral College which awarded Bush the presidency despite having lost the popular vote by more than half a million votes.

Green parties in US local politics

From 1986, when a single green candidate stood for election in the USA (Greg Gerritt in Maine), US Greens have always been most active and most successful in local and regional elections, but even here progress has been slow. In 1990 there were just fifteen lower-level green candidates, in only six states. Ten years later there were 270 candidates in

32 states, the District of Columbia, and American Samoa, for local, state, and congressional office; these included thirteen candidates for the US Senate and 49 for the US House of Representatives. Greens won no congressional or statewide offices in 2000, but 33 Greens did manage to win local elections, bringing the parties total to 80 elected positions, on municipal councils in sixteen states. Most were in California, where five small cities elected Green mayors (Nevada City, Sonoma, Santa Monica, Santa Cruz, Sebastopol). Green Party activist Michael Feinstein, mayor of Santa Monica, was the single highest vote-getter in that Pacific coast city's 2000 elections, as Art Goodtimes, running for re-election to the San Miguel County Board of Supervisors, in Colorado, was that election's most popular candidate. In one California city, Sebastopol, Greens also held a majority of Council seats, as they previously did in Arcata.

In 1992 voters on the Big Island of Hawaii elected green candidate Keiko Bonk to the County Council, the first Green in the USA to win a partisan race against both a Democrat and a Republican. New Mexico's capital city of Santa Fe twice elected the Green Party's Fran Sena Gallegos to its municipal court in 1996 and 2000, the first green jurist in the country, and in 2000 two greens Cris Moore and Miguel Chavez sat on the Santa Fe City Council. Elizabeth Horton-Sheff was elected in 1999 to the City Council in Hartford, Connecticut's capital city. And, in a high-profile defection from the Democratic Party, newly elected Matt Gonzalez, member of the San Francisco Board of Supervisors, joined the Green Party in 2000. One of eleven Supervisors governing a city of 746,000 people, he thus represented the largest green constituency in the USA. By March 2001, eleven green candidates had filed for city and state elections, in California, New Jersey, Minnesota, Mississippi, and Pennsylvania (Feinstein 2000, Rensenbrink 1999).

References

Association of State Green Parties,
  URL: http://www.greenparties.org
Feinstein, M. (2000) 'Green Party Election History, US – 1986–2000' at

URL: http://www.feinstein.org/greenparty/elections.html.
Rensenbrink, J. (1999) *Against All Odds: The Green Transformation of American Politics*, Raymond, ME: Leopold Press.
Winger, R. (2000) *Ballot Access News*, San Francisco: Committee on Free and Open Elections.

Further reading

Bookchin, M. (1982) *The Ecology of Freedom: The Emergence and Dissolution of Hierarchy*, Palo Alto: Cheshire Books.
Green Party platform (ASGP) at
  URL: http://www.gp.org.
Green Party of California at
  URL: http://www.greens.org/cal/.
Green Party of Texas at
  URL: http://www.txgreens.org/.
Green Parties world wide at
  URL: http://www.greens.org.
Green Parties of North America at
  URL: http://www.greens.org/na.html.
Martin, L. (2000) *Driving Mr Nader: The Greens Grow Up*, Raymond, ME: Leopold Press.
Nader, Ralph and LaDuke, Winona at
  URL: http://www.votenader.org.
  URL: http://www.greens.org/winona/.
Spretnak, C. and Capra, F. (1986) *Green Politics*, Santa Fe: Bear & Co.

TONY AFFIGNE

Green Party, UK

The British Greens are Europe's oldest Green Party, founded in 1973. Hampered by an electoral system extremely disadvantageous to small parties, the Greens have never managed to gain parliamentary representation at national level. The party achieved its most notable result in the European Elections of 1989 when it polled 14.5 per cent of the vote. After a return to the political fringe for most of the 1990s, the introduction of proportional representation for elections to the European Parliament, the Scottish Parliament and the local London Assembly led to the electoral revival of the party. The Greens successfully contested all these elections in 1999 and 2000.

In the UK party political register, one party is registered under the name 'The Green Party', but, in terms of their respective party constitutions, there are three completely independent parties: the Scottish Green Party, the Green Party of Northern Ireland and the Green Party of England and Wales.

History

The British Greens were founded in 1973 by a small circle of individuals in Coventry. Named 'People', the party first remained very small. After a change of name to 'Ecology Party' in 1975, party fortunes improved with creditable performances at the 1979 General and European elections, leading to a major membership influx. Renamed 'Green Party' in 1985, the party remained a stable if electorally marginal force throughout the 1980s. The sudden rise of environmental issues in Britain in the late 1980s was one major factor behind its electoral success of 1989. The period of 1989 to 1992 gave the party unprecedented media coverage which was often dominated by reports on the internal conflicts in the party. A disappointing 1992 General Election and the exodus of many leading members was associated with a decline of the party in the 1990s (see **Parkin, Sara**). The electoral successes of 1999 and 2000 have again increased the political visibility of the party.

Ideology

The founders of the party were strongly influenced by the ecological 'doomsday' scenarios of the early 1970s. The *Blueprint for Survival* and Edward **Goldsmith**'s 'survivalist' thinking was the dominant ideological force of the 1970s. While its 'authoritarian' elements were challenged by members with a more 'leftist' view of ecological problems, the new leadership of the late 1970s brought more pragmatic and less apocalyptic approaches to the fore. After 1979, the party attracted many new members whose approach was strongly influenced by 'anarchist', 'alternative' views of green politics (see **anarchism/eco-anarchism**. The main dividing line in the party concentrated on the question of strategy and internal organization: with the 'anarchists' arguing for more decentralization and a focus on social movements rather than elections, the 'electoralists' wanted to turn the party into an effective electoral organization. Unlike many continental green parties, the British Greens never had important factions advocating traditional left wing or marxist ideas associated with a 'statist' left. While the 'anarchists' in the party sought to associate the party with the political 'Left', the pragmatic 'electoralists' generally distanced themselves forcefully from any such notion. After strong internal conflicts in the 1980s and early 1990s, the importance of internal ideological divisions appears to have declined substantially.

As governmental responsibility at national level is as yet a remote possibility, the ideological identity of the British Greens still has a strongly 'fundamentalist', utopian and 'counter-cultural' flavour; the maintenance of an 'alternative' green life-style remains an important feature of party culture (see **counter-culture**.

Policies

The construction of a comprehensive political programme as the foundation of the creation of a 'green', sustainable society has always been one of the key aims of the party. Most of the party's creative energy has gone into the design not just of policy frameworks but details of many individual policies. The first comprehensive statement of party policy, the 'Manifesto for a Sustainable Society' (MfSS), was passed in 1975; it has been amended numerous times but has remained the party's fundamental programme ever since. The 1975 MfSS was heavily influenced by the 'limits to growth' discourse of the early 1970s (see *Limits to Growth*). The creation of a sustainable society was seen as a necessity to avoid the apocalyptic collapse of industrial society. One of the first policy innovations was the adoption of the idea of a '**basic income**' scheme to guarantee a basic social security in the face of the coming major structural changes.

Over the years, the comprehensive range of policies contained in the MfSS has been continually supplemented and up-dated. There are few policy issues that have been the subject of sustained internal conflict within the party. There has been a very broad consensus on key green demands such as the rejection of all nuclear technology; the decentralization of society and political life, and the creation of an environmentally sustainable and socially just society. Amongst the issues that have sparked internal debates have been drugs policy and Europe. The 'legalization of cannabis' has been one issue that was close to the heart of those in the party who came into the greens out of the 'hippie' and other alternative life-style movements; the policy was seen as unwise and dangerous by those who wanted to give the party a more professional media image. Another issue that has seen party divisions is Europe. While criticism of the **European Union** (EU), its political structure and many of its policies, is shared by most Greens, the party has been fairly divided on how to deal with the EU. All recent reforms, such as the Maastricht Treaty, have been rejected, but the party has shied away from advocating a position of Britain leaving the EU altogether.

Organization

The founders of the party gave the party a fairly traditional structure, with a 'National Chairman' elected by a national party congress, presiding over a 'National Executive Committee'. But quickly ideas associated with the concept of 'grassroots' **democracy** gained greater currency. The party constitution, first codified in 1977 and amended numerous times in subsequent years, set up a system of collective leadership with safeguards such as strict term limits built in. From 1982, the national party was represented by three 'co-chairs', emphasizing the absence of a 'party leader'. Between 1979 and 1991, major internal conflicts raged about internal organization, but radical proposals from either 'extremes', advocating the effective disbandment of the national party or the installation of a single party leader, failed to get sufficient support. In 1986, an initiative by some leading party activists to organize a campaigning organization for party modernization called 'Main-green' led to a strong backlash against a supposed 'elite' take-over and quickly petered out. A more

determined initiative to change the party's internal structure arose after the 1989 European elections success. A constitutional reform programme named 'Green 2000' was proposed, calling for the creation of a 'Green Party executive' (GPEx), headed by a single chair, to take over the day-to-day running of the party. GPEx was to be advised by a 'Green Party Regional Council' (GPRC) meeting more infrequently. To improve the party's media presence, two 'principal speakers' were to be elected. Furthermore, term limits for party office holders were to be abolished and the annual conference was to become a conference of representatives elected by local parties, replacing a system where any member attending the national conference had a vote. The Green 2000 reform was supported by many prominent activists, but was vehemently opposed by the decentralist wing of the party. Mobilizing many of the new members who had recently joined, Green 2000 managed to win the decisive conference vote in September 1991 to approve the reform package virtually unchanged. The new internal structure was in place before the May 1992 General Election, but the hopes of some of its protagonists that it would pay immediate dividends in terms of improved media coverage, a respectable election result and a stop to the rapid decline of party membership was not fulfilled. Internal conflict and personality clashes reached a new height after the election, with many leading pro-2000 activists retiring from party activity in the process, accusing the decentralists of sabotaging the working of the new internal structure. While some observers saw this change as a 'fundamentalist' take-over of the party, the Green 2000 internal structure was not radically changed in subsequent years. A term limitation for office holders was reintroduced, but with a shortage of activists willing to take on national party offices, its handling has been more relaxed than before, with exceptions being possible. Also the delegate conference was abolished again, a move of little political consequence given the small size of the membership, with competitive elections of conference delegates in party branches having always been quite rare. Since 1998, a new constitutional working party has considered various proposals to change the current structure, in particular in view of the rather uneasy relationship between GPEx and GPRC, but none of the reform proposals managed to achieve a majority at the 2000 annual conference.

Membership

The number of members of the party has fluctuated quite widely over the years. In the first years, national party membership remained very low. At the time of the launch of the 1979 General Election campaign, with the aim of fielding more than 50 candidates in order to qualify for a public election broadcast, the party only had 650 members. The 1979 election campaign brought many thousands of new members into the party, with national membership reaching a peak of almost 6,000 in 1980. Membership declined to about 2,000 in the mid-1980s, but picked up again steeply at the end of the decade. In 1988 and 1989, membership rose dramatically, reaching an all-time high point of more than 18,000 in November 1990. The subsequent decline was, however, just as dramatic, with the combined membership of all UK green parties falling back to around 5,000 in the mid-1990s.

The social make-up of green party members does not appear to have fluctuated much over the years. Membership surveys in the late 1980s and early 1990s show members to be mainly in their 30s and 40s. Education levels are substantially higher than those of the average population, with 67 per cent of 1990 members holding or studying for a university degree. Most members are in professional occupations, with teaching being a particularly popular career. In comparison with the general population, manual and clerical workers are heavily underrepresented. Self-employment, often in 'green' areas, is also a popular occupational choice.

Electoral performance

The British Greens have had to survive in a very difficult institutional structure. While the formal constitution of parties faces no real constraints in Britain, small parties are confronted by a series of other obstacles. Financially, no state support for small parties is available; to the contrary, the system of submitting deposits for each candidate fielded imposes a substantial financial burden; as a result, the party was never able to field a full slate of candidates in a General Election. The dominant electoral system used, the 'first-past-the-post' majority voting system in single member constituencies, makes it extremely difficult for small parties to gain representation. Not surprisingly, perhaps, the Greens have not done well in General Elections, never coming even close to having an MP elected to the House of Commons. The only successes in national elections have been in elections to the European Parliament. In 1989, the Greens benefited from a combination of factors, including a very high salience of environmental issues and the weakness of their main rivals, the Liberal Democrats, to score their best result ever, with 14.5 per cent of the popular vote. But it was only after the introduction of a form of proportional representation for European and regional elections, that the Greens managed to turn their public support into representation. In **Scotland**, the Greens scored 3.6 per cent in the first elections to the Scottish Parliament in 1999, with Robin Harper elected to the parliament. In the European Elections of the same year, the Greens polled 5.8 per cent in the UK, resulting in the election of the party's first two MEPs, Jean Lambert and Caroline Lucas. Also in the high-profile London local elections in May 2000, the Greens did well, attracting around 11 per cent of the top-up vote, and had three London Assembly members elected.

Voters

Given the poor showing of green candidates in general elections, British elections studies offer no information on the background of actual and potential green voters. The only information available derives from the European Election studies that were carried out in 1989, 1994 and 1999. All surveys confirm that environmental concern is associated with green voting; green voters also tend to be younger and well educated; unlike in some European countries, the role of left-wing orientation and post-material values has been less pronounced in Britain (see **Inglehart, Ronald**). In particular the 1989 green voter in Britain was quite different from the typical continental green party supporter: the Greens attracted support from all political tendencies, including Conservatives. This underlines the impression that the 1989 vote was essentially a protest vote, although concern about environmental issues also played a major role. In subsequent European elections, green voters have tended to be more left-leaning, thus converging on the green voting patterns more commonly seen in continental Europe. In national opinion polls, the Greens throughout the 1990s could never get above the 2 per cent level, indicating that the number of committed green voters is quite small. While this makes it unlikely that the Greens will be able to mount any significant challenge at a General Election, the party is capable of motivating its core supporters as well as other environmentally minded voters of predominantly left-wing persuasion to cast a green vote at European, local and regional elections.

See also: environmental movements; green parties, US; Grünen, Die; political opportunity structures

Further reading

Bennie, L. (2001) *Understanding Political Participation: Scottish Green Party Membership*, Aldershot: Ashgate.

Bennie, L.G. Franklin, M.N. and Rüdig, W. (1995) 'The Ideology of the British Greens', in W. Rüdig (ed.) *Green Politics Three*, Edinburgh: Edinburgh University Press, pp. 217–39.

Burchell, J. (2000) 'Here Come the Greens (Again): The Green Party in Britain During the 1990s', *Environmental Politics*, 9(3), Autumn: 145–50.

Faucher, F. (1999) *Les habits verts de la politique*, Paris: Presses de Science Po.

Green Party website at
URL: http://www.greenparty.org.uk.

McCulloch, A. (1992) 'The Green Party of England and Wales: The Early Years', *Environmental Politics*, 1: 418–36.

Northern Irish Green Party website at
URL: http://www.belfast.co.uk/nigreens.

Rootes, C. (1995) 'Greens in a Cold Climate', in D. Richardson and C. Rootes (eds) *The Green Challenge: The Development of Green Parties in Europe*, London: Routledge, pp. 66–90.

Rüdig, W. (1996) 'Green parties and the European Union', in Gaffney, J. (ed.) *Political Parties and the European Union*, London: Routledge, pp. 254–72.

Rüdig, W and Lowe, P (1986) 'The "Withered" Greening of British Politics: A Study of the Ecology Party', *Political Studies*, 34: 262–84.

Rüdig, W., Bennie, L.G., Franklin, M.N. (1991) *Green Party Members: A Profile*, Glasgow: Delta Publications.

Rüdig, W., Franklin, M.N., Bennie L.G. (1996) 'Up and Down with the Greens: Ecology and Party Politics in Britain, 1989–1992', *Electoral Studies*, 15: 1–20.

Scottish Green Party website at
URL: http://www.scottishgreens.org.uk.

WOLFGANG RÜDIG

green political theory

Green political theory covers a diversity of different ethical and political principles, schools and theorists which share a common concern about the normative dimensions of the relationship between humans and **nature** as well as relations between people within society. That is, green political theory covers two broad and interrelated areas: that relating to the organization of human societies and that relating to how those societies relate to the natural world.

Often wrongly confused with ecologism, and the debate between **environmentalism and ecologism** more generally (Dobson, 2000), green political theory properly speaking is not a narrowly ideological view associated exclusively with the views, principles and beliefs of self-acknowledged 'green' theorists or parties or environmental movements. While of course, green political theory is based on the latter, it is not 'centred' exclusively on these ideological 'ecological' positions (Barry, 1999a). Ideological accounts or schools of green political theory include: **social ecology** (Bookchin, 1980), **anarchism/eco-anarchism** (Carter, 1999), **deep ecology** (Sessions, 1995), **ecofeminism** (Mellor, 1997; Salleh, 1997), **ecosocialism** (Benton, 1993), green liberalism (Wissenburg, 1998; Barry and Wissenburg, 2001), **bioregionalism** (Sale, 1980).

That green political theory introduces some new features to political theory is something all self-professed green political theorists acknowledge. Examples of this include Brian Baxter's statement that, 'it is now intellectually unacceptable to develop political theories in which the sole focus of concern is human well-being and values, ignoring the issues which greens have pushed to the fore concerning the well-being of other species, and the biosphere in general' (1996: 68). While for Tim Hayward,

> *The most distinctive green idea is that of natural relations* These are of numerous kinds: there are natural relations of biological kinship between humans, on which familial and social relations are supervenient; between humans who are not kin, too, relations are naturally mediated, for instance in the sense that reproductive and productive activities occur in a natural medium; such activities normally involve modifying the natural environment in some way, and all humans, individually and collectively, have relations to their environment.
>
> (1996: 80; emphasis added)

The 'newness' of green political theory can be assessed by the following:

- The introduction of social-environmental relations as a proper and central subject of political normative analysis;
- The introduction of new criteria for criticizing the existing social order, prescribing some of the underlying principles of the 'good society' and suggestion how to get from the 'unsustainable' present towards a more sustainable society;
- The extension of the scope of political normative analysis to include: non-humanity and the natural world, future generations, non-resident aliens in other countries, and inclusion of an environmental dimension to the discourses and politics of **distributive justice**. A shorthand way of expressing this is that green political theory extends the discourse of justice to cover: interspecies, intergenerational, international/ global and social relations between humans and the non-human world and between humans.

Barry (1999b) has listed some of the basic and novel features of green political theory. These include:

1 'Overcoming the separation between 'society' and 'environment', (which includes extending environment to include the human, built environment)
2 Appreciation of the *biological embodiedness* and *ecological embeddedness* of human beings and human society
3 Viewing humans a species of natural being, with particular species-specific needs and characteristics
4 Accepting both internal and external natural limits, those relating to the particular needs and vulnerable and dependent character of 'human nature', and external, ecological scarcity in terms of finite natural resources and fixed limits of the environment to absorb human-produced wastes
5 As a critical mode of political theory, green political theory criticizes not just 'economic growth' but the dominant industrial model of '**development**', 'modernization' and **progress**
6 Claims that how we treat the environment is a moral issue, and not just a 'technological' or 'economic' one. This ranges from claims that the non-human world has **intrinsic value**, to the idea of **animal rights**
7 Prescriptive aspects: restructuring social, economic and political institutions to produce a more ecologically sustainable world
8 'Act local, think global': ecological interconnectedness and interdependence which transcends national boundaries.
9 Futurity: time-frame of green social theory is expanded to include concern for future generations, i.e. concerns of **intergenerational justice**
10 Scientific: based on ecological science (but also other natural sciences such as biology and physics)'.

(Barry, 1999b: 187)

Green political theory, on the interpretation expressed here, requires a *naturalistic* perspective which has two main components (Barry, 1999a; 1999b; Midgley, 1983, 1995; Clark, 1995). First, it is a naturalistic social theory in that it explicitly recognizes the natural environmental contexts, preconditions, opportunities and constraints on human activity. Second, as a naturalistic social theory it recognizes the centrality of internal human nature, of seeing humans as natural beings with particular modes of flourishing, like other natural beings.

For Ted Benton (1991), a recognition of the problems with the separation of 'society' and 'environment' and the other related distinctions between 'mind' and 'body', 'human' and 'non-human' requires the integration of the biologically based life sciences and the social sciences. For him, 'The task for any proposed re-alignment of the human social sciences with the life sciences can now be seen as providing conceptual room for organic, bodily, and environmental aspects and dimensions of human social life to be assigned their proper place' (1991: 25). This integration, as he is quick to point out, *does not* mean the reduction of one to the other. At the same time, as materialist eco-feminists point out, there needs to be a recognition of the biological reality and needs of human beings a central part of which would oblige the re-orientation of social and political theory, politics and policies towards issues around *reproduction*, bodily and environmental vulnerability, care and nurture and not just *production* (Barry, 1998; Mellor, 1997; Salleh; 1997).

The integration of biological and ecological insights produces in green political theory a form of social theory which begins from acknowledging human biological embodiedness and ecological embeddedness (Benton, 1993). Green political theory thus focuses on an explicit recognition of the human body and its organic needs, and fully acknowledges human limits, dependency and neediness. Such a social theory would see the bodily vulnerability of humans as an essential and indispensable political and ethical context or background condition. In terms of ecological embeddedness, green political theory accepts ecological limits and parameters to collective human activity. As Lee puts it, given the ecological facts of the world, and our dependent relationship with it, 'Any adequate social/moral theory must therefore address itself to these characteristics [of the world] and the character of the exchange [between humans and nature]. If it does not, whatever solution it has to offer is of no relevance

or significance to our preoccupations and problems' (1989: 9).

See also: anarchism/eco-anarchism; anthropocentrism; bioregionalism; Bookchin, Murray; distributive justice; deep ecology; eco-centrism; eco-feminism; eco-socialism; environmental ethics; environmental justice; environmental movements; environmentalism of the poor; liberalism/liberal democracy; social ecology

References

Barry, J. (1999a) *Rethinking Green Politics: Nature, Virtue and Progress*, London: Sage.

—— (1999b) *Environment and Social Theory*, London: Routledge.

Barry, J. and Wissenburg, M. (eds), (2001) *Sustaining Liberal Democracy*, Basingstoke: Palgrave.

Baxter, B. (1996) 'Must Political Theory Now be Green?', in I. Hampshire-Monk and J. Stanyer (eds) *Contemporary Political Studies*, Belfast: Political Studies Association.

Benton, T. (1991) 'Biology and Social Science: Why the Return of the Repressed Should be Given a (Cautious) Welcome', *Sociology*, 25(1).

—— (1993) *Natural Relations: Ecology, Animal Rights and Social Justice*, London: Verso.

Bookchin, M. (1980) *Towards an Ecological Society*, Montreal: Black Rose Books.

Carter, A. (1999) *Towards a Radical Green Political Theory*, London: Routledge.

Clark, S. (1995) 'Enlarging the Community: Companion Animals', in B. Almond (ed) *Introducing Applied Ethics*. Oxford: Basil Blackwell.

Dobson, A. (2000) *Green Political Thought*, London: Routledge, 3rd edn.

Hayward, T. (1996) 'What is Green Political Theory?', in I. Hampshire-Monk and J. Stanyer (eds) *Contemporary Political Studies*, Belfast: Political Studies Association.

Mellor, M. (1997) *Feminism and Ecology*, Cambridge: Polity Press.

Midgley, M. (1983) *Animals and Why They Matter*, Harmondsworth: Penguin.

—— (1995) *Beast and Man: The Roots of Human Nature*, London: Routledge, revised edn.

Sale, K. (1980) *Dwellers in the Land: The Bioregional Vision*, New York: Secker and Warburg.

Salleh, A. (1997) *Eco-feminism as Politics: Nature, Marx and the Post-modern*, London: Zed Books.

Sessions, G. (ed.) (1995) *Deep Ecology for the Twenty-First Century*, Boston: Shambala Press.

Wissenburg, M. (1998) *Green Liberalism: The Free and the Green Society*, London: UCL Press.

Further reading

Baxter, B. (1998) *Ecologism: A Defence*, Edinburgh: Edinburgh University Press.

Catton, W. and Dunlap, R. (1980) 'A New Ecological Paradigm for a Post-Exuberant Sociology', *The American Behavioural Scientist*, 24(1).

Dickens, P. (1992) *Society and Nature: Towards a Green Social Theory*, Hemel Hempstead: Harvester Wheatsheaf.

Eckersley, R. (1992) *Environmentalism and Political Theory: Towards an Ecocentric Approach*, London: UCL Press.

—— (1996) 'Green Political Thought', in R. Paehlke (ed.) *Encyclopedia of Environmental Conservation*, New York: Garland Press.

Goodin, R. (1992) *Green Political Theory*, Cambridge: Polity.

Hayward, T. (1995) *Ecological Thought: An Introduction*, Cambridge: Polity.

Lee, K. (1989) *Social Philosophy and Ecological Scarcity*, London: Routledge.

Martell, L. (1994) *Nature and Society: An Introduction*, Cambridge: Polity.

Paehlke, R. (1989) *Environmentalism and the Future of Progressive Politics*, New Haven: Yale University Press.

JOHN BARRY

green revolution

Green revolution is a term referring to the application to **agriculture** of science-based technologies, with the objective of maximizing yield. The green revolution of the 1960s and 1970s involved the development of new strains of crops, the use of high levels of artificial fertilizers, **pesticides** and weed-killers, and an increased mechanization of farming. While an increase in production (particularly of wheat and rice) did occur, serious concerns were raised about the contamination of food, impact on local and regional ecology, and the social impact of industrialized **agriculture** on small producers unable to access the capital necessary to make use of the new techniques. A second green revolution is predicted to occur as a result of the genetic modification of crops to enhance growth-rate and also resistance to drought, disease or predators (see **genetic engineering, crops**). Genetic techniques are also being developed for application to livestock. These developments have raised significant concerns regarding the dangers of releasing genetically modified material to the wild and also about the dependence of farmers on the producers of modified seeds, many of which are genetically engineered to be infertile.

ALISTAIR McCULLOCH

Greenpeace

Greenpeace is a citizen's action organization founded in 1971 in British Columbia, Canada in order to oppose underground nuclear bomb testing in Alaska. Since that time it has grown into an international organization with headquarters in Britain, France, Germany, the Netherlands, Australia, New Zealand, Denmark as well as Canada. In the USA it has six regional offices. Greenpeace has adopted many additional environmental causes since its founding. It continues to advocate nuclear disarmament and protection of the ocean ecosystem by eliminating toxic dumping there. It also has initiated campaigns to save whales, dolphins, kangaroos and other species.

Greenpeace has adopted the tactic of direct action by its membership as opposed to traditional lobbying activities of more mainstream environmental groups. Rather than lobbying for passage of a new law, its members take personal action by demonstrating against projects, boycotting products, and intervening directly against companies and governments that engage in environmentally damaging activities. It is probably most famous for sending its small rubber inflatable boats into the path of **whaling** vessels to deter them from their prey. In 1987 Greenpeace established a research station in **Antarctica** to investigate the condition of that subcontinent and the impact of human activities on the ecosystem there.

Greenpeace tracks ships that are armed with nuclear weapons and informs host countries when they dock in their jurisdictions. Greenpeace vessels try to prevent disposal of radioactive and other toxic materials in the oceans. Various governments have retaliated against Greenpeace protests. In 1980 **Spain** seized the **Rainbow Warrior** because it had interfered with whaling and held it for five months. British seamen attempted to sink the *Zodiac*, and the USSR towed the *Sirius* out of Leningrad. Members of the French Directorate General of External Security blew up the *Rainbow Warrior* when it was berthed in Auckland harbour, **New Zealand**, killing a Greenpeace member. Two French government employees were tried and sentenced to ten years, but they were later released to France due to economic and political pressure.

Greenpeace relies entirely on voluntary donations from members and solicitations of the public by them. Its organizing principle is decentralization, with important decisions made at the grassroots chapter level. Hence, it has a diverse membership with some groups more militant than others. Some members are dedicated to **deep ecology** while others have a more shallow commitment to ecological values.

See also: non-violent direct action

Further reading

Greenpeace International at
  URL: http://www.greenpeace.org.

LETTIE McSPADDEN

greenwashing

Greenwashing, greenscamming and greenspeak are all different terms for public relations efforts to portray an organization, activity or product as environmentally friendly.

Greenwash derives from the term whitewash and indicates that organizations using greenwash are trying to cover up environmentally and/or socially damaging activities, sometimes just with rhetoric, sometimes with minor or superficial environmental reforms. Similarly greenscamming indicates an element of fraud and deception and refers to the practice of using environmental names for groups or products that are not environmentally friendly. Greenspeak is a more neutral term meaning environmental language, jargon and terms. It is sometimes used to indicate environmental language that lacks substance, is not genuine or is merely empty rhetoric. Greenspeak is also used by anti-environmental groups to derogatively refer to arguments made by environmentalists.

Environmental public relations, or greenwash, has been a response to the rise of environmental concern, particularly in the late 1980s. Many firms responded with green marketing campaigns in an effort to portray their products as environmentally friendly and capitalize on new markets created by rising environmental consciousness. Green imagery was used to sell products and caring for the environment became a marketing strategy. For example, plastics once advertised for their throwaway convenience were now touted as recyclable.

Green marketing was often augmented with public relations strategies to give corporations an environmentally friendly persona. By 1995 US-based firms were spending about $1 billion a year on public relations advice on how to green their own image and deal with environmental opposition. Today public relations and marketing firms in many countries perform similar services.

The attempt to provide a 'green' and caring image for a corporation is a public relations strategy aimed at promising reform and heading off demands for more substantial and fundamental changes and government intervention. Public relations experts advise how to counter the negative perceptions of business, caused in most cases by their poor environmental performance. Rather than substantially change business practices so as to earn a better reputation many firms are turning to PR professionals to create one for them. This is cheaper and easier than making the substantial changes required to become more environmentally friendly.

One of the ways PR experts enhance the image of their clients and show that they care is by emphasizing their positive actions, no matter how trivial, and down playing any negative aspects, no matter how significant. Some companies make the most out of measures they have been forced to take by the government, making it seem that they have undertaken the improvements because they care about the environment. Companies that have poor environmental records can also improve their image and increase their sales merely by using recycled paper in their products or making similar token adjustments.

Another way for corporations to show they care about the environment, even if they don't care enough to make major changes to their business practices, is to donate money to an environmental group or to sponsor an environmental project. Such donations can also have the additional benefit of co-opting and corrupting environmentalists. Consultancies and perks for individual environmentalists also work wonders for getting a favourable hearing.

As well as funding genuine environmental groups, these corporations also set up anti-environmental front groups that pose as environmental groups adopting environmental names, sometimes with the similar acronyms or logos as their environmental foes to add to the deliberately fostered confusion (see **anti-environmentalism**).

Corporations have also turned their attention to the next generation through the development and distribution of 'educational' material to schools. The potential to shape environmental perceptions and improve corporate images at the same time attracts many customers to the firms designing educational materials for corporations. These materials inevitably give a corporate view of environmental problems and portray activities such as clear cutting forests, coal **mining** and nuclear energy as environmentally friendly (see **nuclear energy/nuclear waste management**).

Sponsorship and advertising still plays a major role in greenwashing, particularly sponsorship of environmental events such as **Earth Day** or Clean Up days and television documentaries on the environment. Similarly companies make use of press releases and video news releases to ensure that the mass media report and emphasize their environmentally beneficial activities rather than their damaging activities.

Further reading

Beder, S. (1997) *Global Spin: The Corporate Assault on Environmentalism*, Devon: Green Books.

Bruno, K., Karliner, J. and Srivastava, A. (2000) 'Exposing Corporate Greenwash', Transnational Resource and Action Center,
URL: http://www.corpwatch.org/climate/kit/index.html.

Greer, J. and Bruno, K. (1996) *Greenwash: The Reality Behind Corporate Environmentalism*, Penang, Malaysia: Third World Network.

Stauber, J. and Rampton, S. (1995) *Toxic Sludge is Good For You! Lies, Damn Lies and the Public Relations Industry*, Monroe, ME: Common Courage Press.

SHARON BEDER

Groenen, De

The party *De Groenen* was founded in the **Netherlands** in December 1983 by members of regional green groups and former members of the Political Party of Radicals (see *GroenLinks*). It took part in parliamentary elections in 1986, 1989, 1994 and 1998, without ever winning more than 0.4 per cent of the vote: not enough for a seat. It did slightly better at European elections in 1984 and 1994 (though not enough to win a seat) and at local elections in larger cities. Unlike its major competitor *GroenLinks* the Greens refused to identify with the left. Members of the Greens were more often ecocentrists and more religious than those of *GroenLinks* (see **eco-centrism**)

Further reading

Lucardie, P., Voerman, G., and Van Schuur, W. (1993) 'Different Shades of Green: A Comparison between Members of Groen Links and De Groenen', *Environmental Politics* 2(1): 40–62.

PAUL LUCARDIE

GroenLinks

GroenLinks (Green Left) started in 1989 as an alliance between the Communist Party of the Netherlands (CPN), the Pacifist Socialist Party (PSP) and the Political Party of Radicals (PPR). Before the general elections of September 1989, it was joined by the ailing Evangelical People's Party (*Evangelische Volkspartij*, EVP) and by independent members from various social movements. On 24 November 1990 *GroenLinks* was founded as a political party, at a congress open to members of all groups involved. In 1991 CPN, PPR, PSP and EVP dissolved themselves.

The PSP had been established in 1957 by opponents of the Cold War; in the 1960s it evolved into a libertarian socialist party of **New Left** persuasion. An even more pure New Left party was the PPR, founded in 1968 by radical dissidents from the Catholic People's Party and from the two major Protestant parties in the Netherlands. Already in the 1970s it criticized economic growth and nuclear power. During the 1960s and 1970s the CPN was a traditional Marxist–Leninist party; but in the early 1980s young reformers introduced feminist and New Leftist ideas. The EVP was set up in 1981 by Protestants who regarded the new Christian Democratic party as too conservative but the PPR as too radical and too secular. Ideological convergence between the four parties facilitated their rapprochement during the 1980s. They began to co-operate at the local level and at the European level for the first time in 1984. Electoral decline and pressure from **new social movements** reinforced the trend towards co-operation.

In 1991 *GroenLinks* adopted a manifesto, or 'programme of starting points' (*Program van Uitgangspunten*). The main principles of the party were defined here: **democracy**, ecological balance, and a just distribution of power, knowledge, wealth, work and income in the Netherlands and in the world as a whole. In its election platforms the party called for democratic reforms, a more liberal immigration policy, more part-time work, a (modest) negative income tax, more welfare, more foreign aid, **eco-taxes**, a transition from industrial to organic **agriculture** and no more expansion of airports and air travel.

GroenLinks had a slow electoral start. In 1989 it attracted 4.1 per cent of the popular vote, enough for six seats in parliament; its predecessors had received 3.3 per cent, but only three seats, in 1986. In 1994 it lost 0.6 per cent of the vote and one seat. As a result, the party leader Ina Brouwer – a former Communist – resigned and was succeeded by Paul Rosenmöller, until 1989 a trade union leader who had never belonged to one of the founding parties. His personal popularity contributed to electoral successes in the late 1990s: 7.3 per cent and eleven seats at parliamentary elections in 1998, 11.9 per cent and four seats at European elections in 1999. The party appealed to former supporters of the Labour Party and the leftwing liberal Democrats 66, who were probably disappointed by the compromises the latter two parties had made in a coalition with the conservative Liberal Party since 1994. At the national level, *GroenLinks* remained in the opposition, whereas it participated in the local government of major cities like Amsterdam, Rotterdam and Utrecht.

Membership had declined from 15,900 in 1990 to 12,000 in 1997, then rose to 13,900 by 2000. The organization combined elements of a **new politics** party with characteristics of a minor mass party: major decisions were taken by party congress, which is since 1995 open to all members provided they are registered at a local branch; a membership vote was held only once.

See also: Groenen, De; Netherlands, the

Further reading

Cordier, T. (1996) 'Cleavages in Green Parties: The Cases of the Dutch, French and German Greens', *Innovation*, 9(4): 491–507.

GroenLinks (1992) *Program van Uitgangspunten*, Amsterdam: GroenLinks.

Lucardie, P., Van Schuur, W. and Voerman, G. (1999) *Verloren illusie, geslaagde fusie? GroenLinks in historisch en politicologisch perspectief*, Leiden: DSWO Press.

Lucardie, P., Van der Knoop, J., Van Schuur, W. and Voerman, G. (1995) 'Greening the Reds or Reddening the Greens? The Case of the Green Left in the Netherlands', in Wolfgang Rüdig (ed.)

Green Politics Three, Edinburgh: Edinburgh University Press.

Lucardie, P., Voerman, G. and Van Schuur, W. (1993) 'Different Shades of Green: A Comparison between Members of Groen Links and De Groenen', *Environmental Politics* 2(1): 40–62.

Voerman, G. (1995) 'The Netherlands', in D. Richardson and C. Rootes (eds) *The Green Challenge. The Development of Green Parties in Europe*, London and New York: Routledge.

PAUL LUCARDIE

Gruhl, Herbert

b. 22 October 1921, Gnaschwitz, Germany; d. 26 June 1993, Regensburg, Germany

Politician, writer

Herbert Gruhl grew up in a farming family. After the Second World War, he earned his doctorate at the Free University in Berlin. He joined the Christian Democrats (CDU) and was elected to the *Bundestag* in 1969 (serving until 1980). There he chaired his party's environmental working group. In 1975 his book, *Ein Planet wird geplündert* (A Planet is Plundered) became a bestseller, and he co-founded the Bund für Natur- und Umweltschultz (later **BUND**). Alienated by the CDU's fixation on economic growth and industrialism, Gruhl resigned and formed Green Action Future (GAZ).

During 1979–80, Gruhl played a major role in the launching of the Greens (*Die **Grünen***). He became one of their co-speakers, and the GAZ was disbanded. However, Gruhl, a 'values' conservative, became disenchanted by the leftist contents of the Greens' programme. In 1981 he left the party and formed the conservative Ecological Democratic Party (ÖDP), which has won scattered local council seats in southern Germany. When its activists began distancing themselves from his increasingly ethno-nationalist views, Gruhl left the party and formed Independent Ecologists of Germany in 1990. His last book, *Himmelfahrt ins Nichts* (Ascension into Nothingness) (1992) reflected Gruhl's growing pessimism about the prospects for saving the planet.

Further reading

Olsen, J. (1999) *Nature and Nationalism: Right-Wing Ecology and the Politics of Identity in Contemporary Germany*, New York.: St Martin's Press.

E. GENE FRANKLAND

Grünen, Die

The formative period for *Die Grünen*, the German Green Party was 1977–80. The primary issue that mobilized electoral alliances of student leftists, environmentalists, and local citizen activists was nuclear power. In 1977, green candidates won local council seats, providing the momentum for the formation of state parties. Soon to follow was a national green alliance of groups and parties which won 3.2 per cent of West Germany's votes in the 1979 European Parliament elections. On 13 January 1980, this alliance, joined by additional groups, officially launched the Greens as a national party. Its founders, ranging from radical left to radical right, shared a deep contempt for the Bonn party cartel. They agreed on four pillars for the Greens: grassroots **democracy**, social justice, **ecology**, and nonviolence. But they began to splinter when it came to spelling out the federal programme. The party's conservatives led by Herbert **Gruhl** became disgruntled (and by 1981 most had quit the party). During 1979–80 green candidates had won seats in two West German states, but the result in the September 1980 *Bundestag* election was only 1.5 per cent of the votes. The Greens' campaign had been overshadowed by the polarizing contest between Social Democratic (SPD) Chancellor Helmut Schmidt and his Christian Democratic (CDU/CSU) challenger Franz Josef Strauss, a right-wing conservative.

During 1981–3, the Greens won seats in four more state parliaments. Once elected, Greens acted as the 'fundamental opposition:' no coalitions, no alliances, and no deals with the major parties; and they engaged in unorthodox behaviour inside parliament and direct actions outside parliament. Nationally the Greens, with passionate leading figures, like Petra **Kelly**, were emerging as a radical movement party that rejected West Germany's established order of: representative democracy and passive citizenship, economic growth with nuclear energy and **consumerism**, and loyal membership in NATO with its policy of nuclear deterrence (see **nuclear energy/nuclear waste management**). Furthermore, the Greens took up the causes of immigrants, women, homosexuals, and varied disadvantaged groups. Some political scientists (Kaelberer, 1992) have explained the Greens' emergence in terms of a generational shift toward 'post-materialist' values (see **Inglehart, Ronald**). Others have emphasized the role of unique historical circumstances (Markovits and Gorski, 1993) and of the **political opportunity structures** of West Germany (Kitschelt, 1986) in the early success of the Greens. In 1983, as the political arm of the eco-**peace movement**, the Greens won 5.6 per cent of the vote, becoming the first new party to win seats in the *Bundestag* since the early 1950s. Four years later, the Greens did even better by winning 8.3 per cent of the vote. Also during the decade, they (twice) won seats in the European Parliament as well as in eight of the eleven West German state parliaments, and the party's membership grew from 18,000 to 40,000.

However, electoral success brought organizational stress. During their 'anti-party' phase (1980–3), the Greens had devised rules to hinder both the emergence of a strong party leadership and the dominance of the movement-party by parliamentarians. For example, the Greens had three federal co-speakers, who were non-salaried and limited to serving no more than two consecutive two year terms. The co-speakers had very little decision-making power and had a headquarters staff of around 20. The new party's ethos of amateurism was also reflected in its rules to check the development of a political class of green parliamentarians. For example, the party required the midterm rotation of parliamentary seats, obliged parliamentary members to follow party resolutions or resign, and forbad parliamentary members from simultaneously holding party leadership offices. Most of the anti-oligarchical rules were modified or abandoned by the end of the decade because of operational difficulties.

From the outset, the Greens had been a pluralistic party, whose factions fought vigorously

in public. Even after the departure of the eco-conservatives, eight distinctive 'currents' could be identified nationally within the Greens (Raschke, 1993). As an extra-parliamentary movement-party, the Greens could more easily accommodate ideological diversity than as a parliamentary opposition party forced to move beyond the symbolic to the concrete (the second phase of their history, 1983–90). Once the Greens had become a relevant parliamentary party at all levels of West German government, the opportunity to share power began to stress their movement-party identity. Thus, the factional cleavage between the *Fundis* (fundamentalists) and the *Realos* (realists) was born in the mid-1980s, becoming so deep that it threatened the unity of the federal party in the late 1980s. (One should note that there were distinctive groups within each wing as well as nonaligned groups.) In simple terms, *Realos* favoured reforms via junior partnership with the SPD, which had first materialized in Hesse where a SPD/Green coalition existed during 1985–7 (and 1991–9). The radical ecologists and eco-socialists who were labelled *Fundis* (by others) downplayed parliamentary work and rejected coalitions with the SPD in favour of extra-parliamentary activism to transform societal power relations. In the late 1980s, while the SPD was renewing its leadership and borrowing many green ideas, the Green Party was immobilized by factionalism at the federal level. Caught off balance by German unification and unable to mount an effective campaign, it was voted out of the *Bundestag* in December 1990.

This unexpected electoral defeat shook the Green Party from top to bottom and set the national stage for its revival as a reformist opposition party (the third phase of its history, 1990–8). In April 1991, a coalition of *Realos*, moderates, and undogmatic leftists at the Neumünster conference pushed through structural reforms to make the party more professional. For example, the number of co-speakers was reduced to two and term limitations dropped, and a new state council, replacing the activist-dominated federal executive committee, increased the federal role of state party leaders and parliamentarians. (The anti-elitist rule separating parliamentary seat and party leadership office survived narrowly.) In the aftermath of Neumünster, the last prominent *Fundis* resigned, and subsequently intra-party relations became more civil. In 1993, the 36, 200 western Greens and the 2,200 easterners of Alliance 90 (*Bündnis 90*), which in contrast to the Greens had won seats in the 1990 *Bundestag* election, merged as *Bündnis 90/Die Grünen*. There was a symbolic change in the basic agreement signed by the two partners: 'grassroots democracy' (a pillar of the West Greens since 1980) was deleted. The principle had suffered from its perceived misuse by the *Fundis*, but also the Greens with thousands of public office-holders in Germany had grown accustomed to representative democracy. Compared to 1990, the Greens' 1994 *Bundestag* campaign was professionally planned and executed. The Greens won 7.3 per cent of the vote and 49 seats making them the third largest parliamentary party, but they were back in the opposition.

The new *Bundestag* parliamentary group became the green power centre at the federal level. Its co-speaker Super-*Realo* Joschka **Fischer** was treated by the media as the *de facto* chair of the Green Party. Polls indicated that Fischer had a more positive image than a number of major party leaders. In addition, a new generation of Greens with the policy savvy to tackle the complexities of taxes, budgets, and social insurance emerged in the *Bundestag*. The Greens closed ranks inside and outside parliament to present themselves as 'the' party of ecological and social reform. During 1994–8, the party membership grew to 50,000. And the Greens saw their electoral share of the votes increase in a series of state elections during 1995–7. Increasing contacts with corporate executives, union leaders, and church officials confirmed the Greens' 'established' status. Yet, despite the efforts of Fischer and his allies to move the party toward a more realistic foreign and security policy, from their view the prerequisite for sharing national power with the SPD, the party's 1998 electoral programme continued to articulate green aversion to NATO and the use of military power.

In early 1998, SPD/Green coalitions governed five of the sixteen German states, and national polls indicated a 10 per cent support level. However, a series of tactical errors (such as calling for raising

the price of gasoline to 5 DM per litre in 10 years) and renewed *Realo*-Left factional quarrels translated into losses in state and local elections, and put the party on the defensive throughout the *Bundestag* campaign. Ultimately Greens closed ranks around a toned down short programme. In September 1998, the Greens won 6.7 per cent of the vote (0.6 points less than 1994), just enough to remain the third strongest parliamentary group. The results in the *Bundestag* election and in the autumn eastern state elections showed the Greens failing to win 5 per cent anywhere in the former East Germany. The social structural profile of the West green strongholds has changed little through the years: large cities or university towns, above average educational levels, and high levels of secularization. In 1998, green voters were again disproportionately under 45 years old, but erosion of support among those 18–24 continued. As in 1994, the Greens had the more support among young women than young men. Through the years, the Greens have maintained a quota system guaranteeing that at least half of green parliamentarians and party leaders are women.

Due to the SPD's gains especially in the East, a workable red-green majority emerged. A coalition was quickly negotiated, and the fourth phase of the party's history began. The Greens received three ministries: foreign (Joschka Fischer), environment (Jürgen **Trittin**), and health (Andrea Fischer). The coalition's first year was rocky: battles within the SPD over economic policy, between the SPD and the Greens over nuclear policy, and within the Greens over NATO's air war against Serbia. During this period the party suffered setbacks in each of the state elections held and lost a couple thousand members. *Realos* pressed for further structural reforms, and at the March 2000 Karlsruhe conference some were passed, such as a new party council (half of whose members were parliamentarians and ministers) with decision-making power. But the major holdover from the movement-party phase, the federal rule separating parliamentary seat and party leadership office survived. The Left placed higher priority on programmatic renewal. In 2000, the coalition seemed to be getting its act together: it agreed upon phasing out nuclear power, reducing taxes, and reforming the pension system. Despite the more positive record of the coalition, the Greens' support in the national polls averaged only 5–6 per cent.

The prospects of the Greens are uncertain. In recent years their national politicians have shown discipline in keeping the SPD–Green coalition alive despite policy compromises that touch on the party's identity. In recent years extra-parliamentary critics have begun to ask what does the party stand for besides 'power' and what is 'green' about the Greens? The formidable challenge facing the small party is to demonstrate competence and reliability as a coalition junior partner, but also to sharpen its profile *vis-à-vis* a senior partner, who has alternatives (particularly the Free Democrats) in terms of coalition formation. Despite periodic speculations about the CDU–Green option, the Greens in the near future will have only the choice between renewing the SPD–Green coalition or going into opposition at the federal level. But to even have this choice, the party will have to better address the issue concerns of voters, especially those aged 18–24. In an era of increasing electoral volatility, a party with a support level barely above the 5 per cent threshold for representation faces a perilous future.

References

Kaelberer, M. (1992) 'The Emergence of Green Parties in France and Germany', paper presented at the German Studies Association annual meeting, Minneapolis, 1–4 October.

Kitschelt, H. (1986) 'Political Opportunity Structure and Political Protest', *British Journal of Political Science* 16 (1): 57–83.

Markovits, A. and Gorski, P.S. (1993) *The German Left: Red, Green and Beyond*, New York: Oxford University Press.

Raschke, J. (1993) *Krise der Grünen: Bilanz und Neubeginn*, Cologne: Bund-Verlag

Further reading

Frankland, E.G. (2000) 'Bündnis '90/Die Grünen: From Opposition to Power' in D. Conradt, G.R. Kleinfeld, and C. Soe (eds) *Power Shift in Germany*, New York: Berghahn, pp. 80–97.

Frankland, E.G. and Schoonmaker, D. (1992) *Between Protest and Power* Boulder, CO: Westview Press.

E. GENE FRANKLAND

H

Haavisto, Pekka

b. 23 March 1958, Helsinki, Finland

Politician

Pekka Haavisto became the first green minister at
the national level in Europe after the set up of the
broadly-based 'rainbow government' following the
Finnish parliamentary elections in March 1995. He
held the Environment and Development Co-
operation portfolios. After being editor of three
ecologist magazines during the 1980s, he was one
of the founding members of Green League.
Member of the City Council of Helsinki (1988 –
95), he was also Member of Parliament from 1987
to 1995. He chaired his party from 1993 to 1995.
Not elected to the parliament in 1999, he left the
national arena to lead the United Nations
Environmental Programme of the Balkans Task
force (1999–2000).

CÉDRIC VAN DE WALLE

Hardin, Garrett

b. 21 April 1915, Dallas, Texas, USA

Ecologist

Garrett Hardin is an American ecologist who has
written extensively on the political and ethical
implications of ecological carrying capacity. He is
best known for his 1968 article 'The Tragedy of the
Commons', published in *Science* (162:1243–48), and
for a series of articles on human population
growth. Both topics draw ethical and political
prescriptions from the ecological concept of
carrying capacity. Carrying capacity is a measurement of the total number of human, animal and
plant organisms that can coexist within an
ecosystem without making energy demands that
exceed biophysical limits. This calculation must
reflect the sustainable yield rate for key plant and
animal species, that is, the number of plants,
wildlife or fish that can be removed each year
without compromising the population's ability to
regenerate itself.

Hardin was a founder of the 'neo-Malthusian'
school in human **ecology**, which argued that
human population would inevitably outstrip the
carrying capacity of the planet, and which argued
for draconian measures to reverse population
trends (see Hardin, 1974; 1993). However, the
work on human population growth is at best
loosely related to his seminal statement of the
incentive problem for the management of **common pool property resources**.

In Hardin's original analysis, 'the common' was
understood as a pastoral range with open access for
grazing. Hardin argued that pastoralists would
inevitably overgraze open access range systems
because individual users cannot capture the
benefits of voluntary conservation. If one herder
limits the number of animals allowed to graze,
another herder will graze more. Carrying capacity
will be exceeded and the resource will be ruined
anyway. From any individual's perspective, one
should exploit the resource as aggressively as
possible over the short run, for it will be

unavailable in the long run, no matter what one does. Ironically (hence Hardin's use of term 'tragedy') it is collectively irrational for commoners to overgraze, for this results in the collapse of a potentially renewable resource.

Ecologists quickly applied the analysis to the tendency to overfish natural **fisheries**, and the failure to conserve use of groundwater. The term 'common pool resources' denotes any open access resource system that is potentially vulnerable to the tragedy of the commons. Economists such as John Baden recognized that Hardin's tragedy of the commons has the logical structure of a game theoretic problem called 'the **prisoners' dilemma**'. The two problems have been theoretically linked ever since. Since individual action fails to produce a collectively rational result in the Prisoners' dilemma game, it is used as a paradigm example of the problem of market failure for natural resource policy (see also **paradigms**).

Hardin, Baden and many of the early analysts of common pool resources argued that a system of private **property rights** would resolve the tragedy of the commons. If users of a common pasture are given exclusive access to part of it, they will benefit from conservation and will thus have an incentive to keep total animal populations within the system's carrying capacity. The privatization solution is less aptly suited to management of fisheries and aquifers, which cannot be parcelled out in acre plots, and it presupposes a political system for administering property rights, in any case. Nevertheless, Hardin and Baden's work sparked great enthusiasm for schemes that would impose systems of tradeable property rights on surface and groundwater and on access to hunting, fishing and even airborne pollutants.

In the 1980s, analysts conducting ethnographic research on traditional users of common pool resources suggested that Hardin's original analysis of the problem was flawed. Instead of driving these resources beyond carrying capacity, fishing and herding peoples often develop co-operative management schemes. These schemes often include procedures for monitoring and enforcement, but do not rely on private property rights or on a formal state apparatus. Theorists such as Elinor Ostrom, Daniel Bromley and Bonnie McCay proposed that local, co-operative institutions could alleviate the tragic depletion of common pool resources. Their work supports the view that local empowerment of stakeholders can be an effective tool for natural resource management.

See also: Malthus, Thomas

Select bibliography

Hardin, G. (1974) 'Lifeboat Ethics: The Case Against Helping the Poor', *Psychology Today*, September.
—— (1993) *Living Within Limits: Ecology, Economics and Population Taboos*, Oxford: Oxford University Press.
Hardin, G. and Baden, J. (eds) (1974) *Managing the Commons*, San Francisco: W.H. Freeman Co.

Further reading

Bromley, D. (1989) *Economic Interests and Institutions*, New York: Basil Blackwell.
Grant, W.E. and Thompson, P.B. (1997) 'Integrated Ecological Models: Simulation of Socio-Cultural Constraints on Ecological Dynamics', *Ecological Modeling* 100: 43–59.
Ostrom, E. (1992) *Governing the Commons*, Cambridge: Cambridge University Press.

PAUL B. THOMPSON

hazardous and toxic waste management

By-products are an inevitable feature of industrial production. As production has increased and globalized over time so has the creation and accumulation of waste materials. Greater understanding of and concern for the environmental and human health impacts of exposure to some of these waste products has made their handling, treating, transportation, trading and disposal prominent political issues (see **health and the environment**).

The classification of industrial waste materials as hazardous varies from country to country and some are, of course, more toxic or hazardous than others.

A vast array of industrial waste materials are deemed to be hazardous. The category includes: discontinued products such as those made from **PCBs**; used products containing metals such as lead or mercury (see **lead poisoning** and **mercury poisoning**); used chemicals such as solvents or acids; chemicals created as by-products such as **dioxin**; used equipment such as the spent uranium rods from nuclear reactors or flat batteries; used fuel such as ash from coal-fired power stations and non-toxic but potentially hazardous by-products of **mining** such as rubble. Not all hazardous waste originates from conventional industrial production. Other sources include: waste from hospitals which may contain disease-carrying organisms; military waste such as scrapped missiles and household waste such as sewage.

Waste disposal can be by incineration, burial underground in landfill sites, or through dumping at sea. Some waste can escape disposal by being reprocessed or recycled, prompting some countries to rid themselves of it by exporting it. All disposal methods carry the potential for environmental pollution. Incineration can release carcinogenic and toxic fumes into the atmosphere. Landfill sites, which account for most household waste, can release toxins into soil and nearby water sources. Dumping at sea is the usual fate of industrial waste and this has the greatest international ramifications since it can include particularly toxic substances and can become a transboundary pollution issue. Seas and sea life can be poisoned directly in this way and humans then poisoned indirectly via water or foodstuffs.

Recognition of such forms of pollution has prompted industrialized countries to develop hazardous waste management programmes over the last 30 years. Most developed countries passed their first hazardous waste laws in the 1970s. West Germany introduced one of the earliest pieces of such legislation in 1972, American legislation was initiated in 1976 and by the 1990s most developed countries had in place extensive legislative frameworks on the transport, treatment and disposal of hazardous waste. National programmes do, however, vary in their favoured methods of disposal and in the emphasis given to minimizing waste creation and to **recycling**.

In the international arena, the dumping of hazardous waste at sea is one of the oldest areas of environmental policy-making (see **ocean dumping**). The 1972 Oslo Convention was the first regional anti-dumping agreement, committing North Sea states. Later that year an instrument covering all global seas, known commonly as the London Dumping Convention (LDC), was signed by thirteen states initiating a regime to which by 2000, 77 states were signatory. The original Oslo Convention did not prohibit the dumping of radioactive waste, but this was included by the LDC, alongside other industrial wastes and sewage sludge. The LDC outlaws the dumping of certain wastes, including oil, heavy metals and high-level radioactive materials above 'trace' levels and regulates the dumping of less hazardous materials, including low-level radioactive waste, by a permit system. The LDC was strengthened by the 1996 Protocol which prohibits the dumping of all radioactive and industrial waste and also bans the practice of waste incineration at sea. The 1996 protocol was, by 2000, yet to enter force and, even assuming that this occurs, would still be weakened by the fact that abstainers, including France, Belgium and the UK, would not be bound by the agreement. This feature of the regime is the focus of criticism from environmental NGOs.

Some regional regimes have more rigorous rules than the LDC. The Helsinki Convention, originally signed in 1974, was updated in 1992 and now outlaws all dumping in the **Baltic Sea** and has provisions curbing the dumping of wastes in national and international waters. The South Pacific Forum took action in 1995 to prohibit the importation of radioactive and other wastes and, in the same year, the Barcelona Convention extended the Mediterranean countries' dumping convention of 1976 to include the prohibiting of waste incineration at sea.

The vast majority of marine pollution comes from land-based sources, including waste discharges into rivers and coastlines. This is far less well-regulated that that from ships, platforms and aircraft covered under the LDC and regional dumping regimes. The modest and non-binding 1985 Montreal Guidelines provide the only global standards, although they were boosted by Chapter

17 of UNCED's **Agenda 21** on the Protection of the Oceans. This paved the way for the Global Programme of Action for the Protection of the Marine Environment from Land-Based Sources (GPA). The GPA, signed by 108 states and the EC in 1995, is not a regulatory regime in the manner of the LDC but has facilitated co-operation and information exchange co-ordinated by **United Nations Environment Programme** (UNEP) and centred on a GPA office in The Hague. The GPA's chief regulatory aim is to strengthen existing regional regimes that deal with land-based pollution. Amongst such Regional regimes, the Mediterranean countries signed a land-based sources protocol to the Barcelona Convention in 1980 and OSPARCOM, at its 1998 Ministerial Conference, declared an intention to eliminate all sources of North Sea and North East Atlantic pollution by 2000.

The most extensive international legal provisions regarding hazardous waste concern the issue of its transboundary movement. The strengthening of domestic hazardous waste management laws in developed countries in the 1980s, coupled with the continual increase in the generation of waste, spawned a growth in the trading of waste materials. Some developed countries, such as the UK, have actively imported hazardous waste for reprocessing, but concerns have focused on the trend for developed countries to export such materials to **less developed countries**, attracted by the comparative gains in disposal costs. The 1989 **Basel Convention** has emerged as a global regime for this issue, centred on the rule of Prior Informed Consent, which ensures importing states are properly notified of the nature of the hazardous material they are receiving.

Two international regulatory instruments go beyond Basel in controlling the trade in hazardous waste between some countries. The Lome Convention, a periodically reviewed extensive trade agreement between the **European Union** and a number of African, Caribbean and Pacific (ACP) countries, prohibits completely the export of certain hazardous wastes to the ACP countries. The 1991 Bamako Convention also prohibits the exporting of hazardous waste to African countries,

including within the definition all waste substances banned in the exporting country.

The Basel Convention has yet to embrace an embargo on the export of hazardous wastes, despite support for this from a number of states and extensive NGO lobbying. Such a development is possible in future and a further strengthening of the regime may occur if a proposal to grant United Nations Environment Programme (UNEP) powers to co-ordinate a global environmental enforcement agency is agreed. Such a body would help combat the significant problem of the evasion of the Basel Convention provisions by smuggling waste, mis-labelling containers or falsifying documentation. Such a development could, of course, radically transform a range of international environmental conventions.

See also: international environmental law; nuclear energy/nuclear waste management

Further reading

Moyers, B. (1991) *Global Dumping Ground: The International Traffic in Hazardous Waste*, Cambridge: Lutterworth.

O'Neill, K. (1998) 'Out of the Backyard: The Problems of Hazardous Waste Management at a Global Level', *Journal of Environment and Development*, 7(2): 138–63.

Probst, K. and Bierle, T. (1999) 'Hazardous Waste Management: Lessons from Eight Countries', *Environment*, November, 41(9): 22–30.

PETER HOUGH

health and the environment

Health is a state of well-being in body and mind, and environment is the physical surroundings and conditions that affect the life of an organism. Thus it is clear that the environment is responsible for the state of well-being of an organism, with the possible exception of genetically determined illness. Equally, different organisms have different environments, although these environments usually overlap. They also interact with each other in ways that are insufficiently well understood to predict outcomes when change is introduced.

Although this entry is defined by the interaction between the environment and human health, actions taken by humans will have effects upon other organisms. The impact of the environment upon health comprises those aspects of human health, including **quality of life**, that are determined by physical, chemical, biological, social and psychosocial factors in the environment. The parameters of the subject also include the theory and practice of assessing, correcting, controlling and preventing those factors in the environment that can potentially affect adversely the health of present and future generations. Environmental Impact Assessment (EIA), is the formal process used to predict the environmental consequences of a proposal or decision to introduce legislation, to implement policies and plans, or to undertake development projects.

EIA was first introduced in the USA in 1969 as a requirement of the **National Environmental Policy Act** (NEPA). Since then, an increasing number of countries have adopted EIA, introducing legislation and establishing agencies with responsibility for its implementation. In the UK the super-ministry the **Department of the Environment, Transport and Regions** (DETR) has been responsible for assessment.

EIA has mostly been applied to individual projects and has led to extensions such as health impact assessment and social impact assessment. Recent developments include cumulative effects assessment and strategic environmental assessment – the latter concerned with environmental assessment at the level of policies, programmes, and plans. The term Environmental Assessment is sometimes used as an umbrella term for these various approaches, but it is also used as an alternative for EIA. In some cases, social and economic impacts are assessed as part of the process.

Environmental health services are those services which implement environmental health policies through monitoring and control; promoting the improvement of environmental parameters; and encouraging the use of environmentally friendly and healthy technologies and behaviours. They also have a leading role in developing and suggesting new policy areas.

Health hazards can present themselves to us in various media e.g. air, water, food. The influence they can exert on our health is very complex and may be modulated by our genetic make up, psychological factors, and by our perceptions of the risks that they present. These can be general environmental health hazards, extremes of climate, occupational hazards, hazards associated with food, machinery, and transmitted disease. Health effects from economic and social consequences of environmental change are also factors.

Associations between an exposure and an adverse health effect do not, on their own, prove that the former is the cause of the latter. Many other non-causal associations could explain the findings. These concerns explain why the language in this context may well be 'hedged' despite suggestions from other sources that some postulated causal associations had been proven. This is the difficulty that environmentalists, environmental lobby groups, and others who are concerned that humans are damaging the biosphere, have in proving links.

Obvious environmental sources of ill health in humans are **air pollution** and **water pollution**. Radon gas emissions are a significant naturally occurring danger to human health. Most other forms of air pollution, such as photo-chemical smogs, are the result of human activity and cause serious respiratory disorders. Acute instances caused by accidental release of chemicals into the atmosphere can be deadly, but in most cases disperse quickly. Release of chemicals such as CFCs alter the environment and thus may in the long term damage human health (see **ozone depletion**). Examples of water pollution that affects human health include, nitrates (the salts of nitric acid) in drinking water which can cause a disease in infants that sometimes results in death, and pollution by faeces containing harmful viruses and bacteria.

Without knowing how toxic they are to the biosphere and to mankind in the long run, every day a very large number of artificial substances pollute the environment. A lack of precise and exhaustive knowledge about the consequences of all these actions and their combined effects is a dangerous deficit. How long the ecological systems can withstand this burden is unknown.

DAVID CARLISLE

Henderson, Hazel

b. 1933, Bristol, UK

Environmental activist, thinker

Originally from Bristol in the UK, Hazel Henderson is based in Florida, USA. She has described herself as unschooled, unchurched and uninstitutionalized, arguably perfect training for her role as an internationally recognized futurologist, syndicated columnist and consultant on **sustainable development**. She has advised on sustainable development in over 30 countries, served on the US Congress Office of Technology Assessment Advisory Council from 1974–80 and on many boards including the Clavert Social Investment Fund, Cousteau Society, Council on Economic Priorities and the Worldwatch Institute. Henderson has declared an end to 'flat earth' economics and in her famous three-layer cake with icing model of the economy showed how the market system is only an icing resting on the layers of public, co-operative, household and natural economies. Her books include *Creating Alternative Futures* (1978), *The Politics of the Solar Age* (1981, 1993), *Paradigms of Progress* (1991). Her most recent is *Building a Win-Win World* (1996).

MARY MELLOR

Hetch Hetchy Dam

Hetch Hetchy, once a valley of great beauty and grandeur near California's Yosemite National Park, became the site of the first important confrontation in America between supporters of an aesthetic approach to wilderness preservation and those who espoused a utilitarian view. The main protagonists were John **Muir**, who advocated the aesthetic approach, and Gifford **Pinchot**, who was the best known spokesperson for utilitarian use. The main issue was a source of water for the growing city of San Francisco. After a heated national debate that reached the US Congress, a dam was constructed, the valley flooded, a water and power supply secured, and an area of pristine wilderness lost forever. However, one key point about the debate was that it occurred at all at this time in the nation's

history. Indeed, Hetch Hetchy still serves as an example of two of the important divisions that exist in the American environmental movement.

WARREN VANDER HILL

human rights

The relationship between human rights and the environment has a number of related themes which demonstrate interdependence between the two areas of international law. The first theme is that a safe and ecologically sustainable environment should be a fundamental human right. Some recognition has been given to this in soft, that is non-binding, international law. Principle 1 of the 1972 Stockholm Declaration links the exercise of other human rights to basic environmental health (see **Stockholm Conference**). It declares that people have a 'fundamental right to freedom, equality and adequate conditions of life in an environment that permits a life of dignity and well-being'. Paragraph 5 of the 1989 Hague Declaration acknowledges that environmental degradation can undermine the 'right to live in dignity in a viable global environment'. Principle 1 of the 1992 Rio Declaration proclaims that people have the 'fundamental right to ... an environment of a quality that permits a life of dignity and well-being' (see **Rio Conference 1992**). It suggests also that people are at the centre of concerns for **sustainable development**. These are, however, non-binding agreements and they are primarily declarations of environmental principles, not human rights principles.

A second theme is that environmental degradation, and the processes which cause it, undermine other fundamental human rights. For example, the consequences of environmental degradation can include *inter alia* loss of land and home, increased poverty, food insecurity and malnutrition, and severe health risks (including death; see **health and the environment**). Practices as varied as the export and dumping of toxic wastes, the destruction of forests for timber, the construction of dams (and the involuntary removal of peoples often associated with them) also directly and indirectly undermine the social and economic rights of local peoples and communities (see **dams/hydroelectric power**). In this respect human rights to a safe environment have become closely linked with international calls for indigenous rights, particularly land rights, intellectual property rights and cultural survival.

A third theme is that it is often difficult for citizens and non-government organizations to raise environmental concerns in countries in which civil and political rights – such as rights of association, freedom of expression and a fair judicial system – are weak or effectively non-existent. A fourth theme draws international attention to the extent to which the human rights of those fighting for environmental protection are deliberately violated. Environmental activists in many countries have been subject to violence and arrest and, in some cases, death for protesting against environmentally destructive practices by governments and **multinational and transnational corporations**. This particular concern has brought environment and human rights NGOs together to pursue campaign activity. Amnesty International and the **Sierra Club**, for example, have joined forces to mobilize the Just Earth! campaign. Other organizations such as EarthRights International and Global Witness focus specifically on the connection between human and environmental rights and seek to expose violations of such rights.

A number of United Nations documents have been central to advancing the debate on the relationship between human rights and the environment. The 1993 Draft Declaration on the Rights of Indigenous Peoples, drafted under the auspices of the United Nations Sub-Commission on Prevention of Discrimination and Protection of Minorities (a sub-commission of the Commission on Human Rights) pays considerable attention to the relationship between indigenous rights and environmental rights (see **indigenous peoples**). The Sub-commission on Minorities was re-designated the Sub-Commission on the Promotion and Protection of Human Rights in 1999. A report by United Nations Special Rapporteur, Fatma Zohra Ksentini, on the relationship between human rights and the environment was presented to the Sub-Commission in 1994. It included a Draft Declaration of Principles on Human Rights and the Environment which recognized that 'human rights violations lead to environmental degradation and that environmental degradation leads to human rights violations'. The rights enumerated in the Draft Declaration included those of participation in environmental decision-making and access to full information, and freedom from discrimination through the differential impacts of environmental degradation. In December 1998, the Secretary General submitted a short report on the question of human rights and the environment to the Commission on Human Rights. Although the Secretary General had, in 1997, requested information from a wide range of UN bodies on this issue, only two (the Food and Agricultural Organization and the **United Nations Environment Programme**) had replied by the date of the report.

Some international agreements, such as the 1989 United Nations Convention on the Rights of the Child, refer to environmental rights. Attempts have also been made· to include the right to a healthy and viable environment in the European Convention on Human Rights. In general, however, international human rights law has yet to formally recognize a right to a safe and sustainable environment.

Further reading

Obiora, L.A. (1999) 'Symbolic Episodes in the Quest for Environmental Justice', *Human Rights Quarterly*, 21 (2): 464–512.

Sachs, A. (1996) 'Upholding rights and environmental justice' in L.R. Brown *et al.* (eds) *State of the World 1996*, New York: W.W. Norton & Co.

Shelton, D. (1991) 'Human Rights, Environmental Rights and the Right to Environment', *Stanford Journal of International Law*, 28 (1): 103–38.

'Statement of the International People's Tribunal on Human Rights and the Environment: Sustainable Development in the Context of Globalization', (1998) *Alternatives*, 23 (1): 109–147.

Tracy, C. (1994) 'The ·Roots of Influence: Nongovernmental Organizations and the Relationship Between Human Rights and the Environment', *Journal of International Law and Practice*, 3 (1): 21–46.

LORRAINE ELLIOTT

human scale technology

The term human scale technology was popularized by Kirkpatrick Sale in his work *Human Scale* (1980). The thesis is that size matters, and 'Bigness' in itself is a problem both in its impact on the environment and society. Scale is a condition that can determine whether a **technology**, building, government or corporation does good or evil. In western culture bigness is almost always preferred to something smaller. But Sale argues there can be greater value in smaller institutions, and increased size does not necessarily yield more human satisfaction. At some point economies of scale become diseconomies of scale. Larger cities, institutions, infrastructure at some point begin to contribute negatively to human well-being. Bureaucracies become more entrenched and the system becomes more inefficient and requires additional energy beyond what could be predicted in straight-line projections. Further, community and **democracy** suffer as institutions grow beyond some undefined human scale balance point.

Further reading

Sale, K. (1980) *Human Scale*, New York: Coward, McCann and Geoghegan.

THOMAS LOWE

humanism and the environment

Within environmental thought, definitions of both humanism and environment are strongly contested. For our purposes here, however, the latter term may be categorized as referring to the realm, whether natural or artifactual, large or small-scale, in which human and other organic life is in some sense set and/or from which it derives primary experiential stimuli, resources and the conditions for ongoing existence. Whilst this definition is terrestrially focused, leaving the wider area of cosmological environment out of immediate concern, it serves to suitably indicate the area primarily covered by environmental issues in international politics. Definition of the term humanism is more complex and immediately

necessary. The term originated from the medieval humanismus, meaning an education based on history, moral philosophy, poetry, rhetoric and grammar, and centrally concerning Greek and Roman classics. In modern environmental thought, however, the term has been used as an often confusing shorthand for a constellation of traditions derived from **Enlightenment** humanism, notably: (i) a belief in the moral centrality of humans, and human perspectives and interests; (ii) a belief in reason and scientific method as a means of discovering objective truth; (iii) belief in human autonomy and reason as basic, definitive aspects of human experience and existence; (iv) a further commitment (often linked to (iii)) to the notions of human moral equality and autonomy as basic to society's proper ethical foundations. The status of green thinkers as both inheritors and critics of the Enlightenment heritage renders their relationship to all of these elements, but especially (i) to (iii), consistently problematic, and numerous critiques of Enlightenment humanist traditions conflate and combine these elements in different ways. Humanism conceived as in (i) is most often attacked, largely by equating it with **anthropocentrism**, and here the primary critique comes from supporters of **deep ecology**.

Defenders of the humanist heritage here can use several responses, some mutually supporting. One option is to recast the notion of human centrality in less morally exclusive terms by distinguishing strong from weak anthropocentrism, in which the latter fits with ecological values; this is compatible with the claim that the attack on humanism is too broadly targeted, and should aim rather at the narrowness of prevalent humanist conceptions of value and/or the economistic and instrumentalist bias in some Enlightenment values. Defenders of humanism in the pragmatist tradition may also argue that the non-anthropocentric values that humanism supposedly ignores can be captured through a downgrading or obliteration of the anthropocentric/non-anthropocentric divide (Weston, 1992) or a consideration of long-term convergence on shared goals (Norton, 1991). Enrichment of Enlightenment humanism's values can also be recommended by invoking pre-Enlightenment virtues of **stewardship**. Further defence of humanism emanates from **social ecology** and **eco-socialism**, each of which associates the root causes of environmental destruction with social practices of hierarchy and **capitalism** rather than with humanism as such. Thus varied humanisms rooted in pragmatism, stewardship, anarchism and Marxism have sought to embody environmental values whilst deflecting the deep ecology critique. These defences lead to further tensions associated with the concerns of humanism in senses (ii) and (iii), in which scientific method, reason and autonomy are promoted. Criticism of scientific method has included attacks on the atomist and mechanistic **paradigms** with which modern science developed and calls for a new scientific paradigm. Linkage of humanist science's assumptions to normative concerns came early with attacks on the arrogance of humanism (Ehrenfeld, 1978), connecting an inflated role of reason in modern humanism to the hubristic view that all problems are scientifically soluble. Ehrenfeld argued for a greater integration of reason and emotion, and later Greens have similarly associated themselves with different conceptions of rationality.

Criticisms of atomism in scientific method connects to the tension over the concerns of humanism in sense (iv) via the role of autonomy in moral theory. Whilst Greens often stress individual liberties, many follow a socialist lead by affirming the place of autonomy as necessarily embedded in a web of natural and social relations. On the reformist side, however, strongly individualistic assumptions are manifest in **free market environmentalism**. Belief in equality is less problematic, at least on the green left, where economic equality and the linkages between equality and liberty are emphasized and discussion of the compatibility of liberalism with green thought is ongoing (see **liberalism/liberal democracy**).

References

Ehrenfeld, D. (1978) *The Arrogance of Humanism*, New York: Oxford University Press.

Norton, B.G. (1991) *Toward Unity Among Environmentalists*, Oxford: Oxford University Press.

Weston, A. (1992) *Towards Better Problems: New Perspectives on Abortion, Animal Rights, the Environment and Justice*, Philadelphia: Temple University Press.

Further reading

Barry, J. (1999) *Rethinking Green Politics: Nature, Virtue and Progress*, London: Sage.

Brennan, A. (1988) *Thinking About Nature: An Investigation of Nature, Value and Ecology*, London: Routledge.

Capra, F. (1985) *The Turning Point*, London: Flamingo.

Mathews, F. (1991) *The Ecological Self*, London: Routledge.

PIERS H.G. STEPHENS

Illich, Ivan

b. 1926, Vienna, Austria

Social philosopher, activist

One of the most innovative and profound critics of western, consumer society and a forerunner of many ecological ideas and policies. He sprang to public prominence with the publication of his best-selling, radical and provocative books such as *Deschooling Society* (1971), and *Tools for Conviviality* (1973), which articulated many ideas and proposals close to both the counter-cultural movement of the 1960s and of the nascent green movement, especially the latter's defence of **civil society** (see also **counter-culture**). One of this central themes is the ways in which modern, 'advanced' industrial societies have systematically disempowered individuals and communities, promising wealth, comfort and security, but leading to mass poverty, inequality, dependency on institutions and experts, and insecurity and unhappiness. What he calls 'radical monopolies' (both state and market based) have lead to this situation in central areas of everyday life, such as education, health, transport and energy consumption.

JOHN BARRY

India

India is a country of great diversity and with a population exceeding one hundred million: it is also the largest **democracy** in the world. India has witnessed the birth, rise and fall of many a civilization and empire. Colonial rule altered the environment in India and for the first time forests all over India were brought under the government. To further their trade and commercial interests, the British government encouraged forestation, replacing rich forests with monocultures and the natural resources were used to serve the interests of the Empire. Prior to the consolidation of India as a single political entity by the British, such resources by and large were not under any centralized control. After the British left, the forests continued to be treated in the same fashion (Gadgil and Guha, 1992).

The challenge facing India in terms of environment and **development** is enormous. Increasing population, the destruction of natural resources, the challenge to maintain and increase food output without degrading the environment and the necessity to modernize industry to control pollution: these are some of the issues that offer no easy solutions. The studies done by Tate Energy Research Institute indicate a grim picture if steps are not taken to ensure that development is not at the cost of environment. It is not that the government is unaware of these facts. But its efforts are inadequate. Still, there are signs of hope and all is not lost as there is a growing awareness about these issues at all levels. There are many success stories where people have demonstrated that environmental issues can be tackled effectively.

Environment and development debates

After India gained Independence in 1947, there was much hope that the new independent India would make rapid progress and poverty soon would be banished. The government headed by Jawaharlal Nehru opted for a socialist vision, in which the public sector would play a pivotal role and the private sector would also have a role in development. Inspired by the Soviet model and Fabian Socialism, Nehru planned for an India where **industrialization** and modernization would transform the country from an agrarian backward economy to an industrialized modern economy. Few opposed such a vision and those who opposed it were marginalized. Gandhians, like Kumarappa, who cautioned against Nehru's vision, wrote about alternative models of development based on the ideas of Mahatma **Gandhi**. As a result industrialization with utter disregard for environment, massive dams and other projects which displaced thousands of people were the norm, and until the 1970s the environment did not figure in the development debate. At the **Stockholm Conference** held in 1972, poverty was seen as the worst form of pollution and until the mid-1970s there were no stringent laws or mechanisms to control pollution. Only in the mid-1970s were laws on controlling **air pollution** and **water pollution** enacted and boards constituted to implement them. India opted for modern seed varieties, fertilizers, chemical-intensive agriculture and the widespread use of tractors for boosting agricultural output and largely followed the principles of the **green revolution** in agriculture. The **Bhopal disaster** in 1984 was an eye opener, for it showed that neither the government nor the company cared for pollution prevention and neither had the capability to handle such a disaster.

In the early 1980s the Delhi-based NGO, Center for Science and Environment brought out reports which for the first time documented the state of the environment in India. In the debate over the 'Statement on Scientific Temper', which was supported by many scientists and issued in 1981, it became clear that a section of academics and activists were questioning the dominant development model. Issues like equity and victims of development were discussed. Scientists like A.K.N.

Reddy and C.V. Sheshadri tried to develop appropriate technologies (see **appropriate technology**). Groups like Kerala Sastra Sahitya Parishad (KSSP) were also involved in environmental issues. The development model was questioned on one hand by NGOs and on the other hand by academics like Ashis Nandy, Rajni Kothari, and groups like Patriotic and People Orientated Science and Technology, and the Bhopal disaster made many lawyers take active interest in environmental issues. This led to rethinking Gandhian ideas, the role of traditional science and technologies, particularly in health, **agriculture** and irrigation, and the development of alternatives to the green revolution. Various movements and struggles at the grassroots level challenged the received wisdom on development. Thus when the Save Narmada Campaign (see **Narmada Valley development programme**) was launched in 1987 the milieu was conducive not only for supporting it, but also for a debate on displacement, rights and development. In the early 1990s the Indian government opted for relaxing controls on investment and opened up the economy for liberal foreign investment and numerous projects were set up. Whether liberalization *per se* would harm the environment is a difficult question.

To say that the debate has been influenced by the real conditions and struggles of the marginalized groups rather than by abstract notions of **environmental justice** and **environmental ethics** is no exaggeration. This does not mean that scholars and activists are unaware of philosophical issues or environment and ethics interface. Although there is no consensus on environment and development, the debates over the past two decades have had a major role in creating awareness among the public, and environmental issues are getting the profile they deserve. But often words are not translated into practice and the will to tackle environmental issues seems lacking amongst the powers that be.

Struggles and movements

Although India does not have organizations like **Sierra Club**, **Environmental Defense Fund**, **Greenpeace** or **Friends of the Earth** which have thousands of members and mobilize money and resources for struggles and campaigns, there are active environmental movements and non-governmental organizations and there are ongoing struggles all over India. **Chipko Andolan Movement** and Narmada Andolan are two well-known environmental movements. There is also an alliance called National Alliance of Peoples' Movements which includes many environmental movements and organizations. The struggles in India are often struggles for asserting basic rights, to protect sources of livelihood, and to ensure that the public interest is not sacrificed in the name of development. In the early 1950s there was a short-lived struggle against the hydroelectric project built by Tatas in Maharastra. From the 1950s to the 1980s thousands of people were displaced in the name of development projects ranging from dams, hydroelectric projects, thermal power stations to industrial sites, but the opposition was weak, isolated and did not get widespread attention. It is only since the 1980s that development-caused displacements and environmental problems have attracted widespread attention. For example, the movement against the Narmada Valley development programme focused attention on the displaced populations and the heavy price paid by them. In fact only as a result of this movement was there a nationwide debate on the rehousing and rehabilitation of displaced populations and policies were subsequently revised. However, this does not guarantee that there will not be forced displacements in the future.

In the early 1980s the Silent Valley Project was abandoned as it would have destroyed an ever-green rainforest area in Kerala. This was due to the campaign by Kerala Sastra Sahitya Parishad and environmentalists (Zachariah and Suryamoorthy, 1994). In the 1980s and 1990s courts often passed orders when cases were brought about pollution and environmental destruction on account of development projects. These cases were often filed as public interest litigations and forced the state to take certain steps which would not have been taken but for the intervention of the courts. For example, it was only after the court intervened that steps were taken to ensure that rivers in Tamil Nadu state were not polluted by tanneries. Similarly it was the Supreme Court of India which made the government ensure that the Taj Mahal at Agra was not damaged due to pollution from foundries. But such interventions are not without problems. For example, when the Supreme Court ordered that 8,378 industrial units in Delhi be closed and relocated elsewhere, it was labourers who were the worst hit (Delhi, 1997). Environmental justice for the poor would mean that their livelihoods are not sacrificed for the sake of the environment. But this is not a question of jobs versus environment, for what is lacking is an effective implementation of laws as well as using environment-friendly technologies. For example, in the case of the leather industry, both the government and the industry could have found solutions before the courts intervened. Only after political pressure did the industry and the government plan to set up effluent treatment plants. However, it has to be remembered that it is workers who are affected when units are closed for violating environmental laws. Working conditions are bad, the industry does not adhere to laws, and the government is often indifferent. Thus, one cannot expect the workers alone to suffer in the name of environmental protection. In the case of the fishing industry, the struggles were against trawlers, and traditional fishermen had to fight to ensure that mechanized trawlers did not plunder the resources of the seas (see **fisheries**). So a ban on using trawlers for some months was imposed to ensure that during the breeding season fish were not caught by the trawlers. This had a positive impact (Kurien, 1993).

There have been conflicts over rights to traditional sources of livelihood of the forest-dwellers and people in the nearby areas *vis-à-vis* the rights of the state to protect forests. By law the state has control over the forests and in the name of conservation access to forests was denied, and people were banned from gathering forest produce or wood for fuel. But over the years there has been a move to ensure that stakeholders are involved in conservation and in this perspective conservation and people are not pitted against each other (Kothari *et al.*, 1996). Joint **forest management** schemes in which village communities are involved in the protection of forests and have a share in the benefits, have been put into practice in many states.

India has also seen many innovative experiments in natural resources protection, regeneration and **sustainable development**. These include regulating grazing, building check dams, water-harvesting systems, developing agro-forestry and afforestation. In many villages NGOs have done commendable work in sustainable development. When in 2000 many states experienced droughts it was found that villages that had check dams, rainwater harvesting systems, and used traditional technologies for catching and storing water could cope well or were not affected much by the drought. Two academics who have done much work in sustainable development in India have suggested that there should be a cyclical system of development and involvement of people for sustainable development to become a reality (Chopra and Kadekodi, 1999).

The 1990s saw struggles against new development projects and, despite much opposition, the Dabhol Power Project has been commissioned. The Narmada Bacho Andolan (NBA) is continuing the struggle and it is more than a decade old by now. The NBA was the first to mobilize international opinion against the Project and for the first time in India the **World Bank** agreed to appoint a panel to examine the project and its implementation. Greenpeace has opened an office in New Delhi and is working with groups on trade in toxic wastes and pollution issues (see **hazardous and toxic waste management**). There is much scope for interaction and co-operation between groups in India and environmental movements elsewhere.

Environmental history and environmental politics

Apart from NGOs like the Center for Science and Environment, and research centres like the Tata Energy Research Institute, there is an active community of environmental scholars and activists in India. Thus debates on environment are often intense and it is not unusual to find voices that go against conventional wisdom. The debates have been enriched by scholars like Gail Omvedt and Bina Agarwal who have tried to bring in *dalit* (the 'untouchables' caste) and feminist perspectives on environmental issues. Omvedt, for example, has

been critical of attempts to provide solutions that ignore caste relations in India. After the publication of Guha's *Unquiet Woods* (1989) there was much interest in environmental history. In recent years many scholars – Mahesh Rangarajan, Ravi Rajan, Nandini Sundar, Sumit Guha, Sivaramakrishnan, to name a few – have published volumes on **environmental history** in India. Some academics are researching the movements and ongoing struggles as well. The irony is that it is often only the English-speaking population in India that has access to these debates and scholarly writings, as English still continues to be main language for such debates.

Most political parties in India do not have any clear-cut idea about environmental issues, and by and large they are in favour of industrialization and development. Apart from mouthing slogans or expressing concern for the environment once in a while, they have no concrete plans on these issues. Thus while a local branch of a political party may oppose a plant or project, the central leadership may not be against it. In some cases, like the Narmada Project, there is a consensus cutting across party lines about such projects. For example all the political parties in Gujarat are committed to this project. Similarly all the parties support nuclear power as a solution for the energy crisis (see **nuclear energy/nuclear waste management**). And there is no green electoral constituency in India. Thus often it is the pressure from NGOs, peoples' movements, directives from courts or international agencies or donors that results in policy changes in environmental and developmental issues rather than action by political parties.

In global negotiations the Indian government often takes a position that is critical of the North. And in this it is NGOs like the Research Foundation for Science, Technology and Natural Resources Policy (RFSTNRP), CSE, TERI that are more vocal and play a major role in shaping public opinion or in bringing issues to the public's attention. India is a signatory to the Convention on Biodiversity but has yet to pass laws that govern **biodiversity** and prevent biopiracy. India often demands that the developed nations should transfer environmentally friendly technologies and they should not expect countries like India to sacrifice their development for the sake of protecting the global environment (see **technology transfer**). Although many NGOs agree with this view they point out that blaming the North is insufficient as the policy measures of the government often promote growth at the cost of environment and environmental policy aims such as the **polluter pays principle** are not implemented. For example, the government heavily subsidizes growth in sectors such as forestry (Gadgil and Guha, 1995)

India ranks low in terms of the UN's Human Development Index and despite decades of planning and development, the absolute number of people in poverty has not decreased. The nexus between poverty and environment is complex. To view this as a vicious cycle: poverty – environmental degradation – more poverty, is not only misleading but also fails to understand the complexity of the issue (Nadkarni, 2000). Gagdil and Guha (1995) have broadly classified Indians as omnivores, ecosystem people and ecological refugees. The poor in India fall in the last two categories. Gadgil and Guha have made this observation in the context of **ecology** and equity in India. But the issue is more complex than this and **globalization** and the consequent opening up of the Indian economy has brought new questions and challenges. It is true that globalization may bring pressures to produce more environmentally friendly goods and the use of better technologies. However, it may also put more pressure on the environment as more mega development projects will also be implemented. The trade and environment debate illustrates the different perspectives of the **North/South divide** in this. While most environmental NGOs welcome the use of trade sanctions to protect turtles, the NGOs in India oppose it. They feel that turtles should be protected but that to use the environment as a pretext for restricting imports is not justified. In issues like clean development mechanism, joint implementation under the Kyoto Protocol, using bioprospecting for biodiversity conservation, NGOs in India are often at odds with views of many NGOs in developed nations (see **Kyoto Conference/Protocol**; **biopiracy/ bioprospecting**).

The future of the environment in India depends on what is done in the next few decades. But until some concrete measures are taken the signs do not augur well either for the environment or for its people. For example **air pollution** is taking its toll on peoples' health in cities like New Delhi (see **health and the environment**). In the decades to come India may witness more struggles and also more environmental policy initiatives. There are enough indications that what lies ahead is going to be more complex and more challenging than in the past. But it is not going to be a continuation of past policies where the environment was sacrificed on the altar of development.

References

Chopra, K. and Kadekoli, K. (1999) *Operationalising Sustainable Development*, New Delhi: Sage.

Delhi, J.A.M. (1997) 'Order That Felled A City', *Economic and Political Weekly*, June 28.

Gadgil, M. and Guha, R. (1992) *This Fissured Land: An Ecological History of India*, New Delhi: Oxford University Press.

—— (1995) *Ecology and Equity*, London: Routledge.

Guha, R. (1989) *The Unquiet Woods:Ecological Change and Peasant Resistance in the Himalayas*, New Delhi: Oxford University Press.

Kothari, A, Singh, S and Suri, S (eds) (1996) *People and Protected Areas: Towards Participatory Conservation in India*, New Delhi: Sage.

Kurien, J. (1993) 'Ruining the Commons: Overfishing and Fisher Workers' Actions in South India', *The Ecologist*, 23(1).

Nadkarni, M.V. (2000) 'Poverty, Environment, Development: A Many-Patterned Nexus', *Economic and Political Weekly*, April 1.

Zachariah, M. and Sooryamurthy, R. (1994) *Science For Social Revolution*, New Delhi: Sage.

K. RAVI SRINIVAS

indigenous peoples

The category of 'indigenous' peoples is not sensibly defined by hard and fast parameters that can be presumed to apply in all contexts, but is an appellation that evokes broadly comparable experiences of history, power and difference. Some 350 million people are claimed as indigenous by the International Work Group for Indigenous Affairs. For people who identify themselves positively as indigenous, academic argument about niceties of definition matter far less than the recognition of common disadvantage in a range of life contexts including political representation, **environmental justice**, and individual and collective **human rights**, even though these experiences vary immensely when comparing the formations of indigeneity in different continents. That there is great diversity between indigenous peoples reflects both the tenacity of locally distinctive lifeways, and variable relationships to socio-political contexts of colonial encounter with their diverse dynamics of economic, environmental and ethnic marginalization. The tendency of environmentalists to treat indigenous people as a singular 'Other', whether scathing or respectful of their relationships to **biodiversity**, needs to be questioned by attending to the historical representation of the native knowledge systems, and the debates on human-environmental interaction within anthropology.

Colonialism impacted massively on the people now recognized as indigenous in terms of settlement patterns, plantation and extraction economies, and the spread of diseases, alternating structures of community and livelihood (Wolf, 1982). The systematic study and appreciation of indigenous societies outside evolutionist mindsets concerning 'the primitive' only began in earnest after the First World War with the new methodology of intensive anthropological fieldwork, aimed at seeing the world 'from the native's point of view'. Knowledge achieved by participation in indigenous lifeways effectively dispelled the colonial era's speculative concerns with imagined passages from magic and religion to science, and of unilineal stages of economic evolution from hunting and gathering, through pastoralism and **agriculture** to industrial production. Rather than confining 'totemic' thought to pre-logical identifications of humans with animals, anthropologists discovered both practical rationales for cultural valuations of natural species, and the sophisticated logical possibilities that animals and plants afford for thinking about biosocial difference. And instead of

the idea that simple technologies condemn people to hunt, gather or cultivate in desperate existences of hardship and toil, systematic data on subsistence patterns revealed that the combination of ecological knowledge, skill, and co-operative labour released people to spend more time at leisure and in non-subsistence cultural activities than the average factory worker.

After colonialism, however, modern **technology transfer** remained the dominant **paradigm** for post Second World War **development** policies up to the 1970s, which perceived 'indigenous' culture (of course used here more broadly than referring simply to Indigenous Peoples) as a barrier or constraint to innovation through capitalized inputs and private property systems. In parallel to development modernization, nature conservation policies based on models of **national parks** as wilderness sanctuary imposed modern designs for maintaining enclaves of authentic biodiversity separated off from human intervention. Human economy had to be technologized, and nature de-humanized, leaving nowhere for indigenous people to turn. Many were displaced from their lands in both scenarios.

From the 1980s, critics of both development and conservation policies produced a body of literature, within an empirical populist paradigm though considerably influenced by Levi-Strauss's concept of 'the science of the concrete', demonstrating both the cultural specificity and inappropriateness of applications of western science in non-western environments, and the locally attuned value of much indigenous knowledge (e.g. Richards, 1985). In conjunction with the attention paid to knowledge, the populist paradigm advocated 'participatory' processes of including local/indigenous people in the planning and implementation of development and conservation projects, giving rise to terms such as Indigenous Technical Knowledge, and Community Forestry. Participation has not, though, proved an unqualified success as long time frames for change are needed, and many local/indigenous people recognize that overall contexts of political marginalization, cultural discrimination, and ecological injustice persist. Participatory concepts, such as national park buffer zones, offer intermediate spaces for legitimate local use purposes between strictly protected areas of **nature** and unbridled human activity. They demonstrate the pragmatic unfeasibility of 'fortress conservation' in areas where non-local authorities are surrounded by poor indigenous populations who rely on commons for many resources, but also perhaps indicate the fragmented viability of the concept of pure nature in the era of 'reflexive' or 'post' modernity. It is probably no simple coincidence that at the same time **biodiversity** is increasingly recognized outside 'wilderness' and within environments of explicit human engagement, such as the cultivation of distinctive varieties of crops (agro-biodiversity) by local communities in specialized ecological contexts such as mountains, or forest-savannah interfaces.

Environmental theory has held a singular fascination with representations of indigenous peoples for the richness of their mythological portrayals of human-environmental intimacy, for holistic models of super-natural interconnection between **landscapes** and species, and for culturally elaborated declarations of respect towards encompassing powers obliging humans to reciprocate or acknowledge their dependence on a greater sentient partnership. The issue of whether indigenous people can be said to practice sustainable livelihoods, or to conserve the environment intentionally is more fraught. Generalizing from a limited range of genuinely in-depth studies, in which optimal conditions for comparative assessment do not pertain due to factors of displacement, demographic fluctuation, and external interventions would be unwise. Ethnographic studies that have attempted to answer this question tend to answer that if conservation is practised it is not that of 'scientific' conservation (Ingold, 2000). The framing of the question is fundamentally mistaken, as a generalized conceptual entity of the environment, let alone one in need of being conserved, is an alien concept to people whose very engagement with their lifeworlds precludes the distanced perspective that has made the environment a 'transcendental object' in the structure of western thought. Attempting to introduce environmental awareness among indigenous people can lead to insurmountable problems of cultural translation, as Milton demonstrates commenting on the Mende people of the Gola Forest region of Sierra Leone:

'The Mende were not in a position to protect the forest, not only because it was not property, but also because the forest, in their view, cared for and supported *them*' (Milton, 1996:126).

Given the contingency of the category of indigenous people on the historical conditions of colonialism, it has to be asked whether this identity will continue to serve as a salient gathering place for diverse communities to find a voice for articulating collective experience and projects. Some conclude that the post-colonial context of environmental politics demands, and is giving rise to, wholly new associations of interests and hybrid alliances, which the primordial connotations of the indigenous cannot effectively participate in. The problem with this formulation, though, is that it over-essentializes what are processual, heterogeneously constituted qualities of identity among indigenous people. Many indigenous people happily live with hybridity and invention in their daily lives, and often in ritual through the transformative, translocal spirit quests of shamans. Ingold even suggests the idea of indigenous people as holding to an intrinsic and primordial relationship with land and territory *transmitted through the principle of descent* is nothing less than a contradictory effect of the need to negotiate with the dominant discourses of the state and its legal principles of property relations (2000: 133). The relational qualities of native identity and environmental dwelling thereby lose out to the linear, inherited, genealogical fixity of the colonizing culture, which treats the land as a surface to be occupied, rather than a source of vitality for those who live on it. Similar advantages present themselves to emphasizing recognized principles of descent in relation to state and international legal systems, such as reserved entitlements to education, welfare, and intellectual **property rights**.

See also: biopiracy/bioprospecting; culture and the environment; environmental justice; land reform; noble savage, myth of; wildlife management

References

Ingold, T. (2000) *Perception of the Environment: Essays in Livelihood, Dwelling and Skill*, London: Routledge.

Milton, K. (1996) *Environmentalism and Cultural Theory*, London: Routledge.

Richards, P. (1985) *Indigenous Agricultural Revolution*, London: Hutchinson.

Wolf, E. (1982) *Europe and the People Without History*, Berkeley: University of California Press.

Further reading

Descola, P. and Palsson, G. (eds) (1996) *Nature and Society*, London: Routledge.

Gupta, A. (1998) *Postcolonial Developments*, Durham: Duke University Press.

Levi-Strauss, C. (1966) *The Savage Mind*, Oxford: Oxford University Press.

Posey, D. *et al.* (1999) *Cultural and Spiritual Values of Biodiversity: A Complementary Contribution to the Global Biodiversity Assessment*, United Nations Environment Programme, London: Intermediate Technology Publications.

BEN CAMPBELL

Indonesia

A seminar on 'Environmental Management and National Development' held in May 1972 in Bandung can be considered the first event signalling the beginning of environmental awareness in Indonesia. This seminar was part of national preparations for the First World Environmental Conference held in Stockholm in June 1972.

In 1972, Indonesia set up an inter-departmental committee to formulate a programme for all environmental policies. The programme was set out in the 1973–8 'Guidelines on State Policy' and in the 'Second Five Year Development Plan' (1974–9). In 1975 the Commission for Inventory and Evaluation of Natural Assets was established, followed by the State Ministry for the Supervision of Development and the Environment in 1979. The Minister of Internal Affairs supported the environmental effort by establishing the Population and Environment Bureau within the Provincial Secretariat.

In 1981, to encourage public awareness of environmental issues, the Government introduced the *Kalpataru* Award. This prize is awarded annually to individuals or communities who are judged to have taken exceptional initiatives in environmental care without expectation of financial reward or prestige. The Act No. 4/1982 regarding the 'Basic Provisions for Environmental Management' is considered to be one of the most important pieces of legislation, since it is the basis of several provisions and regulations concerning the environment (see **environmental management**). It emphasizes that people and their actions constitute one component of the environment. Another milestone is the enactment of Government Regulation no. 29/1986. This is the Environmental Impact Management Analysis (AMDAL), a directive for assessing any development project that is likely to have significant environmental impact. The Environmental Impact Management Agency (*Bapedal*) was set up in 1990 to monitor and control development activities which have a significant effect on the environment. Other significant regulations concerning the environment are the Environmental Quality Standards (1990), Waste Water Quality Standards (1991) and Spatial Planning Regulations (1992). Due to the increasing complexity of population and environment problems, the State Ministry for the Environment was established in 1993.

Most issues of **sustainable development** in Indonesia, having economic, ecological and sociocultural aspects, are related in one way or another to the management of land. Land-related issues of efficiency, equity and **sustainability** have become increasingly important as a result of growing population pressure and changes in the natural environment and in economic activity. The conversion of upland forest to agricultural use, the rapid expansion of urban areas and the spread of industrial companies in and around urban areas are some examples of the above issues in Java.

Since the late 1960s, the Government of Indonesia has encouraged the exploitation of commercial timber resources by issuing forest concessions. Government regulation of selective forest concessions, combined with careful logging and replanting programmes, aims to allow the production forests to be managed sustainably. However, this commercial exploitation of timber resources has contributed to the loss of forest cover and increasing concern over the rate of deforestation (see **forest management**).

Examples of environmental issues involve major agricultural and mining projects. A huge agriculture project in Kalimantan aimed to convert 5.8 million hectares of peat moss land into paddy field farmland. Although Regulation No. 24/1992 has defined the above location as a protected area, this project was started in 1996 without any detailed feasibility study or Environmental Impact Management Analysis report as required by Regulation No. 29/1986. Two Presidential Decrees were enacted to support the above project. Although only three per cent of the project was realized, further studies reported massive environmental destruction including the disappearance of 28 wild animal species, land and **water pollution**, increased potential for both flooding and forest fire, and increased impact on **global warming**. Other negative impacts were uncertainty of life prospects for the migrants who have already moved in from Java to manage the project, and accelerated deforestation due to the usage of channels built for this project for transporting logs.

The Freeport Mine in Irian and the Pulp and Rayon factory in North Sumatra are two other cases creating major environmental problems. Although some local communities and non-government organizations have raised objections, the Soeharto government approved foreign investment in both projects. The current Wahid government is trying to amend the contracts of both investments to achieve better environmental outcomes.

Despite the legal apparatus described above, it is obvious that in Indonesia the political role is still dominant in the decision-making process. Many environmental issues are still questioned by the community and remain unresolved. Its centralized system of government, regulatory inconsistency and the injustice or weakness in law enforcement practices can be considered as the main causes of Indonesia's environmental problems.

See also: development; forest management; mining; Stockholm Conference

References

World Bank (1994) *Indonesia: Environment and Development*, Washington DC: World Bank.

Further reading

TEMPO (Selected investigation report) (1999) *Dari Skandal ke Skandal*, Jakarta: Pusat Data Analisa Tempo.

ISPURWONO SOEMARNO

industrialization

Industrialization is a socio-economic process, originating in the UK in the mid-nineteenth century, characterized by the development of new techniques of mass production through the application to manufacturing of science, **technology**, new forms of energy and rational principles of organization. The period during which production and economic primacy passed from **agriculture** to industry, together with its associated socio-technical changes, is known as the Industrial Revolution.

The first industry to be reorganized along industrial principles was the textile industry of Scotland and the North of England which saw the development of a number of manufacturing innovations which, when combined with the development of steam-powered engines, led to vast increases in productivity, the rapid decline of home-working, and an increase in the size of factories. As inventions were made in other industries, towns and cities based on industrial production grew very rapidly in size and were linked to one another and the ports, first by canal and then by the new steam-powered transport system, the railway. These developments led to the concentration of the industrial workforce within these urban areas, the growth of a new, working **class**, and the emergence of a new class of environmental problems.

These developments spread throughout western Europe and also to the USA where systems of mass production were subject to a higher level of rationalization through the work of Frederick Taylor whose techniques led to an increased degree of specialization of labour. Taylor's ideas were further refined by Fayol who enunciated the principle of the chain of command, that is, each employee receives orders from only one superior. The objective of the industrial process, that high volumes of output be achieved through the rational application of management principles to integrate the production of a standardized product reached its apogee in 'Fordism', the label given to the principles underlying the Ford Car Company's production-line.

In summary, then, industrialization involves specialization of labour and division of process into simplified tasks, simplification and standardization of products and components, the development of specialized machines, and integrated planning of the production process. As a result of its perceived benefits, this idealized model of the production process became the basis of the model of **development** both aspired to and imposed upon the Third World.

Industrialization has unquestioningly led to the improvement of the standard of living of a significant proportion of the world's population. It has, however, been criticized from a variety of perspectives and has been blamed for many of the negative aspects of contemporary society. Criticisms have tended to focus around six general areas, the first of which is that of natural resources.

As noted, industrialization has led to significant increases in the output of manufactured goods. However, this increase in output has been associated with significant increases in the rate of use both of primary raw materials as inputs to the manufacturing process and also of fossil-fuels as an energy source for production and **transportation** (see **fossil fuels**).

Second, increased production has led to an increase in the amount and type of pollution created. This takes the form of waste material which is not, for whatever reason, used as an input to a further process and which must either be disposed of in a specific place (through, for example, landfill), or released into the general biosphere (as, for example, is the case with waste gases from fossil-fuelled transport). Thus, blame for

air and land pollution, **global warming** and **ozone depletion** have all been laid at the door of industrialization. These issues of pollution have been intensified in the large urban areas which developed as a result of industrialization. Over the period to 1980, these areas had tended to develop around concentrated areas of industrial production and also required extensive transport systems. As a result, the worst manifestations of pollution tended to be found in these areas.

Fourth, this tendency to uproot and concentrate population in large urban areas has been held by some to increase the degree of anomie present in the population, leading to a breakdown in traditional social bonds, resulting in what *A Blueprint for Survival* (1972) predicted would be the collapse of society.

Industrialization's requirement for specialization of task has been held responsible for a process of labour de-skilling which, echoing some of Marx's earlier writings, is claimed to result in the failure of the individual to be able to express themselves (and so grow to their full potential) through the activity of producing (or work).

Finally, the requirement that there be significant concentrations of capital in order that the investment required for industrialization can be made has led to concerns about control and power. These have centred around either the power of the state (in socialist countries), the power of monopolies and industrial cartels (in capitalist countries) or the inability of the Third World to chart it own course through dependence on the richer countries of the World.

See also: capitalism; globalization; progress

ALISTAIR McCULLOCH

Inglehart, Ronald

b. USA

Academic

Since 1978 Ronald Inglehart has been Professor of Political Science at the University of Michigan, where he has also been the Programme Director of the Center for Political Studies, Institute for Social Research. During his distinguished academic career, Inglehart has focused on cultural changes and their political consequences.

Beginning with an article in 1971 and elaborated upon in numerous articles and books through the years, Inglehart has argued that the value priorities of western populations have been changing because of the entry into the electorate of the postwar generation of citizens who in their formative years experienced relative peace and prosperity. These new middle-class citizens have shifted their emphasis to 'higher order' values, such as self-actualization, and away from traditional materialistic concerns about economic and physical security. Barring some economic disaster or societal breakdown, these 'post-materialists' are expected to retain their basic value priorities through the life cycle, differentiating them from other generations. In other words, Inglehart's theory of value change is based on two hypotheses: scarcity (individuals place greatest subjective value on vital things in shortest supply) and socialization (individuals' basic values reflect the societal conditions they experienced as pre-adults).

Although the levels have varied between countries, numerous empirical studies have found that supporters of the green movement and parties when surveyed have tended disproportionately to express 'post-materialist' values. There have been many academic critiques of Inglehart's theory and methodology, which he has continued to refine through the years. However, his term 'post-materialist' not only pervaded the social science literature of the 1970–90s, but found its way into the vocabulary of European journalists and green politicians themselves. Inglehart's research in subsequent years has extended to many non-western countries. Since 1988, he has chaired the steering committee of the World Values Survey, whose three waves have gathered data on public values in 60 countries.

Select bibliography

Inglehart, R. (1971) 'The Silent Generation in Europe: Inter-generational Change in Post-industrial Societies', *American Political Science Review*, 65: 991–1017.
—— (1990) *Culture Shift in Advanced Industrial Society*, Princeton: Princeton University Press.
—— (1997) *Modernization and Post-modernization: Cultural, Economic and Political Change in 43 Societies*, Princeton: Princeton University Press.

E. GENE FRANKLAND

Inspectorate of Pollution

Her Majesty's Inspectorate of Pollution (HMIP) was created in April 1987 through the amalgamation of four existing inspectorates for **air pollution**, **hazardous and toxic waste management**, radiochemicals, and aspects of **water pollution**. Important functions remained outside HMIP and it was essentially part of a longer process of structural and procedural transition. Under the Environmental Protection Act 1990, HMIP became responsible for the implementation of a system of integrated pollution control. It can also be seen in the context of a transformation of the British regulatory approach away from informality and administrative discretion towards a more legalistic approach (see **regulatory approaches**). The transition from a fragmented organizational pattern to an integrated agency for pollution control was completed when HMIP was incorporated into the **Environment Agency** in 1996.

ALAN GREER

intentional communities

Intentional communities are *groups of people with shared values who have chosen to live together in order to achieve common goals*. These goals might include spiritual purity, friendship and love, social equality, economic sharing, artistic expression, **stewardship** of the earth, political change, or community itself. Intentional communities have sometimes been called 'communes', implying collective ownership of property; 'colonies', referring to their origins in and ties to some larger entity; 'cooperative communities', to suggest their primary behavioural norm, 'alternative communities', reflecting their divergence from mainstream culture, 'experimental communities', to stress their innovative character, or 'ecovillages', epitomizing a growing global environmental consciousness. Many intentional communities are rural and agricultural, while others are urban, centred in a single large house, several neighbouring homes, or a co-housing complex of shared and private space.

Christian communitarians cite the example of Jesus and his followers, among whom 'all that believed were together, and had all things common' (Acts 2:44). Historical examples of intentional community include medieval European religious orders, Tibetan Buddhist monasteries, and the American communalists that impressed Marx and Engels: the Ephrata Society, Shakers, Harmonists and New Harmonists, Zoarites, Oneida Perfectionists, Fourierist Phalanxes, and Amana Inspirationists. Some historical cases span centuries and persist to the present, notably the Anabaptist Hutterians, Bible–communist farmers who originated in sixteenth-century Europe, came to North America in the nineteenth century, and grew to 40,000 members in almost 400 colonies by 2000.

Intentional communities number in the tens of thousands around the world today. Relatively large and long-lived ones include 250 socialist kibbutzim in Israel, 200 spiritual Emissary groupings and two dozen Twelve Tribes of Israel communities around the world, dozens of Catholic, liberation-theology 'base communities' in Latin America, and more than a dozen Christian Camphill communities in Ireland, the United Kingdom, and North America. Australia, New Zealand, the United Kingdom, and the western USA contain hundreds of highly diverse intentional communities.

Intentional communities commonly criticize society for its poverty, crime, sin, violence, competitiveness, corruption, oppression, alienation, **consumerism**, and ecocide. They suggest, and embody, solutions such as non-competitive values, shared ownership, rule by consensus, spiritual discipline, hands-on education, and **ecological economics**. They expect a higher level of personal interaction and responsibility for the common good than does the surrounding society. They draw a clearer distinction between residents and non-residents than do the citizens of most small towns. Intentional communities offer an intimacy that attracts some people while repelling others. Most welcome prospective visitors who

contact them ahead of time, and many have websites.

Despite shared features, intentional communities differ dramatically from one another. Most are small, with only a handful of residents; by contrast, Sunrise Ranch (Colorado) has about 100, and an Israeli kibbutz may have over 500. Some, like the Hutterian colonies, are strictly religious, while communes of the Federation of Egalitarian Communities are secular. Gender-role distinctions vary from minimal at Twin Oaks to moderate at The Farm to pronounced at many religious communities. Even among Catholic communities, liberation-theology villages engage in dramatic political action, whereas most convents and monasteries remain politically aloof. Property is owned collectively among Hutterians and kibbutzniks, whereas co-housing residents own their own homes, appliances, and vehicles. Decision-making is authoritarian at Padanaram, formally democratic among Emissaries, and consensual at Alpha Farm, Oregon.

Citing tragedies such as Jonestown and the Branch Davidian holocaust, some observers view intentional communities as 'cults', a pejorative term implying manipulative leadership, groupthink, and unhealthy isolation from the outside world. While this characterization is true of some intentional communities, it is untrue of most. In fact, a strong trend among contemporary communities is toward greater internal diversity, privacy, individual freedom, and connection with mainstream society. What is beyond dispute is the wide range of material and cultural contributions such communities have made to the outside world, from Owenite public libraries, Shaker furniture, Oneida silverware, and Amana refrigerators, to more recent communitarian innovations in **organic farming**, holistic health, natural birth, and solar technology.

Influenced by the work of Rosabeth Moss Kanter, scholars used to judge intentional communities as 'successes' or 'failures' according to their size and longevity. Today most analysts accept Pitzer's (1997) concept of communalism as a developmental phase in some larger movement, often originating in spiritual or political beliefs and eventually evolving beyond communal living for most members. In an age of environmental crisis, social malaise, and the breakdown of traditional communities, the experience of intentional communitarians may be worth close examination.

See also: co-operatives; counter-culture; New Age; new social movements; social economy, informal activity in

References

Pitzer, D. (ed.) (1997) *America's Communal Utopias*, Chapel Hill, NC: University of North Carolina Press.

Further reading

F.I.C. (2000) *Communities Directory: A Guide to Intentional Communities and Co-operative Living*, Missouri: FIC: Rutledge.

MICHAEL S. CUMMINGS

intergenerational justice

'We do not inherit the earth from our parents, but borrow it from our children'. This native American Indian saying captures the central moral idea embodied in claims of intergenerational justice. The idea that we owe those who come after us an environment and environmental resources that are no worse (or better) than those we inherited, is something that is central to environmental politics, both in theory and practice (de-Shalit, 1993). Claims of intergenerational justice are at the heart of such central concepts, practices and policy proposals as **sustainable development**, **environmental ethics**, **stewardship**, and policies and statements regarding our environmental obligations to those who come after us can be found in the manifestos and programmes of green parties and **environmental movements** worldwide.

While swathes of forests have been sacrificed in the philosophical, ethical and policy implications and demands of intergenerational justice, there are three core issues that need to be stressed. The first is that future generations stand in a position of vulnerability *vis-à-vis* those presently living, in that decisions taken now can result in future genera-

tions inheriting an environment and environmental resources which can result in them having lower standards of living than they otherwise would have. The second is that, unlike previous human generations, this present one has the capacity to greatly affect the environment in ways previous generations were unable to, largely due to developments in science, **technology**, and economic organization. Third, this present generation has the knowledge that the environment is being radically altered as a result of the technological, economic, social and political decisions and modes of interaction with the environment. And with this power and knowledge comes responsibility for those yet to be born who will (for better or worse) have to live with the environmental consequences of decisions taken today. This responsibility is what we owe future generations, what, as a strict matter of justice between generations, are our environmental 'duties' and 'obligations' corresponding to the 'rights' of those not yet born.

Intergenerational justice is often used as the 'applied ethical' basis for environmental politics and policies, since while it is anthropocentric, it can both create a 'convergence' between 'anthropocentric' and 'ecocentric' ethical positions and thus forge 'unity among environmentalists' (Norton, 1991), and more importantly, create support among the public for environmental policies (especially sustainable development), since unlike ecocentric arguments based on the **intrinsic value** of nature, intergenerational justice is a familiar and widely understood and supported idea (Barry, 1999). As such, intergenerational justice remains one of the most powerful and practical ethical bases for environmental politics and policies.

See also: anthropocentrism; deep ecology; distributive justice; eco-centrism; environmental justice; green political theory

References

Barry, J. (1999) *Rethinking Green Politics: Nature, Virtue and Progress*, London: Sage.
de-Shalit, A. (1993) *Why Posterity Matters*, London: Routledge.

Norton, B. (1991) *Toward Unity Among Environmentalists*, Oxford: Oxford University Press.

JOHN BARRY

intermediate technology

Coined by E.F. Schumacher in his classic work *Small is Beautiful*. From his experience in **India**, Schmuacher came to appreciate the futility of introducing large-scale western **technology** into remote rural areas. Local farmers could not fuel nor maintain such equipment. Even if initially the technology was made available through a grant process. Schumacher's idea was to develop equipment and technology more suited to the infrastructure of local areas. He formed the Intermediate Technology Group in London and developed tools and technology which were more affordable, easier to maintain and required lower energy to operate than previous large-scale western products. Some saw this as an effort to supply third-world economies with inferior goods, and Schmuacher spent considerable effort to demonstrate that this was not the case. The technology he advocated was simply at a different scale and more in touch with the realities facing many poor rural areas.

Further reading

Schumacher, E.F. (1973) *Small is Beautiful*, New York: Harper Colophon.

THOMAS LOWE

International Atomic Energy Authority

The International Atomic Energy Authority (IAEA) was established under the auspices of the United Nations on 29 July 1957 as a means of implementing the 'Atoms for Peace' initiative presented to the UN General Assembly by American President, Dwight Eisenhower, in December 1953. As the main inter-governmental agency for scientific and technical co-operation in the nuclear field the IAEA operates in five main

areas guided by a Board of Governors. These are safeguards and physical protection; nuclear safety; nuclear energy (see **nuclear energy/nuclear waste management**); technical co-operation; and nuclear sciences and applications. The IAEA is thus responsible for both development and regulation in the nuclear sphere. Twenty-two governors are elected via the General Conference of the 130 member nations. The remaining 13 members are nominated by the Board. The promotion of nuclear energy systems in Africa and the technical adequacy of IAEA inspection regimes to prevent nuclear proliferation have been subject to much criticism (see *http://www.sipri.org*). Other activities include the medical and agricultural uses of nuclear techniques and the promotion of nuclear energy as a means of preventing **global warming**. These activities are covered in the journal *International Atomic Energy Bulletin*.

IAN WELSH

International Convention on the Law of the Sea

The United Nations Convention on the Law of the Sea was signed in 1982 after nearly a decade of negotiations by the third UN Conference on the Law of the Sea (UNCLOS III). This comprehensive treaty covers (and codifies) virtually every aspect of international maritime law, including territorial jurisdictions, navigation, **fisheries**, pollution, and seabed mining. For example, it defines national rights in *territorial seas* (up to 12 nautical miles offshore) *contiguous zones* (12 to 24 miles), and *exclusive economic zones* (24 to 200 miles). During the **Reagan** administration the USA refused to sign the Convention because of disagreements over control of seabed mining. The treaty entered into force 16 November 1994 and has 133 parties, but the USA remains outside it.

Further reading

Galdorisi, G. and Vienna, K. (1997) *Beyond the Law of the Sea*, Westport, CT: Praeger.

NORMAN J. VIG

international environmental law

Most environmental problems have become global in recent years, and there is a growing body of international law that attempts to deal with them on an international level. Transboundary pollution problems were the first manifestation of the internationalization of environmental policy. In industrialized Europe, where countries are small and share resources intimately, conflicts have often arisen about responsibility for polluting shared waterways or migrating **air pollution**. The simplest and first level at which such conflicts can become legal issues is in the national courts of one of the countries involved in the dispute. A country seeking redress of grievance is not usually confident of a foreign system's courts, and such disputes have been more often settled through bilateral diplomatic negotiations.

The clear alternative to bilateral and regional agreements is the International Court of Justice (ICJ) in the Hague, Netherlands, to which any nation is permitted to bring grievances against any other. In 1974 Australia and New Zealand sued there to prevent France from conducting more atmospheric nuclear tests on French-owned Pacific islands near them. The ICJ voted eight to six to support Australia and New Zealand, but France simply refused to acknowledge the authority of the court. Since there is no enforcement mechanism available to the ICJ there was no recourse for the litigants. Eventually France changed to conducting underground tests as other nuclear powers had, but whether this stemmed from this law case or international public opinion is unknown, and the ICJ decided that the case had become moot.

The major obstacle to all such attempts at making international legal cases out of environmental issues is the concept of national sovereignty to which all independent nation states subscribe. This first principle of international law enables all nations to claim the right to exploit their own resources on their own territory in any manner they see fit.

Many multinational treaties, agreements, and protocols have been designed to control the shared use of such international **common pool property resources** as the oceans, the ozone layer, **biodiversity**, and the global climate. The International Maritime Consultative Organization (IMO) was organized in 1948 to economic purposes and took on environmental issues later. It has numerous regulations about the appropriate behaviour for all ships at sea including deliberate discharges of oily wastes and accidental spills from tankers. There is, however, no mechanism for monitoring or enforcing this agreement; hence, it depends on voluntary implementation by the countries under whose flag the ships operate.

More recent international agreements have taken place since the 1960s. In 1972 in Stockholm, Sweden (see **Stockholm Conference**) a **United Nations Environment Programme** (UNEP) was established with headquarters in Nairobi, Kenya. All signatories pledged their support of any projects established there, but help was only forthcoming from nations whose governments agreed voluntarily. In 1987 a number of industrialized nations agreed in Montreal to limit and eventually phase out their production of ozone-destroying chloroflourocarbons (CFCs; see **ozone depletion**). Enforcement occurred in those countries where the government agreed to take necessary steps, but developing countries whose governments felt it was their turn to get the benefits of modern **technology** simply did not sign the protocol. Even more divisive was the agreement by 150 nations at the 1992 Earth Summit in Rio de Janeiro to try to stabilize the production of greenhouse gases such as carbon dioxide (see **Rio Conference 1992**). This was only possible because no legally binding targets or schedules were set for any countries, and none of the developing nations agreed to participate.

Ironically international law sometimes prevents countries from taking steps to avoid degrading the environment as they perceive it. The **World Trade Organization**, for example, can impose trade sanctions to prevent countries like the USA from boycotting such products as shrimp caught without sea turtle excluder devices that would reduce the kill of this **endangered species**.

There has been considerable movement on the global level by all nations, but the principle of national sovereignty pervades all such talks, and indeed has been written into the protocols along with the admonition that all nation states should strive to develop their natural resources without causing harm to any other countries.

See also: global warming; ocean dumping; oil pollution

References

Australia v. France (1974) ICJ Reports, 57 ILR 350–600, 253.

Carroll, J.C. (ed.) (1988) *International Enviornmental Diplomacy*, Cambridge: Cambridge University Press.

Kamieniecki, S. (ed) (1993) *Environmental Politics in the International Arena*, Albany, NY: State University of New York Press.

LETTIE McSPADDEN

International Monetary Fund and neoliberalism

Neoliberalism represents commoditization as the route to freedom and prosperity. The 'neo' denotes its origins in eighteenth-century liberalism, which justified the **enclosure** of common land as natural, while representing any resistance as unnatural interference in the market. According to neoliberal ideology today, environmental resources are endangered because no one has a self-interest to protect them, so the solution is to assign ownership or money values to this **natural capital**. In a similar vein, global marketization is promoted as essential for **progress**: 'Markets promote efficiency through competition and the division of labour', according to the International Monetary Fund (IMF).

Since the 1980s such ideology has served as a weapon for an overall neoliberal agenda. This aims to undermine the gains of previous struggles which had won social and environmental protection, to fragment any collective resistance, to enclose present-day commons, and thus to subordinate all resources to commodity exchange. This agenda found a great opportunity in the 1980s debt crisis.

Amidst intense social stuggles in the 1970s, governments had borrowed more funds in order to finance increases in wages and services, e.g. through subsidies and construction projects. By the late 1970s southern countries faced a 'balance of payments' deficit for many reasons – e.g. because their main exports suffered a world decline in prices, while oil imports became more expensive. As these countries could no longer service the debt (repay even the interest), their currency lost value, and they were denied credit for further imports.

Jointly with the **World Bank**, the IMF used the 'debt crisis' in order to impose neoliberal policies. 'Growth-orientated loans' were granted to countries which accepted the 'conditionalities' of **structural adjustment programmes** (SAPs). Indebted governments were required to reduce spending, to privatize industry and services, to cheapen labour, to open up markets to **multinational and transnational corporations**, to relax controls on capital movements, to weaken environmental and labour protection laws, to devalue their currencies, etc. Fees were imposed for health and education services, local industries were driven out of business, many jobs were lost, and rural people lost their access to cultivable land.

In general such policies have helped employers to extract more labour (both paid and unpaid) in return for less income paid to people, who have been thrown into greater competition against each other. People now had to pay for public services which they previously obtained free of charge, and had to pay more for food, so they had to find extra sources of income. Such pressures provided new opportunities for capitalist development and profit-extraction. This 'economic growth' provided a facade of prosperity for widespread immiseration. In revolt against these attacks, 'IMF riots' erupted and met armed repression in many countries in the 1980s.

Governments also underwent pressure to change land use – from subsistence farming to export crops, e.g. coffee and cotton. In the name of 'efficient' resource use, the enclosure of common lands has been extended beyond **agriculture**, to mineral deposits and forests. In some places, logging companies had customarily discussed and negotiated the terms for wealth-extraction with local people. Through SAPs, however, the relatively 'high-value' areas were assigned to companies and the 'low-value' areas to local people. Thus they are excluded from the best forest areas and from further negotiation about their needs.

In the late 1990s IMF policies faced increased criticism and protest. Some G7 governments took up critics' arguments – e.g. that the debt is unpayable, and that reducing poverty is more important. In response, the IMF and World Bank finally conceded that some debts to them should be partly cancelled.

At the same time, the IMF sought to shift responsibility for its neoliberal policies to national governments. Under the new procedure, each indebted government must devise a Poverty Reduction Strategic Paper (PRSP). Once approved by the IMF and World Bank, this Paper would provide the framework for spending any funds received from donors. Indebted countries understood that IMF approval would depend upon the PRSP incorporating the familiar criteria of the earlier SAPs: for the donors, any increase in the nation's social budget would be regarded as endangering 'economic growth'.

Eventually some NGOs moved beyond earlier proposals that the IMF and World Bank be reformed, towards proposals that they be abolished. Moreover reparations were demanded for the '**ecological debt**', i.e. for the environmental harm caused by IMF policies in southern countries In sum, the fundamental issue is not debt remission – but rather the power to reverse past damage and to decide on resource use in the future.

Further reading

Chossudovsky, M. (1996) *The Globalization of Poverty: Impacts of the IMF and World Bank Reforms*, London: Zed.

Dalla Costa, M.R. and Dalla Costa, G. (eds) (1995) *Paying the Price*, London: Zed.

Focus on the Global South (2000) *Prague 2000: Why We Need to Decommission the IMF and the World Bank*, Bangkok: Focus on the Global South, URL: http://www.focusweb.org; see also South-ernPeoples' Ecological Debt Creditors' Alliance, URL: http://www.cosmovisiones.com/Deuda Ecologica.

George, S. (1991) *The Debt Boomerang*, London: Pluto Press.

Goldman, M. (ed.) (1998) *Privatizing Nature: Political Struggles for Global Commons*, London: Pluto.

International Monetary Fund (2000) *Globalization: Threat or Opportunity?* Washington, DC: IMF.

Messkoub, M. (1992) 'Deprivation and Structural Adjustment', in M. Wuyts, M. Mackintosh and T. Hewitt (eds) *Development Policy and Public Action*, Oxford: Oxford University Press, pp.175–98.

LES LEVIDOW

international non-governmental organizations

It is estimated that there are now over 100,000 non-governmental organizations (NGOs) working in some capacity for environmental protection. The growth in internationally orientated environmental NGOs from the 1970s onwards in particular, coincided with, as well as contributed to, the rising profile of a range of global environmental threats including climate change, **ozone depletion** and loss of **biodiversity**. The majority of INGOs are still based in the North where there are the resources to fund active campaigns and maintain a transnational presence across a range of issues, even if many groups have offices in a number of developing countries. Among the more prominent are **Greenpeace** International, World Wildlife Fund (see also **World Wide Fund for Nature**) International and **Friends of the Earth** International. Rather like **multinational and transnational corporations**, these groups have a headquarters as well as national branches in a number of countries.

There are also a number of international umbrella and coalition groups focused around single issues. The global **Climate Action Network** (CAN), for example, brings together most international NGOs that are active on climate change. CAN was created in 1989, prior to the Second World Climate Conference by 63 NGOs from 22 countries under the initial guidance of groups such as **Environmental Defense Fund** (EDF) and Greenpeace International. Within this global umbrella, there are also regional level groupings such as Climate Network Europe and Climate Action Network Latin America, as well as national level offices such as CAN-UK. Being part of these international networks allows NGOs to pool resources and expertise and generate pressure greater than the sum of the parts.

It is for the influence of these organizations in raising awareness, providing expertise to policy-makers, and acting as watchdogs of industry and government in monitoring compliance and expos-ing malpractice, that people credit INGOs with a number of successes in the environmental policy area from getting the ban on **whaling** and the ivory trade to helping to bring about the phase-out of CFC use and the international regulation of the trade in hazardous wastes (see **hazardous and toxic waste management**). INGOs also played a prominent role in the Rio process, so much so that critics argued that they were co-opted by the process by lending legitimacy to the process (through participating in it and generating popular interest in it) but not being granted many concessions in return (see **Rio Conference 1992**). This experience has also raised concerns, as elsewhere, about who INGOs represent and on whose behalf they speak when they exercise this influence. Internationally organized and well-resourced NGOs constitute a very small fragment of a large and diverse **civil society** whose concerns are rarely heard, let alone represented at the international level. In recent years interna-tional NGOs have become more sensitive to concerns that they fail to represent the concerns of smaller NGOs and neglect the **development** side of environmental issues.

The failure to date of the Rio negotiations to produce substantial policy change on the environ-ment has, however, heightened a trend among some INGOs towards targeting the private sector in their campaigns rather than relying upon governments to direct environmental reform. The power of multinational and transnational corpora-tions, in particular, with production structures that span the globe and access to capital which is increasingly mobile, and whose investment deci-sions have enormous implications for natural resource use patterns, make them important

subjects of campaigns by INGOs. This strategic turn to working with and against business is witnessed in the growth of agreements and informal types of regulation of the private sector through codes of conduct, **stewardship** regimes and shareholder activism.

INGOs will clearly continue to play a key part in environmental policy in a number of ways, setting the agenda through awareness raising and media publicity, participating in international negotiations with legal and scientific expertise and acting as watchdogs, pressuring governments and corpora-tions to honour commitments to protect the environment. Their importance to the evolution of environmental politics to date and ability to shape the contours of future action for the protection of the environment should not be under-estimated.

Further reading

McCormick, J. (1989) *The Global Environmental Movement*, London: Belhaven Press.

Wapner, P. (1996) *Environmental Activism and World Civic Politics*, Albany: State University of New York Press.

PETER NEWELL

intrinsic value

Intrinsic value theory is primarily used in green politics to denote and postulate forms of value in **nature** that are distinguishable from, opposed to, or not reducible to anthropocentric or instrumental values, and which thus oppose the conceptions of value predominant in conventional economic theory (see **anthropocentrism**). Whilst modern intrinsic value variants are traceable to G.E. Moore's *Principia Ethica* (1903), the term has been adopted distinctively in **environmental ethics** by supporters of **deep ecology** and **Leopold**'s 'land ethic'. Though multiple variants are used, the term broadly indicates values which (i) are ends in themselves rather than means to ends, or (ii) are located within an object due to that object's properties, or (iii) are objective in that they are independent of valuer's evaluations.

Further reading

O'Neill, J. (1993) *Ecology, Policy and Politics: Human Well-Being and the Natural World*, London: Routledge.

PIERS H.G. STEPHENS

Irish Green Party

The Irish Green Party (*Comhaontas Glas*) was established in 1981 as the Ecology Party of Ireland in response to a perceived need for a political party that would address environmental issues. It changed its name to the Irish Green Party in 1986. The party's guiding principles include that society should not have a destructive impact on the environment; that conservation of resources is vital for the **sustainability** of society and the Earth; that political, social and economic decisions should be taken at the lowest possible level; that world peace overrides commercial and national interests and that there should be a redistribution of the world's resources to counter poverty. In 1989 the first Green Party member was elected as a TD (*Teachta Dála*/member of parliament). Two party members were elected to the European Parliament in 1994 and representation in *Dáil Éireann* (parliament) increased to two in 1997.

NIAMH MURNAGHAN

issue attention cycle

Economist Anthony Downs, author of 20 books, most notably *An Economic Theory of Democracy* (1957) and *Inside Bureaucracy* (1967), in 1972 formulated the 'issue attention cycle', which has been often cited in studies of public opinion and environmental policy. Down's basic point is that a subjective cycle of interest and boredom rather than an objective evaluation of problems has been historically reflected in public policies. There are five general stages in the cycle: (1) pre-problem; (2) alarmed discovery/euphoric enthusiasm; (3) costs realization; (4) gradual decline; and (5) postproblem. Although one can observe the cycle in other western democracies, America's cultural traits and commercial broadcast media have tended to exaggerate its curve. Downs advanced reasons why the cycle might not fit environmental concerns as well as other policy concerns. Utilizing questions about the salience of issues, studies have found a pattern suggestive of the issue attention cycle in 1960s–70s data. However, since then 'the environment' has turned out to be an evolving composite of specific issues, so that as one ebbs, another waxes. Questions probing the strength of opinions have revealed short-term ups and downs, but also evidence of long-term growth in public support for environmental values.

See also: public opinion and the environment

Reference

Downs, A. (1972) 'Up and Down with Ecology: The Issue Attention Cycle', *Public Interest* Summer: 38–50.

E. GENE FRANKLAND

Italian green parties

Political ecology emerged in **Italy** in the 1970s. The most important experience had been the **antinuclear movements**. An embryonic Italian green party was founded in 1984 as the expression of the environmentalist movement. The following year the green lists stood for election in 12 regions, obtaining 648,832 votes. In November 1986, after the regional elections, a national organization of a federal kind was set up, the *Federazione Nazionale delle Liste Verdi*. Seventy lists joined the Federation at the outset.

In the 1987 general elections, support for the green lists grew to reach 2.5 per cent of votes. Fifteen green deputies entered parliament for the first time. In the second half of the 1980s, after the **Chernobyl** accident, attention to environmentalist issues grew in Italian public opinion. The activists of the green lists and of the **environmental movement** were committed to mobilization on various issues. In November 1987, three referenda against the development of the nuclear programme were approved by more than 70 per cent of voters. These results brought about the abandonment of the nuclear programme in Italy. The Italian Greens saw an increase in their popularity and support. New green lists were founded locally. The lists of members of the National Federation increased to 219 in 1988 and 420 in 1990.

A few deputies elected in the lists of *Democrazia Proletaria* and the Radical Party left their respective parties and promoted the constitution of the '*Verdi Arcobaleno*' (The Rainbow Greens). Two rival green lists were presented at the 1989 European elections, and both achieved good results. The Federation of the Green Lists obtained 3.8 per cent of votes, the Rainbow Greens almost 2.4 per cent. The overall result – 6.1 per cent of votes – was the peak of suppport that had until then been reached in Italy.

The Rainbow Greens and the Federation of the Green Lists merged to become '*Federazione dei Verdi*' in December 1990. The figure of the speaker assumed an increasingly important role after the election of Carlo Ripa di **Meana**, a former Socialist Party member, who had been EC Commissioner and Italian Minister of Environment. The rapid institutionalization of the movement created serious difficulties for the Italian Green Federation. In the 1992 general elections electoral support dropped to 2.8 per cent, less than half the level achieved three years previously.

The crisis of the traditional Italian political parties exploded between 1993 and 1994, and profoundly changed the political scene. A new electoral system of three quarters majority forced the Greens to enter the left-wing coalition. In 1993 Green MP Francesco Rutelli was elected Mayor of Rome. But in the 1994 national elections, won by the centre–right formation led by Berlusconi, the Greens obtained only 2.7 per cent of votes and got 17 seats in Parliament. In the 1996 elections, the Greens did not succeed in improving their electoral support. But taking part in the centre–left coalition led by Prodi (*L'Ulivo*), they increased their representation in parliament to 29. The victory of the coalition provided the opportunity for the Greens to enter the government: Edo Ronchi became Environment Minister.

In order to strengthen their political role, the Italian Greens speeded up the process of their transformation into a party. The forms of recruit-

ment changed. In 1996 national membership was introduced, with the promotion of specific campaigns. Membership had risen from a few thousand to over 23,000 in 1999. There were over 800 local groups throughout Italy. But their strength was only apparent. Membership increased, but active grassroots participation fell. The European elections of June 1999 showed the political and organizational fragility of the Italian Green Federation. Votes dropped to 1.8 per cent. The Greens suffered from competition with the Radical Party and with a new formation (*I democratici*), promoted by Romano Prodi. Nor did the Green Federation achieve wide support from the environmental movement.

In July 1999 the Green Federation dissolved national organs and decided to set up the constituent process of a new political entity. Grazia Francescato, a former spokesperson of the World Wildlife Fund (WWF) led the refoundation of a political organization that sought on the one hand to rediscover the original roots in the environmental movement, and on the other to revitalize direct participation within the party and its ability to mobilize public opinion outside (see **public opinion and the environment**). Classical ecological questions (**sustainable development**, opposition to **biotechnology**, **animal rights**, etc.) became the focus of initiatives, and the Seattle mobilization against the **World Trade Organization** (WTO) was taken as a reference model.

See also: new social movements; political opportunity structures

Further reading

Biorcio, R. and Lodi, G. (eds) (1988) *La sfida verde. Il movimento ecologista in Italia*, Padova: Liviana.

Diani, M. (1995) *Green Networks. A Structural Analysis of the Italian Environmental Movement*, Edinburgh: Edinburgh University Press.

ROBERTO BIORCIO

Italy

Italy, or the Italian Republic to give the country its official name, is the central peninsula of the

Mediterranean. It is a narrow and mountainous country with no part of its landscape further than 150 miles from the sea. Italy's capital is Rome and the climate is typically Mediterranean. A clear distinction exists between the prosperous north of the country, which is deeply rooted in continental Europe, and the southern part of the peninsula which includes Sicily and Sardinia.

Economic conditions in the south have always been more difficult than in the north. In recent years there have been calls for autonomy for the Lombardy region by the politicians and industrialists of the Northern League. This dissatisfaction relates to many aspects of life in the south, not least to the high levels of corruption in business and public life and the low amount of tax revenue which the southern part of the country contributes to the overall economy. Since 1945 the country has developed from being mainly agricultural in character to become a major industrial power and an importer of labour. A large public sector and a tradition of family-owned businesses have long been characteristics of Italian economic life but the 1990s saw the progressive privatization of much of the country's industry.

Italy is a country with few natural resources and a difficult transport system. Mineral assets are small while the country is highly dependent on imports of oil and the use of coal for its energy consumption. This results in high levels of sulphur and carbon dioxide in the atmosphere. The nuclear power option was dismissed in 1987 after a national referendum rejected it. Italy's national energy policy is to be found in a series of National Energy Plans. Air pollution and water pollution are the two major environmental issues with which the country has to deal. **Air pollution** is a particular problem in the major Italian cities. Emissions from vehicles cause considerable air pollution while bans on traffic in larger cities have become commonplace. Italy's cultural infrastructure, particularly its ancient monuments and works of art, has been extensively affected by pollution.

Water pollution has long been a problem in Italy. The high **dioxin** levels present in the Venice Lagoon, mainly caused by the nearby Enichem petrochemical plant, are well known but similar pollution problems have arisen in other regions. Moreover, Italy has long had a tradition of its waste treatment plants not working efficiently. In recent years water pollution laws have been enacted in an attempt to regulate the discharge of effluents and dangerous substances.

Only fairly recently has public opinion in Italy recognized the extent of the country's environmental problems and there now exists a general desire to see the environment improved (see **public opinion and the environment**). Although Italy has extensive legislation in this field, it is unsystematic and extremely disjointed. The relevant laws are scattered through decrees, regulations, local legislation and laws. Implementation both at local and governmental levels has been a significant problem. At local level a large number of regional authorities have responsibilities for the enactment and regulation of statutory provisions and permits while frequently there is an overlap between the functions of local and central government causing confusion as to allocation of responsibilities.

Greater co-operation is required between central and local government together with stronger penalties for breaches of the law that are enforceable. In many regions there is no proper surveillance network to warn of potential problems. Even with the growth of **European Union** environmental legislation, Italy has been slow to conform to EU law and has probably the worst record of any member state in enforcing EU Directives on environmental matters.

In theory, responsibility for environmental matters rests with the Ministry of the Environment established in 1986. In practice only a few areas, mainly in connection with air and water pollution and natural reserves, are within the exclusive remit of this department. In the majority of cases the ministry has to liaise with other departments. The government department has few resources, is under-staffed and considered of minor standing compared with the established and larger ministries. Central government tends to set policy at national level while the regions prepare implementation plans. The government in Rome has the authority to exercise default powers if the regions fail to comply with overall policy.

See also: Italian green parties; Seveso disaster

Further reading

Lewanski, R. (1998) 'Italy: Environmental Policy in

a Fragmented State', in K. Hanf and A. Jansen, *Governance and Environment in Western Europe*, Harlow: Addison Wesley Longman.

DOUGLAS WOOD

J

James Bay hydroelectric project

The rivers flowing into James Bay, located at the southern edge of Canada's Hudson Bay, are the site of one of the world's largest hydroelectric developments. The area is rich in wildlife and traditional home to the Cree. In the early 1970s, the first phase of development flooded 7044 square miles of land. The environmental legacy has included methylmercury contamination: in the mid-1980s, Cree individuals were found to have high levels of mercury, up to 20 times above acceptable levels in some cases (see **mercury poisoning**). A coalition of Canadian and American aboriginal and environmental groups opposed plans to proceed with another major phase of development in the late 1980s and early 1990s. The campaign contributed to the New York Power Authority's decision in 1992 to cancel a multi-billion-dollar energy contract with Hydro-Quebec. The loss of important customers, an energy glut, and pressures to perform environmental assessments for new dams convinced the Quebec government to suspend the development in 1994 (see **dams/hydroelectric power**).

Further reading

Hornig, D. (ed.) (1999) *Social and Environmental Impacts of the James Bay Hydroelectric Project*, Montreal and Kingston: McGill-Queen's University Press.

ELIZABETH MOORE

Japan

Modern environmental history in Japan can be divided into three periods: the initial policy response to serious pollution problems, the stagnation of environmental policy due to economic recession, and the engagement in global environmental issues of the 1990s. Among Japanese environmental actors, the most powerful have been the developmental offices of government, followed closely by the mass media, while the less powerful have been the citizen movements. Japanese environmental politics has occurred within the context of the traditional religion and the natural philosophy of the country. Both Buddhism and Shinto, the state religion, maintain that the natural state of the environment plays a fundamental role in one's spirituality. Recently the role of philosophy and religion has come under question as to its relevance in coping with modern environmental dilemmas (see **religions and the environment**). Thus, as in western industrial societies, Japanese citizens are turning not to religion, but to government for environmental policy solutions.

The first **environmental movements** in Japan appeared shortly after the Second World War and persisted until the late 1960s. These movements were reactions to Japan's new-found economic and industrial growth. The rapid **industrialization** and the resulting air and **water pollution** led to the spread of Itai-Itai disease, Kumamoto–Minamata disease, Niigata–Minamata disease, and Yokkaichi asthma. These, becoming known as the four major 'harm events', spurred anti-pollution movements at all levels of government. The victims embarked upon legal actions, and their quest also for full-scale anti-pollution measures was supported by public opinion (see **public opinion and the environment**). As a result, the national government was forced into reforms at the so-called 'Pollution Diet' (Parliament is named the 'Diet' in Japan), where fourteen pollution acts were passed in 1970. The Environmental Agency, a national agency comparable to the U.S. **Environmental Protection Agency**, was established in 1971. Its mission is to create, implement, and enforce environmental regulations. Morever in 1973, the world's first programme ever enacted to compensate the victims of environmental atrocities, the Pollution Related Health Damage Compensation Law, was established.

Despite the new environmental concerns, Japan's environmental progress would slow greatly with the onset of the energy crises of the 1970s (see **energy crisis**). These crises led to the stagnation of the thriving Japanese economy and eventually to a severe economic recession. As a result of the slowing economy, Japan was forced to ease industrial environmental standards to facilitate economic growth. This easing of air and water quality standards was reflected in the revision of the Pollution Health Damage Security Method, which had been implemented to police industrial polluters. The enactment of the Environmental Impact Assessment Act, which the Organization for Economic Co-operation and Development (OECD) had urged in 1974, was delayed in Japan until 1997.

The 1990s saw Japanese environmental policy change once again with surging international environmental issues, such as **global warming** and **ozone depletion** and CFCs. The new political concern with global problems was largely due to the 1992 Rio Earth Summit and the media attention that it garnered (see **Rio Conference 1992**). Not only did journalists' coverage of environment go up rapidly, but also new social movement-type environmental groups began to form and have some influence (see **new social movements**). There was an attempt to use the referendum at the provincial level in response to

environment problems. The Earth Summit spawned such Japanese environmental innovations as the 'Basic Law for the Environment', which sought to promote sustainable and effective environmental policy. The Kiko Forum established in 1997 provides a public forum for citizens to discuss the effects of climate change and global warming. The Forum also encourages local initiatives to combat climate change and global warming.

The Japanese green movement has emerged at both the national and local levels. At the national level it has received a push from such governmental departments as: the Ministry of International Trade, the Ministry of Construction, and the Ministry of Health and Welfare. These departments are now working together to establish and implement environmental guidelines to aid in their respective activities and to provide for **sustainable development** in the future. At the local level city planners throughout Japan are establishing environmental standards that new parks, roads, and sewerage constructions must follow. Newly elected and aspiring public officials have run or are running on pro-environment platforms. The increased citizen activism is reflected in **NIMBY** movements regarding waste disposal and power plant construction. Housewives have been particularly successful in establishing **recycling** and safe food campaigns in their neighbourhoods. However, such grassroots movements are sporadic, and there is not yet an equivalent of a national umbrella organization to co-ordinate the activities of citizen action groups like the **BBU** in Germany. Polls in the 1990s indicated that public interest in environmental issues was continuously rising. On the other hand, participation in the Japanese affiliates of international groups, such as **Greenpeace** and **Friends of the Earth**, has remained low during the decade.

Central to the growth of the Japanese green movement has been the role of the mass media, whose editors and reporters can take small isolated environmental issues and turn them into national political topics (see **mass media and the environment**). By doing this the mass media are 'greening' the policy agenda of Japanese government. For example, the 'Pollution Diet' and its aftermath was the subject of intense media coverage. And in the early 1990s, Japan's three big nationwide newspapers devoted many features to the global environmental issues. In the second half of the 1990s, the media made dioxin pollution a major national concern in Japan (see **dioxins**).

Finally, there are some students and politicians who have advocated a greater emphasis on traditional religion and philosophy in protecting the natural environment. However, such a revival of a Japanese version of **deep ecology** has not been embraced by influential environmental policy actors, rather these actors, including the media, have put their emphasis on **ecological modernization** and sustainable development.

See also: Japanese nuclear power industry; mercury poisoning

Further reading

Broadbent, J. (1998) *Environmental Protection in Japan: Networks of Power and Protest*, Cambridge: Cambridge University Press.

Miyamoto, K. (1991) 'Japanese Environmental Policies since World War II', *Capitalism, Nature, Socialism: A Journal of Socialist Ecology*, 2(2).

Peng-Er, L. (1999) *Green Politics in Japan*, London: Routledge.

Schreurs, M.A. (1997) 'Japan's Changing Approach to Environment', *Environmental Politics*, 6(2).

Terada, R. (1964) 'Changing Characteristics of Japan's Environmental Movements since the 1970s', in Korean Sociological Association (ed.) *Environment and Development: A Sociological Understanding on the Better Human Condition*, Seoul: Seoul Press.

MASATSUGU MARUYAMA

Japanese nuclear power industry

According to a Japanese atomic White Paper in 1998, at that time 52 nuclear reactors were operating. After America and France, the Japanese nuclear power industry is the third most productive in the world, producing 45,000,000 kilowatts annually. Moreover, according to the mid-range forecast of the electric power industry in 2000, 13 more reactors will be constructed by 2010.

The development of nuclear energy use in Japan has outstanding characteristics compared with other advanced nations. First, it has the historical experience of being bombed by atomic weapons. The Japanese postwar constitution explicitly abandons research and development of atomic energy for military purposes. Therefore, atomic energy use was developed exclusively for civil energy purposes. The state organization, the Atomic Energy Commission, was created to oversee and plan nuclear energy development.

Second, all processes, from fuel procurement to radioactive waste, are regulated by the state. However, this regulation is not always effective. For example, the nuclear quango, *Donen*, produced a false report regarding an accident at the Monju fast-breeder reactor in 1995. And again in 1997, failure to comply with state directives caused a fire in the asphalt fixation processing facilities of low radioactive waste (see **nuclear energy/nuclear waste management**). Moreover, in 1999, the JCO Uranium Conversion Company which owned and managed the Tokaimura nuclear power site, caused Japan's worst nuclear accident which resulted in the death of two employees and the exposure of over 400 local people to radiation. Although the direct cause lay equally in the unlawful working practices (employees failed to measure radioactivity leakage), it is also the case that the original manufacturing process did not incorporate a fail-safe design. As a result of this serious breach of management and safety regulations, the government produced a White Paper in 2000. Faced with strong public criticism, the Nuclear Safety Commission had to apologize for its failure to apply safety regulations.

Third, in the process of this atomic policy-making, there are two opposing interest groups. One group is composed of research institutes relating to the Science and Technology Agency, whose purpose is the development of the domestic nuclear energy industry. The other is the union of the Ministry of International Trade and Industry and the power companies, which generates nuclear electricity using imported technology. The latter group is exposed to market pressures and is consequently conscious about the cost efficiency of atomic energy. However, for the former, cost implications are not an issue. It is this group that adheres to research and development of fast-breeder reactors, which have been abandoned by most other industrialized countries.

Because nuclear energy development is supported strongly by the state, the anti-nuclear movement has faced difficulties (see **anti-nuclear movements**). In Japan, because the legal basis of opposition to nuclear power is based on issues of land ownership and a right to fishery compensation, the movement's scope is limited to a narrow area (see **land reform**; **fisheries**). In an attempt to 'buy off' opposition to nuclear power development, the Japanese government promised various subsidy grants. However, this situation changed after the **Chernobyl** nuclear accident. As a result of the public concern about nuclear power, there was a dramatic increase in the number of citizens who believed that the risks far outweighed the benefits. In 1998, a planned nuclear power plant at Maki resulted in large-scale opposition by citizens living in the vicinity. In February 2000, the governor of Mie Prefecture expressed opposition to the construction plan. This was the first time a governor had registered doubt about the construction of a nuclear power plant. Interestingly, the power company did not dare to attempt a counterattack, in the light of an increasingly sceptical, worried and hostile public. The nuclear power industry in Japan is legally protected and supported as a monopoly. However, from 2000 market competition was introduced, albeit incomplete, causing nuclear power companies to take the cost of the generation of electricity much more seriously than before.

Further reading

Koich Hasegawa (1999) 'Global Climate Change and Japanese Nuclear Policy', *International Journal of Japanese Sociology*, 8.

Lesbirel, S.H. (1998) *NIMBY Politics in Japan: Energy Siting and the Management of Environmental Conflict*, Ithaca: Cornell University Press.

Low, M.F. and Yoshioka, Hitoshi (1989) 'Buying the "Peaceful Atom": The Development of Nuclear Power in Japan', *Historia Scientiarum*, 38.

MASATSUGU MARUYAMA

Jefferson, Thomas

b. 13 April, 1743 Goochland (now Albemarle county), Virginia, USA; d. 4 July 1826 Monticello, Virginia

Politician

The third President of the USA and author of the US Declaration of Independence, Thomas Jefferson established land-use policies that continue to influence American and Canadian environmental politics to this day. Jefferson believed that a settled **agriculture** of independent freeholders was the most secure foundation for a democratic state (see **democracy**). As President, he negotiated the Louisiana Purchase in order to secure US farmers' opportunity for westward expansion. Jefferson's faith in the political loyalty of independent owner operators was based on his view that farmers' interest in retaining their title to land would make them unlikely to support fiscally or militarily unsustainable initiatives. Furthermore, those with land-wealth would be less likely to abandon the government in times of trial. Jefferson's ideas led to the US Homestead Act that transferred public lands to agricultural users at bargain rates, and to the American conception of private **property rights** that extend almost despotic control of land to owner-operators involved in food and fibre production.

Further reading

Onuf, P.S. (ed.) (1993) *Jeffersonian Legacies*, Charlottesville: University Press of Virginia.

PAUL B. THOMPSON

K

Kelly, Petra Karin

b. 19 November 1947, Günzburg/
Donau, Germany; d. 1 October 1992,
Bonn

Movement activist, Green Party politician

Petra Kelly lived her childhood in Germany as
Petra Karin Lehmann. Her mother divorced and
remarried US Army Colonel John E. Kelly. The
family moved to the USA, where Kelly spent her
adolescent years. In 1970 she received her B.A.
cum laude from American University. During her
studies, Kelly worked in the Democratic presidential campaigns of Robert F. Kennedy and later
Hubert H. Humphrey, and experienced the US
civil rights and anti-war movements. In 1971 she
earned a master's degree in political science at the
University of Amsterdam. During 1972–83, she
worked as a policy analyst for the European
Community. Her young sister, Grace, died in
1970 after battling cancer for three years, prompting Kelly to found the Grace P. Kelly Foundation in
1973 to support research on childhood cancer.

During the 1970s, Kelly (a member of the Social
Democratic Party) became disgruntled with her
party's priorities under Chancellor Helmut
Schmidt. She redirected her energy into **environmental movements** and later the **peace movement**. As a member of the executive of the **BBU**
(the Federal Association of Environmental Citizen
Initiatives), Kelly dealt with international contacts.
More than anyone else, she came to embody the
'eco-pax' movement (centred on the politics of life)

which was to surge in the early 1980s in West
Germany. Kelly emerged at the top of the
candidate list for the 1979 European Parliament
election of the Green Alliance (SPV), which
received 3.2 per cent of German votes (but no
seats). She was one of the founders of *Die **Grünen***
in January 1980, which she described as 'a non-
violent ecological and basic-democratic anti-war
coalition of parliamentary and extra-parliamentary
grassroots orientated groups'. Kelly was selected as
one of its three federal speakers (1980–2). Her
peace activism at home and abroad brought her
international recognition, including: the Right
Livelihood Award in Stockholm 1982, and the
Peace Woman of the Year Award in Philadelphia
1983. Her first book, *Fighting for Peace*, was
published (in English) in 1984, and several others
were to follow.

The Greens were elected to the *Bundestag* in
1983, and Kelly was selected as one of their
parliamentary group's three speakers (1983–4). She
served on the *Bundestag*'s Foreign Relations Committee. In 1985, Kelly was the only green
parliamentarian to refuse to 'rotate' at midterm
(give up her seat to a successor on the party list) as
mandated by the federal party's rules. Nevertheless,
she was re-nominated to a safe list position in
Bavaria and won a seat in the 1987 *Bundestag*
election. Kelly had no power within the factionalized parliamentary group; however, her international activism for peace and human rights
continued unabated. In 1990, she unsuccessfully
pursued a safe list position for the 1990 *Bundestag*
election, but in the end, no seats were won by West

Greens because of their failure to clear the 5 per cent threshold. In 1991, her candidacy for co-speakership of the Green Party received feeble support; ironically a few months later, *The Sunday Times* (London) portrayed her as one of the 1000 prime movers of the twentieth century. In 1992, she took up the new challenge of editing the environmental magazine of the private SAT 1 television channel. Around 1 October 1992, Kelly was shot dead by her long-time companion, Gert Bastian (a former Bundeswehr general, peace activist, and parliamentary member of the Greens) who then committed suicide. Their isolation from the Bonn scene was graphically illustrated by the fact that nobody had expressed concerns about their disappearance – their bodies were not discovered for almost three weeks.

Kelly was easily the leading figure of the Greens during the movement–party phase of their history (1980–3). It is not too much of an exaggeration to say that during this early period she and the Greens were largely synonymous, at least in the media's eyes. In the 1983 campaign she was, as a 'hope carrier' of the young generation, a significant asset for the party. Long after her influence within the party had waned in the mid-1980s, she exerted international influence in the green movement (which necessitated the assignment of additional staff to her even though she was not part of the parliamentary group's leadership). Kelly was obviously more interested (and skilful) in extra-parliamentary politics, which she described as the more important 'standing leg' of the green movement–party. She declared in 1982, 'Parliament is not a goal but part of a strategy. We are the anti-party party ... the most important thing is to work at the grassroots' (Mettke, 1982). Kelly also publicly worried that the Greens might become too electorally successful and turn into a power hungry/compromising party like the others. Once the Greens had been elected to the *Bundestag*, some colleagues began to view Kelly as a self promoter, whose real cause was herself. Her refusal to rotate provided confirmation for this perception.

Kelly showed no reluctance in staging media events also when visiting East Germany. For example, she not only demonstrated in Alexander-platz, but also, when she met East German Communist leader Erich Honecker, she wore a shirt with the forbidden 'Swords into Ploughshares' logo. Kelly's energetic support of East German dissidents began early and continued despite complaints from within the parliamentary group. She also supported those seeking change in Communist China, and especially in Tibet. As peace activist, Kelly was vocal in her criticisms of NATO's nuclear deterrence strategy and US imperialism in the world, but as a **human rights** activist, in contrast to many left-wing Greens, she was equally critical of the repressive regimes in the Communist Bloc.

Kelly was a fundamentalist (*Fundi*), who argued that there must be no compromises of basic principles. She was often critical of the realist (*Realo*) wing of the party, who seemed fixated on having a green minister(s) in an SPD/Green government, such as was formed in 1985 in Hesse over her objections. She saw life on earth as imperilled by nuclear weapons and environmental pollution, necessitating a fundamental change in society (Beck, 1992). However, Kelly did not participate in the factional warfare between the *Realos* and the *Fundis* that absorbed so much energy among the Greens at the federal level during the second half of the 1980s. As in her foreign policy orientation, Kelly was nonaligned within the party, not bound by factional or parliamentary discipline; only thus could she speak out and work for what she believed was right.

References

Beck, M. (1992) 'Umkehr, das war ihre Botschaft' (Interview with Marieluse Beck regarding the death of Petra Kelly) *die tageszeitung*, 21 October 1992, p.2.

Mettke, J.R. (1982) *Die Grünen: Regierungspartner von morgen?*, Reinbek: Rowohlt.

Further reading

Gottschlich, J. and Sontheimer, M. (1992) 'Zärtlich und zugleich subversiv', *die tageszeitung*, 21 October 1992, p.3.

Kelly, P. (1984) *Fighting for Hope* London: Chatto & Windus.

Parkin, S. (1994) *The Life and Death of Petra Kelly*, London: HarperCollins.

E. GENE FRANKLAND

(eds) *The Global Environment: Institutions, Law and Policy*, Washington, DC: CQ Press.

NORMAN J. VIG

Kyoto Conference/Protocol

The Kyoto Conference (December 1–10, 1997) was the third conference of parties (COP 3) to the United Nations **Framework Convention on Climate Change** (UNFCCC). It resulted in an agreement (the Kyoto Protocol) establishing quantified targets for reduction of emissions of six 'greenhouse gases' (GHGs) by developed countries (Annex I parties) by 2008–12. The USA had resisted fixed targets for reducing GHGs prior to the conference, but in a dramatic intervention by Vice President Al Gore the USA agreed to reduce its emissions 7 per cent below 1990 levels, while the **European Union** agreed to an 8 per cent reduction and **Japan** 6 per cent. **Less developed countries** are not obligated to limit their GHGs under the agreement.

In March 2001, President George Bush withdrew the USA from the Kyoto Protocol's implementation.

Further reading

Molitor, M. (1999) 'The United Nations Climate Change Agreements' in N. Vig and R. Axelrod

Kyshtym nuclear accident

Before **Chernobyl**, the 1957 'Kyshtym' atomic accident, involving the explosion of a high-level radioactive waste tank in the Urals region in western Russia, was the cause of the most significant, unplanned radiological contamination incident worldwide. The explosion took place on 29 September 1957 at the '*Mayak*' Production Association at the Chelyabinsk-65 closed military city ('ZATO') in the South Urals, about 1,450 km east of Moscow and 180 km south of Yekaterinburg, capital of the Sverdlovsk Oblast (district). 'Mayak', ironically, is the Russian term for 'beacon to the future'. The accident in the *yushka* (waste tank) led to widespread regional radio-toxic contamination. Local people were not informed of its occurrence until two weeks later, despite the atomic authorities knowing that to be effective evacuation was needed within 36 hours. Details first emerged in the Viennese paper *Die Presse* (17 March 1959), but were suppressed by the western nuclear authorities and the CIA for fear of undermining public support for nuclear power.

DAVID LOWRY

L

labour/trade unions

The relationship between green ideas and the labour movement is manifold and not straightforward. Trade unions organize workers at the work place and represent their interests in society. From this social structural position, trade unions are concerned with job security, economic prosperity and growth. This position may make them hostile to green ideas of zero growth and pollution protection. However, the labour movement also embodies the ideas of social progress, equality and emancipation. The latter ideas may form a potential for an alliance between green actors and trade unions and may also be the driving force for environmental positions of trade unions (Offe, 1985).

The position of trade unions is not unified. There are some general differences among trade unions: business unions (unions that principally sell their service to members), organizing workers in the energy or production sector, are by and large hostile to green claims whereas social unions (unions that have a societal utopia) are more sympathetic (see **utopia/ecotopia**). This conclusion has been arrived at in studies on US trade unionism and has been confirmed in comparative studies (Siegmann, 1985). However, in Europe further division lines are essential for the ecological position of trade unions. Left-leaning trade unions such as the CGT in France as well as social-democratic unions under strong corporative arrangements as the ÖGB in Austria and the LO in Sweden are more hostile to green demands than other unions. Some unions, such as the CFDT in France, may even serve as a breeding ground for ecological ideas (Touraine *et al.*, 1987). The factors influencing trade unions are their membership base and above all their ideology (Jahn, 1993).

Although blue-collar trade unions are more opposed to green ideology than white-collar unions, trade unions' ideology, as outlined above, is an intervening variable. For instance, the German Metal Workers' union has been the driving force of environmental concerns within the German labour movement. But the **political opportunity structures** of a country are also crucial. If labour is strong with its own ideology as in Austria and Sweden, trade unions are closed to environmental concerns. If the labour movement needs an alliance partner as in Germany, trade unions may be more active in supporting the green agenda.

This leads us to another important aspect. The policy of trade unions is connected with the policy of social democratic or labour parties. If these parties are in opposition, it is by and large easier to be open for environmental concerns than if these parties are in government. Thus, the action space of trade unions is dependent on the position of social democratic and labour parties and vice versa.

Green issues are not easy for trade unions. Since closing down polluting industries, phasing out of **nuclear energy** or preventing new technologies such as gene-technology costs jobs, trade unions are sceptical of green demands. Trade unions are in a dilemma: on the one hand, they represent workers and are concerned with job security; on the other hand, they represent also the interests of workers for a clean environment. In general, green issues seem to be more acute in white-collar trade unions than in blue-collar unions. Opposing attitudes on environmental issues have led to severe conflicts in several white-collar trade unions in Sweden and Germany (Jahn, 1993).

Concepts such as **sustainable development** and **ecological modernization** help trade unions to bridge the gulf between economic and environmental principles. These concepts combine the promotion of environmental ideas with claims for economic growth and technological progress. This compromise formula has led to an increasing openness of trade unions for ecological issues. However, this strategy also implies that green actors give up their ideological core claims.

Under the banner of sustainable development – often translated by trade-union activists to sustainable growth – and ecological modernization, environmental regulation is becoming more common in industrial relations in many industrial societies. Even more so, since enterprises and business associations also agree to aspects of sustainable growth and ecological modernization.

See also: green bans; new social movements

References

Jahn, D. (1993) *New Politics and Trade Unions. An Organization Theoretical Analysis of the Debate on Nuclear Energy in Swedish and German Trade Unions*, Aldershot: Dartmouth.

Offe, C. (1985) 'New Social Movements: Challenging the Boundaries of Institutional Politics', *Social Research* 52 (4): 817–68.

Siegmann, H. (1985) *The Conflict Between Labor and Environmentalism in the Federal Republic of Germany and the United States*, Aldershot: Gower.

Touraine, A., Wieviorka, M. and Dubet, F. (1987) *The Workers' Movement*, Cambridge: Cambridge University Press.

DETLEF JAHN

Lake Baikal

Russia's Lake Baikal (Mongolian *Dalai Nor*, 'The Holy Sea') is the world's largest and most ancient fresh-water lake. Formed 30–50 million years ago, it contains some 20 per cent of all fresh-water supplies. The lake is a site of exceptional natural beauty, and scientific and cultural importance. Two-thirds of the 2,400 plants and animals living in the lake are unique, including the nerpa, the planet's only freshwater seal. The estimated four miles of sediments beneath the lake floor provide a detailed picture of global climate change over the millennia.

While not a problem on the scale of the **Chernobyl** or **Aral Sea** disasters, numerous major threats to the lake's ecology exist, notably industrial and municipal wastewater emissions, uncontrolled logging, and airborne pollution from nearby cities. The Lake Baikal basin was designated a World Heritage Property by UNESCO in 1996. However post-Soviet economic decline continues to make adequate protection problematic.

MATTHEW WYMAN

Lalonde, Brice

b. 10 February 1946, France

Politician

A student in Law and Humanities, Brice Lalonde is very active in unions and on the cultural scene (Chairman of **Friends of the Earth** France). In the 1970s, he became involved in political ecology and the Independentist Left, and he was banned from the *Parti Socialiste Unitaire* in 1976. He helped foster environmental awareness in France through the use of the media and collaboration with leading French intellectuals. During the 1981 electoral campaign he stood on an ecological platform without belonging to any political party. He calls himself a 'libéral-libertaire' and has set up a number of alliances with both French left-and right-wing parties. In 1990 he formed his own party ***Génération Ecologie***. Since 1995 his political stance has become unclear and his electoral support has rapidly dwindled.

BRUNO VILLALBA

land reform

Land reform has been an important demand for green parties and **environmental movements**. Yet contradictions between demands to redistribute land more widely and more radical opposition to the concept of land ownership are apparent. Equally while greens have seen land reform as a way of creating a sustainable economy, it has often been conceptualized by **development** economists as a means of launching rapid **industrialization** in developing countries.

Conservative political ecologists such as Garrett **Hardin** and environmental economists have argued that communal or unowned resources, including land, tend to be over-exploited (see **environmental economics**). Radical greens have in contrast argued that private ownership intensifies the drive to commodify and exploit such resources. Forms of self regulation based on communal/unowned land have been promoted as an alternative to both the market and the state as a means of ecological management. Indeed **deep ecology** and other forms of radical ecology are hostile to the very concept of land ownership. The ecologist Aldo **Leopold** promoted a 'land ethic' and radical environmentalists have seen land as sacred and have sought its decommodification.

Green activists have also seen the redistribution of land as important in promoting a self-sufficient alternative to industrial productivism. Marx minutely analysed how the removal of common land or unowned land disposed rural populations and accelerated the creation of an urban proletariat. Green parties and environmentally orientated anarchists from Kropotkin onwards have stressed the redistribution of land as an alternative to **capitalism** (see **anarchism/eco-anarchism**). Land reform has also been seen by Greens as a means of promoting specifically ecological forms of agriculture such as permaculture and organic cultivation. Martinez-Alier in his work *Ecological Economics* (1987) has sought to promote green 'neo-narodnism' situating traditional peasants as the guardians of the land and low energy producers.

Since the nineteenth century environmentalists have sought to improve access to land so that the public can enjoy leisure pursuits such as bird watching and walking. In Britain during the 1930s the British Workers Sports Federation organized mass trespasses on the Kinder Scout Moor in Derbyshire which had been monopolized by private owners for grouse shooting. This campaign of direct action helped to create pressure for the establishment of **national parks** and improved access to land.

Established in Britain in the mid-1990s, The Land is Ours is a social movement organization promoting land reform and ecological agriculture. It has promoted land occupations to pin-point maldistribution of land and neglect. In 1995 it occupied an area of land in Surrey in memory of the Digger occupation of nearby St Georges Hill in 1649. The Diggers was a radical movement during the time of the English Civil War that claimed that land should be held communally. Radical green networks in Europe and North America have also maintained links with movements in the south of the globe such as the Brazilian Sem Terra and the Mexican Zapatistas that act for the landless (see **Zapatistas/Chiapas**).

See also: indigenous peoples

References

Martinez-Alier, J. (1987) *Ecological Economics*, Oxford: Basil Blackwell.

Roberts, A. (1979) *The Self-Managing Environment*, London: Allison and Busby.

Shoard, M. (1997) *This Land is Our Land*, London: Gaia.

URL: http://www.oneworld.org/tlio.

'Whose Common Future?' (1992) *The Ecologist*, 22(4).

DEREK WALL

land use regulation/planning

The **development** of land raises a wide range of human and physical issues, and so has been the subject of legislation in many countries. A central consideration in planning is the value of a parcel of land, and the way in which conversion to a new use may increase its value. Typically, land which is in a low intensity use, such as amenity or **agriculture**, will greatly increase in value if it becomes available for housing, industry or commerce, and if it possesses suitable physical qualities (e.g. high bearing capacity, good drainage) and locational qualities (e.g. adjacent to a town centre or motorway access).

Generally the development of land has an impact on the environment (e.g. habitat destruction), community (e.g. pressure on services) and economy (e.g. creation of jobs). Consequently, many countries have ensured that land development can only take place subject to certain 'rules of transference'. The usual effect of these rules is that the right to develop land is 'nationalized', that is, conversion of land to urban–industrial uses cannot be undertaken without local political approval. A number of variants on this approach prevail globally, ranging from confiscation or nationalization of the land itself, through to the payment of full compensation to owners for the loss of development rights. Even in liberal democracies, the state often has the legal right to acquire private land compulsorily if there are perceived to be overriding benefits to the wider community.

Land use planning is generally implemented through the production of area-based plans and the regulation of individual site-specific development proposals in accordance with these plans. Planning is undertaken by professionals ('officers') with a training in design, aesthetics, land law, civil engineering, social science and natural science. In liberal democracies, planners' decisions are moderated by politicians ('elected members'), who are the ultimate arbiters of officers' recommendations. Planning often operates at the local level, but local plans and decisions are usually subject to regional and national approval, and higher-level authorities may moderate plans and decisions in the wider public interest. For both plans and individual proposals, there are usually opportunities for specific consultees to make comments relevant to their particular interests (e.g. for wildlife conservation organizations to comment on nature conservation impacts), and for the general public to comment on issues of personal concern.

There are two principal theoretical perspectives on planning: one regards the physical nature of competition for sites with specific qualities; the other relates to the political nature of power relations between different interest groups. On the one hand, therefore, land may be represented as a scarce physical resource for which users compete, and where state officials intervene in the marketplace to ensure that land use changes are reasonably rational and consonant with the best interests of society. Reflecting this perspective, town and country planning legislation tends to be most strongly developed in densely populated industrialized countries, such as the UK and the **Netherlands**. On the other hand, planning practice may be seen as a contested territory between actors with differential political influence, so that the role of planners ranges from one of sanctioning investors' interests, to acting as advocates on behalf of disadvantaged sections of the community.

Rydin (1998) has identified a number of theories of planning which reflect different points along the technical–political spectrum; these theories should be seen as complementary rather than mutually exclusive. Early planning theories tended to be based on 'environmental determinism', whereby planners' skills were employed to design technical solutions to the physical use of urban spaces. Later analyses gave prominence to planners' influence on the formulation of public policy and the management of urban areas; however, these tended to assume a fairly uncomplicated link between the formulation and implementation of policy, and so are described as 'naïve public administration'. Subsequent interpretations comprised those of: 'organization theory' (planners as networkers, negotiating with interested parties over resource allocation); 'liberal political economy' (applying decision-making techniques to ameliorate market failures); 'radical political economy' (planners as agents of a capitalist state facilitating supply-side economics); 'political sociology' (planners acting as urban gatekeepers, exercising their limited powers over the allocation of goods and the reduction of inequalities); 'new right' (planners setting market signals to encourage economic investment); 'new left' (planners facilitating the active involvement of different sections of local communities); and an 'institutional approach' (relating theories of structuration to sectional interests in the development process). Latterly, there has also been great interest in the ability of planning to stimulate debate within neighbourhoods about alternative futures, involving planners in the facilitation of a collective and democratic approach to design. This type of approach places great emphasis on deliberative and inclusive processes, such as community conferences, focus groups and citizens' juries.

There are several ways in which planning legislation can be framed in order to achieve its objectives. In Britain, and in many Commonwealth countries which modelled their legislation on Britain, the solution has been to withdraw landowners' automatic rights to development. ('Development' is narrowly defined, and refers to the transformation of land from agriculture or forestry to industrial, residential, commercial, transportation, mining or amenity use, or changes in the use of 'developed' land.) In this legislation, a land use plan is drawn up by officers, in consultation with local communities, approved by local politicians and, directly or indirectly, sanctioned by national government. Subsequently, any further development is approved (by locally elected members, acting on the advice of officers) insofar as it accords with the policies and proposals of the adopted plan. Plans may be subject to public examination or local **public inquiry**, whilst individual applications may be considered at a public inquiry if an applicant appeals against a decision or central government 'calls in' a controversial application. In these instances, an inspector appointed by central government presides over the proceedings. Owners of land with development potential receive no recompense from the state if they are denied 'betterment' opportunities (i.e. windfall gains in the value of land allocated to development). In several countries (e.g. the USA) the approach is less flexible, and a 'zoning plan' is produced, so that proposals gain relatively automatic approval provided they meet pre-specified criteria for a particular zone. In these circumstances, if planners wish to protect land for public amenity, they may need to persuade owners to forego the future possibility of 'betterment' and offer them compensation, through schemes such as 'transfer of development rights'. In **New Zealand**, the Resource Management Act has sought to stream-

line a range of planning and zoning procedures so that these can be used flexibly in order to promote the achievement of an integrated environmental 'bottom line' rather than rely solely on compliance with regulations.

Land use planning can contribute to the attainment of **sustainable development** objectives. In particular, it can promote settlement patterns which minimize unnecessary traffic generation, re-use **brownfield sites**, improve **quality of life**, protect cultural and **natural capital**, and favour environmentally-efficient buildings. Planners can also help reduce natural resource depletion by controlling mineral extraction and supporting the use of 'secondary' aggregates (i.e. those which are re-cycled from demolished and dismantled buildings, roads, etc.). More generally, planners can pursue environmental aims directly though the safeguard of amenity land from development, and indirectly through partnerships to promote conservation and recreation interests in town and country. Planning legislation often includes provisions for environmental impact assessment, which ensure that proposals with potentially serious ecological consequences are subjected to a more comprehensive review.

See also: land reform; takings; urbanization

Reference

Rydin, Y. (1998) *Urban and Environmental Planning in the UK*, London: Macmillan

Further reading

Cullingworth, J.B. and Nadin, V. (1997) *Town and Country Planning in the UK*, London: Routledge.

Johnson, W.C. (1997) *Urban Planning and Politics*, Chicago: American Association of Planners.

Kenny, M. and Meadowcroft, J. (eds) (1999) *Planning Sustainability*, London: Routledge.

Selman, P. (2000) *Environmental Planning*, London: Sage.

PAUL SELMAN

landscape

With its origins in the eighteenth century, landscape differs from other terms describing the natural world in often being associated with and/or conveying a particular aesthetic (and spatial) appreciation of **nature**, hence its relation to the tradition of 'landscape painting'. In particular, the idea of landscape conveys a natural vista from a distinctly human and social perspective. Thus, landscape is often not a neutral description of 'natural', but a value-laden account of how nature ought to be seen or regarded. A good example of this is the accounts of 'lifeless' or 'deserted' landscapes Europeans gave when they first encountered the Americas and Australia, often completely omitting/denying the fact that these environments were already inhabited by **indigenous peoples**. In keeping with its aesthetic and prescriptive origins, landscape is often associated with the intentional transformation and arrangement of nature in accordance with some human design, as in 'landscape gardening'. Following on from this, another sense of landscape is that it refers to 'domesticated nature' rather than 'wilderness'.

JOHN BARRY

Lannoye, Paul

b. 22 June 1939, Sprimont, Belgium

Politician

Paul Lannoye has been a key figure of Belgian environmental politics since the 1970s (see **Belgium**). Until 1986, he also pursued a scientific career as a physicist. In 1976, he founded the Belgian section of **Friends of the Earth**, and was particularly active in the **anti-nuclear movements**. He played a key role in several progressive and green initiatives and lists in the 1970s, which eventually led to the creation of **Ecolo** in 1980. From 1980–3 and from 1985–8, he was member of the Executive committee and spokesperson of Ecolo, and was elected to the Senate in 1987. Since 1989 he has been a Member of the European Parliament, re-elected in 1994 and 1999. He was also the co-president of the **Green Group in the European Parliament** from 1992 to 1994 and from 1999 onwards, and has mainly dealt with energy-related issues, genetic engineering and various aspects of consumer protection.

BENOÎT RIHOUX

Larzac Plateau

Located in the Aveyron department of the Midi-Pyrénées region in **France**, this rural area, made up of limestone plateaux (Causses), was rapidly depopulated in the 1960s. In 1971, the military authorities planned to extend one of their bases which was located in Larzac. Farmers there rejected the project. Between 1971 and 1981 when President François Mitterrand scrapped the project, there was constant opposition. Public pressure led to impressive demonstrations (for example, on 25 and 26 August 1973, when 60,000 people demonstrated), which brought together anti-military and non-violent groups (Community of the Arch, Lanza del Vasto), but also environmental and **anti-nuclear movements**. Almost all left-wing, far left and anarchist organizations were also present. The '*Lutte*' has enabled the setting up of numerous networks, which still today provide links between the former members of the organizations involved.

BRUNO VILLALBA

Latin American environmental politics

Environmentalism is the expression of conflicts of interest and power strategies for the sustainable management of environmental goods and services, and for the social appropriation of **nature**. Environmental politics embrace three different complementary instances: a) government and governance institutional settings for environmental administration and conflict resolution; b) environmentalism within political parties; and c) the field of social conflict in the appropriation of nature where social actors engage in movements and actions related to **ecological debt**, **environmental justice**, ecological distribution and **democracy**. The first level will be referred to as environmental policies, the second as green party politics, and the third as political ecology.

In the field of environmental policies, since the 1970s Latin American countries have been evolving in the design of different institutional arrangements to address issues of environmental quality, conservation of **biodiversity**, and sustainable management of natural resources. From the first Ministry of the Environment established in Venezuela in 1978, today all countries of the region have national environmental agencies with different institutional designs and degrees of intervention in national **development** policies. They vary from Ministries of the Environment and Natural Resources (in some cases linked to other government sectors) in Argentina, Bolivia, **Brazil**, Colombia, Costa Rica, Cuba, Ecuador, El Salvador, Nicaragua, **Mexico**, Uruguay and Venezuela; Secretaries of State for the Environment and Natural Resources in Dominican Republic, Honduras and Paraguay; National Authority of the Environment in Panama; National Council of the Environment in Peru and National Commissions of the Environment in Chile and Guatemala. These Ministries include in their structures national institutes in charge of developing and enforcing environmental laws and instruments for **sustainable development** planning and monitoring, and general attorney bureaus to address and solve environmental conflicts. The governments of Latin America and the Caribbean have established since 1980 a Forum of Ministers of the Environment with the co-operation of the Regional Office for Latin America and the Caribbean of the **United Nations Environment Programme** to set and co-ordinate an action plan for the Latin American and Caribbean region integrating their main common issues with the global environmental agenda.

After the Earth Summit in Rio de Janeiro in 1992 (see **Rio Conference 1992**), participation and consensus became key words for every project related to sustainable development. Thus, the Earth Council launched a process to integrate different stakeholders in the implementation of **Agenda 21** and in national policies for environmental protec-

tion and sustainable development. National (Consultative) Councils for Sustainable Development (NCSD) have been established worldwide, with eleven such councils in Latin America (Argentina, Bolivia, Brazil, **Chile**, Cuba, Dominican Republic, El Salvador, Honduras, Mexico, Nicaragua and Panama). With different missions, composition and operative structures, NCSD has promoted dialogue and debate of relevant interest groups to integrate economic, environmental and social dimensions of **sustainability** into national policy-making; consultation and participation of academia, business, industry, parliamentarians and NGOs, as well as regional and local governments, are contributing to a more democratic political culture in the decision-making process and planning for sustainable development. Local Agenda 21 programmes are also generating multi-stakeholder processes for the diagnosis and resolution of environmental conflicts and the participatory planning of sustainable development projects.

Environmental politics are not only expressed in the participation of multi-stakeholders in policy-making and in the implementation of sustainable development programmes, but are reflected also in the ways and degrees in which environmental issues penetrate the institutional political structure. The greening of politics and policies has led to the emergence of green parties and to the internalization of environmental issues in other parties, in congress and in actual government programmes. In the last decade, green parties have been established in countries like Brazil, Mexico and Chile. However, green parties have remained marginal and unsuccessful in gaining electoral support and political power. Green parties are linked and recognized by the *Federación de Partidos Verdes de las Américas*; however in countries like Mexico, they have little support and legitimation from the environmental movement and the academic community. Green parties have been unable to build a political discourse to integrate economic, political, social and cultural demands that would attract the electorate in search of fresh political alternatives. Green parties have remained minority sectoral groups that are viewed as conservationists with no clear proposals regarding employment, income distribution, poverty alleviation or other pressing social issues such as corruption, efficiency and transparency in governance, national and personal security, **human rights** and political participation.

In Mexico the Greens, coming from a non-governmental organization (NGO), were rejected from the start by the environmentalist community. They ran as the principal and most visible ally of the National Action Party (PAN), which won the presidential elections in 2000. However, the distance between the party and **civil society** ecologists became an impediment for the Green Party to gain power over the Ministry of the Environment in the new government, which took power in December 2000. In Brazil, the most prominent leaders of environmentalism in the political parties have actually developed outside the Green Party which has little political presence.

In the arena of environmental politics and political ecology, the social environmental movement reached its peak in the 1980s and into the 1990s, ecologists from academia and NGOs have taken positions in government, politics and business; in Brazil, Chile and Mexico, leaders of the environmental movement became high ranking government officials and ministers of the environment. However, the movement has undergone fractioning, disarticulation and decomposition, while being absorbed by an institutionalized process of participation in the sustainable development agenda. Environmentalism in Latin America is shifting from middle-class urban ecological groups to a multi-stakeholder social movement that integrates ecological and cultural demands; it is leading to a politics of difference and diversity linked to the emergent environmental rights of grassroots organizations and **indigenous peoples**. From the politics of consensus and participation promoted by environmental policies, political ecology expresses the conflict and claims emerging from the increasing environmental costs imposed on social groups by the dominant patterns of unsustainable development. They reflect the difference between environmentalism of 'post-materialism' (see **Inglehart, Ronald**) and **environmentalism of the poor**. Latin American environmentalism encompasses the extension of liberation theology to ecologism and the shift of the pedagogy

of the oppressed to popular ecological education, as well as a **critical theory** of **social ecology**, eco-Marxism and political ecology (Leff, 1994); it includes such networks as the Latin American Consortium of Social Ecology (CLAES), the Latin American Consortium of Agroecology and Development (CLADES), and the Environmental Training Network for Latin America and the Caribbean.

Environmental politics is expressed in the demands and struggles of peasant and indigenous peoples like the *seringueiros* (rubber tappers) movement of Chico **Mendes** and the network of community-based extractivist reserves of the Amazonian Working Group in Brazil. It is mobilizing the indigenous peoples throughout the Latin American region, from the Seris in the northern arid lands of Sonora, Mexico, to the Mapuches of Argentina and Chile, including the Co-ordination of Indigenous Peoples Organizations of the Amazonian Basin (COICA) and the Negro communities of the Pacific Coast in Colombia, which are reaffirming their identities and reorganizing for the management of their natural and cultural heritage, including their forests and inherited resources. The field of political ecology has expanded to peaceful armed popular movements, such as the Zapatistas in Chiapas Mexico (see **Zapatistas/Chiapas**) and the Green Army of the Indigenous Peoples of the Ecuadorian **Amazonia** which struggle for the preservation of their ecosystems and for a sustainable development based on the harmonious coexistence of diversity in a globalized world. It is slowly extending to large peasant organizations like the landless movement in Brazil.

Some international environmental organizations, such as **Greenpeace**, Rural Advancement Foundation International (RAFI) and Genetic Resources Action International (GRAIN) have a strong presence in Latin American environmentalism. This is a movement that goes beyond demands against biopiracy and ecological damages and for the distribution of benefits from bioprospecting and **eco-tourism** in the new geopolitics of economic–ecologic **globalization** (see also **biopiracy/bioprospecting**). It is a struggle for reappropriation of their patrimony of natural and cultural resources and for the construction of an environmental rationality (Leff, 1995; 2000).

References

Leff, E. (1994) *Ecología y Capital. Racionalidad Ambiental, Democracia Participativa y Desarrollo Sustentable*, Mexico: Siglo XXI/UNAM.

—— (1995) *Green Production. Towards an Environmental Rationality*, New York: Guildford.

—— (2000) 'Sustainable Development in the Developing Countries: Cultural Diversity and Environmental Rationality', in K. Lee *et al.* (eds) *Global Sustainable Development in the 21st Century*, Edinburgh: Edinburgh University Press.

Further reading

Boff, L. (1995) *Ecologia: Gritos da Terra, Gritos dos Pobres*, Sao Paulo: Atica.

Escobar, A. (1997) 'Cultural Politics and Biological Diversity: State, Capital and Social Movements in the Pacific Coast of Colombia', in R. Fox and O. Stern (eds) *Between Resistance and Revolution*, New Brunswick: Rutgers University Press.

García-Guadilla, M.P. and Blauert, J. (eds) (1992) *Environmental Social Movements in Latin America and Europe: Challenging Development and Democracy*, special issue of *International Journal of Sociology and Social Policy*, 12(4–7), United Kingdom: MCB University Press.

Grueso, L., Rosero, C. and Escobar, A. (1998) 'The Process of Black Community Organizing in the Southern Pacific Coast of Colombia', in S.E. Alvarez, E. Dagnino and A. Escobar (eds) *Cultures of Politics/Politics of Cultures: Revisioning Latin American Social Movements*, Boulder: Westview Press.

Gudynas, E. and Evia, G (1991) *La Praxis por la Vida. Introducción a las Metodologías de la Ecología Social*, Montevideo: CLAES/Nordan.

Leff, E. (ed) (1998) *Los Problemas del Conocimiento y la Perspectiva Ambiental del Desarrollo*, Mexico: Siglo XXI, 2000.

Leis, H. (1999) *A Modernidade Insustentável*, Petrópolis: Vozes.

ENRIQUE LEFF

lead poisoning

Lead (Pb) is a metallic element which combines to form many compounds such as salts, and is very toxic to most biological systems. Small doses can cause altered behaviour in humans, large doses can result in paralysis, blindness and death. Pregnant women are particularly vulnerable, when even small amounts can affect the foetus. Lead poisoning in children can damage the brain, kidneys, and nervous system, even low levels can cause learning and behavioural problems. High levels can result in retardation, convulsions and coma. Poisoning can result from inhalation or ingestion of substances containing lead. Common sources are from paint used on dwellings, furniture, and toys, although Britain has no legislation limiting lead additives, it is no longer found in the majority of domestic paints. Other sources include water from lead pipes, contaminated soil and emissions from internal combustion engines using fuel containing lead additive (tetraethyl lead).

DAVID CARLISLE

Leopold, Aldo

b. 11 January 1887, Burlington, Iowa, USA; d. 21 April 1948, Baraboo, Wisconsin

Forester, wildlife ecologist, environmental writer

Aldo Leopold combined successive careers in the US Forest Service and as professor of wildlife management at the University of Wisconsin with an extraordinary ability to articulate the conservation issues of his day and point the way to the future. He is best known as a leader of the movement for wilderness preservation, as the father of the profession of **wildlife management** in the USA, and as the author of *A Sand County Almanac* (1949), an environmental classic that offers the clearest expression of his land ethic philosophy.

Leopold developed his powers of observation, his ethical sense, and his love of 'things natural, wild, and free' in the bluffs and bottomlands of the Mississippi River near Burlington, Iowa, where he grew up. Upon earning a master of forestry in 1909 at the Yale Forest School, he joined the new US Forest Service, leading reconnaissance on the Apache National Forest in Arizona Territory. He rose to supervisor of the Carson Forest in New Mexico by age 25, then began organizing game protective associations and laying the groundwork for a new profession, game management, modelled on the profession of forestry. As assistant district forester in the south-west (1918–24), he also developed ecological analyses of soil erosion, fire, and watershed problems and a rationale for the designation in 1924 of the Gila Wilderness Area, the prototype for a system of undeveloped preserves that was given force of law in the Wilderness Act of 1964 and has grown to nearly a hundred million acres.

Leopold left the Forest Service in 1928 to conduct game surveys, develop an 'American Game Policy' (1930), and write the first text, *Game Management* (1933), for the new profession, then accepted a professorship at the University of Wisconsin where he devoted himself to research on applied **ecology** and wildlife management on farms and other private land. A prolific writer of more than 500 articles, reports, and books, he addressed many of the conservation issues of his day, progressing from a utilitarian emphasis on rational control and efficient management of resources to an ecological conception of naturally self-regulating systems and a conviction of human responsibility for the restoration of land health.

In the last decade of his career Leopold turned increasingly to writing natural history vignettes and philosophical essays encapsulating a lifetime of observation, experience, and reflection about the relationship of people and land, making the case for what he termed a land ethic – 'A thing is right when it tends to preserve the integrity, stability, and beauty of the biotic community. It is wrong when it tends otherwise.' He incorporated his best essays in a book ultimately published a year after his untimely death in 1948 fighting a grass fire on the sand county farm he restored to ecological integrity. He left his wife, Estella Bergere, and five children, Starker, Luna, Nina, Carl, and Estella, all of whom became noted naturalists and three of whom won election to the National Academy of Sciences, an unprecedented achievement for siblings.

A Sand County Almanac, with its keynote essay, 'The Land Ethic', began steady sales that escalated after the ecological awakening of the late 1960s. The book has come to be widely regarded as the most influential American environmental classic of the twentieth century. After decades of distrust of Leopold's legacy by most natural resource professionals and public land agencies bent on more intensive management, Leopold's land ethic philosophy by the 1990s came to be acknowledged by the US Forest Service and other federal and state agencies as the inspiration for a new emphasis on ecosystem management for the twenty-first century. More important, his insistence on our individual responsibility as 'plain member and citizen' of the land community has inspired and guided countless conservation efforts on private lands and in local communities.

Further reading

Flader, S.L. (1974) *Thinking Like a Mountain: Aldo Leopold and the Evolution of an Ecological Attitude Toward Deer, Wolves, and Forests*, Madison: University of Wisconsin Press, 1994.

Flader, S. and Callicott, J.B. (eds) (1991) *The River of the Mother of God and Other Essays by Aldo Leopold*, Madison: Wisconsin Press.

Meine, C. (1988) *Aldo Leopold: His Life and Work*, Madison: Wisconsin Press.

Meine, C. and Knight, R.L. (eds) (1999) *The Essential Aldo Leopold: Quotations and Commentaries*, Madison: Wisconsin Press.

SUSAN L. FLADER

less developed countries

The poorer nations of the world are regularly lumped together in the international press with the terms 'Third World', the 'South', and 'Less Developed Countries' or its abbreviation 'LDCs'. These terms reflect a desire to simplify the complexities of the world and to find a shorthand or time-saver for the 'have' nations in thinking about and interacting with the 'have-not' nations. The terms also provide alternatives to thinking of the world's poorer nations as individual sovereign states or voicing the one distinction that holds any meaningful difference: the nations of western

Europe, **Japan**, and English-speaking North America and the South Pacific are richer and all the other many nations of Asia, Africa, Latin America, and the Caribbean are poorer.

The poorer majority of the world's nations exist as a collective entity only within the language of the world's elites, those who have defined that majority by what they are not. This linguistic counter-distinction is a rhetorical artifact of Cold War competition between the communist and capitalist blocs. A plethora of either/or distinctions – **capitalism/communism**, freedom/equality, West/East – emerged into the language of politics and press to identify the competing sides. As this competition grew increasingly global the two sides sought allies among the world's poorer nations. In the 1960s many of the poorer nations wishing not to take sides in the competition loosely grouped themselves into a 'non-aligned movement' seeking an alternative 'third way' to both the capitalist West and the communist East. Academics and the press within the USA quickly labelled the nations of this movement the 'Third World', arrogating to the richer capitalist nations the label of 'First World' and casting that of 'Second World' on to the communist nations.

The term 'Third World' has never been embraced by the poorer nations to which it refers, but 'Third World' nonetheless remains commonly used by those living and working elsewhere. In politics and academia 'Third World' has been recognized as prejudicial and, especially since the end of the Cold War, increasingly irrelevant. It has been partially replaced by 'Less Developed Countries' or the abbreviation 'LDCs'. While prejudice is also inferred from this term, it has the advantage of reflecting quantifiable and meaningful distinctions between the richer and poorer nations. The distinctions are demographic and economic statistics commonly including per capita income, literacy rates, life expectancy, infant and childhood mortality, and often several others.

Because of their severe **famines** and armed conflicts during the 1970s, it was further suggested that the poorest of the poorer nations should be separately identified as a 'Fourth World'. This trend toward rank-ordered enumeration halted with the formation of the 'Group of Seventy-Seven', a consultative union of the world's poorest nations, but the rhetorical imprecision continued. By the end of the twentieth century, even the Group of Seventy-Seven included 133 nations.

To avoid prejudicial implications of 'third', 'fourth', and 'less', yet another collective term, 'South', has also been used. While 'South' may be more value neutral, it is not especially accurate. Its factual inaccuracies include the presence of the richer nations of Australia and New Zealand south of the equator and, more significantly, the presence of the great majority of the world's poorer people north of it. And the term 'South' again defines the world's poorer nations by what they are not: not on the average as far north as western Europe, North America, or Japan. The more geographically accurate 'Equatorial' and 'Tropical' never gained favour.

The difference all these terms seek to rank, compare, or obscure is the prevalence of poverty. Poverty obviously is more prevalent in the poorer nations. More importantly, as Indira Gandhi, late Prime Minister of **India** and leader of the non-aligned movement observed, 'Poverty is the greatest environmental threat'. Poverty means continuing population growth and deforestation in the Tropics, plus the associated soil erosion, scarcity of water, and loss of **biodiversity**. It promises a greater likelihood of conflict over resources and all the misery that brings. Perhaps the elites of the world, the richer nations and the richer people of the poorer ones prefer euphemisms to reality, but the question is whether they can afford them.

See also: distributive justice; North/South divide; population movement and control; sustainable development; World Bank

Further reading

Gonzalez, A. and Norwine, J. (eds) (1998) *The New Third World*, Boulder, CO: Westview Press.

Mason, M. (1997) *Development and Disorder: A History of the Third World since 1945*, Hanover, NH: University Press of New England.

PAUL CHANDLER

liberalism/liberal democracy

Liberal democracy is a system of political institutions combining elements of liberalism and **democracy**. Liberalism is a theory with three levels: philosophical, political and economic. Philosophical liberalism presumes (1) the existence of an irreducible plurality of views on the good life, as a fact of political or ethical life; (2) moral equality of individuals; (3) moral priority of the individual's fate over that of more abstract entities (family, state, ideals); and (4) neutrality with regard to individual plans of life and theories of the good on the part of the state, either as a political necessity or as a moral virtue.

Political and economic liberalism translate these ideas into institutions and rules. The former distinguishes between the public sphere of politics and state, and the private sphere of individuals, **civil society** and economy. Economic liberalism, of which **capitalism** is an incarnation, defends **property rights** and freedom of trade as necessary conditions for the realization of individuals' plans of life.

Philosophical liberalism can be subdivided in a classic and a social tradition, both of which can be traced back to John Locke and the early **Enlightenment**. In the classic tradition, the state exists to protect the individual's natural rights, in particular those to property, from interference by others (negative freedom). It is to remain neutral with regard to religious and ethical theories of the good. These are seen as purely individual convictions, by some even as expressing 'preferences' external to the individual's self. On the most radical interpretation of classic liberalism (libertarianism), collective actors like the state can limit individual freedom only when and while the affected individual agrees voluntarily.

The social liberal tradition expects the state to impartially promote the individual quest for the good life. On this view, negative liberty is only one means of advancing autonomy, next to for instance equality and social or **distributive justice**. Hence, freedom can be limited. For social liberals, a (hypothetical) consensus among reasonable and impartial individuals is a necessary condition for the justification of principles, policies and institutions.

Liberal democracy is characterized by political liberty (individual negative freedom), political democracy (the voting system), economic liberty (freedom of enterprise) and economic democracy (a free market). Since democracy allows a choice for undemocratic or illiberal policies, liberal democracies constrain it through constitutions and counterbalancing powers. Liberalism is a procedural theory, liberal democracy a procedural practice: they do not prescribe any specific theory of the good or ideal society, but merely exclude some practices as illegitimate. Consequently, they offer limited room for incorporating elements of **green political theory**.

All forms of liberalism, for instance, allow **free-market environmentalism** and **green consumerism**, either as preferences or in the pursuit of autonomy. Liberalism's insistence on the protection of individual freedom offers additional opportunities for individuals or collective agents to combat potential environmental and health hazards like pollution. (See also **business and the environment**; **ecological modernization**). Classic liberalism often defends private property of resources as justified provided 'enough and as good' is left for others; here, the argument of scarcity can be used in defence of the environment. In social liberalism, the drive for equality and social justice can vindicate **eco-taxes** and restrictions on trade, production and consumption. Finally, it can be argued that the environment is a precondition of life, hence that its protection is an indispensable side-constraint on individual rights and freedoms.

Yet the protection of the environment is nearly always a contingent interest for liberalism, only important when serving human interests. Since liberalism is inspired by **anthropocentrism**, what room it leaves for an appreciation of **nature** in itself lies in the sphere of individual preferences. Nature is a collection of resources, unprotected against transformation into artifice. Moreover, it is a collection of resources for humans only, not for nature itself (although liberal thinkers increasingly consider **animal rights** defensible). Additionally, green political theories advocate a unique ecologically desirable society and way of life, which cannot be squared with the liberal requirement of neutral

or impartial government. Finally, liberal democratic institutions are themselves often obstacles for
ecological politics: constitutions are highly conservative, institutions can be remarkably resilient to
change, and existing democratic procedures are
more fit to record preferences than to discuss and
develop them.

Further reading:

Barry, J. and Wissenburg, M. (eds) (2001) *Sustaining Liberal Democracy*, London: Macmillan.

Doherty, B. and De Geus, M. (eds) (1996) *Democracy and Green Political Thought*, London: Routledge.

Nozick, R. (1974) *Anarchy, State, and Utopia*, New York: Basic Books.

Rawls, J. (1972) *A Theory of Justice*, Oxford: Oxford University Press.

Wissenburg, M. (1998) *Green Liberalism*, London: UCL Press.

MARCEL WISSENBURG

life cycle assessment

Life cycle assessment (LCA) is a process to evaluate
the environmental burdens associated with a
product, package, process, or activity by identifying
and quantifying energy and material use and
environmental releases throughout the life cycle.
A product's life cycle begins with the initial
acquisition of raw materials from the ground or
water and continues through all stages of processing, manufacturing, distribution, transportation,
consumption/use, and final disposal. LCA can
assist organizations with environmental improvements. The stages in LCA are set out in ISO 14040
as: scoping and goal definition; inventory analysis;
impact assessment classification – group parameters in impact categories; characterization –
quantify risk of impact categories; valuation –
compare characterizations; improvement assessment. Problems in LCA include defining system
boundary, defining the functional unit for compar-

ison, obtaining consistent data and the inherent
subjective choices involved in the process.

ROD S. BARRATT

Limits to Growth

In 1972, a team of scientists from Massachusetts
Institute of Technology (MIT) led by Donella
Meadows and Dennis Meadows, produced for the
Club of Rome (a futuristic association of scientists,
technocrats, and politicians from 25 countries) the
global computer model 'World 3'. The team
utilized the systems dynamics method, which goes
back to the 1940s and Jay Forrester's digital
computer and information-feedback applications
in studying social systems. Their research provided
the basis for *The Limits to Growth* (1972), which not
only became a seminal study, helping to give birth
to **ecological economics**, but also made head-
lines in the world news media, provoking a debate
on exponential growth and the finiteness of the
earth's resources that has echoed ever since.

The Limits to Growth is concerned with five factors
that will ultimately limit growth: population,
agricultural production, natural resources, industrial production, and pollution. The study reached
three major conclusions. First, within less than a
hundred years given no major changes in traditional physical, economic, or social relationships,
the global industrial system will run out of
resources and collapse. Second, piecemeal approaches to solving particular problems, such as
even doubling the resource base, will not be
successful in preventing the collapse. Third, the
collapse can be avoided only by immediate self-
restraint on population and economic expansion;
otherwise, growth will stop catastrophically when it
collides with the natural limits of the earth.

The computer model of the MIT study was
vigorously critiqued by other scientists, and its
uncomfortable conclusions provoked editorial reactions to its doom-saying (see **doomsayers**).
Nevertheless, *The Limits to Growth* (which became a
bestseller) had a major influence on the thinking of
the international environmental movement which

was surging about the same time. In 1992, the team produced a sequel, *Beyond the Limits*, which argued that 'the global industrial system had already overshot some of the earth's vital ecological limits and could collapse by the middle of the next century – unless we commit ourselves to sweeping systemic changes...'.

References

Meadows, D.H., Meadows, D.L, Randers, J. and Behrens III, W.W. (1972) *The Limits to Growth*, New York: New American Library.

Meadows, D.H., Meadows, D.L., and Randers, J. (1992) *Beyond the Limits* Post Mills, VT: Chelsea Green Publishing Co.

E. GENE FRANKLAND

Love Canal

From the 1920s to 1950s, an abandoned canal in Niagara Falls, New York, USA served as a repository for both municipal waste, and hazardous industrial waste from the Hooker Chemical and Plastics Company. Over 20,000 metric tons of highly toxic chemicals, some contaminated with chlorinated **dioxins**, were dumped in the canal. By the late 1970s a local public health emergency became apparent: incidences of cancer, birth defects and other serious maladies were well above the national average. After numerous investigations and lawsuits, the parent company of Hooker Chemical agreed to pay over $250 million in damages to local residents. Clean-up activities lasted several years.

The Love Canal disaster set the foundation for federal environmental regulations such as the Comprehensive Environmental Response, Compensation and Liability Act ('**Superfund** Law').

Further reading

Love Canal Homeowners Association (1998) *Love Canal Chronological Report, April 1978 – January 1980*, Niagara Falls, NY: Love Canal Homeowners Association.

JOHN PICHTEL

Lovins, Amory B. and Hunter

Amory B. Lovins: b. 13 November 1947, Washington, DC, USA

Hunter Lovins: b. 26 February 1950, Middlebury, Vermont, USA

Energy researchers and consultants

Amory and Hunter Lovins are the cofounders of the Rocky Mountain Institute, a non-profit resource centre in Old Snowmass, Colorado and work together as analysts, consultants, and lecturers on energy and resource policy. From their research and educational foundation, they and their staff investigate efficiency issues and propose solutions which have a firm base in reality. One example is 'hypercar', an ultra-light-weight, hybrid-electric vehicle. The Lovins have received a great deal of support for their alternative 'soft path' approach to using energy-efficient technologies to meet future demands (see **soft energy path**). In recent years, they have also devoted a good deal of attention to research on water, **agriculture**, forests, sustainable corporations, economic renewal, and global security.

WARREN VANDER HILL

Luddites

The term Luddites refers to the workers and their families who protested against the introduction of new machines and practices in English factories by breaking machines and threatening mill owners. Their activity was concentrated in the East Midlands, West Yorkshire and North Cheshire between 1811 and 1812. Historians of the movement since E.P. Thompson have mostly accepted his characterization of Luddism as a revolt against the violation of the moral economy as a result of the introduction of modern **capitalism**. In the mid-twentieth century 'Luddite' became a derogatory term for unthinking opposition to progress. In fact the Luddites were not against new **technology**, only against technology that caused poverty. In the 1990s green radicals such as Kirkpatrick Sale, Challis Glendinning and Wendell **Berry** aligned themselves with the Luddite heritage by adopting a neo-Luddite manifesto. Its first principle was: opposition to technologies based upon rationality as the key to human potential, material acquisition as the key to human fulfilment and technological development as the key to social progress. The programme also included dismantling nuclear, computer and television technologies and the creation of new technologies by those who use them and are affected by them.

BRIAN DOHERTY

Luxembourg

The Grand Duchy of Luxembourg is a very small (2,586 km^2) and densely populated country (more than 420,000 inhabitants). It is also quite diverse in geographical terms. The northern part of the country (the *Oesling*) is covered by forests and much less populated, whereas the central and southern parts (the *Gutland*) are much more densely urbanized. Only a small south-eastern strip still features heavy industries, whereas the bulk of the country's economic activity consists in a thriving tertiary sector, concentrated in and around the capital city of Luxembourg.

Before the 1970s, environmental issues were not on the agenda. Yet, quite large nature protection organizations already existed for decades, such as the *Ligue Nationale pour la Protection des Oiseaux*. The first major environmental dispute arose in the mid-1970s, around a joint Luxembourg–German nuclear power plant project in Remerschen, in the Moselle valley. Eventually, the project was abandoned, but, along with other large infrastructure projects, it played a key role in the emergence of various ***Bürgerinitiativen***, quite similar to the German context. At the 1979 legislative and European elections, an ephemeral list called *Alternativ Lëscht – Wiert Iëch!* (Alternative List – Defend Yourselves!) was fielded, with very modest results. Two years later, the French decision to build a very large nuclear power plant in Cattenom, right near the border, acted as a further catalyst for the creation of a broader and quite influential environmental organization, the *Mouvement écologique*, maintaining links with several parties but remaining politically neutral.

In June 1983, activists from various *Bürgerinitiativen* and left-wing groups set up the *Gréng Alternativ Partei* (GAP), in the mould of the German ***Grünen***. At the June 1984 legislative and European elections, it obtained an encouraging 5.2 per cent and 2 national MPs. Shortly thereafter, after a bitter factional debate between a more participationist and a more 'alternative' wing, one of the two MPs and leading figure of the party, Jupp Weber, left the party but remained an independent MP. In June 1987, he launched a more moderate green party, the *Gréng Lëscht-Ekologësch Initiativ* (GLEI), reinforcing his personal popularity after the 1987 local elections.

At the 1989 legislative elections, both the GAP (4.1 per cent) and the GLEI (5.9 per cent) obtained 2 MPs, and decided to form a common parliamentary group along with the Communists. This allowed the Greens to initiate a modest professionalization process. During the next few years, the two parties converged increasingly, and presented a single list at the 1994 elections, making a breakthrough both at the national (11.5 per cent, 5 seats) and European (10.9 per cent, one seat) levels. The two parties eventually merged into *Déi Gréng* in early 1995. A few months later, the sole MEP Jupp Weber once again left the party and kept his European seat. This didn't prevent the Greens from consolidating as the country's fourth political force, obtaining good results at the local elections, and confirming their status at the June 1999 national (9.1 per cent, 5 seats) and European elections (10.7 per cent, one seat) in spite of the presence of a competing green list headed by Jupp Weber.

In the meantime, quite a few major environmental issues have been on the agenda. Many of them have had to do with the increasing pressure of car traffic, as more than 70,000 people (more than one-third of the country's total workforce) commute daily from nearby Belgium, France and Germany to businesses and supranational organizations in and around the capital city of Luxembourg. The country also happens to be a transeuropean crossing point for road traffic, draining a massive number of 'petrol tourists' (coming to or passing through Luxembourg in order to purchase cheap petrol). This has regularly been the source of a smog problem, noise pollution, but also of – much disputed – motorway projects throughout the country. The proximity of the Cattenom nuclear power plant is also still an issue, in spite of the elaboration, in 1986, of a national emergency plan.

Since the 1980s especially, the volume and diversity of environmental pieces of legislation and regulations have increased tremendously, ranging from water protection, **forest management**, waste management, regulation of economic activities, country planning, etc. The first 'environment' ministerial portfolio was introduced in 1974. From 1999 onwards, there is not only one minister in charge of these matters, but also a Secretary of State.

BENOÎT RIHOUX

M

Maathai, Wangari

b. 1940, Nyeri, Kenya

Environmental activist

Wangari Maathai was born in Kenya in 1940, studied in Kansas, Pittsburgh and Munich, gaining her doctorate from Nairobi University in 1971 where she became professor of anatomy. Through the National Council of Women of Kenya, she launched the Kenyan Green Belt movement on World Environment Day, 5 June 1977. A woman-based grassroots movement of nurseries distributed trees to villages to re-forest the country. By the mid-1980s there were 600 tree nurseries involving 2–3000 women. Eventually twelve African countries became involved in planting millions of trees. Wangari Maathai's active involvement in environmental protest and Kenyan politics, where she stood for President, led her to be subject to house arrest, a banning order and serious physical attack. She has been a member of the Women's Environmental and Development Organization (WEDO), the UN Advisory Board on Disarmament and received the alternative Nobel Prize the Right Livelihood Award in 1984, **United Nations Environment Programme** (UNEP) Global 2000 Award and the Goldman Environmental Prize.

MARY MELLOR

mad cow disease/BSE

BSE (Bovine Spongiform Encephalopathy), commonly called 'Mad Cow Disease', is a disease of cattle, and is characterized by the sponge-like appearance of the brain at post mortem examinations. It is an example of a policy disaster. Current UK Treasury estimates are that costs stand at £4.5 billion, and that does not include the cost of a possible epidemic of New Variant Creutzfeldt Jacobs Disease. Scientific advisory committees have played a leading role in advising both the UK government and the **European Union**, a paradox when science has failed to provide any answers. The cause, transmission and linkages are still unknown nearly fifteen years after the first official case in 1986.

DAVID CARLISLE

MAI

In 1998, after over three years of negotiation, member countries of the Organization for Economic Co-Operation and Development (OECD) failed to conclude a Multilateral Agreement on Investment (MAI). This agreement was supposed to give foreign investors significant new rights and to put disciplines on countries hosting the investment. Some of these rights and disciplines reached further than the many existing bilateral investment treaties. Developing countries were supposed to accede to the MAI without being allowed to the negotiation table. Negotiations failed due to internal disagreement among negotiating partners and the rising tide of opposition from both non-governmental organizations as well as parliaments from OECD countries. The major point of critique was that the MAI would give too much power to **multinational and transnational corporations** at the expense of sovereign nation-states.

ERIC NEUMAYER

Malthus, Thomas

b. 13 February 1766, Wooten, Surrey, England; d. 23 December 1834, Haileybury

Academic

Thomas Malthus was educated at Cambridge and became Professor of Political Economy and History at Haileybury College, London. Although Malthus made important contributions to the theory of rent he is most famous for his principle of population which states that, unchecked, population grows geometrically while the means of subsistence grows arithmetically (see **population movement and control**). The checks were mostly unpleasant: **famine**, war, plague and general misery. Only the proprietary class might practice moral restraint. Malthus's population theory inspired Darwin's theory of evolution and John Stuart **Mill**'s theory that the economy would reach a steady state. It strongly influenced British social policy towards the poor in the nineteenth century. Neo-Malthusian variations of his theory are frequently incorporated in theories dealing with economically **less developed countries** and in ecological economic thinking about *Limits to Growth*.

Further reading

Malthus, T.R. (1963) *An Essay on the Principle of Population*, Homewood, IL: Richard D. Irwin, Inc.

STANLEY R. KEIL

mangroves

Mangroves exist only in the equatorial region. They are beautiful coastal forests, which resist salinity, protect the coast against sea-level rise, and are an essential habitat for fish production. In many places, local inhabitants use their products (fish and shells, some wood) for direct consumption and also for small-scale markets. In the last 20 years there has been an assault on the mangroves in different countries by the export shrimp-farming industry. Commercial shrimps are grown and fed (with nutrients, antibiotics) in ponds built after cutting the mangroves, thereby depriving poor local people (mainly women) of their livelihood, and destroying the ecosystem. Strong social conflicts, sometimes resulting in deaths, have taken place between local users of the mangroves, and commercial shrimp farmers in Honduras, Ecuador, Sri Lanka, **Philippines** and Thailand. In **India**, the Supreme Court has banned industrial shrimp aquaculture within the country's coastal regulation zone. IsaNet (International Shrimp Action Network) linked together and provided information to local NGOs in the late 1990s.

JOAN MARTINEZ-ALIER

Marsh, George Perkins

b. 15 March 1801, Woodstock, Vermont, USA; d. 23 July 1882, Vallombrosa, Italy

Conservationist and author

George Perkins Marsh is generally regarded as the father of the **conservation movement** in the USA. The author of the prophetic book, *Man and Nature*, published in 1864, Marsh was one of the first Americans to challenge the nineteenth century's zeal for unchecked **development** in virtually every area. A century ahead of his time, Marsh alerted his readers to the problems of food shortages, overpopulation, and chemical pollutants while advocating game preserves, wilderness preservation, and intelligent planning for land use (see **land use regulation/planning**). Many of Marsh's views were based on his extensive travels and observations of other cultures, especially during his period of service as US Ambassador to Turkey (1849–57) and Italy (1861–82) as well as his fluency in 20 languages. Among his avid readers was John **Muir** who said that Marsh inspired him to become a conservationist.

Further reading

Curtis, J. (1982) *The World Of George Perkins Marsh, America's First Conservationist*, Woodstock, VT: Woodstock Foundation.

WARREN VANDER HILL

Marshall, Robert

b. 2 January 1901, New York City, New York, USA; d. 11 November 1939, En route to New York

Wilderness preservationist

Robert ('Bob') Marshall was born to great wealth in New York City but became one of the most zealous advocates for wilderness preservation in the first decades of the twentieth century. A person who early on fell in love with camping and hiking and the preservation of wild places, Marshall was the chief founder and financial supporter of the Wilderness Society (founded 1935) established to fight for the preservation of primitive areas. An explorer, mountaineer, and back packer as well as the holder of a Johns Hopkins' doctorate in plant pathology, Marshall was an enthusiastic supporter of the view that wilderness was needed for aesthetic reasons as a counter to the sameness and boredom of urban society. The Bob Marshall Wilderness area in northwest Montana, one of the jewels of this American system, is named in his memory.

Further reading

Glover, J.M. (1986) *A Wilderness Original: The Life of Bob Marshall*, Seattle: Mountaineers.

WARREN VANDER HILL

mass media and the environment

Prior to the late 1960s, concerns about the environment were expressed by relatively few scientists and members of conservation groups. Since then, however, environmental issues range high on the public and political agenda. The mass media were instrumental in sensitizing large segments of the populace for environmental matters, spurring the spread and activities of newly created environmental groups, and pressing political decision-makers to tackle environmental problems.

Most of our knowledge about environmental problems stems from the mass media rather than first-hand experience. Major environmental disasters have become household names to symbolize the potentially destructive forces of modern civilization. The **Santa Barbara oil spill** (California, 1969), the **Exxon Valdez oil spill** (Alaska, 1989), the polluted soil at **Love Canal** (New York, 1978), the emission of hazardous chemical substances in the **Seveso disaster** (Italy, 1976) and the **Bhopal disaster** (India, 1984), and the **Three Mile Island accident** (Pennsylvania, 1978) and **Chernobyl** (Ukraine, 1986) involving nuclear power plants are a just a few of the many examples that, via the mass media, have influenced our perception of the precarious impact of humans on **nature** and thereby, on humankind itself. The media not only provide us with dry factual knowledge but also with powerful images that appeal to our emotions, such as the dying of an oil-soaked bird on a seashore or the deformation of a baby as a consequence of severe chemical or radioactive pollution.

While vivid images of environmental degradation and destruction may dominate our visual memory, the media offer more than pictures of environmental disasters. They are the main channel to popularize scientific knowledge about the causes and consequences of environmental problems. While probably only a small minority of people have read Rachel **Carson**'s *Silent Spring* and various publications of the Club of Rome, many more have learnt about these writings in the media. Also, common knowledge about environmental groups and environmental policies, ranging from the local to the international levels, is usually drawn from the media. Finally, the role of the media is not restricted to transmitting information. Media are not simply mirrors but also creators and moulders of reality. They select and stress certain aspects; they evaluate and comment; they take a stance and sometimes even become a conflict party. In general, most media are supportive to the environmental cause and tended to present environmental groups in a favourable light.

Unlike face-to-face communication within and between small groups, most types of mass media, namely newspapers, magazines, journals, radio, television, video, and film, are characterized by a structural asymmetry: Relatively few professional 'producers' offer information, opinions and entertainment to a large audience ('the mass') which, for the most part, remains a passive recipient. Also, more recently, the internet has become an important mass medium. In this particular case, communication may take a more reciprocal form so that, in principle, every participant can also be a provider of information.

Newspapers and other print media tend to report routinely on the environment. Some newspapers even devote particular sections to environmental matters, though not necessarily on a daily basis. Moreover, there exist specialized popular journals such as *National Geographic* in the USA, *The Ecologist* in Britain, and *Natur* in Germany, which focus to some extent, or even exclusively, on the environment. In addition, most of the large environmental groups – e.g. the worldwide operating **Greenpeace**, the **Sierra Club** in the USA, and the **Royal Society for the Protection of Birds** in Britain – have their own journals which, in some cases, have a circulation of several hundred thousands of copies.

Alongside the print media, radio and television also cover environmental issues as a potential topic in their daily news. In addition, special documentaries, features, and series may be devoted to aspects of the environment. Television is particularly important in displaying popular series about wildlife, which often, as a side effect, convey a message about threats to the environment and the need to react. Also, some commercial movies, though usually in a more entertaining than informative fashion, have dealt with environmental problems. For example, the fictional film *China Syndrome* (1979)

focused on the threat of a meltdown of a nuclear reactor (see **nuclear energy/nuclear waste management**. *Silkwood* (1983) tells the real story of a trade unionist who mysteriously died in a car accident when she was on her way to deliver proof to a reporter that quality-control records of nuclear fuel rods at the plant were being doctored (see **Silkwood, Karen**). *Erin Brockovich* (1999), a more recent film, portrays an assistant in a small law firm who successfully fights against a large corporation that causes severe environmental damage to its neighbourhood.

Increasingly, the World Wide Web has become an important medium for environmental activities. First, it is a cheap and efficient way to find information about environmental problems and groups. Second, it is used as a channel for communication and mobilization of environmental groups, particularly when these act transnationally. The web played a key role for protest campaigns that, for example, brought together a worldwide coalition to fight the Narmada River dam system in **India** (see **Narmada Valley development programme**). It also served to organize the December 1999 protests against the **World Trade Organization** meetings in Seattle. For some environmental groups such as **Climate Action Network** and EarthAction, the web has become the cornerstone of its activities. It not only links their partner groups across the globe but, in some instances, serves as the very medium of expressing dissent when, for example, thousands of e-mails are sent to protest against an environmental polluter.

While the media's key functions are information and entertainment, its role is not necessarily restricted to these tasks. Intentionally or not, mass media may influence behaviours of individuals, groups and institutions, thus becoming a catalyst or even an agent of social and political change. Because of this pivotal role, environmental associations, pressure groups, corporations, political parties, and public administrations attentively watch how the media covers environmental issues and eagerly try to get their message across. This often includes taking a proactive role by seeking contact with journalists, providing them with background information, distributing press releases, organizing press conferences, and launching action which is likely to attract media attention. Greenpeace is probably the group which was most successful in putting both certain environmental issues and its own trademark on the public agenda. It carefully selects issues that are both highly symbolic and winnable, such as the killing of seal babies. By staging spectacular actions that, based on the image of David versus Goliath, Greenpeace not only attracts attention but also sympathy and financial support.

While it is certainly correct to stress the media's contribution to raise environmental awareness and institutionalize environmental policies, the role of the media is not without problems. First, following their criteria of newsworthiness, the media tend to highlight certain environmental issues while downplaying or completely neglecting others which, from an ecological viewpoint, are probably more urgent. Whereas groups such Greenpeace enjoy public attention due to their well-designed campaigns and spectacular stunts, others have difficulties in getting media coverage and finding volunteers to perform the more cumbersome and mundane routine tasks of environmental protection. Related to the selectivity of the media, is the phenomenon of media issue as emphasized by Anthony Downs (1972) (see **issue attention cycle**). Regardless of the persistence of a particular environmental problem, the media may lose their interest in this issue and turn towards matters that appear more attractive to them. Second, the media tend to simplify environmental problems and conflicts; thereby misrepresenting reality or creating the false image that quick and easy solutions are at hand. Third, the way in which media report environmental problems and activities may have negative consequences for the actors involved who, in their interest in getting media coverage, adapt to the criteria and mechanisms of the media at the expense of other considerations. For example, the media privilege organizations with clear-cut structures and recognizable leaders, preferably prominent figures, over the informal, decentralized and more egalitarian structure of many grassroots groups. Finally, the media may create the overly optimistic impression that environmental crusaders and watchdogs are everywhere and effectively put pressure on corporations and governments while these may react only symbolically.

References

Anderson, A. (1997) *Media, Culture and the Environment*, London: UCL Press.

Chapman, G., Kumar, K., Fraser, C. and Gaber, I. (1997) *Environmentalism and the Mass Media*, London: Routledge.

Downs, A. (1972) 'Up and down with ecology – the "issue-attention cycle" ', *Public Interest* 8(28): 38–50.

Hansen, A. (ed.) (1993) *The Mass Media and Environmental Issues*, Leicester: Leicester University Press.

LaMay, C.L. and Dennis, E.E. (eds) (1991) *Media and the Environment*, Washington, DC and Covelo, CA: Island Press.

Lowe, P.D. and Morrison, D. (1984) 'Bad news or good news: environmental politics and the mass media', *Sociological Review* 32: 75–90.

Mazur, A. (1985) 'The Mass Media in Environmental Controversies', in A. Brannigan and S. Goldenberg (eds) *Social Responses to Technological Change*, Westport und London: Greenwood.

Neuzil, M. and Kovarik, W. (1996) *Mass Media and Environmental Conflict: America's Green Crusades*, London: Sage.

Further reading

Gamson, W.A. and Modigliani, A. (1989) 'Media Discourse and Public Opinion on Nuclear Power: A Constructionist Approach', *American Journal of Sociology* 95(1): 1–37.

Gitlin, T. (1980) *The Whole World is Watching: the mass media in the making and unmaking of the New Left*, Berkeley: University of California Press.

Hilgartner, S. and Bosk, C.L. (1988) 'The Rise and Fall of Social Problems: A Public Arenas Model', *American Journal of Sociology* 94(1): 53–78.

DIETER RUCHT

Max-Neef, Manfred

b. 26 October 1932, Santiago, Chile

Economist

Manfred Max-Neef came to world-wide prominence as an advocate of 'human scale development'. He was trained as an economist at the University of Chile. After working for Shell in the 1950s, he spent many years teaching and researching at a range of North and South American universities and international organizations. In the 1980s, Max-Neef developed his ideas about an 'alternative' approach to **development** and founded an independent think-tank in Santiago, the Centre for Development Alternatives (CE-PAUR). He also published two widely acclaimed books, *From the Outside Looking In: Experiences in 'Barefoot Economics'* (1982) and *Human Scale Development* (1986) and, in 1983, was awarded the Right Livelihood Award, also described as the 'Alternative Nobel Price'. In 1993, Max-Neef stood as an independent candidate in the Chilean Presidential elections, supported by a range of groups associated with various radical causes, in particular ecology and minority rights. Max-Neef polled a very respectable 5.6 per cent of the vote. He refused to become involved in party politics afterwards, and rejoined academic life as Rector of the Universidad Austral de Chile in Valdivia.

See also: human scale technology

WOLFGANG RÜDIG

McDonald's/'McLibel'

In September 1990 the McDonald's Corporation issued libel writs against five members of a small green anarchist group **Greenpeace** London (GL) who they believed had been distributing a leaflet entitled 'What's Wrong with McDonalds?'. The leaflet alleged that McDonald's promoted an unhealthy diet, exploited children, ill treated its workers, damaged the environment and abused animals. Between 1994 and 1996 two members of GL who refused to apologize, Helen Steel and Dave Morris, were taken to court in the UK's longest libel trial by the fast food corporation. In June 1997 the pair were ordered to pay £60,000 damages to McDonald's but several of the claims of the leaflet they distributed were held not to have been libellous. They refused to pay and a worldwide campaign against the corporation has continued.

See also: anarchism/eco-anarchism

DEREK WALL

Meana, Carlo Ripa di

b. 15 August 1929, Pietrasanta, Italy

Politician

Carlo Ripa di Meana was European Commissioner for the Environment, Minister for the Environment in **Italy**, and speaker for the Italian Greens (see **Italian green parties**). As a member of the Socialist Party, he was deputy in the European Parliament from 1979 to 1984. During 1989–92 Ripa di Meana was European Commissioner for the Environment. After this experience, he became Minister for the Environment in the government led by Giuliano Amato (1992–3). Then he left the Socialist Party and joined the Italian Greens. In March 1993 Carlo Ripa di Meana was elected speaker for the *Federazione dei Verdi*. He led the party for four years, when the Greens took part in the centre–left coalition and entered the Prodi government. In 1994 Ripa di Meana was deputy in the European Parliament for the second time and contributed to the activities of the Green Group within the Parliament.

See also: Green Group in the European Parliament

ROBERTO BIORCIO

Mendes, Chico

b. 15 December 1944, Xapuri, Acre, Brazil; d. 22 December 1988

Environmental activist

The short life of Francisco 'Chico' Alves Mendes Filho was devoted to leading the Brazilian rubber tappers' fight to defend the Amazon Forest against exploitation by powerful and wealthy land speculators and ranchers. Mendes was born into poverty on a rubber estate in northwest **Brazil**. Forty-four years later, on 22 December 1988 he was assassinated, leaving a wife and two children.

Chico Mendes received no formal education and became a *seringueiro*, a rubber tapper at the age of nine. Traditionally rubber tappers and their families were at the mercy of a system of debt bondage, but during the 1960s and 1970s this system faced collapse in Xapuri. Ranchers from southern Brazil began to buy up rubber estates and clear vast areas of the forest for cattle grazing. Many tappers and their families were forcefully, often brutally evicted. Others retreated deeper into the forest to continue their work, only to be exploited by local merchants. Ruthless exploitation became a dominating force in existence; resistance to it the focus of Mendes' life. From his endeavours emerged the concept of 'extractive reserves', which are legally protected forest areas held in trust for people who live and work on the land in a sustainable manner.

Early in the 1970s, the Xapuri Rural Workers' Union was founded, and Mendes was elected its president. As exploitation and conflict intensified, the Union developed the technique of the *empate* or 'stand-off'. During the dry season ranchers hire labourers to clear the forest for pasture. Just before the rains come in September the cleared areas are fired. Faced with eviction, the rubber tappers assembled at sites about to be cleared, preventing the clearing and persuading the labourers to lay down their chainsaws. During the 1970s and 1980s the forests of the upper Acre valley were the scene of numerous *empates*. In 1985, Mendes and other leaders founded the National Council of Rubber Tappers (CNS) and gained increasing international support for their cause and passive resistance demonstrations. The movement was recognized as a force not only for social justice, but also against environmental destruction. The rubber tappers were able to propose a socially equitable and environmentally **sustainable development** policy for the region based on securing and improving their way of life, rather than official investments in ranching and colonization projects that would lead to disaster both for them and for the forest (Gross, 1989: 2). In 1988, responding to ever increasing international pressure and support for the cause, the Brazilian Government established the first ever extractive reserve.

Chico Mendes played a crucial role in negotiating with governments, with the **World Bank** and the Inter-American Development Bank. In addition to a great deal of respect and support, Mendes won two international prizes for his efforts. Yet as rewards and support increased, so too did risk to the rubber tappers. The political power of the landowners was formidable. Their movement, the UDR (Rural Democratic Union), successfully defeated land reform proposals in the Constituent Assembly. In April 1988 it formally set itself up in Acre and the number of hired gunmen and assassinations increased.

Chico Mendes was well aware of the threat to his own life; perhaps he foresaw his death. In a letter written shortly before his assassination by the son of a local cattle rancher, Darli Alves da Silva, Mendes wrote: 'If a messenger from heaven came down and guaranteed me that my death would help to strengthen our struggle it would even be worth it. But experience teaches us the opposite ... I want to live' (Mendes, 1989: 6).

Perhaps the most significant element of the legacy of Mendes is the enhanced power and voice of the organizations associated with him and the rubber tappers' cause – the National Council of Rubber Tappers and the Amazon Work Group from whose membership emerged a new generation of environmental leaders and activists. In Acre, Mendes's co-campaigners won important elective offices. Such political successes for the Mendes cause have transformed national debate in Brazil on the Amazon region. The political conditions for potential change have never been better as state and federal policies which promote and support **sustainability** are framed. The poverty, degradation and destruction of **Amazonia** are amongst the greatest socio-environmental challenges of the present day; challenges brought on to the world's political stage and the agendas of non-governmental organizations as a result of various significant influences. The charismatic and courageous leader of the Brazilian rubber tappers union must surely be one of the most significant of all.

See also: environmental justice; rainforests

References

Gross, T. in Mendes, C. (1989) *Fight for the Forest,*

Chico Mendes in His Own Words, London: Latin American Bureau (Research and Action) Ltd.

Mendes, C. (1989) *Fight for the Forest, Chico Mendes in His Own Words*, London: Latin American Bureau (Research and Action) Ltd.

Further reading

Branford, S. and Glock, O. (1985) *The Last Frontier: Fighting Over Land in the Amazon*, London: Zed Books.

Reukin, A. (1994) *The Burning Season: The Murder of Chico Mendes and the Fight for the Amazon Rain Forest*, New York: Plume.

JOY A. PALMER

mercury poisoning

The element mercury (Hg) has various chemical forms that determine its toxicity. Most toxic are forms such as methylmercury, which can combine with proteins, etc. and 'bioaccumulates' in fish through the food chain. Between 1932–68, the Chisso Corporation discharged mercury compounds into Minamata Bay in **Japan**. People whose diet included fish from the Bay developed symptoms of methylmercury poisoning characterized by instability of the neck, convulsions, and severe neurological and mental impairment. Cats that ate fish suffered similarly. The illness became known as 'Minamata Disease'. Chisso denied that its processes produced methylmercury, and produced evidence that it was using relatively harmless inorganic mercury. Apparently Chisso identified methylmercury compounds in the drain from its process and its toxicological studies produced similar findings to the Minamata disease pattern. These results were kept confidential. After three decades of legal proceedings, over 5,000 victims of Minimata Disease received financial compensation in 1995.

ROD S. BARRATT

Mexico

Mexico's commitment to environmental protection can be traced to the 1972 **Stockholm Confer-**ence on the Human Environment in which Mexico participated as a host country for one of the preparatory meetings. Serious attention to environmental matters is associated with the presidency of Miguel de la Madrid (1982–8) which established the environment as a national ministry and undertook a major revision of the national environmental law, which entered into force in 1988. Under the De la Madrid administration environmental progress was hampered, however, by the profound economic shock brought on by the contraction of world petroleum prices after 1979. De la Madrid's successor, Carlos Salinas de Gortari (1988–94), is notable for a number of high-profile environmental initiatives, including upgrading technical norms and standards for environmental regulation, a popular **air pollution** abatement campaign in Mexico City aimed mainly at vehicular pollution, and various conservation activities, as well as associating Mexico with several international treaties on the environment, including the Convention on International Trade in Endangered Species (**CITES**) and the **Montreal Protocol**. In 1992, pressed by environmentalists in debate on the North American Free Trade Agreement (**NAFTA**), Salinas reorganized Mexico's environmental administration and joined several NAFTA side-agreements, including the North American Agreement on Environmental Co-operation, an agreement establishing two linked binational agencies, the Border Environment Co-operation Commission (BECC) and the North American Development Bank (NADBank), and strengthened environmental protection along its US border through the Border XXI Program.

Under the 1988 environmental law, environmental protection in Mexico remained highly centralized though Mexico is a federal system. The national environmental ministry, known as the Secretariat for Environment, Natural Resources, and Fisheries (SEMARNP), established in 1992, is chiefly responsible for implementing the environmental law. Since 1992, SEMARNP has been headed by environmentalist Julia Carabias. Carabias, however, sits astride a number of powerful and independent agencies, some of longstanding and nearly independent policy authorities such as the National Water Commission and the Fisheries

Department, with mandates favouring **development** over environmental protection. Other nearly independent agencies include the National Institute for Ecology (INE), a think tank for developing environmental standards and policy strategies, and the Federal Attorney General for the Environment (PROFEPA), with primary responsibility for judicial enforcement of the nation's environmental laws. Further complicating matters is SEMARNP's acknowledged weakness in budgetary matters in the context of national economic contraction precipitated by the 1994 devaluation of the Mexican *peso*.

There is little question, however, that NAFTA has pushed Mexico's environmental agenda forward, ensuring that the environment would not be neglected by the Ernesto Zedillo administration (1994–2000). The environmental performance review of the Organization for Economic Co-operation and Development (OECD) gives Mexico credit for improving overall expenditure on environmental protection, harmonizing environmental standards and programmes, and strengthening environmental enforcement. **Development** is particularly strong along the border; the Mexico–USA, Border XXI Program has stimulated inter-agency and binational co-operation and directed much-needed financing to environmental infrastructure development with emphasis on water provision and waste-water management. In 1996, an important revision to the environmental law provided greater opportunity for public participation in policy-making and implementation as well as promoting and strengthening the administrative role of Mexico's states and local governments in environmental protection.

Environmental protection in Mexico has been strengthened by the growth of environmental organizations and citizens groups. Over 600 environmental groups are active nationwide, and many of these are associated with several national associations of environmental groups. The Mexican Green Party (PVEM) has survived over a decade in Mexican electoral politics, though it remains a small parliamentary faction with little over 1.5 per cent of the vote nationwide. Through its congressional delegation it has been a player in a few high profile environmental victories, however,

most notably a decision in February 2000 to deny Mitsubishi Inc. a permit to build a massive salt refinery near birthing grounds of the Mexican Grey Whale off the Baja California coast. In the momentous 2000 presidential elections, the PVEM joined a presidential alliance with Vicente Fox, the winning presidential candidate and official representative of Mexico's centre-right National Action Party (PAN). The PVEM is credited with pushing Fox's electoral platform to include greater emphasis on the environment comprising better environmental enforcement, commitment to Mexico's international environmental commitments, and defence of Mexico's rich natural resources. The PVEM gained 16 lower house seats in the Chamber of Deputies and 6 seats in the Mexican Senate that may give it a tie-breaker role in Mexico's emerging coalition politics at the level of the national legislature.

See also: Partido Verde Ecologista de Mexico

Further reading

Mumme, S. and Lybecker, D. (2000) 'Environmental Capacity in Mexico: An Assessment', in J. Janicke and W. Weidner (eds) *National Environmental Policies*, vol. 2, Berlin: Springer Verlag.

Organization for Economic Co-operation and Development (1998) *Environmental Performance Review: Mexico*, Paris: OECD.

STEPHEN MUMME

militarism and the environment

There are numerous connections between militarism and environmental problems. For example, military expansion often leads to war, which is highly damaging environmentally. The costs of expanding, even of maintaining, a credible military threat have increased Third World debt, as well as raising the interest rates to which debt repayment is subject (and Third World debt is argued to be a major cause of environmental destruction). Furthermore, the opportunity costs of military expansion are severe. For example, direct global military expenditure exceeds $1,000 billion per annum, and, per capita, less is spent by governments on health, education or environmental protection than they spend on their military. This emphasis on perceived military requirements is mirrored in research expenditure, with most research being conducted because of its military implications. This, of course, reduces the funding available to, amongst other things, research into environmentally benign technologies. Most importantly, the perception by governments that they need to spend so much on their military necessitates a highly productive (and thus resource- and energy-consumptive) economy to provide the taxable surplus needed to pay for military personnel, weaponry and research. And such economies are widely regarded as the direct cause of most major environmental problems. It is not surprising, therefore, that many political ecologists see militarization as a principal cause of environmental problems and view an opposition to militarization as absolutely essential for the attainment of an environmentally benign society.

ALAN CARTER

Miljöpartiet de Gröna

The Swedish environmental party (*miljöpartiet*) was created in 1981 in the wake of the referendum on **nuclear energy**. In 1985, it added 'green' (*de gröna*) to its name in order to emphasize its connection to other green parties around the world. At the outset, the party was most successful on the local level, winning seats in over 100 municipal councils in the elections of 1982 and 1985, while failing to attain the four per cent of the votes necessary to enter the national parliament. In 1988, the party passed the four per cent barrier and won 20 seats, becoming the first new party in the parliament in 70 years. The party, which has been strongly opposed to Swedish membership in the **European Union**, won four seats in the elections to the European parliament in 1995. After the 1998 national elections, the Greens have served as a support party to the minority social democratic government.

ANDREW JAMISON

Mill, John Stuart

b. 20 May 1806, London, England;
   d. 7 May 1873, Avignon, France

Philosopher

John Stuart Mill was a quintessential philosopher of classical liberalism who defended individual liberty via a reformulated version of utilitarianism rather than claims of natural rights. The son of the utilitarian philosopher James Mill, John Stuart Mill's writings display a number of themes relevant to green thought: in the *Principles of Political Economy* (1848) he combines belief in moral **progress** with the only classical liberal argument for a steady-state economy, *On Liberty* (1859) positively supports liberty and social toleration by appeal to the value of diversity, whilst *The Subjection of Women* (1869) makes implicit appeal to the idea of an expanding circle of moral considerability.

See also: liberalism/liberal democracy

PIERS H.G. STEPHENS

mining

Each of the forms of mining involves removing large amounts of material lying above the mineral that is of no value to the miner. Once this overburden material has been removed and disposed of, the mineral can then be extracted and sold for profit. These types of mining are highly destructive to the immediate local environment. Microclimate, vegetation regimes, ground-water systems are all destroyed in the process of overburden removal and mineral extraction. Most jurisdictions now require some type of reclamation of the sites, but in the past many of them were abandoned after the mining operations were complete. This has left tens of thousands of dangerous and non-productive landscapes for future generations to cope with. Current reclamation practices require replacement of soil and overburden, some type of vegetation to be replanted and monitoring of the site for environmental hazards.

Further reading

Brookings, D. (1990) *Mineral and Energy Resources: Occurrence, Exploitation, and Environmental Impact*, London: Merrill Publishing.

THOMAS LOWE

monkey-wrenching

The website of **Earth First! (US)** defines monkey-wrenching as 'unlawful sabotage of industrial extraction/development equipment and infrastructure, as a means of striking at the Earth's destroyers at the point where they commit their crimes'. Dave **Foreman** and other founders of Earth First! (US) were inspired by Ed **Abbey**'s *The Monkey Wrench Gang* (1975), which celebrated in fiction the actions of four saboteurs of the roads, dams and bridges which were eroding the wilderness areas of Utah. Sabotage of this kind is usually 'neither condemned nor condoned' by Earth First!. The Earth Liberation Front is more openly supportive of sabotage. It was this group that claimed responsibility for the arson attack on ski lodges at Vail, Colorado, in 1998 which caused $12 million of damage which it justified as an effort to defend the last habitat of the lynx in Colorado. Although the media and security services have sometimes defined monkey wrenching as **eco-terrorism**, with the exception of the independent activity of the Unabomber, there has been very little violence against people. Most eco-sabotage is carried out on an *ad hoc* basis by small groups. Because it is usually intended to be a means to defend wilderness it is more common in North America than in western Europe.

BRIAN DOHERTY

Montreal Protocol

The Montreal Protocol on Substances that Deplete the Ozone Layer (1987) is an international agreement pursuant to the Vienna Convention for the Protection of the Ozone Layer (1985). It established the first binding targets for reducing production and use of chemicals damaging to the stratospheric ozone layer. All parties to the agreement were required to reduce their consumption of chlorofluorocarbons (CFCs) by 50 per cent by 1 July 1998, but **less developed countries** (LDCs) such as **China** and **India** refused to join. Subsequent protocols signed in London (1990) and Copenhagen (1992) required total phase-out of CFCs by 1996 for developed countries; brought additional chemicals under control; and established differentiated responsibilities and financial and technical assistance to enable LDCs to participate. The Protocol is considered a model for international environmental diplomacy.

See also: ozone depletion

Further reading

Benedick, R.E. (1991) *Ozone Diplomacy: New Directions for Safeguarding the Planet*, Cambridge: Harvard University Press.

NORMAN J. VIG

MOVE

The MOVE organization, based in Philadelphia, is a radical mainly African American group, which fuses religious and political themes, including **deep ecology**. MOVE, which is not an acronym but signifies the organization's commitment to radical change, has a history of conflict with the US authorities. In 1985 a MOVE communal household was bombed by the FBI after a lengthy siege. Six adult MOVE members were killed along with five children. A MOVE supporter and writer Mumia Abu-Jamal, a former member of the Black Panther Party, has been imprisoned on death row since 1981. Sentenced for the murder of a city policeman, many believed that his conviction is unjust. European green parties and **Earth First! (US)** have contributed to the campaign for Mumia to receive a retrial. MOVE members believe that racial injustice, social inequality, environmental damage are products of the 'reform world system' which must be swept away via a green revolution. MOVE are deep ecologists with network links to Earth First! and African American militants. Their fusion of pagan themes and Christianity suggests a milieu shared with other black green radicals including the Mother Earth sect from Trinidad and Jamaican Rastafarianism.

DEREK WALL

Muir, John

b. 21 April 1838, Dunbar, Scotland;
   d. 24 December 1914, Los Angeles,
   California, USA

Preservationist and author

A gifted writer and founder of the **Sierra Club** (1892), John Muir was one of America's leading advocates of the preservationist approach to wilderness conservation. He is also considered to be the 'father' of his country's **national parks**.

John Muir's family emigrated from Scotland to rural Wisconsin in 1849 and homesteaded in the wilderness, a difficult life indeed for young John and his seven siblings. In addition to the hardship of frontier life, John's father raised his children guided by an ethic of stern Calvinism, but allowed John enough freedom to begin a lifelong interest in mechanical inventions.

In 1861, Muir went to the University of Wisconsin to study geology and chemistry and began a long friendship with Ezra Carr, one of his science professors. Carr introduced him to the geological theories of Louis Agassiz which were to become an important part of Muir's later research and writing on the Sierra Mountains.

Two years later, Muir began walking trips through Canada and the Midwest, eventually going to Indianapolis where he worked in a carriage factory. In 1867, while working on a machine belt, a file pierced his eye leaving him totally blind. During his recovery from the accident, he decided that if he regained his sight, he would devote his life to nature study. Once his eyesight returned, he set out to walk to Florida with an ultimate goal of going on to South America. Keeping extensive notes in a journal as he travelled, Muir got as far as Cuba, but eventually decided to head for Yosemite, arriving in 1868 in an area with which he would be associated for the rest of his life.

In this California nature paradise, Muir worked at a sawmill, a cattle ranch, and eventually as a tourist guide while spending much of his spare time exploring the Sierras. He also began a lifelong career as a nature writer, selling pieces on the West's scenic grandeur to *Harper's*, *Century*, and the *National Geographic*. While many of these essays were on Yosemite, he also wrote accounts of his travels in Utah, the Northwest, and Alaska. Financially secure because of his literary success, Muir married Louie Strentzel in 1880 and, through her father's land holdings, began a successful vineyard.

Muir's career as a national leader in wilderness preservation actually began when he and *Century* magazine editor, Robert Underwood Johnson, camped in Yosemite in 1889 and were appalled by the damage sheep ranching and lumbering had done to the area. Muir now devoted his literary talent and organizational zeal to a successful campaign to save Yosemite. In 1890, it became the country's second national park.

Throughout the 1890s and the administration of Theodore **Roosevelt**, Muir, Johnson, and their associates, many of them members of the Sierra Club, which Muir founded in 1892, led a successful national crusade to preserve wilderness. Perhaps Muir's finest hour was Roosevelt's presidency. Muir and Roosevelt camped in Yosemite and, of course, Muir used the opportunity to lobby the President for more national parks and forest reserves. He was successful as Roosevelt created several more national parks, set aside millions of additional acres as national forests, and approved legislation to establish national monuments.

In the last years of his life, Muir finally had the opportunity to tour the Amazon and Africa. By this time he was always greeted as 'John-o'-the-Mountains', an adored person whose long-bearded visage was almost a national trademark. Still, his final fight on behalf of the mountains and valleys he loved, the attempt to prevent the damming of Hetch Hetchy Valley near Yosemite, was unsuccessful, though it became a part of a debate that brought the views of both aesthetic and utilitarian conservation into the national arena (see **Hetch Hetchy Dam**).

Further reading

Fox, S.R. (1981) *John Muir and His Legacy: The*

American Conservation Movement, Boston: Little Brown.

Muir, J. (1912) *The Yosemite*, San Francisco: Sierra Club Books; repr. 1992.

Wilkins, T. (1995) *John Muir, Apostle of Nature*, Norman, Oklahoma: University of Oklahoma.

WARREN VANDER HILL

multinational and transnational corporations

Perhaps more than any other trend, the growth in multinational corporations (MNCs) has come to symbolize what people like and fear about **globalization**. Operating globally and bringing goods to new areas of the world, as well as bringing about great improvements in **technology**, for some, MNCs are key actors in delivering **sustainable development**. For others, the mobility of capital and the internationalization of production that make international investment possible, give companies unprecedented freedoms to locate their businesses where it is most profitable to do so, often at the expense of communities and environment.

A couple of statistics demonstrate why people are concerned about the power of MNCs. The combined revenues of General Motors and Ford, the two largest automobile companies in the world exceed the combined gross domestic product (GDP) for all sub-Saharan Africa and over 51 of the largest one hundred economies in the world are corporations. Multinational companies are, therefore, increasingly central to environmental decision-making and resource use behaviour. This reflects the importance of their investment decisions for the **development** paths pursued by countries, the ecological impact of the volume of trade and transfer of goods around the world which they administer, as well as the ecological impact of production processes.

Cynicism about the environmental impact of companies and concern about the power they wield in international affairs has promoted many companies to demonstrate their commitment to environmental protection and the possibility of reconciling profit maximization with the goals of sustainable development. The extent to which businesses have made genuine attempts to lessen the impact of their activities on the environment has been a matter of some debate. Initially businesses sought to resist environmental measures through forming lobbying groups to fend off legislation damaging to their interests. From the early 1990s however, many businesses began to play a more proactive role in the debate seeking to shape rather than directly obstruct the inevitable flurry of environmental regulations. In addition other companies have sought to exploit new market niches in green technology and the demand for 'green' products. However, while greening has taken place in some areas of companies' activities, environmental concerns have yet to penetrate key strategic areas, let alone address questions of overall material consumption.

Of particular concern has been the failure of international agreements to regulate companies responsible for ecological degradation. The issue of transnational corporation (TNC) regulation was conveniently dropped from the United Nations Conference on Environment and Development (UNCED) agenda at the insistence of the USA in particular (see **Rio Conference 1992**). An international code of conduct to regulate the activities of TNCs has been on the international agenda since the 1970s. The United Nations Centre for Transnational Corporations was set up in 1973 to perform this task, but after two decades of failed negotiations, the Centre was closed in 1993 and has been replaced by the Division on Transnational Corporations and Investment located within the United Nations Conference on Trade and Development (UNCTAD). In place of binding commitments at the international level, there has been a growth in voluntary agreements, self-monitoring, and the proliferation of **sustainability** audits of corporations by external consultants. The best known voluntary guidelines on the environment are those endorsed by the International Chamber of Commerce (ICC) known as the *Business Charter for Sustainable Development*, a document of 16 principles produced prior to UNCED. At the same time, during the UNCED negotiations, TNCs successfully presented themselves as part of the solution to environmental problems, arguing that only they have the necessary capital, technology and expertise to deliver positive environmental change. Their role in all of these key areas, necessary for the successful implementation of international environmental agreements, has elevated them to the status of partners alongside governments. Businesses are, therefore, centrally involved in the setting of standards and targets for environmental protection (see **business and the environment**).

The darker side of this special relationship, is the significant impact of business lobbying on government environmental policies (see **Global Climate Coalition**). They are involved in drawing up environmental agreements, and often sit on government delegations at international negotiations. Governments' reluctance to impose restrictions upon the companies they depend upon for investment is heightened in a context of globalization where capital mobility and the internationalization of production permit companies greater freedom to choose where to base their business. This makes it costly for states to adopt unilateral and regional environmental measures in the absence of similar measures by rival states and firms for fear of industry relocation.

Concern about the power of TNCs also centres on the powers which international agreements confer upon multinational enterprises. The allocation of trade-related intellectual **property rights** (TRIPs) to companies through the **World Trade Organization** TRIPs agreement allows companies to patent biological materials that affect people's livelihoods in direct and potentially detrimental ways. Moves to negotiate a Multilateral Agreement on Investment (MAI), currently stalled, but certain to return will also affirm the entry and exit options of MNCs in choosing where to invest (see **MAI**). Negotiated amid an extraordinary degree of secrecy, this agreement embodied the right of TNCs to invest anywhere in the world on equal terms with national and local business. The agreement would allow TNCs to sue governments for profits lost through laws which discriminate against them. The agreement would have been binding for 15 years after withdrawal and a country must give five years' notice that it wants to leave the agreement. It was little surprise, therefore, that the agreement provoked such a strong NGO campaign. According to NGOs, the agreement would elevate

corporations to the status of 'supercitizens' free from the normal obligations of citizens in relation to the environment. The agreement is part of a broader trend in which regional trade organizations also permit companies to challenge governments and local authorities about restrictions on their activities. Within the North American Free Trade Agreement (**NAFTA**) two Mexican authorities are currently being sued by US companies that were prevented from establishing toxic waste dumps in Mexico. In broad terms, these patterns imply a growth in the power of TNCs and a reduction in restraints upon the terms of their investment. TNCs are said to wield power without responsibility on the basis that while they are often as powerful as states they are less accountable.

While accounts about the enormous power and wealth of companies are common place, what is often overlooked is the role of counter-balancing norms and expectations which surround company conduct on environmental and social issues, that have grown up in the past few years together with softer forms of regulation including codes of conduct and **stewardship** regimes (such as the Forestry Stewardship Council). Companies increasingly operate in a global environment which means they are not insulated from the evolving norms and expectations about their social and environmental obligations, diffused through the activities of **international non-governmental organizations**. Companies are increasingly expected to operate according to a 'triple bottom line' of financial performance, environmental sustainability and social justice. Pressure upon companies to introduce new standards and regulations on the environment, albeit often informal and voluntary in nature, and to improve their reporting and environmental auditing has changed the way the companies operate. Companies recognize that partnerships and agreements with NGOs are often more desirable than formal regulation by governments which is backed by law and sanction. While much progress has undoubtedly been made by some MNCs in ensuring that their investments do not undermine efforts to protect the environment, the continued activities of many others do much to discredit the 'greening' that has taken place and will provide the impetus for continuing calls for strengthened national and international regulation of the environmental and social impacts of MNCs.

See also: greenwashing; international non-governmental organizations

Further reading

Fischer, K. and Schot, J. (eds) (1993) *Environmental Strategies for Industry*, Washington: Island Press.

Karliner, J. (1997) *The Corporate Planet: Ecology and Politics in an Age of Globalization*, San Francisco: Sierra Club Books.

Murphy, D. and Bendell, J. (1997) *In the Company of Partners*, Bristol: Policy Press.

Newell, P. (2000) 'Globalization and the New Politics of Sustainable Development' in J. Bendell (ed) *Terms of Endearment: Business, NGOs and Sustainable Development*, London: Greenleaf.

Schmidheiny, S. (1992) *Changing Course: A Global Business Perspective on Development and the Environment*, Cambridge, MA: MIT Press.

PETER NEWELL

Mumford, Lewis

b. 19 October 1895, Flushing, New York, USA; d. 26 January 1990

Urban and social theorist, historian

In the course of six decades, Lewis Mumford produced 30 books on an astonishingly wide range of areas. In his popular histories of **technology**, (prefiguring Ivan **Illich**), Mumford argued that human societies should not passively submit to technological change but technology should be controlled and shaped by human beings. In urban studies, he became a powerful critic of twentieth-century urban sprawl and the rise of the modern 'megamachine'. In philosophy, his claim that nature is marked by interdependence, co-operation and 'immanent purpose' significantly influenced the thinking of Murray **Bookchin**. It is his utopian vision, however (see **utopia/ecotopia**), that self-realization could only occur with participation in a democratic community in balance with the natural world that truly reveals him as one of the forefathers of **social ecology**.

Further reading

Miller, D.L. (ed) (1999) *The Lewis Mumford Reader*, Georgia: University of Georgia Press.

DAMIAN WHITE

municipal solid waste

Municipal solid waste (MSW) can be defined in several ways. For example in the **European Union** it is described as waste from households and wastes generated by offices, shops etc., that are similar in nature and composition to household wastes. In the USA a slightly wider definition is used and MSW is taken to mean the combined household and commercial waste generated in a given municipal area. Within Europe and the USA the amount of commercial waste classified as MSW varies, so care must be taken when comparing information on waste across national boundaries. The main waste materials produced by households in developed countries are paper and cardboard, kitchen and garden waste, glass, metals and plastics. Commercial waste tends to contain higher proportions of paper waste and smaller amounts of kitchen and garden-type waste than household waste.

STEPHEN BURNLEY

N

NABU

The Nature Protection Association Germany, NABU (Naturschutzbund Deutschland), is one of the major environmental pressure groups in Germany, with more than 260,000 members (2000). The association emerged out of a long tradition of campaigning for the protection of birds. The first national bird protection group in Germany was founded in 1899 under the name *Bund für Vogelschutz* (Association for Bird Protection, BfV). This organization became the dominant organization for bird protection in Germany throughout the twentieth century. One of its main tasks was the purchase and management of natural bird habitats. Since the late 1960s, the BfV gradually widened its scope of activities. In 1990, a merger of the West German bird protection association with nature protection groups from East Germany under the new name, *Naturschutzbund Deutschland*, signalled the final departure from the narrow scope of bird protection. In the 1990s, the group campaigned on nature protection, with a strong emphasis on lobbying and media relations, and covering a broad range of environmental topics.

WOLFGANG RÜDIG

Nader, Ralph

b. 27 February 1934, Winsted,
   Connecticut, USA

Consumer advocate, lawyer, author

After earning degrees from Princeton University and Harvard Law School, Ralph Nader practised law in Hartford, Connecticut. In the mid-1960s, he rose to national prominence by successfully targeting giant General Motors for producing the Corvair, an automobile 'unsafe at any speed'. This became the title of his first book, with fourteen others to follow. 'Citizen Nader' went on to found over fifteen public interest groups dealing with consumer protection, environmental quality, health, regulatory reform, energy, and disability rights. His crusade for corporate accountability attracted dynamic young professionals, who became known as 'Nader's Raiders'. His and their efforts have contributed to the passing of a number of laws.

Nader was nominated as the presidential candidate of the US Greens in 1996. It was a low budget campaign that won less than 1 per cent of the vote. In 2000, he was again nominated by the Greens. Nader declared, 'I am running for President in order to mobilize citizens who are ... disgusted by the single-party corporate system, who have withdrawn from political activity because they believe it too seedy, too corrupt, or irrelevant'. A number of former 'Raiders' urged suspension of his campaign; they feared that Republican George W. Bush would be its prime beneficiary. Rejecting the lesser of two evils argument and urging supporters to vote for their principles, Nader ended up with only 3 per cent of the vote. However, he drew enough votes away from Democrat Al **Gore** in pivotal Florida to elect Bush, a conservative lacking environmental and consumer protection credentials. Nader has remained committed to building a grassroots progressive alternative to the forces of 'oligarchy'.

See also: green parties, US

Reference

URL: http://www.votenader.org.

E. GENE FRANKLAND

Naess, Arne

b. 27 January 1912, Oslo, Norway

Philosopher

Best known today as the founder of **deep ecology**, Arne Dekke Eide Naess was born into an affluent family, the youngest of four children. His love of **nature** began early with an enduring interest in mountaineering, but although the youthful intellectual influences of Spinoza and **Gandhi** were later to help frame his ecological concerns, as was the thought of his friend Peter Wessel Zapffe. His initial philosophical grounding was with the logical empiricism (positivism) of the Vienna Circle, amongst whom he moved from 1934–5. After his inaugural dissertation for the Norwegian Academy of Sciences in 1936 he attained a research appointment in psychology at the University of Berkeley, California from 1938–9, then returned to the University of Oslo where he was appointed as a full professor in 1939, at 27 the youngest in Norway. Here he started reforming Norwegian University education, encouraging interdisciplinarity, diversification and tolerance. These values, along with Naess's adherence to Gandhian ideals, were tested by the Nazi occupation of Norway from 1940, and Naess helped the Norwegian resistance whilst retaining his commitment to non-violence (see **non-violent direct action**).

After the war, Naess helped to organize structures to trace missing Norwegian prisoners and their torturers, and this effort, along with his resistance record, intellectual profile and long-standing support for peace causes, led to his being appointed leader of a UNESCO project to resolve the dispute between East and West over the meaning of the term **democracy** in 1948. The

published results of this brought controversy from which Naess stayed aloof, instead investing his pay in the first Norwegian mountaineering expedition to the Himalayas, which he led in 1950. He continued to focus on philosophy of science and communication, critically reflecting on the empiricism that had underpinned his thought and founding the journal *Inquiry* in 1958. A number of the perspectives reached at this period, notably his notion of a plurality of 'total views', were later to feed into his accounts of deep ecology and ecosophy (see **eco-philosophy/ecosophy**), but it was not until 1968, when Naess published his thoughts on Pyrrhonian scepticism, that he gave up both his primary commitment to empiricism and his professorial chair to devote more attention to the nascent movement of ecologism (see **environmentalism and ecologism**). His path from the peace to ecology movements thus anticipated that trodden by many later greens, and despite the disputes between the emphases of **deep ecology** and **social ecology**, Naess regards the peace, ecology and social justice movements as operating in concentric circles (see also **peace movements**).

In some ways the linkage between engagement and distance found in Naess's thought on scepticism surfaces in his later deep ecology, in which identification with very different life forms is significant for transcending the immediate ego in favour of a notion of realization of the wider Self (Naess 1987), but his ecological commitment first bore intellectual fruit in 1973, when Naess published 'The Shallow and the Deep, Long-Range Ecology Movements: A Summary'. This influential paper, distinguishing anthropocentric resource environmentalism (see **anthropocentrism**) from the radical ecological approach of **eco-centrism**, coined the term 'deep ecology' and resulted in Naess's name being primary in the resultant philosophy and movement. Its themes were taken up by George Sessions and Bill Devall in the USA from 1977, and as interest grew, Naess and Sessions drew up an 8-point platform for the deep ecology movement (Sessions and Devall, 1985), regularly revised since; his ideas also deeply influenced **Earth First!** (**US**). Naess himself, however, distinguishes his own personal philosophical variant of deep ecology, Ecosophy T (named after Tvergastein, his Norwegian mountain cabin) from the broader deep ecology *movement*, maintaining in the latter case that his only claim is to the terminology and that the real originator was Rachel **Carson** (Rothenberg, 1993).

Naess was awarded the Sonning Prize for contribution to European culture in 1977 and the Mahatma Gandhi Prize for Non-Violent Peace in 1994. He remains an active thinker and campaigner, and a new selection of his work is forthcoming from the deep ecology scholar Harold Glasser.

References

Devall, B. and Sessions, G. (1985) *Deep Ecology: Living as if Nature Mattered*, Salt Lake City: Peregrine Smith Books.

Naess, A. (1973) 'The Shallow and the Deep, Long-Range Ecology Movements: A Summary', *Inquiry*, 16.

—— (1987) 'Self-Realization: An Ecological Approach to Being in the World', *The Trumpeter*, 4.

Rothenberg, D. (1993) *Is It Painful to Think?: Conversations with Arne Naess*, Minneapolis: University of Minnesota Press.

PIERS H.G. STEPHENS

NAFTA

The North American Free Trade Agreement (NAFTA) linking the USA, Canada, and **Mexico** represents an important environmental milestone insofar as the agreement contains important environmental-related elements and a 'side agreement' that addresses additional pollution control and natural resource management issues. NAFTA has been called the 'greenest' trade agreement ever negotiated, and its environmental elements remain an important model for integration of environmental sensitivities into trade policy. Prior to the launch of the NAFTA negotiations, environmentalists had not perceived much of an intersection between trade and environmental policy-making. The prospect, however, of linking countries at quite disparate levels of development raised a number of environmental questions including: (1) fears of spill-over pollution into the USA from increased Mexican industrial activity, particularly along the contaminated US–Mexican border; (2) concerns that high US–Canadian standards of environmental protection would be lowered as part of a NAFTA-driven harmonization process; (3) doubts about the rigour of Mexico's environmental standards and enforcement programme leading to a fear that Mexico might emerge as a 'pollution haven' luring investment and jobs on the basis of lower environmental compliance laws and the possibility of environmentally derived competitiveness opportunities; and (4) distress over the closed nature of trade negotiations and the perceived lack of transparency in trade policymaking more generally.

The parties to NAFTA responded to the environmental concerns that were raised with a number of initiatives. The USA (and ultimately Canada and **Mexico** as well) undertook a series of environmental reviews of the prospective NAFTA, seeking to identify the full spectrum of possible pollution and natural resource effects from a more open North American marketplace. In addition, the US **Environmental Protection Agency** and its Mexican counterpart developed an 'integrated border environment plan' that catalogued the pollution control and natural resource management issues arising along the three thousand kilometre US–Mexico border. Finally, the trade treaty negotiators addressed the environment both within the Agreement itself and through the negotiation of a parallel track 'side agreement' (The North American Agreement on Environmental Co-operation) that commits the NAFTA parties to an ongoing programme of environmental co-operation. Substantively, trade-related environmental concerns are addressed in a number of places in the NAFTA agreement itself. First, the 'Preamble' calls on the parties to pursue their programme of trade liberalization so as to promote **sustainable development** and to strengthen development and enforcement of environmental laws and regulations (see **environmental law and litigation**). This commitment to environmental protection as a goal within the trade policy process has now been replicated in other agreements such as the 1994 Uruguay Round multilateral trade negotiations that led to the creation of the **World Trade Organization**.

Second, the NAFTA parties committed (Article 104) to a provision that ensures that major environmental agreements with trade provisions would be given precedence if there ever were a conflict between a party's obligations under the environmental treaty and the NAFTA. This provision responded to environmentalists' concerns that trade principles might 'trump' environmental goals if there were not an express provision to uphold environmental commitments. NAFTA's sanitary and phytosanitary provisions declare that each country retains the unrestricted right to set and maintain environmental health and safety standards so as to achieve whatever level of risk management the nation chooses. Although NAFTA requires that any sanitary and phytosanitary standards be based upon scientific principles and be derived from a **risk assessment** appropriate to the circumstances, the NAFTA language represents a more flexible approach than is found in the General Agreement on Tariffs and Trade (GATT).

NAFTA's investment chapter (Article 114) provides that each country remains free to adopt and enforce any environmental measure it deems necessary to ensure that new investments within its territory do not degrade the environment, so long as any such measures are applied in a non-discriminatory fashion. To diffuse the pollution haven concern, the Agreement suggests that it is inappropriate for parties to encourage or seek to retain investments by relaxing environmental standards or enforcement.

NAFTA's dispute resolution provisions also provide a greater degree of environmental sensitivity than is found in traditional trade agreements. Parties to a dispute may request the convening of a board of scientific or technical experts to advise a dispute settlement panel (Article 2015). In addition, where a challenge has been made to environmental standards, the NAFTA rules provide that the burden of proof lies on the challenger to the standard (Article 723). NAFTA's environmental side agreement commits the parties to a regime of environmental collaboration and the support of an institutional structure to manage issues that arise at the intersection of trade and environmental policy. These collaborative efforts are co-ordinated by the North American Commission for Environmental Co-operation (CEC). The CEC has three components: a three-person 'Council' made up of Cabinet-level environmental officials from each NAFTA country, a 'Joint Public Advisory Committee' comprising of 15 non-governmental representatives (five each from Mexico, Canada, and the USA), and a Secretariat based in Montreal.

See also: globalization; World Trade Organization

Further reading

Beaulieu, A. and Johnson, P. (1996) *The Environment and NAFTA: Understanding and Implementing the New Continental Law,* Washington: Island Press.

Esty, D. (1994) *Greening the GATT: Trade, Environment, and the Future,* Washington: Institute for International Economics.

—— (1994) 'Making Trade and Environmental Policies Work Together: Lessons from NAFTA', *Aussenwirtschaft* (The Swiss Review of International Economic Relations) 49: 59–79.

North American Free Trade Agreement (8 December 1992) Canada–Mexico–US, 32 ILM 289.

DANIEL C. ESTY

Narmada Valley development programme

The massive project in India to harness the Narmada river and its tributaries, flowing across three states Madhya Pradesh, Maharastra and Gujarat originated in the late 1940s. The project envisages building 30 large, 135 medium and 3000 small dams, making it the largest project of its kind in **India** (see **dams/hydroelectric power**). While all the usual benefits of such projects are claimed by its supporters, opponents question not only the benefits but also the way such projects are implemented without examining alternatives. In 1987 the Narmada Bacho Andolan (NBA Save Narmada Campaign) was launched and it brought into focus issues relating to the displacement, rehabilitation and the rights of the people. Since then the process is an on-going struggle being fought in different fora. The **World Bank** appointed a commission which found that rehabilitation is far from satisfactory. NBA argues that alternatives are not examined by the government and the drought-prone areas of Gujarat would not benefit from the project. Apart from the protracted legal battle, and struggles of various kinds, NBA is also involved in experimenting with alternative technologies for the tribal communities affected by this project.

K. RAVI SRINIVAS

National Audubon Society

The National Audubon Society, named after ornithologist and wildlife artist John James Audubon (1785–1851), was founded in 1905, to 'conserve and restore natural ecosystems, while focusing on birds and other wildlife for the benefit of humanity and biological diversity'. Headquartered in New York City, the Audubon Society has 300 full-time staff members and a national dues-paying membership of about 550,000. As a conservatory agency, it has established 100 wildlife sanctuaries and nature centres across the USA. For example, it is currently working to preserve Spring Creek Prairie, a 610-acre, rare, tall-grass prairie outside Lincoln, Nebraska, and the Wind River Forest, an old growth forest located in the Pacific Northwest. The Audubon Society has been active in lobbying for the passage of environmental legislation. It points to legislative achievements such as: the **Everglades** Restoration Act, the Tropical Migratory Bird Act, and the Conservation Funding Act.

Further reading

National Audubon Society (15 March 2001) *About Audubon* and *Conservation and Action* at URL: http://www.audubon.org.

JON E. FITCH

National Environmental Policy Act

The National Environmental Policy Act (NEPA) of 1969 became a 'cornerstone' of modern environmental law in the USA. It grew out of the realization that not only the substance of federal policies, but also the process of decision-making within federal agencies was sorely in need of change. US observers have long noted how regulators tend to be 'captured' over time by regulated interests, with the result that public interests are put at a tactical disadvantage. NEPA was an attempt to reinvigorate existing federal agencies with a new mandate to consider the environmental consequences of their programmes and projects, and, if the agencies failed to comply, to provide a legal basis for environmental groups to use the courts to enforce consideration.

In contrast to the **Clean Air Act**, NEPA (as originally written) was a simple and brief law. Its most important provisions were Section 101 and Section 102. The first advanced a broad policy commitment for the federal government to maintain conditions of environmental harmony; however, judges have not seized upon its broad intent as the basis for overturning specific agency decisions. On the other hand, Section 102, which requires that all federal agencies inform themselves about the environmental consequences of their actions to 'the fullest extent possible', soon became the primary focus of the judges in the wave of 500 cases in the four years after NEPA's enactment. Sections 201–207 established the **Council on Environmental Quality** to advise the President on environmental issues and to review the agencies' environmental reporting. These reports were soon to be known as 'environmental impact statements' (or EIS for short).

NEPA was not a particularly controversial bill. It received little media coverage and passed virtually unanimously. Apparently many Congressmen viewed it as a more or less symbolic act that might do some good. The task fell to the federal courts to determine what the law actually would mean in practice. For example, how major and significant would federal actions have to be to trigger a fully fledged EIS, and how detailed would it have to be in order to be adequate under the law? In the early 1970s federal court cases, most notably *Calvert Cliffs Co-ordinating Committee v. Atomic Energy Commission* (1971), judges took seriously the 'fullest extent possible' wording of Section 102 and made the EIS requirement a time-consuming exercise which each agency must follow to inform itself about the possible environmental impacts of projects. Federal agencies not deemed in compliance with NEPA, found their projects halted by injunction. In the mid-1970s, a legislative backlash against NEPA emerged as Congressmen sought (mostly unsuccessfully) to exempt pet projects from the force of the law. More significantly, US Supreme Court rulings, most notably in *Vermont Yankee Nuclear Power Corporation v. Natural Resources Defense Council* (1978), showed more deference to the agencies' discretion in determining how they responded to NEPA procedurally.

In recent decades the number of NEPA suits has declined. The most visible NEPA case in the 1990s was *Public Citizen v. US Trade Representative* (1993). In this case, several environmental groups attempted to derail the North American Free Trade Agreement (**NAFTA**) because the federal government had filed no environmental impact statement. Although these groups won at the federal district court level, the federal appeals court ruled that NEPA did not apply to the Trade Representative of the President, because trade law gives exclusive authority to the Presidency (which is not a federal agency).

Studies have indicated that few NEPA cases that have been appealed to the Supreme Court have resulted in a victory for the environmental side. On the other hand, the EIS requirement can be still seen as essential in improving agency decision-making by forcing the consideration of alternatives, including those advanced by outsiders. Critics argue that the EIS requirement has taken on the character of a routinized paper chase. Yet environmentalists vehemently oppose any legislative effort that seeks to undermine the EIS process. Thirty years later it remains an invaluable tool to force agency attention to their objections and to slow the process of decision-making so that a less environmentally threatening alternative has a

chance. Many states and localities in the USA, as well as foreign countries, have incorporated environmental impact analysis, inspired by NEPA into their own laws.

Further reading

More, T.M. and Brooks, R.O. (1987) *Green Justice: The Environment and the Courts*, Boulder, CO: Westview Press, pp. 60–72.

Smith, Z.A. (2000) *The Environmental Policy Paradox*, 3rd edn, Upper Saddle River, NJ: Prentice-Hall, pp. 56–62.

E. GENE FRANKLAND

national parks

The world's first national park, Yellowstone National Park, was established in 1872 in the northwest corner of Wyoming, USA, as a 'public park or pleasuring ground for the benefit and enjoyment of the people'. The US Congress intended to set aside a territory noted for its spectacular natural wonders and protect it from commercialization and privatization. The concept of preserving a natural area for the enjoyment of its citizens was unique to the USA but has proven to be a valuable influence throughout the world (Nash, 1982). Since 1872, the concept and role of national parks has been modified and adapted to fit the cultural and economic values of 143 nations. By 1997, the **World Conservation Union** (IUCN) listed 3,384 national parks.

Little formal protection was provided for natural areas until European royalty began to maintain hunting preserves for food and sport. The concept of preservation was largely utilitarian and dedicated to the benefit of nobility or state. For instance, Peter the Great forbade the use of oak trees in selected areas to ensure a steady supply of timber for the growing Russian navy, and early American towns passed ordinances protecting forests and waterways (*c.* 1700s). The concept of preserving large tracts of land is first attributed to George Catlin, a Philadelphia artist travelling throughout the western USA. In 1832 he wrote that a 'Nation's Park' should be established for future ages and proposed that an immense preserve be established on the Rocky Mountain front range containing indigenous people as well as native wildlife. However, until the late 1800s the dominant philosophy throughout the world was that natural resources existed for exploitation.

The wonders and curiosities of the Yellowstone area were documented throughout the nineteenth century. Finally, with the support of railroad companies and the assurance by promoters that the land was of little agricultural value, Congress established Yellowstone National Park in 1872. Several nations soon followed suit. Australia designated the Royal National Park in 1879, Canada designated Banff National Park in 1885, and New Zealand designated Tongariro National Park in 1894.

The movement to establish national parks resulted from a combination of several social forces and changing values. One changing value in the late nineteenth century was an emerging appreciation for an increasingly scarce commodity – wilderness. Wilderness preservation is rooted in the romantic/transcendental movement that valued the sublime qualities of wild nature and described natural objects as a terrestrial manifestation of God (see **Romanticism**). John **Muir** (1838–1914) became an articulate and effective proponent of the spiritual values of nature preservation. Coincidentally the progressive **conservation movement** surfaced in the early 1900s among resource managers and government officials. Despite the growing movement to preserve natural areas in their own right, most legislation was passed with utilitarian values. Often protected sanctuaries were perceived as valuable for society such as a source of game or water to areas outside park boundaries.

Tourism began to play an increasing role as a value of national parks (see **tourism, environmental impact of**). In 1916, the US National Park Service (NPS) was created in the US **Department of Interior** to 'conserve the scenery and the natural and historic objects and wildlife therein ... unimpaired for the enjoyment of future generations'. Stephan Mather (the first US NPS director) promoted tourism as a means of increasing awareness of national parks, generating

revenue through admission fees and, indirectly, securing Congressional appropriations. Tourism and visitation dominated the US National Park System at the expense of scientific and preservation values (Sellars, 1997).

In the early part of the twentieth century, North American and European interests established several more national parks. The potential economic, scientific and spiritual benefits of national parks contributed to their appeal throughout the world. South Africa established Kruger National Park in 1926 from a game reserve, Belgium established Albert National Park in the Belgian Congo in 1925 (dedicated to scientific research and closed to tourists), and Japan established a national park system in 1931.

National parks grew rapidly after the Second World War and international organizations emerged to promote and inventory protected areas by supporting conferences and research. In 1948, the United Nations Educational, Scientific and Cultural Organization (UNESCO) ratified the IUCN and charged it with preserving the world's biotic environment. The First World Conference on National Parks was held in Seattle, Washington in 1962. In the 1950s and 1960s national parks increasingly reflected the unique cultural distinctions of each nation. For instance, although providing some public access for recreation, Great Britain's national parks may include private land and restrict development to preserve the character of the human as well as natural **landscape**.

By the late 1960s the international community recognized the increasing diversity of protected areas throughout the world and initiated a system of definitions and categories. National parks were defined at the IUCN Tenth General Assembly in New Dehli, **India**, as places where ecosystems are not materially altered by human exploitation and occupation, the highest competent authority has taken steps to protect the area from exploitation, and where visitors are allowed to enter under special conditions. The most recent definition is an IUCN Category II Protected Area – a protected area managed mainly for ecosystem protection and recreation. It is a natural area of land and/or sea, designated to (a) protect the ecological integrity of one or more ecosystems for present and future generations; (b) exclude exploitation or occupation inimical to the purposes of designation of the area; and (c) provide a foundation for spiritual, scientific, educational, recreational and visitor opportunities, all of which must be environmentally and culturally compatible (IUCN, 1994). Other categories have evolved since the original 'national park' concept of 1872 and are defined by IUCN as; (i) scientific preserves that exclude tourists; (ii) unmodified wilderness areas; (iii) natural monuments protected for specific features; (iv) habitat/species management areas; (v) protected landscape/seascapes distinguished for the qualities produced by human–nature interaction; and (vi) areas managed mainly for the sustainable use of natural ecosystems.

One criticism of the early national park movement is that parks were wildlands devoid of people. 'Imperial' forces (wealthy or powerful nations and individuals) denied **indigenous people** access to traditional sources of food and shelter. The lack of sensitivity to indigenous people either on the parklands or nearby, contributed to a hostile opinion of park goals and subsequent threats to personnel and poaching of wildlife. Some nations incorporated indigenous people into the national park with the stipulation that they do not 'significantly modify the natural environment' (e.g. Taman Negara (est. 1938) in Malaysia, and several national parks in India). Most nations now consult with local people before establishing a park.

In the later part of the twentieth century Central and South America have experienced a rapid increase in parks. For instance, Costa Rica established Santa Rosa and Volcan Poas National Parks in 1969 and, in 1997, listed 22 national parks. Forces that played a significant role in establishing parks in Central and South America include a small but growing number of nationals sympathetic to the preservation of natural or cultural heritage, the expanding influence of North American conservation organizations, **debt-for-nature swaps** and finally, the promise of economic benefit from tourism.

Tourism was often the substitute for traditional means of employment or resource gathering from the territory protected by the national park. A side effect is that tourism is becoming a significant threat to the integrity of national parks throughout the world. Increased traffic has forced North American parks to shift to mass transit, and on some African parks, the presence of people has altered the behaviour of animal life. Other nations worry that the local infrastructure will not support mass visitation nor will smaller wild areas remain 'wild'.

Principles of **conservation biology** were increasingly applied in the 1990s highlighting the scientific value of relatively undisturbed natural areas. Conservation biology dictates that to protect ecosystems and areas that are often the last refuges for **endangered species**, the territory should be as large as possible and follow natural boundaries (e.g. divides, meteorological distinctions, watersheds). Many managers are concerned that park boundaries are permeable or ill designed. To address these concerns, parks have been expanded, or trans-boundary 'Peace Parks' have been established to co-ordinate preservation efforts. Additional threats to national parks include **air pollution, biopiracy/bioprospecting, water pollution**, war, **famine, mining, exotic species** and **agriculture**.

Despite continued population and political pressure to develop or utilize natural resources, national parks continue to be established and expanded in all nations. Proponents emphasize the contribution that national parks can make to the economy, and to the preservation of endangered species and vanishing 'wild' areas.

See also: environmentalism and ecologism; Romanticism

References

IUCN (World Conservation Union) (1994) *Guidelines for Protected Area Management Categories*, Commission on National Parks and Protected Areas with the assistance of World Conservation Monitoring Centre. Gland, Switzerland: IUCN.

Nash, R. (1967) *Wilderness and the American Mind*, New Haven: Yale University Press; 3rd edn, 1982.

Sellers, R.W. (1997) *Preserving Nature in the National Parks: A History*, New Haven: Yale University Press.

DAVID OSTERGREN

National Trust

The National Trust was founded in 1895 and has the function of acquiring and preserving historic buildings and scenic areas. It has become the largest private landowner and voluntary organization in Britain, and has more members than all of the political parties combined. Issues facing the Trust at the beginning of the twenty-first century concern its organizational oligarchy and passive membership, and its objectives which some regard as too general, varied and ill defined.

The National Trust was created by a number of Victorian philanthropists, most notably Octavia Hill, concerned with preserving the environment as an amenity to which people could escape from the squalor and grime of urban and industrial Britain. Various statutes have shaped the role of the Trust, the first in 1907 protecting the inalienability of its property. The Trust now owns '240,000 hectares of land, nearly 600 miles of coastline and some 164 historic houses, plus castles, mills, churches, gardens, prehistoric sites and parks' (Walker, 1999). The Trust also has an imposing headquarters next to the Home Office in St James's in London, fifteen separate regional offices in England, Wales and Northern Ireland (Scotland has its own separate National Trust) and employs 2,000 full-time and over 4,000 part-time and seasonal staff.

The largest constituent parts of the Trust's tax-free income of about £170m in 1996–7 were from membership subscriptions (30 per cent), and legacies (16 per cent). The Trust also receives public money from the Heritage Lottery Fund and the Ministry of Agriculture. There have been substantial increases in membership over recent years, rising from 170,000 in 1969 to 950,000 in 1980 and 2.2m by 1995, figures that compare favourably with other environmental groups. While the Trust does engage in primary pressure group activity, designed to secure legislative change through influencing decision-makers, it is the 'selective incentives' it can offer to members – in particular free access to properties it owns – which probably hold the key to its impressive number of members (Olson, 1965).

Despite its supposedly democratic constitution, the Trust has been criticized for its oligarchical decision-making structure. Reflecting, perhaps, a national problem of declining political participation, the Trust's membership is very passive, with few voting in the organization's elections and, as a result, there is an ever-present danger of capture by a highly organized minority interest using the Trust to impose its will. Anti-nuclear campaigners have attempted to use the Trust in this way, but the classic case concerns the issue of blood sports.

As an important owner of land, and because of its charitable status, which necessitates the election of a ruling council, the National Trust has been an important arena in the on-going political battle over blood sports. Opponents of blood sports, led by the League Against Cruel Sports, have, since the 1930s, tried to get hunting banned on Trust land. It was not until the 1990s, however, that the Trust's membership voted to ban deer (but not fox) hunting, a decision later confirmed by the ruling council. This decision severely restricts most of the West Country deer hunts and puts their future in doubt. Under the auspices of an organization called the Friends of the National Trust (FONT), the blood sports lobby has sought to reverse this decision, and prevent fox hunting from being banned too, by electing its supporters to the Trust's ruling council. There has been relatively little success so far but the campaign goes on.

A final issue is that the National Trust's responsibilities are varied and, some would suggest, too great and unwieldy for one organization to cope with effectively. There is a world of difference between managing a historic house, on the one hand, and important sites of nature conservation, on the other, and there can also be conflicts between the management of countryside as amenity and as a site of scientific importance. There has been a gradual shift in the Trust's work in recent years towards countryside management in particular and to broader environmental issues in general. While this is to be welcomed on environmental grounds, it has been suggested that the Trust's resources are being spread too thinly and there is too much reliance on enthusiastic amateurs.

References

Olson, M. (1965) *The Logic of Collective Action*, Cambridge, MA: Harvard University Press.

Walker, D. (1999) 'Charitable Status', *Guardian*, 28 October.

Further reading

Hobson, D. (1999) *The National Wealth*, London: Harper Collins.

National Trust website at URL: http://www.nationaltrust.org.uk.

Waterson, M. (1994) *The National Trust. The First Hundred Years*, London: BBC Books.

ROBERT GARNER

National Wildlife Federation

The National Wildlife Federation (NWF) was founded in 1936 by J.N. 'Ding' Darling (as the General Wildlife Federation). Since then, NWF has grown to 4 million members, making it the largest US environmental group. Its agenda is determined by representatives from 46 state and territorial affiliates. The NWF describes itself as a 'big tent' of diverse people, supporting 'common sense initiatives' to restore and protect wildlife. Interestingly, studies have found more of the membership identifying as Republican than Democratic. Its state affiliates have attracted enlightened outdoors people: hunters, fishermen, and campers. Its national leadership has been rated by observers as among the most effective in lobbying Congress on environmental issues. Despite the NWF's boast about being 'the nation's premiere grassroots conservation organization', it generally follows an insider strategy, seeking to convey to elites an image of mainstream respectability and professional competence. Among its many recent activities have been efforts to restore grey wolves and grizzly bears to their original habitats, to save the **Everglades** eco-system, and to protect South Dakota **wetlands**.

Reference

National Wildlife Federation website at

URL: http://www.nwf.org/nwf.

E. GENE FRANKLAND

natural capital

Natural capital is an extension of the traditional economic notion of capital to include the stock of **renewable and non-renewable resources** of the earth. Natural capital provides the flow of life-support services and raw materials necessary for human activity. Just as a stock of factory machinery provides a flow of furniture, a stock of trees produces a flow of goods in the form of lumber and new trees and a flow of services in the form of oxygen, erosion control, wildlife habitat, genetic information, etc. If, as critics note, our social accounting system ignores natural capital it underestimates our wealth while simultaneously overestimating our income by not charging for depreciation and depletion of natural resources.

Reference

Prugh, T. (1999) *Natural Capital and Human Economic Survival*, Boca Raton: Lewis Publishers.

Further reading

Jansson, A. Hammer, M., Folke, C. and Costanza, R. (eds) (1994) *Investing in Natural Capital: The Ecological Economics Approach to Sustainability*, Washington, DC: Island Press.

STANLEY R. KEIL

Natural Resources Defense Council

The Natural Resources Defense Council (NRDC) was founded in 1970 as a non-profit organization in the state of New York 'to safeguard the earth: its people, its plants and animals and the natural systems on which all life depends, in ways that advance the long-term welfare of present and future generations'. The NRDC has currently about 400,000 members nationwide and an operating budget of $30 million. Its primary role is as a legal counsel; thus, it has often sued the government and polluting industries since 1970.

The NRDC works 'to foster the fundamental right of all people to have a voice in decisions that affect their environment and to break down the pattern of disproportionate environmental burdens borne by people of color'. The NRDC has worked to hold the **Environmental Protection Agency** accountable for the enforcement of federal environmental laws, aided in the passage of the **Clean Water Act**, and successfully lobbied for the removal of lead in US gasoline. Although focused on US issues, the organization has on occasion taken up environmental causes in other countries, most recently in Canada and Mexico. Currently the NRDC is working to prevent the Bush administration from opening the Arctic National Wildlife Refuge for oil exploration.

Further reading

Natural Resources Defense Council. 'Natural Resources Defense Council', *about us.* at URL: http://www.nrdc.org.

JON E. FITCH

nature

Nature is a notoriously difficult word to define. Meanings range from indicating all that exists, as in the 'natural world' i.e. external nature, to meaning the essence and potentiality of something, as in an 'entities nature', i.e. internal nature. Nature can mean the opposite of anything human, or human made, thus referring to the non-human world and its entities and processes, and thus is related to concepts such as environment, **landscape**, ecosystem and so on. At the same time, nature can also mean the opposite of anything 'artificial', as in 'naturally produced' food. Nature and its derivatives are very powerful terms loaded with normative significance, such that when one describes something as 'natural' or 'unnatural' one is making a very strong claim regarding its normative rightness. Related to this 'nature' is often counterposed against 'nurture'. Thus nature, like so many other

terms in environmental politics initially seems to be a purely descriptive concept, but turns out to have an intrinsically normative and prescriptive character.

JOHN BARRY

Nature Conservancy

The Nature Conservancy, first incorporated in 1951 under the name of the Ecological Society of America, is dedicated to finding and protecting the best examples of every type of ecosystem in the natural world. It is supported by dues paid by over 1 million individual members as well as corporate associates, and prides itself in its non-confrontational approach to conservation. The Nature Conservancy obtains its land holdings from charitable contributions from individual landowners, especially those who wish to see their holdings kept in a natural state after their deaths. Its professional staff of naturalists maintains and manages more than 71 million acres in North and South America, the Carribean, Asia and the Pacific Rim. The Nature Conservancy advocates public ownership and preservation of natural areas in the form of parks and wildlife preserves and refuges. It occasionally turns over some of its nature preserves to government agencies for management and regularly partners with national and state agencies in developing plans for managing their own natural areas. It conducts extensive trips to rare ecological systems in order to educate the public about the value of preserving habitat for rare and **endangered species**.

LETTIE McSPADDEN

net energy

A concept brought to the attention of academics largely through the work of H.T. Odum. Net energy can variously be described as: the energy remaining after energy has been expended to make a given energy source available for use; energy out minus energy in; energy available for end use; net energy is similar to net profit. Net energy analysis requires consideration of the entire system needed to explore, mine, produce, transport and convert a given energy resource. When energy sources are viewed in this manner a much more accurate representation can be given of their potential to serve human needs and minimize environmental impact of energy use. Decision-makers should find this concept useful when evaluating proposals for future energy-resource development. It makes little sense to expend energy to develop energy resources that will in themselves be negative in net energy yield. It also becomes apparent that high energy systems cannot be run on low quality energy resources.

Further reading

Odum, H.T. and Odum, E. (1981) *Energy Basis for Man and Nature*, New York: McGraw Hill.

THOMAS LOWE

Netherlands, the

Located at the mouth of the Rhine, Meuse and Schelde, the Netherlands is the most densely populated country in Europe, sixteen million inhabitants living on less than 15,000 square miles of land: more than 1000 on a square mile. Only 12 per cent of the land has not been cultivated or built up in some way. Yet even those 'natural' **wetlands**, marshes, sand dunes and (relatively small) forests are planned and controlled. Almost two-thirds of the country's surface is used for **agriculture**. Dutch agriculture, and in particular livestock-farming, has become very productive and export-orientated, but also expensive in ecological terms: causing water depletion, pollution by **pesticides** and a manure surplus. Other important sectors of the economy are also orientated towards export or transport: the harbour of Rotterdam is the largest in the world, and Schiphol Airport tries to be a European 'mainport'. Several **multinational and transnational corporations** have been founded in the Netherlands: Shell ('Royal Dutch'), Unilever, Philips, Heineken. Most of them cause some pollution; 'clean' industries in the 'new economy' (information technology, entertainment) are as yet relatively under-represented.

Environmental problems can be attributed not only to agriculture and industry, but also to the relative wealth and density of the Dutch population: traffic density and high energy consumption. On top of these self-created problems, the country 'imports' pollution from its industrialized neighbours: Germany, Belgium and (indirectly, through the rivers Rhine and Meuse) France and Switzerland.

Since the early 1970s, old and new environmental movements have tried to politicize these problems, sometimes quite successfully. Organizations like **Greenpeace**, the World Wildlife Fund (see **World Wide Fund for Nature**) and the Society for the Preservation of Natural Monuments claim together more than two million members – more than the Dutch Federation of Trade Unions can muster. Admittedly, most of these members remain passive, preferring donations to direct action in the street. Only the **anti-nuclear movements** managed to mobilize fairly large numbers of demonstrators in the late 1970s and early 1980s. It proved successful in the long run: in 1994 the Dutch parliament decided to close down the remaining nuclear power station in the country.

In tune with the corporatist and consociational Dutch political culture, the minister who is responsible for the environment aims at regular consultations with leaders of the environmental organizations. In 1971 a General Directorate for Environmental Affairs was established and added to the portfolio of the Minister of Health. Since 1982 it has been part of the department of Housing, Physical Planning and Environment. In 1989, a Directorate of Nature Management (*Natuurbeheer*) was created within the Department of Agriculture and Fisheries. Also in 1989 the Minister of Housing, Health and Environmental Affairs presented a National Environmental Policy Plan, in order to 'bring environmental problems under control within a period of 20 to 25 years'. The Plan was approved by parliament in 1990 – but only after a serious conflict within the governing coalition – and revised in 1993 and 1998. The revisions were no less ambitious than the original version. To achieve its aims, the government would try to negotiate covenants or voluntary agreements with organizations of employers, farmers, truckers, car-drivers and so on. Only if this failed would it introduce regulation or tax incentives. This approach proved successful in part: **air pollution** was reduced and more waste recycled, while nature reserves and **national parks** were allowed to expand. However, the government had to admit by 1998 that the problems caused by agriculture and cars were not really 'under control', that CO_2 emissions continued to increase and **biodiversity** continued to decline.

Obviously, the impact of environmental organizations on government policy is limited, given the counterpressure from economic interests. Most political parties try to balance or 'aggregate' these conflicting interests, though the balance is never even. The best ally of the environmental movement is no doubt Green Left (**GroenLinks**) – if we ignore the small party The Greens (*De **Groenen***), which is not represented in the (decisive) lower house of parliament. Another environmentalist party is the Reformed Political Federation – a small social conservative party based on the Bible. More doubtful allies are the leftwing liberal Democrats 66 (D66) and the Labour Party (*Partij van de Arbeid*, PvdA): internally often divided about sensitive environmental issues, they tend to lean more towards economic interests at the end of the day. That tendency was even stronger among the Christian Democrats (*Christen Democratisch Appèl*, CDA), at least until they were sent to the opposition benches in 1994. The staunchest ally of business interests is no doubt the Liberal Party (*Volkspartij voor Vrijheid en Democratie* VVD), even if it has produced two outstanding ministers of environmental affairs. In 1997, some car drivers lost faith in the Liberals and founded their own party (Mobile Netherlands, *Nederland Mobiel*), which won three seats at provincial elections in 1999 and might enter parliament in the twenty-first century.

Further reading

Lucardie, P. (1997) 'Greening or Ungreening the Netherlands', in M. Jacobs (ed) *Greening the Millennium?: The New Politics of the Environment*, Oxford: The Political Quarterly/ Blackwell, 183–191.

Minister van VROM (1989) *National Environmental Policy Plan: To Choose or to Lose*, The Hague: SDU.
Organization for Economic Co-operation and Development (1995) *Environmental Performance Reviews. The Netherlands*, Paris: OECD.

PAUL LUCARDIE

New Age

New Age refers to a kind of spiritual 'seeker' or the ideas they propound. First emerging in the late 1960s, the New Age movement is an eclectic mix of eastern and western spiritual traditions and practices along with positive thinking and psychological personal growth techniques. Seekers combine these in their quest to find the 'true self' or more authentic modes of experience. A key tenet of New Age thought is that from lots of personal changes in consciousness will come a new era of ecological renewal and social harmony. In the 1960s to the 1980s, this was known as the 'Age of Aquarius'. Since the 1990s such a belief has become less common and groups and individuals in these milieux have become less likely to refer to themselves as 'New Age'. Thus, some academic commentators have suggested that the term is outdated, and that 'expressive spirituality' is a more appropriate term.

BENJAMIN SEEL

New Economics Foundation

The New Economics Foundation (NEF), a leading independent think-tank, promotes a 'new economics' founded upon social justice and environmental **sustainability**. It originated from 'The Other Economic Summit' (TOES) in 1986, an annual coalition of non-governmental organizations (NGOs) which shadows the major G7/8 summits taking a critical stance against conventional economic agendas. NEF's work combines research, policy guidance and advocacy, training, and action with organizations putting 'new economics' ideas into practice. In 1996 NEF's *UK Index of Sustainable Economic Welfare* showed that despite rising incomes, recent environmental degradation and growing inequality led to falling levels of welfare. NEF's particular interests include: devising community indicators of **sustainable development**; measuring social capital; developing techniques for participation and community visioning; introducing and developing community currencies in the UK, from Local Exchange Trading Schemes (LETS) to Time Banks; promoting and benchmarking community finance initiatives (credit unions, microcredit etc.) to tackle social exclusion; and pioneering Social Auditing methods to facilitate greater corporate accountability.

GILL SEYFANG

New Left

The term New Left (*Nouvelle Gauche, Neue Linke, Nuova Sinistra, Nieuw Links*) refers to different political movements (in countries like the USA, Great Britain, France, Germany, Italy and the Netherlands) during the 1960s that shared certain characteristics:

- rejection of the Cold War and a critique of both the American and the Soviet model;
- search for a libertarian as well as communitarian utopia (see **utopia / ecotopia**);
- participatory **democracy** as an end in itself as well as a model of organization;
- affinity with the **counter-culture** and with **post-materialism** (dominant culture was criticized as materialist, consumerist, technocratic);
- a preference for direct action, spontaneity and voluntarism;
- solidarity with ethnic minorities, women, and the Third World.

After 1970 the New Left disintegrated into factions: some turned into terrorist groups, others infiltrated established parties or joined **new social movements**; again others founded green political parties.

PAUL LUCARDIE

new politics

Green parties and **environmental movements** have been conceptualized as manifestations of a distinct new politics. The new politics has been seen by its advocates amongst both academics and activists to include a novel ideology, innovative forms of organization, a new constituency of voters and to be based upon fresh political cleavages in society. The new politics is closely linked to conceptions of **post-modernism**, post-Marxism and post-materialism (see **Inglehart, Ronald**). In turn critics of the new politics thesis argue that none of its manifestations are entirely novel and the 'old' politics of left and right has not yet been transcended by the rise of green parties and **new social movements**.

The new politics has been conceptualized as promoting an innovative political discourse whose features include environmental concern, anti-productivism and an antipathy to centralized power. Post-materialist values including anti-productivism have been identified as specifically novel by academic commentators (O'Neil, 1997). The new politics has also been conceptualized as promoting distinctly new forms of organization. Typically *Die* **Grünen** were described by the late Petra **Kelly** as an 'anti-party party'. Practices such as decentralized power structures and the rotation of elected representatives have been endorsed.

Extra-parliamentary action has also been supported by European green parties, while new social movements (NSMs) in turn have been seen as part of the new politics. While it is difficult to define a generic new social movement, theorists emphasize 'the largely cultural character of new social movements, their loose organizational structure, and their emphasis upon life-style, rather than conventionally political issues', (Scott, 1990:14). The new politics has in turn been based on the support of a new constituency of voters and activists, according to some theorists. This new middle class is apparently well educated, prosperous, youthful and likely to be found amongst those working in the professional sections of the public sector. Above all, advocates of the new politics thesis believe that the emergence of green parties is based upon a new cleavage in national politics. Rather than positioning parties on a left/right continuum, a division between 'old' and 'new' or materialist and post-materialist groupings may be more appropriate. The new politics has been widely seen as originating in the student protests of the late 1960s, followed by the establishment and growth of small 'left libertarian' parties and ultimately distinct green parties.

The discourse of the new politics articulates with wider discussion of post-materialism, post-modernism and post-Marxism. Inglehart has argued that a 'silent revolution' is transforming politics with materialistic motivations giving way to new concerns. The new politics can also be seen as evidence of the breakdown of a Marxist grand narrative which conceptualizes political cleavages as based on divisions between distinct social classes. Struggles to abolish **class** inequality may be supplanted by fears that **capitalism** and the state are colonizing the lifeworld. New social movements can be seen as providing a new form of agency distinct from the working class.

In turn critics argue that the concept of new politics is both empirically and theoretically flawed. Certainly notions of novelty have been criticized and relativized. Steinmetz suggests, sardonically, that a 'cottage industry has grown up around the project of proving that the new social movements were really not so new after all' (1994: 179). Much of the new politics 'new' discourse is 'old'; social movements have mobilized around women's and environmental issues since the nineteenth century at least. The revolt against the colonization of the lifeworld can be traced via Marcuse and Bloch to Marx and earlier social critics like Carlyle who predate Marx. Anarchism as well as libertarian forms of Marxism have clearly influenced the apparently new forms of political organization (see **anarchism/eco-anarchism**).

In turn while green parties are apparently new, other 'new' parties are rather 'old'. The Pacifist Socialist Party of the Netherlands was created in the 1950s and during the 1940s the Commonwealth Party in Britain championed a number of new political themes such as environmental protection and grassroots **democracy**. Kitschelt (1993) argues that green parties are distinct left libertarian parties incorporating a politics of redistribution. During the late 1990s green parties have moved in a more realist direction and become incorporated within social democratic coalition governments in a number of western European

states. In turn the very notion of 'new politics' as green politics is being replaced by the new 'new politics' of the Third Way with social democratic parties moving to the centre or right.

References

Kitschelt, H. (1993) 'The Green Phenomenon in Western Party Systems', in S. Kamieniecki (ed.) *Environmental Politics in the International Arena*, New York: State University of New York Press.

Scott, A. (1990) *Ideology and the New Social Movements*, London: Unwin Hyman.

Steinmetz, G. (1994) 'Regulation Theory, Post-Marxism and the New Social Movements', *Comparative Studies in Society and History*, 36 (1): 176–212.

O'Neil, M. (1997) *Green Politics and Political Change in Contemporary Europe*, Aldershot: Ashgate.

DEREK WALL

new social movements

New social movements (NSMs) is a term frequently employed to refer to the range of social movements that emerged in the advanced industrial societies since the 1960s and especially in the 1970s and 1980s. Usually included are the environmental, anti-nuclear, peace and women's movements (see **environmental movements**; **anti-nuclear movements**; **peace movements**; **eco-feminism**).

The term has its origins in the 'European' approach to social movement theory developed by, amongst others, Alain Touraine, Alberto Melucci and Claus Offe. NSM theory is most articulately (and controversially) expressed by Touraine. Touraine sought, in a series of works, to identify in the plethora of social and political struggles the germ of *the* new social movement which will have the pivotal role as the agent of social and political transformation in the social and political **development** of the post-industrial society analogous to that which Marxists ascribed to the labour movement – the prototypical 'old' social movement – in industrial society.

Other writers with similar theoretical ambitions were more catholic and saw the new social movements collectively as embodying a qualitative change in social and political relationships as well as promising social and political transformation (Offe, 1985). NSMs were characterized as fluid, open, inclusive, non-doctrinal, non-ideological, socio-cultural rather than political, uninstitutionalized, self-limiting in their radicalism, and committed to **non-violent direct action**. Emphasizing personal autonomy and identity rather than centralized control, they typically involved *ad hoc* mobilizations rather than formal membership organizations and political parties. In all these respects they were supposed to be distinct from the 'old paradigm' politics and social movements that preceded them (see **paradigms**).

They were distinct, too, in the kinds of issues they embraced, the values they embodied, and the social constituencies they mobilized. The issues of peace, the environment, **human rights**, and unalienated forms of work displaced those of economic growth and distribution, military and social security, and social control. These new issue preferences reflected new value priorities. The materialist concerns with economic well-being and physical security were subsumed by 'post-materialist' concerns with personal autonomy and identity, and aesthetic and intellectual interests (see **Inglehart, Ronald**). In their critique of the allegedly purely instrumental rationality of conventional politics and older social movements, NSMs raised the standard of a transcendent and emancipatory politics rooted in the commitment to substantive rationality.

The bearers of these new values and interests were the new middle classes, the increasingly highly educated and relatively affluent people employed in the new, largely public sector, professional, administrative and higher technical occupations spawned in the course of the transition to the **post-industrial society**. However, although the NSMs had a clear class base, they were claimed to be movements *of* a class rather than *for* that class, to represent the pursuit of universal human interests rather than sectional or selfish interests, and in this they were supposed to have a different relationship to class and class interests than the 'old' movements.

NSM theory was developed as a theory of and for the advanced industrial societies of western Europe but, no doubt because of its theoretical ambition and its political promise, it was enthusiastically embraced by students of political and social change in places such as Latin America where **industrialization** was at a relatively early stage and where the social and political preconditions of the emergence of NSMs were underdeveloped or precarious (Foweraker, 1995).

The version of NSM theory that had most influence – because it was allied with the revival of interest in the **critical theory** of the Frankfurt School and the influential work of Jürgen Habermas – suffered from the extent to which it abstracted and generalized from the peculiar single instance of West Germany in the late 1970s and early 1980s. Not the least peculiarity of the West German case was the near identity, in that period, between the radical ecological and peace movements. Such ideas found some resonance in places such as Australia where an 'ecopax' movement, in a country quite remote from the front line of the Cold War, conjoined anti-nuclear and other environmental issues under the leadership of a **New Left**. It was much more problematic elsewhere in western Europe where the peace and environmental movements generally strove successfully to maintain identities separate from each other and from the left. In Britain, it was argued, NSMs were conspicuous by their absence or, at best, their weakness in a country where opposition was still dominated by the political agenda of the old left.

Its application to the USA was particularly controversial because there the 'old' social movement of the industrial working class was only weakly developed. Moreover, social and political structures there had long been so permeable that social mobility and the political incorporation of organized interests had been relatively normal. Thus, whilst since the early 1960s in the USA, there had been no shortage of social movements that were temporally new, there was less presumption that they, individually or collectively, promised a qualitative transformation of the social and political order. US political culture had long been more participatory than that of western European societies such as Germany and Austria in which, especially in the period from the Second World War to the late 1960s, citizens had been notably more reluctant to participate in politics in any but the most conventional ways. As a result, social movements (other than the labour movement) had been a more normal feature of political and social life in the USA and so the developments in and after the 1960s appeared less novel than in western Europe.

Even in Europe, however, the question was asked: what was 'new' about the new social movements? The more closely they were inspected, the more completely most of the claims for the novelty of the NSMs collapsed. The women's movement, the environmental movement and the peace movement all had historical precedents in most industrialized countries. Earlier social movements (including, at least in its early stages, the labour movement) could be shown to have been motivated by a transcendent moral idealism rather than narrowly instrumental rationality, and the claim that it pursued universal human interests had also been made by the socialist movement. The numbers of the highly educated might be unprecedented, but intellectuals and students had always been prominent in social movements.

Gradually, the theoretical and political ambitions of NSM theory subsided and the term 'NSM' came to be used, in Europe as well as in the USA, simply as a convenient shorthand to denote the collectivity of individual movements that emerged from the 1970s onwards and of which the environmental, anti-nuclear, peace, feminist and solidarity movements were the most nearly universal. (The student and anti-war movements of the late 1960s, which were in many ways the origins of ideas about NSMs, are sometimes regarded as precursors rather than NSMs themselves.)

This, however, leaves unexamined the question of whether there is indeed something qualitatively different about the NSMs that warrants the use of the label. The NSMs rose on the surge of protest that began with the student movements of the mid to late 1960s, and they were at least novel by the standards of western liberal democratic states in the years following the Second World War (see **liberalism/liberal democracy**). Their novelty consisted in the extent to which they reflected and translated into politics the social changes of an era of unprecedented prosperity unprecedentedly widely shared and derived from the long economic boom of the years of postwar reconstruction. The extent to which they were rooted in long-term secular social change is evident in the remarkable extent to which they were able to survive and indeed to develop during and beyond the years of recession and economic insecurity that followed.

If they are no longer so prominent a feature of western societies it is principally because so many of their aspirations and so much of their style has been incorporated into the political mainstream. The theorists who, in the 1960s and 1970s, saw the rise of protest as a crisis of democracy have been confounded by the ability of liberal democracies in Europe as in North America to accommodate new demands for participation by hitherto under-represented sections of society, to embrace new or newly urgent issue agendas such as those of feminism and environmentalism that some had thought to represent fundamental challenges to the capitalist order, and to adapt to an expanded repertoire of citizen participation that included the hitherto unconventional tactics of protest as well as the strictly conventional ones of electoral and interest group politics. The continuing vitality of the impulses which fed the NSMs can be seen in the resurgence of protest that occurs when governments fail to respond to the concerns of their educated and 'post-materialist' citizens (see **Inglehart, Ronald**).

The great survivor among NSMs – the modern environmental movement – is qualitatively different from its predecessors in the range and integration of its ecological concerns and in the diversity of its forms of organizations and action. More widespread higher education has enhanced the skills and self-confidence of populations, and knowledge itself has changed. Even as ever more potent **technology** has facilitated the more complete subjugation of **nature**, so understanding of the ecological interdependence of humanity and the rest of the natural world has grown. For the first time in history, there is widespread concern that humanity may fall victim to an ecological catastrophe of its own making. Touraine (1983) identified the ecology movement as the only one among the NSMs that had the potential to be *the* structurally transformative movement of the post-industrial society because it was the one most clearly focused upon the central contradiction of modern capitalist industrialism: technocracy (power exercised in the name of knowledge). Its persistence when the other NSMs have come and gone suggests that he was right.

See also: eco-feminism; new politics

References

Dalton, R.J. and Kuechler, M. (eds) (1990) *Challenging the Political Order: New Social and Political Movements in Western Democracies*, Oxford: Polity.

Foweraker, J. (1995) *Theorizing Social Movements*, London: Pluto.

Maheu, L. (1995) *Social Movements and Social Classes*, London: Sage.

Offe, C. (1985) 'New Social Movements: Challenging the Boundaries of Institutional Politics', *Social Research*, 52: 817–67.

Touraine, A., Hegedus, Z., Dubet, F. and Wieviorka, M. (1983) *Anti-nuclear Protest: The Opposition to Nuclear Energy in France*, Cambridge: Cambridge University Press.

CHRIS ROOTES

New Zealand

New Zealand's geographical features contribute to its 'clean and green' image. But underneath this lies a reality of environmental degradation, a dominance of economic interests, weak environmental policy performance, and a long up-hill struggle of the **environmental movement**. In the late 1990s, however, New Zealand entered a new phase of environmental politics as a change in the electoral system offered scope for stronger expression and influence of environmental interests in the political arena.

Given its relative isolation in the South Pacific, scenic beauty, and sparse population, New Zealand is often pictured as one of earth's natural wonders. But images are misleading. Many indigenous species of plants and animals have become extinct or are in decline, largely as a result of the reduction of forest cover, the draining of **wetlands**, and the introduction of predators and pests. Resources, including land, **fisheries**, and timber, often have been exploited with little consideration for ecological consequences. Although the scale of environmental pollution may be small compared to highly industrialized nations, it is serious in places. In many instances, the extent of environmental problems is not known, as a system of environmental monitoring and reporting was not established until the 1990s.

In the 1960s, concern about the decline of indigenous forests, wildlife, and the despoliation of scenic values gave rise to a strong **conservation movement**. In 1972, rising concerns about the social, cultural and environmental effects of unmitigated economic growth led to the establishment of the world's first national-level green party (see **Values Party**). In 1985, the bombing, in Auckland's harbour, of **Greenpeace**'s flagship the *Rainbow Warrior* by the French secret service, further boosted support for the environmental movement. In 1987, the strength of the anti-nuclear feeling led to the adoption of legislation to declare New Zealand a nuclear-free nation.

Growing support for environmental issues contributed to a reform of environmental institutions in the 1980s, including the establishment of a Ministry for the Environment (the main environmental policy agency), a Parliamentary Commissioner for the Environment (an independent environmental 'watchdog'), and a Department of Conservation. In 1991, the Resource Management Act was adopted, integrating an array of fragmented environmental legislation, devolving much responsibility for environmental decision-making to local and regional government, and proclaiming the sustainable management of natural and physical resources as its purpose. In 1995, the Government introduced the 'Environment 2010 Strategy', formulating the general principles and objectives of its longer term environmental policy.

Although these developments suggest that environmental interests gained considerable influence during the 1980s and 1990s, they need to be seen in a wider context. Environmental reform was just one element of a broad programme of fundamental change inspired by neoliberal ('New Right') ideology that left no area of the state and public policy untouched. Although efficiency, transparency, and accountability were the guiding principles underlying the reforms, the first priority of governments was creation of an open and minimally regulated economy to encourage investments and economic growth.

Consequently, the environmental reforms have had little effect in terms of addressing or reducing the main sources of environmental pressure. Environmental concerns are poorly if at all integrated into the energy, transport, and **agriculture** sectors, responsible for many of the environmental pressures. Environmental agencies have been hamstrung by underfunding and weak government commitment. **Development** is hindered only when opponents can prove that 'environmental bottomlines' are likely to be transgressed, a very difficult task given the inevitable uncertainty associated with environmental issues, and the inequality of resources between proponents of development on the one hand, and public and environmental groups on the other.

In 1996, the electoral system was changed from a 'first-past-the-post' system to a system of proportional representation, enabling for the first time the representation of the Green Party in Parliament, be it in a coalition with other small parties ('The Alliance'). In 1999, the Green Party contested the elections independently, gaining more than 5 per cent of the vote and 7 (of the 120) seats in Parliament, giving it a strong basis for increasing the political weight of environmental concerns within the minority centre–left (Labour–Alliance) government.

Further reading

Bührs, T. (2001) 'New Zealand', in: M. Jänicke and H. Weidner (eds) *National Environmental Policies. A Comparative Study of Capacity-Building*, vol. 2, Berlin: Springer.

Bührs, T. and Bartlett, R. (1993) *Environmental Policy in New Zealand. The Politics of Clean and Green?*, Auckland: Oxford University Press.

Gleeson, B. (1996) 'The Perils of Market Envir-
onmentalism: The New Zealand Experiment', *Environment and Planning A*, 28: 1910–16.

Organization for Economic Co-operation and Development (1996) *Environmental Performance Reviews*, Paris, NZ: OECD.

TON BÜHRS

newly industrializing countries

The term 'newly industrializing countries' (NICs) became widely used during the 1970s when the traditional industrial powers of Europe and North America were challenged by imports from Asia, eastern and southern Europe and a number of other developing countries. The rise of the Japanese economy posed the greatest threat to the established industrial powers, although Japan is usually not included in the official classifications of NICs.

Usage of the term NIC is problematic because different institutions have different definitions of the term and consequently the number of countries classified as NICs can vary from source to source. As Turner (1982: 5–6) noted, the definition of NICs could sometimes encompass no more than six to eight countries but at other times it could cover up to 20 countries. For instance, the OECD (Organization for Economic Co-operation and Development), which selected a number of criteria such as an expanding share of industrial employment, published a top list of 10 NICs in 1979 including Singapore, South Korea, Hong Kong, Taiwan, **Brazil**, **Mexico**, **Spain**, Portugal, Yugoslavia and **Greece**. Britain's Foreign and Commonwealth Office compiled a considerably larger list, which included, amongst others, Israel, Malta and Iran. As an added difficulty, countries classified as NICs have partly changed since the 1970s with newcomers such as Malaysia.

Notwithstanding any conceptual problems, the industrial production of NICs, particularly from East and South East Asia, has quickly expanded since the 1960s. For instance, between 1963 and 1994, South Korea's and Taiwan's share of world manufacturing output rose from 0.1 per cent each to 2.7 per cent and 1.2 per cent respectively (Dicken 1998:30). Since much of this expansion was achieved through a shift towards export-orientated **industrialization**, the NICs' share of world manufactured exports is even higher.

The success of NICs can partly be ascribed to their ability to attract foreign investment thanks to low wages as well as little or poorly enforced legislation in the area of labour rights. Lower wages as well as lower labour standards rendered some NICs a preferred location for labour-intensive industries such as clothing manufacturing. Due to savings on operational costs, many **multinational and transnational corporations** have relocated some of their manufacturing plants from developed countries to NICs or shifted to sourcing their supplies from NICs.

The success of NICs has also sometimes been ascribed to their liberal economic policies with regards to foreign investment and trade. However, such a view is largely inaccurate since the most successful NICs such as South Korea and Taiwan owe much of their economic success to initial government intervention in the economy including a devaluation of the country's currency, preferential treatment of national firms (e.g. preferential access to credit) and strong educational policies. In South Korea, for instance, certain industries were initially reserved for the national business conglomerates, or chaebol, which were able to expand without the competitive threat of established foreign firms. In general terms, Dicken (1998:126) argued that one common feature of NICs was the principal role of the state administration in their economic **development**, although specific government policies varied widely between countries.

The success of NICs was, nonetheless, accompanied by some difficulties such as rising foreign indebtedness and rapid **urbanization**. Furthermore, many countries developed their economies at the expense of the environment, leading to deforestation and the related problems of soil erosion and flooding; **air pollution**; and other environmental problems (see **forest management**). As conventional measurement of economic growth such as GDP (gross domestic product) does not take ecological losses into account, the high GDP rates of growth of some NICs are somewhat deceptive because they do not consider the related

social cost such as health costs and environmental clean-up costs for future generations (see **green accounting**).

Despite the rapid economic growth of NICs, industrial production has remained concentrated in the old industrialized countries. At the end of the twentieth century, roughly four-fifths of world manufacturing production was still located in North America, western Europe and Japan (Dicken 1998: 27).

References

Dicken, P. (1998) *Global Shift: Transforming the World Economy*, London: Paul Chapman, 3rd edn.

Turner, L. (1982) 'Introduction', in L. Turner and N. McMullen (eds) *The Newly Industrializing Countries, Trade and Adjustment*, London: Allen and Unwin.

Further reading

Bello, W. and Rosenfeld, S. (1990) *Dragons in Distress: Asia's Miracle Economies in Crisis*, San Francisco: Institute for Food and Development Policy.

Brohman, J. (1996) 'Postwar Development in the Asian NICs: Does the Neoliberal Model Fit Reality?', *Economic Geography* 72: 107–130.

Douglass, M. (1994) 'The "Developmental State" and the Newly Industrialized Economies of Asia', *Environment and Planning A* 26: 543–66.

J. GEORGE FRYNAS

Nigeria

Nigeria, Africa's most populous country (with more than 100 million people), is a leading exporter of crude oil, which is its major source of wealth and, on the other hand, of anxiety and ecopolitical conflicts. The country's diverse ecological **landscape** also generates other significant problems that have far-reaching consequences for public policy.

The discovery and exploitation of crude oil in the Niger Delta area of south-eastern Nigeria more than 50 years ago has led to the nation's economy systematically acquiring a monocultural base.

Hence, from a 30 per cent average in the late 1960s, crude oil exports have risen to account for 85–95 per cent of the country's external revenue in the past 30 years. Nigeria's total proven reserves of oil in the Niger Delta is estimated to be 16–17.9 billion barrels (1.8 per cent of proven global reserves) (see Robson, 1999: 380).

Like most developing countries, Nigeria's oil industry is dominated by expatriate **multinational corporations** (MNCs) (Shell, Mobil, Chevron, Agip, Elf, etc.), who carry out the prospecting, exploitation, and production activities (see **multinational and transnational corporations**). Over the years, a great deal of harmony of interests has prevailed between Nigerian government and the MNCs. Given its weak and dependent position in the global circuit of commodity and capital production, the role of the Nigerian state has largely been one of fostering hospitable conditions (mainly through legislation) for the operation of the MNCs in the oil sector.

The longstanding business understanding of the state and the MNCs has been increasingly challenged by the **indigenous peoples** of the Niger Delta, who among other things, protest the cumulative degradation of their environment following the activities of the oil companies. The different stages of oil extraction, namely seismic survey, drilling and processing stages, cause severe ecological damage to the host communities. For instance, the vibrations of the explosives used in seismic surveys when the MNCs make initial underground explorations for oil formation can collapse several buildings and crack the walls and foundations of many others. The drilling process releases toxic wastes, which pollute the soil, fishing waters and traditional livelihood of the local people. During the processing phase when the black crude is processed into oil, water and gas, leakage of pipes and spillage are frequently reported in the oil settlements in the course of pumping oil into evacuation tanks or transporting it to the seaports. The effluent water (usually containing oil and soluble pollutants) is released into the surroundings, which further devastates the environment. The gas component is usually flared at the flow stations. The flares adversely affect the ecosystem owing to exposure to light intensity and

excessive **global warming**. A major adverse effect of the gas flaring is the **acid rain** in Iko of Akwa Ibom State.

Almost every community in the Niger Delta suffers at least one oil-related ecological hazard or another. The situation tends to be compounded by the reluctance of some of the oil companies to introduce environment-friendly technologies and measures. Consequently, most of the MNCs provide paltry or no compensations to local people for damaged buildings, livelihood, or for desecrated shrines, forests and totems. Sometimes, the MNCs pay their compensations into the wrong hands (usually community leaders), who often misappropriate the monies at the expense of the masses who actually suffer most of the environmental hazards. This invariably exacerbates the situation.

Similarly, the far-reaching socio-economic disruptions and polarization brought by the MNCs to the communities enrage the grassroots population. Oil extraction activities in these local communities usually lead to a massive influx of company workers into the rural setting (mostly expatriates and Nigerians of other ethnic origins). The monthly wages, purchasing power, life-style and residential quarters of these oil workers are almost of western standards. This leaves a detestable pill of socio-demographic duality in the mouths of the indigenous people. Although the oil communities often derive significant benefits (arguably inevitable fallouts) from this global capital network such as provision of public infrastructure (roads, potable water etc.), employment of casual labour and booming of petty trading, the negative **externalities** and social cost, particularly in terms of prostitution of girls and women, disruption of family life, and rising rates of localized inflation and crime are enormous.

Furthermore, the social provisioning of the oil companies is hardly adequate for the host communities and it is rarely extended to the surrounding communities, which also suffer heavy ecological damage; the resulting agitations for compensation and provision of infrastructure are endless. These agitations, which have grown more violent than ever during the past fourteen years of severe economic hardship caused by the **World Bank**'s **structural adjustment programmes**, have resulted in more disruption of oil activities, pollution due to sabotage of oil pipelines and loss of human life.

Distressed by the growing undermining of oil activities and the national economy as a consequence of these violent protests of oil communities, the state has occasionally responded by using military violence. The climax of the state's violent campaign was the 1995 militarization of the crisis-torn Ogoniland, which culminated in the execution of Ken Saro-Wiwa and eight other Ogoni environmental rights activists by the late Nigerian military dictator, Sani Abacha (see **Ogoni People**). This incident outraged the international community and earned Nigeria limited sanctions from the West.

Nigerian governments, past and present, have hardly disputed the fact that the oil-producing communities of the Niger Delta are comparatively disadvantaged in spatial **development** terms and suffer parlous environmental degradation. Governments have also instituted various development agencies to redress these plights. Consequently, both the national and concerned subnational governments have, since the 1990s, established different environmental protection agencies to enforce legislation for a sustainable and healthy environment in the Niger Delta.

Despite these measures, both environmental and humanitarian conditions in the Niger Delta remain largely deplorable. The real problem of environmental protection and **sustainable development** in the Niger Delta lies in the institutional and positional weaknesses of the state to enforce (existing) environmental legislation (both municipal laws and international standards) with the aim of effectively and responsively regulating the operation of the powerful MNCs, and their interactions with oil communities.

Beyond oil-induced ecological problems, Nigeria has one of the highest levels of municipal waste pollution (both organic and inorganic) in Africa and this phenomenon is related to the proliferation and growth of urban centres following the oil wealth. Hazardous emissions from medium and small-scale industries form the bulk of the toxic wastes in big cities like Lagos, Port Harcourt, Warri, Ibadan and Onitsha. The ecological risks of toxic wastes in Nigerian cities are greatly heightened by the lack of waste treatment, poor drainage systems and the reliance of a large proportion of the urban population on shallow wells for drinking water. Furthermore, poor **municipal solid waste** management and lead emissions from vehicles add to the urban environmental hazards. Municipal solid waste generation in most Nigerian state capitals and commercial centres averages more than 95,000 tons per year. The lack of sanitary landfills and adequate disposal systems means the wastes are dumped on open sites and rivers. As such, they pose a serious health risk to the people. Vehicular emissions are of a profound health concern because lead (the emitted substance) contributes to mental dysfunction and the concentration of lead in Nigerian gasoline is one of the highest levels in the world (0.74 mg/l) (World Bank, 1995: 11). See also **lead poisoning**.

There are significant non-industrial environmental problems in Nigeria, mostly related to its **biodiversity**. They include water hyacinth proliferation along the Atlantic coast, deforestation and soil erosion in the southern parts of the country and desertification in the north. Since it was discovered in the Lagos sea coast in the late 1980s, water hyacinth, an exotic weed, has expanded throughout the Nigerian coastal region, closing many creeks and impeding water transportation and fishing. This has adversely affected the livelihood of many of the coastal communities. Government and local agencies have employed mechanical and manual harvesting techniques to clear water hyacinth but the enterprise has proved relatively expensive and ineffective.

Deforestation has mainly resulted from game hunting (for animal protein), unbridled logging and most critically, the extensive nature of small-scale agriculture (shifting cultivation), an activity that also contributes to flooding and soil erosion. The Nigerian **mangroves** and **rainforests** have enormous biodiversity significance and they hold a large number of threatened and **endangered species**, particularly mammals. The Government Forestry and Agricultural Departments, however, lack the resources to protect the rapidly depleted forest resources (see **forest management**).

Finally, desertification, a growing problem that has exposed several communities in different parts of northern Nigeria to the devastation of the north-east (**Sahel**) winds, is attributable to the combined effects of pastoralism and the encroachment of the Sahara desert on arid and semi-arid areas. Within the past decade the government has embarked on a massive tree-planting campaign and prohibition of tree felling in endangered areas to stop the problem.

See also: oil pollution; sub-Saharan Africa

References

Robson, E. (1999) 'Commentaries – Problematizing Oil and Gender in Nigeria', *Gender, Place and Culture*, 6(4): 379–90.

World Bank (1995) *Defining an Environmental Strategy for the Niger Delta*, vol. 1, Washington: The World Bank.

Further reading

Gupta, A. and M.C. Asher (1998) *Environment and Developing World*, Chichester: John Wiley & Sons.

Inyang, L.D. and. AwakEssien, H. S (eds) (1995) *Topical Issues in the Nigerian Oil and Gas Industry*, Uyo-Nigeria: Universal Communications Ltd.

KENNETH OMEJE

NIMBY

The not-in-my-backyard (NIMBY) syndrome reflects the increasingly common pattern of strong public opposition to proposals to site new waste disposal facilities in neighbouring areas. This response is regularly found for proposed facilities involving a wide range of waste types (radioactive, hazardous, biomedical, and solid) and waste disposal technologies (landfill, incineration, treatment). It has resulted in extreme difficulty in many political jurisdictions in finding a place to manage wastes.

Any benefits to be derived from a new facility are likely to be widely distributed. By contrast most costs and risks related to facility operation will be concentrated upon a particular community and its neighbours. Such an imbalance provides considerable incentives for potential site communities to take aggressive political action, including litigation, appeal to administrative bodies, media outreach, or direct political protest. Local, grassroots organizations often form quickly in such circumstances, galvanizing public opposition in relatively short amounts of time.

BARRY G. RABE

noble savage, myth of

The 'noble savage' appears in Jean-Jacques Rousseau's *Discourse on the Origins of Inequality* referring to people who, in a state of nature, 'do not know good and evil', but whose 'peacefulness of passions and ignorance of vice keep them from doing ill'. This mythical construction contrasts with Hobbes's characterization of life in the state of nature as 'poor, solitary, nasty, brutish and short'. The Rousseauian idea has resonances for contemporary ecological thinkers who believe that more harmonious and less exploitative ways of living are exemplified in traditions of **indigenous peoples** whose relations to one another and their natural environment have not been corrupted by modern '**development**'. The empirical basis of this belief, however, appears questionable in the light of evidence from archaeology and anthropology; and while there are certainly aspects of indigenous people's ways that more 'developed' societies could profitably learn from, the 'ecologically noble savage' is essentially a myth. Still, as myths do, it may encapsulate a guiding idea 'with a power beyond the rational and limited impact of the literal'.

TIM HAYWARD

non-renewable resources

Non-renewable resources exist in given stocks in given places. They make up part of the **natural capital** endowment of the earth. The endowment of a non-renewable resource is measurable usually in terms of mass or volume although neither of these may be known with certainty. Geologists distinguish between measured, inferred, and speculative stocks of these resources. They are also called 'depletable' resources since withdrawals from the stock lead eventually to their exhaustion. Two types of non-renewable resources can be distinguished, those that are recyclable (e.g. metals and water) and those which are not (e.g., **fossil fuels**, radioactive isotopes). Since **recycling** can never be complete, it only extends the time before exhaustion. While the stock of a non-renewable resource is finite, the flow is a matter of economic demand and public policy.

Further reading

Tietenburg, T. (2000) *Environmental and Natural Resource Economics*, New York: Addison Wesley Longman, 5th edn.

STANLEY R. KEIL

non-violent direct action

Non-violent direct action (NVDA) by environmentalists includes the kind of civil disobedience where arrests are anticipated and even desirable, but it is also broader. It can include **monkey-wrenching** and protests in which activists seek to evade arrest. **Greenpeace** carries out the first kind of action; radical environmentalists such as Sea Shepherd and the networks of **Earth First!**, mainly the second type of action (see also **Sea Shepherd Conservation Society**). Non-violent direct action has also been used by established environmental movement organizations (EMOs) such as the **National Trust** (in the nineteenth century) and **Ramblers' Association**, and also by local environmental campaigners in the North and South. It has often been defined as a key characteristic of **new social movements**. Most often, however, it has been associated with the most radical green groups.

Attempts to generalize about NVDA by radical greens are difficult. Groups who use this form of action can be found throughout northern and eastern Europe, but are strongest and have greatest impact in English-speaking countries, notably the USA, Australia, Britain and Ireland. But even

where there has been most mutual influence there are differences. In the USA and Australia the defence of wilderness has been the primary *raison d'être* for Earth First! and similar groups. In Britain and the rest of Europe, anti-capitalist urban protest has been more important and direct action in rural areas has more often been alongside existing local environmental campaigns. Yet these differences seemed less important when at the end of the 1990s protests were mounted by groups in all these countries against the effects of global trade and neoliberal **capitalism**.

One issue common to environmental direct action groups in the USA, Australia and Britain is debate about the appropriateness of the commitment to non-violence. The death of a protester who fell from a walkway on a tree at the Headwaters camp in Oregon in 1998 fuelled an already live debate in the US movement. In Australia a shift towards more militant direct action in which those responsible do not necessarily accept the traditional roles of civil disobedience has been noted. In Britain, protests in the City of London against capitalism on 18 June 1999 marked a turning point in that some activists fought openly with police. In Germany in the 1980s there were conflicts between groups from local communities opposed to nuclear power plants at Wackersdorf and Gorleben and other more militant anti-nuclear movement protesters over violence by the latter (see **Gorleben controversy**; **anti-nuclear movements**).

Direct action is the defining characteristic and purpose of Earth First! and similar radical environmental groups. These groups are distinct from most other **environmental movements**, first because they justify their protest as a strategy for bringing about comprehensive social and political change towards a radical green society. Second, their protest actions are rooted in an alternative culture. This is manifested in their clothes, their ecological lifestyle, the rejection of dominant values and institutions and their non-hierarchical form of organization. Third, they reject the existing environmental pressure groups as inadequate or insufficient to deal with the environmental crisis. Those who initiated NVDA groups did so as a result of disillusionment with the compromises made by pressure groups. They argue that when pressure groups accept compromises to achieve partial gains they help to legitimize policies and a decision-making process that favours **development** over the environment. Fears over the loss of assets from court actions or the loss of support from cheque-book subscribers, make it difficult for EMOs to take radical action. For instance, Greenpeace has had to back away from NVDA actions on occasion when threatened with legal action. The style of organization adopted by NVDA groups is intended to offset the limitations of the EMOs. By maintaining a decentralized and informal organization, NVDA groups have no resources which could be targeted by their opponents and which might limit their ability to act. Moreover, where action is the responsibility of the individual or a small groups it is the individual rather than the organization who has to take responsibility for the consequences. Fourth, for radical environmentalists, individual moral obligations to do what is right count for everything, political obligation to the state counts for little or nothing. Although the heritage of **Gandhi** and Martin Luther King is acknowledged, the NVDA of radical environmental groups is more confrontational than earlier forms of civil disobedience. King's emphasis on upholding the law and American and Christian values is not echoed by many contemporary environmental NVDA activists. Radical environmentalists often see themselves as acting consciously in opposition to dominant values that help to sustain environmental destruction. Illegal action is justified both because the political, social and economic system itself is illegitimate and because it is seen as the most effective means to achieve change.

See also: anti-roads movement

Further reading

Seel, B., Paterson, M. and Doherty, B. (eds) (2000) *Direct Action in British Environmentalism*, London: Routledge.

BRIAN DOHERTY

North Africa and Middle East

Any attempt to address the Middle East and North Africa from an environmental perspective cannot but note the disparity between political borders and the physical environment. Ranging from Turkey in the north, to Iran in the east, Egypt in the south and Morocco in the west, the area crosses continents and climatic zones. However, in terms of human impact on the natural environment, one can identify some common characteristics. Due to the geography of the area and its arid and semi-arid conditions, human settlements have concentrated along river banks, sea and gulf coasts and valleys, thereby intensifying the impact of population pressures, **agriculture** and rapid **urbanization** and **industrialization** (see also **population movement and control**). The resulting problems are mainly water shortages and salinization and soil degradation.

Regional problems

Agricultural development prompted by growing population and the desire to reduce dependency upon food imports and to increase crop yields for export, has expanded irrigation and **pesticide** use. In Tunisia, for example, the absence of reliable rainfall increasingly forces farmers to turn to irrigation. However, the consequence of this has been a rapid increase in the salt content of water which, in turn, has led to increased salinity of soils, a process which will eventually lead to their sterility. In Tunisia this accounts for as much as one per cent per annum of the country's fertile land (Chourou, 1995: 77). Salinization due to irrigation has been a problem in the Nile, Tigris, and Euphrates basins for thousands of years, but the scale and rate of damage is increasing.

Fertilizers and pesticides threaten groundwater in Israel and Egypt. They may also play a large part in alluvial soil pollution in Egypt by heavy metals. In Lebanon, the unregulated use of pesticides and other hazardous agricultural chemicals has caused serious damage to the soil, human health and wildlife and a similar situation exists in Iran (Jabbra and Jabbra, 1997: 3–7).

In North Africa, the increase in the human population has required growing numbers of livestock, which in turn are exploiting more range land and forest areas (Swearingen and Bencherifa, 1996: 6). Under the combined effects of natural and human factors, Tunisia has been losing about 18,000 ha of productive land every year (Chourou, 1995: 76). In Lebanon and Israel, increased urbanization is a central cause of the decreasing area of agricultural land, encouraged by the high prices offered by developers.

Urbanization and rapid industrialization, coupled with population growth, have caused a growing problem of urban and industrial waste. As a consequence of land-based polluted discharges, the Black Sea is becoming a cesspool. The Israeli government is concerned about sewage pollution in the Sea of Galilee, a problem compounded by pollution introduced by the Jordan river from the north. In Egypt, experts have claimed that a large percentage of untreated waste is discharged into the Nile, irrigation canals and drainage ditches, and the harbour of Alexandria is under increasing environmental stress (Jabbra and Jabbra, 1997: 3–5). The fragile coastal systems and **coral reefs** of the Gulf of Aqaba are threatened by sewage from Aqaba and particularly Eilat, maritime activity in both harbours and tourism (see **tourism, environmental impact of**). Conflict among the bordering nations has contributed to these problems by preventing co-operation on marine conservation projects (Amer, 1993).

The Arabian gulf is one of the busiest oil transport water arteries. Half of the world's oil passes through its bottleneck, the Hormuz Strait, and oil is the sea's prime pollutant. Pollution of the Tigris river by untreated domestic and industrial waste on its way from Turkey, through Iraq, contributes to the already polluted Gulf as do increased production and use of plastic in the Gulf states (Jabbra and Jabbra, 1997: 3–4). The Gulf states have ratified several protocols to protect their marine environment from pollution and its lethal effects. However, full implementation has been hindered by weak national institutions (Al-Awadhi, 1997: 157). The Dead Sea, a unique salt-lake, lying currently at 411 metres below sea level is constantly breaking its own record – its level is dropping by up

to a metre every year. Areas surrounding the Sea itself, much of which are pristine nature reserves, are being threatened by plans for expanding heavy industry, tourism initiatives, and transportation infrastructure planned by Israelis, Palestinians, and Jordanians. Finally, a number of the region's countries border the Mediterranean on its southern and eastern shores and contribute to the sea's growing pollution. In consequence, they are also committed to the Mediterranean Action Plan.

National capabilities

While certain basic environmental problems are similar, national capabilities to deal with them differ greatly. By the simple measure of per capita GNP, countries range from the richer oil producing countries of the Gulf, and industrialized Israel, to poverty stricken Yemen. Countries also differ widely along the human development index (Wilson, 1995: 9–13). The latter distinction could explain some of the disparity in environmental awareness, which is usually linked to a certain level of **development** and education.

The pollution caused by the Gulf War prompted some of the local governments, such as the United Arab Emirates (UAE) and Oman, to respond by stepping up their efforts to protect the environment. The UAE's environmental protection law, which was drafted in 1998, is a comprehensive attempt to deal both with requirements and with the need for adequate enforcement. Since then, one of the government's projects had been to encourage the establishment of a **coastal zone management** plan. In contrast, environmental legislation in Saudi Arabia has been slow in coming and even where laws and regulations exist, they have not always been enforced properly (Smith, 1999: 33–6). Lack of enforcement is characteristic of most of the region's governments. Lack of resources has limited environmental protection in Jordan and Egypt. Iranian environmental protection laws are ineffective due to lagging **technology**, budgetary constraints and general non-compliance (Jabbra and Jabbra, 1997: 9), nor has Morocco's environmental policy been able to keep pace with the emerging challenges (Weidnitzer, 1995: 67). Lebanon has faced similar problems.

However, it has been relatively successful with educational measures (Masri, 1997: 105).

The development of environmental non-government organizations (NGOs) in the Middle East has been rather slow compared with other areas of the world, due in large part to the political conditions in the region. Environmental activism has gained momentum only towards the end of the twentieth century (Amer, 1993: 487–8). By the mid-1990s approximately 120 environmental NGOs had formed in Lebanon, most of which were local (Masri, 1997: 107). Israel also underwent an expansion of activity in the NGO sector during the 1990s. In the late 1990s **Greenpeace** Mediterranean set up offices in Turkey, Lebanon and Israel and has been active in protesting against waste incinerators and coastal pollution.

Jordan is particularly notable for organized citizen groups active in inducing national awareness of environmental problems and promoting public demands for their solutions (Jabbra and Jabbra, 1997: 8). In Egypt, however, it was the state that first demonstrated interest in environmental issues (Gomaa, 1997: 5). Similarly, the first approaches towards the development of an environmental policy in Morocco came chiefly 'from the top'. However, the decentralization policy initiated in the mid-1970s has successively broadened the scope of action open to civic initiatives. However, the capacity of organizations to mobilize broad segments of the population remains low (Weidnitzer, 1995: 72–4).

Water and conflict in the Middle East

Access to water has always been a key environmental factor in the politics of the region (see **water politics**). The Tigris and particularly the Euphrates rivers have been a bone of contention between Turkey, Syria and Iraq. The filling of the Ataturk Dam had already caused tension when, in 1990, Turkey blocked the flow of the entire Euphrates for one month. In 1975, the filling of Tabqa dam's reservoir in Syria provoked an aggressive response from downstream Iraq. It was only through Soviet and Saudi mediation that potential violence was prevented (Hillel, 1994: 106–8). Perhaps even more contentious is the

Jordan River, the catchment of which is shared by Syria, Lebanon, Israel, Jordan and the West Bank. It has prompted continuous conflict and contributed indirectly to the 1967 war. Possession of the Banias (one of the river's main sources which has its headwaters in the Golan plateau) is in dispute between Israel and Syria (Hillel, 1994: 156–8).

Examples of rivalries over groundwater also abound. One case is the Damman aquifer, which underlies parts of the Arabian peninsula along the Persian Gulf. A similar rivalry exists between Saudi Arabia and neighbouring Jordan over the fossil waters of a desert aquifer underlying their border area. Perhaps even more fateful – though not as immediate – is the rivalry over groundwater that is threatening to develop between Egypt and Libya in what the Egyptians call the Western Desert. Finally, one of Israel's main supplies of fresh water is the mountain aquifer, the catchment area of which lies in the mountainous territory of the West Bank (Hillel, 1994: 194–209). Israel's control of Palestinian water sources coupled with a large gap between Israeli and Palestinian water consumption is one of the more poignant aspects of the Israeli occupation of the West Bank since 1967.

See also: dams/hydroelectric power; militarism and the environment; oil pollution

References

Al-Awadhi, B.A. (1997) 'Regional Instruments for the Protection of the Marine Environment in the Arabian Gulf', in J.G. Jabbra and N.W. Jabbra (eds) *Challenging Environmental Issues*, Leiden: E.J. Brill.

Amer, O. (1993) 'An Agenda of Co-operation Among Non-Governmental Organizations in the Gulf of Aqaba-Bordering States', in D. Sandler, *et al.* (eds) *Protecting the Gulf of Aqaba*, Washington DC: Environmental Law Institute.

Chourou, B. (1995) 'The Dilemma Between Environmental Protection and Economic Development: Tunisia as a Case Study', in E. Watkins (ed.) *The Middle Eastern Environment*, Cambridge: St Malo.

Gomaa, S.S. (1997) *Environmental Policy Making in Egypt*, Cairo: The American University in Cairo.

Hillel, D. (1994) *Rivers of Eden*, New York: Oxford University Press.

Jabbra, J.G. and Jabbra, N.W. (1997) 'Challenging Environmental Issues: Middle Eastern Perspectives', in J.G. Jabbra and N.W. Jabbra (eds) *Challenging Environmental Issues*, Leiden: E.J. Brill.

Masri, R. (1997) 'Environmental Challenges in Lebanon', in J.G. Jabbra and N.W. Jabbra (eds) *Challenging Environmental Issues*, Leiden: E.J. Brill.

Smith, P.A. (1999) 'Protecting the Arab Environment', *Middle East*, 286: 33–6.

Swearingen, W.D. and Bencherifa, A. (1996) 'Introduction: North Africa's Environment at Risk', in W.D.Swearingen and A.Bencherifa (eds) *The North African Environment at Risk*, Boulder, CO: Westview.

Weidnitzer, E. (1995) 'Environmental Policy in Morocco: Institutional Problems and the Role of Non-Governmental Organizations', in E. Watkins (ed.) *The Middle Eastern Environment*, Cambridge: St Malo.

Wilson, R. (1995) 'Measuring Living Standards in the Middle East', in E. Watkins (ed.) *The Middle Eastern Environment*, Cambridge: St Malo.

MEIRA HANSON

North/South divide

The economically developed countries of the global North (so named because most of them are in the northern hemisphere) and the developing countries of the global South have traditionally had major differences over national and international environmental objectives. The North has tended to stress environmental protection and the problem of population growth, whereas the South has focused on economic **development** and the responsibility of the North for much past and ongoing global environmental damage. This divergence of views was manifested at the 1972 **Stockholm Conference** on the Human Environment, where the agenda of the North prevailed. In contrast, the 1992 Earth Summit was characterized by discussions of **sustainable development**, and hence was an effort to bridge the divide between countries concerned mostly with environmental goals (the North) and those con-

cerned with their citizens' economic welfare (the South) (see **Rio Conference 1992**). While international environmental protection efforts and sustainable development have in some ways bridged the divide, differences prevail. The South remains (justifiably) concerned about economic development, although many countries are taking action to preserve the environment, especially when local and national effects are severe. The North, for its part, seeks assurance that assistance for sustainable development has positive environmental impacts, and it still rarely admits responsibility for past environmental harm.

PAUL G. HARRIS

Norway

Environmental politics in Norway have been characterized by a unique combination of strong state involvement and vibrant local activity, as both the corporatist policy system and populist political traditions have come to be mobilized in the cause of environmental protection. In the 1960s, environmental issues became a part of a widespread movement of opposition to the **European Union**, which inspired a particular form of locally based activism in defence of rural communities, as well as the so-called **deep ecology** of the philosopher Arne **Naess**. As in the other Nordic countries, Norway has developed a substantial state policy sector for environmental protection, and, in the 1990s, has devoted especial attention to international issues and the fostering of **sustainable development**. In the 1980s, the former prime minister Gro Harlem **Brundtland** chaired the World Commission on Environment and Development, which has helped give the quest for sustainable development a special importance in Norway.

ANDREW JAMISON

nuclear energy/nuclear waste management

The control of nuclear fission to produce weapons, create new elements and materials for medicine and research, and electric power, is one of the great achievements of science, engineering, and **technology** in the twentieth century. It is, however, in the words of Alvin Wienberg, a 'Faustian bargain' with trade offs that range from the potential destruction of thermonuclear weapons to the risks of low-dose radiation exposures. The abrupt rise and decline of nuclear science and technology has no true historical analogy. To understand it we must look to the internal dynamics of the nuclear enterprises, the type of risks they pose to human beings and the environment, their management, and the social responses.

The USA provides the most comprehensive source for examining this historical process. Nuclear industrialization began during the Second World War with the secret development of the world's first atomic bombs. In August 1945 two Japanese cities, Hiroshima and Nagasaki, were bombed. The Soviet Union conducted its first atomic test in 1949. The resulting Cold War competition produced tens of thousands of nuclear weapons. These programmes greatly expanded scientific knowledge and control over nuclear technology but also produced the hazards of weapons, radioactive materials and wastes. Military developments preceded and supported civilian uses. The US Navy developed the first nuclear-powered submarine, the Nautilus, by 1954. This design, a pressurized light-water reactor, was adapted for civilian nuclear power in the USA and became the dominant model worldwide.

A December 1953 'Atoms for Peace' proposal by President Eisenhower encouraged an intense period of speculation on possible civilian uses. Electric power generation would be cheap and plentiful, trains, buses, and cars would run for years on small nuclear power units, and nuclear-powered rockets would be used to explore outer space. Nuclear explosions could release oil and gas trapped in geologic formations, dig new canals for shipping, blast out new harbours, and reshape mountains and the **landscape**. All these suggestions were grounded in applications from the US nuclear weapons programme and all were examined with major funded research programmes. The US federal government put special emphasis on nuclear power. It financed engineering and tech-

nical developments, created an insurance programme (The **Price–Anderson Act**), and promoted nuclear power. The period 1967–74 saw a tremendous national commitment to new nuclear power plant siting and construction with over 200 sites selected for new nuclear power stations.

Government and industry studies forecast 2000 US reactors by the end of the twentieth century. The US **Atomic Energy Commission** (AEC) operated the weapons programme, provided for nuclear scientific and technological research, served as the federal regulatory agency, and promoted military and civilian development. But the Commission struggled with the inherent contradictions of developing, promoting, and regulating. Internal advisors and external critics raised questions about safety, decision processes, public and government oversight, and the acceptability of programme outcomes. Congress belatedly acted in 1974 to reassure the public, abolishing the AEC. The Nuclear Regulatory Commission was created to regulate civilian nuclear technologies and by 1978 the US Department of Energy (DOE) was created and assumed direction of the weapons complex and research at the national laboratories.

Nuclear fission using uranium inevitably produces plutonium, which from any source can be used to build nuclear weapons. The creation of plutonium makes weapons proliferation a legitimate concern. Despite extensive attempts to separate civilian and military nuclear uses in the public mind, the links remains. The nuclear power industry added to the public's concerns. The **Three Mile Island accident** in March 1979 presented the spectacle of lost control over a huge power reactor. As the nation watched, more than 50,000 people fled from the surrounding area. Over the following years, public opposition grew while economic and management problems plagued the industry. More than a hundred planned nuclear power plants were cancelled, abandoning hundreds of millions of dollars in 'sunk costs', and new orders ceased. The technical, managerial and social problems were often recorded in economic terms. The Washington Public Power Supply System defaulted on bonds worth $2.25 billion in 1983, the nation's largest public bond failure to that date. Troubled plants like Rancho Seco in California, and Trojan in Oregon shut down early. Diablo Canyon, California experienced extraordinary cost overruns. In New England the Seabrook project was the focus of public controversy, opposition, and civil disobedience for years. Most remarkable was Shoreham, New York where a $5.5 billion dollar investment in a completed nuclear power plant with an operating licence was decommissioned before it went into production. Other countries had their problems.

The most serious nuclear power accident of the twentieth century took place in 1986 at the Soviet **Chernobyl** complex in the Ukraine. The public went from two-thirds' support in the mid-1960s to two-thirds' opposition by the 1980s, where it continues to the present. The entire range of industrial efforts that supported nuclear development was focused on production often at the expense of **health and the environment**. Eventually there were a series of revelations about radioactive contamination and exposures from **mining** and milling, processing nuclear materials, weapons testing, waste disposal, worker conditions, and experiments on civilians and military personnel. These problems were created by past management choices that discounted protection of public health and the environment to meet production goals, often with full awareness that the public would not agree with such choices if it knew.

During the last decades of the twentieth century public values shifted and the standards for judging nuclear projects became more stringent. Environmental concerns rose to prominence and led to the passage of the **National Environmental Policy Act** (1969). Environmental impact statements focused on public health and environmental risks and were established as a decision tool for public hearings. Trust and confidence in government and the nuclear industry decreased while support for anti-nuclear groups grew along with the effectiveness of these groups at the local, state-regional, and national levels. There was a major shift in estimating nuclear hazards during the 1970s. The earlier approach was to make assurances of safety for nuclear facilities even to the extent of preparing for 'worst case scenarios'. However, the increased size of nuclear power reactors meant that the potential

harms from worst case scenarios grew to frightening dimensions and this approach was viewed as a pubic relations disaster by federal and industry officials. The development of a risk-based approach to decision-making emphasized that the probability of worst case scenarios was very unlikely. This approach was meant to blunt public concerns about possible but unlikely outcomes. But the adoption of risk as the conceptual framework for radiation management decisions had unexpected results, what might be called 'blowback' in the language of Cold War espionage. This approach relied upon complex, expert-driven processes. It tried to limit concerns to calculations of the probability plus the consequences of an event, and then it tried to ignore or denigrate the resulting adverse public risk responses. As a result, the public was not convinced by **risk assessment** methods; to the contrary the public reduced its trust in the expert's work and discounted it. The public's concept of risk was broader and more inclusive than that presented in risk assessments. The blowback was that the public began to view nuclear managers, regulators and proponents as unworthy of public trust and as additional but unacknowledged sources of risks to public health and the environment.

The inability of officials, experts and managers to address public concerns about health and environmental issues crippled the future of nuclear power and stigmatized nuclear technology. In a unique way a brilliant science and technology was created with the promise of great power and wealth but then failed because it lost public support. A further question asks if this experience is the prototype for public responses to developments in chemistry and biology.

See also: anti-nuclear movements; British nuclear power industry; French nuclear power industry; German nuclear power industry; International Atomic Energy Authority; Japanese nuclear power industry; Kyshtym nuclear accident; mass media and the environment; Russian nuclear power industry; technology assessment; technology transfer; Yucca mountain and nuclear wastes

Further reading

Carter, L. (1987) *Nuclear Imperatives and Public Trust:*

Dealing with Radioactive Waste, Washington, DC: Resources for the Future.

Dunlap, R.E., Kraft, M.E., and Rosa, E.A. (1993) *Public Reactions to Nuclear Waste: Citizens' Views of Repository Siting*, Durham, NC: Duke University Press.

National Research Council. Committee on Risk Characterization (1996) *Understanding Risk: In-forming Decisions in a Democratic Society*, Washington, DC: National Academy Press.

Slovic, P. (2000) *Perception of Risk*, London: Earth-scan.

Weart, S. (1988) *Nuclear Fear: A History of Images*, Cambridge, MA: Harvard University Press.

JAMES FLYNN

O

ocean dumping

The disposal of waste into the oceans and seas has occurred ever since humankind started to create waste streams. For centuries it was assumed that the wastes would be dispersed/diluted in a huge volume of moving water contained in the oceans. But since industry started to produce much larger volumes of wastes, it has become increasingly accepted that the discharge of liquids and dumping of solids needs controlled regulation. Regional regimes have been created to implement and refine controls, one of which is the OSPAR convention for the Protection of the Marine Environment of the North East Atlantic, created in 1992 out of the merger of the 1972 Oslo Convention and 1974 Paris Convention. OSPAR's contracting parties have a legal obligation to take all possible steps to prevent and eliminate pollution and to take the necessary measures to protect the maritime area against adverse effects of human activities to safeguard human health, and to conserve marine ecosystems. OSPAR has been particularly influential in setting limits on radioactive discharges from Europe's nuclear reprocessing plants at **Sellafield/Windscale** (UK) and La Hague (France), although both countries subsequently expressed reservations on the ministerial decision taken in Sintra, Portugal in July 1998 which set the framework for the discharge limits. Environmental groups such as **Greenpeace** International and World Wildlife Fund (WWF) have active campaigns on protection of the oceans (see also **World Wide Fund for Nature**).

DAVID LOWRY

Odum, Eugene

b. 17 September 1913, Lake Sunapee, New Hampshire, USA

Ecologist

Eugene Odum was educated as a typical field naturalist but he laid the foundations for a new turn to theory and experimental methods of larger-scale **ecology**. His ecosystem approach influenced the environmental movement from the 1970s on. At the University of Georgia, Odum attracted large grants from the **Atomic Energy Commission**. They enabled him to study the pathways of radioactive isotopes in the environment from one organism to another. He was thus able to study food chains in a quantitative way. Odum is the author of a well known textbook, *Fundamentals of Ecology*, first published in 1953. For more than 25 years, it was *the* textbook of ecology. In it, Odum hinted at a relationship between the diversity of an ecosystem and its ability to withstand outside perturbations. Though this relationship was later increasingly rejected, it appealed to many because of its intuitive insight into the supposedly cybernetic character of ecological 'systems'. The so-called 'stability-principle' informs nature conservation practices to this day.

CHUNGLIN KWA

Ogoni People

Ken Saro-Wiwa (1941–95) was a renowned creative writer, publisher, television producer,

360

environmentalist and leader of the Ogoni People of Niger Delta, **Nigeria**. He was the founder of the radical Movement for the Survival of Ogoni People (MOSOP). Under the auspices of MOSOP, Saro-Wiwa campaigned on both local and international fronts for the right of self-determination of the Ogoni People, whose natural environment is severely polluted and despoiled by the side-effects of oil extraction (see **oil pollution**). The Ogonis are one of the smallest of Nigeria's 250 ethnic groups, with a population of only 500,000 out of Nigeria's more than 100 million people. MOSOP's campaign for self-determination and the sovereignty of Ogoniland under the leadership of Saro-Wiwa was a direct affront to the Nigerian government whose major source of revenue is crude oil from the Niger Delta. Saro-Wiwa and eight other MOSOP activists were executed in November 1995 following a widely flawed trial by a special military tribunal over charges of murdering four supposedly conservative Ogoni activists.

KENNETH OMEJE

oil pollution

Crude oil (or petroleum) is a hydrocarbon material of ancient animal and vegetable origin. By processing, crude oil can be converted, amongst other things, into gasoline, kerosene, lubricating oil, fuel oil, asphalt and paraffin. As liquid and gaseous hydrocarbons are closely related, the word petroleum is sometimes used to refer to both petroleum and natural gas.

Until the late nineteenth/early twentieth century, crude oil had a limited use in different cultures, amongst others, as a medicine, a flammable product for military purposes and a source of illumination. In the course of the twentieth century, crude oil became the world's most important source of energy and assumed an important role in international relations.

The significance of the oil industry for environmental politics stems partly from the fact that oil operations pose a threat to the environment at each stage of the supply chain – exploration, production, transportation and refining. During exploration for oil, environmental threats include clearance of land which can lead to a long lasting or permanent loss of vegetation and drilling activities which can lead to the release of drilling fluids. Oil production activities can have an adverse impact on the environment through damage from leaking pipelines or atmospheric emissions from the flaring of gas, a by-product of oil production. During transportation, tankers release oil into the sea in the course of pumping out bilge-water or unloading the cargo. The pollution from refineries can include the release of waste water containing oil residuals, solid waste disposal and atmospheric emissions.

Public awareness of the adverse impact of oil operations was further heightened by major environmental disasters. These included, above all, oil tanker accidents such as the **Exxon Valdez oil spill** off Alaska in 1989 and 'well blow-outs', for example, when Mexico's Ixtoc 1 oil well blew out and released an estimated 3 million barrels of oil into the Gulf of Mexico in 1979. Although the spilled oil can degrade relatively fast, the adverse impact of such accidental oil spills can be considerable, including ecological effects such as soil and water contamination, loss of birds or loss of habitat for aquatic life forms; and economic effects such as losses to tourism and fishing (see **tourism, environmental impact of; fisheries**).

In response to the harmful impact of oil, environmental pressure groups have campaigned on the oil pollution issue since at least the 1920s when groups such as the National Coast Anti-Pollution League in the USA and the **Royal Society for the Protection of Birds** (RSPB) in the UK lobbied for oil pollution legislation. With the general rise in environmental awareness around the world, combined with a proliferation of accidental oil spills and increased evidence of oil pollution, the controversy over the oil industry has further increased in recent decades. The oil pollution issue was taken up by major non-governmental organizations as exemplified by **Greenpeace**'s high-profile campaigns in 1995 on the decommissioning of the Brent Spar platform in the North Sea and on environmental devastation of the Niger Delta (see also **Brent Spar controversy**). Furthermore, the oil industry faced the emergence of international networks and pressure groups focused specifically on oil, above all **Oilwatch**, and popular movements in developing countries which opposed oil operations, most notably, the Movement for the Survival of the **Ogoni People** (MOSOP) in Nigeria under the leadership of Saro-Wiwa.

The first major international regulatory attempt to reduce oil pollution dates back to the draft Washington Convention produced by the world's first oil pollution conference in 1926 which dealt with oil pollution at sea. However, early international oil pollution control measures, most of which focused on pollution from shipping, proved largely ineffective as a result of a combination of factors including the lack of political will and the reluctance of major oil companies. Encouraged by rising public concern over oil pollution from the 1960s and the 1970s, nations came to agree to specific oil-related international treaties such as the 1969 Intervention Convention on Civil Liability for Oil Pollution Damage, which provided for the liability of a ship owner for oil pollution, and general treaties with application to the oil industry such as the 1973 International Convention on Marine Pollution, which covered oil pollution at sea. At the same time, national legislatures passed laws to curb oil pollution backed by enforcement agencies such as the **Environmental Protection Agency** in the USA. Furthermore, as a reaction to public pressures and in order to stave off further government regulations, oil companies were prepared to voluntarily introduce some pollution reducing measures and to establish industry-wide agreements such as a mutual insurance scheme called OPOL (the Offshore Pollution Liability) to meet claims for pollution damage and clean-up costs.

While some of the adverse ecological effects of oil operations were minimized as a result of public pressure and environmental regulations, environmental devastation from oil operations has remained an important concern, particularly with regards to exploration and production activities in developing countries as exemplified by **Nigeria**. For instance, gas flaring in Nigeria was more significant as a percentage of total gas production than elsewhere in the world. According to the **World Bank**, up to 76 per cent of the associated gas from oil wells was flared in Nigeria in 1995, as compared with 0.6 per cent in the USA and 4.3 per cent in the UK (Frynas, 2000: 178). Nigeria also had reportedly in excess of 300 oil spills per year in the early 1990s (Frynas, 2000: 165), which was considerably greater than the frequency of oil spills in the developed world.

In addition to the ecological hazards in the course of oil operations, end-user consumption of oil – like the other **fossil fuels** – is an important contributor to **global warming**. In global climate-change policy, oil was often targeted to a lesser extent than coal because of its relatively lower carbon intensity. In a comparison with natural gas, oil generates roughly 30 per cent more carbon dioxide for every unit of energy produced, while coal produces almost 60 per cent more carbon dioxide (Rowlands, 2000: 346). The contribution of oil to global warming was, nonetheless, considerable because of the absolute quantities of oil consumed. According to the *BP Statistical Review of World Energy* (2000), total world consumption of oil was 3462.4 million tonnes in 1999, compared with coal consumption of 2129.5 million tonnes oil equivalent, natural gas consumption of 2063.9 million tonnes oil equivalent and nuclear energy consumption of 650.8 million tonnes oil equivalent. North America and Europe accounted for more than half of the world's oil consumption, which highlighted their contribution to global warming.

Despite international commitments to reduce carbon dioxide and other gas emissions starting with the **Framework Convention on Climate Change** in 1992, the world's oil consumption continued to increase from 3163.5 million tonnes in 1992 to 3462.4 million tonnes in 1999 (*BP Statistical Review of World Energy* 2000). Any measures to reduce oil consumption were hampered by powerful opposition of certain governments and inter-governmental organizations such as the **Organization of Petroleum Exporting Countries** (OPEC) as well as **multinational and transnational corporations** and industry lobby groups such as the **Global Climate Coalition**.

At the 1999 levels of oil production, the world's estimated oil reserves will last for another 40 or so years if production were to remain at these levels, with the Middle East accounting for almost two-thirds of the world's proved oil reserves (*BP Statistical Review of World Energy,* 2000). Nonetheless, as large new oil reserves could be added in future and there could be unforeseen events such as further advances in oil technology, the world's oil reserves might last considerably longer – provided that the use of fossil fuels such as oil remains widely acceptable.

See also: air pollution; energy crisis; Kyoto Conference/Protocol; ocean dumping; Sandoz spill; Santa Barbara oil spill; water pollution

References

BP Statistical Review of World Energy (2000) London: BP Amoco.

Frynas, J.G. (2000) *Oil in Nigeria: Conflict and Litigation between Oil Companies and Village Communities,* Münster/Hamburg: LIT.

Rowlands, I.H. (2000) 'Beauty and the Beast? BP's and Exxon's Positions on Global Climate Change', *Environment and Planning C* 18: 339–54.

Further reading

Clark, R.B. (ed.) (1982) *The Long-term Effects of Oil Pollution on Marine Populations, Communities and Ecosystems,* London: Royal Society.

Hartshorn, J.E. (1993) *Oil Trade: Politics and Prospects,* Cambridge: Cambridge University Press.

Hyne, N.J. (1995) *Nontechnical Guide to Petroleum Geology, Exploration, Drilling and Production,* Tulsa, OK: PennWell.

Ketola, J. (1998) 'Why Don't the Oil Companies Clean Up their Act? – The Realities of Environmental Planning', *Long Range Planning* 31(1): 108–119.

Pritchard, S.Z. (1987) *Oil Pollution Control,* London: Croom Helm.

J. GEORGE FRYNAS

Oilwatch

The arrival of the oil and gas extraction industry in tropical countries has given rise to environmental and **human rights** problems, because of the poverty of many of those countries, the presence of tribal peoples who often claim indigenous territorial rights, and the peculiar ecology of humid tropical areas. Oilwatch is a non-government organization network which was founded in Ecuador at the end of 1995 by Accion Ecologica together with some 20 other organizations from Latin America, Asia and Africa. Oilwatch is different from other environmental networks, in that it is a South–South, tropical network, with supporting offices in Europe and the USA. Both local arguments and global greenhouse arguments are used to back its main platform, a moratorium on oil and gas exploration in tropical **rainforests**. It has been very active in the late 1990s in the conflicts between oil companies and the Ogoni and Ijaw in the Niger Delta (see **Ogoni People**), in the conflict between Occidental Petroleum and the U'Wa in Colombia, and in the Chad–Cameroon proposed oil pipeline. Oilwatch publishes a newsletter, *Tegantai,* in Spanish, English and French.

JOAN MARTINEZ-ALIER

organic farming

Organic farming is a counter-movement to industrial-chemical **agriculture** which it criticizes for diminishing soil fertility, biological self-regulation, and food value; it opposes synthetic fertilizers, **pesticides**, herbicides and fungicides, and genetically modified organisms (GMOs). It was pioneered in Europe from the 1920s to 1940s. Small numbers increased somewhat with environmental and alternative movements in the late 1960s. By 1986, there were 7,000 organic farmers in Europe. In 1992, reform of EU **common agricultural policy** brought support for ecologically sound practices. These regulations accelerated conversion dramatically: in 1995, about 3 million hectares, in 1999 2.2 per cent of the cultivated area in the EU. In North America there is similar market growth but legislation is lagging; in the USA, the Organic Foods Production Act of 1990 still was not implemented by 2000. Advocates of organic farming point to the unsustainable character of conventional farming and argue that small-scale, intensive organic production holds more promise for Third World populations than large-scale industrial agriculture.

VOLKMAR LAUBER

Organization of Petroleum Exporting Countries

The Organization of Petroleum Exporting Countries (OPEC) was founded in September 1960 by Iran, Iraq, Kuwait, Saudi Arabia and Venezuela as a cartel of oil-producing countries in order to co-ordinate the petroleum policies of its members. Throughout the 1970s, OPEC policy led to massive increases in oil prices, most notably a fourfold increase in oil prices between October and December 1973. OPEC was also successful in encouraging nationalization policies of member countries. OPEC's founding members were later joined by other developing countries. However, the major oil exporting developed countries failed to join. This partly explains the relative decline of OPEC's power since the 1970s. OPEC's threat to international oil supplies and oil price rises played a part in prompting the governments and corporations of developed countries to increasingly back the development of new sources of energy including natural gas, nuclear energy and **renewable energy**.

See also: nuclear energy/nuclear waste management

J. GEORGE FRYNAS

ozone depletion

The ozone layer is a thin layer of the gas O_3 in the stratosphere, 10 to 50 kilometres above the earth's surface. It prevents up to 99 per cent of the sun's ultraviolet B radiation from reaching the earth's surface, and was thus important to the development of life on earth. Ozone molecules are constantly formed and broken down by reacting with ultraviolet radiation, but until recently the overall composition of the ozone layer has been relatively stable. Its depletion by human-made substances beginning in the twentieth century may have serious environmental impacts.

Chlorofluorocarbons (CFCs) are a class of organic chemicals composed of carbon and some combination of chlorine, fluorine, and hydrogen. They are non-toxic and stable. Invented in 1928 and hailed as miracle chemicals because of their safety and ease of manufacture, they became widely available beginning in the 1950s. Initially they were used as alternatives to the flammable chemicals previously used for refrigeration. They also gained widespread use as cleaning agents, blowing agents, and propellants.

Their stability is what contributes to their ability to harm the ozone layer, because it allows them to drift to the upper atmosphere before decomposing. As hypothesized in 1974 by F. Sherwood Rowland and Mario Molina (who won a Nobel Prize in 1995 for their work), chlorine from CFCs is able to break down ozone in the stratosphere. CFCs and other ozone-depleting substances, in the presence of ultraviolet radiation, eventually decompose to include a chlorine free radical, which reacts with ozone to create an oxygen molecule and chlorine monoxide. The chlorine molecule can then repeat the process, causing a chain reaction in which one chlorine atom can destroy thousands of ozone molecules. Nitrogen, and bromine can have a similar impact. Additional substances, such as halons (used as a fire suppressant), and methyl bromide (used as an agricultural fumigant) were also found to deplete the ozone layer. Some of the substances used initially as substitutes for CFCs, such as hydrocholorofluorocarbons (HCFCs), also damage the ozone layer, although less dramatically.

Scientific investigation of the ozone layer first found evidence of damage to the ozone layer in 1985 over **Antarctica**. This seasonal thinning by up to 50 per cent of the ozone layer at the end of the southern hemisphere winter came to be known as the 'ozone hole'. This 'hole' has been detected every year since then and has increased in size. Special conditions over the poles make this dramatic thinning of the ozone layer more likely than at other latitudes, as ice clouds formed during the dark winter combine with the return of sunlight to create a vortex that traps chlorine. Seasonal ozone thinning in the **Arctic** of an average of fifteen, but as high as 60, per cent has been found as well. The ozone layer at other latitudes also decreased an average of about five per cent, with greater decreases detected in some locations. This decrease in the amount of ozone has led to a corresponding increase in the amount of ultraviolet radiation reaching the earth. It is likely the increased ultraviolet radiation due to a depleted ozone layer causes increased skin cancer, cataracts and immune system problems in humans, genetic damage to plants, and harm to the aquatic life forms at the bottom of the food chain. Other environmental impacts are expected as well.

International efforts to protect the ozone layer, primarily the **Montreal Protocol** and its amendments, have resulted in decreased emission of many ozone-depleting substances. The ozone layer will not respond as quickly. Because of the stability of ozone-depleting substances, they can remain in the stratosphere for a century or longer. While the amount of ozone-depleting substances in the stratosphere was expected to peak in 2000, they will continue to damage the ozone layer for years. The long residence time of these substances in the atmosphere, the special provisions under the Montreal Protocol that allowed developing countries to increase their use of ozone-depleting substances until they were required to begin some control measures in 1999, and an international black market in CFCs that increased their use above what control measures specified suggests that ozone depletion will be a long-term phenomenon.

Further reading

Le Prestre, P.G., Reed, J., and Morehouse Jr, T.E. (eds) (1998) *Protecting the Ozone Layer*, Boston: Kluwer Academic Publishers.

Makhijani, A., and Gurney, K.R. (1995) *Mending the Ozone Hole*, Cambridge: MIT Press.

Ozone Secretariat, United Nations Environment Programme (1999) *Synthesis of the Reports of the Scientific, Environmental Effects, and Technology and Economic Assessment Panels of the Montreal Protocol*, Nairobi: UNEP.

ELIZABETH R. DeSOMBRE

P

Pakistan

With a population of 152.33 million and a 3 per cent annual population growth rate, making it the sixth most populous nation in the world, Pakistan ('land of the pure') faces tremendous environmental challenges. While Pakistan was part of colonial India before the 1947 partition, the British instituted policies of extracting natural resources that, compounded by the unequal relations of trade, led to environmental degradation. After gaining independence in 1947, the Pakistani government has further entrenched the models set under colonialism.

In the 1960s the Pakistani government launched the **green revolution** in order to increase the agricultural yield. The increased use of agro-chemicals and chemical fertilizers and heavy application of water, which accompanied the green revolution, led to a deterioration of soil structure and the contamination of ground and surface water, adversely affecting plant growth and health of wildlife and rural populations. In the 1980s the **structural adjustment programmes** in Pakistan brought about adverse effects on environment.

Pakistan faces severe environmental problems. **Water pollution** is perhaps the most serious pollution issue in Pakistan. Industrial wastewater pollution and domestic wastewater pollution have contributed to the contamination of groundwater, leading to the spread of water-related infections. At present, patients with water-related diseases occupy more than 40 per cent of the hospital beds in Pakistan. Only 80 per cent of the urban and 45 per cent of the rural population has access to clean water.

Motor vehicle emissions, urban and industrial **air pollution**, and marine and coastal zone pollution form the other major pollution problems. With rapid **urbanization**, the number of motor vehicles has rapidly increased in cities. The absence of emissions regulations and the lack of enforcement of regulations have led to the present situation where 90 per cent of total emissions of hydrocarbons, aldehydes and carbon monoxide are produced by motor vehicles. With only 3 per cent of industrial plants treating their wastes according to the accepted international standards, industrial air pollution, which is concentrated in the urban areas, is on the rise. The coastal environment has changed over time because of the massive take-off from the Indus River for irrigation and extensive pollution from Karachi, one of the most polluted cities in the world. Commercialization and mechanization of fishing has led to over-fishing, causing a rapid depletion of **fisheries** stock.

Deforestation, soil erosion, waterlogging and salinity and agricultural chemicals are also major issues of concern. Deforestation has resulted from poor **forest management** and population pressure upon forests. The forest cover in Pakistan has shrunk from a high of 14 per cent in 1925 to 5 per cent in 2001. Deforestation and overgrazing has resulted in an increase in soil erosion, leading to a decrease in the depth, fertility and productivity of soil. Waterlogging and salinity are also major issues of concern. With 90 per cent of the total area of Pakistan either arid or semi-arid, the loss of land due to salinity or waterlogging is crucial. Due to the canal irrigation system, the water containing dissolved salts from the lower parts of the soil profile seeps and evaporates from the surface, leading to a continually rising salinity.

The Pakistani government has adopted policies to guard against environmental degradation. In 1983, the government of Pakistan enacted the Pakistan Environmental Protection Ordinance (PEPO), leading to the creation of the Environmental Protection Council (EPC). The EPC works to control pollution and preserve the living environment. In 1986 the National Conservation Strategy (NCS) was initiated and it resulted in the formation of the Environmental Protection Agency (EPA), the main government agency dealing with environmental protection. In 1997, the government of Pakistan passed a more comprehensive act, the Pakistan Environment Protection Act (PEPA), to protect and salvage the environment.

Pakistan also has a fledgling environmental movement, which works to hold the government accountable. The nuclei of this movement are the green non-governmental organizations and community-based organizations. Kalabagh dam, a project on the Indus River that will lead to the displacement of 83,000 people, is the major point of contention between the government and the Pakistani environmental movement. While Punjab, the dominant province in Pakistan, supports the project, the provinces of Sindh and NWFP oppose this project (see **dams/hydroelectric power**).

Further reading

Faruqee, R. (1996) 'Role of Economic Policies in Protecting the Environment: The Experience of Pakistan', *The Pakistan Development Review*, 35(4): 483–506.

Hasan, A. and Ali, A.A. (1992) 'Environmental Problems in Pakistan: Their Origins and Development and the Threat that they Pose to Sustainable Development', *Environment and Urbanization*, 4(1): 8–21.

Khan, F.K. (1991) *A Geography of Pakistan: Environment, People and Economy*, Oxford: Oxford University Press.

AMANDEEP SANDHU

paradigms

A paradigm may be thought of as a particular lens or pair of spectacles through which different humans view their world. The term came into use as referring to the scientific community in Thomas Kuhn's *The Structure of Scientific Revolutions* (1962). Kuhn used the term to describe how the scientific enterprise evolves and changes focus. A particular contextual approach and worldview (a paradigm) underlies scientific research in most fields and structures the assumptions of participating scientists. Scientific advances in the field follow, guided by the paradigm, until anomalous results accumulate to the point where researchers begin to question their assumptions. When further progress along these conventional lines of enquiry stalls and the anomalies continue, some scientists begin to question the underlying paradigm guiding the discipline as a whole. They proceed to formulate a new paradigm which has greater explanatory power to re-interpret the anomalies.

Environmentalism is a new paradigm which allowed early activists and writers such as this author to re-contextualize all human activities on Planet Earth as anthropocentric (see **anthropocentrism**). The concept of paradigms was also powerfully explanatory in the deliberations on science and **technology** policy in the US Congress and the Nixon and Carter Administrations. This helped illustrate the societal transition then beginning, as the Industrial Age of **fossil fuels** gradually became questioned (due to concerns about depletion, petroleum availability and pollution). The anthropocentric paradigm of mainstream economics rendered this great transition invisible due to incorrect pricing and investment models. The **environmental movements** pressured politicians and academics to examine and reformulate these often invisible paradigms.

Gradually, spearheaded by the US Office of Technology Assessment, many additional studies (all archived on CDs from the US Government Printing Office) were able to document the alternative approaches to energy: solar, wind, tidal, biomass and other renewables, as well as redesign of industrial production for take-back, re-manufacturing, re-use and **recycling**. Alternative macro-economic policies were also driven by paradigm shifts: such as shifting taxes from payrolls and incomes to waste, depletion, and pollution; removing tax breaks and subsidies from unsustainable practices and industries, and the paradigm shift implied in the concept of **sustainable development**. Even the heated debates over new paradigms help move academia, business, media politics and eventually societies toward more ecologically informed policies.

In our new century, the sustainable development paradigm will continue reformulating economics and **capitalism** toward its new sub-fields of **ecological economics**, social economics and evolutionary economics. This sustainable development paradigm is driving practical alternatives: socially responsible investing, green and ethical mutual funds and unit trusts, all of which as of 2000, accounted for some 10 per cent of US capital markets, some $2 trillion of assets. Even the money paradigm itself is now challenged by the re-birth of barter (in high tech computer-based electronic terms).

As we move further into the new economy of networks and information, knowledge is being accepted as a key factor of production, and auditors are trying to account for such intellectual capital. Some governments are at last realizing that they must fully account for their ecological and social assets in their national accounts (see for example, the Calvert–Henderson Quality of Life Indicators).

Many other environmentalist writers and activists have emphasized paradigms and their role in changing perceptions and policies. For example, Stephanie Mills, Ernest Callenbach, William Irwin Thompson, Charlene **Spretnak**, Ziauddin Sardar, Carolyn Merchant and Joanna Macy also interweave ecological paradigms with those of **environmental ethics**, feminism, peace and critiques of materialist technology and economics. Many scientists originally trained as physicists, engineers, and mathematicians, including Buckminster Fuller, Fritjof **Capra** and Amory **Lovins** expanded their analyses to embrace **ecology**. Biologists Lynn Margulis, James Lovelock, Mae Wan Ho, John Todd, Elisabet Sahtouris and Paul and Anne **Ehrlich** followed Rachel **Carson** and also expanded their disciplines to include ecology. Sociologists including Elise Boulding, David Loye and Riane Eisler emphasize ecological and evolutionary perspectives. To sum up, paradigms are powerful!

Reference

Kuhn, T. (1962) *The Structure of Scientific Revolutions*, Chicago: University of Chicago Press.

HAZEL HENDERSON

Parkin, Sara

b. 1946, Aberdeen, Scotland

Environmental campaigner, author

Sara Parkin grew up in Scotland and Coventry. During 1967–74 she was a nurse at the Royal Infirmary of Edinburgh. In 1977 she joined the Leeds Ecology Party. In 1979 she ran for parliament and soon joined the Party's national council. After moving to Lyons, France, she became the Party's international liaison secretary and was involved with the world-wide development of green parties. During 1985–90, she served as the co-secretary of the European Greens. With her media skills, Parkin became one of the prominent figures of the UK Green Party (as it was known after 1985). Following the Greens' 15 per cent of British votes in the 1989 European Parliament election, she and other 'electoralists' sought to rationalize the Party's structure and encourage more professional behaviour. Reforms were resisted by the 'anarchists' and 'lefties' among its activists (see **anarchism/eco-anarchism**). In 1992 she resigned as Chair of the Party, in frustration over its inability to mature as a political force. After leaving the Greens, Parkin has been active in the Real World Coalition, 30 UK groups seeking to encourage **sustainable development**. In 1996, she co-founded the **Forum for the Future**, which takes 'a positive, solutions-orientated approach' to environmental problems. Parkin has written numerous articles and several books.

See also: Green Party, UK

Further reading:

Parkin, S. (1989) *Green Parties: An International Guide* London: Heretic Books.

E. GENE FRANKLAND

Partido Verde Ecologista de Mexico

The *Partido Verde Ecologista de Mexico* (PVEM) – Green Ecology Party of **Mexico** – was founded in 1988 and gained federal recognition in 1991. PVEM's programme emphasizes environmental protection and education, and the rights of Mexico's **indigenous peoples**. By the July 2000 elections, PVEM had grown strong enough to be junior partner in a victorious national electoral alliance. The *Alianza por el Cambio* (Alliance for Change), linking *Partido Verde* with the much larger, older, and more conservative PAN, *Partido de Accion Nacional*, ousted Mexico's 70 year old ruling regime, wresting control of the national executive away from PRI, the *Partido Revolucionario Institucional*. PVEM's 6 per cent of the July 2000 vote was sufficient to elect 32 Greens to the Chamber of Deputies (Congress), including five senators, up from 8 seats in 1997. Six weeks later in the state of Chiapas, scene of the 1994 Zapatista rebellion, PVEM joined an eight-party opposition coalition to bring down the PRI-controlled state government, replacing it with one pledged to reconciliation and implementation of existing peace accords between the government and the area's Lacandon Mayan people (see **Zapatistas/Chiapas**).

TONY AFFIGNE

PCBs

PCBs, the acronym for polychlorinated biphenyls, are a group of synthetic organic chemical compounds produced for a range of industrial purposes. The chief industrial value of PCBs, their chemical stability, also serves to render them a hazard since they are highly persistent in the environment and bioaccumulate as they move up the food chain. The production of PCBs began to be phased out domestically in developed countries in the 1970s, but their persistence and presence in old industrial materials has necessitated continued political action, particularly on the international stage. PCBs are included amongst the hazardous chemicals subject to the 1998 Rotterdam Convention, committing exporting states to notify importing authorities of the nature of the chemical entering their country. PCBs are also amongst the 12 persistent organic pollutants (POPs) identified by the **United Nations Environment Programme** (UNEP) in 1995 and due to be eliminated from production by a Convention in Stockholm in 2001.

PETER HOUGH

peace movements

Peace movements played a significant role in many western European democracies in the 1980s, and in some countries in the 1950s and 1960s as well. Peace movements protested against nuclear weapons and other aspects of security policy in the Cold War context. 'Peace' became a **new politics** issue in the 1970s and 1980s, nuclear pacifism helped define post-materialism (see **Inglehart, Ronald**), and peace movements belonged to the **new social movements**. In some countries, peace movements had significant effects on security policy itself, occasionally blocking the adoption of new weapons systems and often making governments more wary of proposing new weapons systems in subsequent years. Peace movements also strongly influenced the security policy platforms of left-of-centre parties. In some countries, peace movements provided a strong impetus to the formation of green political parties as well, for example *Die* **Grünen** in Germany. In Germany, this reshaped the party system and resulted in new SPD/Green governing coalitions in various states (*Länder*) and in the federal government following the 1998 elections.

European peace movements were cyclical in nature, alternating high mobilization with long periods of latency. Peace movements' mobilization capacity depended on highly variable aspects of their **political opportunity structures**. Favourable political opportunities included a salient nuclear issue on the active political agenda, developments in the international arena which enhanced the credibility of movement positions, government security policy that failed to address popular fears adequately, and high levels of 'protest potential' in society. However, even when many of these factors were present, national traditions and the shape of national party systems depressed mobilization in some countries. In the 1980s, political opportunities were more favourable than at any other time of the Cold War. NATO's proposal to station new missiles made nuclear weapons highly salient. International developments, moreover, lent peace movement positions greater credibility than earlier. Arms control and detente had helped alleviate popular fears of the Soviet Union, and the public preferred these policies to military confrontation. At the same time, many Europeans questioned American leadership, especially given the perceived military adventurism of the early **Reagan** presidency. In many countries, the governing parties failed to address popular fears of nuclear annihilation. In addition, high protest potential had developed in society at large, as witnessed by the new social movements of the 1970s.

In many countries, peace movements typically relied organizationally on *ad hoc* coalitions composed of numerous pre-existing organizations. Peace movements in the 1980s drew their organizational strength from the dense networks of autonomous extra-parliamentary groups generated by the new social movements of the 1960s and 1970s. These networks also forged links to dissident groups within parties, churches, and unions. In Germany, for example, the peace movement's 'Coordinating Committee' provided the movement's diverse political coalition with a national leadership structure based entirely on the extra-parliamentary arena. Local groups and regional networks provided additional avenues for grassroots mobilization. In the 1970s, *Bürgerinitiativen* (citizen action groups), including environmental groups represented in the **BBU**, had helped pave the way for such grassroots mobilization in the 1980s. Petra **Kelly**, one of the German movement's most telegenic leaders, came to the peace movement via the environmental movement.

Peace movements' ideology included rejection of nuclear weapons, preserving peace through detente and arms control, and nuclear-free zones in Central Europe. In addition, various groups from the **New Left** linked other concerns to more narrowly defined 'peace' issues. Third World groups opposed new missiles because they allegedly reflected American imperialism, and 'grassroots revolution' groups linked security questions to socio-economic change and radical **democracy**. In addition, environmentalists and women joined the peace movement when they perceived that nuclear weapons threatened the environment and that the military reinforced patriarchy.

In the 1990s peace movements were less visible. Clearly, their political opportunity structure had changed radically with the end of the Cold War. In addition, peace-keeping missions challenged them ideologically, for they had to face the issue of whether to use force to end genocide or for some other inherently desirable end.

Further reading

Carter, A. (1992) *Peace Movements: International Protest and World Politics since 1945*, London: Longman.

Cooper, A. (1996) *Paradoxes of Peace: German Peace Movements Since 1945*, Ann Arbor, MI: University of Michigan Press.

Klandermans, B. (ed.) (1991) *International Social Movement Research*, vol.3, *Peace Movements in Western Europe and the United States*, Greenwich, CT: JAI Press.

Marullo, S. and Lofland, J. (eds) (1990) *Peace Action in the Eighties: Social Science Perspectives*, New Brunswick, NJ: Rutgers University Press.

Meyer, D. (1990) *A Winter of Discontent: The Nuclear Freeze and American Politics*, New York: Praeger.

ALICE H. COOPER

Peoples' Global Action

The Peoples' Global Action (PGA) is an alliance of grassroots movements challenging the **World Trade Organization** (WTO) and other free trade organizations. The PGA was constituted during a conference in Geneva, in February 1998;

world peoples' movements from all over the globe were invited. The PGA is said to be an instrument for communication and co-ordination of resistance to the global market, not an organization. Besides rejecting trade liberalization, the main characteristics of the alliance are (i) a rejection of all forms of domination; (ii) confrontation rather than lobbying; (iii) non-violent civil disobedience; and (iv) acting in accordance with a philosophy based on decentralization and autonomy. During the WTO ministerial conference in Geneva in May 1998, the first co-ordination of local struggles took the form of simultaneous demonstrations on all continents.

See also: globalization

Further reading

Levidow, L. (2000) 'Peoples' Global Action: A Brief History', *Race and Class*, 41(1): 92–9.

SVERKER CARLSSON

pesticides

Pesticide is a term that is applied generically to any product used to control or eradicate unwanted insects, rodents, fungi, or weeds. The range of such products is immense, with the dominant portion of the contemporary market comprising synthetic compounds (e.g., **DDT**) derived through chemical processes. A much smaller segment comprising organic products derived from plants, trees, or parasites (e.g., nematodes).

Prior to the 1940s most pesticides were based on arsenic, copper, and lead, toxic poisons that were difficult and even dangerous to apply (see **lead poisoning**). They required frequent applications to ensure effectiveness, and their residues on food products raised continual questions about consumer safety. A much smaller range of prewar pesticides was based on pyrethrims derived from flowers, but most of this supply was cut off during the Second World War.

Wartime pressures for increased agricultural production and the need to control the spread of diseases in combat theatres, not to mention secret biological and chemical warfare research, led to the development of a broad range of new synthetic compounds. After the war these new products, best exemplified by DDT, were quickly adapted to the civilian market, with dramatic effects. Compared to prewar pesticides, the new compounds were apparently nontoxic, inexpensive, effective on a wider range of pests and diseases for a longer period of time, and easy to apply. Widespread use of the new pesticides enabled public health officials to control vector-borne diseases such as typhus and malaria, helped farmers boost crop production at lower costs, and, generally made everyday life more bearable for many people. Moreover, the new compounds contributed to the **green revolution** that enabled **less developed countries** to feed their own burgeoning populations.

However, indiscriminate use of the new chemicals throughout much of the postwar era eventually produced unforeseen consequences. By the late 1950s wildlife biologists in North America and western Europe began to link pesticides such as DDT to noticeable drops in the reproductive rates of many bird populations, in particular raptors. Public health experts grew alarmed at the degree to which residues of these chemicals accumulated in human tissue, and especially in children. Their concerns were aimed not at toxicity, but at more subtle long-term effects, such as cancer. But these side-effects emerged gradually, making it difficult for public health and wildlife advocates to challenge the pro-pesticides perspective promoted by agricultural and chemical interests.

Public concerns about health and environmental consequences crystallized in the early 1960s, beginning with the publication of *Silent Spring* (1962) by Rachel **Carson** (see **health and the environment**). In fact, Carson is credited with providing the intellectual basis for the **environmental movements** that emerged in the early 1970s throughout North America and western Europe. By the late 1970s pesticides manufacture and use was subject to greater regulatory oversight, although overall chemical use continued to boom.

Today policy-makers in developed nations struggle to balance continued dependency on chemical pesticides with public health and environmental concerns. To do so, they juggle competing needs: safeguarding the public against diseases; providing inexpensive but safe food; reducing farm labour costs; ensuring environmental safety and public health; protecting wildlife. Unlike many other environmental hazards, pesticides produce positive benefits for many. They are, depending on your perspective, bad things that can do good or good things that can do bad.

In **less developed countries**, the imperative to address proximate problems of disease and adequate food production frequently overshadows more distant environmental and health concerns. However, even here pesticides use has global implications in the form of the so-called 'circle of poison', whereby pesticides exported to and used in nations where regulation is less stringent or non-existent come back in the form of residues on imported fruits and vegetables.

The twenty-first century is touted as the age of **biotechnology**. In this regard, advances in genetic engineering may transform pest control (see **genetic engineering, crops**). Pest-resistant plant strains may reduce reliance on chemicals and thereby alleviate the environmental and public health threats posed by them. However, just as with DDT and its kin, new technologies invariably produce unexpected consequences, so the conflicts embodied in the debate over pesticides are likely to persist.

See also: agriculture; Basel Convention; Carson, Rachel; chemical industry; DDT; genetic engineering, animals; genetic engineering, crops; hazardous and toxic waste management

Further reading

Bosso, C. (1987) *Pesticides and Politics: The Life-Cycle of a Public Issue*, Pittsburgh: University of Pittsburgh Press.

Carson, R. (1962) *Silent Spring*, Boston: Houghton Mifflin.

Hough, P. (1999) *The Global Politics of Pesticides: Forging Consensus from Conflicting Interests*, London: Earthscan.

Wargo, J. (1996) *Our Children's Toxic Legacy: How Science and Law Fail to Protect Us from Pesticides*, New Haven, CT: Yale University Press.

CHRISTOPHER J. BOSSO

Philippines, the

The Philippines is a cluster of more than 7,100 islands 800 kilometres east of the Indochinese coast of mainland Asia. Its total coastline of 36,298 kilometres encloses a combined land area of around 30,000,000 hectares. Mountainous and volcanic, the country is rich in forest, mineral, aquatic and other natural resources. The climate is tropical. Population is 75 million (2000), concentrated on the coastal regions and valleys of the 11 largest islands. The country is a major centre of **biodiversity**: 13,500 species of plants and 170,000 species of animals. Many are found nowhere else on the planet: 44 per cent of flowering plants, 44 per cent of birds, 64 per cent of mammals, 68 per cent of reptiles, and 78 per cent of amphibians.

Beginning in 1565 and for more than 300 years, Spain extracted wealth from the resource-rich islands and their people through feudal taxation, forced labour, natural resource extraction, and the conversion of native food farms into vast plantations of sugar, tobacco, abaca, banana, coconut, and other export crops. The nature abuse that began during this period persists today. In 1898, although it had just declared independence from Spain, the Philippines was annexed by the USA. After a brutal war of conquest, the USA set up a network of military bases and its own colonial administration, intensifying the extraction of resources, particularly through logging, **mining**, and plantation **agriculture**.

Postwar independence found the economy relying heavily on natural resources exploitation but failing to take off. The sixth postwar president, Ferdinand Marcos, declared martial law in 1972. Marcos rewarded loyal officers with logging concessions, depleting further the country's dwindling forest ecosystems. He intensified chemical agriculture through the **green revolution** and invited more foreign industries, accelerating toxic contamination. The 1986 'people power' uprising re-established a constitutional regime. The US military bases closed in 1991, leaving a deadly legacy of toxic dumpsites that had not been neutralized or cleaned up by 2000.

Post-Marcos administrations continued exploiting the country's natural resources for foreign exchange and uncritically attracting foreign investments. Those that came often turned out to be industries that were unwelcome at home due to their pollutive emissions. **Indigenous peoples** are disappearing due to encroachment of their ancestral lands and the intrusion of a market-orientated consumerist culture. This is tragic because their ancient knowledge might hold the key to future survival on a threatened planet.

Some 24 million hectares (80 per cent) of the land used to be forest-covered. Now, only 800,000 hectares of these original ancient forests remain. More than 1.6 million hectares of biodiversity-rich ecosystems are directly under threat. Mining applications in 2000 of 6.8 million hectares (21.6 per cent) exceeded the 5.6 million hectares (18.6 per cent) of remaining forests, mostly secondary growth. Logging and mining continue unabated, destroying an estimated 180,000 to 550,000 hectares of forests per year.

Millions of tons of topsoil are lost annually due to industrial activities, creeping **urbanization** and soil erosion. In arable lands, soil fertility is declining due to unecological farming methods. The use of chemical fertilizers, for instance, rose from 76.5 kg/ha in 1980 to 119.3 kg/ha in 1996. Pesticide residues, mountains of garbage and other toxic matter are also contaminating the soil (see **pesticides**).

The country is losing its water sources and watersheds to industrial and commercial activities such as logging, mining and the dispersal of industrial plants into the countryside, which led to poisoning and siltation. The worst dump toxic wastes directly into rivers and lakes. A 1990 survey of 69 rivers, for instance, found 17 per cent 'grossly polluted'. Even the country's vast underground water and marine resources are showing signs of overexploitation.

Air pollution from transport and industrial sources is very serious in Metro Manila, where 80 per cent of residents are exposed to levels of total suspended particulates that exceed the standards. In other major cities, air quality is deteriorating significantly. Air pollution is also serious around power plants, cement plants, chemical plants and similar pollution sources. A Clean Air Act passed in 2000 bans incinerators, the first such ban in the world. The Philippines is an archipelago and gets hit by some 20 typhoons annually. Thus, it is very susceptible to sea level rise and climate change caused by **global warming**.

The Philippines has an active green movement. An organization called the Philippine Greens, founded in 1996, keeps the movement alive through organizing and mass campaigns on mining, clean air, genetically modified organisms, zero-waste, pollution, and other ecological issues. As of 2001, though, the Greens have not established any major presence in national or local governments.

References

Tabao, M.L. (2000) 'The State of the Nation 2000', *Haring Ibon*, 2 (2), July–September:12–16.

The Philippine Environmental Quality Report 1990–1995 (1996) Department of Environment and Natural Resources, Environmental Management Bureau: 1–379.

The World Bank (2000) 'Philippines Environment Monitor', July: 1–37.

ROBERTO VERZOLA

Pinchot, Gifford

b. 11 August 1865, Simsbury, Connecticut, USA; d. 4 October 1946, New York City

Forester and conservationist

Gifford Pinchot was America's first trained forester, the first head of the US Forest Service, the principal adviser to President Theodore **Roosevelt** on conservation issues, and an important advocate of utilitarian conservation.

Pinchot was born into a family of great affluence, part of a group who formed an American aristocracy by the middle of the nineteenth century. Young Gifford's views about **nature** were initially formed by family vacations, his father's reflections on the importance of natural history and conservation, and the outdoor life of the American sportsman with his bamboo fly rod and finely tooled shotgun.

Like many in his social **class**, Pinchot was determined to devote his life to important public service. Educated at the finest private schools and Yale, Pinchot early on took his father's advice about becoming a forester, a profession unknown at the time in America. At Yale, he took a rigorous science course, but his real education began during post-graduate work at the French National Forestry School in Nancy. Here he learned first hand about the European view of the planned use of forests and forest products, a philosophy that was to influence profoundly his professional life and the **conservation movement** in the USA.

Pinchot returned to the USA in 1890, a time when most Americans, especially in the western USA, still believed in the 'myth of unexhaustability'. Simply stated, there was no reason to conserve resources because they would never run out. **Development** was part of **progress**. However, the following two decades were to witness the first great challenge to this 'myth' with Pinchot playing a leading role.

For much of the 1890s, Pinchot worked as a forester for the Vanderbilt family at their Biltmore estate in North Carolina and as a successful private consultant out of offices in New York City. However, his desire to help shape national forest policy took a critical turn in 1898 when he was appointed head of the Division of Forestry in the Department of Agriculture, a position that was little more than a public relations assignment but, for the aggressive Pinchot, a window of opportunity, especially after Roosevelt became President in 1901. A personal friend of Pinchot, Roosevelt was an outdoor enthusiast who shared Gifford's conservation views. Together, they would help shape a national environmental agenda that is still important today.

Pinchot's first goal was to convince Roosevelt to transfer the nation's forest reserves from the Department of the Interior to Agriculture which the President did in 1905, renaming the reserves 'National Forests' under the direction of the US Forest Service and Gifford Pinchot. Now in charge of millions of forest acres, primarily in the west, Pinchot became the focal point of the long-raging national debate over the use of these resources. On one hand were advocates of unrestricted use; on the other, were such as John **Muir**, who favoured preservation largely for aesthetic reasons. Pinchot tried to steer a middle course and convince a sceptical public that the resources were better off under the government's scientific management which would produce timber for future generations. Such a 'middle way' was clearly impossible in such controversies as the construction of the **Hetch Hetchy dam**, but Pinchot was firm in his utilitarian convictions alienating some in both groups in the process. The debate continues!

In 1908, Roosevelt and Pinchot convened the first White House Conference on the Conservation of Natural Resources and, the following year, Roosevelt created the Natural Conservation Commission with Pinchot as its chairman. These events were the high point of Pinchot's influence on the federal level.

In 1909, W.H. Taft became President and one year later he fired Pinchot following a disagreement with his Interior Secretary. For the rest of his life, Pinchot remained active in numerous conservation organizations and taught for a time at the Yale School of Forestry which his father had founded. He was often mentioned as a possible candidate for national office or for a cabinet position and served two terms as a reform-orientated Governor of Pennsylvania (1923–7; 1931–5). He spent his last years working on his autobiography, *Breaking New Ground*, published after his death in 1946, but by that time the American conservation movement had moved on to the philosophy of such people as Aldo **Leopold** who set forth an ecological perspective and an attendant ethic of man–land relationships. In this context, Pinchot's career becomes an important bridge from a pioneer past to an ecological present.

See also: forest management

Further reading

Pinchot, G. (1946) *Breaking New Ground*, New York: Harcourt, Brace.

WARREN VANDER HILL

policy networks

Policy networks are clusters of public and private sector actors connected to each other by resource dependencies, such as information, expertise, money and legitimacy. One can distinguish two main types of network. A *policy community* has a closed membership, usually a government ministry/agency and a handful of privileged producer groups, who regularly interact and share common views about a policy sector. The exclusion of environmental and consumer groups typically results in stable policy outcomes that reflect the interests of the powerful producer groups within the policy community, such as farmers, energy producers or road builders. The more open *issue network* has many competing groups and fluctuating membership, offering more opportunities for environmental interests to be represented. Governments consult rather than bargain with different interests, and policy outcomes are less stable and predictable.

See also: agriculture; car industry; chemical industry

NEIL CARTER

political action committees

Political action committees (PACs) are formed by interest groups such as corporations and labour unions to contribute funds to candidates and political parties (see **labour/trade unions**). US law restricts the amount a business, union, or association can give, so PACs are formed to avoid the limits. The first major PAC was formed by organized labour in 1943. PACs were encouraged by the Federal Election Campaign Act of 1971 and its 1974 amendments, which sought to curb the abuses of the Watergate scandal. PACs exist both at the federal and the state levels, where state law limits contributions to state and local candidates. PACs have come under recent criticism for driving up the cost of campaigns and for 'buying' access to office holders. In 1997–8 no environmental PAC was ranked in the top 50 for federal expenditures.

Further reading

State Capital Law Firm Group (1996) *Lobbying, PACs, and Campaign Finance: 50 State Handbook*, Eagan, MN: West Publishing.
US Federal Election Commission at
    URL: http://www.fec.gov.

RAYMOND H. SCHEELE

political opportunity structures

The much contested concept of political opportunity structures has become central to the comparative study of social and political movements. First employed by Eisinger in his attempt to explain differences in the development of urban politics in the USA by reference to the divergent political structures of cities, the term acquired wide currency following its application by Kitschelt (1986) to the comparison of **anti-nuclear movements** in **France**, Germany, **Sweden** and the USA.

For Kitschelt, political opportunity structures (POS) function as filters between the mobilization of a movement and its choice of strategies and its capacity to change its environment. The crucial dimensions of political opportunity structures are the openness or closedness of states to inputs from non-established actors and the strength or weakness of their capacities to deliver the effective implementation of policies.

Kitschelt hypothesized that, depending on their openness or closedness on the input side, and their strength or weakness on the output side, states encourage movements to adopt strategies which are either assimilative or confrontational. States which are open and weak (e.g., USA) invite movements to work through the multiple points of access provided by established institutions, but where systems are closed and strong (e.g., France), movements are likely to adopt confrontational, disruptive strategies.

Although Kitschelt's approach developed a clear, economical account of the impact of state structures upon political challengers, it conflated genuinely structural features of political systems with aspects of them which, because they change relatively quickly and are themselves shaped by institutional arrangements, are more properly recognized as contingent or conjunctural features of those systems.

Subsequent attempts to clarify the concept (Tarrow, 1994; Kriesi *et al.*, 1995) distinguished between the formal institutional structure of the state, the informal procedures and prevailing strategies used to deal with challengers, and the configuration of power and alliances in the party system, but still, confusingly, described contingent constellations as 'structures'.

Another weakness of the POS approach was its susceptibility to what Tarrow (1994: 90) termed 'the seductions of statism' – the tendency to treat state structures and official responses to actors as timeless and undifferentiated. In fact, states and different state institutions treat different social movements and movement organizations in different policy areas differently both generally and at different points in time (Rootes, 1997). The complexity of state structures and the contingent and conjunctural aspects of state responses to collective action compromise attempts to advance global characterizations of even relatively formal institutional structures.

The POS approach also neglected the sociologically crucial consideration that different individuals, groups and classes of actors are differently resourced for different kinds of political action. Thus, it overlooked the most salutary lesson of **resource mobilization theory** (RMT) while faithfully reproducing its chief limitation – the assumption that calculative rational choice is the basis of action. Thus, like RMT, the POS approach neglected the ways in which actors' tactical and strategic preferences are dictated by their values and discounted the affective or emotional satisfactions of collective action.

The concept of political opportunity structure was overloaded by being extended beyond those elements of the environment of collective action which are genuinely structural to others which are contingent or simply conjunctural. Because the development of collective action is a dialectical process, it is unrealistic to expect a structural theory of such action to have great predictive power. As Tarrow observed, it is the non-structural dimensions of the political context which appear most consequentially to shape opportunities for political challengers.

Nevertheless, the concept of political opportunity structure, stripped of its excess baggage, has heuristic value, especially in the initial stages of comparative research. If we are unable to propose a systematic theory of the impact of political context upon collective action, there are many aspects of the context of collective action in which scrupulous investigation might discover pattern, but it is neither necessary nor desirable to label everything which displays pattern as 'structure'.

Recent writers are acutely conscious of the problems that careless use of the term 'political opportunity structure' has caused, but their remedy – the use of the term 'political opportunity factors' or simply 'political opportunity' – simply avoids the issue and, in so doing, risks returning us to the situation where the proposition that the development and outcomes of social movement mobilizations are the product of political opportunities is a simple tautology. What would then be lost is the potentially useful – and testable – proposition that the formal structure of political opportunities (political institutions) is a powerful determinant of social movement development. The great merits of the POS approach are that it identifies phenomena where there is genuine and consequential cross-national variation and that it encourages sociologists to take institutional structures seriously.

See also: environmental movements; new social movements

References

Kitschelt, H (1986) 'Political Opportunity Structures and Political Protest: Anti-nuclear Movements in Four Democracies', *British Journal of Political Science*, 16: 57–85.

Kriesi, H., Koopmans,R., Duyvendak, J.W. and Giugni, M. (1995) *New Social Movements in Western Europe: A Comparative Analysis*, Minneapolis: University of Minnesota Press; London: UCL Press.

Rootes, C. (1997) 'Shaping Collective Action: Structure, Contingency and Knowledge' in R. Edmondson, (ed.) *The Political Context of*

Collective Action, London and New York: Routledge, pp. 81–104.

Tarrow, S. (1994) *Power in Movement: Social Movements, Collective Action and Politics*, Cambridge: Cambridge University Press.

CHRIS ROOTES

polluter pays principle

The polluter pays principle (PPP) was adopted in 1972 as one of the fundamental principles of environmental policy by the Organization for Economic Co-operation and Development (OECD), an intergovernmental organization for industrial countries. Its initial meaning was that, when countries require that their industries control their pollution, the cost of the control should be paid by the industries and not by the public sector. The rationale for PPP was threefold: it promoted economic efficiency by allocating costs to the generator of them; it gave a financial incentive to polluters to reduce their pollution; and it prevented trade distortions from government subsidies, which may have been more motivated by industrial protectionism than a desire for environmental protection. Later PPP also came to mean that polluters should bear the cost of their pollution damage. While PPP, in both meanings, is still in practice honoured as much in the breach as in the observance, it is regularly cited as a rationale for imposing particular environmental policies, especially **eco-taxes**.

PAUL EKINS

POLYCHLORINATED BIPHENYLS *see* PCBs

population movement and control

An increasing and mobile human population affects virtually every environmental challenge of the twenty-first century, from energy use and climate change at the international level to local efforts to build sustainable communities and constrain urban sprawl. A larger number of human beings typically translates into greater demands for energy, water, land, food, shelter and other critical resources. Yet environmentalists and scholars have disagreed about the importance of population issues as well as the most appropriate policy actions that might be taken. Some environmental scientists such as Paul **Ehrlich** have written and spoken frequently on the need to limit population growth, but others have argued that **technology** and human consumption are more important influences on environmental quality.

The politics of population policy is also affected by the historically low visibility of the issue on policy agendas, the complexities of projecting population growth and its impacts over a period of several decades or more, and the difficulties faced in resolving moral, cultural, and religious differences intimately related to decisions on reproduction and migration. Population policy and politics tend to reflect the unique demographic circumstances within each nation in addition to the pronounced differences in growth rates between industrialized and developing nations. Disagreements between industrialized and developing nations were prominent at the 1974 and 1984 international conferences on population and development held under United Nations auspices. Yet at the 1994 International Conference on Population and Development (ICPD) held in Cairo, Egypt, a new level of global consensus on population growth and its effects was evident.

In October 1999 the world crossed an important symbolic threshold as the population reached 6 billion people, up from a mere 2.5 billion in 1950. The global growth rate has been declining slowly over the past two decades and by 2000 it stood at about 1.3 per cent a year. That is down from 1.7 per cent just since 1992. At a 1.3 per cent growth rate, the world adds about 79 million people annually. Even with declining fertility rates, the United Nations' medium, or most likely, projection indicates a world population of 6.9 billion people by 2010 and 9 billion by 2050. Most of the anticipated growth (about 95 per cent) is expected to occur in developing nations. These kinds of projections depend on key assumptions made about economic and social development, the availability of family-planning programmes, and the extent of contraceptive use. Social development, such as improved education, a higher status for women and greater gender equity, better reproductive health care and nutrition, adoption of old age security programmes, and economic reforms are all as important as provision of family planning services. These kinds of measures were strongly endorsed at the 1994 ICPD.

In many nations, the combination of such social and economic **development** and family planning programmes has produced striking declines in fertility levels. These include Cuba, Sri Lanka, South Korea, Thailand, Tunisia, Singapore, **Mexico**, **Indonesia**, and **China**. Yet other nations have exhibited far less progress toward lower growth rates. In addition, migration from the countryside to urban areas continues as a major worldwide trend, leading to overcrowded and severely polluted 'mega cities'.

The USA stands in sharp contrast to the prevailing pattern in developed nations, which have an average growth rate of only 0.1 per cent a year. That has been the rate in northern and western Europe, for instance, with eastern Europe recording a slightly negative rate in the late 1990s. The US rate has been close to 1.0 per cent a year, in large part because of a high rate of immigration as well as higher fertility rates. Given these trends, the US Census Bureau projects a continuing high rate of growth, with the nation expected to reach 404 million by 2050 and 571 million by 2100. These are middle-range projections from the nation's 275 million base population in 2000. According to a 1997 National Academy of Sciences study, about 60 per cent of this anticipated growth is attributable to the nation's immigration rate, among the highest in the world. Fierce debate has surrounded the immigration issue within the USA, with the environmental community deeply divided over it.

Equally important, however, has been the ongoing debate over whether population growth, including immigration, is as important as the prevailing patterns of consumption, pollution, and waste, particularly within rich industrialized nations. Industrialized nations consume a far greater proportion of the world's resources and have a much higher per capita impact on the environment. For instance, the richest one-fifth of the world's nations controls about 85 per cent of the global income and consumes about 60 per cent of its energy and three-quarters of its paper, chemicals, iron, and steel. They are also responsible for more than 90 per cent of industrial and hazardous wastes produced and about two-thirds of greenhouse gases (see **global warming**).

For these and other reasons, both within the USA and worldwide, scientists differ in their assessment of what population growth and immigration rates mean for use of natural resources such as energy, water, and land, and increased pollution, and for impacts on protection of biological diversity and other environmental concerns (see **biodiversity**). There are also varying analyses of whether the world can meet the challenge of feeding, housing, clothing, and otherwise providing for the manifold needs of an expanding population and rising expectations for economic development. Those who favour taking action on population growth through public policy argue that without great advances in technology, substantial improvement in efficiency of resource use, and significant moderation in consumptive lifestyles, most environmental problems will likely grow worse. Optimists on population trends, such as the late Julian **Simon**, have exhibited greater faith that these kinds of technical advances and changes in human behaviour will occur and thus minimize adverse environmental and resource impacts.

Such scientific and political disagreements have provided few incentives for policymakers to give population issues the serious consideration that they merit. Yet public policies can help both rich and poor nations attain a better future than these demographic projections suggest is otherwise likely. The 20-year programme of action approved at the 1994 ICPD called for a tripling of the amount the world spends on population policies such as voluntary family planning programmes, from $5 billion (US dollars) spent in 1994 to $17 billion by the year 2000 and $22 billion by 2015.

Delegates to the ICPD argued that with such financial support the world's population could be kept below UN medium projections. Yet the low salience of population issues will likely constrain the willingness of most nations to commit funds at this level. Controversies over population programmes, particularly those that are considered to be coercive, may further limit financial assistance. For example, following the 1984 UN conference on population in Mexico City and concerns expressed over China's population policy, the USA cut all funding for UN population programmes. That policy lasted through the presidencies of Ronald **Reagan** and George Bush and was reversed only at the beginning of Bill Clinton's presidency in January 1993. Annual battles in the US Congress over funding for international population assistance testify to continuing political conflict over such programmes.

The generally weak support for population policies is striking in light of the widespread use of the concept of **sustainable development**. **Sustainability** has emerged as perhaps the most compelling way to describe the long-term agenda for environmentalism and environmental policy. Even with considerable variation in the definition of sustainability, the linkage to population growth is manifest. Sustainability must include the enduring capacity of a given ecosystem to support the demands that its human population imposes on it – for example, in providing food, clean water, shelter, energy, and other essential services.

By the late 1990s, these kinds of considerations, in addition to increasingly obvious diminishment of the **quality of life** in many urban areas, sparked a worldwide movement toward creating sustainable communities. Within the USA, there was no mistaking a sharp rise in public support for limiting urban sprawl and creating more 'livable' communities. The Clinton White House strongly endorsed such measures and promoted a series of federally sponsored programmes designed to help states and communities preserve open space, ease traffic congestion, and promote sensible growth. Such a focus on liveable communities, better planning, and public involvement in local decision-making should make sustainability an even more attractive goal in the years ahead. The message here may be that at least some elements of population growth and migration may be resolved more effectively and democratically at the local level where the consequences of such population changes are most evident.

See also: United Nations Fund for Population Activities; Zero Population Growth

Further reading

Cohen, J.E. (1995) *How Many People Can the Earth Support?*, New York: Norton.

Kraft, M.E. (1994) 'Population Policy', in S. Nagel (ed.) *Encyclopedia of Policy Studies*, New York: Marcel Dekker, 2nd edn.

Mazmanian, D.A., and Kraft, M.E. (eds) (1999) *Toward Sustainable Communities: Transition and Transformations in Environmental Policy*, Cambridge, MA: MIT Press.

Tobin, R.J. (2000) 'Environment, Population, and the Developing World', in N. Vig and M. Kraft (eds) *Environmental Policy: New Directions for the Twenty-First Century*, Washington: CQ Press.

MICHAEL E. KRAFT

Portuguese Green Party

Created in 1982, *Os Verdes*, the Portuguese Green Party, got its first seat at the national level in 1983. In 1987, it accepted the invitation of the Portuguese Communist Party to form an electoral coalition, the United Democratic Coalition (CDU), to assure its representation at the national and local levels. *Os Verdes* benefited from this pragmatic strategy and won two seats in the national parliament. The same alliance was used at the local and European level for all the following elections and *Os Verdes* assured the same representation in the national parliament. Nevertheless the party remains weakly organized and run by a small elite. The development of *Os Verdes* was constrained by several factors. The post-dictatorship politics focused primarily on democratic consolidation and economic modernization based on the European integration process, limiting the growth of post-materialism to a minimum (see **Inglehart, Ronald**). Portuguese politics is also characterized by a strong bi-partisanship and a constraining electoral system for small parties.

CÉDRIC VAN DE WALLE

post-industrial society

As a form of 'social forecasting', the term post-industrial societies involves the claim that certain societies have moved (or are in the process of moving) from industrial societies to a new post-industrial era. It is argued that 'industrial societies' are based on hierarchically organized manufacturing industry, involving standardized mass production where the industrial worker is of central importance and the labour party a central political actor. In contrast, post-industrial societies are characterized as based on decentralized service industries and diversified 'knowledge centred' production. 'Knowledge workers' are often seen as the centrally important workers, and social movements the new political actors. Sociologist such as Daniel Bell and Alain Touraine became the main propagators of this body of ideas in the 1960s and 1970s. Green thinkers (such as Schumacher, **Gorz** and **Bookchin**) also selectively incorporated some of these notions into their own work.

Further reading

Frankel, B. (1987) *The Post Industrial Utopians*, Oxford: Polity Press.

DAMIAN WHITE

post-modernism

Post-modernism refers to the crisis of authority of modern culture from the 1960s. In the arts post-modernism points to the culture of a media-saturated consumer society, where media images have become more real than lived reality. Initially applied to architecture, post-modernism broke down the division between high art and mass culture, using a pastiche to rapidly cannibalize previous art works or art forms. Advertising is the perfect post-modern art form, where all other representations are referred to ironically in the production of simulacra (images that relate only to other images). In philosophy and social science, post-modernism is associated with the collapse of grand narratives of historical **progress**, scientific rationality, universal ethics and individual identity.

Post-modern social science presents multiple ethical viewpoints, and humans with multiple, shifting identities. Post-modernism may be a shallow consumer culture or the possibility of new identities and new politics.

See also: counter-culture; new social movements

DERRICK PURDUE

precautionary principle

Set against continued concerns over environmental impact, policy-makers have sought to develop ways of dealing with the hazards associated with modern societies. One such approach has been the notion of the precautionary principle. The precautionary principle has its origins in the German environmental movement although it became enshrined in Principle 15 of the Rio Declaration of 1992 (see **Rio Conference 1992**).

At its core lies the notion that, if there is potential for harm in an activity, then a full discussion of the acceptability of that risk should be encouraged by policy-makers. Within this process, the nature and frailty of any evidence should be open to informal public debate. However, despite its obvious merits, the use of the principle is shrouded in conflict and disagreement. At its simplest, the precautionary principle can be seen to involve taking preventative action in the absence of any proof of harm. Even this represents a major shift in the thinking of policy-makers, as previous practice has invariably required proof of harm as a precursor to policy shifts. Within many environmental and risk debates, the notion of a burden of proof has been a powerful element in undermining many of the concerns expressed by environmental groups.

One of the most systematic attempts to define the principle can be found in the so-called Wingspread Statement. What is significant in such definitions of the principle is that the notion of a scientific burden of proof is no longer a requirement in the prevention of potentially hazardous activities from taking place. In elaborating on the detail of the principle, Raffensperger and Tickner (1999) observe that it can be seen to consist of four core elements. The first is the notion that preventative action should be taken in advance of any scientific proof of harm and often before clear causality is established. Second, the principle is often seen to advocate that the risk generators (and not those who are the potential victims) should be faced with the burden of proof. Third, policymakers should always consider a range of alternative actions when evidence of harm materializes. It is possible that the solutions to the problem can create even greater hazards. Finally, the decision-making process surrounding policy-making should be open and democratic and should include all parties who might be affected by the activity.

Because of the ambiguity surrounding the concept, the precautionary approach has attracted considerable criticism from certain quarters, who see its use as a heavy-handed response to the alarmist views of environmental activists. More muted criticisms have also been made. Giddens (1999), for example, has argued that the use of the principle can serve to stifle innovation due to the inherent difficulties involved in balancing costs and benefits associated with scientific advances. The recent debates in the UK over genetically modified foods illustrate the nature of that dilemma. Morris (2000) has pointed to the argument that the use of the principle might serve to undermine legal certainty by allowing intervention from bureaucrats and administrators. In contrast, members of the **environmental movements** see the core of the principle as a powerful guiding concept, not least because it challenges the domination of scientific expertise within debates on hazard.

A significant criticism surrounding the principle concerns the lack of a universally accepted definition of what the term means in practice. At its core lies the notion that sufficient consideration should be given to the potential risks that are inherent in a proposed policy and that these should be set against the benefits that arise from the activity. Herein lies the potential for conflict however, and the principle seems destined to remain shrouded in controversy. Industrial groups are clearly concerned about the implications that a strict interpretation of the principle would have on their competitiveness and profitability. Similarly, the vague nature of the principle also brings with it problems surrounding implementation and enfor-

cement. Unless the principle is firmly grounded within a regulatory framework and is rigorously enforced, it could remain little more than an abstract concept around which heated debates will continue to occur.

See also: environmental ethics; cost-benefit analysis; genetic engineering, crops; risk assessment; risk society; Stockholm Conference; sustainability; sustainable development

References

Giddens, A. (1999) *Runaway World. How Globalization is Reshaping Our Lives*, London: Profile Books.

Morris, J. (2000) 'Defining the Precautionary Principle', in Morris, J. (ed.) (2000) *Rethinking Risk and the Precautionary Principle*, London: Butterworth-Heinemann, pp. 1–21.

Raffensperger, C. and Tinkner, J. (1999) 'Introduction: To Foresee and Forestall', in Raffensperger, C. and Tinkner, J. (eds) *Protecting Public Health and the Environment. Implementing the Precautionary Principle*, Washington DC: Island Books, pp. 1–12.

DENIS SMITH

Price–Anderson Act

The Price–Anderson Act, amending the Atomic Energy Act, was passed by the US Congress in 1957 to encourage the commercial production of nuclear power by limiting the financial liability of persons or companies responsible for a nuclear accident. The Price–Anderson Act limited nuclear power industry liability to (originally) less than $600 million per nuclear accident, to be covered from a combined insurance pool. In case of costs beyond these limits, governmental subsidies would cover damages.

Although environmentalists opposed the continuation of special treatment for the nuclear power industry, in 1988 the Price–Anderson Act was amended and re-authorized by Congress to extend indemnification protection to the Department of Energy and its contractors. Plant operators' liability in case of nuclear accident is now limited to less than $10 billion (which would cover only a fraction of the costs of a Chernobyl accident in the USA). The Bush Administration favours renewal of the liability limits in 2002. Otherwise, in Vice President Cheney's words, 'nobody's going to invest in nuclear-power plants'.

Reference

'Special Report: Nuclear Power' (2001) *The Economist*, 19 May, p. 26.

Further reading

The Nevada for Nuclear Projects. *Insurance Coverage for Nuclear Accidents: Price–Anderson Act Re-Authorization* at
URL: http://www.state.nv.us/nucwaste/trans/prand01.htm.

JON E. FITCH

prisoners' dilemma

Two people are questioned, in separate cells, about crimes they have committed together. The police already have enough evidence to convict them both of a minor crime, and, if either confesses, to a much more serious one as well. Each prisoner is given the option of confessing to the serious crime. It is made clear that, if just one of them confesses, he will be pardoned while the other will be jailed for 25 years. If both confess, each will receive 10 years. If both remain silent they will each receive 2 years (the going rate for the lesser crime). Each prisoner concludes that, whatever the other decides, the rational course of action would be to confess to the more serious crime, thereby saving them 15 years in prison. However, it is also true that this course of action will bring about an outcome that is worse for each prisoner than if both had decided to stay silent. This is the 'prisoners' dilemma', and it has been applied to environmental problems by a number of scholars seeking to understand the absence of norms which would prevent the depletion of natural resources, such as **fossil fuels** and **fisheries**.

ED PAGE

progress

Related to terms such as **development**, modernization, evolution, a core meaning of progress is that it conveys a sense of movement to some higher or better stage or state. Progress usually refers to the western-centred idea, associated with St Augustine, referring to the (linear) evolution of (western) society from ignorance, material poverty and insecurity to rationality, affluence and security. 'Progress' in modern debates is most often associated with the development of a capitalist industrial economy and society within a globalized economic system, and a liberal democratic state (see **capitalism**; **globalization**; **liberalism/ liberal democracy**). In environmental political debates, critics of this notion of progress point out that the cost of this progress is the destruction of the natural world, increasing inequality and poverty (both between and within societies) and a dramatic decrease in the **quality of life**. At the same time there are those who argue that what is needed is not a rejection of progress, which is a politically powerful idea, but a redefinition of it which incorporates environmental goals and values.

JOHN BARRY

property rights

Property rights are a bundle of rights guaranteed by the government. They give to individuals the right to exclude others from their land and to dispose of and use their property in a manner that suits them. Although some philosophers such as John Locke argued that property rights preceded government and were absolute, it is difficult to imagine how these rights could be exercised without an enforcement mechanism provided by a protective state. In practice these rights have always been circumscribed in some manner. Traditionally governments have used the power of eminent domain to seize private property for the public good and convert it to some public use such as roads and other societal infrastructures. The private owners are compensated at 'fair market value' but they have no choice in the decision to sell.

At the same time that people want government to intervene to assure them of their property rights, they also expect the authorities to ensure the value of their land by controlling conditions external to their land that may affect it. Zoning ordinances are one method by which governments protect property owners who wish to prevent loss of value of their own land by being located near an undesirable or 'dirty' land use, such as a garbage dump or industrial plant. Historic preservation districts also restrict the way in which owners can modify the appearance of their buildings.

Such land-use restrictions apply to all property owners in the same area equally, and this inevitably leads to conflict (see **land use regulation/ planning**). Property owners generally argue that they should be allowed to use their own land for the 'highest and best' use for which it is appropriate. This is often defined as the most profitable for themselves. Inevitably some property holders will wish to use their land in a manner that their neighbours deem undesirable. An individual home-owner may wish to raze a historic building and replace it with a larger house; his neighbours, however, may want to preserve the historic atmosphere of a bygone era. An individual farmer may seek to sell his farm to a local developer, while his neighbours want to continue to farm their lands without complaints from residential neighbours. This brings the government's two tasks into direct confrontation: the demand for maximum freedom for the individual landowner, and the community's demand for homogeneity.

Judicial interpretation of property rights has waxed and waned in history. At the turn of the twentieth century the courts tended to empathise with property owners who complained against government intervention in the use of their lands. As societies adjusted to the welfare state, judges became more sympathetic to the claims of communities to control their environments. However, in the late twentieth century a revived property rights movement asserted itself in many countries. As populations became denser and governments increased their efforts to preserve some natural

areas, many landowners launched successful efforts to get the courts to overturn such regulations. In the USA for example, the Supreme Court created a rule of thumb that in order for cities or towns to prevent a given land use, the government had to demonstrate the value to the community outweighed the loss to the individual property owner.

See also: land use regulation/planning

Further reading

Ely, J.E. (1992) *The Guardian of Every Other Right*, New York: Oxford University Press

Locke, J. (1967) *Second Treatise on Government*, in P. Laslett (ed.) *Two Treatises of Government*, Cambridge: Cambridge University Press, 2nd edn.

Dolan v. Tigard (1994) 114 S.Ct. 2309

Lucas v. South Carolina Costal Council (1992) 112 S. Ct. 2886.

LETTIE McSPADDEN

public inquiries

The basic principle of a public inquiry is to allow all parties affected by or with an interest in a proposed project or activity a chance to put forward their point of view; before permission is granted or once it has been refused. Public inquiries may be held following an appeal by the public against a decision by a local Planning Authority, or an appeal arising from the Environmental Protection Act, the Transport and Works Act, or the Water Resources Act. The Planning Inspectorate is the prime source of impartial expertise for resolving disputes about the use of land, natural resources and the environment. A public inquiry may also result when the Secretary of State for the Environment, Transport and the Regions 'calls-in' a planning application for his own determination where there is considered to be a major public interest. Disadvantages include the considerable time taken to present evidence, cross examine witnesses and produce a report.

NICOLE DANDO

public opinion and the environment

It is difficult to assess the true dimensions of public opinion on environmental protection issues, much less the connections between expressed opinion and policy outcomes. First, fluctuations in public attention to environmental issues may mask deeper, less transient values. Second, but not necessarily contrary to the first point, the depth of public support for environmental protection may run shallow when other, more proximate priorities dominate public concerns. As a result, even strong diffuse support for environmental protection may not translate easily into directive support for green candidates or policies.

Fluctuating issue saliency

The apparent temporal saliency of an issue – where it seems to stand on an attentive public's stated list of priorities – can fluctuate tremendously. For one thing, public opinion polls often rely on open-ended 'most important problem' questions to measure issue salience. Yet exclusive reliance on such measures can understate general public support for environmental protection for two reasons.

First, environmental protection issues rarely reside atop the public's agenda for action, particularly when compared to such perennial concerns as economic well-being, crime, and national security. Second, public perceptions about most important problems are shaped markedly by mass media coverage of events or crises (see **mass media and the environment**). In essence, measures of issue salience are headline sensitive. As a result, it is relatively easy to assess the dimensions of public opinion under conditions of high issue salience. For example, during the 1980s a series of dramatic industrial accidents – e.g., the deadly release of chemical gas at **Bhophal**, India in 1984, the core meltdown at the **Chernobyl** nuclear power plant in 1986, and the massive **Exxon Valdez oil spill** off Alaska in 1988 – crystallized worldwide mass public concern about environmental protection and health issues. However, by the late 1990s the absence of dramatic focusing events, at least in the developed world, translated into lower environmental issue salience in Europe and the Americas.

Absent such agenda-setting events, policy-makers may interpret low temporal issue salience as equivalent to low public support for environmental protection. However, doing so can result in a salience trap where low temporal issue salience actually masks more latent environmental values. In the USA, for example, Republicans regained control over the US Congress in 1995 for the first time in 40 years. At this time only 1 per cent of Americans in a Gallup Poll cited the environment as the 'most important problem', down dramatically from 11 per cent in 1992. Given their electoral successes, and faced with apparently low public concern about the environment, the new Republican majority believed that voters would support major changes in American environmental policy. Yet the attentive public soon reacted negatively to perceived reversals in longstanding environmental policy directions. Voters who had expressed theoretical support for less government and a streamlining of bureaucratic rules none-theless expected the continuation of an energetic national government role in protecting the environment. Indeed, while there was little public urgency about environmental issues, most Americans continued to believe that the nation needed to take some additional actions to address environmental problems. Faced with a public backlash, Republicans abandoned much of their deregulatory agenda. In general, momentary fluctuations in mass public attention to environmental issues can understate more consistent long-term support for environmental priorities, particularly when citizens are faced with explicit choices.

In the USA, a January 1998 Pew Charitable Trust poll asked Americans to indicate the level of priority the nation should give to environmental protection. Given a forced-choice option, 53 per cent said it should be a top priority, while another 37 per cent said it should be a lower but still important priority. More telling, when these respondents were asked to pick among alternative uses for a federal budget surplus, the single greatest option (33 per cent) was 'for increased spending on domestic programmes such as health, education, and the environment'. Another useful indicator in the US context is a CBS News/New York Times poll question that gauges agreement with the statement that 'protecting the environment is so important that the requirements and standards cannot be too high, and continuing environmental improvements must be made regardless of cost'. By the 1990s, most Americans agreed to some extent with what is a rather absolutist view.

Similar, if not higher levels of support for environmental values are found across nations. A 1992 Gallup survey of environmental attitudes in two dozen nations found widespread support for a stronger environmental protection ethic. More important, the survey found 'little difference in reported levels of environmental concern between people of poor, less economically developed nations and those of the richer, highly industrialized nations'. (Dunlap, Gallup, and Gallup, 1993) This finding is vitally important inasmuch as many if not most of the world's worst examples of environmental degradation now arise in **less developed countries**.

In general, as Dunlap (1995) argues, issue salience fluctuates but overall public concern endures to the point that support for environmental protection can be regarded as a consensual issue which generates little open opposition. Citizens in most societies regard environmental problems as serious and believe that too little progress has been made in resolving them. Moreover, deep public concern about environmental issues has endured – even increased – regardless of fluctuating temporary issue saliency, a level of persistence attributed in part to the universal impacts of environmental problems.

The strength of environmental support

Even so, the strength of concern about the environment can vary profoundly within mass publics. While it seems clear that in most nations diffuse support for better environmental protection has increased across all societal cohorts, such support still typically runs stronger among younger, more educated, and more urban individuals, but noticeably weaker among their older, less educated, and more rural counterparts. These differences among social groups can have telling political

results. For example, in some countries older and more rural voters often wield disproportionate political clout in legislative elections. However, age by itself is not necessarily predictive, nor is locale. Support for environmental values may depend as much on the nature of the perceived problem or threat. In this regard, the more localized and immediate the threat the more it is likely to generate concern across social groups.

Although support for environmental values increasingly seems to transcend social divisions, education by itself does seem to matter. Better-educated individuals regardless of gender, locale, or overall ideological orientation typically express stronger concern about the environment. Education also correlates with greater overall attention to public issues, which by itself also leads to a stronger focus on environmental issues.

Beyond rough demographic differences, there are also limits to how far citizens are willing or able to go, particularly when faced with stark, if sometimes false, choices between long-range, often intangible environmental improvements and more immediate, and often very tangible costs. Strong generalized support for environmental protection does not preclude voters from voting against green candidates or from defending local industries regardless of their adverse environmental impacts. Simply put, environmental priorities compete with other, often more salient concerns during election or policy debates, particularly when issues are posed in stark, zero-sum terms. Citizens may believe in the abstract that they can have both economic growth and a cleaner world, and in theory are willing to pay higher taxes for environmental protection, but are understandably reluctant when their livelihoods might be at stake.

Thus, as with public opinion generally, diffuse public support for environmental protection rarely translates automatically into directive support for specific public policy outcomes. Effective political institutions and enlightened political leaders are necessary to connect opinion with outcome.

References

Dunlap, R. (1995) 'Public Opinion and the Environment (US)', in R. Paehlke (ed.) *Conserva-*

tion and Environmentalism: An Encyclopedia, New York: Garland: p. 536.

Dunlap, R., Gallup, G., and Gallup, A. (1993) 'Of Global Concern: Results of the Health of the Planet Survey', *Environment* 35: 11.

Further reading

Bowman, K. and Ladd, E. (1995) *Attitudes toward the Environment*, Washington, DC: American Enterprise Institute.

Downs, A. (1972) 'Up and Down with Ecology: The Issue-Attention Cycle', *Public Interest*, 28: 38–50.

Dunlap, R. (1991) 'Public Opinion in the 1980s: Clear Consensus, Ambiguous Commitment', *Environment*, 33: 286.

Kempton, W., *et al.* (1995) *Environmental Values and American Culture*, Cambridge, MA: The MIT Press.

Mitchell, R. (1990) 'Public Opinion and the Green Lobby: Poised for the 1990s?' in N. Vig and M. Kraft (eds) *Environmental Policy in the 1990s*, Washington, DC: CQ Press: p. 84.

Moore, D. (1995) 'Public Sense of Urgency About Environment Wanes', *The Gallup Poll Monthly* (April): 17–20.

Pew Research Center (1998) 'Education, Crime, Social Security Top National Priorities Spending Favored Over Tax Cuts or Debt Reduction', *National Issues Index*, (January) at URL: http://www.people-press.org/jan98que.htm.

Saad, L. (1995) 'Welfare, Federal Deficit Emerge as Public Concerns', *Gallup Poll Monthly* (January): 6–8.

Times–Mirror Organization (May 1995) *The Environmental Two-Step: Looking Back, Moving Forward*, Washington, DC: Roper Starch Worldwide: p. 2.

CHRISTOPHER J. BOSSO

Q

quality of life

A person's, or population's, quality of life can be understood as that which makes their life go as well as possible. The simplicity of this definition masks the fact that there are several competing theories of what makes a life go well, as well as profound difficulties associated with finding an appropriate metric by which we might compare the quality of life of different people, or populations. Much recent debate, for example, has focused on whether welfare, resources, or basic capabilities should be used to construct indices designed to measure the quality of life of different populations. In environmental political debates quality of life arguments are used to criticize dominant views of human well-being which focus on 'quantitative' measurements such as wealth, income and employment.

ED PAGE

387

R

Rainbow Warrior

In 1978 **Greenpeace** undertook its first sea-going campaign against Spanish and Icelandic whalers in a north seas fishing trawler named the *Rainbow Warrior* (see **whaling**). The vessel derived its name from a North American Indian legend which prophesies that 'when man has destroyed the world through his greed, the warriors of the rainbow will arise to save it again'. The *Rainbow Warrior* sailed around the globe campaigning against environmental atrocities.

In 1985 the *Rainbow Warrior* began its Nuclear Pacific Peace Voyage in Auckland, **New Zealand**. The plan was to take part in a protest against French nuclear testing in the South Pacific. In the harbour of Auckland, French agents bombed the ship, sinking it and killing one crew member. In 1987 the French Government was ordered by New Zealand courts to pay Greenpeace US$8.16 million in damages, which allowed Greenpeace to purchase and launch the *Rainbow Warrior II*.

Further reading

'Greenpeace' (24 January 2001) *About the S/V Rainbow Warrior* at
  URL: http://www.greenpeace.org/~comms/ rw/rwabout.html.

JON E. FITCH

rainforests

Tropical rainforests contain Earth's greatest measured terrestrial **biodiversity** and are home to many small, ancient, nomadic societies of **indigenous peoples**. Rainforests also exist in temperate **New Zealand** and the northern Pacific coast of North America, but most of the world's humid, high, multiple-canopy forests lie within the Tropics. Over half the area of these forests occurs in **Amazonia**, most of that in **Brazil**. A bit occurs in the Americas around the Caribbean Basin, the Paraguay–Parana Basin, and in the Mata Atlântica on Brazil's south-east coast. Another quarter of these forests are scattered from Myanmar, through Indochina, **Indonesia**, and the rest of the archipelago to New Guinea and north-east Australia. About one-fifth is found in Africa in the Congo Basin, its surrounding highlands, and along the Gulf of Guinea littoral.

Tropical rainforests are the source of most of the Earth's fresh water, produce much of its breathable oxygen, and represent a vast reserve of largely untapped genetic capital. These biologically highly productive but fragile ecosystems remain largely intact, mainly due to their low human population density. For example, the population density of Amazonia is only 50 per cent greater than that of the Sahara Desert. Both regionally and worldwide the greatest threat to tropical rainforests is their conversion to subsistence agricultural uses by the land-hungry poor, especially in Africa and the fragmented Caribbean and largely destroyed Mata Atlântica forests. Here human population density is much higher.

Secondary threats to tropical rainforests vary by region. Export timber sales and conversion to forest plantations are significant in the Asian forests. Fuel uses, plantation conversion, and civil conflict cause much rainforest loss in Africa. All these threats exist in the American rainforests. Also in the American forests, especially in those more heavily impacted areas, a follow-on use to subsistence agricultural conversion is a further conversion to extensive cattle pasturage. In the 1980s rainforest preservation joined the list of goals of organized environmentalism (see **environmentalism and ecologism**). Environmentalists' public rhetoric often cited the aspects of biodiversity, oxygen and water production, and 'lost' cures for cancer and other frightening maladies. In the late 1980s the aspect of cattle production on the already disrupted ecosystems of Central and South America was the focus of a widely publicized boycott of Burger King Restaurants organized by Rainforest Action Network (RAN) using free mailing lists from other sympathetic tax-exempt environmental groups like the Earth Island Institute, **Friends of the Earth**, and **Sierra Club** in the USA. In addition to direct mailings, RAN purchased full-page advertisements in several major US newspapers attacking the 'hamburger connection' to tropical deforestation. The advertisements' selective statistics made Burger King Restaurants fearful of adverse customer responses and they eventually agreed to cease purchases of Central and South American beef.

Except among urban, educated elites, the response in Central and South America to the RAN campaign was almost universally negative. The Costa Rican Minister of Agriculture noted that his country could not afford to compete financially in a publicity war with American environmental groups. Brazilian scientists asserted that if RAN and other groups were truly worried for the rainforests, they would use their money to help Brazil and other tropical nations toward **development**. This response became more general and widely shared by the time of the 1992

Earth Summit in Rio de Janeiro (see **Rio Conference 1992**). Indonesia, Malaysia, Zaire, and most other nations with tropical rainforests asserted their sovereignty over these resources and refused to discuss their disposition with other, especially First World nations. As its Foreign Minister stated, 'Brazil will not see itself turned into a nature preserve for the rest of humanity'.

While they object to First World and other nations dictating what is to be done with their tropical rainforests, many Third World nations nonetheless have taken independent and collective steps to protect these ecosystems. Common methods include **debt-for-nature swaps**, laws against felling native tree species and clearing non-planted forests, tax incentives to create private biological reserves and creation of new public parks and reserves. Still, as long as these nations' people remain in poverty, they will look upon their tropical rainforests as the most promising way to a better life.

See also: Brazilian Green party; Central American environmental politics; forest management; Latin American environmental politics

Further reading

Nations, J. and Kromer, D. (1983) 'Tropical Rain-Forests and the "Hamburger Society" ', *Environment*, 25(3) April: 12–20.
Parker, J. (1999) *Rainforests*, Brookfield, CT: Copper Beech Books.

PAUL CHANDLER

Ramblers Association

Founded in 1935, the Ramblers Association (RA) has 130,000 members and a federal structure which is rooted in Victorian social reform movement. Its principal income is from subscriptions, charitable tax relief and regular grants from a hived-off trading arm, Ramblers Association Services. In the popular imagination, the campaign for open access to all uncultivated land, mass trespassing and a handful of members with communist sympathies, has given the Association the reputation of striking at the very heart of private **property rights**. By contrast, RA officials claim this is a misleading notion based on the canonization of mere titillation as history. Walking for pleasure in open countryside is an innocent occupation: the Association works consensually in well-established political fora. Nevertheless, a hero of Trollope neatly summarizes the situation: 'land gives so much more than rent. It gives position and influence and political power, to say nothing about the game.'

PENELOPE LAW

Reagan, Ronald

b. 6 February 1911, Tampico, Illinois, USA

Politician and actor

Ronald Reagan, the fortieth President of the USA and Governor of California (1967–75), helped bring the post Second World War American environmental movement to an abrupt turning point, especially in the use of the Federal government as a change agent for environmental progress. Advocates of a strange combination of corporate socialism and libertarianism, Reagan and his followers championed a conservative Republican view that came out of the opportunism of the American Sun Belt. Reagan accomplished this significant redirection largely through his appointments to important Federal agencies and the judiciary as well as budget allocations. All of this was explained by Reagan's desire to get the government 'off the backs of the people'. The electorate responded by giving him high approval ratings. In short, the Californian's two terms as President gave the environmental movement the most organized opposition it had ever faced (see **environmental movements**).

WARREN VANDER HILL

recycling

The environmental problems generated by our consumer societies require immediate measures

that respect the principles of long-term **sustainability**. However, in response to the rising amount of wastes (on average, per capita arising municipal wastes increased by 26 per cent between 1970 and the late 1980s in the Organization for Economic Co-operation and Development [OECD]) various (mostly end-of-pipe) waste-management strategies have been advocated, while a real questioning of what constitutes 'wastes' is still desperately needed. In Europe, a Strategy for Waste Management (SEC [89] 934), adopted in May 1990, established a hierarchy of preferred methods of disposal. Thus,

- the reduction of wastes can be achieved by using **technology** that requires less material and produces less waste, and by producing longer lasting products with lower pollution potential;
- re-use can be promoted – returnable bottles, re-usable packaging;
- recovery consists in finding beneficial uses for wastes and includes material recycling, composting and energy recovery (producing energy either by burning wastes or by using landfill gas);
- the disposal of wastes, finally, can be done by incineration or landfill.

Waste minimization is the preferred solution. However, it does not sit easily with the existing social habits of western societies. In parallel, industrialized countries have been encouraged, if not legally obliged (European Framework Waste Directive Dir. 75/442 as amended in 1991) to recycle and re-use wastes as raw materials.

Recycling, although only in third position in the hierarchy, has widespread support. The giant German recycling industry and its advanced technology is promoted as an example of environmentally friendly practices; and 'western' environmental groups promote it and are supported by grants provided by the Governments who enjoy the reward of being seen as green. In most OECD countries, although recycling rates for (increasing) households' wastes need to be improved, those for industrial processes are generally high. Recycling processes (collection of wastes, processing and re-processing of recyclable materials) are highly regulated and the legal texts also provide information concerning the targets to be reached. Thus, the EC packaging directive's recovery target is 50–

65 per cent for packaging, with a recycling target of 25–45 per cent, and a minimum of 15 per cent for each material by 2010.

In our economies, recycling is viewed as important for three reasons:

1 It allows us to reduce our need for virgin materials.
2 Significant energy savings can be achieved by re-processing waste materials, compared with the production of the equivalent virgin material.
3 Recycling reduces the environmental damage that waste disposal on landfill creates.

But the practical realities of recycling are not clear cut. Aluminium drink cans, for instance, seem worthwhile items since their recycling is financially viable and only takes 5 per cent of the energy compared to making the aluminium from bauxite ore (excluding transport considerations). On the other hand, the recycling of steel, paper, plastic, and glass are much less straightforward and more costly. Moreover, questions are raised about the existence of markets for recycled goods. Thus, once all the factors are taken into account, recycling can actually take more energy than the use of virgin or renewed resources.

In developing countries, where wastes generally consist of vegetable matter which can be composted, the issue of recycling is different altogether. Recycling is automatically implemented, in particular in big cities, where whole communities of people (have to) support themselves as dump scavengers and recyclers.

Therefore, although energy recovery and composting are two important forms of 'recycling', only in a few developing countries can we see official figures on the rates of recycling of wastes such as paper (e.g. 25 per cent in Morocco, 37 per cent in Colombia).

The issue of wastes has grown as a striking illustration of the North–South economic and environmental differences (see **North/South divide**). The disposal crisis has, in effect, created an active international trade in wastes, where the North is looking for countries poor enough to want to accept trash for dumping fees. Although many poor countries are increasingly reluctant to landfill imported wastes, this being partly due to the trade

of hazardous wastes which has to be regulated (in 1993, South Africa was the only country in Africa which did not ban imports of hazardous wastes; see **South African environmental politics**; **hazardous and toxic waste management**), there is a now growing interest in shipping wastes to the Third World for recycling.

New insights in waste disposal can provide solutions that are better adapted to our long-term needs. Energy recovery, as well as a new conception of wastes that questions the production and consumption processes in **life cycle assessment** terms and in view of using wastes as inputs, could solve problems related to material recycling and markets all at once. Such illustrations can be found in the 'industrial symbiosis' system in Kalundborg, Denmark, or in sustainable agricultural processes in industrialized and developing countries.

SANDRINE SIMON

regulatory approaches

Regulatory approaches to environmental issues range from highly decentralized to completely centralized controls. They also range from negative sanction policies (compensation, fines, imprisonment, or taxes) to positive sanction policies (subsidies and moral suasion). The way in which a policy is written may also differ greatly from the way in which it is enforced.

Decentralized policies are those that allow the directly affected parties to work out a solution for themselves either through informal negotiations or through the more formal intervention of the courts. Decentralized approaches have the advantage that the parties directly involved are likely to know the most about damages and abatement costs. This approach can be based on common or statutory laws which establish liability and often provide guidelines for judges and juries in determining appropriate compensation for injured parties. Liability may be determined under doctrines of negligence or of strict liability. In the first instance polluters are not held liable if they take appropriate steps to avoid damage. In the second polluters are held liable for damages regardless of circumstance.

The purpose of liability laws is not simply to

compensate victims but also to get would-be polluters to make careful decisions. But this depends on their knowing that they will be held liable for damages. There are a number of shortcomings to relying on liability to regulate polluting behaviour. Damages must be established and a clear set of perpetrators must be identifiable. The critical factors are: i) where the burden of proof lies; ii) the standards that must be met to establish proof; and iii) the transaction costs of gathering evidence, reaching agreement, and enforcement. In many countries the standards of proof required by the courts may be more than current science can supply.

The historically most common form of centralized environmental policy is the 'command and control' (CAC) approach. In order to bring about behaviour thought to be socially desirable political authorities may simply mandate the behaviour in law and then use whatever enforcement machinery is necessary to get people to obey the law. Generally the law establishes a set of performance standard of various types to bring about improvements in environmental quality. There are three broad types of standards: ambient quality, emission levels, and technology. Technology standards specify techniques, practices, and specific devices that polluters must adopt and maintain. Catalytic converters and stack-gas scrubbers are examples.

An ambient standard is a 'never to be exceeded' concentration for some pollutant at a particular location. Such standards may be measured in parts per million (ppm) or micro-grammes per cubic metre. Emission levels are limits on the maximum volume of pollution that can be emitted per unit of time and may be measured in pounds, tons, etc. In the 1960s some national governments set ambient standards for many air and water pollutants and expected local governments to convert these standards into emission limits for individual polluters. Attempts to enforce the emission standards set under this approach were often thrown out of court because there was insufficient scientific information about the linkage (transfer coefficients) between emissions at one location and ambient quality at other locations. It became necessary to give emission standards legal standing separate from ambient standards to make them enforceable.

By the 1970s it was clear that standards-based command and control policies were resulting in long legal battles, delays in enforcement, perverse incentives regarding research and development of new pollution-control technologies and were proving to be far from cost-effective. Economists have long been advocating policies that incorporate economic incentives (see **environmental economics**). These policies include emission taxes, abatement subsidies, transferable discharge permits, and deposit/refund schemes. The advantage of these policies is that firms are given more flexibility to seek the least-cost solution to their emissions problems. These policies have gained limited acceptance in some countries. Taxes may be imposed on all emissions or may be combined with an emission standard and imposed only on excess emissions. In the latter case taxes are being used to decriminalize excess emissions while simultaneously giving polluters an incentive not to delay compliance with the standard. Transferable permits may be tradeable in local markets or in national markets. Both taxes and emission permit trading can be made sensitive to local conditions if transfer coefficients are known.

See also: eco-taxes; tradeable emission permits

Further reading

Field, B. (1994) *Environmental Economics: An Introduction*, New York: McGraw-Hill.

Stavins, R. (1989) 'Harnessing Market Forces to Protect the Environment', *Environment* 31(4–7): 28–35

Organization for Economic Co-operation and Development (1992) *Climate Change: Designing a Practical Tax System*, Paris: OECD

—— (1992) *Climate Change: Designing a Tradeable Permit System*, Paris: OECD.

STANLEY R. KEIL

religions and the environment

When the religions which are currently called 'world' traditions (for example, Jewish, Hindu, Buddhist, Christian, Islamic, Sikh and Bahai) began, environmental issues were not the major pre-occupation that they are today. However, people from these faiths, along with those from indigenous religious traditions and new religious movements, are now demonstrating that they have either scriptural teachings, doctrines or practices which are supportive of environmental concerns and actions. In this way environmental concerns are paralleled by other issues, such as those focusing on the place of women. These issues are part of a new global perspective, a concern for the whole planet and its communities who are seen as interdependent. Economic issues, issues of population control, and matters of justice are all bound together with those focusing on the environment.

Attitudes and ideals which Hindus might present as aspects of their tradition on which to build an environmental awareness are wide-ranging. At the beginning of a dance, the Hindu dancer makes a gesture of respect (*namaskaram*) towards the earth and asks her forgiveness for trampling on her. This sense of respect is also extended to the cow who is protected as a symbol of life which gives so much to human beings. This protection may have economic roots since the cow traditionally provided not only milk but dung which is dried for burning, and the oxen to work the land, pull carts and carry loads. **Vegetarianism**, which is often linked in people's minds with environmental concerns, is seen as a significant spiritual practice for Hindus and for many arises out of the teaching that the eternal *atman* (self or soul) is present in all living things. This means that trees and bushes can also be the object of veneration and protection. The Hindu tradition is not anthropocentric and therefore does not see the natural world as the possession of human beings to use for their own satisfaction (see **anthropocentrism**). However, modern **India**, which is predominantly Hindu, does have severe environmental problems because of the pressures of a growing population as well as industrial exploitation. But an expert in Indian law reports that, 'The Indian higher judiciary has taken a lead in developing a uniquely Indian environmental jurisprudence which is fed by Hindu notions of an overriding order to which all life forms are subject' (Menski, in Morgan and Lawton, 1996: 51).

A fundamentalist Buddhist belief is that human and all other forms of life are part of an interdependent chain, and abstaining from harming other living things (*ahimsa*) is the first precept undertaken by Buddhists. The economist and environmental thinker E.F. Schumacher was impressed by Buddhist ideas and pointed out that, 'Man is the child of nature and not the master of nature' (1984: 84). He writes about the Buddha's attitude to all sentient beings, but especially to trees, as reverent and non-violent and some Buddhist monks in northern Thailand, where forests and the local communities dependent upon them are being destroyed, have engaged in social action to try to stop this exploitation. If one watches Zen monks meditate on a garden of rocks and sand, seeing it as a microcosm of the universe, and also observe them sweep leaves from moss gardens with great gentleness so that the moss is not damaged, and then use the leaves to fuel the fires for bath water, one has a sense of an attitude where human beings live in harmonious respect for the natural world. Not all Buddhists are vegetarians but an attitude of mindfulness and responsibility towards taking any life to sustain one's own is encouraged. The Tibetans have a wise saying that not too much of anything that is precious should be taken from the earth, as then its quality fades and the earth is destroyed.

The heartland of the Sikh tradition is the agricultural area of the Punjab in India. Many Sikhs there are farmers and were involved in the **green revolution** which began in the 1960s and which welcomed chemical fertilizers and modern **technology**. The full consequences of this, both economically and environmentally, are not yet fully known or acknowledged, but may present a future challenge. The Ari Granth 16 says 'the food which causes pain to the body and breeds evil in the mind is baneful', and contemporary Sikhs, particularly in the West where there is debate over issues such as **factory farming**, food additives, genetically modified crops and BSE (see **mad cow disease/BSE**), may avoid meats or other foods on the basis of this teaching as well as adopt traditional Indian attitudes towards any foods which are thought to encourage unwelcome character traits.

Members of the Jewish tradition point out that there is a great deal of teaching in the Torah and Talmud on which Jewish **environmental ethics** can build. Human beings are seen as partners with God in the creating of their world and its environment and should in this responsibility show it every respect. Examples of teaching are that land should be left fallow one year in every seven (Exodus 23: 10–11), and in the modern state of Israel those working the land in the religious kibbutzim will suspend produce trays above the soil for that sabbatical year because of a lack of space. Trees should not be harvested for profit until their fourth year (Leviticus 19: 20–25), and there is a special 'New Year for Trees' (*Tu B'Shevat*) Festival in Israel when trees are planted, including many given as gifts from abroad for special occasions such as bar Mitzvahs, birthdays or weddings. This is a great aid to reforestation as well as being a long-term commemoration of individual lives and events. Jewish teaching also makes provision for war and postwar situations when it is required that the environment should be damaged as little as possible in any conflict (Deuteronomy 20: 19–20).

So-called 'Christian' countries have been particularly involved in the last centuries' movements of colonialism, **industrialization** and global economics and these are inextricably linked with environmental exploitation. It has been suggested that Christian attitudes towards the natural world have contained too much sense of a God-given 'dominion' over and permission to 'use' the world, which derives from Christian use of the Genesis story, and that this has caused or allowed exploitation and the initial impetus in the experimentations of scientists for narrowly human purposes. A seminal and much debated article by Lynn **White** Jr in 1967 entitled, 'The Historical Roots of our Ecologic Crisis' suggested that Christians needed new **paradigms**. There is now much more emphasis on human **stewardship** over the rest of creation and that humans are part of rather than the lords of other living beings. Christians often focus on figures such as St Francis and his deep sense of brotherhood and sisterhood with the natural world and on the world as itself as a sacrament, a means of grace. They might highlight Jesus's affirmation of the 'lilies in the field' in comparison with human

activity. Many Christians are members of organizations such as **Friends of the Earth**, **Greenpeace** and the movement for alternative technology and are active in finding ways of living that do not harm or exploit the environment.

Muslims have a strong sense that the whole universe, sun, moon, stars, trees, birds and flowers are God's creation and 'signs' of His being, and that humans are *khalifa*, vice-regents under God with responsibility to care for what God has made. Muslims teach that they should be neither wasteful nor extravagant and should share with their fellow Muslims and others in need, hence the centrality of almsgiving. Muhammad is said to have chastised a man who ill-treated his camel and Muslims believe that their responsibility of care for other living things, for trees and water supplies will be taken into account on the day of judgement. The concepts of unity (*tawhid*) and harmony are very important and human beings have a particular responsibility to acknowledge the unity of all life under God and maintain a harmony in society and with the natural world. This may be lived out in a variety of ways, from the Indonesian sufi who collects pieces of wood from garbage heaps and carves them with Qur'anic calligraphy to those who make sure that in times of war the land is left so that the next season's crops can be planted.

It is often thought that those who belong to so-called indigenous religious traditions have maintained a sense of the sacredness of nature and humans as part of the natural world more strongly than have the so-called 'world' religions. Many religious people acknowledge how much they have come to respect and learn from the attitudes of first peoples of North America for example. There are now many self-styled animists among the ecology-warriors at demonstrations against new roadways. These people say they believe that 'everything that is, lives, and everything that lives is holy'. These approaches are also part of contemporary paganism, but not all pagans wish to see themselves as 'religious'.

See also: anthropocentrism; environmental ethics; indigenous peoples; New Age

References

Morgan, P. and Lawton, C. (eds) (1996) *Ethical*

Issues in Six Religious Traditions, Edinburgh: Edinburgh University Press.

Schumacher, E.F. (1984) *Small is Beautiful*, London: Fontana.

White, L. Jr (1967) 'The Historical Roots of our Ecologic Crisis', *Science*, 155: 1203–7.

Further reading

Breuilly, E. and Palmer, M. (eds) (1992) *Christianity and Ecology*, London: Cassell.

Kahlid, F. and O'Brien, J. (eds) (1992) *Islam and Ecology*, London: Cassell.

Klostermaier, K. (1973) 'World Religions and the Ecological Crisis', *Religion*, 3:2.

Prime, R. (1992) *Hinduism and Ecology*, London: Cassell.

Regenstien, L.G. (1991) *Replenish the Earth*, London: SCM Press.

Rose, E. (ed) (1992) *Judaism and Ecology*, London: Cassell.

Tucker, M.E. and Williams, D.R. (eds) (1997) *Buddhism and Ecology*, Cambridge, MA: Harvard University Press.

PEGGY MORGAN

renewable energy

Renewable energy harvesting exploits the day-to-day energy income from the sun, avoiding the need to extract the stored energy content found in **fossil fuels**, and offers the option of centralized *or* distributed placement of facilities for resource conversion. Forms of renewable energy include wind power, biomass, low-head hydroelectrical, ground-source conversions and **solar energy**, thermal and electrical.

Wind as an energy source is continually renewed. Wind energy can be captured to yield two classes of useful energy supply: mechanical pumping or electrical generation. Pumping is achieved with low-speed devices, electrical production with high-speed devices. Wind machines can be noisy and must be located, for safety purposes, at some distance from nearby buildings.

Biomass includes cord wood, wood pellets, paper pellets, and switch grass. These products can be burned in fireplaces, stoves, furnaces or boilers as a primary fuel or as a fuel amendment – e.g., combined with coal. Their combustion releases pollutants, CO_2 (carbon dioxide), SO_2 (sulphur dioxide), NO_X (nitrous oxides). Although the release of CO_2 can contribute to the greenhouse effect, the CO_2 released by the burning of biomass fuel can be offset by the sequestration of similar amounts of CO_2 by the concomitant and/or subsequent growth of plant matter – analytically, a zero net load on the atmosphere. Nonetheless, the combustion of biomass still releases SO_2 and NO_X which can contribute to **acid rain**; additionally, some heavy metals can be precipitated into the ash, which can contribute to contamination of the solid-waste stream. For this energy source, issues of reliability and transportation efficiency can be raised. Growing season production and rate of growth may not readily match the times of need and/or rates of consumption. Temporary storage may be required. When large acreage of distributed production must be brought to centralized points of end use, the energy extraction can be offset by energy consumed in the moving of this bulk material.

Low head hydro is a form of electrical production at point-of-use. Typically, a waterfall of less than 20 feet or a stream flow at a minimum of 30 gallons per minute is sufficient to turn small-scale turbines. The capacity and consistency of such electrical generation typically matches well the times of need and rates of consumption for the point-of-use end-user; grid-based transmission loss is virtually non-existent.

In contrast, conventional electrical energy production is achieved with turbines spinning at high speed, generating power in large centralized facilities, which gain their dependability through a reliance on the predictable flow of large volumes of water held in a reservoir. The highly centralized placement of such large-scale hydro-electric dams necessitates connection over considerable distance to the end-user and is inefficient, since line losses are experienced (see **dams/hydroelectric power**).

Ground source energy exploits the capacity of the Earth's mantle to store thermal energy. Specifically, soil can hold heat; in fact, soil temperatures remain very stable during the seasonal cycles whereas ambient air temperature can fluctuate substantially. Placement of heat-exchange coils in the soil can be used to extract energy during the heating season and to discharge (sink) energy during the cooling seasons.

Solar energy from the sun can be used as a thermal source, an illumination source and/or an electrical generation source. Direct or indirect thermal heating of spaces in buildings can be achieved with proper placement of windows. During winter heating seasons these windows can receive full sun; during summer cooling season, shading devices over such windows can block out the unwanted solar gain. Solar radiation (as direct beam and/or a reflected skyvault brightness) can be used to light buildings by properly placing skylights, roof monitors and/or window-integrated light shelves in the building shell. The use of such daylighting offsets the need for electrical lighting.

Solar radiation also can be converted directly to electrical power using photovoltaic cells. Batteries are used to store the electrical production, which occurs when the sun is shining, for use when the sun is not available. The electrical energy is stored in batteries as a direct current potential; it must be converted if used to power alternating current appliances.

Use of these forms of renewable energy involves the balancing of individual interests with group interests. Concerns include atmospheric loading, surface **water pollution**, and/or micro climatic changes, as well as resource-based rights – solar, wind and water access.

Further reading

Berger, J. (1997) *Charging Ahead: The Business of Renewable Energy and What It Means for America*, New York: Henry Holt.

Cole, N. and Skerrett, P.J. (1995) *Renewables Are Ready: People Creating Renewable Energy Solutions*, Lebanon, NH: Chelsea Green.

Johansson, T., Kelly, H., Reddy, A., Williams, R. and Burnham, L. (eds) (1993) *Renewable Energy: Sources for Fuels and Electricity*, Washington, DC and Covelo, CA: Island Press.

ROBERT J. KOESTER

resource mobilization theory

Social movement theorists from the USA, who were concerned to challenge the then dominant assumptions that social movements were spontaneous and disorganized, developed resource mobilization theory (RMT) in the 1970s. They argued that social movements usually arose out of pre-existing networks that provided the resources in time, money or social networks necessary to produce new mobilization. Such campaigns required systematic organization and rational planning to develop. Successful social movements were those best able to mobilize resources, and find influential allies. Good leaders, or political entrepreneurs prepared to take risks were central in this process. In explaining why social movements arise it was not the power of the issue or the emergence of new ideas that was central but the emergence of new political opportunities, the tactics of political leaders and the effectiveness of the movement's organization in generating mobilization.

According to RMT single social movement organizations should be understood as part of a 'social movement industry' in which different organizations co-operate and compete. According to this logic, organizations seek niches in the market and adopt strategies in response. **Environmental movements** seek to develop their own brand identities to remain distinctive. For instance, if **Greenpeace** gave up on high visibility protest it would be likely to undermine its subscription base.

In explaining how movements develop, RMT gives priority to the need to mobilize resources. Initially RMT advocates offered a general model in which institutionalization was part of the normal cycle of successful social movements and a sign of maturity. Hierarchical organization was more efficient than participatory organization and moderate groups were likely to have wider support and be able to amass more resources and achieve more political influence than more radical groups. RMT works well as a framework for understanding the institutionalization of professionalized EMOs (environmental movement organizations) such as the **Sierra Club** or Greenpeace. Yet critics argued that this general model failed to pay sufficient attention to the ideology of groups. Those with more radical ideas were not necessarily less effective than more moderate groups, but they made choices about how to act that were consistent with their ideology. For radical environmental groups hierarchies were part of the problem and challenging hierarchies was part of the solution to the environmental crisis. As a result RMT theorists have tended to accept that the appropriateness of action will depend on a group's ideology.

RMT is based upon the assumption that rational action involves the calculation of personal costs and benefits by individuals before they act. This calculation affects both why people join movements and how movement organizations develop. Organizations need to provide individuals with selective incentives that would not be available if they did not join. Organizations are also most likely to achieve their aims if they seek to minimize internal disagreements and maximize their influence upon policy-makers. Criticisms made of rational choice theory also apply to RMT. For instance, it is difficult to show that action in pursuit of collective goods such as the environment is based upon self-interest. Environmental movements provide no real material rewards for those who take part in their actions. Nor, contrary to the expectations of RMT, are environmental protests mobilized from above by EMOs. Critical events seem to generate most protest activity and most action is by local groups, or **non-violent direct action** (NVDA) networks, independent of the major EMOs. The membership of formal organizations tends to rise after protests die down. So protests are not a result of members providing more resources to the movement, but rather might be seen as a more limited and distant kind of commitment, which becomes more attractive when protest is in abeyance.

RMT works well as a framework for understanding the institutionalization of professionalized EMOs such as the Sierra Club or Greenpeace. These groups have invested more in research, media and marketing in order to maximize their influence upon the policy process. The analysis of the use of resources can also be applied to all environmental campaigns. However, while useful in explaining social movement organizations it is not a general theory of social movement action. Social movements are not equivalent to organizations. Although organizations may be part of a movement, they also include informal networks linking groups and individuals. Furthermore, action by environmental activists cannot be explained solely by calculations based upon individual interest. Instead resource mobilization theory needs to be used alongside consideration of the identity that governs the appropriateness of action and gives it meaning.

See also: Friends of the Earth; National Audubon Society; political opportunity structures

Further reading

Morris, A. and Mueller, C.M. (eds) (1992) *Frontiers in Social Movement Theory*, New Haven: Yale University Press.

Zald, M.N. and McCarthy, J. (eds) (1987) *Social Movements in an Organizational Society*, New Brunswick, NJ: Transaction Books.

BRIAN DOHERTY

restoration, ecological

Ecological restoration is the name given to the intentional restoration or repair of an environment, place or some other aspect of the environment back to its original condition and character before it was transformed or disturbed by human settlement or productive activity. Much of the debate around ecological restoration centres on the practical and philosophical implications of trying to create or 'fake' **nature** (Elliott, 1982). Some hold that a restored **landscape** is less 'valuable' than a 'natural' one, since the former is analogous to a copy of the latter. Once humans restore landscapes their value is diminished relative to the 'original'. However, while there is philosophical debate concerning ecological restoration, there is no suggestion that it ought not to be done. Where there is doubt as to whether it ought to be done is where claims of future restoration of ecosystems or landscapes are used to justify present ecological disruption.

References

Elliott (1982) 'Faking Nature', *Inquiry*, 25.

JOHN BARRY

Rhine River Commission

The International Commission for the Protection of the Rhine (ICPR) was established on 11 July 1950 in Basel, Switzerland, and consists of five member states: Germany, the Netherlands, Luxembourg, France, and Switzerland. The ICPR was created to address the increasing levels of pollution found in the Rhine due to rapid **industrialization** and population growth. The commission has since evolved into an international conservation agency concerned with the ecological rehabilitation of the entire Rhine River.

The mission of the ICPR is to provide for **sustainable development** of the entire Rhine ecosystem, guarantee it as a source of safe drinking water, improve the sediment quality of the river, and provide for environmentally sound flood protection. In order to achieve these goals the ICPR has established the Ecological Master Plan for the Rhine River, which calls for the restoration of the entire Rhine River Valley.

Further reading

International Commission for the Protection of the Rhine (5 March 2001) *History* and *Characteristics of the Rhine* at
URL: http://www.iksr.org/icpr/welcome.html.

JON E. FITCH

Rifkin, Jeremy

b. 1945, Chicago, USA

Activist and social critic

Jeremy Rifkin is the President of the Foundation on Economic Trends located in Washington, DC. An economics graduate of the Wharton School of the University of Pennsylvania, he is widely known as an activist and social critic. He is the author of over ten books ranging from energy and environmental concerns to issues on food supply and genetic modification. His timely publications address the future and unintended consequences of **technology** and modifications to the earth's natural systems. An excellent speaker, he raises fundamental questions and proposes radical solutions to the problems he confronts.

Rifkin's questioning of new technologies and well-accepted assumptions makes him a highly controversial figure. He has lectured at over five hundred universities and has testified before the US Congress on various governmental policies. As a result of his work he has been recognized as one of the most influential people in the USA in helping shape public debate.

Further Reading

Rifkin, J (1992) *Beyond Beef: The Rise and Fall of the Cattle Culture*, New York: Dutton.

THOMAS LOWE

Rio Conference 1992

The United Nations Conference on Environment and Development (UNCED), often referred to as the Earth Summit or the Rio Conference, took place in Rio de Janeiro, Brazil, in June 1992. The Summit was hailed as a key opportunity to save the planet from environmental destruction. Yet from the outset, it was clear that the conference would fall far short of that aim. This entry describes and explains the background to the conference; considers the agenda of the conference, and examines the role of the parallel NGO conference; looks at the UNCED agreements; and assesses whether the UNCED really did set us on a the path to sustainable development.

The UNCED conference was attended by representatives of over 170 states. A parallel NGO conference attracted over 20,000 people representing over 600 NGOs. UNCED took place amid great fanfare; and there were great expectations of the conference. Yet even before the conference took place, northern and southern governments had different views on what the conference should be about. At the most general level, southern governments perceived the challenge in terms of a **development** crisis, while their northern counterparts preferred to see the problem as an environmental crisis. The concession from the North was to hold a conference on environment and development. Thus, **environmental management** and **sustainable development**, two sides of the same coin, were to be addressed together. Thus the concerns of the northern industrialized states and the southern developing states would both be attended to. Why did UNCED take place when it did, in the way it did, amidst great publicity and hype?

To understand UNCED, we have to go back at least 20 years previously, and see how interest was developing in environmental problems and also in sustainable development in all corners of the globe.

The **Stockholm Conference** in 1972 represented a milestone in the history of environmental concern, even though the concerns expressed there were mainly those of developed industrialized states. At Stockholm, there was the recognition of the legitimate place of environmental issues in international relations. Also, the clear link between environment and development was established in a public international forum. The **United Nations Environment Programme** (UNEP) was established as an outcome of Stockholm.

Thereafter, there was a steady build up of interest in regional, international, then global, environmental problems, especially within certain international institutions, and amongst grassroots groups. Over the 1970s and 1980s, there was a spread of environmental awareness worldwide, as green ideas were taken up at the level of citizenry. Non-governmental organizations, green movements and green parties sprung up in the North, South, East and West. A series of environmental disasters and incidents heightened awareness. At the level of international institutions, UNEP played a catalytic role in mobilizing interest, awareness and concern within UN agencies. During the 1980s there was a proliferation of environmental funds and facilities in various multilateral organizations.

The second half of the 1980s saw the reduction in superpower tensions, and the negotiation of arms reduction agreements between the USA and USSR. The changing nature of the superpower relationship created the political space for issues hitherto classified as low politics to assume a more important role. President Gorbachev, impelled by domestic economic difficulties, took advantage of the opportunity to promote internationally his new conception of global security, in which the environment, disarmament and economy were inextricably linked. The passing of the Cold War presented an opportunity for discussion of global problems that depend on international co-operation if they are to be addressed with any possibility of success. The environment was high on the list.

The **Brundtland Commission** of 1987 had highlighted the importance of sustainable development, that is development that meets the needs of present generations without compromising the ability of future generations to meet their needs. The idea that growth is necessary for environmental protection and sustainable economic development was accepted by governments, and the outstanding issues concerned how best to achieve this. Market-based instruments were winning the day over more traditional standard-setting controls. With the passing of the command economies in eastern Europe and the former USSR, there seemed to be a growing global acceptance of what global sustainable development required.

The challenge for Rio was to take the world back from the brink of environmental disaster by promoting the principle of global **sustainability** over parochial state interest. It was hoped and expected then that Rio would result in global agreements that would put the entire world on a more secure footing towards sustainable development. However, the opinions expressed at the parallel or 'alternative summit' were far less optimistic about what Rio could realistically achieve.

The Rio Conference was preceded by a series of preparatory committees where agreements were largely negotiated in advance. These were mostly interstate affairs, though there was an opportunity for some NGOs to participate in some of them. Ultimately, five key agreements resulted from UNCED: The **Framework Convention on Climate Change**; the Convention on Biological

Diversity; **Agenda 21**; the Forest Principles; and the Rio Declaration. Unfortunately these for the most part lacked binding quality. Moreover, the record of rich country commitments contained within these agreements was very poor. President Bush's comment just before UNCED that the US lifestyle was non-negotiable was borne out in the lack of specific policy commitments in all the UNCED agreements, the lack of new finance, the lack of far-reaching **technology transfer**, and the wholesale omission of attention to and targets on fundamentals like debt repayment and terms of trade.

One of the issues highlighted by the alternative summit was that of agenda-setting. Whose interests did Rio really represent? Who had been involved in drawing up the agenda? Why were certain fundamental issues, for example, consumption and population, omitted from the agenda? Why was there no discussion of desertification? And even more fundamentally, why was there no place for a discussion of what constitutes unsustainable development? For many in the alternative summit, the Rio conference, in avoiding discussion of environmental degradation that ensues from routine processes of modernity itself, was missing the point. The link between environment and development was there on paper and in rhetoric, but it was never really on the conference agenda in a serious way. How can **global warming**, deforestation and **ozone depletion** be discussed outside the context of industrial development and modernization? (See also **forest management**.)

Politicization in the run up to Rio shaped and constrained the agenda. Some believe that the involvement ·of **multinational and transnational corporations** (TNCs) in contributing to the funding of the conference, for example through the Business Council for Sustainable Development, also gave them undue influence on the framing of the global environmental challenge, which was in fact a development challenge. Maurice **Strong**, who ran the Conference on behalf of the UN Secretary General had close ties with the business community. In the run up to Rio, those transnationals were able to present themselves as legitimate players alongside national governments. They publicly signed up to the notion of sustainable development, but the mechanics of how this might be achieved – other than the magic of the market – were not discussed. Moreover, in the huge Agenda 21, all references to transnationals were deleted.

On balance, UNCED did help to give the environment higher diplomatic profile. However, the conference did not do much to put the globe onto a more sustainable footing. While there were tangible outcomes, such as the creation of the **Commission on Sustainable Development**, these, like the conference itself, have not lived up to expectations. Short-term state interest, plus the profit motive which drives transnational corporations, have impeded the development of the truly global response required to tackle long-term environmental/developmental problems. Moreover, critics fear that UNCED contributed to the legitimation of a notion of sustainable development which is inherently flawed.

See also: global environmental governance; North/South divide

Further reading

Chatterjee, P. and Finger, M. (eds) (1994) *The Earth Brokers: Power, Politics and World Development*, London: Routledge.

Grubb, M. (1993) *The Earth Summit Agreements London*, Royal Institute of International Affairs/ Earthscan.

Kenny, M. *et al.* (1996) 'Debate: Re-evaluating Rio', *New Political Economy* 1(3): 399–417.

CAROLINE THOMAS

risk assessment

In its ideal form, risk assessment can be seen as a multi-disciplinary decision-making tool that allows policy-makers to make informed judgements concerning the nature of the hazard inherent within a given activity. Risk assessment is a broad term that includes the process of risk analysis (concerned with the identification and quantification of risk) and the process of risk acceptability and management. There are often inherent tensions between these two elements of risk assessment and this, ultimately, centres on the relationship between scientific and public expertise and the legitimacy of knowledge.

Figure 1 shows the main components of the process of risk analysis.

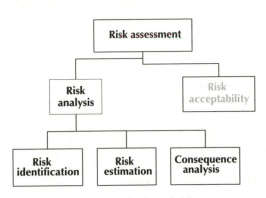

Figure 1 Rowe's categorization of risk assessment: risk analysis
Source: adapted from Rowe, 1977

Criticisms centre on the nature of the evidential basis for risk estimation and the willingness of 'experts' to accept a risk in the absence of any proof of harm. This so-called 'burden of proof' has been an important factor in affecting the willingness of many within the expert community to accept as legitimate any calculation of risk that is not built upon a priori evidence (usually considered in terms of evidence of harm rather than a proof of safety).

Where the process of risk assessment does prove to be problematic is in terms of the acceptability of the risks identified (especially in terms of the relevance of the probabilities ascribed to the hazard) and the relative weights that should be given to the views of the (legitimated) experts compared to those who are deemed to be a risk. This has proved to be an area of considerable controversy and some have argued that the views of local publics should be given much greater weight in debates concerning hazard, in a process often termed as 'participatory risk assessment' (see Fischer, 1990, 1995; and also Irwin, 1995; Irwin and Wynne, 1996). The process of risk acceptability centres around the relationship between the perceptions held by the various participants in the

debate, the ways in which those risks are evaluated and, subsequently, traded-off against other criteria (Figure 2). In the early years of debates on hazard, the view taken by industry was often that the public operated on a 'deficit model', that is they had insufficient knowledge (and information) upon which to judge the nature of the risk. Those members of the corporate (and often the governmental) technocracy, on the other hand, were deemed both to be trained in the use of risk techniques and to have sufficient knowledge and experience to judge the hazards in a non-emotive manner. Clearly, such a dichotomous position is no longer legitimate and there have been many cases of hazard where the views of local publics and their associate experts have been proved to be more accurate than those of the legitimized body of expertise. This raises a number of important questions about the nature, legitimacy and dissemination of knowledge and the manner in which decisions on hazard are ultimately taken. In more recent years there have been calls for a more precautionary approach to dealing with risk, particularly in the wake of the **Three Mile Island accident**, **Bhopal disaster** and **Chernobyl** and this raises important questions about the communication of risk and the dissemination of knowledge.

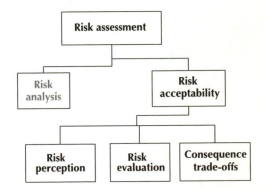

Figure 2 Rowe's categorization of risk assessment: risk acceptability
Source: adapted from Rowe, 1977

The process of risk assessment will ultimately be an effective policy-making tool only if it is open, transparent and recognizes that different forms of knowledge and expertise exist. Ultimately, a failure to move towards a more participative form of discourse around risk will render the process politically sterile.

See also: Alarm UK; Brent Spar controversy; civic science; environmental ethics; global environmental governance; mad cow disease/ BSE; precautionary principle; risk society; Seveso disaster; technology assessment

References

Fischer, F. (1990) *Technology and The Politics of Expertise*, Newbury Park: Sage.
—— (1995) 'Hazardous Waste Policy, Community Movements and the Politics of Nimby: Participatory Risk Assessment in the USA and Canada', in F. Fischer and M. Black (eds) *Greening Environmental Policy. The Politics of a Sustainable Future*, London: Paul Champan Publishing, pp. 165–82.
Irwin, A. (1995) *Citizen Science*, London: Routledge.
Irwin, A. and Wynne, B. (eds) (1996) *Misunderstanding Science?: The Public Reconstruction of Science and Technology*, Cambridge: Cambridge University Press.
Rowe, W.D. (1977) *The Anatomy of Risk*, New York: Wiley.

DENIS SMITH

risk society

Ulrich Beck (1992) uses the idea of risk society to denote an epoch in which qualitatively new types of risks – which are not limitable, not accountable, not compensatable or insurable – come to dominate social debate. In risk society, politics has a new orientation – to the distribution of threats rather than of goods – and a new character, for while threats can be hard to pin down as calculable risks, equally unpredictable are the alliances of resistance to them which can be formed. If ecological movements highlighting threats have been unexpectedly successful in recent decades, what remains is the need to transform an apocalyptic view of threats so as to discern opportunities for action. If threats are necessarily perceived through multiple media of representation, in law, science, public relations and politics – with all the possibilities of manipulation this entails – then a key factor in reducing them is a more transparent regime of accountability, which Beck sees as involving the expansion of **democracy** into previously walled-off areas of science, **technology**, and industry.

References

Beck, U. (1992) *Risk Society: Towards a New Modernity*, London: Sage.

TIM HAYWARD

Robertson, James

b. 1928, UK

Writer

James Robertson is an 'eminently reasonable revolutionary' and leading figure in the 'new economics' movement in the UK. Robertson's career included working in the Cabinet Office in the 1960s, and since then, over 25 years as an independent writer and thinker on alternative social and economic **paradigms**, continuing the work of his friend E.F. Schumacher. His work on a range of issues promotes a 'SHE' (sane, humane, ecological) future, encompassing ecological tax reform, multiple currencies, citizen's income, diversified forms of work and livelihoods ('future work'), decentralized energy and transport, and new conceptions of wealth ('future wealth'). He has advised policymakers in the UK, and in 1997 briefed the European Commission on 'The New Economics Of Sustainable Development'. In the 1980s he set up The Other Economic Summit, and subsequently the **New Economics Foundation**. Robertson, together with his wife Alison Pritchard, produced the *Turning Point 2000* networking newsletter from 1976 till 2000.

See also: basic income; sustainable development

GILL SEYFANG

Robin Wood

Robin Wood is an environmental, non-governmental organization with strongly ecologist leanings. Founded in 1982 as a splinter group of **Greenpeace** Germany, the group shares the anti-nuclear stance and direct action emphasis of its parent organization, but rejects the centralized and hierarchical structures. In the early years the thematic focus was on **acid rain** and dying forests in Germany, later the perspective widened to indigenous forests and logging world wide (see **forest management**). Other campaigning topics now include **transportation** and energy policy. Structurally, the emphasis is on regional action groups (currently about 20, all located in major cities), setting their own agenda. Specialist groups (tropical forests, transportation, energy) prepare and co-ordinate national campaigns. In the late 1980s professional administration and fundraising methods boosted the membership and budget, but Robin Wood was never intended to become a mass organization. Since the early 1990s the membership has declined slightly (and in 2001 was around 2,500 members).

INGOLFUR BLÜHDORN

Romanticism

As a literary and philosophical movement, Romanticism was initially fuelled by the work of **Rousseau** in France, Goethe in Germany and the poets Coleridge and Wordsworth in Britain. Emphasizing the role of spontaneity, imagination and personal feeling in creativity as well as liberty of individual expression and an aesthetic concern for unspoilt nature and rural tradition, it flourished in western Europe and America from the 1750s to approximately 1870. Its defence of individuality, celebration of the authentic feeling of the common person and often melancholic appreciation of vanishing **nature** made Romanticism politically radical, and it can be seen as proto-green in linking these themes. Though often regarded as anti-rationalist, romantic thinkers sometimes attempted

to reconcile the traditional western cultural split between feeling and reason, as evidenced by Goethe's attempts to reintegrate emotion into scientific method.

PIERS H.G. STEPHENS

Roosevelt, Theodore

b. 27 October 1858, New York, USA;
d. 6 January 1919, New York

Politician

Theodore Roosevelt was a nationalist, reformer, philanthropist, and naturalist who utilized his political power as New York governor and US President to advance progressivism's conservationist cause of wisely managing natural resources. His personal affinity with **nature** extends to his childhood and emerged early in many of his written works and support for conservationist organizations like the Boone and Crockett Club. His gubernatorial efforts to preserve forests, manage **development**, and fight pollution continued this focus. The presidency enabled him to promote federal **stewardship** of the country's natural resources through programmes like the 1902 Newlands Act establishing major western irrigation projects and the creation of 51 wildlife refuges. He doubled the number of **national parks** to ten, preserved over 150 million acres of national forestland, and utilized the 1906 Antiquities Act to preserve 18 national monuments including the Grand Canyon. He also advanced conservation with the restructuring of the National Forest Service under Gifford **Pinchot** and promoting conferences. After his presidency, he continued his efforts through leading scientific expeditions to Africa and Brazil.

Reference

Brands, H.W. (1997) *Theodore Roosevelt: The Last Romantic*, New York: Basic Books.

ERICH G. FRANKLAND

Rousseau, Jean-Jacques

b. 1712, Geneva, Switzerland; d. 1778, Ermenoville, Paris, France

Philosopher

Going against the grain of **Enlightenment** thought, Rousseau was one of the first to reverse the view that the 'Natural' was inferior to the 'Artificial', that a less complex and 'advanced' society was necessarily inferior to an advanced civilized society such as those which existed in eighteenth-century Europe. Rousseau questioned the 'progressive' character of civilized society as representing an advance over previous stages of human social evolution. His critique of the 'artificial', and laying the blame of social ills on the corrupting effects of 'civilization', constitutes one of the first critiques of the Enlightenment from a green perspective. In this he anticipated a key aspect of the romantic critical reaction to the industrialism of the nineteenth century, and his critique of modernity and its conception of **progress** is something that is at the heart of the later emergence of green thought in the twentieth century.

See also: noble savage, myth of; Romanticism

JOHN BARRY

Royal Society for the Protection of Birds

The Royal Society for the Protection of Birds is Europe's largest conservation organization. Its origins are Victorian; it has a million members, 250,000 acres of nature reserve, and national and international offices including one in Brussels. Over time, its style has fluctuated from a radical to a consensual one. It is active in legislative, executive, judicial and electoral processes and has an outstanding legislative record as an agent of influence, a channel of representation, a source of information and expertise, and communicator to specialized sectors of society. On an executive level, through grants and contracts, it has become an officially recognized partner of government in the formulation and administration of public money. It is not only an accepted and valued political participant in, but almost indistinguishable from government itself. In 1985, the government of Ghana and the Society, a key partner of BirdLife International, signed an agreement to conserve seashore birds and their Ghanaian habitat. Its future challenges include **sustainable development** and effective mobilization of its mature and conservative membership base.

PENELOPE LAW

Ruckelshaus, William

b. 24 July 1932, Indianapolis, Indiana, USA

Politician, administrator

William Ruckelshaus grew up in a family active in the Indiana Republican party. He received degrees from Princeton University and Harvard Law School. His first experience with environmental policy came as the Deputy Attorney General assigned to the Indiana Board of Health in the early 1960s. In 1965, he won a seat in the Indiana House of Representatives, and became its Majority Leader. After losing a US Senate race in 1968, he took a legal post in the Nixon Administration. In 1970 Ruckelshaus became the first Administrator of the **Environmental Protection Agency** (EPA), where he served until 1973. He was a high profile Administrator, who was not reluctant to initiate legal actions against big polluters. Ruckelshaus returned to private life, and became the Senior Vice President of the Weyerhaeuser Company, a large timber corporation (cited by the EPA for **air pollution** and **water pollution** violations). In 1983 Ruckelshaus began a second term as EPA Administrator. He restored the morale of the agency after the turmoil associated with his predecessor Anne **Burford**, and removed the EPA as an issue of Republican vulnerability before the 1984 presidential campaign. He returned to private life in 1985, and later became the Chief Executive Officer of Brown Ferris Industries, which manages solid wastes throughout the country.

Further reading

URL: http://www.epa.gov/history/publications/ruck/.02htm.

E. GENE FRANKLAND

Russian Federation/Former Soviet Union

Proponents of the socialist economic system that existed in the Soviet Union until 1991 hoped that it would prove a superior form of economic organization. The planned economy would be more efficient and fairer than **capitalism**, and also more rational, since planners would be able to take account of **externalities** in their decision such as environmental pollution. However the reality was very different. The policy of growth at all costs made the Soviet Union into one of the most polluted countries on the planet. By 1991 when the communist system collapsed, some experts estimated that 45 regions constituting more than three per cent of the total land area had experienced 'catastrophic' (i.e. irreparable) environmental damage. The 15 Soviet successor states inherited this appalling legacy, and possessed very limited resources to deal with it.

Ideological, cultural and political origins of Soviet environmental destruction

A number of theoretical aspects of Marxism–Leninism were significant in shaping Soviet attitudes to the natural environment. In the materialist view of history, **progress** was inevitable, and the final goal of human history, **communism**, determined. Full communism would be a situation of abundance. Underlying this was an assumption of inexhaustible natural resources. Historical progress and technological advance would overcome any problems of scarcity. New resources would constantly become available. Marx's labour theory of value held that a commodity (including all natural resources) was worthless until labour is added to it. Thus in socialist economies energy supplies were always cheap and plentiful, and natural resources such as water were virtually free. Little or no attention was paid to conservation, and industries were highly wasteful.

The superiority of the socialist system would also be reflected by its ability to reshape the natural environment on a massive scale. The Soviet period saw a number of seemingly impossible 'victories' over nature: the Belamor Canal from the **Baltic** to the White Sea, 140 miles tunnelled through ice and rock in 20 months (at the cost of countless prisoners' lives); the Great Stalin Plan for the Transformation of Nature; the Virgin Lands scheme; construction of the Baikal–Amur mainline railway; the irrigation of the Central Asian desert that culminated in the **Aral Sea** disaster. There were even plans to divert the Great Siberian rivers southwards.

This preoccupation with bigness was also applied to industrial **development**. The Soviet Union was to have the largest chemical plants and biggest power stations. Industries were to be concentrated together in 'territorial production complexes' (thus concentrating their polluting effect). Daring and scale were much more important than the usefulness of a new project. The stress was always on extensive rather than intensive growth, that is on using more resources rather than on using existing ones more efficiently.

A number of features of the system of economic planning contributed to the problem. The concentration on gross output at all costs meant that enterprises had no incentive to pay attention to objectives other than production. The deliberate policy of full utilization of resources meant that outdated machinery was rarely replaced: to stop using it threatened achievement of targets. The planned economy was averse to innovation. To introduce more efficient (or environmentally friendly) machinery or processes threatened the plan targets on which wages and bonuses depended. State ownership effectively meant no ownership, with nobody taking responsibility for damage to the environment.

In the famous saying, the USA had a military industrial complex, the Soviet Union *was* a military industrial complex. The defence industry was allocated around a quarter of national income, and operated in conditions of total secrecy. Nuclear, chemical and biological waste was casually discarded, and even the existence of such waste was a state secret.

The nature of the Soviet political system was the heart of the problem. Its essence was the absence of politics. Decision-making was by a small clique of senior Communist Party officials, among whom environmental interests were unrepresented. Means for criticizing or reversing official decisions were very limited. The priority was always more production, especially in the areas of heavy industry and military hardware. So while there were laws and regulations guarding against pollution, these were not properly applied, and enforcement efforts were drastically underfunded. Often the same ministry that was responsible for production was responsible also for checking that rules were obeyed, with predictable consequences.

Air

The quality of the air in many cities of the former Soviet Union remains dire. The main pollution sources are heavy industry and cars. Dramatic falls in production in the 1990s as well as some switching from coal to natural gas for energy production led to significant declines in emissions of polluting substances. Greenhouse gas emissions are typical: for example, Russian CO_2 emissions decreased by 37 per cent between 1990 and 1996, but Russia and Ukraine between them were still contributing more than 8 per cent of world energy-related carbon dioxide emissions (OECD, 1999: 192). In terms of air quality, it was still estimated that, for the Russian Federation, two-thirds of the population lived in places where maximum allowable concentrations of air pollutants were exceeded at some points in the year. Around one-third lived in cities where these were exceeded by ten times or more (OECD, 1999: 57). Respiratory diseases, **lead poisoning**, congenital defects, blood diseases and cancers were all inevitable consequences. It wasn't just human beings who suffered: there were severe problems of **acid rain** in several regions.

Water

The former Soviet Union is blessed with abundant water resources, but these are largely concentrated in the north and east, away from heavily populated areas. Consequently, some parts suffer from periodic shortages. The most serious problems are in Central Asia, where the overuse of the major rivers has led to the Aral Sea catastrophe.

Virtually all rivers, lakes and inland seas in the former Soviet Union as well as many ground water supplies and coastal areas are moderately, some heavily, polluted. Causes vary from location to location. Most water treatment facilities are inadequate or outdated, meaning that sewage from municipalities and wastewater from industry is released incompletely or not at all treated: only about 10 per cent was fully treated in Russia in 1996 (OECD, 1999: 76). Standards are in any case often ignored. It is estimated that around 30 per cent of **pesticides**, fertilizers and defoliants end up in rivers, lakes and reservoirs. Pollutants include petroleum products, heavy metals, phenol, organic substances, nitrogen compounds and sulphates. Particularly critical groundwater and river contamination from industrial effluents has occurred in among others the Donbas, southern Urals and lower Volga regions.

Thermal pollution from nuclear power stations severely disrupted the ecosystems of many rivers and lakes. The **Kyshtym nuclear accident** poisoned nearby rivers and lakes, and other nuclear plants discharged (either directly or by seepage from underground stores) substantial amounts of radioactive waste into the Tom and Yenisey rivers. The former Soviet Union's continental seas and many of its other coastlines are severely contaminated. Some experts in the mid-1990s expected the Black Sea to have just 10–15 years more life. In contravention of the 1972 London Convention, the Soviet Union dumped nuclear waste in the Barents and Kara and in the Far Eastern seas, a practice that Russia continued in the 1990s.

Governments in many Soviet successor states simply could not guarantee safe drinking water to their citizens. Some smaller towns had no running water supplies at all. In Russia at the end of the 1990s, around half the population consumed water that failed to meet some standards (OECD, 1999: 75). Cardio-vascular, gastro-intestinal, kidney and urinary disorders were common, and the risk of cholera epidemics was high. Pollution or eutrophication of water resources, as well as the practice of creating large numbers of dams and reservoirs on major rivers and (often illegal) overfishing, put major pressure on fish stocks. The population of (caviar-producing) sturgeon in the Volga, for example, was decimated. Drastic quotas have had to be introduced for all inland and coastal sources.

Land

Soviet agriculture suffered greatly from the passion for the technological quick fix. The virtual elimination of private **agriculture** after Stalin's collectivization of agriculture in the 1930s created an ownership structure, in the system of state and collective farms, which proved hopelessly inadequate from the point of view of soil conservation and husbandry. State ownership meant in effect no ownership and frequently negligent practices.

Responses by the leadership to the severe problems of Soviet agriculture included mechanization, chemicalization and irrigation. Each brought its own environmental problems. Gigantomania meant that communist tractors and farm machinery had to be the world's biggest. If capitalist tractors had wheels, so must Soviet ones, regardless of the fact that caterpillar tracks distribute weight more evenly. Consequently soil compaction became a major issue. Similarly Khrushchev's campaign to chemicalize agriculture from the 1960s concentrated on Soviet fertilizer output, rather than the more important issue, its application. Thus fertilizers and **pesticides** were often used excessively or inappropriately, seriously contaminating farmland and surrounding water supplies. While their use has declined in the 1990s, residues remain a significant problem, and many foodstuffs are seriously contaminated. Similarly, expansion of the amount of irrigated land in southern parts of the former Soviet Union in the 1970s and 1980s was carried out without regard to long-term consequences, and frequently led to severe waterlogging, salinization and erosion.

Adding to the pressures on soil resources were industrial emissions and wastes, which led to many instances of excessive concentrations of nitrates, chlorides and fluorine, as well as several heavy metals, oil and petrochemicals. The **Russian nuclear industry**, both directly through accidents and indirectly through nuclear waste disposal, added to the pressures. Another disastrous legacy of the Cold War was the problem of stockpiles of chemical and biological weapons. No less than 53 cities in the former Soviet Union produced, tested or stored chemical weapons. Russia formally declared in the mid-1990s that she possessed 40,000 tonnes of these (mostly nerve gases such as sarin), but some activists estimated that as many as half a million tonnes more had been buried or dumped at sea in the postwar period. Furthermore, by the end of the 1990s, half of all agricultural land was eroding or considered highly susceptible to soil erosion (OECD, 1999: 109). Regions where the humus content was not declining steadily were the exception, and by some estimates Soviet farmland was scarred by a million kilometres of ravines and gullies (Peterson, 1993: 97). Poor agricultural practices had combined disastrously with a natural environment that in any event was prone to wind and water erosion.

Forests

One-third of the former Soviet Union, including 47 per cent of Russia, is forested. This represents about one-fifth of the world's forested area, although substantially less biomass, since tropical forests are much more abundant. Most of this resource is located in remote areas of Siberia and the Far East with fragile environments and low growth potential. Russia's forests and taiga, as well as being a significant carbon sink, are home to 300 species of birds, 100 species of mammals, over 40,000 types of insects and 15 species of reptiles.

In the Soviet period, the timber industry tended to treat forests as an abundant resource to be exploited as intensively as possible. This happened most heavily in the more accessible parts of European Russia, meaning that forest cover in much of the land west of the Urals decreased by half or more (Pryde, 1995: 55). The amount of logging in Russia decreased very substantially in the post-communist period, to about one-third of 1990 levels, due to economic decline and increases in fuel and transportation prices. However, inadequate funding for reforestation and illegal logging meant that accessible resources continued to be depleted or even exhausted. Overcutting of mature trees, a rise in the number of forest fires, and dieback and disease as a result of **air pollution** all remained significant ongoing issues.

Desertification

Around ten per cent of the former Soviet Union consists of deserts and semi deserts. In 1970, only around a tenth of this was true desert, but by 1990, the proportion was 20–30 per cent and rising: a man-made catastrophe of spectacular proportions (Golitsyn, 1993: 38). Rapidly expanding deserts included much of Central Asia, the Tengiz region of Kazakhstan on the Caspian Sea coast, and the Kalmyk steppes in southern Russia, the first man-made desert in Europe. By the mid-1990s over 80 per cent of Kalmykia's territory was in the grip of desertification, and almost half was either severely or very severely affected. Surrounding areas were increasingly vulnerable.

Among the causes of this was reckless year-round pasturing of cattle, which had previously been done on a seasonal basis. This degraded the quality of vegetation cover and exacerbated erosion. Overuse of water for livestock, removal of trees for firewood, and large-scale development of heavy industry in the context of highly vulnerable ecosystems all contributed to the disasters. Equivalent pressures were also placed on the Russian **Arctic**, where tundra was greatly affected by industrial development and overgrazing by reindeer.

Biodiversity

Russia is estimated to be home to 7 per cent of the world's **biodiversity** of mammals, 8 per cent of birds, and 8 per cent of trees. Rather less is known about insects, lower plants, and aquatic life. Much of the country remains true wilderness, containing many vast, unique ecosystems such as **Lake Baikal** and many forest or Arctic locations.

The Russian Red Book, where **endangered species** are recorded, identified 415 endangered animal species and 533 threatened species of plants

(OECD, 1999: 107). Of endangered vertebrates, around 14 per cent were globally endangered. These included such well-known examples as, in the Arctic, the Siberian crane, snow goose, red-breasted goose, wild reindeer, polar bear; in the Far East the Siberian tiger and snow leopard; in Kalmykia the saiga antelope; and offshore several species of whales. Hunting and poaching of the rarer species were an increasing problem through the 1990s.

Not all the news was bad. A system of *zapovedniki* (nature preserves) had predated the Russian revolution, and was expanded throughout the Soviet period. As of 1999, Russia had 98 genuine wildernesses in which economic activity of any kind was prohibited, as well as 34 **national parks** and a number of other protected areas, together amounting to around 5.5 per cent of her land area. Other ex-Soviet republics had similar systems. Despite severe underfunding, conservation efforts had led to some significant achievements. This was in no small part due to the efforts of a number of committed and ecologically aware Soviet scientists and ecologists (Weiner, 1999).

Conclusions and future prospects

The evidence of the Soviet experience, then, is that the centrally planned economy is disastrous for the natural environment. The fundamental problem with central planning was that, while it paid lip service to conservation in the form of numerous laws and decrees, economic actors always knew that the priority was something else: output at any cost. Plan fulfilment was what people's wages, life chances, and under Stalin often even their lives depended on. This led to a destructive treadmill of production for its own sake, where natural resources were used to build machines that were used to extract more natural resources. Bureaucrats responsible for environmental protection were subordinate to producers as a deliberate choice.

The Soviet experience is also an object lesson in humankind's ability to blind ourselves to the long-term consequences of our actions. Environmental damage became a state secret, because it undermined the image of communism as a superior system. Such arrogance directly created many public health disasters, with life expectancy plummeting at rates unprecedented in peacetime in many parts of the former Soviet Union (see **health and the environment**). The combination of high **technology** and political dictatorship is literally a poisonous one.

In some ways, post-communist economic collapse has been good news for the environment. Drastic falls in production also meant less environmental damage. However, serious lack of investment in, for example, pollution control technologies meant that any economic recovery in the former Soviet Union would simply see old problems reasserting themselves. Russian industry, for example, became *less* energy efficient in the 1990s.

Increased openness to the outside world, and increased tolerance of internal political pluralism clearly had positive consequences. Foreign governments and non-government organizations, where operating sensitively, helped in a number of areas. Local political activism successfully halted a number of potentially damaging proposed industrial developments. Devolution of environmental responsibility to regional governments often led to greater sensitivity to local needs. Environmental legislation was tightened.

However severe doubts remained. Environmental issues were not high on the political agenda, as symbolized by Russian President Boris Yeltsin's decision to downgrade the Ministry for Environmental Protection to a State Committee. Environmental expenditure was slashed. The priority was economic recovery at all costs. Russian and other former Soviet green parties were universally unsuccessful. Russian officialdom harassed and prosecuted environmental activists for drawing attention to, for example, nuclear waste dumping by the Russian military. The official mindset remained attached to the conquest of nature.

See also: Russian green parties and movements

References

Golitsyn, G.S. (1993) 'Ecological Problems in the CIS During the Transition Period', *RFE/RL Research Report* 2 (2): 33–42.

OECD (1999) *OECD Environmental Performance Reviews: Russian Federation*, Paris: Organization for Economic Co-operation and Development.

Peterson, D.J. (1993) *Troubled Lands: the Legacy of Soviet Environmental Destruction* Boulder: Westview. also available on line at URL: http://www.rand.org/centers/cre/troubledlands/.

Pryde, P.R. (ed.) (1995) *Environmental Resources and Constraints in the Former Soviet Republics*, Boulder, CO: Westview.

Weiner, D.R. (1988) *Models of Nature: Ecology, Conservation and Cultural Revolution in Soviet Russia*, Bloomington: Indiana University Press.

Further reading

Bridges, O. and Bridges, J. (1996) *Losing Hope: the Environment and Health in Russia*, Aldershot: Avebury.

Edberg, R and Yablokov A. (1991) *Tomorrow Will Be Too Late*, Tucson: University of Arizona Press.

Feshbach, M. (1994) *Ecological Disaster: Cleaning Up the Hidden Legacy of the Soviet Regime*, Washington, DC: Twentieth Century Fund Press.

Feshbach, M. and Friendly, A. (1993) *Ecocide in the USSR: Health and Nature under Siege* New York: Basic Books.

Weiner, D.R. (1999) *A Little Corner of Freedom: Russian Nature Protection from Stalin to Gorbachev*, Los Angeles: University of California Press.

MATTHEW WYMAN

Russian green parties and movements

Independent environmental groups emerged as the former Soviet Union liberalized under Mikhail Gorbachev. Environmental activism flourished in 1989–91, then atrophied in the chaotic reform period of the 1990s. In the post-Yeltsin era relatively small groups of dedicated Greens have fought uphill battles against government obstructionism and public indifference.

In the Soviet totalitarian state only organizations closely monitored by the Communist party were allowed. The first voluntary Greens emerged in 1986, after the **Chernobyl** disaster, and soon hundreds of mostly local ecology groups were engaged in lobbying and protest actions across the USSR. One green movement formed in 1986, the Socio-Ecological Union (SEU), survives as Russia's primary umbrella organization for ecologists. The SEU acts as a clearing-house for a large number of regional and local groups within Russia – the Baikal Ecological Wave, the Union for Chemical Security, and Green Don, for example – and counts as members ecology groups from the former republics and from western Europe. The SEU oversees implementation of environmental legislation, monitors health conditions, and helps local ecology groups publish newspapers.

Moscow's Ecological Federation originated in the late 1980s. This confederation of ecological groups consists largely of middle-aged, well-educated Muscovites who monitor the city's environmental efforts and provide support to local movements. As with many of Russia's green movements, this group has limited resources, weak organization, and minimal access to the mass media. *Ecojuris*, which claims to be Russia's first public interest law firm, maintains a database of environmental legislation and has brought cases against the Russian government (see **mass media and the environment**). Significantly, women are very active in Russia's ecology movements – the SEU and *Ecojuris* are both headed by women, and their memberships are heavily female.

One of the country's best funded and best organized ecology groups is **Greenpeace** of Russia. Founded by Greenpeace International in 1990, Greenpeace Russia has a small, full-time professional staff and 10–15,000 dues-paying members. Greenpeace Russia has focused its efforts on contesting nuclear power, promoting disarmament, protecting Russia's forests and waters from depletion, and opposing trade in toxic substances.

While the international connection has made Greenpeace Russia more prominent and better organized than its purely Russian counterparts, it has fuelled suspicion that environmental activists are working against Russia's national interests. The trials of Aleksandr Nikitin and Grigorii Pasko, military officers who co-operated with Norway's Bellona Foundation and Japanese ecologists respectively to oppose nuclear dumping, illustrate the Russian government's continuing obsession with foreign subversion. Encouragingly, the courts dismissed charges against both activists. However, statements by President Vladimir Putin that spies would not be allowed to use environmental issues as cover for subversion portend tougher official restrictions on green activism. This may explain why Greenpeace Russia and ecology groups in many of Russia's 89 provinces failed in their attempt to force a referendum on the dissolution of the State Committee on Environmental Protection and government plans to import nuclear waste. Russia's Central Electoral Commission ruled late in 2000 that nearly 700,000 of the 2.5 million signatures collected by Russia's Greens were invalid; two million signatures are needed to mandate a referendum according to Russian law.

Ecological parties have not had much success in Russian electoral politics. The largest, Cedar (the Ecological Union of Russia), led by Anatolii Panfilov, received a miniscule 0.76 per cent of the party list vote for the Duma (lower house of parliament) in the 1993 elections. The party did somewhat better in 1995, getting 1.39 per cent of the party list vote, but still did not win any seats. In the 1999 elections, however, factional infighting led some of Cedar's top representatives to withdraw from the electoral bloc just before the election, resulting in the party's disqualification. There are also localized green parties scattered throughout the Russian Federation, but few are politically influential.

Obstacles to a more successful ecology movement in Russia include the continuing economic crisis, public apathy, a bureaucratic culture that does not welcome citizen initiatives, and a weakly developed legal system. Those few citizens who voice ecology demands must contend with arrogant bureaucrats who resist public input as unwarranted interference by amateurs. Green activism is seen as interfering with foreign investment projects and jeopardizing the profits of Russia's wealthy oligarchs. President Putin's decision in 2000 to eliminate the State Committee on Environmental Protection and the Forestry Service, and fold its environmental duties into the Ministry of Natural Resources, will likely reduce state responsiveness to environmental initiatives. Overall, the weak showing of Russia's green movements and parties reflects the country's weak **civil society**.

See also: Aral Sea; Chernobyl; Kyshtym nuclear accident; Russian Federation/Former Soviet Union; Russian nuclear power industry

Further reading

Hertsgaard, M. (18–25 September 2000), 'Russia's Environmental Crisis', *The Nation*, 8: 22–4.

Pickvance, K. (1998) *Democracy and Environmental Movements in Eastern Europe: A Comparative Study of Hungary and Russia*, Boulder, CO: Westview Press.

Ruffin, M.H., McCarter, J. and Upjohn, R. (1999) *The Post-Soviet Handbook: A Guide to Grassroots Organizations and Internet Resources in the Newly Independent States*, Seattle: University of Washington Press.

Yanitsky, O. (2000) 'Russian Greens within a Risk Society: A Structural Analysis', Helsinki: Aleksanteri Institute, Finnish Centre for Russian and East European Studies.

Ziegler, C.E. (1991) 'Environmental Politics and Policy under *Perestroika*', in J.B. Sedaitis and J. Butterfield, (eds) *Perestroika from Below: Social Movements in the Soviet Union*, Boulder, CO: Westview Press.

CHARLES ZIEGLER

Russian nuclear power industry

The Russian nuclear industry represents one of the most disturbing legacies of the Cold War. Countries of the former Soviet Union boast crumbling and under-funded networks of atomic power stations, reprocessing plants, nuclear weapons factories and waste storage facilities, scores of institutes and thousands of underemployed and badly paid nuclear scientists. A further legacy is an environment severely, and in some places irreparably, damaged.

Once the Hiroshima and Nagasaki explosions had demonstrated the technical feasibility of nuclear weapons, Stalin stopped at nothing to acquire them for the Soviet Union. The first Soviet atomic bomb was tested in 1949, and the first hydrogen bomb in 1953. A network of 13 secret cities known only by their postal codes and entirely closed off to the outside world was created to produce nuclear weapons, whatever the cost to the environment and to human health.

Exploitation of civil nuclear power, too, was a major priority of the Soviet Union in the postwar period. 'Communism equals Soviet power plus electrification of the whole country' was one of the best-known early Bolshevik slogans (see **communism**). Abundant power would be the panacea for many problems of social and economic **development**. 'Let the atom be a worker, not a soldier' was the rallying cry. Soviet leaders wanted to show that a socialist society could use a technology, that the capitalist West had used for mass destruction, to work wonders with.

The Soviet Union opened the world's first civilian nuclear power station at Obninsk, near Moscow, in 1954. By the mid-1980s, Russia had around 30 operating nuclear power stations, and the Ukraine some fifteen. Plants were usually located near to population centres to minimize losses from long distance transmission. As well as fission, fusion and breeder reactors, other developments included atomic icebreakers and submarines. Nuclear devices were exploded for underground oil and gas exploration, the creation of underground storage space and even to create canals and reservoirs (described as 'correcting the mistakes of nature'). Food was irradiated as a means of preservation, and livestock irradiated to increase productivity. This all took place in an environment of total secrecy, where safety standards were lax, leading to literally thousands of accidents. The authorities failed to inform the population about life-threatening problems associated with nuclear power such as the consequences of the **Kyshtym nuclear accident** in 1957, a dramatic illustration of the dangers of combining advanced technology with political dictatorship.

Contributors to current radioactive pollution problems in countries of the former Soviet Union include power plants and research centres, intercontinental ballistic missile (ICBM) testing sites, surface and underground bomb and accident residues (including catastrophic damage from the Kyshtym and **Chernobyl** disasters), uranium mining and processing facilities, (often secret) radioactive waste burial sites and spent reactors from ships and submarines. By 1999 the Russian nuclear industry had generated an estimated one billion tonnes of high and low level nuclear waste. It has been estimated that Russia has released into the environment around 1.7 billion curies of radiation (the equivalent of 60 Chernobyls).

The consequences of Chernobyl led to a temporary end to the expansion of the nuclear industry. However, in the context of severe economic crisis, many Soviet successor states have now adopted programmes to develop nuclear power further, in the context of a depletion of other energy resources west of the Ural Mountains. Ukraine in particular wishes to avoid dependency on Russia for energy supplies. A major energy crisis has forced Armenia to reopen the nuclear power station at Medzamor, located in an earthquake zone. Lithuania cannot afford to replace the giant Ignalina reactor that provides 80 per cent of her electricity. Russia is constructing small floating nuclear stations meant to serve as cheap power sources for remote towns, but possibly leak prone and vulnerable to terrorists. All this is occurring in the context of a financial crisis that leaves safety regimes unenforced and workers unpaid and disillusioned. A large amount of weapons grade fissile material is scattered throughout the former Soviet Union, and considered vulnerable to theft. In these circumstances, politicians and the nuclear industry find it inconvenient to draw attention to the alarming evidence of the health consequences of radioactive pollution on former Soviet territory (see **health and the environment**).

Further reading

Holloway, D. (1995) *Stalin and the Bomb: The Soviet Union and Atomic Energy 1939–1956*, New Haven: Yale University Press.

Josephson, P. (1999) *Red Atom: Russia's Nuclear Power Program from Stalin to Today*, New York: W.H. Freeman.

Quester, G. (ed.) (1995) *The Nuclear Challenge in Russia and the New States of Eurasia*, Armonk: M.E. Sharpe.

MATTHEW WYMAN

S

Sagebrush Rebellion

Federal environmental regulations and western anti-federal sentiment provide the context for the emergence of the Rocky Mountain West Movement, or the Sagebrush Rebellion, in the late 1970s. Led by the powerful livestock lobby, the rebels were concerned about growing limitations on their use of federal lands. Primarily, the rebels focused on the passage of favourable state legislation transferring jurisdiction of federal lands, especially those under the Bureau of Land Management (BLM), to state governments. Also, they worked to raise funds for likely legal challenges and to sway public opinion (see **public opinion and the environment**). In 1979, symbolic success was obtained when Nevada's legislature awarded the state jurisdiction over BLM lands. This was replicated in Arizona, New Mexico, Utah, and Wyoming, but it failed elsewhere in the region. **Reagan**'s 1980 election and his appointment of James **Watt** as Interior Secretary resulted in efforts to deregulate, devolve control to states, and to dispose of federal western lands. Watt's privatization efforts were opposed by Sagebrush rebels who preferred that these lands be under sympathetic state control. The rebellion fizzled out in 1983, but the rebels re-emerged within the **wise-use movement**. The 2000 election renewed their hopes, especially after the confirmation of the pro-development Gale Norton as the new Interior Secretary.

See also: Department of the Interior

Further reading

Cawley, R.M. (1993) *Federal Lands, Western Anger*, Lawrence, KS: University Press of Kansas.

ERICH G. FRANKLAND

Sahel

The combined effects of drought, **famines** and desertification on human and ecological life mostly characterize Sahel Africa. The name Sahel is derived from the Arabic word for 'border' and refers to a vast area of semi-arid to arid lands forming the southern borders of the Sahara desert. Six West African countries properly belong to the Sahelian Belt – Burkina Faso, Chad, Mali, Mauritania, Niger and Senegal. Other adjacent countries like Cameroon, Central African Republic, Ghana and **Nigeria** whose northern fringes are affected by drought, famine and desertification (the dominant characteristics of the Sahel) are often classified as belonging to the Belt. Food production in the Sahel (mainly cereals and livestock) depends largely on shallow seasonal rains, which in recent years are rendered increasingly unreliable by climatic change. As such, food deficits and famine are often widespread in the subregion.

See also: sub-Saharan Africa

KENNETH OMEJE

Sandoz spill

On 1 November 1986 a fire started at the Sandoz plant in building 956, containing 1250 tonnes of chemicals. An estimated 10,000 – 20,000 cubic metres of water were used to extinguish the fire, far beyond the capacity of on-site water retention facilities. Most run-off drained into the Rhine with some seepage into the ground. **Pesticides** in the run-off killed most aquatic fauna downstream of Basle, and the river bed was contaminated with mercury for 15 km downstream (see **mercury poisoning**). Pollution reached the Rhine Delta in the Netherlands. The self-cleaning capacity of the river enabled a fishing ban to be lifted in July 1987. The most difficult remediation was the fireground.

The Swiss had a proud record of industrial safety, but their hesitancy in passing on information caused diplomatic ill-feeling between neighbouring governments. The incident also demonstrated that fire safety and environmental protection could no longer be viewed separately.

See also: Rhine River Commission

ROD S. BARRATT

Santa Barbara oil spill

On 29 January 1969, a Union Oil platform stationed 6 miles off the coast of Santa Barbara, California, experienced a natural gas blowout that led to the release of over 3 million gallons of crude oil. Approximately 800 square miles of ocean and 35 miles of coastline were contaminated. The accident – and its heavily televised effects on birds and marine mammals – galvanized US public action on environmental issues. Within days of the spill, mobilization by citizen activists, the news media, and political leaders had brought the issue to international attention. Environmental historians credit the spill with influencing US passage of the **National Environmental Policy Act** (NEPA) and other key environmental laws. Although the long-term ecological effects of the spill appear to be less destructive than initially feared, its political and economic consequences continue to be felt in the way oil and gas facilities are sited and regulated in many parts of the world.

See also: oil pollution

Further reading

Steinhart, J, and Steinhart, C. (1972) *Blowout: A Case Study of the Santa Barbara Oil Spill*, Belmont, CA: Wadsworth.

LAMONT C. HEMPEL

Scotland

Scotland, with a population of just over 5 million, has not been particularly fertile ground for environmental politics. The Green Party has existed in Scotland since 1979, and the Scottish Greens formally gained their independence from their UK (English, Welsh and Northern Irish) counterparts in 1990. However, the Greens in Scotland have never achieved more than 1 per cent of the vote in a General Election; nor have they made any significant impact at the local government level. Britain's first-past-the-post electoral system has made it very difficult for small parties, and in the Scottish arena the existence of a nationalist party (Scottish National Party), which attracts up to a third of the vote, creates a crowded party system. As might be expected in the case of a rather unsuccessful green party, the Scottish Greens have never attracted more than a few hundred members.

Except for a brief period at the end of the 1980s, the Scottish public have shown little interest in green issues, and less so than residents of more affluent parts of the UK. Furthermore, the main political parties in Scotland (including the nationalists) have pursued a materialist agenda, concentrating on traditional measures of economic performance. The nuclear issue is one that has a relatively high profile in Scotland, with nuclear military sites at Rosyth, Holy Loch and Faslane, and nuclear power stations at Dounreay, Hunterston, and Torness, and studies of public opinion reveal that Scots tend to be more supportive of unilateral nuclear disarmament than the rest of the UK (Brown *et al.*, 1998: 164). However, evidence suggests that attitudes towards nuclear issues are often human-centred, and these issues are perceived as separate from other environmental issues (see Pattie *et al.*, 1991). All in all, despite being a country of extensive natural beauty and resources, Scotland has not been at the forefront of green politics.

At the beginning of the twenty-first century, however, there are some signs of increased interest in environmental issues. The devolution programme of the Labour Government, and the setting up of a new Scottish Parliament may revitalize the green agenda. The first elections to the Parliament in May 1999 were contested under the more proportional Additional Member System (AMS). This resulted in the election of the Scottish Green Party's Robin Harper who attracted 6.91 per cent of the vote in the area around Edinburgh. Significantly, Harper was the first green to be elected to a national-level Parliament in Britain. (Two English greens were elected to the European Parliament one month later.)

Key areas of devolved responsibility include health, education, housing, transport and the environment (see **health and the environment**; **transportation**). This suggests that the new Parliament has real potential to influence progress towards **sustainable development** in Scotland. In the first year of the Parliament there have been high profile debates on genetically modified foods and areas of legislation have included land reform, new transport plans and national parks. Other initiatives have included setting up a Wave Power Commission to explore the generation of electricity from waves. Furthermore, the Scottish Parliament provides a range of opportunities for environmental pressure groups. **Friends of the Earth** (FoE) Scotland, for example, is an influential lobby group. The Scottish Parliament, with its committee structure, consultation exercises, and public petitions, provides an important channel for such group activities.

Nevertheless, moves towards a green agenda in Scotland should not be exaggerated. As Kevin Dunion (1999), Director of FoE Scotland, argues there are clear limits to **sustainability** in a small country. The UK (Westminster) Parliament controls economic and energy policy, and the **European Union** (EU) and international agreements set the broader framework. Moreover, the Scottish

Parliament may resist environmental initiatives of these institutions if there are perceived costs in the form of lost jobs. The future of environmental politics in Scotland remains unpredictable.

See also: Green party UK; nuclear energy/ nuclear waste management

References

Brown, A., McCrone, D. and Paterson, L. (1998) *Politics and Society in Scotland*, London: MacMillan, 2nd edn.

Dunion, K. (1999) 'Sustainable Development in a Small Country: The Global and European Agenda', in E. McDowell and J. McCormick (eds) *Environment Scotland: Prospects for Sustainability*, Aldershot: Ashgate.

Pattie, C.J., Russell, A.T. and Johnston, R.J. (1991) 'Going Green in Britain? Votes for the Green Party and Attitudes to Green Issues in the Late 1980s', *Journal of Rural Studies*, 7(3): 285–97.

Further reading

McDowell, E. and McCormick, J. (eds) (1999) *Environment Scotland: Prospects for Sustainability*, Aldershot: Ashgate.

LYNN G. BENNIE

Sea Shepherd Conservation Society

The Sea Shepherd Conservation Society was established as a splinter group from **Greenpeace** International by the Canadian Paul Watson in 1977. Watson felt that Greenpeace's approach was too moderate and he advocated stronger forms of direct action against whalers and seal-culling ships. During the early 1980s Sea Shepherd members sank five illegal **whaling** ships. Other Sea Shepherd campaigns have targeted caribou and wolf hunts. International law has been used to legitimize such acts. During the early 1990s Sea Shepherd helped resource **Earth First! (UK)** by lending the network a number of its speed boats which were used in rainforest actions on the

Thames (see **rainforests**). Sea Shepherd has maintained links with **animal rights** organizations and Earth First!

DEREK WALL

Sellafield/Windscale

Sellafield/Windscale in Cumbria is one of the oldest and most controversial nuclear plants in the world. Since its creation as a Ministry of Supply project in 1947 Windscale and Calder Works has been central to the British State's civil and military nuclear aspirations. As ultimate owner and regulator of the site, the UK has been drawn into intense political conflicts with both citizens and other governments over the environmental and radiological consequences of nuclear reprocessing.

Windscale was initially the site for the two air-cooled piles, chemical separation plant, nuclear waste and plutonium storage facilities needed to produce Britain's atomic bomb. Built to exceedingly tight schedules amidst intense secrecy, Windscale was fully operational by the end of 1951 and Britain's first atomic bomb was detonated at Woomera, Australia in 1953. Upon its creation, in July 1954, the UK Atomic Energy Authority (UKAEA) assumed responsibility for Windscale. Four further gas-cooled Magnox reactors were built at Calder Hall, officially opened as 'power stations' by the Queen in 1956; the reactors produced weapons-grade plutonium.

In 1957 Windscale came under intense scrutiny following a fire at the No.1 pile. The fire raged out of control for two days before being extinguished with water amidst scientific speculation that this may result in an explosion (see *http://www.lakestay.co.uk*). The resultant inquiries revealed substantial shortcomings in both operational and radiological protection procedures and laid the foundation for contemporary regulatory structures in the UK. Throughout the late 1950s radioactive discharges from Windscale were kept higher than necessary to yield data on environmental uptake. Windscale became the site of the proto-type Advanced Gas Cooled Reactor (WAGR) which was adopted for the UK's second nuclear power programme. The UKAEA's advocacy of the AGR was based on *its* interpretation of data from WAGR and *its* commitment of capital to an AGR fuel fabrication plant prior to the reactor's adoption.

Windscale's reprocessing activities were transferred to British Nuclear Fuels Ltd (BNFL) following its creation in 1971. BNFL set out to make Windscale the biggest international commercial nuclear fuel cycle centre. The Thermal Oxide Reprocessing Plant (THORP) was central to this plan. Following intense public and media debate about whether Britain should become the world's 'Nuclear Dustbin' a **public inquiry** was announced in December 1976. The Windscale Inquiry lasted 100 days and the Inspector's report, published in 1978, recommended giving THORP the go-ahead. BNFL's rationale for THORP was a buoyant, long-term world market in plutonium to fuel Fast Breeder Reactors. Government backing for THORP created tensions following the International Nuclear Fuel Cycle Evaluation (INFCE) that signalled a shift away from reprocessing, particularly in the USA.

The Windscale Inquiry unified environmental and anti-nuclear groups within the UK but the outcome polarized those advocating continued participation within such events (notably **Friends of the Earth**) and those advocating direct action (notably *The Ecologist* and **Greenpeace**). Direct action was subsequently used to oppose the construction of reactors in Scotland and England. After decades of nuclear secrecy the Windscale Inquiry provided a public focus for a range of issues associating Windscale, and the nuclear industry more generally, with: leukaemia clusters; the proliferation of nuclear weapons; radioactive contamination; terrorist attacks; leaks; occupational health risks; and transport hazards – debates that continued to unfold (see **health and the environment**).

Windscale's routine discharges of radioactivity, leaks and accidents remained a source of growing public, regulatory and political unease into the 1980s. Following intense negative publicity, BNFL announced in 1981 that Windscale would henceforth be known as Sellafield. A 1983 Yorkshire TV documentary into the leukaemia cluster at Seascale prompted a government inquiry just as public beaches in the area were closed for nine months due to radioactive contamination. The 1984 Black Report confirmed the presence of a cluster but did not demonstrate a direct link with Sellafield. Post-**Chernobyl** monitoring of the Cumbrian fells in 1986 revealed a significant 'footprint' of previously unacknowledged contamination from Windscale. In 1989 epidemiological work claiming to demonstrate a link between male occupational exposure to radiation and leukaemia in resultant progeny precipitated further studies. The so-called Gardener hypothesis was subsequently disclaimed and the intervening death of its originator left such dismissals substantially unchallenged.

Constructing and commissioning THORP added to BNFL's difficulties illustrating how changing political and public climates can jeopardize projects with long lead-times. THORP, originally estimated at £600 million, was not completed until 1992 costing £2.85 billion. Public consultation exercises during the licensing and discharge authorization process revealed considerable opposition with 63 per cent of responses opposed to the plant. A site licence, stipulating lower overall discharges but increased emissions for isotopes produced by THORP, was granted in 1993 with commercial operation being sanctioned in 1997.

The decision was controversial as world uranium prices had more than halved, uranium demand was at a postwar low, FBRs had been abandoned and the end of the cold war removed military demands for plutonium. Reprocessing also generated more nuclear waste, added to waste disposal costs and lost significant support amongst electricity utilities. BNFL secured contracts for the fist ten years of THORP. Customers for the second ten-year, profit-making, period proved more difficult with **Japan** investing in domestic reprocessing capacity and Germany deciding to phase out nuclear power and abandon reprocessing (see **German nuclear power industry**; **Japanese nuclear power industry**).

The initial operation of THORP also intensified international pressure upon the British State to close Sellafield. Discharges of key radioactive isotopes, particularly Tehnetium 99, concentrated in seaweed and lobsters redoubled the efforts of the Irish and Nordic Governments to close the plant within the context of EU food radiation standards. BNFL's attempts to utilize their plutonium stockpile by using it in nuclear fuel resulted in international embarrassment. Acting independently, like the UKAEA with AGR fuel, BNFL commissioned a demonstration mixed-oxide (MOX) fuel facility to put plutonium beyond the reach of terrorists whilst providing a significant source of foreign income. Upon arrival in Japan it became clear that safety certification procedures for the first 'commercial' shipment had been falsified. Following extensive negotiations, throughout which BNFL paid for access to British Embassy resources including diplomatic status, it was agreed to return the fuel to the UK at a cost of £40 million. The resultant inquiry into the 'safety culture' of Sellafield revealed a positive risk disposition amongst the work force and acts of sabotage within the waste vitrification plant. The British government postponed plans to privatize BNFL until after another general election whilst reaffirming its commitment to restoring commercial confidence in the company.

Throughout the postwar era the civil and military nuclear ambitions of the British state have been intertwined at Windscale. The close association between Windscale, BNFL and the British State has continually generated tension and conflict within Whitehall as military and economic priorities have been set against environmental and human health concerns. By consistently shrouding Sellafield under a cloak of military and commercial secrecy the British State continues to contribute to the lack of transparency underpinning public and political opposition to Sellafield.

See also: British nuclear power industry; British regulatory agencies; non-violent direct action; nuclear energy/nuclear waste management

Further reading

Arnold, L. (1992) *Windscale 1957: Anatomy of a Nuclear Accident*, London: Macmillan.

Aubrey, C. (1993) *THORP: The Whitehall Nightmare*, London: Jon Carpenter.

Beral, *v* and Romar E. (1993) *Childhood Cancer and Nuclear Installations*, London: BMJ.

Welsh, I. (2000) *Mobilising Modernity: The Nuclear Moment*, London: Routledge

Wynne, B. (1982) *Rationality and Ritual: The Windscale Inquiry and Nuclear Decisions in the UK*, British Society for the History of Science: Chalfont St Giles.

IAN WELSH

Seveso disaster

The 1976 leak at a chemical plant in the Milan suburb of Seveso was a landmark incident in the history of environmental pollution regulation. A cloud of Trichlorophenol (TCP) and **dioxin** TCDD formed around the plant, although no acknowledgement of this was made to nearby villages for four days. Within three weeks animals and crops had died, 30 people were hospitalized and one person had died whilst, in the long term, a significant increase in birth defects was recorded. The disaster had profound political effects. The plant was owned by a Swiss company, prompting fears that they had exploited laxer safety standards in Italy. A so-called 'Seveso Directive' was quickly drafted by the European Community (82/501/EEC) tightening safety standards and making provision for notifying local populations of accidents.

See also: community-right-to-know laws

PETER HOUGH

Shiva, Vandana

b. 5 November 1952, Dehra Dun, India

Physicist, writer and environmental activist

Vandana Shiva has made a leading contribution to the feminist and environmental critique of Third World development, both as a writer and an activist. A physicist by training, she has drawn analogies between the reductionist nature of western science and capitalist **development** in their combined exploitation of women and **nature**. She is also known for her critique of **green**

revolution technologies and their effect on local **agriculture** and for her support of grassroots movements in India such as the **Chipko Andolan Movement**. According to Shiva, the task of redefining development as the production rather than the destruction of life, ties feminism and **ecology** in a political project to promote the indigenous knowledge of women who through their work as subsistence farmers reproduce and conserve **biodiversity**. To this end, Shiva has worked with local communities creating seed banks and protecting intellectual **property rights**. Vandana Shiva won the Right Livelihood Award (known as the alternative Nobel Prize) in 1993 for her work connecting environmentalism and feminism.

See also: biopiracy/bioprospecting; ecofeminism

MEIRA HANSON

Sierra Club

The Sierra Club is a non-governmental organization based on voluntary membership and dedicated to preserving natural areas in the USA and educating the public regarding the value of those areas. It was founded by John **Muir**, who spent much of his adult life exploring the Sierra Nevada Range of mountains in California and convincing the public and government officials to preserve as much of it as possible.

The Sierra Club charter, modelled on that of the eastern Appalachian Mountain Club, states that its purpose is to:

explore, enjoy and preserve the Sierra Nevada and other scenic resources of the United States and its forests, waters, wildlife, and wilderness: to undertake and to publish scientific literary and education studies concerning them: to educate the people with regard to the national and state forests, parks, monuments, and other natural resources of scenic beauty and to enlist public co-operation in protecting them.

The Sierra Club has grown from a small California based organization dedicated to introducing people to the Sierra Nevada to a national organization with hundreds of local chapters with their own individual causes designed to preserve natural resources in their areas. It has established 12 regional offices, including one in Canada. It is a major player among conservation organizations that lobby regularly in Washington and state capitols for preservation policies.

The first meeting of the club was held in San Francisco in 1892 after John Muir enlisted the help of science professors from the University of California. In 1890 Muir had convinced President Theodore **Roosevelt** to make the Yosemite Valley into a national park (see **Muir, John**). He and the Sierra Club failed, however, to obtain the same protection for the Hetch Hetchy Valley which became a water reservoir for San Francisco (see **Hetch Hetchy Dam**). John Muir remained as president until his death in 1914, using trips he planned and led into wilderness to introduce the public and political leaders to the wonders of **nature**.

Originally allied with naturalists in the federal government, such as Gifford **Pinchot**, the Sierra Club came to adhere to a preservationist stance on wilderness areas as opposed to the more pragmatic conservationist attitude of the Forest Service to utilize natural resources for the 'greatest good for the greatest number'. While many early outings were rather elaborate affairs involving pack animals and considerable equipment, the club's leadership came increasingly to argue for visitors to wilderness to tread lightly and make no impact on fragile ecological systems.

In 1952 David **Brower** became the first professional executive director of the Sierra Club and remained in that capacity until 1969 when differences over administrative issues with the volunteer board of directors forced him out. During that time the club's mission came to emphasize political activities over the traditional outings sponsored for the membership. The Sierra Club led many of the early struggles against major reclamation projects in the west that reduced the quality of natural free-flowing streams.

Today it lobbies against the **Department of the Interior**'s programme of leasing public lands for mineral exploration and grazing cattle and the US Forest Service's policy of allowing timber companies to clear cut national forests. It opposes most efforts of the National Park Service to extend accessibility and modern accommodations in the national parks. It was instrumental in the effort to prevent flooding part of Dinosaur National Monument in Colorado. It lobbied with other conservation groups for the Wilderness Act of 1964 and became so involved in supporting political candidates who would advocate its causes in government that the Internal Revenue Service withdrew its tax exempt status in 1969. Later a Legal Defense Fund was created as a tax exempt entity in order to fund research and take some of the club's causes to court.

It has sued agencies from the Corps of Engineers to the Department of the Interior in order to force them to abide by the **National Environmental Policy Act** and write impact statements about their proposed projects. When the federal government has slowed its efforts to enforce pollution control regulations on violators, the Sierra Club has sued in the name of the public to enforce the law. It continues to have a separate Committee on Political Education (SCOPE), a political action committee that selects candidates to endorse and help run their campaigns through grassroots volunteers, as well as contributions (see **political action committees**).

It is a politically active organization that continues to inspire its membership through extensive trips that it plans and runs into wilderness and other natural areas throughout the USA.

Further reading

Culhane, P. (1981) *Public Lands Politics*, Baltimore, MD: Johns Hopkins Press, Resources for the Future.

Fox, S. (1981) *John Muir and His Legacy: The American Conservation Movement*, Boston, MA: Little Brown.

LETTIE McSPADDEN

Sierra Club *v.* Morton

Sierra Club v. Morton, 405 US 727 (1972), is a landmark case in which the US Supreme Court set the conditions to be met by an environmental group seeking access to the federal courts. In accordance, the Court ruled that the Sierra Club did not have 'standing to sue' US Secretary of the Interior, Rogers Morton, in the Mineral King Valley case, but its reason for the denial accelerated the trend toward a broadened interpretation of standing in environmental cases. Litigation became an indispensible tool of the American environmental movement in the 1970s (see **environmental law and litigation**).

Mineral King Valley is located in the Sierra Nevada Mountains of California on national forest lands adjacent to the Sequoia National Park. A $35 million ski resort complex to accommodate 14,000 daily visitors, proposed by Walt Disney Enterprises and approved by the US Forest Service, would threaten the area's quasi-wilderness quality. Alleging that this development would violate federal laws and regulations protecting **national parks**, forests, and wildlife refuges, the Sierra Club filed a lawsuit in 1969. It obtained an injunction in the US District Court that blocked the construction of an access road and high voltage power line across the national park to the development site in the national forest. However, the US Court of Appeals overturned the lower court by ruling that the Club lacked standing.

In reviewing the case, the Supreme Court declared, 'Aesthetic and environmental well-being, like economic well-being, are important ingredients of the quality of life in our society'. Therefore, it concluded that relief for non-economic as well as economic injury from an agency's decision could be sought in the federal courts. The Sierra Club, citing its 'special interest in conservation', relied on the judicial review provision of the Administrative Procedures Act (APA) for standing. However, the Supreme Court upheld the Court of Appeals because the Club had made no effort to demonstrate that actions by Morton *et al.* would cause any of its members 'injury in fact'.

In a historic dissent, Justice William O. **Douglas** urged that environmental objects, such as valleys, rivers, forests, and meadows, be given legal standing, just as inanimate objects, such as ships and corporations, already have. He argued that 'those people that have a meaningful relation' to an environmental object (e.g., members of the Sierra

Club) must be able to serve as 'its legitimate spokesmen' in the courts 'before these priceless bits of Americana are forever lost'.

The practical implication of *Sierra Club v. Morton* was that environmental groups should include allegations of specific harm in legal complaints. Renewed litigation delayed Disney's project until 1978 when the US Congress resolved the issue by passing legislation to incorporate Mineral King Valley into Sequoia National Park, precluding the ski resort complex.

The case was cited as a precedent in *United States v. Students Challenging Regulatory Agency Procedures* (1973), where the Supreme Court held that standing is not to be denied because many share the injury, and that the (low) magnitude of injury makes no difference as long as there is injury in fact. It was also cited in *Duke Power Company v. Carolina Environmental Study Group* (1978), where the Supreme Court held that standing is not to be denied when there is a 'substantial likelihood' of environmental injury despite a tenuous connection between the injury and the claim on its merits.

By the end of the decade, environmentalists had initiated more federal environmental cases than had industry and government combined, and the Sierra Club had initiated more cases than any other environmental group. During the 1980s, the federal courts generally continued to interpret standing broadly in environmental cases.

In the early 1990s the Supreme Court, whose ideological character had been changed by the appointments of President Ronald **Reagan** and President George Bush, signalled a turn to a more restrictive interpretation of standing. In *Lujan v. National Wildlife Federation* (1990) the **National Wildlife Federation** had attested that its members' recreational use of federal lands would be adversely impacted if the Bureau of Land Management (BLM) opened them to **mining**. However, the Court ruled that the group's affidavits were defective because they did not allege use of the particular acreage to be reclassified within a vast tract of land, and that even sufficiently specific affidavits would not have provided standing to challenge the BLM's land programme as a whole.

In *Lujan v. Defenders of Wildlife* (1992), the environmental group had sought to force the US

Department of Interior to apply the **Endangered Species Act** (ESA) to overseas developmental aid programmes that threaten rare species. Despite the ESA's explicit provision for such citizens' suits, the Court ruled that the Defenders of Wildlife did not have standing because its members failed to demonstrate 'imminent' injury to their specific interests. In his dissent, Justice Harry Blackmun denounced the majority opinion as a 'slash and burn expedition through the law of environmental standing'.

Although not all environmental lawyers would agree with Blackmun's ominous assessment, it is clear that American environmentalists will confront additional requirements to obtain 'standing to sue' as federal judges depart from the well-worn path followed since Mineral King Valley.

See also: environmental movements

Further reading

Findley, R.W. and Daniel, A.F. (1991) *Environmental Law in a Nutshell*, St Paul: West, 3rd edn.
Hoban, T.M. and Brooks, R.O. (1996) *Green Justice: The Environment and the Courts*, Boulder: Westview, 2nd edn.
Valente, C.M. and Valente, W.D. (1995) *Introduction to Environmental Law and Policy*, St Paul: West.

E. GENE FRANKLAND

Silkwood, Karen G.

b. 19 February, 1946, Longview Texas, USA; d. 13 November, 1974, Crescent, Oklahoma

Chemical technician and activist

Karen Silkwood has become the focus for conspiracy theories and **anti-nuclear movements** because her mysterious death was ruled an accident by federal authorities. Her demise fuelled speculation because of narcotics found in her system, suspicious dents on her automobile, and the absence of incriminating documents she was purported to be carrying. Interest in her death has obscured her work exposing the plutonium processing operation at the Kerr–McGee owned Cimarron Nuclear Facility in Oklahoma where she worked. As a chemical technician (since 1972) and later activist/leader (from 1974) of the Oil, Chemical and Atomic Workers' Union at the plant, Silkwood helped compile information exposing health, safety, production violations as well as the possibility of missing plutonium. Her death prompted an Atomic Energy Commission investigation, the plant's closure in 1975, and increased focus on industry working conditions. The contamination of her body and belongings with plutonium prior to her death led to a civil lawsuit which was settled out of court in 1986 for $1.3 million.

Reference

Rashke, R. (2000) *The Killing of Karen Silkwood: The Story Behind the Kerr–McGee Plutonium Case*, Ithaca, NY: Cornell University Press, 2nd edn.

ERICH G. FRANKLAND

Simon, Julian

b. 12 February 1932, New Jersey, USA; d. 11 January 1998, Maryland

Economist

Julian Simon studied at Harvard and the University of Chicago. Before becoming a professor of business management, he ran his own mail-order firm and advertising agency. Simon spent his academic career at the University of Illinois and the University of Maryland. He also became a Senior Fellow at the libertarian Cato Institute. Simon was a prolific writer, with over 20 books – most notably *The Ultimate Resource* (1981) and *The Resourceful Earth* (1984) with Herman Kahn – and 200 professional articles to his name. His primary interest was the economic effects of population changes (see **population movement and control**).

Simon waged intellectual wars against environmentalists who worried about the 'population bomb'. He viewed world population growth as positive. His thesis was that human minds are the ultimate resource, and the more, the better. Accordingly, he advocated economic and political freedom to allow those minds to innovate. Thus Simon maintained that the economy will not run out of resources, the environment will become cleaner, and people will become healthier. Because of these trends, it would make no sense to conserve for the sake of future generations since they are going to be far better off than we are. In short, Simon saw no need to worry about **sustainability**.

Further reading

Simon, J. (1996) *The Ultimate Resource 2*, Princeton: Princeton University Press.

E. GENE FRANKLAND

Singer, Peter

b. 1946, Melbourne, Australia

Philosopher, environmental and animal activist

Peter Singer has been described as having more positive influence on the world than any other living philosopher. His book *Animal Liberation* (1975) has been translated into fifteen languages, sold half a million copies, and is known as the Bible of the Animal Liberation movement. Singer argues that it is wrong to cause millions of animals the most terrible suffering in **factory farms** for the sake of a trivial difference in taste to our meals, and that it is wrong to allow people in poor countries to die of starvation, when we could prevent their deaths by making donations which do not represent unbearable costs to ourselves. In so doing, he develops a number of arguments which conclude that most of us should, like him, become vegetarians and donate – with some flexibility depending on our circumstances – at least 10 per cent of our incomes to charities like Oxfam that assist the world's poorest people.

PAULA CASAL

snail darter case

The snail darter case (*TVA v. Hill* [1978]) is the most famous US Supreme Court case involving the **Endangered Species Act** (ESA) of 1973. The small fish had been discovered in the Little Tennessee River, and placed on the **endangered species** list. Since 1967 the Tennessee Valley Authority (TVA) had been at work on the Tellico dam (which was 80 per cent completed) on the river. Hiram G. Hill, Jr, a University of Tennessee law student, sued to stop the dam before it submerged the only known stream where snail darters lived (see also **dams/hydroelectric power**). The legal action was joined by sportsmen, archaeologists, farmers, and Cherokees opposed to the flooding of 16,500 acres.

The federal district court agreed that the dam threatened the species with extinction, but allowed it to go forward because Congress had continued its funding despite the species' peril. But the court of appeals overturned the lower court's decision. TVA appealed to the Supreme Court, which ruled that the dam's completion would violate the ESA so the $100 million project had to be halted. Congress amended the ESA to create a 'God Committee' to review such controversies; it decided against the dam on economic grounds. In 1979, Tennessee legislators attached a rider exempting the Tellico Dam to an appropriations bill, which Congress passed. The dam was completed. However, colonies of snail darters were later found elsewhere. The Fish and Wildlife Service now lists the snail darter as threatened (rather than endangered).

Reference

Hoban, T.M. and Brooks, R.O. (1987) *Green Justice*, Boulder: Westview Press, 2nd edn, pp. 26–37.

E. GENE FRANKLAND

social ecology

Social ecology is often counted among the main varieties of political theories which focus on environmental issues, including **deep ecology**, **bioregionalism** and some forms of **eco-feminism** and liberalism (see e.g., Eckersley 1992 and **liberalism/liberal democracy**). Principally, it is a form of dialectical naturalism most closely connected with the work of Murray **Bookchin** and his Institute for Social Ecology, founded in

1974 in Plainfield, Vermont (USA). So closely connected is social ecology with Bookchin's work that the two are often thought of as co-extensive. Only in the 1990s did several theorists, most notably John Clark (1997) and David Watson (1996), challenge the hegemony of Bookchin's influence over the theoretical foundations of this school of thought.

Bookchin's social ecology is grounded in the notion that domination, as applied to **nature**, is incoherent. One makes a category mistake when one says that humans dominate **nature**. Rather, domination is a human–human relationship. Bookchin maps from prehistory to the present different forms of hierarchy that have evolved over time – gender, race, **class**, age, etc. He then claims that this history of human–human domination helps to create forms of society which are incompatible with environmental **sustainability**. These claims justify for Bookchin a form of anarchism demanding a decrease in state power and in turn a dismantling of institutions that enable domination and create ecologically unsustainable societies (see **anarchism/eco-anarchism**).

In the mid-1980s, spearheaded largely by Bookchin's efforts, a debate emerged between social ecology and deep ecology, which, for a time, shaped the theoretical ground of alternative visions of a more stable environmental future in North America. This often divisive clash between rival political theorists and activists spilled over into the pages of organizational newsletters and popular leftist magazines. Bookchin argued throughout this debate that deep ecology represented an individualistic, mystical, and irrationalist departure from social, democratic and rational forms of political ecology. Regardless of one's views about which side of this debate was correct, or indeed whether it was an important debate to engage in at all, it is clear that one of Bookchin's contributions to this exchange was to elevate its intensity through accusations that deep ecology entailed forms of fascism and primitivism reminiscent of Nazism.

John Clark links such arguments by Bookchin to what he perceives to be the general decline in interest in social ecology. In turn, Clark and others also emphasize the 'internal' debates which have emerged among social ecologists, largely due to Bookchin's attempts to push away competing expressions of the view. To overcome both the external and internal sectarian fights with which social ecology has become involved, Clark and others have formed competing versions of social ecology which challenge the basis of Bookchin's divisions between his work and competing environmental theories.

For example, Clark argues that the roots of social ecology are older than Bookchin's work, going back to figures such as the Russian anarchist, biologist and geographer Peter Kropotkin (1842–1921), the French geographer Elisee Reclus (1830–1905), the Scottish botanist and social thinker Patrick Geddes (1854–1932), and the American historian and social theorist Lewis **Mumford** (1895–1990). As such, Clark argues that social ecology in Bookchin's form is a continuation of the communitarian, organicist and regionalist dimensions of the history of ecological thought. Drawing from these sources and others, Clark attempts to broaden social ecology to include robust conceptions of the role of spirit in political ecology which opens up the possibility of a rapprochement between social ecology and deep ecology.

The future of social ecology remains unclear. In contrast, the influence of deep ecology in environmental circles appears to remain viable in part because of the proliferation of different varieties of deep ecology in different parts of the world (a proliferation encouraged by Arne **Naess**, the principle theorist of this school of environmental thought). But because of Bookchin's strong rejection of alternatives to his version of social ecology, active interest in social ecology may only continue as long as environmentalists and environmental theorists remain interested in the work of Bookchin. It is quite possible that the term 'social ecology' may shortly cease to refer to an identifiable political theory or school of environmental thought, and instead become a short-hand term for any environmental work that takes social issues into consideration. Tom Athanasiou's *Divided Planet: The Ecology of Rich and Poor* (1998) has in this sense been hailed as a landmark work of 'social ecology', while it is arguably the case that the claims made therein are only tangentially related to Bookchin's theoretical work.

References

Athanasiou, T. (1998) *Divided Planet: The Ecology of Rich and Poor*, Athens, GA: The University of Georgia Press.

Clark, J. (1997) 'A Social Ecology', *Capitalism, Nature, Socialism*, 8(3):3–33.

Eckersley, R. (1992) *Environmentalism and Political Theory*, Albany, NY: State University of New York Press.

Watson, D. (1996) *Beyond Bookchin: Preface for a Future Social Ecology*, Brooklyn, NY: Autonomedia.

Further reading

Bookchin, M. (1982) *The Ecology of Freedom*, Palo Alto, CA: Cheshire Books.

—— (1995) *Re-Enchanting Humanity*, London: Cassell.

Clark, J. (2000) 'The Matter of Freedom: Ecofeminist Lessons for Social Ecology', *Capitalism, Nature, Socialism*, 11(3); 62–80.

Light, A. (ed.) (1998) *Social Ecology after Bookchin*, New York: Guilford.

ANDREW LIGHT

social economy, informal economic activity in

The central problem with summarizing informal economic activity in the social economy or third sector is one of definition. The felling of many forests has produced two main competing approaches. The concept of the social economy originates from parts of southern Europe in the nineteenth century, while the non-profit sector idea emanated from the USA. The latter is narrower in scope and is associated with the studies coordinated by Johns Hopkins University (Salamon and Anheirer, 1997).

The differences between the two are complex, involving such issues as whether organizations are exempt from taxes; how they use surpluses or profits; how far membership is restricted or open; and whether the main motivation is altruism or self-interest. All this, together with problems in translating the two terms, has led many to fall back on the simple idea of a third sector operating between the traditional public and private sectors. The topic is best understood in terms of examples. These include community businesses, food and housing **co-operatives**, credit unions, community windfarms, **recycling** schemes, community development trusts, environmental improvement projects, wildlife organizations, social housing bodies, sustainable communities, and a huge range of self-help and mutual aid organizations. The third sector is analogous to where the sea meets the land. A greater variety of species inhabits the inter-tidal zone than any other habitat on the planet.

The above examples focus on activities at the level of the county or the city and below, down at the urban neighbourhood or village. Other examples could be given for the types of organization that operate at the national, and supranational levels. The 1980s and 1990s also saw considerable growth of similar organizations in the Third World (Defourny *et al.* 1999). Here, initiatives were linked to churches, unions, and supranational northern non-governmental organizations (NGOs), and drew from local traditions of self-help and mutual aid. However, many greens would argue that, by taking an organizational focus, the approaches discussed above do not cover all that greens draw in under the umbrella of informal economic activity. One of the criticisms that greens have of contemporary society is the way work is conventionally defined only in terms of paid employment. Greens include unpaid voluntary work in the third sector, also looking after children and housework.

From a green perspective, third sector organizations are important because they create opportunities to put green ideas into practice. Apart from work, they relate to needs not wants; they frequently adopt holistic approaches to these local problems, integrating the economic, social and environmental dimensions; they operate around interpretations of participatory **democracy**; and they develop small-scale, decentralized approaches outside the state in **civil society**. Interestingly, they often develop these ideas without using the language of green ideas or **sustainable development**. Some argue that, in the face of **globalization**, they offer a route to greater local self-reliance (Douthwaite, 1996). Because they educate and inspire others, they are seen as part of the greens' extra-parliamentary strategy to transform society.

Despite difficulties in evaluating their contribution, it is now increasingly accepted by writers and policy-makers unconnected with green thinking that these organizations deliver much that is useful. Such arguments led the European Commission, in the late 1990s, to survey the contribution of the social economy and analyse ways of promoting it further. But policy-makers confront a paradox. On the one hand they want to intervene and inject resources in a targeted way. On the other, they are forced to recognize that many third-sector organizations do not trust the state. They succeed partly because they have emerged spontaneously from civil society and retained their autonomy and independence, as with the Local Employment and Trading Schemes (LETS).

Some state strategies are based around creating legal and financial frameworks that remove obstacles and provide incentives (Belgium, Italy), or amend tax details (USA). Others are based around empowerment programmes that offer funding, advice and support to promote community development organizations. In order to address the problems implicit in top-down participatory programmes, this activity is often handed over to other third-sector bodies operating at arms length from the state.

See also: civil society; green political theory; sustainable development

References

Defourny, J., Develtere, P and Fontenau, B. (eds) (1999) *L'Economie Sociale au Nord et au Sud*, Brussels: de Boeck.

Douthwaite, R. (1996) *Short Circuit: Strengthening Local Economies for Security in an Unstable World*, Totnes, Devon: Resurgence.

Salamon, L. and Anheirer, H. (eds) (1997) *Defining the Non-Profit Sector: A Cross-National Analysis*, Manchester: Manchester University Press.

STEPHEN C. YOUNG

sociobiology

The concept of sociobiology was first made prominent by the entomologist Edward O. Wilson. Wilson claimed that the social behaviour of all animals, including human beings, could be shown to be genetically based and thus explicable in terms of the Darwinian account of adaptation based on natural selection. This implied that, since human social behaviour is studied by the various social sciences, the latter should be integrated into biology. Critics reply that the human behaviour in question is mainly, or entirely, the product of culture, not of genes. Sociobiology has, however, inspired evolutionary psychology, which similarly seeks to identify universal features of human emotion and intellect and explain them in evolutionary terms.

BRIAN BAXTER

soft energy path

Soft energy path is a term coined by Amory **Lovins** in his various works regarding soft and hard energy paths. Lovins defines the hard energy path as one based on the unforgiving energy resources of nuclear and high fossil fuel consumption (see **fossil fuels**). The soft energy path is based on energy income from solar, wind, biomass conversion and other low impact energy technologies. Lovins envisions a transition where nuclear, coal and petroleum are phased out over time. As this occurs the softer energy resources begin to come on line and sometime in the twenty-first century the soft energy path will have been established. Lovins quantifies the economics, scale, socio-political and equity outcomes of hard versus soft energy paths, and makes the case that the soft energy path is much more desirable from an environmental perspective. He also projects tremendous energy savings available through conservation not only by using less energy, but by matching the type of energy used with a specific energy task.

Further reading

Lovins, A (1977) *Soft Energy Paths*, San Francisco: Friends of the Earth.

THOMAS LOWE

Soil Association

The Soil Association was established in 1946 to promote **organic farming**. This is now done via research, advice, publications, and partnerships with councils, groups and others to develop more sustainable local food economies. The Association started its certification scheme in 1972 to promote organic standards. Recommended, permitted, re-stricted and prohibited practices are defined with regard to crops, livestock, and other products. By 1999 about 80 per cent of UK organic food was marketed with the Association's symbol. This all adds up to an ambitious approach to **sustainable development**, focusing on the links between the health of the soil, plants, animals, humans and the biosphere. In the early 1990s the Association was a peripheral organization. However, the food scares, the surge in demand for organic food, and farmers wanting to switch to organics all gave it a broader lobbying and campaigning role, as over genetic engineering (see **genetic engineering, crops**). It also became more active outside the UK as a prominent member of the International Federation of Organic Farming Movements.

STEPHEN C. YOUNG

solar energy

Solar energy as it radiates from the sun passes through the Earth's atmosphere driving climatic change by affecting the temperature of land, water, and air. Solar energy can be a thermal resource, an illumination resource, an electrical generation resource, and/or can affect the growth of plants which can be used as food, fuel, and/or fibre.

The sun's radiant energy is universally available; it can be harvested directly or indirectly. Direct harvesting occurs in plant growth – as carbon is fixed and oxygen released during the photosyn-thetic process and/or in the warming of material surfaces – whether the skin of living creatures, the soils of the Earth, the shells of buildings or the pavement of streets and walks. Indirect harvesting occurs in the capture of the hydrologic cycle – the power in flowing streams and rivers, the capture of variable windflow, and/or by the incineration of plant fibre as a fuel.

One of the unique characteristics of the thermal measure of the sun's radiant energy is that generally it is in diffuse, low-density concentration; moreover, some 50 per cent is lost to filtration, reflection and atmospheric absorption. As a result, only 221 (British thermal units) BTUs per ft^2 on average reach the Earth's surface. Such energy density can be used for space and hot water heating, but higher resulting temperatures are needed to meet other demands. As a result, solar concentration – by mirrored reflection or lens transmission – is used to focus a large aperture of incoming radiation onto a smaller area for a magnification effect.

The capture of solar radiation as useful thermal energy is achieved by a passive or active conver-sion. Passive solar conversion involves the use of the sun's energy to warm materials directly; solar radiation passing through a window can heat the interior surfaces of a room; that same energy shining onto an opaque, translucent or transparent container can heat water therein. The air bubble in a room and the water in a holding tank, each, will experience turbulent internal flow as a result of the build up of thermal gradients. This is referred to as a stack flow or thermosyphoning effect and can be used to advantage in assisting the more complete distribution of the thermal energy in the respective fluid.

Active solar conversion involves localized har-vesting of the energy for use in other locations or at other times – sometimes achieved with a natural thermosyphoning effect and at other times assisted by mechanical pumping of the exchange fluids. Solar collectors are used to perform this thermal capture and redistribution; they are categorized as flat plate or concentrating, low temperature or high. Low temperature collectors use an exchange medium, such as air or water to move the thermal energy to temporary remote storage; under cold ambient conditions, a glycol–water mix is used; high temperature systems use liquid metals.

The capture of solar radiation as useful electrical energy is achieved by photovoltaic conversion. In this technology, silicon wafers, when exposed to radiation from the sun, experience a flow of electrical current. Solar cells made of such wafers can be gathered into panels and those into arrays to build up a large collection area and a corresponding leveraging of electrical current flow for powering tools, appliances and/or lighting. Storage of a large electrical harvest from the sun for later use requires banks of batteries, but in experimental form has been achieved using mechanical pumping of water to an elevation sufficient to establish a store of potential energy – which when drained by the pull of gravity can power electrical generators or other mechanically driven devices.

Photovoltaic panels can also be integrated with glazing systems to allow, simultaneously, the production of electricity and the daylighting of interior space. This integration can offset the need for electrically powered lighting devices during daylight hours and enable such devices to be supplied at night with electric power harvested during the day.

Use of these forms of solar energy involves the balancing of individual rights with group rights typically achieved with legislation prescribing the group interrelationships needed to assure individual solar access.

Further reading

Crosbie, M. (ed.) (1997) *The Passive Solar Design and Construction Handbook*, New York: John Wiley & Sons

Hastings, S.R. (ed.) (1995) *Solar Low Energy Houses of IEA Task 13*, London: James & James (Science Publishers) Ltd.

Lasnier, F. and Ang, T. (1990) *Photovoltaic Engineering Handbook*, Bristol: Adam Hilger.

Strong, S. and Scheller, W. (1994) *A Solar Electric House: Energy for the Environmentally-Responsive, Energy-Independent Home*, Lebanon, NH: Chelsea Green Publishing Company.

Winkelmann, F. and Selkowitz, S. (1986) *Energy and*

Buildings, Berkeley: Lawrence Berkeley Energy Laboratory Daylighting Group.

ROBERT J. KOESTER

South African environmental politics

South Africa faces a dilemma it shares with most third-world countries. It faces mounting environmental pressures of many sorts. However, because of its poverty, it lacks the resources to make a major effort to alleviate them. That said, its situation is also unique in one key way. Its environmental problems and possible solutions have both been deeply shaped by the legacy of apartheid. South Africa's environmental problems affect Blacks far more than Whites in ways that far exceed the impact of environmental racism in the USA.

The segregation policies of the apartheid era had devastating environmental consequences. The rural homelands created early in the twentieth century only allowed Blacks to live in limited areas, because Whites wanted the best agricultural land for themselves. To cite but the most glaring statistic, in white areas, there were six Whites living on each square kilometre of crop and pasture land, but almost 109 Blacks living on the same amount of land in the former homelands. Similar statistics can be found for almost every other indicator of the quality of the environmental or energy use. Over the years, water and fuel shortages, overfarming, and population growth have taken their toll on the ecosystems of the already marginal soil the Blacks depended on (see also **population movement and control**).

Those environmental and economic pressures, in turn, there led millions to move to shantytowns in the 'townships' that surrounded all the major cities. These, too, were typically built on marginal land (e.g., subject to flooding). Existing environmental problems there, too, were magnified by the social impact of apartheid, including overcrowding, the lack of running water and sewerage, and the deficient health-care system. Again to cite but one example, Black South African children were seven times more likely to die of acute respiratory disease than their European counterparts. There was one more consequence in the townships; the over-crowding, poverty, and isolation contributed to the violence that characterized life in them both under apartheid and today.

For good or ill, building a society that treats Blacks and Whites equally will have environmental consequences. The South African energy mono-poly, Eskom, estimates that electricity consumption will double in the next generation, as power is supplied to the 80 per cent of the Black population that was not connected to the grid when apartheid fell in 1994.

Ironically, too, today's democratic South Africa can benefit from the wealth generated under apartheid and the goodwill the new government has generated abroad to make some major progress on a number of issues. To be sure, South Africa lacks the resources to fully address its environ-mental problems. Nonetheless, it has to be pointed out that the apartheid regime did establish a number of game parks and reserves covering more than 70,000 square kilometres or about six per cent of the total land. At the time, they were available only for Whites to enjoy; now, however, they are open to all.

More importantly, both the wealth and the isolation of the regime following the imposition of sanctions beginning in the 1970s led the old regime to launch some innovative programmes on the environmental and energy fronts. In particular, it developed one of the world's most extensive synthetic fuels programmes once it began encoun-tering serious difficulties in getting petroleum products on the world market. Thus, the state-owned, apartheid era companies such as Sasol have developed state of the art coal to natural gas facilities which can generate the equivalent of upwards of 200,000 barrels per day of petroleum.

The government has made some promising decisions that, again, build on the wealth and technological developments of the apartheid years. For instance, the government plans to use **solar energy** to provide electricity to hundreds of thousands of new homes as well as schools and clinics over the next 20 years, thus limiting the environmental consequences of connecting millions of people to the electrical grid. More generally, it is estimated that South Africa could easily improve its

energy efficiency by a factor of three by making technologically easy transitions such as shifting more to the use of natural gas rather than coal.

Finally, because of the nature of the remarkable transition to majority rule, South Africa benefits from unusual goodwill and funding from the international business and NGO (non-governmen-tal organizations) communities. Global organiza-tions such as the **World Wide Fund for Nature** have major South African operations, and there are dozens of South African-only NGOs, most notably the Endangered Wildlife Trust. It is not just the liberal NGO world. The state-owned Eskom builds all of its new electrical lines in ways that are friendly to the blue crane, an **endangered species**. In sum, the South Africans have made considerable progress in protecting and then rebuilding populations of species that are seriously endangered elsewhere on the continent, including the crane, the black rhinoceros, and wild dogs.

See also: development; eco-tourism; in-dustrialization; wildlife management

Further reading

Holt-Biddle, D. (2000) 'Ground Force: Wildlife Conservation in South Africa', *Geographical*, 72: 36–56.

Homer-Dixon, T. (1999) *Environment, Scarcity, and Violence*, Princeton: Princeton University Press.

Hudak, A.T., (1999) 'Rangeland Mismanagement in South Africa', *Human Ecology: An Interdisciplin-ary Journal*, 27: 55–81.

Scholand, M (1996) 'Re-energizing South Africa', *World Watch*, 9: 22–9.

Thompson, L. (1995) *A History of South Africa*, New Haven: Yale University Press, revised edn.

CHARLES HAUSS

South East Asian environmental politics

The environmental issues of the South East Asian region bring into sharp relief the tensions between environmental conservation and eco-nomic **development** and international versus domestic political demands. The rapid economic growth of the East Asian economies has brought significant changes to the surrounding nations. These changes are a byproduct of both the incorporation of South East Asia into the East Asian economy and attempts by South East Asia to emulate this rapid development.

The consequences of large dam projects are a major source of debate in the region. As a major benefit, dams offer energy via hydroelectric power that can be put to increased **urbanization** and development projects (see **dams/hydroelectric power**). Perhaps more significantly, dams are engineering endeavours that can be viewed as symbols of the nation. The construction of dams is framed as a matter of national pride, to prove that indigenous engineers are just as capable as westerners. While the construction of a dam is a great technical achievement that can build a sense of nationhood, the social and environmental consequences are much more tangible, especially for the local communities whose lifestyles are disrupted. Local concerns are often pushed aside for the building of a dam that will serve national interests. The inherent irony is that the attempt by a national government to build an object of national pride will disenfranchise many of the individuals that the national government wanted to reach.

The Mekong Basin in particular has been a focal point for discussions over dam projects since the 1950s. The lower Mekong river region is seen by and large as an untapped resource. The Mekong Commission established in 1957 was reformulated in 1995 as the Mekong River Commission, continuing its mandate of co-ordinating dam projects for the lower Mekong. The Commission consists of the governments of Thailand, Laos, Vietnam, and Cambodia, but it is funded via the **United Nations Development Program**, as well as bilateral donations. The Mekong situation highlights another level of negotiation (and obstacle) in the dam issue. Local, national, and now international factors must be considered regarding this river system that crosses several national borders.

Many nations in the region have put greater thought and effort into developing their tourism industry. In particular, **eco-tourism** has become one of the most rapidly growing sectors of the economy in the region. Vietnam expects an increased number of visitors from the USA as relations between the two countries are normalized. Since 1980, **Indonesia** has embarked on a concerted effort to attract more eco-tourists, establishing several **national parks** in some of the more remote areas of the country, the most notable being Komodo National Park, home to the famed dragon.

It remains debateable as to whether eco-tourism projects can completely avoid problems of cultural dislocation and environmental degradation and still become profitable ventures. Increased numbers of visitors mean greater monetary benefit, but they also mean a greater impact on the environment. It is impossible to circumvent all impacts on traditional cultures, no matter how hard officials and visitors might try. Not only human communities, but natural ecosystems are affected. There is some concern that the feedings of Komodo dragons for the benefit of tourists has made some of the reptiles dependent on the food.

The most significant single environmental issue in the region may be deforestation (see **forest management**). Perhaps no other issue highlights the tensions between developed and developing countries so well. Although much of the clearing is due to increased domestic demand for timber, the major causes of deforestation in the region are international ones. First, the forests have been cleared to make way for cash crop **agriculture** such as sugar. Second, the timber itself is a major export of the region, most notably to **Japan**. Japan has been able to conserve most of its own forests by importing the overwhelming majority of its timber. Japan is the world's leading importer of tropical timber, mostly from South East Asia. Though Japan has some of the strongest domestic environmental regulations, especially in conservation, it has been able to maintain those regulations by externalizing many of its environmental impacts to other countries.

Further reading

Dauvergne, P. (1997) *Shadows in the Forest: Japan and*

the Politics of Timber in Southeast Asia, Cambridge, MA: MIT Press.

Hirsch, P. and Warren, C. (eds) (1998) *The Politics of Environment in Southeast Asia: Resources and Resistance*, London: Routledge.

Parnwell, M. and Bryant, R. (eds) (1996) *Environmental Change in South-East Asia: People, Politics and Sustainable Development*, London: Routledge.

ERIC SHIBUYA

Spaceship Earth

The metaphor of the planet Earth as a spaceship originated in the mid-1960s during the era of the US space programme (see **whole earth photograph**). Its first use is attributed (by Barbara Ward) to Adlai Stevenson, the US ambassador to the UN, in a speech to the Economic and Social Council in Geneva on 9 July 1965. He referred to the earth as a little spaceship on which we travel together, 'dependent on its vulnerable supplies of air and soil'. This metaphor was quickly adopted by others, including Barbara Ward and Kenneth Boulding in 1966, and Buckminster Fuller (1969), Paul **Ehrlich** (1971), and Garrett **Hardin** (1972). Boulding used the spaceship imagery to present early ecological arguments for **Limits to Growth** based on his **ecological economics** systems theory.

HORACE HERRING

Spain

In 2000, after 15 years of green attempts at getting elected to regional or the national Parliament, the Spanish Greens were rewarded with the regional environmental ministry in the government of the Balearic Islands, held by Margalida Rosselló. This was something, but not much. Moreover, she was elected (together with Joan Buades) to the regional assembly not on a purely green list but in a coalition with the post-communist party. There have been a handful of green city councillors (Ricardo Marqués in Seville, Pep Puig in Barcelona), also elected in coalition with other parties. Despite the system of proportional representation which in the provinces of Madrid and Barcelona

allows election with only 3 per cent of the vote, no green has ever been elected to the national parliament. And no green list has been successful for the European Parliament, though less than 2 per cent is necessary to get one deputy. The multiplication of green lists (including some ludicrous ones) dispersed the green vote, which in total reached around 3 per cent nationally. After the mid-1990s, Spanish Greens gave up trying on their own. Perhaps there is not enough electoral space for the Greens in a country with relatively strong Communist and post-communist parties plus left-wing nationalist parties in some regions. Maybe the **environmental movement** in Spain was too weak, or perhaps it never put its heart into electoral politics.

As in other countries, there have been two main trends in Spanish environmentalism (Fernández, 1999). The conservationist trend has a European symbol in the national park of Doñana in the Guadalquivir Delta (see **national parks**). Joaquin Araujo is the best-known representative of this trend. An early wildlife television hero was Rodriguez de la Fuente (who died in Alaska in 1980). ADENA (the Spanish member of the WWF) is the main organization. The second trend was born as an anti-nuclear movement in the late 1960s and 1970s, and also as a movement against industrial pollution still under the Franco regime (before 1975; see **anti-nuclear movements**). In 1969, the deaths in Erandio (near Bilbao) of workers who demonstrated against pollution marked a self-conscious beginning. Of course, antecedents of both currents may be found much earlier. There were deep concerns over deforestation and overfishing in the eighteenth century (*la tierra esquilmada*), there was the conservationism of Pidal in the early twentieth century, there was the cult of the **landscape** in the literary generation of 1898.

One famous episode of urban-industrial protoenvironmentalism was the massacre of 4 February 1888 when many workers and peasants complained against sulphur dioxide produced by the copper mining British Rio Tinto Company. Today's environmental movement in Spain likes to refer back to such history, which includes also the anarchist 'neo-malthusian' movement imported from France around 1900 (Masjuan, 2000). See also **anarchism/eco-anarchism**; **Malthus, Thomas**)

Something of the anarchist ethos pervaded the environmentalists' meetings in the heady atmosphere of the late 1970s, after Franco's death. The best-known activists, then in their thirties, decided at a series of encounters in Cercedilla, Valsain, Daimiel, not to enter electoral politics. Men like Mario Gaviria, Juan Serna, José-Manuel Naredo, Santiago Vilanova, Pedro Costa, Josep-Vicent Marqués, José Allende, all of them anti-nuclear activists, went into slightly different political trajectories. Almost all remained active environmentalists, some devoted themselves to writing and teaching, a few briefly joined the Socialist Party, a few became organic co-operative farmers, at least one tried in the mid-1980s to get one viable green party going, and failed.

While green electoral politics has produced many bitter divisions, the environmental movement as a whole has slowly grown. This has been partly because of external influences. The Spanish branch of **Greenpeace** (started in 1986 by Xavier Pastor) has been successful, with about 75,000 members. Hundreds of local environmental groups belong to an umbrella organization, *Ecologistas en Acción*. New issues (urban sprawl and transport, urban and industrial refuse, inter-basin water transfers) now dominate the environmental agenda. There are still fights over big energy projects (though no nuclear power station has been built in 20 years). There is new knowledge of an action against **transnational corporations** – some like Enron because of what they plan to do in Spain, others like Repsol and Endesa because of what they do in Latin America. International links are still weak. The activists (hundreds of thousands of demonstrators against the National Hydrological Plan in 2001, under the banner *una nueva cultura del agua* proposed by Pedro Arrojo) are more important in environmental politics in Spain than the green party or parties. Often, the movement looks for support from the European bureaucracy. Domingo Jiménez Beltrán, head of the European Environmental Agency, and the 'shadow' environment minister Cristina Narbona, are slowly pushing the Socialist Party (in opposition since 1996) towards environmentally orientated policies.

References.

Joaquín Fernández (1999) *El ecologismo español*, Madrid: Alianza

Eduard Masjuan (2000) *La ecología humana en el anarquismo ibérico*, Barcelona: Icaria

JOAN MARTINEZ-ALIER

Spanish environmental movement

With origins in anti-nuclear and conservationist struggles rather than in a broader counter-cultural milieu, the Spanish environmental movement emerged during the democratic transition in the late 1970s. Its main organizational features include a non-violent culture, anti-partisan sentiments, and a commitment to internal **democracy** and local autonomy (influenced by Iberian libertarian traditions and nationalism). Subsequent growth produced many new local groups but few and scattered economic resources. During this period, the movement's agenda expanded to include pacifist, environmental quality and health issues, partly thanks to the successful foundation of **Greenpeace** (by far the largest group in 2000 with 75,000 members). Localism has curbed professionalization and restricted mobilizations to numerous local, reactive conflicts, limiting the movement's influence on policy. In the late 1990s, it gained political leverage through a dense network centralized around a few state-wide organizations and the unification in 1999 of 300 groups in *Ecologistas en Acción* (30,000 members, 250 branches and thousands of volunteers). Other leading organizations include ADENA/WWF (15,000 members) and SEO/Birdlife (5,000 members).

MANUEL JIMÉNEZ

Spanish Green Party

Encouraged by Petra **Kelly**, the Greens (*Los Verdes*) were founded in 1984 during Spain's anti-NATO campaign. They initially lacked the support of the **Spanish environmental movement** or other social movements. Prone to constant splits over the territorial model of organization and electoral strategy, *Los Verdes* have hardly been a significant political force. Territorial fragmentation, together with an unfavourable electoral and party system have kept the green vote consistently below 2 per cent. However, the 1990s saw some organizational growth and a move towards a confederal structure of regional parties, 15 of which, representing 13 of the 17 Spain's Autonomous Communities, joined together in 1998. By then, the first green representatives had been elected to regional parliaments and city councils, often thanks to electoral coalitions with *Izquierda Unida*. In the late 1990s, the Greens switched electoral strategies to run in broad coalitions with the socialists and nationalists. This brought them their first seats in a regional government in 1999 (in the Balearic Islands).

MANUEL JIMÉNEZ

spotted owl controversy

The northern spotted owl is a non-migratory bird native to the old growth forests of Washington and Oregon states in the US Pacific North-west. Necessary for the owls' survival in the wild are large stands of live trees, with multi-layered branches and cavities in which to nest. Also required are dead standing and fallen trees which act as shelter for the owl as well as its prey. In 1986 the northern spotted owl was placed on the **endangered species** list due to habitat loss from excessive logging. As a result, the federal government began restricting logging in a 2,000 acre radius surrounding all known spotted owl nests. This required that at least 500 acres of the largest trees within the restricted zone be left uncut and that no logging occur within 70 acres of the actual nest. Due to these restrictions the timber industry has estimated that since 1987 it has lost over 85,000 jobs. Environmentalists have viewed the northern spotted owl as an indicator species for the health of old growth eco-systems.

Further reading

Hughes, B. (20 February 2001) 'The Northern Spotted Owl, Endangered – Fact or Fiction?' at

URL: http://www.siskiyous.edu/class/geog1a/fall1997/owl.htm.

JON E. FITCH

Spretnak, Charlene

b. 1946, Pittsburgh, USA

Writer

Charlene Spretnak was born in Pittsburg and raised in Columbus, Ohio. She holds degrees from the Unversities of St Louis and California, Berkeley and is on the Faculty of the California Institute of Integral Studies. She was an early and leading exponent of women's spirituality and **eco-feminism** in the USA and co-founded the US Green Committees of Correspondence. Her books include *The Spiritual Dimension of Green Politics* (1986), *The Politics of Women's Spirituality* (ed.) (1982), *States of Grace: The Recovery of Meaning in the Postmodern Age* (1991). In *The Resurgence of the Real: Body, Nature and Place in a Postmodern World* (1997) Spretnak argues that the modern mechanistic and industrialized world has lost touch with its sensuous and elemental roots and lacks a spiritual dimension. She seeks to unite wisdom, intellect and spirit by breaking down the barriers between peoples, while at the same time encouraging diversity and autonomy.

MARY MELLOR

steady-state economy

A steady-state economy is characterized by constant stocks of people and physical wealth maintained at some chosen, desirable level by as low a level of throughput as possible. The throughput provides direct consumption benefits (e.g., food, shelter) and investment in so far as necessary to counteract depreciation of the capital stock. Since the steady state is defined in physical terms there can be growth in economic value. That is, achieving a steady-state economy is not the same thing as the end of economic **development**. For example, as society learns more efficient ways to use energy, the value derived from the flow of energy may increase even though the flow itself does not.

Further reading

Daly, H. (ed.) (1980) *Economics, Ecology, Ethics: Essays Toward A Steady-State Economy*, San Francisco: W.H. Freeman.

Daly, H. (1991) *Steady State Economics*, Washington: Island Press.

STANLEY R. KEIL

stewardship

Often associated with religious and agricultural views and practices, stewardship covers a diverse range of related positions in regard to how humans ought to value and treat the environment. All of the great 'agricultural religions' of the world (Judeo-Christianity, Hinduism, Islam, Buddhism) have a 'stewardship' tradition in which humans are 'stewards' of God's 'creation' – the earth and all that lives on it. However, there are stewardship views of how humans ought to treat the land which are not associated with religious views, such as many aboriginal or indigenous views of the environment, or more modern ones such as **Leopold**'s 'land ethic' (see also **religions and the environment**; **indigenous peoples**). Since humans have neither created nor own the earth, a stewardship view places restrictions on how humans can use the environment. As an ethically based form of agricultural practice, stewardship explicitly recognizes the legitimacy and 'brute fact' that humans must use, transform and otherwise productively engage with the environment. While stewardship has its origins in these agricultural (and religious) relations between humans and the environment (based on direct productive experience of the environment, and often based on ownership of land), the modern use of the stewardship idiom seeks to update it to the current situation where the majority of the world's population live in urban areas, and thus have mediated, non-direct productive experience of the environment.

JOHN BARRY

Stockholm Conference

Arguably the landmark event in the evolution of the international environmental movement, the United Nations Conference on the Human Environment was held in Stockholm, **Sweden** from 5–16 June, 1972. It was attended by representatives from 113 countries, 19 inter-governmental agencies, and 400 other inter-governmental and non-governmental organizations (NGOs). Sparked by concerns in Sweden about the growing problem of acid pollution, it symbolized emerging concerns and public awareness in industrialized countries about the damaging environmental effects of human activities (see **acid rain**).

The conference produced a Declaration, a list of Principles, and an Action Plan. The 26 principles can be broken down into five main groups. These stated that:

1 Natural resources should be conserved, the capacity of the earth to produce renewable resources should be maintained, and **non-renewable resources** should be shared.
2 **Development** and environmental concern should go together, and **less developed countries** should be given every assistance and incentive to promote rational environmental management.
3 Each state should establish its own standards of **environmental management** and exploit resources as it wished, but should not endanger other states. There should be international co-operation aimed at improving the state of the environment.
4 Pollution should not exceed the capacity of the environment to clean itself, and marine pollution should be prevented.
5 Science, **technology**, education, and research should all be used to promote environmental protection.

The Action Plan consisted of 109 separate recommendations, ranging from the specific to the general, and falling into one of three broad groups: environmental assessment, environmental management, and supporting measures. Almost half dealt with the conservation of natural resources, while the rest covered issues relating to human settlements, pollution and marine pollution, development and the environment, and education and information.

The Stockholm Conference had four major results. First, it confirmed a new emphasis on human environment, and on the international dimensions of environmental problems. Before Stockholm, the environment was seen as something separate from humans. Following the conference, there was a broader perception of humans within their environment, and as primary victims of the consequences of environmental mismanagement. Stockholm helped spawn a series of conferences on specific issues such as population (see **population movement and control**), **agriculture**, desertification, and human settlements, and paved the way for the agreement of a series of key **international environmental laws/treaties**.

Second, Stockholm helped encourage a compromise between the different perceptions of rich countries and poor countries. During the preparatory discussions on the conference, less developed countries made clear their view that poverty was a greater concern than pollution, and used their UN General Assembly voting power to encourage industrialized countries to recognize the need to balance the priorities of environmental management with the aims of economic development. For their part, industrialized countries were encouraged to rethink the priorities of environmentalism (see **environmentalism and ecologism**), to take a broader view of the global nature of many problems, and to appreciate how many of these problems – particularly those in poorer countries – were rooted in social and political issues. Before Stockholm, environmental priorities had been determined largely by more developed countries; following Stockholm the needs of less developed countries were added to the mix.

Third, the presence of so many NGOs at the conference – and the part they played in discussions – marked the beginning of a new role for NGOs in the work of governments and intergovernmental organizations. The NGOs had little influence at the conference itself, and have not always since achieved as much influence at UN fora as they might have, but there was a rapid growth in the number and quality of NGOs in the post-Stockholm decade. The conference not only put national NGOs in contact with one another, but emphasized that they faced common problems in their countries which demanded a concerted response.

Finally, the most tangible outcome of Stockholm was the creation of the **United Nations Environment Programme** (UNEP), whose first executive director was Maurice **Strong**, Secretary-General of the Stockholm Conference. UNEP has had limitations and deficiencies, but it was probably the best form of institution possible under the circumstances, and it became the focus of a new interest in global responses to global problems. In 1992, it provided the main organizational focus behind the UN Conference on Environment and Development, held in Rio de Janeiro, which took up many of the themes first explored at Stockholm (see **Rio Conference 1992**).

Further reading

McCormick, J. (1995) *The Global Environmental Movement*, Chichester: John Wiley, chapter 5.

Ward, B. and Dubois, R. (1972) *Only One Earth*, Harmondsworth: Penguin.

JOHN McCORMICK

Strong, Maurice

b. 1929, Oak Lake, Manitoba, Canada

Administrator

Often referred to as the 'custodian of the planet', Maurice Strong has been involved with the **environmental movement** for more than 30 years. Strong first worked as an apprentice in the **Arctic** with the Hudson's Bay Company. In 1947, at the age of 18, he joined the secretariat of the United Nations (UN). In the early 1950s, Strong left his UN position to pursue a career in the private sector and achieved great success in running various energy corporations. He then returned to the UN. In 1972, he organized and chaired the **Stockholm**

Conference (UN Conference on the Human Environment). Strong has subsequently held many notable positions, including the Executive Director of **United Nations Environment Programme** (UNEP), the Secretary–General of the 1992 Rio Earth Summit (see **Rio Conference 1992**), and Senior Advisor to the **World Bank**.

Strong proclaiming himself a 'socialist in ideology and capitalist in methodology' has maintained that only a strong UN will be capable of saving the earth from environmental disaster. He has been labelled as a 'bi-sectoral entrepreneur who uses business success for leverage in politics, and vice versa' (Bailey). Currently Strong is the president of the Earth Council, a coalition which links together national governments, environmental groups, and the private sector in global pursuit of a new developmental paradigm (see **paradigms**).

Further reading

Bailey, R. 'Who is Maurice Strong?'
  URL: http://www.afn.org/~govern/strong.html.
Barkley, D. 'Who is Maurice Strong',
  URL: http://www.endtime.com/03_oldsite/strong.htm.

JON E. FITCH

structural adjustment programmes

During the 1980s, development assistance shifted in emphasis from financing infrastructure and investment, to supporting programmes of growth-orientated policy reform and economic liberalization. Structural adjustment programmes (SAPs) became a condition for **World Bank** lending in much of the world, from Central and Latin America to Africa and Russia. They comprise a set of policies which combine short-term economic stabilization, with long-term adjustment. These cover: deregulation and privatization of the domestic economy (to remove subsidies and 'obstacles' to free trade), fiscal policies to cut public spending, strict monetary policies (maintaining high interest rates), wage and price controls to limit inflation, and devaluation of the national currency to promote exports. Despite securing gains in growth, SAPs have been criticized for their damaging impacts on the poor (in particular women, smallholders and workers), and the environment. The resulting inequality and poverty, only partially alleviated by transitional 'social funds', provokes growing **civil society** activism against SAPs.

GILL SEYFANG

sub-Saharan Africa

Africa south of the Sahara desert, otherwise known as sub-Saharan Africa, is geographically vast, with diverse ecological and socio-economic resources and challenges. With a population of about 614 million people (about 10 per cent of the world total), the region comprises 42 countries on the mainland, plus seven island nations that are off the coastlines of East, West and Southern Africa. In terms of human and economic **development** indices, sub-Saharan Africa is the least developed and poorest region of the world with two-thirds of the population living in rural areas and deriving their livelihood from smallholder, free range agro-pastoral production. Twenty-one of the 30 poorest countries in the world are in this region (World Bank, 1996: 2). Major environmental concerns in sub-Saharan Africa result from heavy reliance on natural capital, land degradation, deforestation, rapid **urbanization**, demographic explosion, and loss of **biodiversity**, compounded by climatic change.

The national incomes of most countries of sub-Saharan Africa depend heavily on their **natural capital** (natural resources), particularly, agricultural production and to a lesser extent, the exploitation of mineral resources. This is largely a consequence of colonial underdevelopment. In countries like Burkina Faso, Eritrea, Ethiopia, Malawi, Tanzania and Uganda, more than 80 per cent of the population are rural dwellers engaged in small-scale **agriculture**. With the exception of a few Southern African countries (Zimbabwe, Botswana and South Africa), where

modern **technology**, large-scale agricultural pro-
ductions are carried out by some minority white
settler populations, much of sub-Saharan African
agriculture relies heavily on crude technology and
rotational bush fallowing (a variant of shifting
cultivation). Rotational bush fallowing has the
disadvantage of requiring larger areas of land for
farming, and coupled with low levels of technology
and farm inputs, the phenomenon results in soil
degradation and food deficits. Some critical factors
that contribute to, or exacerbate the problem of
soil degradation in Africa are uncontrolled grazing
(linked to nomadism and the use of natural
pastures), water erosion, deforestation (loss of trees
and forests mostly related to clearing of agricultural
land and logging), climatic variability and desertification in areas adjacent to the Sahara and
Kalahari deserts.

In recent years, desertification has heightened
the risk of serious droughts in the Sudano-Sahelian
Belt and Horn of Africa. Repeated devastations of
human, animal and plant lives by droughts have
been witnessed in Ethiopia during the past 20 years
and the most recent dimension of the problem,
which was brought to the attention of the
international community by aid agencies in April
2000 puts about eight million Ethiopians under the
threat of severe hunger and starvation (see
famines). The droughts were preceded by three
years of little or no rain in the Horn of Africa.

Whereas the Sudano-Sahelian Belt and Horn of
Africa suffer severe droughts and paucity of rain,
the flooding effects of torrential rain, swollen rivers
and cyclones most dangerously threaten countries
of Southern Africa. Between February and March
2000, different parts of South Africa, Zimbabwe,
Zambia, Madagascar and especially Mozambique
were hit by the worst floods in African contemporary history. Cyclone Eline, heavy rain and
rushing torrents of the swollen Limpopo and
Zambezi rivers devastated and swept away countless buildings, livestock and village settlements into
the Indian Ocean. An estimated one million people
were left homeless by the deluge while the death
toll from drowning is worsened by hunger,
exhaustion and an explosion of filthy water related
diseases (malaria, cholera and diarrhoea). In a
subregion believed to have the largest concentra-

tion of landmines in Africa following a historical
cycle of deadly conflicts, the recent flooding has
dislodged thousands of landmines and carried
them into previously safe areas, thereby posing a
greater danger to human life.

Closely related to the problems of flooding,
desertification and deforestation in sub-Saharan
Africa is the continued loss of natural habitats and
biodiversity. With the exception of a few countries
like Kenya, South Africa and Zimbabwe where
wildlife has been efficiently developed as a major
component of tourism and source of external
revenue (see **eco-tourism**), wildlife conservation
is increasingly neglected in sub-Saharan Africa.
Primates and many of the world's **endangered
species** are eaten as sources of animal protein in
most countries of the region. Other overlooked
aspects of biodiversity in Africa, reports the **World
Bank** (1996:13), include sustainable food production, medicine and ecosystem resilience.

Finally, both **urbanization** and demographic
explosion generate major environmental concerns
in sub-Saharan Africa. This is the most rapidly
urbanizing region in the world and this dynamic,
in the context of the political economy of underdevelopment and poverty, produces some stark
challenges: crowding due to rural–urban migration
for economic opportunities, inadequacy of social
infrastructure and services, municipal waste pollution, and poor environmental health. These
problems are quite evident in such big cities as
Accra, Capetown, Dakar, Lagos, Abidjan, and
Johannesburg (to mention a few). The problem of
rapid urbanization is exacerbated by high population growth rate, which shows a current annual
average of 3 per cent (the world's current highest
regional growth rate). The fast pace of medical
progress and the traditional premium on children
as a form of social capital are two major factors
that have contributed to Africa's demographic
explosion.

See also: Nigeria; South African environmental
politics

Reference

World Bank (1996) *Towards Environmentally Sustain-*

able Development in Sub-Saharan Africa, Washington: World Bank.

Further reading

Middleton, J. (ed.) (1997) *Encyclopedia of Africa South of the Sahara*, vol. 1, New York: Simon & Schuster MacMillan, pp. 549–55.

Mkandawire, T. and Soludo, C.C. (1999) *Our Continent, Our Future*, Dakar-Senegal: CODES-RIA.

KENNETH OMEJE

Superfund

Prior to the Solid Waste Disposal Act 1965 there was no federal legislation addressing the problems of solid and hazardous wastes; they were left to the states and localities, which basically operated 'out of sight, out of mind'. The first significant federal law to pass was the Resource Conservation and Recovery Act of 1976. RCRA is a complex piece of legislation, becoming more complex with its amendments in 1984. At its core has been a federal permit and monitoring system to regulate the operations of hazardous waste sites. However, RCRA did nothing to grapple with the health threats posed by abandoned waste sites and emergency events (see **health and the environment**). The ticking time bomb of hazardous wastes reached the national policy agenda in the late 1970s as a result of media coverage of the disaster at **Love Canal**, New York.

Congress responded to Love Canal by passing the Comprehensive Environmental Response, Compensation and Liability Act of 1980 (CER-CLA), which has been commonly known as 'Superfund'. The nickname is ironic since the Congress compromised the authorized funding down to $1.6 billion in order to get passage prior to Ronald Reagan's inauguration as President (see **Reagan, Ronald**). The funding scheme for Superfund was innovative in that 87.5 per cent of the monies would be derived from new 'feedstock' taxes on the chemical industries. The basic idea of CERCLA was that the federal government would deal quickly with abandoned sites, and then would

recoup its expenses by taking legal action against all responsible parties. In practice, this has not happened and clean up of Superfund sites has taken many years due to engineering studies and litigation. According to the General Accounting Office, there are nationally over 378,000 hazardous waste sites needing remedial action. CER-CLA authorized the **Environmental Protection Agency** (EPA) to draw up a National Priority List (NPL) to focus action on the sites most threatening to public health. The first listing in 1982 included 418 sites; a decade later there were over 1,200 on the NPL.

The most controversial part of CERCLA has been its liability provisions and how they have been applied by the EPA. Responsible parties (generators, transporters, owners, operators, and even bankers) are liable for actions taken before the law came into effect as well as afterwards. They are held 'strictly' liable which means that even if they disposed of the wastes in a legal way at the time, legal action can still be taken against them. Furthermore, their liability is 'joint and several' which means that even a small disposal at a site could translate into responsibility for the entire clean-up (which tends to make the law self-enforcing as the lawyers of one responsible party go after others). CERCLA withstood early challenges in the federal courts (only in the 1990s were there more mixed rulings).

There were many complaints about the implementation of the Superfund programme during the first Reagan Administration. For example, critics charged that the EPA was doing 'sweetheart deals' with corporations to get them off the hook without fully paying for clean-ups, and that Superfund monies were being allocated in a partisan way. Ultimately the EPA head Anne **Burford** was cited for contempt of Congress over failure to provide information relating to these charges, and she later resigned. (Her subordinate, Rita Lavelle, went to jail for perjury.)

In 1986 Congress passed the Superfund Amendments and Re-authorization Act (SARA). It came closer to being a 'Superfund', with $9 billion authorized for remedial actions. The new law was more ambitious and complex. Among the things that it has attempted to do are: to codify the level of

cleanliness required, to accelerate the work schedule on Superfund sites, to require greater public
participation in decision-making about remedial
action, and to allow minimal site contributors to
settle early (and lightly). CERCLA/SARA came up
for re-authorization again in the 1990s. A compromise reform act favoured by environmentalists
and industrialists failed in November 1994 due to
last-minute disagreements among key congressmen. Since then the pace of clean-ups has
accelerated; however, though rarely in the head-
lines, criticisms of the Superfund programme have
come from all sides. During the Republican control
of Congress (1995–), bills have been introduced to
rollback the Superfund law by weakening its
polluter pays principle (leaving the taxpayers
to pick up more of the costs), and by relaxing clean-
up standards. To date, none of these bills have
passed, but with Republicans controlling all
branches of the federal government after January
2001, this could change.

See also: hazardous and toxic waste
management

Further reading

'Cleaning up Hazardous Wastes' (23 August 1996)
  The CQ Researcher, 6(32): 745–68.
de Saillan, C. (1993) 'In Praise of Superfund',
  Environment, 35, (8) October: 42–4.
Probst, K.N. and Konisky, D.M. (2001) *Superfund's
  Future*, Washington, DC: Resources for the
  Future.
Superfund website at
  URL: http://www.epa.gov/superfund.

E. GENE FRANKLAND

sustainability

Sustainability has a number of connected meanings. The first is a sense of futurity, sustaining
something into the future. A second relates to ideas
of supporting and developing some process or
thing. Related to this is the sense of providing the
right or necessary means to support some end,
entity or process. Sustainability is related to the
idea of **sustainable development**, which has

become a central concept in international environmental politics, in that it is taken as a shorthand
way of referring to harmonious, secure, stable and
long-term productive relations between human
society and the natural environment. However,
many environmental activists and writers reserve
sustainability as indicating something more radical
and stronger than the 'reformist' notion of
sustainable development, in the sense that sustainability, unlike sustainable development, incorporates a concern for the natural world as something
more than the just the means to human development ends.

JOHN BARRY

sustainable development

The concept of sustainable development was
originally promoted in the 1987 Brundtland
Report, *Our Common Future*, by the United Nations
World Commission on Environment and Development (WCED) (see **Brundtland Commission**).
A product of international pressure for unified
international action on global environmental
degradation, it has affected development actions
on a global scale. Its aim however, to promote
development that meets the needs of the present
without impinging upon the ability of future
generations to meet their needs, has proven to be
an enormously challenging task.

Sustainable development has been the target of
a wide variety of groups. Given the complexity
which surrounds the concept and its materializa-
tion, critics tried to disentangle the different
dimensions it entails. According to Baker *et al.*
(1997), when the emphasis is placed on the
contestability of the concept, four alternative
frameworks to sustainable development may be
envisaged: the treadmill approach, weak sustainable development, strong sustainable development,
and the ideal model. Ranging from the most
anthropocentric (treadmill) to the most bio/**ecocentric** (ideal) these approaches are representative
of major actor orientations and actions (see
anthropocentrism). More specifically, the ecocentric perspective (ideal and strong sustainable
development) places nature before economic

growth whereas the anthropocentric (weak and treadmill sustainable development) is an interventionist approach to nature, in terms of industrial–economic and technological activities. This proposed frame, as seen below, situates a variety of actors according to the approaches they tend to adopt.

In the treadmill approach, which was especially dominant until the early 1980s, ecosystems are viewed in terms of their utility to producers and production-related agencies. Environmentalists do not adopt this sustained growth approach since it ignores environmental impacts. Transnational corporations and many producers adopt this view in their drive to increase profits, not only in the north, but in the southern and eastern parts of the globe. Even though it promotes economic growth as well, the weak sustainable development approach takes into account ecosystem effects since it views the ecosystem as a measurable resource. In ameliorating the most adverse effects via **environmental management**, it uses tools such as environmental impact assessment, **cost-benefit analysis** and resource accounting. Such an approach is likely to be adopted by the most 'conservative' wings of environmental organizations, who are exclusively concerned with the preservation, for example, of specific wild-life areas or with the passing of a law requiring impact-assessment studies. States and supra-national bodies such as the **European Union** are more likely to take this approach as well, given their sector-driven orientations and the need for only minimal amendments to institutions.

Turning to more biocentric approaches, strong sustainable development is characterized by changes in patterns of production and consumption towards an environmentally regulated economy. Although the overall objective of economic growth remains, strong sustainable development requires policies that maintain the productive capacity of all ecosystem resources, preserving or improving them as needed. Its advocates posit that environmental protection is a precondition of economic development, requiring market regulation, state intervention and the involvement of local communities. This approach is more appealing to ecocentric environmental organizations, grassroots groups, as well as to political ecology groups. Given

the needed institutional restructuring it requires, as well as the integration of environmental policy across sectors, this approach is not as easily adopted by states or supra-state bodies such as the European Union.

Finally, the ideal type aims towards more profound changes at the socio-economic, ideological and political levels. It therefore requires changes in patterns as well as levels of production and consumption to promote and protect **biodiversity**. Its adherents agree that environmental protection demands severe restraints on the consumption of natural resources and economic activities. The most radical environmental groups are likely to adopt this approach which would require drastic restructuring of political, legal, social and economic institutions (Baker *et al.*, 1997; Kousis, 1998).

Discourses in sustainable development

The discourse of sustainable development creates counter-discourses that follow local, regional, or national images of nature. The more the boundaries of legitimate environmental discourse are defined by the dominant discourse, the more local, regional, or national counter-discourses will rise. Alternatively, grassroots groups may initiate sustainable development discourses which in turn lead to counter-discourses from top groups (Kousis and Eder, 2001).

In its formal, institutionalized guise, the discourse on sustainable development is strongly linked with economic growth and the priorities of competition, thereby reflecting concerns of the more advanced economies. Informal activities of smaller scale state and economic interests disclose the existence of a silent un/sustainability discourse, suggesting tolerance of economic priorities (Briassoulis, 2001). Increasing competition on a global scale nevertheless, intensifies both formal and informal economic activities at all levels – such as the illegal dumping of large amounts of toxic/hazardous waste.

At a transnational/global level, this prevailing discourse aims to maintain or improve the economic wellbeing of the powerful North, while at the same time promoting the North's own competitive position *vis-à-vis* other economic blocs (Redclift, 2001). At the nation-state level this discourse reflects spatially and socially limited power relations. Involved groups include business interest groups, civil servants, the government, environmental organizations, a variety of publics, and, if European Union members, European Union agencies (Eder, 2001). Competing claims on the environment are thus evident. On the one hand, environmental activists seek a more sustainable use of local ecosystems. On the other hand, producers and state actors usually pursue vested interests and economic growth. In this context, after the end of the Second World War and the Cold War, the world has been divided decreasingly between national societies and increasingly between organized blocks of national societies. Three worlds of sustainable development, i.e. of shared interests and identities forming the ways of dealing with environmental issues and sustainable development, are proposed by Eder (2001) and described below as the transnational elite world, the nation-state world, and the popular world. The (new) 'transnational elite world' is characteristic of deliberative bodies and councils, green images of business, and **sustainability** discourses translating economic interests into good life metaphors (see **business and the environment**). The impacts of these institutional changes are not yet clear. Here, the involvement of collective actors in transnational negotiation turns environmental issues into public issues which allow policy outcomes to be attributed to these actors, thus creating particular constraints on them. Elite groups organize themselves ever more beyond the national level, e.g. as European groups, as **epistemic communities** or other carriers of an information and knowledge society. Such groups replace the cultural and social hegemony once belonging exclusively to national elites.

The (old) 'nation-state world' embraces corporatist arrangements on environmental issues, state responsibility with intense temporary anti-state actions, and national economic growth minimizing ecological transaction costs (occasionally appearing as **ecological modernization** initiatives), as good life metaphors. In such a world, a strong identification of environmental politics with na-

tional interests drives collective actors to act when these interests are at stake. National groups represent people concerned about their position in an increasingly competitive world, feeling threatened in their relative position between the losers and the winners and striving to protect their individual and collective goods (Eder, 2001).

Strong localism dominates in the 'popular world', with scattered mobilizations, informal economies embedded in a life-world, with nature again a good life metaphor. Here, top-down initiatives such as those by economic, state, or EU bodies, may produce collective action, i.e. local protest and grassroots mobilization. Local groups represent a class of people hit economically and socially by the consequences of the new economic order. This change is reflected especially in the loss of collective goods, such as clean air and clean ecosystems, together with the negative impacts on social life (Eder, 2001).

Thus far, no collective vision exists on how sustainability and **democracy** may unite to surpass the obstacles and to build on opportunities and alliances. Nevertheless, the transition towards strong sustainable development may be enhanced, via local empowerment, intervention programmes aimed at assisting the vulnerable, the willingness of formal governance to collaborate with informal governance, and the promotion of social well-being and ecological integrity (O'Riordan and Church, 2001).

Sustainable development and the environmental movement

The relationship between **environmental movements** and sustainable development has only recently been explored (e.g. Brand, 1999; Viola, 1997). In general, works point to the existence of competing frames of sustainable development, which follow either economic development/modernization orientations, or those of environmental and new social movement contenders (see **new social movements**). Sustainable development discourses expressed by environmental contenders contrast those of the groups they usually challenge, namely state and supra-state agencies as well as economic organizations. Each of the competing interest groups makes a different use of the physical environment, with different implications for local ecosystems, health and economy (Kousis, 1998). It is thus argued that while the state and entrepreneurs seek an economically viable sustainable development, environmental movements usually search for an ecologically and socially orientated sustainable development (Kousis, 1998).

Environmental organizations may adopt weak sustainable development alternatives (see e.g. Brand, 1999), especially in the First World. While promoting economic growth, they take into account ecosystem effects, viewing ecosystems as measurable resources. These approaches may use tools such as environmental impact assessment (EIA), cost-benefit analysis, resource accounting, eco-labeling, and **risk assessment**. The more conservative or professional wings of the environmental movement (e.g. concerned with the preservation, for example, of specific wild-life areas or with the passing of a law requiring EIA) tend to support such schemes. Nevertheless, faith in ecological modernization initiatives is lately subsiding within environmental organizations (Brand, 1999).

Grassroots, ecocentric as well as political ecology groups are more likely to favour strong sustainable development, a more biocentric approach characterized by changes in patterns of production and consumption towards an environmentally regulated economy, requiring policies that maintain the productive capacity of all ecosystem resources – preserving or improving them as needed, while simultaneously addressing pressing social issues (Brand, 1999; O'Riordan and Voisey, 1998). Given the institutional restructuring it requires as well as environmental policy integration across sectors, this approach is not as easily adopted by states or supra-state bodies such as the European Union, nor by environmental organizations (Brand, 1999). Even though local environmental groups tend to adopt confrontational tactics, it is difficult to characterize their views under the strong sustainable development approach, unless this refers to the local level.

Environmental claims made by grassroots environmental protesters may be viewed as parallel to the weak and strong sustainable development approaches, according to a recent study (Kousis *et al.*, 1996). More specifically, the claims made about the

user's responsibility are either radical or moderate. Some believe that eco-intervening activities should be fully stopped, thus approaching a stronger sustainable development perspective, while others believe protective steps should be taken to remedy the problem, as a weaker sustainable development approach would support. The majority of the mobilizers propose the permanent ceasing of source/activities (planned or operating), or the creation, application or implementation of environmental rules and regulations, proper regional/urban planning and less polluting technologies. The mobilizers tend to see three basic types of negative impacts running more or less simultaneously: local ecosystem, public health, and economic impacts, in this order of importance. They relate these to the destruction of the local ecosystem, atmospheric, fresh water and soil pollution. The transition path to sustainable development was long overdue, as these grassroots actions reveal since the mid-1970s. The great difficulties which do not allow for proper problem solving are tightly intertwined with top-down economic and political decision-making power which takes place above community-based residents' and local environmental groups. Consequently, the great majority of these cases have been contending for at least, a weaker, if not a stronger, type of sustainable development, but have basically been alone and not been heard as much as expected by those in power to remedy the problems. The experience they had with their local environment led them to resist negative ecosystem and public health impacts, and envision a more sustainable situation through protest activities.

The cases against conventional sustainable development projects such as protected areas, waste treatment and **renewable energy** plants constitute only about five per cent of all such environmental protest cases (Kousis *et al.*, 1996). For these protesters there are different costs and benefits associated with this type of transitional path to sustainable development. The socio-economic costs centre around the loss of jobs and the loss of the community itself in some cases, as well as the inability to participate in the decision-making which severely affects their daily lives. Other costs incurred are related to public health, experienced or suspected (see **health and the**

environment). The benefits of many of these projects are much greater or exist only for people outside the affected area, such as urban based producers and consumers of toxic-waste producing items. Thus, the transitional path has more grave consequences for example, for people in remote, previously unharmed rural communities where a toxic-waste treatment facility is/will be located. The benefits of such a transitional path accrue in essence to nonlocals (Kousis *et al.*, 1996).

Finally, the more radical grassroots groups and environmental organizations aim for the ideal type of sustainable development, targeting more profound changes at the socio-economic, ideological and political levels. This would require changes in patterns as well as levels of production and consumption to promote and protect biodiversity and would thus require drastic restructuring of political, legal, social and economic institutions.

See also: Agenda 21; anthropocentrism; business and the environment; deep ecology; ecological economics; ecological modernization environmental economics; green accounting; less developed countries; multinational and transnational corporations; social ecology; sustainability; Commission on Sustainable Development

References

Baker, S., Kousis, M., Richardson, D. and Young, S. (1997) 'Introduction: The Theory and Practice of Sustainable Development in EU Perspective', in S. Baker, M. Kousis, D. Richardson and S. Young (eds) *The Politics of Sustainable Development: Theory, Policy and Practice in the European Union*, London: Routledge.

Brand, K-W., (1999) 'Dialectics of Institutionalization: The Transformation of the Environmental Movement in Germany', *Environmental Politics* 8(1): 35–58.

Briassoulis, H. (2001) 'Sustainable Development – The Formal Or Informal Way?' in K. Eder and M. Kousis (eds) *Environmental Politics in Southern Europe: Actors, Institutions and Discourses in a Europeanizing Society*, Dordrecht: Kluwer Academic Publishers.

Eder, K. (2001) 'Sustainability as a Discursive Device for Mobilizing European Publics', in K. Eder and M. Kousis (eds) *Environmental Politics in Southern Europe: Actors, Institutions and Discourses in a Europeanizing Society*, Dordrecht: Kluwer Academic Publishers.

Kousis, M. (1998) 'A Theoretical Exposition of Environmental Movement Research Worldwide: The Challengers, The Challenged, and Sustainable Development', Proceedings of the Second Woudschoten Conference, *Sociological Theory and the Environment*, (eds) A. Gijswijt, F. Buttel, P. Dickens, R. Dunlap, A. Mol, and G. Spaargaren, SISWO, University of Amsterdam.

Kousis, M., Aguilar-Fernandez, S., and Fidelis-Nogueira, T. (1996) *Grassroots Environment Action and Sustainable Development in the Southern European Union*, European Commission, DGXII, EV5V–CT94–0393, 1994–1996.

Kousis, M. and Eder, K. (2001) 'Introduction: EU Policy-making, Local Action, and the Emergence of Institutions of Collective Action, A Theoretical Perspective on Southern Europe', in K. Eder and M. Kousis (eds) *Environmental Politics in Southern Europe: Actors, Institutions and Discourses in a Europeanizing Society*, Dordrecht: Kluwer Academic Publishers.

O'Riordan, T. and Church, C. (2001) 'Synthesis and Context', in T. O'Riordan (ed.) *Globalism, Localism and Identity: Perspectives on the Sustainability Transition in Europe*, London: Earthscan.

O'Riordan, T. and Voisey, H. (1998) 'The Political Economy of the Sustainability Transition', in T. O'Riordan, and H. Voisey (eds) *The Transition to Sustainability: The Politics of Agenda 21 in Europe*, London: Earthscan.

Redclift, M. (2001) 'Sustainability and the North/South Divide', in K. Eder and M. Kousis (eds) *Environmental Politics in Southern Europe: Actors, Institutions and Discourses in a Europeanizing Society*. Dordrecht: Kluwer Academic Publishers.

Viola, E.J. (1997) 'The Environmental Movement in Brazil: Institutionalization, Sustainable Development, and Crisis of Governance Since 1987', *Latin American Environmental Policy in International Perspective*, Boulder, CO: Westview Press, pp.88–112.

Further reading

Baker, S. (2000) 'Between the Devil and the Deep

Blue Sea: International Obligations, Eastern Enlargement, and the Promotion of Sustainable Development in the European Union', *Journal of Environmental Policy Planning* 2(2):149–66.

Buttel, F.H. (1998) 'Some Observations on States, World Orders and the Politics of Sustainability', *Organization and Environment* 11(3):261–86.

Golub, J. (ed.) (1998) *Global Competition and EU Environmental Policy*, London: Routledge.

Jamison, A. (2001) *Ecological Transformations: Sustainable Development, Public Participation, and the Making of Green Knowledge*, London: Cambridge.

Peet, R. and Watts, M. (eds) (1996) *Liberation Ecologies: Environment, Development, and Social Movements*, London: Routledge.

Redclift, M. (1987) *Sustainable Development: Exploring the Contradictions*, London: Routledge.

—— (1992) 'Sustainable Development and Popular Participation: A Framework for Analysis', in D. Ghai and J.M. Vivian (eds) *Grassroots Environmental Action: People's Participation in Sustainable Development*, London: Routledge.

Richardson, D. (1997) 'The Politics of Sustainable Development', in S. Baker, M. Kousis, D. Richardson and S. Young (eds) *The Politics of Sustainable Development: Theory, Policy and Practice in the European Union*, London: Routledge.

MARIA KOUSIS

Sweden

Despite its relatively small population (8 million), Sweden has played an important, and often a leading, international role in many areas of environmental politics and policy-making. The Swedish state was the first in the world to establish an environmental protection agency (in 1967), and the comprehensive environmental protection law, passed by the parliament in 1969, was also among the earliest such pieces of legislation. A particular court of appeals was created for the hearing of environmental cases, and local environmental officials were given greater authority to enforce compliance than was the case in most other countries. In the 1970s, there were also comparatively early efforts by Swedish companies, universities and other research institutions to develop innovative technical solutions to many cases of industrial pollution, as well as to reorient ecological research into more practical and social directions. In 1972, Sweden also played a pioneering role in international environmental politics, by hosting the United Nations Conference on the Human Environment, which led to the creation of the **United Nations Environment Programme** (UNEP).

As in neighbouring **Norway** and **Finland**, the strong interest in environmental issues is due, among other things, to the relatively harsh geographical conditions and the low population density, which have given rise historically to a strong environmental sensibility in the population. The emergence of Sweden as a European great power in the seventeenth century served to establish a legacy of bureaucratic public administration that has continued to dominate the Swedish political culture. Also significant in Sweden is the paternalist character of the state, which has served historically to counter the influence of the aristocracy and the private sector. A unique result is the Swedish tradition of *allemansrätt* (public right), which guarantees free access and public use of the rural countryside environment. There was thus a comparatively early and widespread public response to the international environmental debate literature that followed in the wake of Rachel **Carson**'s *Silent Spring* in the 1960s.

Environmental organizations have played a significant role in Swedish policy-making. The so-called corporatist system of interest negotiations has meant that environmental organizations have been given the right to comment on forthcoming legislation and policy measures, as well as to take part in policy deliberations at different levels of government. Many organizations also receive state subsidies for their activities. In addition, there has been a strong parliamentary interest in environmental issues in Sweden since the 1960s. Largely because of its opposition to **nuclear energy** and its support for stronger environmental protection measures, the agrarian centre party was able to unseat the ruling social democratic party in the 1975 election, and lead a non-socialist coalition government for the first time in 40 years.

These processes of 'incorporation' have not been able to keep environmental politics from taking on more contentious forms. The various components of the highly diverse environmental movement have been influential in Sweden, at least since the debate over nuclear energy in the second half of the 1970s. The inability of the Centre party to convince its coalition partners brought on a 'people's campaign against nuclear energy' and a referendum, which produced a political compromise, by which it was decided that nuclear energy was to be phased out by the year 2010. The polarized mobilization around the nuclear issue led to the creation of a Green Party (*Miljöpartiet de Gröna*) – which entered the parliament for the first time in 1988, and has continued to be influential in parliamentary politics – as well as to an anti-environmental corporate lobby, which continues to campaign for nuclear energy.

In the 1990s, the environmental political agenda in Sweden has largely been redirected to global issues, such as climate change and **biodiversity**, as well as to the integration of environmental protection into economic and social policies in the name of **sustainable development**. Particularly important have been the efforts to establish **environmental management** procedures in companies and to foster environmentally friendly patterns of consumption. In these activities, the large environmental organizations, especially the Swedish Society for the Protection of Nature (*Naturskyddsföreningen*) have played significant roles, as have new, more commercially orientated organizations, such as the internationally active The Natural Step. The country's entrance into the **European Union** in 1995 has also meant that there has been a need to increase international cooperation and co-ordination in policy-making. The Swedish government has supported efforts in environmental protection in several eastern European countries, as well as in international organizations. The 1990s have also witnessed the emergence of a more militant form of environmental activism, particularly in relation to **animal rights**.

Further reading

Jamison, A. (1997) 'Sweden: The Dilemmas of Polarization', in A. Jamison and P. Østby (eds) *Public Participation and Sustainable Development. Comparing European Experiences*, Aalborg: Aalborg University Press.

ANDREW JAMISON

Swiss green parties

Emerging during the 1970s, canton-based Swiss green parties gathered into two loose federations before the 1983 national elections expressing the split between the more radical and alternative groups. In 1987, despite the favourable political context and the huge ecological awareness of Swiss citizens, the Greens, competing in 18 of the 26 cantons, showed disappointing results. The 'moderate' Green Party of Switzerland (GPS) got 9 seats and the 'radical' Green Alliance of Switzerland (GBS) received 3 seats. However, they performed better at the local and cantonal level. In 1990, the GBS decided to merge with the GPS. This unification helped the Greens to consolidate their position as the fifth largest party in 1991. This fusion turned the GPS into a left–green party less appealing for the moderate voters in 1995. In the 1999 national elections the GPS stabilized its position (9 seats).

CÉDRIC VAN DE WALLE

T

takings

Takings doctrine in Anglo-American law is the concept that the government's power to 'take' private property is constrained by the law. Eminent domain allows government bodies to seize privately held land for public purposes, but only if there is fair compensation to the property owner. The takings doctrine argues that the government also 'takes' private property when it regulates the use of the land and prevents the owner from using it in the manner intended, thereby depriving the owner of some of the value of the land. This doctrine has resulted in many law suits in the USA challenging zoning, historic preservation, **wetlands** conservation, and other land-use laws at both the federal and state levels. The federal courts have been receptive to many of the arguments by the resurgent **property rights** movement and have ordered that the government agency either withdraw the regulation or pay the landowner for the value that has been reduced.

See also: land use regulation/planning

LETTIE McSPADDEN

Tasmanian Greens

The Tasmanian Greens were founded in 1989 after five greens (Dr Bob Brown, Dr Gerry Bates, Christine Milne, Di Hollister and Lance Armstrong) were returned to the state's Lower House of Assembly. They twice held the balance of power in the state parliament (1989–92; 1996–8) before the Hare–Clark electoral system was altered in 1998 to favour majority government. The Greens' first foray into politics was in 1972 when they formed the world's first state based green party, the United Tasmania Group (UTG), and opposed the flooding of Lake Pedder. Following the UTG, the Tasmanian Greens campaigned on a broad range of environmental, social, economic, and educational issues. Between 1989 and 1998, they brought previously unknown notions of political transparency and environmental accountability to state development politics.

See also: Australian environmental groups

Further reading

Crowley, K. (1997) 'The Tasmanian State Election 1996: Green Power and Hung Parliaments', *Environmental Politics* 5(3).

KATE CROWLEY

technology

While many (particularly within the **environmental movements**) hold technology responsible for many of the environmental problems we now face, others see technology as the solution to them. Closely associated with scientific knowledge, **development** and **progress**, in terms of how humans view, value and use the environment, technology has long been a centrally important dimension of environmental politics.

For those who see technology as a (if not the) main cause of the environmental crisis, the evidence seems clear enough. They point to technologically caused environmental problems such as:

- large-scale environmental damage caused by 'mega-technological' developments such as dams, road-building schemes, large-scale developments involving deforestation or the destruction of ecosystems (see **dams/hydroelectric power**);
- the widespread use of chemical **pesticides** such as **DDT** and the negative effect these have on wildlife and ecosystems, or in the case of the **Bhopal disaster**, the catastrophic effects (including death and serious illness) of the production of these chemicals on humans;
- the use of **fossil fuels** for energy in causing pollution problems such as **acid rain**, and carbon emissions causing **global warming** and climate change;
- the environmental, health and social damage caused by motor cars (see **health and the environment**; **transportation**);
- the environmental, equity, economic and ethical problems associated with **biotechnology**;
- the environmental and health risks of nuclear power, and cite **Chernobyl** and the **Three Mile Island accident** in support of this claim.
- Technology is a central aspect of the 'growth-mania' intrinsic to capitalist development which requires the consumption of natural resources at an unsustainable rate and the creation of pollution which exceeds the absorption capacity of ecosystems.

While there are a small number of environmentalists who reject modern technology (sometimes called 'neo-**Luddites**'), most tend to see that while technology can be and has been a source of environmental problems, this is not grounds for outright rejection. Rather, most environmentalists see that technology will be needed to identify, cope with or solve some environmental problems. Most favour the development of **appropriate technology** or **human-scale technology** (associated with authors such as **Bookchin**, **Commoner**, **Illich**, **Mumford**, Schumacher and **Shiva**) which

would both be more environmentally sustainable (in terms of sustainable development), and support more egalitarian, democratic and peaceful forms of social relations (see **democracy**).

At the same time, this qualified endorsement of technology as a necessary part of the solution to environmental problems is explicitly against the idea that somehow in principle all environmental problems can be solved by technology. As such this position rejects the ideas of 'technocentrism' and 'technological fix' which basically claim that all environmental problems are at root amenable to technological solutions.

'Technocentrism' as a term is often used within environmental politics to describe a particularly modern view of the environment and our relationship to it, in which our primary relation to the environment is mediated via technology, and that our main interest in the environment is a productive or economic one (O'Riordan, 1981). It denotes a view of the environmental crisis in which technology and technological development can heal, repair or restore the ecological damage caused by environmentally unsustainable or insensitive technology. Now while it is clear that part of the solution to many environmental problems will and does involve technology, the critique of 'technocentrism' is that it denies the non-technological causes of environmental problems as well as non-technological solutions to them. What is meant here is that the causes of most environmental problems involve not simply the application of environmentally damaging technology, but also deeper political, economic, social and ethical causes. For example, the causes of global warming and climate change can either be solved by technological means – the shift to renewable forms of energy and transport – or by addressing the various inequalities involved in the consumption of unequal amounts of fossil fuels and the emissions of unequal amounts of carbon dioxide between a minority of the world's population (those in the affluent 'developed' countries) and the majority (those in the 'developing' world). Thus, taking a technocentric perspective simply 'rules out' any discussion or acknowledgement of the ethical, political and economic inequalities and disparities involved. Equally, a technocentric perspective which focuses exclusively on 'techno-fixes' leaves open the danger of environmental problems being 'solved' undemocratically by unelected scientists, technologists, economists and other 'experts' (Barry, 1999; Beck, 1992).

See also: anthropocentrism; capitalism; car industry; ecological restoration; genetic engineering, animals; genetic engineering, crops; industrialization; risk society

References

Barry, J. (1999) *Rethinking Green Politics: Nature, Virtue and Progress*, London: Sage.

Beck, U. (1992) *Risk Society: Towards a New Modernity*, London: Sage.

O'Riordan, T. (1981) *Environmentalism*, London: Pluto, 2nd edn.

JOHN BARRY

technology assessment

Technology assessment consists of formal and informal procedures for evaluating the social, cultural and environmental impacts, or consequences, of specific technical developments. Particularly important have been the various assessments that have been conducted in relation to **genetic engineering**. The term came into use in the 1960s as a way to characterize new institutional mechanisms that were being proposed to provide advice for policy-makers. One such proposal led to the US Congress establishing the first Office of Technology Assessment, which was subsequently closed in 1997. Organs for technology assessment have since been established in several European countries, where, in recent years, efforts have been made to develop new pro-active, or constructive forms of technology assessment, instead of the typically reactive, or *post facto* forms of assessment that have previously characterized the activity.

ANDREW JAMISON

technology transfer

Technology transfer is the term for the transfer of environmentally sound **technology**, mainly from developed countries to developing countries. According to the United Nations Conference on Environment and Development (see **Rio Conference 1992**), environmentally sound technologies are those which protect the environment, not just by preventing pollution at the 'end of the pipe', but also by requiring less energy/material input with improved efficiency and by enabling the reuse and **recycling** of energy/material wastes. Transfer of these technologies is seen as an imperative, particularly by developing countries, for sustainable **industrialization**. Successful technology transfer depends on building effective capability to give and receive the systems surrounding a particular technology, such as the skills and knowledge for its utilization. It is also widely accepted that the transfer of technology should improve the indigenous competence, rather than exacerbate the technological or financial dependency, of developing countries.

AKI SUWA

Thoreau, Henry David

b. 12 July 1817, Concord, Massachusetts, USA; d. 6 May 1862

Writer

Since the middle of the twentieth century and the advent of **environmental history** as a field of study, Henry David Thoreau has been increasingly identified as America's first environmentalist prophet. Throughout his writings – but particularly within his voluminous *Journal*, later natural history essays, *The Maine Woods* (1864), and his masterpiece, *Walden* (1854) – we encounter an eloquent ecological voice that has influenced and inspired many subsequent environmental advocates and writers, including John **Muir**, Edward **Abbey**, and Wendell **Berry**. Informed by an aesthetic appreciation and holistic reverence for **nature**, Thoreau's writings urge his readers to consider the wisdom of **voluntary simplicity** and wilderness preservation. Most of all, they reveal Thoreau to be one of the greatest harbingers of **ecology**.

Thoreau's growing fame during the twentieth century has led many scholars to acknowledge his full-scale canonization as one of America's leading writers and his emergence as cultural icon. Lawrence Buell notes that Thoreau 'has been canonized as natural historian, pioneer ecologist and environmentalist, social activist, anarchistic political theorist, creative artist, and memorable personality combining some or all these roles' (Buell, 1991: 315). Thoreau's worldwide fame is certainly due in part to the dramatic character of his two-year experiment in living at Walden Pond near Concord from 4 July 1845, to 6 September 1847. In the seven years following his residence in Walden woods, Thoreau revised and greatly expanded his initial manuscript concerning his experiences there to produce *Walden* (1854), the most widely read work among his writings.

Hailed by many as *the* seminal text informing the development of environmental nonfiction in the twentieth century, *Walden* is a multifaceted, highly structured text that belongs to several genres, including moralistic treatise. Among the many didactic messages within *Walden* is its panegyric in favour of voluntary simplicity. Thoreau's plea to simplify our lives is in part an anti-materialistic call to reject a consumptive lifestyle that would enslave one to the acquisition of money and things. In addition, the self-restraint and meditative discipline that Thoreau espouses lead to a philosophy of environmental humility that recognizes humanity's kinship with nature and the human responsibilities growing out of that kinship. In the same light, we may read Thoreau's thoughts on farming in 'The Bean-Field' chapter of *Walden* as an early argument for what is now called sustainable **agriculture**.

Though the final decade of Thoreau's life was dedicated more to ecological inquiry than to preservationist arguments, his aesthetic appreciation and deeply personal love for the non-human led to forthright preservationist statements that criticize the commodification of nature as destroying not only living entities but the human soul as

well. In the final paragraph of 'Chesuncook', first published serially in 1858 and included posthumously in *The Maine Woods*, Thoreau argues for the establishment of 'national preserves' after having observed how even the vast Maine forest had been scarred by logging. His essay entitled 'Walking', most of which is derived from his *Journal* of 1850–1852, presents his most sustained argument for the value of wilderness, and the wildness inherent there. In proclaiming wildness as the source of our vigour, inspiration, and strength, Thoreau provides the ideological underpinnings of the wilderness preservation movement.

To study the history of Thoreau's relationship with nature as reflected in his life and writings is to note a gradual, though irregular, movement from a largely anthropocentric viewpoint to an ecocentric one (see **anthropocentrism**; **eco-centrism**). In so doing, he departs from the conventionally anthropocentric position of Ralph Waldo **Emerson**'s essay 'Nature' (1836), that seminal document of American transcendentalism which essentially denotes nature as the mystical counterpart of the self and, thus, subserving humanity. Unlike Emerson, Thoreau eventually sought to describe the intrinsic worth of nature and to understand the workings of those ecosystems he had studied in the Concord area. As Buell observes, 'over the last dozen years of his life, Thoreau made himself into an amateur field biologist of considerable skill: in botany especially, but also in zoology, ornithology, entomology, and ichthyology' (Buell, 1991: 130). Since the 1940s, with the rise of ecological biology, he has come to be recognized as a pioneering ecologist on the strength of his meticulous studies in limnology and forest succession alone.

Further reading

Buell, L. (1991) *The Environmental Imagination: Thoreau, Nature, and the Formation of American Culture*, Cambridge: Harvard.

Oelschlaeger, M. (1991) *The Idea of Wilderness: From Prehistory to the Age of Ecology*, New Haven: Yale. (See Chapter 5, 'Henry David Thoreau: Philosopher of the Wilderness'.)

Worster, D. (1977) *Nature's Economy: A History of*

Ecological Ideas, New York: Cambridge. (See Part Two, 'The Subversive Science: Thoreau's Romantic Ecology'.)

KEVIN RADAKER

Three Gorges project

The Three Gorges (Sanxia) area of the Chang Jiang (Yangzi) is a spectacular section of China's largest river in the western Hubei province, beginning about 40 km west of Yichang where the stream leaves the mountains and enters the Hubei plain. The three gorges (Xiling, Xia and Qutang) confine the river to a narrow channel by tall, steep rocky slopes extending more than 100 km westward into the eastern Sichuan. The gorges appear to be an obvious location for a very large dam, and the first mention of such a project was contained in Sun Yatsen's 1919 plan to develop China's industry. In 1932 the Nationalist government announced its intent to build a dam in the region, and in 1944 the US Bureau of Reclamation prepared a preliminary construction plan.

After the worst ever flood in the river's middle and lower basin in 1954, Soviet hydro-engineers helped **China** to conduct necessary surveys, and silting and design studies, and the Beijing government set up the Chang Jiang Valley Planning Office which became the project's principal, and steadfast, promoter during the next three decades. The dam was also favoured by ministries of water resources and electric power which also saw the gargantuan project as an outstanding mark of China's technical maturity. The world's largest electricity-generating capacity, effective flood control in the heavily populated Yangzi's basin, and improved navigation as far inland as Sichuan were to be the project's principal benefits.

But the enormous cost of the project was the principal cause for repeated postponement of the final decision to proceed with the construction of the Three Gorges dam. In 1984, after the country's economic situation began improving with the progress of Deng Xiaoping's economic reforms, the State Council approved the construction of a 175-m high dam to start in 1986. But a more relaxed political situation in China of the mid-

1980s led to unexpected public debate about the merits of the project – and to its wide-ranging criticism. In 1986 the Economic Construction Group of the Chinese People's Political Consultative Congress recommended to the State Council and to the Communist Party's Central Committee that the project should not go ahead. A year later an edited book published in Hunan gathered a wide range of arguments against the dam, and in February 1989 an unprecedented alliance of journalists, engineers, scientists and public figures organized a press conference to launch a new book vigorously arguing against the dam.

None of these arguments swayed the leadership. Not long after the Tian'anmen massacre of June 1989 any criticism of the project in Chinese media was strictly forbidden, and Dai Qing, the editor of the 1989 book and the country's best-known female journalist (who trained as an engineer before becoming an environmental activist) was jailed for ten months. Although no criticism of the project appeared in the Chinese media until 1999, Dai Qing continued her campaign against it, both in China and abroad, throughout the 1990s.

The final decision to proceed with the construction was made on 3 April 1992 when the vote to approve the project taken in the National People's Congress (China's normally docile version of a parliament) passed with an unprecedented third of all delegates either abstaining or voting against. At that time the bureaucracies in favour of the project had the strongest possible ally in the country's Prime Minister: for Li Peng, an electrical engineer trained in the Stalinist Russia of the early 1950s, the dam was a most desirable proof of the country's technical prowess.

Some preparatory work at the site had been already done before the final vote; work on the main construction site and on the river's diversion began in 1993. The world's third most voluminous river was diverted from its main channel on 8 November, 1997. The completed dam should be 175 m tall, its reservoir will inundate about 630 km^2 of land and displace at least 1.2 million people. The dam will have about 18 gigawatts (GW) of generating capacity and produce annually 84 terawatthours of electricity. Sanxia would thus become by far the world's largest hydro-station: the

Itaipu project on the Parana between Brazil and Paraguay has 12.6 GW, and the largest Russian and American plants have about 6 GW, as does Egypt's **Aswan Dam** across the Nile.

But the project's progress has done little to eliminate the widespread opposition in China and abroad. A long list of arguments against the dam embraces human, engineering, economic, and environmental considerations. The human impact of the project is unprecedented as the dam's 600 km long reservoir will displace anywhere between 1.2–1.5 million people. Because there is very little suitable (i.e. flat and fertile) land available for their resettlement in the dam's immediate surroundings reclamation has been proceeding on slopes steeper than 25°. In spring of 1999 Zhu Rongji, Li Peng's successor as China's premier and a man who has not shown any enthusiastic support for the project, urged the end to such dangerous practices.

The lagging pace of resettling hundreds of thousands of people and chronic construction problems (including the collapse of a bridge in the resettlement area) led to other official expressions of concern in spring and summer of 1999. The original plan to resettle most of the displaced people close to their former towns and villages is proving to be quite impractical, and more than half a million peasants will have to be moved far from the site, most of them even into other provinces.

The key engineering argument against the Sanxia dam questions the necessity of such a gargantuan project in a country which has the world's largest hydroelectricity-generating potential and hence no shortages of sites where smaller (although in absolute terms still very large) dams could be built at a lesser financial, environmental and human cost. By concentrating on more manageable projects China could rely much more on domestic engineering capability, while most of the electricity-generating equipment needed for the Three Gorges project will have to be imported. And with smaller projects there would be a welcome diffusion of regional economic multiplier effects, an important consideration in a nation which must encourage decentralization in order to prosper.

The official Chinese projection for Sanxia's total cost is *yuan renminbi* (1996) 200 billion, or close to

$25 billion (2000) when converted by the official exchange rate. A quarter of this sum is to be spent on the dam itself and a fifth on the resettlement. But, as we have learned from numerous megaprojects inside and outside China, this total is almost certainly a substantial underestimate, and the final cost may be easily twice as high.

While engineering and economic considerations are undoubtedly important, concerns about the environmental effects of this unprecedented undertaking came eventually to dominate the surprisingly widespread opposition. Environmental risks that have been discussed most frequently include excessively rapid siltation of the reservoir caused by extensive deforestation in the river's upper basin; loss of silt deposition downstream from the dam and possible coastal erosion of the river's delta; flooding of sites containing toxic wastes; fluctuation of water levels at the reservoir's upper end exposing long stretches of the riverbed loaded with untreated waste from Chongqing, a city of more than ten million people; risks of reservoir-induced earthquakes in the seismically active area; dangers of massive rock slides causing the overtopping of the dam; and effects on the river's biota, including such rare species as the white river dolphin. Other concerns range from the loss of one of the world's most spectacular landscapes and tourist attractions to the encroachment of salt water into the Yangzi's delta during the periods of low water flow.

While the environmentalists lost the fight in China, their arguments were critical for shaping Sanxia's perception abroad.

Probe International, International Water Tribunal and International Rivers Network have been among the dam's most outspoken opponents. Governments of the USA and Canada, two of the western world's most experienced builders of large dams, were initially rather enthusiastic supporters of the project. In 1985 a US consortium made up of government agencies and private companies began laying the ground for a joint project with China to build the dam, and in 1986 a feasibility study undertaken by a consortium of Canadian and Chinese institutions and paid for by the Canadian taxpayers through the Canadian International Development Agency, endorsed the official Chinese design. But both governments eventually refused any direct participation in this controversial project, as did the **World Bank**.

Completion of the project is planned for the year 2009, but delays are almost certain. Disclosures made in 1999 about the use of substandard concrete in the dam's foundations, and the necessity to employ foreign quality-control engineers in order to circumvent widespread corruption at the site confirm such a conclusion. But abandoning the project at this relatively late stage is very unlikely. Although opponents of the dam still feel that the government may decide to build a lower dam (165 m) such a decision, while reducing the flooding and population displacement, would halve the amount of planned electricity generation. Only one thing remains certain: the Sanxia dam will continue to be a highly controversial project and a great environmental *cause célèbre* for many years to come.

See also: dams/hydroelectric power

Further reading

CIPM Yangtze Joint Venture (1988) *Three Gorges Water Control Project Feasibility Study*, Montreal: CIPM.

Dai Qing (ed.) (1994) *Yangtze! Yangtze!*, trans. N. Liu *et al.*, London: Earthscan.

Ryder, G. (ed.) (1990) *Damming the Three Gorges*, Toronto: Probe International.

Smil, V. (1988) *Energy in China's Modernization*, Armonk, NY: M.E. Sharpe.

VACLAV SMIL

Three Mile Island accident

The most serious nuclear accident in the USA occurred at the Three Mile Island nuclear station near Harrisburg, Pennsylvania on 28 March 1979. Mechanical failure and operator error combined to create an out of control reaction that melted about 20 per cent of the reactor core within Unit 2. Volatile radionuclides were released into the air. Additional errors caused the release of radioactive water into the nearby Susquehanna River. It is estimated that about one million curies of radionuclides were released from the reactor.

The response of federal and state authorities revealed a lack of preparation for a nuclear emergency. No immediate deaths were noted; however, concerns about birth defects and cancer persist among many local residents. Public trust in the nuclear industry and the Nuclear Regulatory Commission suffered as a result of the accident.

Further reading

Cole, M. (2001) *Three Mile Island: Nuclear Disaster*. Berkeley Heights, CA: Enslow Publishers.

JOHN PICHTEL

tourism, environmental impact of

Tourism's ecological impacts are expected to increase in the next two decades, given the steadily continuing growth of the sector worldwide. The task of estimating all of the impacts created from legal and illegal tourism activities is arduous. Harder to estimate are the more global impacts, related to the transportation of tourists which leads to **air pollution** and **water pollution**. Global impacts also stem from various manufacturing activities of products used in different stages of tourism-associated activities, such as those related to clothing, food and drink, as well as furniture, electrical products, construction and infrastructure material.

Local impacts are usually related to local land traffic and sometimes short distance naval transport, as well as to the construction and operation of related projects. These projects include tourist-catering or hosting facilities/buildings, such as hotels, resort projects, camping, holiday homes, etc., recreational facilities, such as night life/entertainment clubs, aquatic parks, yacht clubs, golf courses, ski areas, rally grounds, other sports areas, and infrastructure projects such as airports, roads, parking areas, and marine-harbours. Additional sources of such ecological damage include water or sand extraction activities, traffic and congestion, waste and sewage problems, and lack of, or non-implementation of environmental protection policies.

All of the above tourism-related sources and activities produce ecological problems including water shortage, marine, fresh-water, coastal, and soil pollution, noise pollution, damage to flora and fauna, and sometimes a general destruction of local ecosystems. These in turn create a wide range of impacts, which include negative aesthetic, cultural, historical, recreational, economic, ecosystem, psychological, and public health impacts.

According to a recent tri-national study of Mediterranean local environmental mobilizations making environmental claims on tourism activities (Kousis, 2000), in almost half of the cases, mobilized locals refer to problems created from already existing facilities or activities, while more than a third react to the siting of planned tourism activities. These cases appear more in urban than in rural areas. The most prevalent form of ecological degradation identified by these local people is general ecosystem disruption, followed by noise, soil, fresh water, marine, and air pollution problems, respectively – linked to traffic, congestion, entertainment activities, solid waste disposal, intensive water extraction, and effluent waste disposal, in that order.

Local environmental protesters argue that the above offences lead to a wide range of impacts. In general, they are mostly concerned about negative ecosystem, public health, aesthetic, recreational and psychological impacts (see **health and the environment**). Ecosystem impacts of particular concern are those related to flora and fauna, coastal zones, forests, land and fresh water, and **wetlands**. Negative ecosystem and public health concerns precede economic ones.

The resolutions proposed by these local people centre on the annulment of planned tourism projects, the creation or implementation of environmental protection rules, the permanent ceasing of tourism activities, or the preservation of wild areas. They are followed by proper regional and urban planning, as well as environmental impact assessment studies. According to the same study, the groups challenged by local environmental protesters, i.e. tourism entrepreneurs, the state, and local government, show a strong reluctance to accept the environmental claims, denying the impacts of their activities, or considering them insignificant.

Even though tour operators and large multinationals appear to be influenced by their clientele's recent pro-environment demands, attempts towards the alleviation of tourism's negative impacts thus far appear meagre since for most production-related agencies, ecosystems are viewed in terms of their economic utility. Hotel and shop owners in host communities, many of which are small to medium family enterprises, are faced with more serious economic dilemmas. Thus, economic growth and profit considerations of these major actors in both host and guest regions appear to be more of an obstacle, preventing the creation and effective application of pro-environment ameliorating measures. States and supra-national bodies such as the **European Union** have only recently begun to show interest in the environmental impacts of tourism. Nature-tourism and agro-tourism initiatives attempt to offer alternatives to the existing patterns of production and consumption. Nevertheless, most forms of tourism are environmentally damaging and a society characterized by **sustainability** would not foster the need for tourism as contemporary societies do.

See also: air transportation and infrastructure; eco-tourism; coastal zone management; transportation

References

Kousis, M. (2000) 'Tourism and the Environment: A Social Movements Perspective', *Annals of Tourism Research*, 27 (2): 468–89.

Further reading

Apostolopoulos, Y., Ioannides, D. and Sommez, S.F. (eds) (2000) *Mediterranean Islands and Sustainable Tourism Development*, London: Cassell Academic.

Mowforth, M. and Munt, I. (1998) *Tourism and Sustainability: New Tourism in the Third World*, London: Routledge.

MARIA KOUSIS

tradeable emission permits

Tradeable emission permits are a mechanism for regulating emissions of pollutants. They involve the allocation of permits to polluting actors (factories, states) who can then trade those permits between them. The system is intended to abate emissions in the most cost-effective manner, as well as perhaps enabling emissions reductions to occur in an equitable fashion. They have been implemented in relation to **acid rain** in the USA, and a system is coming into being in relation to **global warming** at the international level. Criticisms focus on the way the system is alleged to create a 'permit to pollute', or to enable actors to evade their responsibilities to abate their own emissions by buying up permits.

Further reading

Svendsen, G.T. (1998) *Public Choice and Environmental Regulation: Tradable Permit Systems in the USA and CO_2 Taxation in Europe*, Cheltenham: Edward Elgar.

MATTHEW PATERSON

transportation

Transportation is one of the key sectors for meeting the environmental challenge. In the developed world, transport contributes over one-third of all **air pollution**; in cities, road transport is responsible for over 90 per cent of noxious gases (Friends of the Earth Scotland, 1996). Transport is the one area in which greenhouse gas emissions continue to rise in North and South alike (Royal Commission on Environmental Pollution, 1995). Air transportation, in particular, is a fast growing contributor to **global warming** (see also **air transportation and infrastructure**). The car already accounts for the vast majority of journeys in the North and is fast extending its grip globally: by 2001, the global car market is expected to reach 59 million units annually.

In this context, mass transit and public transportation are seen (and marketed) as the sustainable solutions to the demand for mobility. Many cities – including Portland, Oregon and Los Angeles in the USA and Manchester and Sheffield in Britain – reintroduced light rail mass transit schemes in the 1990s. Overall, this has been a success (but see below). In the USA, for example, 9 billion mass transit trips were made in 1999, compared to 6.5 billion in 1972 (Overholsen, 2000). In Manchester, 13.5 million trips were made with the newly established Metrolink light rail system in 1997 (McLaren *et al*, 1998: 112).

However, the heyday of rail-based mass transit was during the period of rapid growth for northern cities (Hall, 1995). Throughout the late nineteenth and early twentieth centuries, suburbs as well as factories were laid out along railway lines (Ward, 1991). Railway tracks opened up new land for **development**. Despite the light rail renaissance of the 1990s, which is likely to continue, the twentieth century as a whole was a period of decline. This decline first set in in the USA, where car manufacturers successfully bought up rail companies in order to shut them down (Sachs, 1992). By the 1960s, car-oriented planning philosophies had become dominant in Europe, too. Therefore, more and more rail services (particularly on suburban and local routes) were shut down. In Britain, the Beeching report of 1963 started a rapid decline, during which one-third of the national rail network was abandoned.

First, buses could provide a public transport alternative. Not being tied to tracks, buses were more flexible. They could reach further out of town and service increasingly less linear development patterns. However, buses, like trains, need economies of scale to function efficiently and profitably. As the century went on, suburban layouts became less dense and more orientated towards the car. Business locations increasingly focused on motorway and Interstate services (and their junctions in particular). Public transport lost out in the process. Low-density suburban development cannot provide enough customers to allow for an efficient bus service. Densities of *at least* 30 households per hectare are required to make the provision of public transport viable (Newman and Kenworthy, 1999). Out-of-town office locations have vast catchment areas (at least a half-hour drive in all directions). Therefore, even though a high number of people may need to get there, it is impossible to put on public transport facilities that cater for everyone. Not enough people want to travel in the same direction.

Due to these dominant car dependent development patterns, attempts at making public transport more competitive with the car have had only limited success (Marshall and Banister, 2000). Public transport improvements can work on key radial routes leading to city centres (which in turn have to be attractive locations that people actually want to travel to). It is these radial routes that the successful American light rail systems serve. And it is on these routes that increased bus frequencies and attractive, modern buses have also resulted in higher patronage levels in Britain, for example (Mittler, 1999). Sadly, not even these increases in public transport uptake are equivalent to a decrease in car journeys. An *increase* in public transport use does not necessarily result in a *decrease* in air pollution. It is one of the iron laws of transportation that providing opportunities for travel creates further demand for travel. If it becomes easier or more convenient to go to point x, more people will make that journey (Sachs, 1992; Engwicht, 1993). The same law applies to travel time: if a journey from A to B becomes faster, this does not result in an (average) individual using less time for travelling purposes overall. If a journey becomes faster, an individual benefiting from that increased time efficiency usually decides to make longer (and sometimes more frequent) trips. An average individual in the North today travels two and a half times the daily distance travelled by an average person in 1950. The number of trips has only increased marginally; and the number of tasks we fulfil through these trips (such as getting to work or to shops) has remained practically unchanged (Friends of the Earth, 1997: 19).

Because of these 'laws of transportation' fast and efficient trains, trams or buses to the city centre simply result in more journeys there. People who did not go to the centre, now decide to make use of it. And, to make matters worse for the environment, while one member of a household may now choose to go to the city centre by public transport, this very act may give another member of that household the opportunity to use the car to go somewhere else (Marshall and Banister, 2000).

Meanwhile, on non-radial routes, *all* public transport systems remain uncompetitive with the car. Unfortunately, it is on these routes that the main growth in traffic takes place. Trips made within cities are getting increasingly complex. Suburb to suburb trips, for example, account for an increasing proportion of journeys. Due to the low densities of suburbs; the need for economies of scale (see above); and the inevitable fixation of public transport to one specific route, public transport will never be able to meet these travel demands.

An increase in public transport services and their quality is thus, despite frequent claims to the contrary, not sufficient to reduce the negative environmental impact of the transport sector (Banister and Marshall, 2000). Public transport cannot provide for the kind of trips that fuel traffic growth; and where public transport is viable and efficient, it often simply contributes to an overall rise in traffic volume. Mass transit and public transport certainly have a role to play in meeting the environmental challenge in the transport sector. Some 20 per cent of the trips made on Manchester's Metrolink, for example, are substitutions for more polluting car journeys. Ultimately, however, less transportation intensive ways of living must be found. Only through the reduction of its volume can the transport sector become environmentally viable.

See also: car industry; urbanization

References

Banister, D. and Marshall, S. (2000) *Encouraging Travel Alternatives*, London: HMSO.

Engwicht, D. (1993) *Reclaiming Our Cities and Towns*, Philadelphia: New Society Publishers.

Friends of the Earth (1997) *Unlocking the Gridlock*, London: Friends of the Earth.

Friends of the Earth Scotland (1996) *The State of Scotland's Air*, Edinburgh: Friends of the Earth Scotland.

Hall, P. (1995) *Cities of Tomorrow*, Oxford: Blackwell.

Marshall, S. and Banister, D. (2000) 'Travel Reduction Strategies: Intentions and Outcomes, *Transportation Research Part A*, 34: 321–38.

McLaren, D., Bullock, S. and Yousuf, N. (1998) *Tomorrow's World*, London: Earthscan.

Mittler, D. (1999) 'Reducing Travel!? A case study of Edinburgh', *Built Environment*, 25, 2: 106–17.

Newman, P. and Kenworthy, J. (1999) *Sustainability and Cities: Overcoming Automobile Dependence*, Washington: Island Press.

Overholsen, D. (2000) 'Mass Transit Regaining its Popularity', *Detroit News*, 28 June.

Sachs, W. (1992) *For the Love of the Automobile*, London: Zed Books.

Ward, C. (1991) *Freedom to Go: After the Motor Age*, London: Freedom Press.

Further reading

Royal Commission on Environmental Pollution (1995) *Transport and the Environment*, London: HMSO.

DANIEL MITTLER

Trittin, Jürgen

b. 25 July 1954, Bremen, Germany

Politician

Jürgen Trittin has been a leading politician of the German Greens, *Die **Grünen***, since 1990. Trittin became involved in radical student politics in the 1970s and joined the Greens in 1980. He quickly rose to prominence in regional green politics and, from 1990 to 1994, was Minister for Federal and European Affairs in Lower Saxony. From 1994 to 1998, Trittin served as co-speaker of the federal Green Party, establishing himself as a powerful, if sometimes controversial, force in federal green politics, representing the 'left' of the party. In 1998, Trittin became one of three green ministers in the SPD/Green government as Minister for the Environment, Nature Protection and Reactor Safety. His main task was to steer through the government's plan to phase out nuclear power. While Trittin lost early battles with Chancellor Schröder to speed up the process, his main achievement was to keep his own party behind the government despite many painful compromises he was forced to make.

WOLFGANG RÜDIG

U

United Nations Development Program

The United Nations Development Program (UNDP) was founded in 1965 with the remit of enhancing international co-operation for social and economic **development**. It focuses its activities in the poorest countries and, following the 1992 United Nations Conference on Environment and Development held in Rio de Janeiro, promotes **sustainable development** and the notion of sustainable livelihoods (see **Rio Conference 1992**). Based in New York, and with a budget of over $2 billion and a staff of over 5,000, its current priorities lie in the areas of capacity building to promote democratic governance, the promotion of national policies to protect the rights and improve the situation of the poor, helping manage the transition from a crisis situation (whether natural or man-made) to normality, the development of ICT (information and communication technology) capacity, the development of clean and affordable energy, and developing responses to the crisis caused by HIV/AIDS.

ALISTAIR McCULLOCH

United Nations Environment Programme

The United Nations Environment Programme (UNEP) was created by the 1972 United Nations Conference on the Human Environment, or **Stockholm Conference**. Headquartered at Nairobi, Kenya, UNEP was intended to operate as the focus of environmental activities, within the UN system. As a 'programme', not one of the autonomous Specialized Agencies, UNEP is itself accountable via ECOSOC to the UN General Assembly. It is a small, non-executive programme relative to the many larger UN agencies. It operates primarily as a data-source and clearing house, with particular responsibility for the development of **international environmental law**. Its focus is facilitative, and quasi-academic. It is not, itself a funding agency for environmental programmes. Measured by its own budget, staffing and limited record of pilot-project research, on these indicators, UNEP is a very modest programme relative to the size and funding of **United Nations Development Program** (UNDP), and the multi-lateral development banks. UNEP's funds are, for example, dwarfed by its erstwhile subsidiary, the **Global Environment Facility** (GEF).

UNEP's Executive Director, Klaus Topfer is the fourth incumbent. His predecessors were Maurice **Strong** the charismatic Canadian who founded the programme in the wake of his Chairmanship of the Stockholm Conference. Egyptian Mostapha Tolba, served four terms, 1975–92, and his tenure effectively defined the purpose and shape of the organization. A Canadian former civil-servant, Elizabeth Dowdeswell served from 1993–8, before being succeeded by Herr Topfer. Klaus Topfer, a former German Minister for the Environment, (1987–94), and prominent CDU politician, served as Chairman of the UN **Commission on Sustainable Development** (CSD), 1994–5. UNEP's Executive Director also holds the rank of UN Under-Secretary General.

UNEP was charged in its earliest days with a controversial dual mandate both to catalyse and to co-ordinate the environmental activities of the UN. The more sanguine contemporary mission statement merely aims to provide leadership and encourage partnership in caring for the environment by inspiring, informing and enabling the nations and peoples to improve their **quality of life** without compromising that of future generations. The earlier dual mandate proved a very mixed blessing. Whilst the mission to catalyse was discharged well within the limited staffing and budget of the programme, the latter, co-ordinating mandate proved an impossible burden. It raised expectations that a small, quasi-academic research-led organization, 5,000 miles distant from the centre of UN decision-making on economic and social matters, could somehow co-ordinate the work of larger, autonomous agencies, such as the **World Bank**, or the UNDP, when none of these organs are themselves constitutionally required to be co-ordinated, by anyone (other than ECOSOC and the General Assembly), and have historically, politically and behaviourially shown no such enthusiasm to relinquish their autonomy.

UNEP developed a reputation for advancing small pilot schemes of research and feasibility studies across a wide range of activities during the 1970s and 1980s. These were funded from the Environment Fund, a voluntary fund in the UN. Other agencies such as UNESCO's Man and Biosphere Programme expended far larger resources on environmental science programmes. Among UNEP's most best-known and best respected programmes were the Global Earth Monitoring (GEMS), and INFOTERRA, which utilized Landsat data for environmental planning and early warning purposes. These essentially global data-gathering exercises relying heavily on NASA and Landsat data typified the consensual, science-driven and functional mandate of the programme. UNEP was also associated in this period with pioneering international law in the fields of chemical transport, the International

Register of Potentially Toxic Chemicals, (IRPTC), international agreements on river management, and with the earliest activities to identify and prioritize the issue of ozone-layer depletion (see **ozone depletion**). UNEP was also one of the founders, with the World Meteorological Organization (WMO) of the late 1980s movement towards identifying and prioritizing the question of climate change, and its role in the Intergovernmental Panel on Climate Change (IPCC), prior to the adoption of the **Framework Convention on Climate Change** (FCCC) at Rio in 1992.

UNEP might be expected to have found its niche in a post-UNCED atmosphere which elevated **sustainable development** to the top of the international political agenda (see **Rio Conference 1992**). In fact, UNEP then suffered a curious and severe decline in fortunes. This had three particular causes. First, having suffered comparative neglect in its formative period, the popularity of the environmental issue and the funds available to advance it were then competed for by larger and more effective multilateral actors. More specifically UNEP became trapped in the system-wide failure of the UN to grasp fundamental structural reform in the post-Cold-War decade. Small, geographically remote and friendless, UNEP was not a high priority. More latterly, UNEP has suffered as the whole **sustainability** project has faltered under the impact of **globalization**, de-regulation and an extraordinary decade of doom-defying economic growth. Moving international opinion from the rhetorical, vote-catching and consciousness-raising phase of environmental politics to the real world of scientific proof, electoral choices and tax-raising is beyond the competence of any single UN agency.

UNEP is organized around a number of different structures and functions. Five functional programmes are responsible for environmental information, assessment and early warning; environmental policy and law; environmental policy implementation; **technology**, industry and economics; and the regional offices. UNEP also supervises the convention secretariats for the **Montreal Protocol**, **Basel Convention**, Convention on the Biological Diversity, **CITES**, and Migratory Species. The third major task is UNEP's role in the **Global Environment Facility**, (GEF). UNEP operates as one of three agencies, the others being the UNDP and World Bank (IBRD), which constitute the partners in the tri-agency GEF.

The political direction of UNEP operates through three tiers. The ultimate Governing Council comprises UN-member states, elected by the UN General Assembly (UNGA), 54 in total. These are elected for two-year terms. Their local diplomatic representatives in Nairobi meet more frequently as the Committee of Permanent Representatives. The environmental enthusiasms and degree of operational latitude afforded to these day-to-day diplomatists varies enormously between members. Newly created to sit between these two layers is the High-Level Committee of Ministers and Officials.

UNEP's funding has always been precarious. The overhead costs of its permanent secretariat are met from UN regular budget. UNEP's projects have relied since the Programme's inception upon voluntary donations. The largest of these form the Environment Fund. Smaller sums are available through trust funds and counterpart contributions. The Environment Fund is the centre-piece of UNEP's development, and since 1992, its decline has equally well measured the diversion of donor-funds to other institutions, the Environment Fund thereafter was halved. The overall UNEP budget continued to decline, from $124 million for the bi-ennium 1994/5, to $87 million for the 1998/9 bi-ennium.

UNEP's future course and effectiveness will depend upon its ability to become indispensible and respected in at least one major activity. It is in the nature of UN bureaucracies to over-extend their claims of juristiction and competence, and to compete with one another rather than to co-operate. UNEP will never succeed in competition for resources and influence against much larger and centrally located actors such as UNDP, the World Bank and the ever-increasingly important **World Trade Organization**, (WTO). It must therefore run another race. UNEP's small quasi-academic nature makes it the natural partner of leading universities, research institutes, and NGOs in the intellectual battle to promote sustainable development in international public policy. In this the quality of ideas produced rests upon the quality of staff who can be attracted and retained.

Further reading

Imber, M. (1994) *Environment, Security and UN Reform*, Basingstoke: Macmillan.

McCormick, J. (1989) *The Global Environmental Movement*, London: Belhaven Press.

Sandbrook, R. (1999) 'New Hopes for the United Nations Environment Programme (UNEP)?', in *Global Environmental Change*, 9: 171–174.

von Moltke, K. (1996) 'Why UNEP Matters', in *Green Globe Yearbook*, Fridtjof Nansen Institute: Oxford University Press, pp. 55–64.

MARK IMBER

United Nations Fund for Population Activities

The United Nations Fund for Population Activities (UNFPA) is the principal UN aid agency responsible for promoting reproductive health, family planning policies and thus, indirectly a larger range of women's health and child-survival issues. Founded in 1969, UNFPA is funded by voluntary donations from the member states. These have averaged $250 million per annum in the last decade. It has become the focus of disputes, in turn, with the Roman Catholic Church, the Iranian government in the 1980s, and, since the 1990s with the US anti-abortion lobby. The last of these has ensured that UNFPA has been subject to deep cuts in its US voluntary contributions imposed by the US Senate. These cuts, of course, have increased the number of poor, third-world women seeking abortion as a result of reduced access to safe and legal contraception.

Further reading

Populi New York:UNFPA (quarterly).

MARK IMBER

urbanization

Cities have always provided their rulers with the challenge to design them in a way that suited their purposes. In the twentieth century, **democracy**, economic crisis, war and reconstruction created modern urban planning. By the close of the century the rise of economic **globalization** and global environmentalism had again reshaped the planning task.

Industrialization resulted in cities containing poverty-stricken parts of the urban environment which became festering pockets of potential epidemic and insurrection. Governments responded by introducing minimal public health, housing and land use legislation, and constructing sewerage and water supply networks. Following the Great Depression and the Second World War 'city (or town) planning' benefited from a political climate distrustful of markets and favouring government intervention. The task of postwar urban reconstruction demanded planning. Urban planning became professionalized and embedded in the institutional framework of most democratic societies.

In the capitalist world urbanization was driven mainly by markets in land and buildings. Under authoritarian communist regimes vast tracts of low cost, often high rise, housing were built to accommodate the workers in state-run industries. In many countries planning was helped by government ownership of land for urban development. Growing populations were accommodated in peripheral suburbs, new planned settlements and sometimes in whole new cities and towns (see **population movement and control**). Conflicts over the urban environment were mediated by land use regulation (see **land use regulation/planning**). **Transportation** infrastructure was added in response to demands to relieve 'congestion' or simply because the private car symbolized **progress**. Access to the non-urban environment and local open space was provided by public parks and 'green belts' where urban **development** was restricted.

In the third quarter of the twentieth century both urbanization and the tasks of urban planning changed. In the developed world economic prosperity and planned reconstruction resulted in elimination of the worst excesses of industrial degradation of urban living environments. While poverty was not overcome, the potential for governments to alleviate poverty seemed to reach limits set by **capitalism**. Destructive urban redevelopment sometimes stimulated strong social opposition (see **green bans**). Environmental pollution became a concern of planning. Environmental protection authorities (see **Environmental Protection Agency**) were established and environmental impact assessment was added to the planners' toolbox.

At the same time the discipline of capital and markets began to be reasserted. The freeing up of capital flows resulting from the demolition of national regulatory barriers created the conditions for the rapid growth of a global financial market dominated by transnational corporate empires, and co-ordinated by the new information technology. Population flows created a cultural mixture in many cities. The primary task of urban planning changed from meeting basic human needs to attracting investment. Attention turned to accommodating new households within the existing boundaries of the city (see **brownfield sites**).

Contemporaneously with the growth of economic globalization under neoliberal regimes, the global environment was placed on the planning agenda in a series of United Nations conferences from the **Stockholm Conference** of 1972 to the Conference on Environment and Development at Rio de Janeiro in 1992 (see **Rio Conference 1992**). The latter produced a moderate manifesto for **sustainable development**, **Agenda 21**, containing specific recommendations on the planning of human settlements to be pursued by local government, thus foreshadowing Local Agenda 21 (LA21) plans. The threat of **global warming** loomed ever larger.

The rise of global environmentalism illuminated the paradox that 'developed' cities with the most 'liveable' local environments also make the greatest negative impact on the global environment, while those with poor local environments make much less of a global impact.

In the developed world, comprehensive planning of cities and urban regions is once again required to alleviate, and if possible eliminate, the social problems caused by overdependence on market solutions. The urgency of these problems is beginning to outweigh the perceived imperative to attract investment. The protection of local urban environmental quality remains a major priority. Acceptance of the idea of cities as consumers of the natural environment, and the need to reduce the level of consumption, has reorientated planning from 'city planning' to 'environmental planning'. At the same time the greatest challenge facing urban planners today is how to accommodate the immense growth of the cities into which capital is now flowing – to a high level of local environmental quality – without destroying the world's environmental heritage, its atmosphere and its **biodiversity**.

Further reading

Hall, P. (1996) *Cities of Tomorrow: An Intellectual History of Urban Planning and Design in the Twentieth Century*, Oxford and New York: Blackwell.

Low, N.P., Gleeson, B.J., Elander, I and Lidskog R. (2000) *Consuming Cities: The Urban Environment in the Global Economy after the Rio Declaration*, London and New York: Routledge.

NICHOLAS LOW AND BRENDAN GLEESON

utopia/ecotopia

A utopia is literally a 'nowhere land', an ideal society in another place, where justice prevails, where people are perfectly content, and from which sadness, pain and violence have been banned. Utopias, although fictions, are characterized by a conviction that the envisioned society will in fact be without problems. Other distinguishing features of utopias are that they are extremely critical in regard to the present society, and contain the 'blueprints' for a completely new state. In ecotopias, a society is portrayed which is ecologically sustainable, and where humanity can live in harmony with nature. The objective of ecotopian writers is the realization of a perfectly 'clean' society that leaves **nature** unharmed, and ensures the lasting physical and spiritual well-being of humankind.

See also: anarchism/eco-anarchism; Blueprint for Survival; Bookchin, Murray; future studies; sustainability

Further reading

Geus, M.A. de (1999) *Ecological Utopias: Envisioning the Sustainable Society*, Utrecht: International Books.

MARIUS DE GEUS

V

Values Party

The world's first national green party, the Values Party was founded at Victoria University, Wellington, New Zealand, on 30 May 1972. Its inspiration was Tony Brunt, a former journalist who was alarmed at the rapid **urbanization** of New Zealand and the increasing materialism of New Zealand society. He saw the contemporary political system as morally bankrupt and wanted to regenerate politics through infusion of nonmaterial values, with particular emphasis on respect for the environment and the rights of the individual.

In essence, the Values Party represented green ecological principles before standard green terminology had been developed. Much influenced by the increasing degradation of the **New Zealand** environment and by the contemporary **Limits to Growth** debate worldwide, the party produced a manifesto for the general election of November 1972 based on the groundbreaking *Ecologist* magazine publication, ***Blueprint for Survival***. Entitled *Blueprint for New Zealand*, it envisaged a society that was 'just, sustainable, community-based, participatory, diverse, co-operative, internationalist, but above all, humanitarian'.

The Values Party was the political product of the ferment of social and cultural ideas of the time. In many ways, it was a New Zealand reflection of the concerns and the interests of the **new social movements** that had become active across the industrialized world as the post-Second World War generation began to challenge the more conservative ideas of the past. In this respect, the party put special emphasis on the rights of women and respect for cultural diversity – Maori in particular. It opposed the Vietnam War and campaigned against French nuclear testing in the Pacific.

In the 1972 general election, standing in 42 out of 87 constituencies, the Values Party gained 2 per cent of the votes but no parliamentary seats. Three years later, standing in all constituencies, it increased its votes to 5.2 per cent, only 0.4 per cent short of the percentage gained by the West German Greens (*Die Grünen*) when making their *Bundestag* breakthrough in 1983. However, under New Zealand's majoritarian (first-past-the-post or FPP) electoral system, the party once again obtained no seats in the national parliament. In this respect, the lack of success of the Values Party in terms of parliamentary representation can be compared with that of other green parties in FPP systems, notably Britain and the USA.

The parliamentary scene in New Zealand continued to be dominated by the Labour Party (1972–5) and the National Party (1975–8). The fortunes of the Values Party declined and after a dismal result in the 1978 general election (2.4 per cent of the votes) it was engulfed by internal wrangling. In the 1981 and 1984 general elections, standing for 17 and 30 respectively, it obtained a mere 0.2 per cent of the votes.

During the 1980s, New Zealand's electoral system became increasingly discredited. In the 1978 and 1981 elections, the Labour Party received more votes than the National Party, but the National Party gained more seats. In 1981, the Social Credit Party gained 21 per cent of the vote but only two parliamentary seats; and in 1984 the New Zealand First Party gained 12 per cent of the votes and no seats. In 1987, the Labour Party leader, David Lange, promised a referendum on proportional representation if Labour were re-elected, but then reneged on his promise. Eventually, two referenda were held, in 1992 and 1993, which brought about a new electoral system, officially known as Mixed Member Proportional (MMP), based on the German Added Member System (AMS).

Under the new electoral system, first used in the election of October 1996, there are 120 seats in the New Zealand parliament, 60 of which are constituency seats elected by the traditional FPP method. Five regional seats are reserved for Maori representatives, and the remaining 55 are filled from the party lists in proportion to the national party vote. To secure representation, a party must either win a constituency or obtain 4 per cent or more of the national vote.

During the 1980s, the Values Party began to reform itself and regain support. In 1986 it renamed itself 'Values, the Green Party of Aotearoa', Aotearoa being the Maori word for New Zealand. In this guise, the revitalized party won 6.7 per cent of the national vote in the October 1990 general election. More importantly for Values, this campaign showed the advantages of forming working relationships with similarly-minded small parties if proportional representation were to be implemented in New Zealand. With this in mind, the leaders of the party entered into negotiations with potential allies.

In December 1991, after tough but amicable negotiations, the party came together with the New Labour Party (a progressively minded splinter group from the Labour Party), the Liberal Party (an analogous splinter group from the National Party), the Democrats (formerly Social Credit), and Mana Motuhake (a progressive Maori party) to form the New Zealand Alliance. An agreement was reached between all five parties based on the principles of 'honesty and accountability'. Each party retains its own integrity, but there is a National Council for the Alliance as a whole, composed of four members of each constituent party. Any two parties acting together can veto any item on the agenda.

Values played a significant part in the policy and organization of the Alliance. It was on a Values' initiative that the parties accepted that the National Council should work by consensus rather than majority voting. A further Values' initiative made it possible for all recognized members of the Alliance to attend National Council meetings as observers. Jeanette Fitzsimons, co-leader of Values, held the important position of Alliance Policy Co-ordinator.

Electorally, the Alliance was an immediate success, gaining 18 per cent of the votes and two parliamentary seats in the 1993 general election, the last to be held under the traditional FPP system. Neither of the two seats, however, fell to Values Party. Subsequently, in the MMP election of October 1996, the Alliance vote declined to 10.1 per cent although their number of MPs actually rose to thirteen, three of whom were from Values: Jeanette Fitzsimmons, Rod Donald, and Phillida Bunkle. The numbers for the other members of the Alliance were: New Labour five, Democrats two, Mana Motuhake two, and Liberals one. In the aftermath of the 1996 election, Values participation in national government as a part of the Labour/Alliance combination seemed possible. However, the leader of New Zealand First Party, which held the balance of power, opted to form a coalition with the National Party.

Dissatisfaction with Alliance decision-making procedures and concern about the lack of 'green' profile in Alliance campaigning led to the party conference's decision in November 1997 to run parliamentary candidates under the party's own name in the future.

See also: anti-nuclear movements; Australian environmental groups and parties; Green Party, UK; green parties, US

Further reading

Parkin, S. (1989) *Green Parties: An International Guide*, London: Heretic Books.

Rainbow, S. (1992) 'The New Zealand Values Party: Challenging the Poverty of Progress 1972–1989', in Rüdig, W. (ed.) *Green Politics Two* Edinburgh: Edinburgh University Press.

Steward, R. (1997) 'Politics in New Zealand from

Beginning to Breakthrough', *Synthesis/Regeneration* 13(7): 11.

Steward, R. (1998) 'Charting Our Own Course', *Synthesis/Regeneration* 16: 19.

Values Party (1972) *Blueprint for New Zealand*, Wellington, NZ: Values Party.

DICK RICHARDSON

vegetarianism

The term vegetarianism covers several ways of abstaining from the consumption or use of animal products. Lacto- and ovo-vegetarianism allow the use of milk and respectively eggs; veganism rejects the use of all animal products; fruitarianism limits consumption to products obtained without killing or exploiting animals and plants. Arguments for vegetarianism vary accordingly. Anthropocentric arguments focus on the aesthetic, economic, agricultural or medical advantages of a meat-free diet (see **anthropocentrism**). Vegans can also object to cruelty to animals (see **animal rights**) including cruelty in the dairy and poultry industry. **Eco-centrism** (see **environmental ethics**) rejects all exploitation of **nature**. Vegetarianism is a form of **green consumerism**, but may be at odds with several strands of **green political theory**: rejecting animal-based clothing, for instance, implies opting for synthetic alternatives requiring a petrochemical industry.

Further reading

Frey, R.G. (1983) *Rights, Killing and Suffering: Moral Vegetarianism and Applied Ethics*, Oxford: Blackwell.

MARCEL WISSENBURG

Verts, les

Although political ecology appeared on the French electoral scene in 1974, it took activists ten years to acknowledge the need for a single permanent national organization. Thus *Les Verts* were founded in January 1984. In the late 1980s, *Les Verts* benefited from the green wave in Europe and since then have claimed about 4,500 members.

The ideal of participative **democracy** which presided over their creation still underlies the party structure. Party members are involved at every stage of the decision-making process. The Federal Assembly of party members is gathered every second year to discuss and adopt the party's policies. The 23 autonomous green regions elect three-quarters of the 120 delegates to the Conseil National Inter-régional. The Parliament of the party, this body meets quarterly to deliberate on policies and strategies. It also elects and controls the executive.

In 1986 *Les Verts* adopted a strategy of autonomy based on a refusal to compromise with parties of either right or left. This attitude contributed to the success of the organization at the end of the decade. As newcomers to the political system they were untarnished by political sleaze and attracted those disappointed with the socialists and conventional parties. However, such a stance became problematic when a rival organization, ***Génération Ecologie***, was set up by Brice **Lalonde**, a former speaker of the ecology movement, then a minister in Mitterrand's government. The environmental constituency was split and *Les Verts* were denounced as dangerous radicals and extremists.

The two parties eventually stood together in 1993 legislative elections but the result was found disappointing and fuelled infighting. Moreover, the leadership of the movement was at stake in the selection of the green candidate for the 1995 presidential elections. Competition between groups and personalities resulted in further splits and, by the mid-1990s, the movement was in electoral terms drawn back to its level of the late 1970s. Dominique **Voynet** was eventually selected as the green candidate and her supporters gained the party majority. In the following years they reunited the movement by welcoming smaller groups and adopted a strategy of alliance with the left. A deal was brokered with the socialist party a few months before the 1997 legislative elections, allowing *Les Verts* to get 7 deputies elected (with 4 per cent of the national vote). Thus, Voynet was appointed Minister for the Environment in the socialist government. Success was confirmed by a good performance at the 1999 European elections (9.5 per cent and 9 MEPs).

Under the leadership of Antoine **Waechter** (1986–93), *Les Verts* had emphasized their environmentalist agenda. Priorities have since shifted. Although the protection of the environment remains important (closure of nuclear power plants, opposition to genetically modified organisms, promotion of **organic farming**, **eco-taxes**), social issues feature more prominently on *Les Verts'* manifesto and the party is campaigning alongside social movements on issues such as homelessness, illegal immigration, social exclusion and reduction of the working week.

The party culture is marked by entrenched anti-leader sentiments, and tensions between the grassroots and the party elite or elected politicians have long plagued the organization. Rather than taking a single leader, *Les Verts* elect four national speakers to promote the image and the policies of the party to the media and the public. The grassroots act as guardians of radicalism. However, since 1997, activists have proven willing to accept a compromise on some issues provided some others are promoted in government. While the Minister is bound by governmental solidarity, deputies have retained a wider autonomy within the coalition and often express dissent. At the local and regional levels, councillors do not follow a uniform strategy but enter *ad hoc* negotiations and occasionally partnerships.

Les Verts have secured their position as the only legitimate representative of green politics in **France**. They have demonstrated that far from being a single-issue party they promote a wider agenda on which social issues and solidarity are prominent. They face the paradox of wanting to remain amateurs while demonstrating their ability to work within the institutions and perform as well as professionals. By 2000 they had elected representatives at all levels of national, regional and local government but their success rests on their association with the left. The question of their autonomy will remain a key variable in determining their future fortunes.

Further reading

Boy D., Roche A., and Jacques le Seigneur V. (1995) *L'Écologie au Pouvoir*, Paris: Presses de Sciences Po.

Faucher, F. (1998) 'Is There Hope for the French Ecology Movement?', *Environmental Politics*, 7(3): 42–65.

—— (1999) *Les Habits Verts de la Politique*, Paris: Presses de Sciences Po.

FLORENCE FAUCHER

voluntary simplicity

This is an essentially American development that arose out of the work of Duane Elgin in the 1970s. Individuals opting for voluntary simplicity make conscious choices to live below their economic means to lessen the impact they make on the environment. This does not mean these individuals live in poverty. The choice involves having fewer material goods, although the quality of the goods they do possess may be of relative high quality. It is closely linked to **appropriate technology** which creates, manufactures and builds goods that have minimum negative impact on the environment, and is referred to by author Edward **Abbey** as 'Positive Poverty'. From the mid-1980s and 1990s the growth of voluntary simplicity was slowed, but began to flourish again in the late twentieth century. The movement continues today largely through a Seattle-based organization called the Simple Living Network, which has a website and numerous publications demonstrating the principles of the group.

Further reading

Elgin, D. (1981) *Voluntary Simplicity*, New York: William Morrow and Company.

Simple Living Network at
    URL: http://www.simpleliving.net.

THOMAS LOWE

Voynet, Dominique

b. 4 November 1958, Montbéliard, France
Politician.

Trained as an anaesthetist, Dominique Voynet was involved in trade-union and associative activities (nature conservancy, anti-nuclear and anti-militarism protest, feminism, humanitarianism) before turning to political activity. A member of the French Greens from 1984, she has held various positions (spokeswoman) and various mandates within the Party (member of Dole municipal council, of the European Parliament in 1989). Partly thanks to the media, she succeeded in uniting around her the green militants (1991–3). In 1993, she won a majority position and consequently the Greens became left-orientated. She was named as the Greens' candidate for the 1995 presidential election (in which she won 3.3 per cent). She was elected as a member of Parliament thanks to the electoral agreement signed with the Socialist Party in 1997. She was appointed as minister for Aménagement du territoire and Environment in Lionel Jospin's cabinet, in June 1997.

See also: Verts, les

DANIEL BOY

W

Waechter, Antoine

b. 11 February 1949, Mulhouse, France

Politician.

Ecologist (Ph.D. in Biology), political militant and leader of cultural associations and life-long pacifist (he refuses to do his military service), Antoine Waechter has a long track record of participating in demonstrations against projects destroying fauna and flora (motorways, nuclear stations). From 1973, he supported various electoral campaigns and become a candidate (and has been so since 1977) at local, national and European levels. He has a resolutely independent vision of **ecology**, beyond any Left/Right division. He was instrumental in the creation of political ecology in France in 1973, with Solange Fernex (*Ecologie et Survie*), and in 1984 participated in the creation of the Green Party, which he chaired between 1986 and 1990. Following a vote of no confidence due to his refusal to accept the party's shift to the left, he left in 1994 and set up the Mouvement des Ecologistes Indépendants. This formation obtained poor results (1.53 per cent) in the 1999 European elections.

See also: Verts, les

BRUNO VILLALBA

Wales, Party of

Established in 1925, the Party of Wales or Plaid Cymru has been associated with the preservation of the Welsh language, culture, and economy. The party has also utilized its brand of nationalism to promote environmental issues. For example, it organized mass protests in the 1950s and 1960s against the Tryweryn reservoir, which submerged parts of Wales to meet Liverpool's water needs. This environmental focus within the party can be traced from its founders to its current leaders. Its environmental interest stems from its largely rural public support, the perception of Wales as an English colony, and its blending of nationalist and post-materialist principles (see **Inglehart, Ronald**). The continued significance of such concerns can be seen in the opposition to incomers (mainly English) taking over Welsh communities, the brief electoral union with the Green Party in Ceredigion and Pembroke North (1992–3) which produced an MP, Cynog Dafis, and the drive to restore the south's former mining areas. The party's political rise, to being only second to Labour in Wales (2001 elections), awards it the opportunity to impact all areas of policy in Wales from three directions (the Welsh National Assembly, the Westminster Parliament, the European Parliament).

ERICH G. FRANKLAND

water politics

As human populations and economies grow exponentially, the amount of freshwater in the world remains roughly the same as it has been throughout history. While the total quantity of water in the world is immense, the vast majority is either saltwater (97.5 per cent) or locked in ice caps (1.75 per cent). The amount economically available for human use is only 0.007 per cent of the total, or about 13,500 km^3 (this comes to about 2300 m^3 per person, a 37 per cent drop since 1970 [United Nations, 1997]). Adding complexity to this increasing scarcity is the fact that almost half the globe's land surface lies within international watersheds, i.e., that land which contributes to the world's 261 transboundary waterways.

The scarcity of water for human and ecosystem uses leads to intense political pressures, often referred to as 'water stress'. Furthermore, water ignores political boundaries, evades institutional classification, and eludes legal generalizations. Water resources have contributed to tensions between competing uses around the globe, from neighbouring irrigators to neighbouring nations; from towns versus **agriculture** to environmentalists versus high-tech manufacturers.

While water quantity has been the major issue of the twentieth century, water quality has been neglected to the point of catastrophe (see **water pollution**).

1 More than a billion people lack access to safe water supplies.
2 Almost three billion do not have access to adequate sanitation.
3 Five to ten million people die each year from water-related diseases or inadequate sanitation.
4 Twenty per cent of the world's irrigated lands are salt-laden, affecting crop production.

Water demands are increasing, groundwater levels are dropping, surface-water supplies are increasingly contaminated, and delivery and treatment infrastructure is ageing. The **World Bank** estimates that it would cost $600 billion to repair and improve the world's existing water delivery systems (United Nations, 1997) These tensions have spilled into violence on occasion, mostly at the intranational level, generally between tribes, water-use sectors, or states/provinces. Examples of internal water conflicts range from interstate violence and death along the Cauvery River in **India**, to California farmers blowing up a pipeline meant for Los Angeles, to much of the violent history in the Americas between **indigenous**

peoples and European settlers. The desert state of Arizona in the USA even commissioned a navy (made up of one ferryboat) and sent its state militia to stop a dam and diversion on the Colorado River in 1934.

While these disputes can and do occur at the sub-national level, the human security issue is more subtle and more pervasive than violent conflict. As water quality degrades or quantity diminishes over time, the effect on the stability of a region can be unsettling. For example, for 30 years the Gaza Strip was under Israeli occupation. Water quality deteriorated steadily, saltwater intrusion degraded local wells, and water-related diseases took a rising toll on the people living there. In 1987, the *intifada*, or Palestinian uprising, broke out in the Gaza Strip, and quickly spread throughout the West Bank. Was water quality the cause? It would be simplistic to claim direct causality. Was it an irritant exacerbating an already tenuous situation? Undoubtedly.

There is some room for optimism, though, notably in the global community's record of resolving water-related disputes. For example, the record of acute conflict over international water resources is overwhelmed by the record of co-operation. The last 50 years has seen only 37 acute disputes (those involving violence) and, during the same period, 157 treaties negotiated and signed. Total numbers of events are equally weighted towards co-operation: 507 conflict-related events, and 1,228 co-operative.

The most vehement enemies around the world either have negotiated water-sharing agreements, or are in the process of doing so as of 2001. Violence over water seems neither strategically rational, hydrographically effective, nor economically viable. Shared interests along a waterway seem to consistently outweigh water's conflict-inducing characteristics (Wolf, 1998).

Furthermore, once co-operative water regimes are established through treaty, they turn out to be impressively resilient over time, even between otherwise hostile riparians, and even as conflict is waged over other issues. For example, the Mekong Committee has functioned since 1957, exchanging data throughout the Vietnam War. Secret 'picnic table' talks have been held between Israel and Jordan, since the unsuccessful Johnston negotiations of 1953–5, even as these riparian nations were in a legal state of war until recently. And the Indus River Commission not only survived through two wars between **India** and **Pakistan**, but treaty-related payments continued unabated throughout the hostilities.

These patterns suggest that one valuable lesson of international waters is as a resource whose characteristics tend to induce co-operation, and incite violence only in the exception.

The greatest threat of the global water crisis, then, comes from the fact that people and ecosystems around the globe simply lack access to sufficient quantities of water of sufficient quality for their well-being.

References

United Nations (1997) *Water in the Twenty-First Century: Comprehensive Assessment of the Freshwater Resources of the World*, Geneva: World Meteorological Organization and the Stockholm Environment Institute.

Wolf, A. (1998) 'Conflict and Co-operation Along International Waterways', *Water Policy*, 1(2): 251–65.

Further reading

Elhance, A. (1999) *Hydropolitics in the 3rd World: Conflict and Co-operation in International River Basins*, Washington, DC: US Institute of Peace.

Gleick, P. (1998) *The World's Water: The Biennial Report on Freshwater Resources*, Washington DC: Island Press.

Postel, S. (1999) *Pillar of Sand: Can the Irrigation Miracle Last?* New York: Norton.

AARON T. WOLF

water pollution

The availability of water resources and the quality of the water are vital to life and to the world's economy. Water resources support **agriculture**, industry, electric power, recreation, navigation, and **fisheries**. They are also distributed around the world in a highly uneven manner. Some nations and regions are rich in water resources and access to clean water while others face a future of dire water scarcity and degradation of water quality. Water pollution refers to degradation of water quality, whether the causes are natural or anthropocentric, and particularly the latter (see **anthropocentrism**).

Water pollution, both from so-called point sources and nonpoint (e.g., agricultural and urban runoff) has been both a public health and ecosystem health concern for much of the past century (see **health and the environment**). It has also been the object of extensive and costly governmental programmes of pollution control. Controversies over such policy efforts have focused largely on the stringency of water quality criteria that are adopted, the level of enforcement of rules and regulations designed to achieve a designated level of water quality, and the costs imposed on industry, states and municipalities, and other regulated parties. Increasingly policy debate has focused on the relative merits of conventional or direct regulation and alternatives involving the use of market incentives, public–private partnerships, and collaboration between regulatory agencies and polluters. In addition, a consensus appears to be emerging that use of comprehensive watershed or river basin approaches, a form of ecosystem management, offers the best hope of addressing both point and nonpoint sources of water pollution.

Public policies directed at water pollution include several relatively distinct programmes dealing with pollution of surface water, groundwater, and drinking water. Surface water includes streams, rivers, lakes, and ponds, and has received the greatest public attention and policy action (e.g., through the **Clean Water Act** in the US). Increasingly, governments have also addressed drinking water (e.g., through the US Safe Drinking Water Act of 1974 and later amendments) and groundwater, which is also a major source of drinking water.

The state of water quality is inherently difficult to determine, in part because of the large number of bodies of water and great variability in their condition. Nonetheless, available evidence indicates that in most industrialized nations considerable progress has been made in reducing water pollution through 'end-of-the-pipe' controls on municipal and industrial dischargers. There has been a major reduction in the raw pollution of surface waters and significant reductions in emissions of persistent toxic organic pollutants and toxic metals such as mercury and lead (see **mercury poisoning**; **lead poisoning**). The US **Environmental Protection Agency**, for instance, reported that by the late 1990s some 64 per cent of US rivers and streams that were surveyed fully supported all uses, such as swimming, fishing, drinking-water supply, and support of aquatic life. About 36 per cent were found to be impaired to some extent, as were about 39 per cent of lakes, ponds, and reservoirs and 38 per cent of US estuaries. These data point to improving water quality while also indicating that major water quality problems remain even after decades of governmental and private cleanup actions.

Water quality experts believe the greatest remaining challenges for surface water (especially in industrialized nations) are largely nonpoint sources, particularly from agricultural runoff such as nutrients from farm fertilizer and animal wastes, **pesticides**, and suspended solids. Urban runoff from rain and melting snow is also significant, and carries a wide assortment of chemicals into local rivers, bays, and lakes, or into groundwater. In addition, concern today focuses on the challenge of dealing with toxic chemicals that enter surface and groundwater, and their effects on human and ecological health.

The newer focus on nonpoint sources of water pollution has brought increasing emphasis by government agencies, environmental scientists, and environmentalists on the use of comprehensive approaches linked to watersheds and river basins. Consistent with these new policy strategies, greater attention has been given to building collaborative partnerships among diverse stakeholders as an alternative to conventional regulation through permitting processes. These partnerships may be crucial to controlling nonpoint sources and to building sufficient support to restore damaged ecosystems.

See also: Environmental Protection Agency; oil pollution; water politics

Further reading

Davies, J.C. and Mazurek, J. (1998) *Pollution Control in the United States: Evaluating the System*, Washington: Resources for the Future.

Freeman, A.M. (2000) 'Water Pollution Policy', in P. Portney and R. Stavins (eds) *Public Policies for Environmental Protection*, Washington: Resources for the Future, 2nd edn.

Kraft, M.E. and Johnson, B.N (1999) 'Clean Water and the Promise of Collaborative Decision Making: The Case of the Fox-Wolf Basin in Wisconsin', in D. Mazmanian and M. Kraft (eds) *Toward Sustainable Communities: Transition and Transformations in Environmental Policy*, Cambridge, MA: MIT Press.

MICHAEL E. KRAFT

Watt, James

b. 31 January 1938, Lusk, Wyoming, USA

Federal administrator and attorney

James G. Watt was US Secretary of the Interior from 1981 to 1983 and a zealous environmental counter revolutionary for the newly elected President Ronald **Reagan**. Watt came to Washington, DC from the leadership of a Denver, Colorado based right wing law foundation though he had worked at the Interior Department in the early 1970s. At the **Department of the Interior** he quickly became the Reagan administration's most outspoken advocate in opposition to the nation's environmental groups. His policies and programmes for his department's areas of responsibility were all focused on his right-wing view of economic growth. With his Christian fundamentalist passion and bulldog-like determination, Watt did all that he could to shift federal environmental power to private interests as a means to further the larger Reagan agenda. By late 1983, Watt had managed to offend a variety of important groups and constituencies on one issue or another and was forced to resign. He returned to the Rocky Mountain area and resumed his advocacy of conservative causes.

WARREN VANDER HILL

wetlands

Intermediate between terrestrial and aquatic ecosystems are **landscapes** that are routinely flooded during some or all of a year. Fluctuating hydrology makes these ecosystems both abundant in life and sensitive to hydrologic disruptions. Collectively known as wetlands, delineations are made on the bases of hydrophytic plant assemblages and undrained hydric soils. Among the most biologically productive landscapes, wetlands are estimated to cover at least 570–778 million hectares worldwide, six to eight per cent of the earth's land surface, although some estimates range as high as 4,462 million hectares (Ramsar Bureau, 2001). Historical misunderstandings of their values to human and natural systems alike contributed to losses of wetlands following transformations of landscapes for **agriculture** and urban land uses.

Wetlands include bogs, marshes, and swamps. A bog is commonly described as 'spongy ground' that is often saturated with water or is poorly drained and contains an abundance of decaying plant matter. Acidic groundwater frequently builds up in such conditions and anaerobic decomposition of organic materials results from oxygen-poor, 'reducing' conditions of saturated soils. Bogs may grade into freshwater lakes in low depressions, which in turn gradually fill in with sediment to become bogs. If supplied continuously with freshwater, bogs may remain for extensive periods of time.

Marshes, by contrast, are wholly inundated by water throughout most of the year to depths of 33–200 cm. They are characterized by a mixed ecology of perennial grasses, forbs, and bushes that support intricate webs of animal life, including aquatic and flying insects, migratory and non-migratory birds, small mammals (e.g., mink, muskrats, otters), reptiles and amphibians, as well as larger foraging mammals (e.g., opossums, moose). The periodicity of its hydroperiod is critical to a marsh, as deeper areas attract dense assemblages of fauna during relatively drier times of the year when water levels are likely to recede. Customarily there is relatively little throughflow of water in marshes.

The principal characteristic distinguishing swamps is their support of woodier vegetation than that found in marshes; these include trees and some shrubs that are adapted to conditions of saturated roots. **Mangroves** and cypress are some of the forest vegetation representative of swamps. Some swamps are actually slow moving streams or rivers; the lower **Everglades** in Florida typifies this.

Other names used to distinguish wetlands include fens and moors (terms most often used in Britain to describe boggy areas of grasses and sedges), bayou (distributary drainage courses, sometimes brackish and often deltaic, typified by North America's lower Mississippi River), prairie potholes (widely distributed depressions found across the North American prairie), and muskeg (alternating depressions and tufts characterized by sphagnum moss in Boreal Canada). Flood plains may be thought of as potential wetlands, although not all flood plains flood each year. Tidal flats represent emergent marine aquatic ecosystems which grade into coastal wetlands. Constructed, or human-made, wetlands include fish and shrimp ponds, irrigated agricultural land, salt pans, reservoirs, gravel pits, sewage farms, and canals. This diversity emphasizes the growing importance for economic uses of wetlands, and recent attributions of ecosystem services places a value of $4.9 trillion annually (Ramsar Bureau, 2001).

International attention to the importance of wetlands was initiated in 1962 at the MAR Conference sponsored by the International Union for Conservation of Nature and Natural Resources (IUCN: see **World Conservation Union**) emphasizing 'reclamation' (destruction) of marshland and wetlands in Europe. A series of meetings led to the Convention on Wetlands, signed in Ramsar, Iran, in 1971. By 2001, 123 signatories designated 1045 wetland sites, totalling 78.6 million hectares for 'conservation and wise use of wetlands and their resources' in the context of globally **sustainable development**. This includes Botswana's Okavango Delta System which at 6.9 million hectares is the world's largest Ramsar site (Ramsar Bureau, 2001).

Wetlands in the USA were estimated at 42.7 million hectares in 1997, a decline by more than half from the area thought to have existed at the beginning of European settlement in North America (Dahl, 2000). Regulation was initiated as part of the **Clean Water Act** involving dredge and fill operations by the US Army Corps of Engineers. Since adoption of the Emergency Wetlands Resources Act (1986), requiring the US Fish and Wildlife Service to conduct status and trend studies of wetlands, the rate of wetland losses declined rapidly compared with previous decades. Important factors affecting this trend were enactment and enforcement of governmental policies to protect wetlands, public education (increasing public perception of wetland values), monitoring, protection, and restoration programmes.

References

Dahl, T.E. (2000) *Status and Trends of Wetlands in the Conterminous United States 1986 to 1997*, Washington, DC: US Department of the Interior, Fish and Wildlife Service.

Ramsar Bureau (2001) *Ramsar Convention on Wetlands*, Internet website at
URL: http://www.ramsar.org.

JAMES EFLIN

whaling

Commercial whaling has taken place since at least 1100, and indigenous whaling since long before that. Whales have been caught for their meat, bones, and the oil in their blubber. Initially, whalers hunted those whales close to their shores using small boats, and towed whales back to land for processing. By the mid-fifteenth century, whalers began to venture far from home in larger boats, eventually establishing permanent whaling stations in the **Arctic**. By the seventeenth and eighteenth centuries whaling vessels traversed the globe.

It was not until the middle of the nineteenth century that human impact on the world's population of whales became apparent. The response of whalers was to improve **technology** so as to be able to find and hunt whales more efficiently. Steam was introduced to power whaling vessels, hand-held harpoons replaced by exploding lances shot from vessels, and blubber processed into oil on the ships. In the twentieth century, the addition of refrigeration increased the length of time vessels could remain at sea.

Concern from the whaling industry about possible depletion of the whales on which they depended for their livelihood led to efforts to regulate whaling. The main agreement currently governing whaling is the International Convention for the Regulation of Whaling, negotiated in 1946. Its objective is the 'proper and effective conservation and development of whale stocks' in order to enable 'the orderly development of the whaling industry'. This agreement regulates whaling through the International Whaling Commission (IWC), in which each member country has one vote. The IWC sets restrictions on whaling each year through the passage of a 'schedule' that denotes how many of which types of whales are allowed to be caught in which areas. Passage of the schedule requires an affirmative vote of three-quarters of the IWC members and then becomes binding on all members, except those who lodge an 'objection' to a regulation within 90 days after it has been passed.

The IWC failed in its initial effort to conserve and develop whale stocks. Its legal requirement to set global rather than national quotas led to a race to catch whales as quickly as possible resulting in the overcapitalization of whaling vessels. The 'race' ended in 1962 when the main whaling countries reached an agreement outside the IWC to divide quotas. The tradition (until 1972) of regulating whale catches by Blue Whale Units (the number of whales equal to the oil in a Blue Whale), a holdover from an earlier era when the main economic use of whales was for the oil they produced, made it difficult to regulate individual species of whales that were more depleted than others. Non-compliance has also plagued the history of whaling regulation, most clearly by the former Soviet Union, which had a systemic programme to misreport numbers and species of whales caught. Quotas were also set higher than the IWC's own scientific committee recommended, because whaling states were not willing to agree to lower limits.

By the last quarter of the twentieth century whale stocks were severely depleted. The idea of a moratorium on commercial whaling to allow stocks to replenish was first proposed in 1972 at the **Stockholm Conference** and passed by the IWC in 1982, to begin in the 1985/1986 season. The moratorium was accomplished with an alliance among those who had come to believe, for **animal rights** reasons, that whales should never be killed, those who believed that whales were too depleted to be taken sustainably, and those who still wished to catch whales but were persuaded (largely by economic or political pressure) to suspend their commercial whaling temporarily. The open membership policy allowed non-whaling states to join the agreement and eventually a three-quarters majority in favour of a moratorium was reached.

During the commercial moratorium some whaling persisted. Subsistence whaling by indigenous populations has always been accepted under international regulation. Whaling for scientific purposes has been explicitly allowed under the agreement, and **Japan** increased its level of research whaling, with the whale meat from the studies sold in food markets. Iceland withdrew from the IWC to preserve its right to catch whales, and Norway resumed commercial whaling in 1993, legally because of its original objection to the moratorium. The debate over whether to end the moratorium has shown the inability of the international community to agree on whether, and under what conditions, whaling should be allowed.

Further reading

Andresen, S. (1989) 'Science and Politics in the International Management of Whales', *Marine Policy*, April 1989.

Friedheim, R. (ed.) (2000) *Toward A Sustainable Whaling Regime*, Seattle: University of Washington Press.

Tønnessen, J.N. and Johnsen, A.O. (1982) *The History of Modern Whaling*, Berkeley: University of California Press.

ELIZABETH R. DeSOMBRE

White, Lynn, Jr

b. 29 April 1907, San Francisco, California, USA; d. 30 March 1987, Los Angeles, California

Historian

Lynn White Jr's significance for environmentalism

stems from his 1967 essay, 'The Historical Roots of Our Ecologic Crisis', in which he argued that western devaluation of **nature** was culturally rooted in Judaeo-Christian religion, primarily due to the assumption of human 'dominion' over Earth in Genesis and the Christian emphasis on the immaterial soul and the afterlife rather than terrestrial and bodily concerns. The article sparked immense debate and helped give birth to a burgeoning new field, ecotheology. In 1973 White, himself a Presbyterian lay preacher, added a second article, 'Continuing the Conversation', in which he nominated Saint Francis of Assisi as representing a different, historically secondary Christian tradition of **stewardship** which he suggested as being more appropriate for Christians to adopt in response to environmental crisis.

See also: environmentalism and ecologism; religions and the environment

PIERS H.G. STEPHENS

whole Earth photograph

The US Apollo space programme in the 1960s provided the first photos of the Earth from space. These offered a perspective on the Earth never before seen: a ball suspended in a vast abyss of darkness. From these images developed the idea of spaceship Earth, a fragile capsule on which we all depended. Stewart Brand, a hippie entrepreneur in California, used the photo as the cover for his very successful *Whole Earth Catalogs* (first published in 1968) which marketed survival and self-sufficiency tools to the emerging US **environmental movement**.

Further reading

NASA's excellent website (*www.earth.jsc.nasa.gov/*) is a very useful resource and contains many images – both moving and static – of the Earth, including the well-known image taken by the Apollo 17 astronauts as they left Earth en route for the Moon in December 1972 (the first time that the trajectory of an Apollo mission enabled a view of the South Pole).

HORACE HERRING

wildlife management

Wildlife management requires the deliberate manipulation of wildlife and the environment, aimed at achieving specific goals that relate to humans and wildlife. The scientific discipline was created in the USA during the 1930s. Aldo **Leopold**, a professor at the University of Wisconsin, is considered to have been its founder. The Wildlife Society, an organization of managers and scientists, was formed in 1937. Wildlife management is an applied discipline which draws heavily on ecological principles. In addition, concepts from the fields of **conservation biology**, animal behaviour, landscape ecology, ecological restoration, human dimensions, **environmental ethics**, conservation genetics, and epidemiology guide its actions. Historically, the profession emphasized the management of game species, primarily mammals and birds. Recently, it has broadened its area of interest to include all life in the wild (see **biodiversity**).

Wildlife management focuses on managing populations of single species and wildlife communities. Goals for managing single species include manipulating populations and environments: (i) to produce sustainable surpluses of species which can be harvested (game species); (ii) to recover species' populations that are in decline and sustain them indefinitely (**endangered species**); or (iii) to reduce species' populations or their activities that threaten human economies (overabundant species). Managing single species involves the concept of density dependence and emphasizes manipulating birth and death rates as well as dispersal of individuals into and out of populations.

The goal of managing wildlife communities is to maintain or preserve the status of the naturally occurring species of an area. Status is usually evaluated by the relative abundance of the species within a community comprising all its natural members. Managing for wildlife communities comprises the vast majority of organisms yet has received the least attention from wildlife managers.

There are three general approaches to managing wildlife communities: (i) the species approach; (ii) the ecological process approach; and (iii) the landscape approach.

The species approach concentrates on managing a single species that affects a wildlife community through some sort of ecological process, such as predation, competition, or disease or parasitism. Examples of this approach include managing viable populations of keystone species, such as black-tailed prairie dogs (*Cynomys ludovicianus*) or Pacific salmon (*Oncorhynchus* spp.), upon which a large array of other species either directly or indirectly depend.

The ecological process approach focuses on ecological processes (e.g., fire, herbivory, hydrological cycles) that shape wildlife communities. Because wildlife communities occur on landscapes that are formed by natural disturbances, the persistence of these communities depends on ensuring these ecological processes still occur. This approach assumes that if ecological processes are properly occurring within natural spatial and temporal limits, then the wildlife community will benefit.

The landscape approach manipulates landscape components in such a way that wildlife communities benefit. **Landscape** components may include size, shape, proximity and diversity of plant communities, as well as human attributes such as roads, cities, agriculture, and other development. For example, in order to maintain songbird communities that depend on late-successional stage forests, forest stands could be managed for old age, large area, increased proximity to each other and minimal edge. A landscape approach emphasizes management at different spatial and temporal scales and requires two basic components. The landscape components have to be managed so as to maintain or simulate internal dynamics of natural systems. Internal dynamics include natural disturbances such as fire and nutrient cycling. Second, management needs to focus on factors external to the patches but that influence internal patch dynamics. These may include such things as pollution, **urbanization** or other human land uses.

Effectively managing for wildlife communities usually requires integrating all three approaches. Traditionally, wildlife management has emphasized single species management. Increasingly, wildlife managers are taking a broader approach and attempting to manage for wildlife communities. This approach is inevitable since there are far too many species to manage them one at a time.

See also: ecology; endangered species; environmental ethics; environmental management; exotic species

Further reading

Bolen, E.G. and Robinson, W.L. (1995) *Wildlife Ecology and Management*, Englewood Cliffs, NJ: Prentice Hall, 3rd edn.

Verner, J., Morrison, M.L. and Ralph, C.J. (eds) (1986) *Wildlife 2000: Modeling Habitat Relationships of Terrestrial Vertebrates*, Madison, WI: University of Wisconsin Press.

RICHARD L. KNIGHT

wise-use movement

Mainly relegated to the USA, the 'wise-use' movement emerged in the late 1980s as the focal point for concerns about **property rights**, access and usage of public lands, and the economic impact of federal policies. In particular, the movement represented the mobilization of resource industries like **mining** companies to retain their privileged access to resources on public lands. The movement drew its impetus from environmentalists' successes, such as the removal of James **Watt** in 1983, social and political pressures stemming from the influx of newcomers, and the growth of political alienation in the American West that had inspired earlier movements like the **Sagebrush Rebellion**. The movement was also encouraged by the rhetoric of new federalism calling for less government and privatization which had been propagated by Presidents **Reagan** and Bush (see also **federalism and decentralization**). The movement started in the American West with conservative populist organizations like the Public Lands Coalition and Communities for a Great Northwest, which focused upon the multiple use of public lands, the socio-economic threats of environmental policy, and perceptions of federal arrogance. The apparent grassroots nature of the movement obscured its backers and most vocal proponents including various resource industries (especially mining and timber), large ranchers, and developers. Nonetheless, it worked to encourage its perception as a movement made up of rational stewards who would manage resources for the good of all.

By 1990 the movement seemed on the verge of coalescing into a potent regional political force with the creation of such influential groups as People for the West! and the Center for the Defense of Free Enterprise. Along with others, People for the West! played an important role in the 1994 federal elections as well as in state and local elections in that decade by getting its members elected as well as advancing its views. The Center's founder and father of the 'wise-use' movement, Ron Arnold, further boosted the movement's appeal by focusing attention on property rights and the belief that environmental zealots were attempting to both eradicate the western lifestyle and destroy the region's economic base. This new focus provided a new venue for the movement – the courtroom – which resulted in a plethora of lawsuits centred on the issue of **takings**. These efforts contributed to the rise of other groups elsewhere in the USA, Canada, and the UK. Most efforts outside the USA have been limited to **forest management** concerns and have drawn few members and little financial support.

For the movement, the expansion of the number of 'wise-use' groups in the 1990s represented the triumph of the people against the denigrations of the environmentalists and the federal government who had belittled the movement and its concerns from the beginning. The expansion drew largely from its corporate backers, which broadened their efforts to include all-expenses-paid junkets for jurists, widescale public relations campaigns trumpeting their environmentalism, and increased contributions to political candidates and parties. The expansion mirrored the supportive reception for the movement's concerns in Congress after 1994, though these legislative efforts were often frustrated by the executive branch elevating Vice President Al **Gore** as the movement's symbolic bogeyman.

The rapid rise of the movement obscured the reality that most Americans, including westerners, failed to join any of the hundreds of groups, did not support many of the movement's candidates or policies, and even formed counter groups to reclaim the movement's issues from its large and powerful supporters (e.g., the creation of the Wyoming Public Land Access Association in 2000). The movement's inability to move much beyond its corporate base has been coupled with its disorganization and absence of leadership. The movement's popular appeal rests mainly with fringe groups like the county movement, the militia groups, and Rev. Moon's American Freedom Coalition. Also, the region's demographics and economies have changed dramatically though anti-government sentiment is still fairly common. The movement faces an uncertain future because of these changes and its very diversity. Its focus on public lands will continue to draw interest in the American West, which possesses the largest percentage of such lands, but its narrow base of the resource elite may limit its future political efficacy.

Further reading

Arnold, R. and Gottlieb, A. (1994) *Trashing the Economy*, Bellevue, WA: Free Enterprise Press, 2nd edn.

Bosso, C. (2000) 'Environmental Groups and the New Political Landscape', *Environmental Policy*, N. Vig and M. Kraft, (eds), Washington, DC: Congressional Quarterly Press.

Pendley, W. (1995) *War on the West: Government Tyranny on America's Great Frontier*, Washington, DC: Regnery.

Switzer, J. (1997) *Green Backlash: The History and Politics of Environmental Opposition in the United States*, Boulder, CO: Lynne Reinner.

ERICH G. FRANKLAND

Women's Environmental Network

Founded in the UK, the Women's Environmental Network (WEN) is an eco-feminist organization representing women's interests on a range of environmental and health issues (see **eco-feminism; health and the environment**). Since 1990 WEN has combined awareness-raising campaigns with lobbying, grassroots activism and consumer advice, in three main areas: waste minimization, environmental pollutants and health, and local sustainable **agriculture**. The first of these addresses consumer waste and packaging, e.g. weighing up the environmental costs of reusable versus disposable nappies; and currently, working with local authorities and businesses to demonstrate an economic rationale for reducing waste in town centres and markets. Second, WEN successfully campaigned against chlorine-bleached paper and sanitary protection, highlighting the danger of dioxin residues (see **dioxins**); hazardous 'para-bens' in deodorants are a current target. Finally, WEN encourages local organic food production by supporting schools and community groups in growing their own produce; and opposes genetic engineering in food and farming (including genetically modified cotton in sanitary protection) on the grounds of public health and environmental concerns (see **genetic engineering, crops**).

GILL SEYFANG

World Bank

The World Bank, as the International Bank for Reconstruction and Development is more commonly known, was established in 1945, and is affiliated with the United Nations. With 181 members, it is the largest international development agency whose primary aim is poverty alleviation and economic growth in developing countries. Since the 1980s, the World Bank has been sharply criticized by environmental and **human rights** organizations, scholars, and grassroots movements for promoting environmentally destructive development. In the 1990s, this criticism was expanded to include the Bank's ignoring of the gender implications of environmental destruction. In response, the Bank has integrated environmental policies into its development agenda, overseen the formulation of environmental policies in countries, and created an Inspection Panel to investigate complaints of human rights violations by Bank projects. It also administers the **Global Environment Facility** that funds environmental projects in developing countries.

The World Bank was the first international development agency to acknowledge the significance of environmental protection, creating the post of Environmental Adviser in 1970. But until the mid-1980s, there was a staff of only five in its Office of Environmental and Scientific Affairs, to review its development projects – *after* they had been approved – for their environmental effects. Thus, no real redefinition of what constitutes **development** took place. The emphasis was on expanding the Bank's portfolio of funded projects with little or no attempt to ensure implementation of its environmental policies, compliance with negotiated agreements, consultation with and involvement of local people most affected by projects, and, certainly, no awareness of the gendered impacts of development projects or environmental destruction. The result was a series of projects, such as the Polonoroeste road building project in **Brazil**, the transmigration project in **Indonesia**, the Trans-Juba cattle project in Sudan, and the **Narmada Valley development programme** in India, among others, that achieved international notoriety both for their blatant violation of human rights of local, often indigenous, people, and for the environmental catastrophes they heralded for the region (see **indigenous peoples**).

The 1980s were also marked by sustained efforts by international environmental organizations to draw attention to the environmental consequences of World Bank projects. Western donor nations responded with increased pressure on the World Bank to improve its environmental record, resulting in a significant shift in Bank policy with the creation, in 1987, of a central environment department and four regional environment divisions. In 1989, the Bank adopted its environmental assessment (EA) policy, now the cornerstone of its environmental policies. EA is now required for all major projects with significant impacts on the environment. Task managers categorize projects according to their potential environmental impact into three categories (A, B, C) with comprehensive EA to be conducted for category A projects and more limited ones for category B. The EA policies cover issues relating to impacts on the physical environment, health, indigenous people, cultural property, and involuntary resettlement. The Bank's own internal review of its EA performance in 1997 revealed that 54 per cent of projects between 1993 and 1995 had 'good' impact assessments, while 32 were rated 'excellent'. In contrast only two were seen as being 'inadequate'. Yet, the review also revealed that public consultation, analysis of alternatives, and supervision of even category A projects remained weak and generally insufficient.

A parallel evolution in Bank policies has been on the issue of women and development, now referred to as gender and development. Although Bank policies endorse gender-sensitive development projects and programmes, and there is some official recognition of the significant role women can play in environmental management, there has been no attempt to include gender issues in its environmental policies. Thus, the Bank continues to ignore an extensive literature on gender and the environment, calling into question its ability to deliver environmentally **sustainable development**.

Despite the reforms it has undertaken, the Bank's commitment to a particular brand of economic development that emphasizes trade liberalization, structural adjustment (despite their specific negative impacts on women and children), and economic reform, has meant that its environmental policies inevitably take second place to its economic policies. Gender policies are not even seriously in the picture where the environment is concerned. Thus, a cleaner, greener Bank is unlikely to emerge until fundamental changes take place in formulating its core policies and priorities.

See also: globalization; International Monetary Fund and neoliberalism; World Trade Organization

Further reading

Kurian, P.A. (2000) *Engendering the Environment? Gender in the World Bank's Environmental Policies*, Aldershot, UK: Ashgate.

Le Prestre, P. (1987) *The World Bank and the Environmental Challenge*, Cranbury, NJ: Associated University Presses.

Rich, B. (1994) *Mortgaging the Earth: The World Bank, Environmental Impoverishment, and the Crisis of Development*, Boston: Beacon Press.

PRIYA A. KURIAN

World Conservation Union

The World Conservation Union or International Union for Conservation of Nature and Natural Resources (IUCN) was established 1948 in Gland, Switzerland, with the 'hopes of developing a just world that values and conserves nature'. The IUCN consists of 78 states, 112 governmental and 735 non-governmental organizations, and approximately 10,000 scientists and experts from 181 countries. The mission of the IUCN is to influence, encourage, and assist societies throughout the world in conserving the integrity and diversity of nature.

The IUCN is widely known for the production of the Red List, which is a comprehensive inventory of the world's plant and animal species. The Red List is compiled by 7000 species-specific experts and consists of eight categories: extinct, extinct in the wild, critically endangered, endangered, vulnerable, lower risk, data deficient, and not evaluated. The Red List is used to influence and aid in the development of national and international conservation policy.

See also: endangered species

Further reading

The World Conservation Union 'IUCN' (5 March 2001) *Mission/Vision* and *2000 Red List* at URL: http://www.iucn.org.

JON E. FITCH

World Health Organization

A body whose roots lie in the League of Nations and earlier conventions to combat specific diseases, the United Nations World Health Organization (WHO) was established as part of the United Nations in 1945. Based in Genva, its objective is to promote the 'highest possible level of health', defined holistically as 'a state of complete physical, mental and social well-being' rather than merely the absence of disease. The organization is active in both capacity building in the area of health and also the development and promotion of standards. Despite its definition of health, the WHO has tended to focus on disease and it has run a number of successful campaigns to eradicate specific diseases. Its most successful campaign resulted in the complete eradication of smallpox, once a major killer, in 1977. Among the major challenges facing the organization in the twenty-first century is that of AIDS, a problem of particular significance in southern Africa.

See also: health and the environment

ALISTAIR McCULLOCH

World Heritage Convention

The 'Convention Concerning the Protection of the World Cultural and Natural Heritage' was adopted by UNESCO in 1972 with the aim of identifying, and thereby protecting, sites identified as being of 'outstanding universal value'. With its genesis lying in international concern during the 1950s and 1960s over danger to a number of high-profile sites including the Abu Simbel temples (Egypt) and the city of Venice (Italy), by 2001, 160 countries had signed up to the Convention. Membership of the Convention imposes a small cost on UNESCO members, raises public awareness of any sites nominated (thereby, paradoxically, increasing tourist attention which often demands further protective measures), and allows countries to draw on financial (for poorer counties) and technical resources to aid preservation. Among the 690 designated sites are the city of Timbuktu (Mali), the Galapagos Islands (Ecuador), the Royal Chitwan National Park (Nepal), Yellowstone National Park (USA), and Stonehenge (UK).

See also: eco-tourism; national parks; tourism, environmental impact of

ALISTAIR McCULLOCH

World Resources Institute

The World Resources Institute (WRI) is an independent scientific and public-policy research institution located in Washington, DC. It was founded in 1982 to bring greater attention to global environmental problems such as natural resource destruction, environmental pollution, and ecosystem degradation. Its mission is to foster environmental protection and **sustainability** through the generation and promotion of scientific knowledge and policy studies that can catalyse public and private action. WRI has grown significantly, and by 2000 it had a staff of over 125 professionals from 20 nations, all connected to an impressive network of scientists, policy specialists, and collaborators in over 50 nations. It is a co-producer of the biennial *World Resources: A Guide to the Global Environment*, a treasure trove of environmental data. It also publishes a diverse collection of studies and reports on global environmental issues, with summaries available at its website *http://www.wri.org.*

MICHAEL E. KRAFT

World Trade Organization

The World Trade Organization (WTO) is an international agency comprising 139 member governments. The WTO was established by the Uruguay Round trade negotiations in 1994 and came into operation in 1995. The purpose of the WTO is to oversee national trade policies and to reduce barriers to commerce among countries. The underlying premise is that by liberalizing trade, governments can promote economic **development**. This premise has drawn increasing challenge during the 1990s from environmentalists who contend that in the absence of appropriate ecological policies, more trade will degrade the environment and can curtail rather than enhance prospects for sustainable economic growth.

As world trade has expanded, the international trade regime has acquired more influence. In 1999, world exports were about $5.5 trillion. The WTO influences governments by its far-reaching rules and by the norms of open markets that it espouses.

Another important influence is the 'accession' process in which applicant governments must buy their way in by making 'concessions' to existing members. For example, **China** made numerous concessions to the USA and the **European Union** in 2000 in an effort to gain membership. Many countries yearn to join the WTO because they want a role in shaping WTO policy and because they perceive that WTO membership can increase inward foreign investment.

The creation of the WTO in 1994 capped almost 80 years of frustrated efforts to establish world trade governance. The first initiative for a World Trade Tribunal came during the Paris Peace Conference following the First World War. In 1927, the League of Nations sponsored a treaty to abolish import prohibitions, but it fell one nation short of ratification. During the drafting of this treaty, the governments recognized that some import restrictions did not need to be abolished and provided an exception for trade measures used to protect animals and plants from disease or extinction. In 1947, 23 countries negotiated the General Agreement on Tariffs and Trade (GATT) to establish rules against certain discriminatory and protectionist government trade policies. The GATT was intended to be auxiliary to the establishment of an International Trade Organization in 1948, but the treaty establishing this agency received insufficient ratifications. During the negotiations for this treaty (1946–8), the governments recognized the link between trade and **nature**, and provided that trade rules would permit intergovernmental agreements relating solely to the conservation of **fisheries**, birds, or wild animals. Over the following decades, the GATT spawned several 'rounds' of trade negotiations and tightened world trade rules. In 1994, GATT member governments agreed to establish the WTO which would incorporate the GATT and add several new agreements that vastly expand the scope of world trade governance.

The Uruguay trade round (1986–94) coincided with the so-called 'trade and environment' debate. The environment was not on the agenda for the round, but by the late 1980s, environmental non-governmental organizations (NGOs) recognized the importance of trade-environment linkages and began to push the GATT to consider the environmental implications of trade. The grassroots concerns about the GATT were heightened by a GATT arbitral panel decision in 1991 in the Tuna–Dolphin dispute. In that case, the panel ruled that the US tuna import ban was a violation of trade rules. The USA was banning tuna from countries (like **Mexico**) whose fishing vessels were killing many dolphins as they dropped nets on tuna. The panel ruled that the GATT did not permit the USA to safeguard foreign dolphins, but this decision provoked such an uproar that it was never adopted by the GATT.

The governments did not add environment to the Uruguay Round agenda, but did set up a Committee on Trade and Environment in the WTO. This Committee has accomplished little since 1995. One problem is that it is composed largely of national trade officials with little understanding or empathy for the environment. The Committee has refused regular participation by the **United Nations Environment Programme** (UNEP), or by NGOs.

The infamous WTO Seattle Ministerial held in December 1999 may be the most serious setback for the trading system in 50 years. Environmental concerns were only one small cause of the failure of the governments in Seattle to agree to launch a new trade round. But many of the protestors on the streets were complaining about the impact of WTO rules and international trade on the environment, and those concerns (whatever their validity) have diminished public support for the WTO in many countries.

The WTO contains several agreements and provisions with potential implications for the environment (WTO, 1999). The GATT bans taxes that discriminate between countries, including, for example, **eco-taxes**, unless they meet narrowly interpreted exceptions. The Services Agreement promotes greater market access for services – including, for example, **eco-tourism** – and also establishes disciplines for transparency in regulations. The Agriculture Agreement imposes limits on domestic support, but provides an exemption for payments under environmental programmes. The Agreement on Subsidies and Countervailing Duties prohibits export subsidies and allows counter-action against domestic subsidies, but the Agreement also declares certain subsidies to be non-actionable including certain assistance to adapt to new environmental requirements. The Agreement on Technical Barriers to Trade promotes the use of international standards and requires that non-international standards use the least-trade-restrictive approach. The Sanitary and Phytosanitary Agreement also promotes the use of international standards and requires that non-international standards be based on a **risk assessment**, have a scientific basis, and meet other stringent tests. The Agreement on Trade-Related Intellectual Property Rights requires that governments have a 20-year patenting system that covers products and processes in all fields of **technology**.

The WTO also establishes a dispute settlement system, which is more sophisticated than those contained in multilateral environmental treaties. By virtue of being members of the WTO, governments agree to allow other governments to lodge complaints against them which will be investigated by an independent panel. The arbitral decision, which may be appealed to the WTO Appellate Body, becomes binding in the sense that governments have an international obligation to comply. When a defendant government flouts that obligation, a winning plaintiff government may seek authority to impose trade sanctions. Today, the WTO dispute process is the most active State-to-State international adjudication.

Trade and environment will continue to be a WTO issue for the foreseeable future. International trade will often affect the environment, particularly in resource sectors such as fisheries and forests (see **fisheries**; **forest management**). Environmental laws and regulations will often affect trade, particularly in areas like **hazardous and toxic waste management**, **recycling**, and the protection of **endangered species**. The management of **global warming** also has many linkages to trade policy (e.g., emissions trading).

As a result of the new attention to trade and environment, several governments have agreed to do environmental impact assessments of new trade negotiations and agreements. The WTO itself has taken no part in these assessments, but the WTO

Secretariat did publish an overall study of trade and the environment in 1999, just before the Seattle meeting. The study points out the ways in which trade can both improve and degrade the environment. The overall conclusion from the study is that if proper environmental policies are in place, greater trade can be supportive of environmental protection. In that sense, there is a link between the WTO Secretariat's view and **free market environmentalism**.

Although the WTO approach to trade policy is multilateral, GATT rules permit regional trade agreements such as the North American Free Trade Agreement (**NAFTA**). Because pollution from Mexico affected the USA, the environment became an issue in the NAFTA negotiations, and the governments agreed to establish a North American Commission on Environmental Co-operation. The Commission established an impressive track record in its first five years, and many NGOs believe that it is a good model for how environmental concerns can be incorporated into proposed regional trade agreements such as the Free Trade Area of the Americas.

It is clear that environmental politics have influenced the trading system. The most important achievement has been to promote WTO transparency. When the NGOs first began looking at the trading system, the GATT was a closed, secretive organization. Environmental pressure was an important factor in opening up the GATT and the WTO. But the WTO still has a long way to go, particularly in providing participatory opportunities for **civil society**.

The establishment of the WTO has also had a significant influence on international environmental politics. Successive directors-general at the GATT/WTO have noted the uncoordinated nature of the environment regime and have argued that **global environmental governance** needs improvement. The gap between the sophisticated dispute settlement on trade and the rudimentary dispute settlement on environment has suggested to many commentators that the environment regime needs to reorganize to look more like the WTO. In late 1999, the WTO and United Nations Environment Programme signed a co-operative agreement. Little co-operation had developed by mid-2000,

but many analysts have endorsed joint efforts by the two organizations to conduct capacity building in developing countries.

References

World Trade Organization (1999) *The Legal Texts. The Results of the Uruguay Round of Multilateral Trade Negotiations*, Cambridge: Cambridge University Press.

Further reading

Sampson, G.P. and Chambers, W.B. (eds) (1999) *Trade, Environment, and the Millennium*, Tokyo: United Nations Press.

Schott, J. (ed) (2000) *The WTO After Seattle*, Washington: Institute for International Economics.

STEVE CHARNOVITZ

World Wide Fund for Nature

The World Wide Fund for Nature (or World Wildlife Fund as it is also known) is a non-profit non-governmental organization whose purpose is to conserve **biodiversity** on the earth. Founded in 1961, the Fund adopted the endangered giant panda as its logo to educate the public about threats to **endangered species** everywhere. The Wildlife Fund has millions of individual contributing members and over 13,000 projects in 157 countries. It works co-operatively with governments on all continents to save endangered species from extinction by setting aside nature preserves and parks where they can survive and reproduce. Although its founders were European and North American conservationists, they early recognized the need to train conservation workers in Asia, Africa and Latin America to maintain the parks and preserves. In 1985 the Fund started the Wildlands and Human Needs programme to create sustainable economies among the people who live near the world's most endangered habitats, recognizing that protected areas cannot survive indefinitely outside a sustainable social and economic system (see **sustainability**). It affiliated with the Conservation Foundation in 1985 and became active in lobbying the international community on a variety of threats to the global environment from such sources as climate change and the thinning of the ozone layer (see **ozone depletion**). It is the world's largest private international conservation organization.

Further reading

URL: http://www.worldwildlife.org.

LETTIE McSPADDEN

Worldwatch Institute

The Worldwatch Institute, established in 1974, is one of the best known US environmental organizations. It is dedicated to fostering the evolution of an environmentally sustainable society, primarily through the conduct of interdisciplinary research and public education (see **sustainable development**).

Worldwatch's annual *State of the World*, its flagship publication, is widely read in college classrooms, and its frequent reports on the environmental conditions and trends receive prominent coverage in the mass media (see **mass media and the environment**). It publishes a bimonthly magazine, *World Watch*, an annual compilation on emerging global trends, *Vital Signs*, and an extensive series of research papers and books on global environmental problems and policy actions. Worldwatch publications are disseminated in as many as 30 different languages.

The organization's Web site (*www.worldwatch.org*) provides a gateway to its many studies, reports, and global environmental issues. Worldwatch's founding president, Lester R. Brown, stepped down in 2000 and became chairman of the organization's board of directors.

MICHAEL E. KRAFT

Wuppertal Institute

The Wuppertal Institute for Climate, Environment and Energy is one of three branches of the *Sciences Centre North Rhine-Westphalia*. It was founded in 1991 and has currently about 120 staff. Major areas of research (departments) are climate politics, material flows and structural change, energy politics, and transport politics. As a major player in the **ecological modernization** discourse, the Wuppertal Institute aims to bridge the conflict between ecological and economic interests, and suggest practicable strategies for the achievement of **sustainability**. Until the end of the 1990s, the institute was led by the distinguished scientist Ernst Ulrich von Weizsäcker. Its publications have had a major impact on German and European environmental politics, not least because in 1998 Weizsäcker and other leading figures from the institute became members of the German *Bundestag*. In particular, issues such as ecological taxation (see **eco-taxes**) and resource and energy efficiency are widely associated with the Wuppertal Institute.

INGOLFUR BLÜHDORN

X

xenotransplantation

Xenotransplantation (XTP) is the use of non-human transgenic and cloned organs and cells for human transplantation (see **cloning**). Demand for tissues is rising because: a) improved techniques means more people are thought to benefit from transplantation; b) a fall in the number of fatal accidents reduces the availability of human organs; c) genetic modification can now be used to lessen immunological incompatibilities between species. XTP is the focus of several related environmental risks. Primarily, debates have centred on the way XTP disturbs the physical, cultural and moral boundaries between species. First, using other species' organs may introduce new diseases into the human population, a concern more acute since the BSE/CJD crisis (see **mad cow disease/ BSE**). Second, transgenics and cloning represents an increasing technical dependence on animals which many find morally objectionable thus heightening tensions between the **biotechnology** industry and **animal rights** organizations

NIK BROWN

Y

Yucca Mountain and nuclear wastes

Located in arid southern Nevada about 110 miles west of Las Vegas, Yucca Mountain is the site favoured by the Department of Energy (DOE) for the permanent storage of US high-level nuclear wastes. The Nuclear Waste Policy Act of 1982 had devised a disposal scheme entailing two sites: one in the east and one in the west. Political opposition killed the plan for an eastern site, and geological factors ruled out two other prospective western sites. In tunnels bored deep into Yucca Mountain, the DOE has maintained that optimal conditions exist for safe storage of nuclear wastes for 10,000 years. Opponents have argued that the mountain is prone to earthquakes, has a geological history of vulcanism, and is more permeable to water than expected. While scientific studies have been underway, congressional allies of the nuclear lobby have sought to authorize an above-ground interim storage facility. Citizen groups have opposed their plan as 'Mobile Chernobyl' since it would mandate thousands of truck- and rail-cask shipments of highly radioactive wastes across 43 states. Accidents would seem inevitable over the anticipated 30 years of shipping. Environmentalists have maintained that the wastes can be stored more safely at the power plants, awaiting the development of technological solutions with lower environmental and financial costs. The election of President George W. Bush has increased the odds that Yucca Mountain will receive nuclear wastes.

See also: hazardous and toxic waste management; nuclear energy/nuclear waste management

Further reading

Flynn, J. Kasperson, R.E., Kunreuther, H. and Slovic, P. (1997) 'Redirecting the US High-Level Nuclear Waste Program', *Environment* 39(3) April: 7–11, 25–30.

E. GENE FRANKLAND

Z

Zahniser, Howard

b. 25 February 1906, Franklin,
  Pennsylvania, USA; d. 5 May 1964,
  Tionesta, Pennsylvania

Environmental lobbyist

Howard Zahniser, a brilliant, hardworking, lobbyist based in Washington, DC and Executive Director of the Wilderness Society, played a key role in the fight for the preservation of American wilderness in the 1950s and early 1960s. He first became nationally prominent as a lobbyist in the fight to prevent a dam and reservoir in southern Utah's Dinosaur National Monument (see **dams/hydroelectric power**). Here he articulated views about the value of wild places and the need for an enduring reservoir of wilderness and defined his mission to work toward safeguarding and extending wilderness designations while developing working alliances with such groups as the **Sierra Club**. However, his tireless advocacy for the Wilderness Act (1964) and the creation of the National Wilderness Preservation System (1964) was his finest hour. His endless work with the US Congress as well as his sincerity, persistence, and ability to work out critical compromises helped to pass this landmark legislation.

WARREN VANDER HILL

Zapatistas/Chiapas

On 1 January 1994, timed to the inauguration of **NAFTA**, the Zapatista National Liberation Army (EZLN) launched a rebellion in the southern Mexican state of Chiapas. EZLN leaders defined their rebellion as an indigenous struggle for land, work, health care, education, independence, **democracy** and justice, following Mexico's *campesino* legacy. Militarily pressed, the Zapatistas withdrew to the Lacandon forest near the border with Guatemala. In February 1996 the government broke with Mexican political tradition by conceding self-determination, municipal autonomy, and natural resource control to Chiapan indigenous communities. Implementation of these San Andres Accords became mired in political infighting. The Zapatistas have since refused to deal with the government, labouring instead to build alliances and fashion a national advocacy movement for indigenous rights and democratization.

See also: indigenous peoples; Mexico

Further reading

Howard, P. and Homer-Dixon, T. (1998) 'The Case of Chiapas, Mexico', in T. Homer-Dixon and J. Blitt (eds) *Ecoviolence*, Oxford: Rowman and Littlefield.
URL: http://www.chiapaslink.ukgateway.net.
URL: http://flag.blackened.net/revolt/mexico.html.
URL: http://www.ezln.org/.
URL: http://www.ciepac.org/.
URL: http://www.laneta.apc.org/enlacecivil.

STEPHEN MUMME

Zero Population Growth

Zero Population Growth (ZPG) is a national US non-profit organization that works to slow population growth and achieve a sustainable balance between the Earth's population and its resources (see **population movement and control**). Its education and advocacy programmes strive to influence public attitudes and public policies on population growth within the USA and globally. ZPG is the only US environmental organization that focuses exclusively on population growth, particularly US growth and its impact on the environment. The organization was founded in 1968 at the height of public concern over US and world growth rates and its origin coincided with the publication of Paul **Ehrlich**'s *The Population Bomb* (1968). Ehrlich has long served as ZPG's honorary president.

ZPG's Web page (*http://www.zpg.org*) provides extensive coverage of population issues and policy actions, and helps to facilitate citizen involvement in the political process. It also includes access to a diverse array of studies and reports on population, family planning, women's rights, and local growth concerns.

MICHAEL E. KRAFT

ZOOS

The keeping of animal collections dates back to Ancient Egypt but the first modern zoos were created from the late eighteenth century. It is estimated that, worldwide, some five million animals are kept in about 10,000 zoos. Zoos have come under increasing challenge in recent years by the animal protection movement and by a general public that feels increasingly uncomfortable about keeping animals in captivity. Advocates of zoos have responded by emphasizing the quality of animal care and the educative and conservation roles played by zoos.

From a strict **animal rights** perspective, zoos are morally illegitimate because captivity deprives animals of the crucial right to freedom. Conversely, if one adopts a strict anthropocentric, or human-centred, perspective, then providing some, however slight, human benefit is gained from keeping animals in captivity, zoos are justified (see **anthropocentrism**). Most of the debate now takes place between these two extremes of the moral spectrum.

The extent to which the needs of captives in zoos can be met is obviously hugely important. This will vary according to particular species and particular zoos. Although it is difficult to measure accurately the level of suffering inflicted on wild animals by captivity, it is clear that for some species, whether because of their size, the complexity of their social lives or their instinctive need to hunt over long distances, it is impossible to cater for their needs. The classic example here is the polar bear which in captivity exhibits signs of psychotic behaviour such as stereotypical pacing and head shaking, as do other species such as big cats, apes and elephants. The needs of other, usually smaller, species, however, are much easier to meet, and relatively minor adjustments to their environments can greatly improve the quality of their lives.

The quality of zoos also varies enormously. Some are undoubtedly extremely poor, whereas some are much more advanced than others in providing large 'naturalistic' environments for their animals. The **European Union** has tried to harmonize the law on zoos but, while this has improved conditions in countries such as Spain, Portugal, Italy and Greece where there was previously no regulatory framework, the standards are set at a relatively low and general level. This may change, however, with a new more rigorous directive, the provisions of which must be adhered to by April 2003. Britain has had legislation specifically regulating zoos since 1981 but the government has recognized the need to improve standards in the run up to the new directive by setting up an advisory body, the Zoos Forum, and introducing new regulations, which came into force in April 2000. For the first time, these emphasize the importance of environmental enrichment and the conservation role of zoos. In most countries, however, there is still no legislation to protect zoo animals, which undoubtedly suffer unacceptably in a variety of ways.

Most reputable zoos now justify their existence primarily through the conservation work they engage in (Tudge, 1992). This raises a moral question, concerning how far conservation work should take precedence over the needs of individual animals in captivity, which again will be coloured by pre-existing moral perspectives. It also raises, of course, the issue of how effective zoos are as agents of conservation. Here, the picture would seem to be mixed.

Some zoos, such as London Zoo, do useful conservation work, whereas many do little or no such work. The creation of gene banks may be vital in future reintroductions. Already, species as varied as the Mongolian wild horse, the European bison and the golden lion tamarin monkey seem to owe their survival to the work of zoos. Reintroductions, however, remain few and far between, and are very expensive; the vast majority of zoo animals are not **endangered species**, and it is questionable whether zoo conservation work, however productive in itself, is really going to have much impact on the protection of the world's **biodiversity** when the biggest problem by far is loss of habitat. This leaves the role that zoos can play in educating visitors about conservation. It may be argued,

though, that this educative role is much better performed by the use of computer technology and the impressive array of wildlife television programmes.

References

Tudge, C. (1992) *Last Animals At The Zoo: How Mass Extinction Can Be Stopped*, Oxford: Oxford University Press.

Further reading

Born Free Foundation website
  URL: http://www.bornfree.org.uk/zoocheck.
Bostock, S. (1993) *Zoos and Animal Rights: The Ethics of Keeping Animals*, London: Routledge.
O'Connell, S. (2000) 'Never Mind the Animals. Can our Zoos save Themselves?' *Independent*, 14 April.

ROBERT GARNER

Index

Page numbers in **bold** indicate references for main entry